NOBODY OF ANY IMPORTANCE: A FOOT SOLDIER'S MEMOIR OF WORLD WAR I

BY SAM SUTCLIFFE

Edited by Phil Sutcliffe

Published by SUTCLIFFE & SON

ii

First published in the UK in 2014 by Sutcliffe as an e-book original.

ISBN 978-0-9929567-2-1

SUTCLIFFE & SON PUBLISHING
Phil Sutcliffe, 26 Kirkstall Road, London SW2 4HF, UK

ALL AUTHOR/EDITOR ROYALTIES FROM THE E-BOOK
VERSION AND ANY ROYALTIES OR OTHER AUTHOR/
EDITOR PROFIT FROM THE PRINT VERSION
OF THIS PUBLICATION WILL GO TO THE RED CROSS.

For the boys of the old Brigade
– and the boys and girls of the new
Brigades too.

In memory of
Philip Broughton "Ted" Sutcliffe
1896-1922
(Sam's brother, Phil's uncle)

"I feel one can say with some conviction that no man should willingly leave his home to fight, wound, maim or kill other men about whom he knows little and whom he certainly does not hate. When all men refuse to commit such follies the foundations of a true civilisation will have only just started to be laid."

Sam Sutcliffe, circa 1974
(extracted from War: The Somme,
Part Five of this memoir)

Charles Samuel Sutcliffe, 1898-1987, photographed in 1919.

*"Ted" Sutcliffe and younger brother Sam. Date uncertain,
but some time after mid-1916 possibly even late 1918.*

CONTENTS

Editor's Foreword viii

PART ONE 1898-1912 1
AT HOME: CHILDHOOD TO LEAVING SCHOOL

Chapter One 3
Chapter Two 8
Chapter Three 17
Chapter Four... 23
Chapter Five.. 32
Chapter Six 45
Chapter Seven 56
Chapter Eight 63
Chapter Nine 74

PART TWO 1912-1914 81
RECRUIT: OUT TO WORK AND OFF TO BE A SOLDIER

Chapter Ten 83
Chapter Eleven.. 93
Chapter Twelve 105
Chapter Thirteen.. 111
Chapter Fourteen 123
Chapter Fifteen 136
Chapter Sixteen.. 149

PART THREE 1914-1915..155
PREPARING FOR BATTLE: KENT, MALTA, EGYPT

Chapter Seventeen..157
Chapter Eighteen 160
Chapter Nineteen..174
Chapter Twenty...182
Chapter Twenty-One..197
Chapter Twenty-Two..207
Chapter Twenty-Three...221
Chapter Twenty-Four...233
Chapter Twenty-Five..241

PART FOUR 1915-1916..259
WAR: GALLIPOLI

Chapter Twenty-Six...261
Chapter Twenty-Seven...276
Chapter Twenty-Eight..293
Chapter Twenty-Nine...301
Chapter Thirty 310

PART FIVE 1916 323
WAR: THE SOMME

Chapter Thirty-One...325
Chapter Thirty-Two...334
Chapter Thirty-Three...344
Chapter Thirty-Four...352
Chapter Thirty-Five..363
Chapter Thirty-Six 374
Chapter Thirty-Seven...387
Chapter Thirty-Eight..394
Chapter Thirty-Nine...398
Chapter Forty..408

PART SIX 1916-1917 415
A PEACEFUL INTERLUDE: FRANCE AND ENGLAND

Chapter Forty-One 417
Chapter Forty-Two 427
Chapter Forty-Three 431
Chapter Forty-Four 445
Chapter Forty-Five 451
Chapter Forty-Six 462

PART SEVEN 1917-1918 467
WAR: THE SPRING OFFENSIVE

Chapter Forty-Seven 469
Chapter Forty-Eight 480
Chapter Forty-Nine 487

PART EIGHT 1918 495
PRISONER OF WAR

Chapter Fifty 497
Chapter Fifty-One 508
Chapter Fifty-Two 519
Chapter Fifty-Three 527
Chapter Fifty-Four 540
Chapter Fifty-Five 550
Chapter Fifty-Six 559
Chapter Fifty-Seven 566
Chapter Fifty-Eight 579

PART NINE 1918-1919 583
HOME AGAIN: THE PEACE BEGINS

Chapter Fifty-Nine 585

Chapter Sixty 597
Chapter Sixty-One 612

Editor's Afterword 615

Afterword Pictures 623

ENDNOTES 629

Editor's Foreword

Sam Sutcliffe, my father, wrote this memoir over several years when he was in his seventies. The first sentence he wrote — or, at least, the first he sent to me — gave me the title phrase, "nobody of any importance", so typical of his own fierce perspective on himself, so true about the way the First World War made a cannon-fodder, amorphous mass out of millions of individual men.

He told me much of his story during the '60s. He spent his days at home, having retired from the small draper's shop he'd run for years with his brother, Alf — because of his age, but also the post-operational pain which afflicted the last 30 years of his life following radical surgery for rectal cancer in 1955.

His retirement had turned our family's life upside down, though not chaotically; as a child I always felt my parents would deal with the difficulties, no matter what. But suddenly they had no income, bar my father's state pension, and problems with the business in the last couple of years before the shop closed had much depleted their small savings. As a result, they came to a big decision. Contrary to lower-middle-class tradition — and neighbouring families' usual practice on our street in New Southgate, north London — my mother got a job (as a GPO telephonist), and my father became a "househusband" long before the term was invented.

So, luckily in the event, we spent far more time together than most fathers and sons are able to, especially during the school holidays. Through my teens, without any restriction on me going out and about with friends, we did the housework together — me being their only child, he taught me how to hoover and dust and polish to my mother's standards — and we often ate our meals together. He helped me with my homework too.

We'd argue about everything under the sun: sex, politics and religion, of course, but we talked about our lives too. My childhood and youth reported as it happened, his recollected from up to 70 years earlier by his astonishing near-total-recall memory. My mates, his mates; my class bully, his class bully; my A-levels, his Battle of the Somme...

After a while, my mother and I started urging him to write it down, above all his First World War experiences. Eventually, some time after they moved from London to Paignton, Devon, in 1968, and got settled in, he made a start.

THE WRITING

Early in Part Two of his memoir, my father broke off to explain to anyone reading exactly how he'd "written" the text so far — he refers to "Tommy" because he started his story in the third person, with himself-as-narrator observing himself-as-Tommy, if you see what I mean: "Here let me say that a lot of Tommy's story was tape-recorded. Its telling was interlarded with comments from me, not to mention his considerable digressions. Usually I just let the tape run on, so much consideration as to what to leave in and what to cut had to precede the typing of the final manuscript [*by me, I think he meant*]. One would not bother readers of fiction with such details, but here we deal with facts and how a rather simple lad lived through a war which wrought death and injury among millions of people."

He bought a second-hand, reel-to-reel machine for the job. He posted the tapes to me, up in Newcastle where I worked as an apprentice journalist on the *Evening Chronicle*. I transcribed them and sent him copies, along with questions when I wasn't clear about something.

He'd expected recording to suit him because he had difficulty sitting. The surgeon had removed his coccyx (the "tail" of the spine), saving his life, yet leaving him with permanent pain. He took morphine and then synthetic substitute analgesics for the rest of his life. So he would lie on his bed and shift this way and that as convenient, the microphone with built-in stop/start switch in his hand, and proceed with relative comfort — at least, in the two-to-four-hour windows the tablets gave him before the pain, which he described aptly as "like someone sticking a bayonet up your backside", got too wearing for clear thought. (A necessarily registered morphine addict, he controlled his intake to the prescribed dosage with immense, almost merciless self-discipline; my mother and I could read the depth of his pain in the frown lines between his eyebrows.)

However, perhaps feeling his spoken style read a little too loose on the page when he saw the transcripts — and also, I think, starting to "find" himself as a wordsmith — from Part Three onwards, he abandoned taping. Instead, he tried typing for the odd hour he could manage sitting in a chair at a table. But then, for the most part, he took to handwriting on pads of lined paper resting on his knee in bed.

And, with his usual determination and attention to detail — the solid detail of facts, the raw detail of acutely remembered emotions — he kept on going for six or seven years through the '70s, from his first toddler memory to the grand commemoration parade after all the World War One peace treaties were finally signed in 1919.

THE EDITING

I think, in the beginning, my father simply started to tell his story. But, as he moved along, he developed his ideas about what he was doing. In another of his step-back comments, in Part Three, towards the end of the Gallipoli campaign, he wrote: "This reminds me to point out that, throughout this narrative of the experiences of a boy during World War I, no books or records have been consulted, no claims regarding accuracy made or verified.

"Hundreds, perhaps thousands of men have written about their wars or, more frequently, about other men's wars. Historians are the blokes who go in for research, who unashamedly pick other men's brains, and omit what they deem irrelevant, or maybe unworthy, or include what they think important or flattering to the Government which commissioned their researches. So, when completed, the monumental work may in essence be an exercise in mind-bending, those who read it may accept conclusions, regarding participants and results, which are inaccurate.

"Else why should many think that Napoleon was a great man, or any other famous General for that matter? A man who issues orders which result in the deaths or woundings of large numbers of his fellows cannot be considered great in any sense of that word. At the low level of the soldier, or of the artisan who helps to construct the shells, bullets, guns, rockets, with which the soldier does the killing or wounding — no credit lies with them either when judged unemotionally. Nor with the parson who blesses their banners or 'war efforts', as politicians describe their activities."

To sum up, he told the truth as he saw it, no more nor less. But he did want me to work on what he wrote, "improve" the efforts of the boy who had to leave school at 14, make it more readable. I'd gone to university, got a literature degree, done my apprenticeship as a journalist — I was qualified, we'd talked about the whole thing for years, we were close, he wanted me to take part in it, I wanted to do it. For a while, we talked about fictionalising it, interweaving short excerpts of a modern lad's life to age 21 — mine, of course — to compare and contrast with his story. I tried, about 200 pages' worth, but my approach felt egocentric to me, and I wasn't up to it anyway.

To my regret, even shame, I left the whole thing, while promising I would come back to it. This must have disappointed my father, but he never badgered me about it and, I think, actually had faith that I would return to the project when I could.

He died, aged 88, in 1987. And I finally got back to editing his manuscript when I semi-retired from freelance journalism. Luckily secure enough, because of my wife Gay Lee's pension from her career as a nurse, I've spent the last 18 months — with the World War I Centenary a looming deadline of Fleet Street-like insistence — almost full-time doing my best for my father's memory and his life as a formidable, rock-like nobody of any importance.

I had the practical skills from magazine and newspaper writing and subediting, but the job presented technical and emotional difficulties I'd never dealt with before. Get right down to it and how far would any change I made change Dad's truth? Well, I tried to avoid causing any such damage, of course, but there's no chance I pulled that off to perfection. And the unedited transcript (in digital form) will, I hope, be available to anyone interested via various archives — or, in return for a £5 donation to the Red Cross, I'll send it to you individually if you email me at philsutcliffe47@gmail.com.

However, I'd like to tell you about three editorial points which illustrate what I ended up doing to my father's words:

* Bearing in mind what my father wrote (above) about the wholly personal experience, totally unresearched nature of his narrative — not to mention his suspicion of historians — I have added nothing to the text and nothing in the footnotes (or, technically, "endnotes") that could be dignified as "research", much less "scholarship". My regular references to Wikipedia as a source show well enough that nothing in-depth is occurring. But the

footnotes are offered as factual or, at times, self-confessedly speculative explanations of anything from archaic/arcane words my father uses, to basic historical or geographical background. I hope they're useful if you use them — but you don't have to!

* Addressing my father's writing style, like any editor of any piece of writing, I could only form an opinion and act on it. Essentially, I think he chose his words particularly well and put sentences together with anything from competence to flair. The exception was a preoccupation with using the passive voice — you know, "dinner was served" instead of the active "they served dinner". It's a true truism that this slows everything down, undermines immediacy, generally cuts the nuts off any kind of storytelling. I don't know why he had that habit: as a practice, from school? and/or from "English" or personal reserve, the instinct to back away from his feelings in some fashion even as he dug deep into his heart and soul for the sweetnesses and the agonies? Whatever it was, I decided readability demanded that whole regiments of sentences be turned around — no, that I turn them around (see what a trap it can be!) — from passive to active. The aim: same words, same meaning, different momentum. But I also decided that in the context of his relationship with the Army, the passive voice had something to say: that the individual soldier is not in control, he is a pawn, a tool, so the impersonality of "we were ordered to" and any number of other passive actions was dead right and I left most of them alone to tacitly create a realistic underlying tone.

* Point of view is where my father's memoir gets wholly "unprofessional" — and I didn't change a thing because the "confusion" seems honest and meaningful. As mentioned above, he started out calling himself "Tommy Norcliffe" and writing about himself from the third-person narrator point of view. Then, in Part Two (Chapter Nineteen), a while after he's lied about his age and enlisted, a transition begins. More or less out of the blue, my father begins to quote "Tommy" as if he'd interviewed him and written down his responses. So Tommy speaks direct and first-person in quotes for two or three pages. Then my father reverts to all-seeing-narrator third-person for a bit... but pretty soon he gives it up and jumps off whatever literary cliff he was teetering on and right into first-person "I" mode from there on for the duration. Perhaps I should have smoothed that out too. But, apart from adding explanatory point-of-view endnotes at the transitional moments for those who didn't read this foreword, I left it as my father wrote it — gut-feeling that it expresses something strong which anyone may care to take their own guess at... But I'd see it as, possibly, his sense of outsider distance from the child, schoolboy, young working lad who grew up in peacetime, and his sense that the real Sam Sutcliffe, including the old man writing this story, began with foot-soldiering through World War I.

AUTHOR'S ROYALTIES

All the author's/editor's royalties for the e-book version of this Memoir — probably 35-45 per cent of the "cover" price, depending on distributor — will be donated to the British Red Cross. I hope some of the distributors may give some or all of their take to the same charity. On the print version, all royalties from commercial vendors plus all "profit" above the cost of printing, postage and packing on copies I sell via Footsoldiersam. blogspot.co.uk or otherwise will go to the Red Cross. As you'll see, they saved my father's life once, at Gallipoli, and, throughout his war, he observes how they and other medics, from surgeons to stretcher-bearers, dedicated themselves to saving lives no matter what the risk. I know my father would be delighted to see a few quid generated by his efforts go towards sustaining an organisation he so admired.

Phil Sutcliffe, July, 2014

PART ONE

1898-1912

AT HOME:

CHILDHOOD TO LEAVING SCHOOL

Chapter One

May I say straight away he became nobody of any importance...

The child, the boy, the youth, the man whose life I am going to talk about, think about, write about... his earliest recollections are of several incidents which occurred in a northern town — a dull, damp, depressing place.

He remembers sitting on the floor of a kitchen with a lady — Mrs Rowbottom he called her — giving him titbits as she proceeded with her cooking. Little sweet pastries. He blesses the memory of Mrs Rowbottom.

He remembers too a shop full of toys, particularly a drum — he was allowed to tap away on this drum... He gathered that his mother owned this toyshop and life at the toyshop went on happily for him...

Except for one strange memory. As he learned how to feed himself and draw crudely with crayons his mother noticed he was left-handed — "cack-handed" she called it. She didn't like it, the boy didn't understand why, but she forced him to change, nagging him, slapping his left hand away from the knife or the jam pot when his mistakes had particularly annoyed her. Of course, he obeyed; he learned to live right-handed. But, for a long time, it felt wrong.

So, 1900 it must have been[1]. The boy aged two, living in Manchester with two brothers, one a couple of years older than him, the other younger, a sister five years older, a mother and father[2] an apparently happy, comfortable home.

He remembers a very pleasant outing, a visit to Belle Vue. Belle Vue — he didn't know what it meant or what it was, but he saw animals there, pretty things called deer. He looked through the railings into their green enclosure... And fireworks, the great firework display... bursting rockets, humming rockets, whistling rockets, a lovely picture in the night. Such little things… they remain with him always.

Then experiences of that sort became all too rare. It would have been a treat to see a smile on mother's face. He seldom saw that these days. He remembered her going round the place singing and generally enjoying life. But all that was fading, replaced by a heaviness, a constant worry and depression — resulting in perhaps rather harsh treatment of the children at times.

The sad situation arose because her father-in-law had died unexpectedly. Not many years out of grammar school, in his early twenties, and there was her husband in charge of this business: a works with a number of employees. A manufacturer of tiles and all sorts of related fittings, kerbs and so forth, fashionable back then. Coloured, beautifully decorated tiles sold all over the country. One large London store placed a regular order.

Unfortunately, due to his youth, pitchforked into becoming head of the family firm — the proprietor — and ill-equipped for the post, he could not exercise control over his two younger brothers. It became known later that they had put stock to wrongful use, disposing of it secretly and taking the money. Incompetence further depleted the firm's stocks when consignments were sent to places where they shouldn't have gone so no payment was received. And the new young boss's mother expected the same high standard of living she had enjoyed when her husband was still alive; large sums of money, which should never have been taken from the business, went to maintaining her in that style. Other members of the family needed allowances too — two young women studied at Girton College, Cambridge, of all places — how expensive that must have been.

Everything pointed towards what eventually happened — financial collapse.

While the father was doing the best he could to cope, the mother tried to keep the family going with some money she put by herself. She started a small retail business in children's toys — the shop the boy remembered — and did quite well for a short time until it was brought to her notice that, with the family firm in a state of suspense pending liquidation, it was wrong for her to conduct a business of any sort, so she had to close it down.

Not knowing where the next meal was coming from taxed her ingenuity to the limit. To provide the bare necessities she even went to work for a manufacturer and wholesaler of men's trousers. She knew very little of this trade. She took samples around the poorer type of men's clothiers and tried to induce them to place orders. She had a little success but, really, competition was so keen that a newcomer didn't stand much chance of opening an account with many tradesmen.

Then, another change. The boy found they were living in a much poorer area. A row of houses, small[3]. Going out of the back door one came to a long, continuous yard common to all the houses. No dividing fences at all. Privies against the yard's rear wall. The people were kindly to him and his brothers and sister. But worry and anxiety hung over all. Each day seemed dark and drab and dull in a heavy way, which only the weather in a Northern industrial town can contrive. So oppressive to a child.

About this time he began to miss his father. "Where's Pa?" he would ask his mother. "Where's Pa?" "Oh, he's gone to London to see what he can do down there and later we shall join him." Sad news, this, for the boy because he really loved his father, even though he'd only seen him at bedtimes. Sometimes father would join the children as they were prepared for bed and the boy remembered a cot in which he had slept in earlier days, made of ironwork, though similar in design to the wooden cots of today. For some reason the boy recalled standing up in it, calling out, "Father! Father!" And father came. Said the things that fathers said to their children and laid him down, comforted. Off to sleep the boy went.

Soon a great bustle of activity. Packing. Everything being loaded into cases, boxes, crates. He saw all this going on and, before very long, off they all went to the big railway station and soon boarded a train. Full of excitement now, of course, headed for London, for the big town where their father was, leaving that drab place. And, on that account alone, feeling much happier than they had done for some time.

At one point on the journey a railway official came into the carriage and inspected tickets. He looked at mother — they were alone in the compartment, mother and the four children — and he said, "I quite understand, short of money, eh? Can't pay for tickets for all of them. Well, where you think it's necessary — and if we stop at a station — put two of the children under the seat... Do as I say. That will help." And so they followed that procedure. As stations approached or the train slowed down, the younger two brothers would pop under the seat.

The boy remembers the clothes he wore that day. He heard later that it was called a Little Lord Fauntleroy Suit. Nice, green material. Green velvet. A long jacket, a belt, knickers to the knee and a hat — a sort of Tam O'Shanter — all of the same cloth. He particularly remembered arriving at the London station and looking at this suit of his and feeling quite proud of it.

They all climbed into a horse-drawn cab at the terminus, their bags piled up beside them, and off through the busy streets — seeing all these carriages and big wagons drawn by numbers of horses. Horses everywhere. Splendid sight. Temporarily at least, life seemed to be on quite a prosperous plane. It wasn't so really, of course. They just had no other means of transporting the family and baggage across London.

They went into a big building, a hotel right down in the East End, a district called the Minories[4]. They were shown to a room with only two beds in it for the five of them. A temporary arrangement mother had made. She said she had rented a flat on the outskirts of the city, but they couldn't move in for two or three days. The excitement of watching the comings and goings occupied the time they remained there. Then once more to a horse-drawn cab — their last ride in such a vehicle for many a day. The journey took an hour or so — the children peering about all the way, everything around them of interest.

The mother had relied on father doing reasonably well on his arrival. The flat had three bedrooms, a sitting room, kitchen and the "usual offices", as the saying went. After a few days, sufficient furniture having arrived from the North, it felt comfortable. They settled down[5].

Sad to say, though, when father arrived his news was not good. Two wealthy friends of his from the time when he too was quite well off had promised to help him — put business his way. On his behalf, they got in touch with firms who required an agent in London. Of these, though, only one, a company based in Germany, had immediately offered him a solid opportunity to work. He'd taken samples of their product around day after day, walked miles, far too many — although, at that time, a great deal of walking was done by people in all sorts of business. Despite some tramways and a few bus services, generally, outside the City of London itself, travel was not so easy.

Anyway, father had secured a number of orders, so a fair amount of commission was already due to him. Accordingly, he requested payment, but it had not been forthcoming. He continued in hope.

Mother was terribly disappointed that he had no money to give her. It meant that supporting the family fell on her shoulders. Certain precautions she had taken appeared to be the only hope of keeping them going. In addition to the furniture, she'd had some valuable glass and chinaware sent down from Manchester. It now reposed in a beautifully made cabinet and, from time to time, she carefully disposed of single articles to a dealer. He must have been a fair-minded man; she said he gave her quite good prices and, with this money, at least a start was made. For a time, at any rate, they were able to live, not well, but adequately.

Chapter Two

At the first opportunity, mother took them to a school. The older brother and sister had, of course, been sent to school in Manchester, but under slightly better circumstances because the parents had been able to pay for their education. In London they attended an ordinary council school — quite a good school, but utterly strange to the boy.

Two of the teaching staff impressed themselves on the lad on the first afternoon and thereafter. The headmistress of the infants' school, Mrs Mortimer, was a large woman, her face rosy, the skin of it rough, a rather forbidding figure. Her eye pierced you. Doubtful whether he ever saw her smile. But she had to be encountered only once or twice a day at most, in assembly and sometimes a special afternoon lesson.

His class spent most of each day with a Miss Tasket and his attention became centred on the little mannerisms she had. When afternoon tea came round — for the teacher only, of course, not for the children — she invariably indulged in two or three biscuits. Fascinating to him was the way in which she carefully chewed them with a rather extensive movement of the lower jaw up and down, up and down. He gazed at her with longing for one of the biscuits. In fact, the whole classful of children would watch her, the liveliness of their interest in the proceedings determined by the state of their tummies. But he came to look forward to the performance as part of the day's entertainment. This movement of the lower jaw... He'd never seen anybody eat quite like this. So carefully.

But it turned out that this orderly first day and the boy's peaceful contemplation of Miss Tasket had given him a false impression of how tranquilly his introduction to schooling in London might proceed.

Within a few days, as the other children grew bolder, whenever Miss Tasket or another teacher called on him to answer a question his accent started to attract adverse attention because it was so different from what all the Cockney kids around him were used to. The trouble really started when, for some reason, he had to say "photograph". With his Mancunian vowels, it came out "phawtawgraph", with a short, hard "a" in the final syllable. They all laughed — many, it seemed to him, with that mean, harsh, forced laugh children produce when they want to wound one of their fellows. "It's 'phoetoegraaph'!" one of them yelled and in a trice the whole class was chanting "Phoetoegraaph! Phoetoegraaph! Phoetoegraaph!" until Miss Tasket exerted her rather languid authority and quietened them, though saying only that the noise must stop without explaining that their mockery was wrong and cruel.

Over the following days, similar derisive eruptions occurred when he'd say "coom" — "Cum! Cum! Cum!" — or "glass" with that short "a" — "Glarss! Glarss! Glarss!" The boy cringed with shame and embarrassment.

At once, and desperately, he tried to change the way he spoke. With his first, momentary, new friend — a forgotten name — he spent an afternoon's play, as it might have been, under a table; he couldn't remember where, but he had a clear picture of it, the thick table legs, the dark shadows, the other lad's Cockney quack, exasperated yet persistent and somehow kind as he repeated time after time "T'ain't plànt, it's plarnt! *Plarnt!*" and "T'ain't bàth, it's barth! *Barth!*" The boy copied him diligently and found he had a good ear. Impelled by raw fear of ridicule, within a couple of weeks — if he measured his words carefully — he could speak with a fairly anonymous middling English accent which, at least, did not provoke mass mockery. At which, mercifully, the other children forgot about him and he returned to the obscurity he craved.

Soon, they all settled down, with the sister in charge of the boys. But gradually the three took to going to school and returning by themselves although they weren't supposed to, especially the youngest boy.

To children, the distance from house to school felt considerable. Down the road, round a corner, round another corner, and they came to a busy main road, the traffic all horse-drawn — horses everywhere, horses pulling small carts, great wagons. Milkmen used them, bakers used them delivering house to house. But the boy took a particular interest in horse-drawn trams. He had never seen anything like them. The horses weren't big really — large ponies you'd call them. Two of them pulled each tram along on its rails, the driver seated at the front, the reins in one hand, a light whip in the other. A conductor on the back collected the fares. The lower deck was glazed, the upper deck open to the sky.

Strange that coming to live in this busy town brought him into contact with animals; not nature in the raw, but nature anyway. Manure constantly cluttered the roads. A deal of urine lay around. The boy and thousands of children like him watched the normal processes of what you might call intake and output and very soon clearly understood what was going on.

These tram drivers, for instance, would be observed closely by the children, especially when they came to a terminus. Our boy would stand there and, if there happened to be a fairly long wait between arrival and departure, watch the driver put the bag of corn or chaff under the horse's nose, pass the strap over its head, and adjust it so that the animal could eat comfortably. He'd see the horse's jaws champing away. Every now and then it would blow hard when the dust got in its nostrils. To see a bucket of water placed in front of one of these ponies, that was worth watching. In went the horse's mouth, a sucking and pumping operation followed, the speed at which the water vanished from the bucket unbelievable.

That was the front end of the animal. The rear held his interest equally. Some horses, he noticed, had one opening just under the tail and some had two. One can't say that the reasons for this were clear to him at first. He knew that if the tail went up and the animal was of the type which had one opening, dollops of manure would issue forth, landing on the road with a series of thuds and what, to him, was quite a pleasant smell. If the animal had two of these openings, if he saw the lower one moving he knew that a jet of water would presently shoot out. It was advisable to step back because, although the water had no bad odour, if one arrived home with shoes and socks soaked with the stuff there would certainly be trouble from mother.

He was learning, all the time learning.

It soon became obvious to him that the animal with only one of these openings must have an outlet elsewhere for the water. On the first occasion it became apparent to him, he watched, with wide-eyed amazement, the emergence from immediately in front of the horse's hind legs a big, long thing from which poured forth a stream of liquid splashing into the road and flowing away along the gutter.

So that explained how the two types of animal urinated and he thought no more about it. But sometimes a horse some distance away would put up his head and neigh loudly, perhaps start to jump about, even lash out with his hind legs, his hooves cracking against the bodywork of the tram or cart. The boy didn't quite understand the reason for this behaviour, although he realised it was connected with some other animal in the vicinity. But it wasn't for him to know that the noisy, frisky animal was disturbed by one of the opposite sex.

It wasn't just horses. One could see cattle driven along a busy road to market, a flock of sheep — just one old man with his stick and a dog controlling them. Butchers bought sheep live at the nearest market and had them driven to their own slaughterhouses.

Animals everywhere...

The lad came into further contact with ponies because his road ended in a low, large field. You went down an embankment and there horses were put to graze. A free feed. Quite a consideration for the owners, no doubt.

Well, one day the children were playing in that field and the horses all gathered into a mob. When that happened, usually there was fighting — they bit each other or, more often, presented their rear ends to their foe and shot out their back legs to catch him a whack in the ribs with their hooves. The children would watch, excited.

But, on this occasion, when the children turned to leave, the mob of horses all followed them from the field up the embankment on to the road. Why they did it, I don't know — unless they thought the children were leading them to food or water — but the children got rather scared. So the sister led them up the pathway to an unoccupied house, thinking the horses would go straight on. But they didn't, they followed the children to the front door. So now you had the children cowering against the door with several of the horses crowded in between the house and the front-yard railings while others waited on the pavement.

How fortunate then that, after a while, their father came home, carrying his customary walking stick. You can picture his astonishment when he saw the children's predicament. In wealthier times, he had owned a fashionable trap drawn by a smart pony — he had aspired to teach it to trot, an ambition of many well-to-do men. So, used to horses and unafraid, he edged his way into the yard and beat the horses off with his stick. Quite a feat. He took the children home.

As winter came on, the poorly surfaced roads frequently became slippery and, on several occasions, the boy saw horses fall down and become tangled in their harness. When this occurred, the driver would climb down as quickly as possible and sit on its head. The first time the boy saw this happen, the horse lay quite still so he thought, "He's finished, he's dead". But he soon realised this was the accepted method of controlling a fallen horse and preventing it from trying to get up while tangled in harness, which might loosen or break the shafts.

At this point, while the driver remained seated on the horse's head, almost any man in the neighbourhood would help to free the beast. Then, with much slipping and sliding on the ice, the poor thing would scramble up — the forelegs first, they'd straighten out, then the hind legs would get a grip on the road and up would come the rear half, and there it would stand, usually quite placid.

The boy noted all these things and gleaned knowledge about life as it went on along the road...

Coming home from school one day, he paused and looked at a man lying on the grass. He had a light, almost yellow pair of shoes on. He was rubbing them with a banana skin. The boy wondered if banana skins were good for cleaning shoes — he never found out.

After a few weeks, he discovered a quicker and more interesting way home, through a large park. He would run along a path uphill, then down, and over a carriage road — a road on which ladies would be driven by their coachmen for an afternoon's outing away from the main road and all the other traffic.

There, the boy had a rather startling experience one day. He had raced up the incline and was making great strides, great speed for him, down the slope. He came to the carriage road looking neither left nor right, expecting nothing, when he ran full tilt into the side of a coach — he grabbed at it, but he could not prevent his head crashing into the side of it and he rebounded clear and fell, blinded momentarily. On recovering to some extent, he felt his sore head, toddled on and managed to get safely home where his sister chided him for being careless and going what she called the wrong way. But she was soon applying cold water to the swelling lump on his forehead, so the incident was forgotten by all, except him.

It's doubtful if his mother ever heard anything about it. She, in common with many busy mothers, reacted violently to any little accidents, any injuries sustained, and the children would think twice before letting her know about anything of that kind, particularly if it was their own fault. If the boy could plant the blame somewhere else it wouldn't matter, of course. If he could say so-and-so — his brother, sister or some other child — had been at fault, he would tell that with joy, with relish, hoping for some sympathy or perhaps even something more substantial by way of compensation or reward.

Still no cash came in to father from the German firm. So mother did various little jobs to augment the sales of china — and then of their good furniture. The children observed that she began to wear, for part of the day at least, a nurse's uniform. She had become a doctor's assistant. An epidemic of smallpox was sweeping the country and occupying the regular nursing services. Pregnant mothers could not be taken into any clinic or hospital and had to be nursed at home, although the risk remained that any kind of visiting health worker might carry this awful disease into their house.

And further trouble did come to the boy's own family. He caught scarlet fever, and soon after that his brothers and sister fell sick too. Mother had to nurse the children and still go out to work. She did it all quite successfully. She had acquired a book published by a firm that made antiseptics; she read it carefully and, sticking closely to its instructions, she never did anything that could bring risk to the women she went out to help. The boy noticed the meticulous care with which she changed from ordinary clothes into her nurse's uniform.

For three or four weeks the children were confined to their home. Mother would give them all the attention possible, leave food, medicines and instructions about what to do with her daughter, and then off she went. They would look out of the window and wave to her as she walked briskly up the street. Then they turned in upon themselves, amused themselves — not always happily, little squabbles occurred — but time passed and they were cured.

Mother saw that living must become very frugal. She devised a system of apportioning food. Bread, for instance. For breakfast, slices were cut and the cheapest sort of margarine spread on them. She gave each child five half slices of bread for breakfast. Dinner comprised the cheaper sort of meat and potatoes, some greens. Five more pieces of bread at teatime.

Jam vanished from the table, except that it might appear once a week. Sometimes not. Beyond that, nothing available for the children. And this had to go on for several years.

So, when one day our boy saw a lad younger than himself sitting on the ground tearing up paper and eating bits of it, he asked him, "Why are you eating paper?" "Because I'm hungry," said the boy. Our lad thought, "Perhaps it would help if I could do the same". He tore up some paper and chewed it, but, oh, it tasted horrible. He never resorted to that again and he didn't hear what became of the little boy who had been eating quite a lot of it.

The family's situation gradually became worse. The flat proved too expensive. The mother arranged to join a family who lived in the house opposite and rent a floor from them.

Life took a change, then — not for the worse by any means as far as the children were concerned. They had the company of the other family's children and their good Cockney parents. Cheerful. Hard up, but happy. A poor, but scrupulously clean home. And the man was a most willing helper. The boy's parents didn't have enough furniture for one of the large rooms, so he quickly re-upholstered an old suite he'd got from somewhere. The skilful way in which he worked and the speed of it fascinated the boy. He sat in the garden watching the man rip the covers and the stuffing off the old chairs, take out the rings, put new webbing straps across the bottom, screw in the springs, then put in the stuffing once more with a new cover of shiny American cloth over it. Apparently, they had a new chair.

But that kindly, strong, active man one day appeared in a very different light to the lad. They had a cat, these people. It was not properly looked after and it made a mess on the floor of the landing upstairs. The boy saw the man grab the cat by the scruff of its neck and rub its nose in the mess, take it to the window on the first floor and throw it out into the garden. The boy understood the man's rage at what had happened, but he thought it very harsh treatment for the poor cat. Still, when he looked out at the garden, there was the cat, frightened, yet none the worse for its adventure. It landed on it's forefeet and went about its business once more.

As they settled in, the boy and his brother began to venture further. Beyond the horses' field they found a disused clay pit filled with water. Old planks and beams floated about in it, left over from previous industrial activity — perhaps brick-making. On this man-made pond, boys became sailors and pirates. They stood on the planks and, holding a piece of wood as an oar, paddled themselves across to the other side. The young brothers watched with admiration. No doubt the water was deep but, if a chap fell in, he could grab a piece of wood and make the shore. Of course, what happened to him when he got home soaked to the skin was entirely his affair.

Tiring of this free entertainment the brothers would make their way home and, en route, our boy would always go to the rail of yet another field where he'd hope to see Daisy, a young cow. Often, she would come over and allow herself to be stroked; he would smell the sweet, grassy breath of her and watch the flies that gathered around her eyes and sometimes beat them off. On one occasion, with no Daisy in sight, there was a horse instead. But what had happened to the poor beast? The lad was shocked when he saw, at the base of the neck where it is broadest, its coat almost in shreds, obviously torn on barbed wire. Mercifully, the owner had already dressed it with some ointment, so this area of torn flesh was a mass of yellow. Something else for him to think about.

A competition between boys became fashionable. It necessitated finding a fairly large smooth stone and a quiet stretch of pavement. Then the boys took turns to skid their stones across the slabs. Wishing to take part, Tommy[6] decided to get some practice. He found himself a suitable stone, an empty pavement and skidded it back and forth, no harm to anybody he thought. But, at one point, looking around he saw two burly men coming towards him. They took hold of him and told him they were policemen in plain clothes and he would be charged with "throwing stones dangerously".

Tommy was scared stiff, of course. He ran home and told his mother what had happened. She was a little worried. It seemed so absurd to hear that two policemen should spend their time looking for such petty misdemeanours as this.

Two days passed with Tommy in a constantly worried, nervous state about this awful crime he had committed. But one day a Sergeant called at the house and mother talked to him for a while. Then she called Tommy in. The Sergeant gave him a lecture on the evils of throwing stones about. He said that, as Tommy had never been in trouble before, and he was aware of the good character of the family generally, on Tommy promising never to do it again, no further action would be taken. You can picture Tommy's relief. The threat of having to go to court was lifted.

Later, his mother told him that, as luck would have it, she had helped the wife of this Sergeant when she was giving birth. This helped considerably when those two plain-clothes constables mentioned the family's name at the police station. The Sergeant took advantage of his rank to hush the matter up.

Chapter Three

In fact, from the boy's point of view, life in general had started to go fairly smoothly. But suddenly a jolt. Father appeared one day and said, "You must say goodbye to your mother for the moment and come along with me. We're off to a different home."

So they set off and walked the quarter of a mile to the end of the road on which they were living — the unbuilt part with fields on either side — and came to the main road where they boarded a horse tram and climbed to the upper deck. For the children, an exciting journey followed. New buildings, new sights. It lasted nearly an hour. Twice the ponies pulling the tram had to be taken out of the shafts and fresh ones installed. It was the custom to change them quite frequently.

The journey finished in what seemed to be a very far away place, a developed suburb eight miles to the north of Central London[7]. Streets of small houses. They walked along until father turned off and led them to a front door at one end of a terraced row. The house was completely empty. At that point, father said, "I shall have to leave you here for a time. I have to see to something. You amuse yourselves."

So now we have three children in an empty house, no food, no warmth, but still the excitement of the new surroundings kept them occupied for some time.

They went to the bedroom at the back and looked out over a small garden. They saw a group of children playing a few doors away and called out to them. By way of response, a boy swung his arm back and threw a stone which hit Tommy on the forehead. A howl of pain, down came the window. Above the pain, fear of the new place and what these children might do. A swelling came up. His brother applied a wet hankie, but the loneliness and anxiety, that wasn't so easily got rid of.

Father didn't reappear and the children felt hungry. No food in the house and no money. They started searching the garden –overgrown with weeds and dumped rubbish. They did discover something that might have been eatable. A piece of bread, green with mould. The boy nibbled at this, but it tasted too horrible.

As darkness fell, the children huddled together in the corner of a room. After what seemed like many hours, a bang on the front door. They rushed down and it was father, in the road behind him a small, horse-drawn van. The driver and father began to unload bedding and a few bits of furniture. Beds were set up: a double bed, a smaller bed, and a cot. Mattresses, sheets, two blankets per bed and a cotton cover, pillows. So, a roof over their heads and a bed to sleep in. But no food still. Cold, sad, nevertheless grateful for their father's presence, they tucked themselves in, quite warm, and went to sleep.

The next day they got dressed and father said, "Well, I must go up to where we lived before. Mother is staying on there for a while to continue with her nursing work and make some money to keep us going until I can work myself. I must see her and get a bit of money to buy some food and bring it to you."Sister started a thorough exploration of the house. The two boys followed her around. She found a sink with one cold-water tap from which they all had a drink. A boiler made of brick and cement with a big metal container for water and a fireplace underneath it. For lighting, gas jets in the back room, the living room, the front room and the passage; upstairs just one, in the largest of the three bedrooms. The boy took stock of the furnishings father had brought along. No floor coverings anywhere. The front room contained a cabinet and a pair of steps, the living room three chairs and one wooden table, the scullery a few pots and pans. Upstairs the three beds. On the landing a large chest covered with hide — a mystery to the children for many a year.

Hungry, fearful, miserable, the children huddled together in one of the beds until, after some hours, father returned. He brought some cheap meat, potatoes and carrots. Although no cook, no handyman at all, he put all these things into a saucepan, boiled them up and shared them out so the children had their first meal. Not a very good one, not a very palatable one, but at least it filled them and warmed them and, with night coming along, they went to bed and forgot all their troubles in sleep.

In the morning, father set off again, but soon returned. He'd had a few coppers left and bought some bread. He showed it to the children, a loaf with a small upper deck and a large lower deck, which could be pulled apart. Not only this, but another piece of bread too. He told them the baker had weighed the loaf and found it not quite up to the two pounds it should have been for tuppence ha'penny. According to custom, he added a piece off another loaf as makeweight. Father cut slices off and handed them round. The children devoured them ravenously before he departed yet again.

They had to amuse themselves for hours around the house and in the rough garden until, towards evening, father turned up, this time with not only bread, meat and vegetables — meat was 2d a pound and the vegetables "a pennorth of pot herbs" — but a real luxury: a cake. One of the people mother worked with had given it to her. They tucked into what they considered a really satisfying meal.

But it was a bleak experience in a bleak house.

While doing what business he could for the German firm — hoping for a lump sum in final payment — father looked for more permanent work. This again entailed a vast amount of walking right across London. He had to arrange to finish up each evening at their previous home and get from their mother money or provisions, anything available to keep the children and himself going.

The boy gradually built up a picture of the area. But he was concerned immediately with four walls, a small railed-in garden, and the terrors which lay beyond.

Of course, changes came. And what a happy day it was for the children when mother arrived. She had visited them quite often, but this time it was for good. It gave them an added sense of security.

And some of the valuable glass and china still remained in the cabinet, so the same dealer who had helped in the past called from time to time and bought one or two pieces. His money helped to maintain some sort of modest supply of food for the family until the day came when father returned home and said he had at last landed a job. It turned out to be a poorly paid one, the fares to the city to come out of the small wage, but at least it assured a regular weekly income and the mother and father could hope to build on it.

With work to go to, after a very frugal breakfast he would set off and walk 15 minutes to the station and then take a train journey into the City of London. If he caught an early train, about 6.15pm, he could travel cheaply. The return ticket had to be bought the previous night, price 2d[8], so his fares for a six-day week (morning only, on Saturday) would cost a shilling — more than could really be afforded, even so.

Now came the question of new schools for the children. Easily solved. An elementary school stood only a 10-minute walk from the house... The two older children fitted into their class quite easily. But Tommy had been to school for only a brief period. Because of the moves from Manchester to London and then from one district to another, he had lost slightly over a year, so he went into the infants' part of the new school. The alphabet, the abacus, and plasticine occupied his days for the first few weeks. Games. Dancing to music on the piano played by the teacher. And the maypole featured quite frequently.

Tommy soon acquired a regular way of living. After his breakfast of bread and margarine and a cup of tea, at 20 to nine he set off for school, ran along with the rest of the children and got there about 10 to. At nine, when a hand bell rang out, the children formed up into double lines, then marched into the assembly hall to a military tune played on the piano. Miss Smith was the pianist, a lady of 30 or so with a mop of curly hair not conforming to the usual fashion of the period. On the highly polished wood-block floor, small white crosses were painted about 30 inches apart. On each one stood a child. They took up the same positions every morning. It had been drilled into them.

They faced the rostrum, a small raised stage with a handrail in front of it, occupied by three persons only. In the middle, the headmistress, a Miss Thomas: a short, sturdy, manly type of woman, ruddy cheeks, bright eyes, certainly knew her job — how to take control of this swarm of children and command silence when silence was needed, singing when singing was required. Everything worked like clockwork, fixing indelibly in Tommy's mind a picture of the hall: the children standing in lines, Miss Thomas's beady eye watching for the movement, the cough, the sniffle which she would not approve... it was really not allowed, you know. The children came to regard the good lady not with fear, but respect, and a wish to please her.

To Miss Thomas's left on the rostrum, Miss Smith — the joy it gave the lad when she played the piano... A feeling when he took his place in assembly each morning that everything was in order, was as it should be.

The brief morning ceremony over, the children formed up again, each class in two lines. Their teachers then lead them off to the strains of another of Miss Smith's stirring marches. In time to the beat — as best they could — they took their places at their desks and faced the teacher. A Miss Booth presided over Tommy's class, a tall, stately lady who usually wore a velvet gown gathered in at the waist. An appearance of depth and stateliness, the ideal matronly figure to command the children's respect. One look from her would subdue even the most difficult child.

When morning school finished, Tom would be allowed to go home for lunch — home now a place where some food could be had, though never a satisfying meal, just enough to keep them going. Perhaps a cheap meat stew with a few vegetables. Puddings were out, of course. Money would never run to that.

Afternoons started at 2 o'clock. To Tommy they always seemed nicer, more friendly, warmer than mornings. He gradually became aware of the children around him in the classroom. To his right, a well-dressed and rather good-looking boy with a quite outstanding name: Nelson-Moxon. How did he come by it? Who were the Nelson-Moxons? What was his family doing in this poor neighbourhood? Nelson-Moxon. Tommy would repeat it to himself while considering these questions. Nelson-Moxon. What a grand name...

To his left a little girl. Bright, rosy cheeks, merry eyes, dark hair... curls across her forehead. Always smiling. They became quite friendly. One day she held out her hand to him and they sat there listening to the teacher, holding hands. But disaster struck. Tommy felt a rumbling in his tummy and soon after that a dampish unpleasant something or other in the seat of his trousers. As realisation of what had happened came to him he freed his hand from the little girl's grip, stood up, dashed down the gangway, out of the classroom, out of the school building, across the playground and the road and into the fields. So to the haven of home. His first romance shattered.

That week when Dad received his first pay packet was long remembered because on the Sunday, very unusually, their mother lit a coal fire in the grate of the kitchen range and they baked rather more potatoes than usual and boiled a small number of haricot beans (hard when bought, they had to be soaked for 24 hours or so before cooking). For this occasion dishes they hadn't used for some time were set out on the table. One for the potatoes, another for the beans, and a larger one for the joint. Mother placed it at the end of the table where father sat. He carved it most carefully, small portions for the children, of course, but the taste of that meat in addition to the beans and the potatoes was a treat.

Chapter Four

Life seemed quite eventful to the young boy from that time on. He learned to read more rapidly than most children do because of the help given him by his sister — even though she only read penny-booklet fairy stories with him — and also, in part, because of a little derision from his elder brother whose reading was well advanced.

Through school, he formed a friendship with two children, Charlie Bolton and his sister, the girl younger than Tommy and the boy older. In fact, the sister played an inadvertent part in easing the shame of his classroom misfortune with the little girl and the rumbling tummy. In the assembly hall one morning, as they all lined up on their crosses, Charlie's sister stood somewhat to his left and ahead of him. He looked at her and noticed a pool of water appearing on the floor around her feet and when he realised what was happening to her he didn't feel so bad about his own ill luck.

On the main road across the field surrounding the school, Charlie's mother kept a small drapery shop. Once, Charlie invited Tommy to step inside. Behind the counter stood two very severe-looking ladies, pale of face and dressed in black. Tommy felt the look they gave him was not very approving and, without a word, he dashed out and, for several years, never set foot inside it again.

Tommy had become conscious of the way he dressed compared to Charlie with his soft collar, good shoes and hose. You could say that class distinction was rearing its ugly head. Then, and on many occasions, he felt inadequate. But he still wished to keep Charlie's friendship. He really loved him and Charlie obviously thought a lot of Tommy.

The cold wind of winter blew around and Tommy's clothing consisted of just a shirt, his jacket and short trousers, socks and short boots. One occasion remained in his memory: facing a strong wind he was brought to a standstill, the freezing cold hitting his body. It really shook him for a moment. But soon he ran on. He and his brother and sister could certainly have done with overcoats — a garment none of them had.

No joy, then, was felt by Tommy or anyone else in the household when, with that standard of living, another child was born, a boy[9]. This must have put off for some time any improvement in conditions for the family.

Tom moved up from the infants into the junior mixed. Girls and boys together in classes learning simple arithmetic and reading. After two years in that class he was presented with a book as a prize. Then the head teacher, a kindly and, as the boy thought, good-looking lady spoke to him, asked his name and so forth, and had a conversation with his class teacher. As a result he moved upstairs to a boys-only department — all ages up to 14 in a series of classes.

There, with space at a premium, the assembly hall had to be used for lessons. Partitions drawn across after assembly screened off two classes. Catching up quickly after his missing year, Tommy bypassed the lowest class. Unfortunately, this meant he never really learnt the geography of Britain, which caused him some inconvenience for years afterwards.

He took a liking to his new form teacher, a young man called Parker, fresh from college. But, shortly, the teacher fell ill and for a couple of days the two groups in the assembly hall joined together and he came under the authority of a very strange man, elderly, with a grey, pointed beard, ruddy face, iron-grey hair and a tongue like a whiplash.

The old boy rambled on, seldom sticking to one subject, telling the youngsters about the Crimean War, the price of tea shortly after it ended — apparently it soared to 8 or 9 shillings a pound and bread went up to a shilling a loaf... and similar bits of fruity information. But regularly, perhaps every ten minutes or less, he would call a lad forward from his desk, instruct him to hold out his hand and wham the cane down on it. Perhaps the boy had been doing something wrong, who knew? But surely that constant procession, wham, howl, surely they couldn't all have been breaking the rules all the time.

No indeed, that old fool was a relic of a previous age of education in this country when it was assumed that all boys were wicked, all boys were bad. Corporal punishment should be administered regularly to keep the little devils in hand.

The stick as a means of maintaining discipline bred no respect in the children. The old boy's nickname, "Dizziba", in those days indicated the first stages of insanity. Even as he walked down the street the bigger lads would yell after him — if they could remain hidden — "Dizziba! Dizziba!" The contrast between that idiot and the young teacher when he returned from his illness was very marked. In most cases, the lads lapped his lessons up. Parker was carroty of hair, pale of face, a jutting jaw, height about 5'10", broad-shouldered — just the type to become a sort of hero to the class. If his legs looked a little bandy, he was always nicely dressed — a rare sight for those boys, a nicely dressed man.

He was so new to the job that he didn't know the golden rule, "nobody allowed outside the grounds during school hours". When the time came for the weekly one hour of physical training, noting that the fields around the school extended for a mile at least in one direction, he took his class out through the gate and organised a game of rounders. But, sadly for us, it wasn't repeated. We heard that the headmaster ticked him off and thereafter that sort of thing had to be done in the playground. They was no sports kit — nobody in Tommy's class could afford it anyway — so their PT comprised just bending and stretching and running around, that sort of stuff; it wasn't too bad.

Occasionally, Tommy would catch sight of his brother, who was two to three classes ahead of him, being both older and remarkably clever. Learning everything rapidly and exceedingly well just came naturally to him. He set a pace in the school which the other lads could not hope to keep up with. But it dawned on Tommy that, as he moved through the school, each master would expect him to follow in his brother's footsteps and match his brilliance. Clearly impossible! He admired his brother, didn't envy him at any time, but probably suffered unnecessary anxiety because of constant comparisons with his talent and performance.

Another year passed and Tommy went on to the next class. He rather feared this because the teacher was a North-Country man, short, wiry, strong, and reputedly rather harsh. But he taught well. He either wrote down or told his boys the things they ought to know and, after a time, he tested them and questioned them and if they didn't know, why didn't they know, huh? He knows over there, why don't you know? Given any suspicion of inattention... out came the stick.

Tommy had only a brief stay with that gentleman because, for some reason, it was decided he should swiftly step up again to the next class — and a teacher of a different type, scholarly, firm, but gentle. The lad who did his best received every encouragement. The teacher selected those he thought the most promising and rearranged the seating to fill one side of the room with the lads on whom he thought it worthwhile to lavish most of his attention.

Finding himself among that top group, Tommy wondered why. He was clean, which was something to a teacher in charge of perhaps 40 small boys but, looking around, he saw that most of them were better dressed than him.

He wore completely home-made clothes. For the first time since they moved to London he had the luxury of a vest, a woollen vest. To make it, mother had cut down an old men's vest. A cotton shirt over that, a white celluloid collar — quite deep and easily washed under the tap, it cost thruppence farthing, no more than that, and no laundry... In addition a sort of jacket; blue, thick, wool cloth, strong and warm — because Tommy's family's next-door neighbour had a son in the navy. He came home once and gave Tommy's mother a complete uniform, a flannel vest, jacket and baggy trousers, in good condition although he'd worn it for some while. Quite a lot of cloth there for her to work on and produce a jacket and knee-length trousers. Of course, the cut wasn't marvellous. The most obvious thing about it was that it was home-made.

The children in Tommy's family had a weekly bath, usually on a Friday evening. Mother boiled water in the large copper and poured it into a galvanised iron hip bath set on the floor in front of the kitchen range. Then she washed each child down. They would sit around in their birthday suits afterwards, the warmth of a good fire there, a pleasant feeling of cleanliness... their garments, roughly made but washed and clean and sweet, ready for them to put on when they wished.

Compulsory school attendance brought together children who otherwise would never have rubbed shoulders. None of their parents well off, though some more so than others, they observed varying standards of cleanliness in their homes. On one occasion Tommy felt a good deal of itching round his body and scratched. Mother noticed and suspected what was wrong. In his vest she found a number of lice. She had never seen them before, but knew about them and wondered where he could have got them from. School? She paid a visit there. "Ah," said that good man, Tommy's teacher. "I'm aware of this already — I found some in my underclothes. We must discover who is bringing them in. I'll confer with my colleagues and we will evolve some plan for finding the carrier."

Predictably, Stinker Jackson turned out to be the one, the host of these wretched lice. Poor Stinker. Even a lad like Tommy could look across at him and see his staring eyes, wide-open mouth, dirt-streaked face, and feel sorry for him and justified in pitying him. Stinker's family relied for their living on keeping pigs. He and his sisters had to work in the sheds, cleaning them out, before they came to school. The smell of the piggery hung about him. By common consent, depending on who was absent with illness, he would occupy the most isolated desk in the classroom. When the lice were discovered, the teacher sent him home with orders to his parents to scrub him up and never let him come back carrying these wretched things again.

The school did try to encourage some universal standards of personal hygiene. Tommy never forgot the day when the head of the junior-mixed department had assembled all classes. There on a small table in front of her she had a long, narrow box and a cup of water. In her hand she held a toothbrush with which she gave a demonstration. In the box was powdered chalk. She dipped the brush in the water, then in the powdered chalk, and carefully brushed her teeth up and down all round and explained the reason for it to the children.

One day a man called at the house and said he represented the sewing-machine company and told mother that if she could possibly spare a shilling a week he would supply her with a machine, introduce her to a firm which made ladies' blouses and dresses, and she could make money by working at home for these people. So it turned out. But they were very elaborate blouses with many tucks and seams and ornamentations, the material velvet or woollen cloth, quite heavy and difficult to work. Each one took a whole day to make up to perfection and the payment on completion would be a shilling. Mother was well and truly in the sweated-labour trade. But there it was, the first shilling was the first payment on the machine. It remained in the family for many years, sewing garments for the children in addition to the work done for the firm.

Now that sewing occupied the greater part of mother's day, an extra burden fell on the daughter. As the eldest, she had to undertake any shopping required, in addition to supervision of the children and the baby — and going to school. In fact, her life became a round of drudgery. But she shouldered her tasks cheerfully at times.

Of course, the conditions under which they lived were not conducive to happiness — a word never used in that household nor in many like it, a state of being with which they were not familiar. One lived. One got sufficient food to keep one going. Frequently, one was hungry. If the children went out for a few hours walking in the open country they might become thirsty. Having no money to buy anything, they would perhaps beg a drink of water from some kind soul they might see in a doorway. They had a sense of lacking many things.

But so too, very often, did their neighbours. They changed quite frequently in those days because people moved house a lot, looking for work. At first, in the house to their right, lived a family called Phillips, the father a brickmaker; in fine weather they were relatively prosperous, but when it turned bad their fortunes sank rapidly. If work became scarce the brickmakers would organise a procession. They'd carry a trade-union banner, one man playing a tin whistle, another an old drum — in fact, they brought out anything that would make a noise and perhaps 200 of them marched through the town, some carrying collection boxes. They would go into shops and ask for a contribution.

But the Phillips family were themselves nice, generous people when they could afford to be. Although, at these times, the father took too much liquor, he interfered with nobody — he would just come home rolling from side to side of the pavement and nobody would see or hear of him for a day or two afterwards. One day, his wife called Tommy over the fence and said, "Here boy, eat this". It was a thick slice of bread liberally covered with butter, real butter — the first real butter he could remember eating…

Soon, though, the Phillipses moved on. The Hills replaced them. A strange mixture they were. The husband was huge, rough-and-ready of manner, probably kind-hearted in his way. Mrs Hill was a little, meek woman. They had several children; one, a girl who looked much like her mother, played the piano quite nicely.

The husband kept a chicken shed in his garden, as did most working-class people back then — but he went in for fighting birds. The fiercer they were, the better he liked them. One cock bird he used to tease. Tommy often saw it fly up towards Mr Hill's face and, when he backed off, it stuck its spurs into the jersey he was wearing. The man enjoyed this sort of rough-and-tumble.

Strangely, the Hills' arrival led to Tommy seeing a dead person for the first time. Mrs Hill suddenly died and, for a reason Tommy never understood, he and his family were invited to go into the front room and gaze upon the body of the woman as she lay in her coffin. No one wished to do this, but it was expected. Tommy looked down and saw this very pale skin like marble. Still. More like a wax model than a human being. He wasn't at all shocked. In fact, he thought how almost-beautiful the little woman looked in death.

Their first neighbours on the other side of their house were totally different. The husband — short, broad-shouldered, with a grey, pointed beard — was German, but spoke English well, with an accent. He had a hobby: growing dahlias. He put in a striking amount of work to produce the flowers he wanted. To start with, he removed the topsoil to spread manure, then re-covered it. The resulting show brought a marvellous mass of colours to an otherwise drab street.

In due course, they moved on, their successors unusually well-to-do compared to most who ever lived in Tommy's street. Husband and wife and a small boy of four or five, they lived and dressed well. The little boy had everything he wanted. Tommy and his brothers and sisters saw this, But they accepted it as being life.

On one occasion, in the evening there came a banging on the front door. Tommy opened it and this woman, her little boy in her arms, rushed in and begged his mother, "Can you help me? The little chap's swallowed a mouth whistle."[10] It was stuck in his throat, impeding his breathing. His mother was frantic, of course. Tommy's mother promptly took hold of the child by his ankles, turned him upside down, and got his mother to give him a smart slap on the back. At once, this expelled the whistle from his throat and, apart from a little soreness, he appeared none the worse. The gratitude of his mother was pathetic to see.

Despite their lack of money, the children found much to excite them in the neighbourhood, especially the terrific activity on the nearby main road out of London[11]. Stacks of wooden blocks and pipes and tall, iron standards appeared, laying by the roadside. Work lasting several years began. Hordes of navvies with pick and shovel dug trenches and laid tramlines in a new road surface made with wooden blocks (replacing the granite chips which had previously done the job).

Following the roadworks led the children to explore further. Much open space lay beyond the new street they lived in; fields and market gardens, a farmhouse with a large barn and pigsty. Tommy liked all the natural smells. Temporarily, they lived at the very edge of the city.

They found brickfields — where Mr Phillips had worked, no doubt. They watched as workers dug up clay and mixed it with water to form a thick mud they called "pug", which they then moulded and baked. The manufacture all took place in the open air.

Then, among the tall grass of the fields around their school, they found kerbs and manhole covers laid at intervals along what had obviously been intended as a road. They learned that, during an earlier boom period encouraged by the extension of the suburban railway line, speculators put up street after street of cheap terrace houses. But the bubble burst and they abandoned the work at whatever point it had reached when the money ran out. You could still walk around streets they had completed, though "To Let" notices stood outside many of the houses. Someone told Tommy the rents ranged from about 6/6 to 8/6 per week, low even for those times.

The children and their friends sometimes repaired to an area of bushes and small trees among the surrounding fields. Christened The Rookery, it became one of their playgrounds. Under one of the bushes they made a secluded home. They would play games around it and then crawl into this shelter in the bush. They spent many happy hours there.

To one side of this Rookery was a huge unfenced area planted with rhubarb. It grew beautifully there, never touched or pilfered by anybody. However, one day a rumour spread among the children of the neighbourhood to the effect that the land had been sold and the owner had decided to give away all the rhubarb — on a certain day everyone could go there and help themselves. Who started this yarn nobody ever discovered, but on the appointed day hundreds of children and some adults too arrived with sacks, bags, and little barrows they had made out of boxes, and they proceeded to pull the entire crop. In a short space of time they'd cleared the whole field. Not a stick of rhubarb left. Tommy ate some of it raw, skinning the sticks... he still remembers the sharp taste of the all-green ones compared with that of the red.

Although their row of houses where the children lived had been completed and the drains and gas pipes laid, the builder still had to suspend operations from time to time — due to lack of money it seemed — and the road itself still hadn't been made up. No footpath, no pavement, no lampposts, no surfaced road, just the rough ground. But the builder was a very nice man, Tommy thought. He'd supervise his men working on the houses at one end of the street, while at the other he collected the rents for the occupied houses.

One day, he very optimistically mentioned to Tommy's parents the possibility that they might want to buy their house. Small hope of that, but it was interesting to note the price he was willing to accept: £150. Externally it was quite a nice-looking, working-class home with a front bay window, its pillars and wide sills of a red stone, which must have been cheap then.

The builder had a large number of horses to pull the carts his men used and he stabled them at the end of the road. Again, Tommy was able to get close to these animals. As a special favour, the builder sometimes allowed him to go into the stable's central cobbled area, sometimes even to clean out the stalls — rake out straw and manure while the horses were out at work, hose down the floors and walls, and refill their mangers with hay or chaff or grain.

That introduced him to an activity which sometimes produced a few pennies. Men who worked their gardens for food or flowers needed manure and sometimes Tommy was able to get a few buckets from the stable. On occasion, the dahlia-loving German next door would purchase their wares. Often, though, it had all been sold to a market gardener on contract, so Tommy and his brother took to scouring the neighbourhood streets to find what their customers wanted. With a bucket and a small shovel they'd set off in the early hours of the morning. A large bucketful of horse manure fetched one penny. A valuable coin.

Chapter Five

Not long after the family's arrival in this growing suburb, it had occurred to mother that church attendance would be good for the children. She probably would not have time for it herself and father would not want to do anything of that sort because the religion to which he had been slightly attached in Manchester was Unitarianism and there was no branch of that somewhat obscure sect nearby. So sister was given the job of seeking out a suitable place where they could go on Sundays.

Somebody told her about a small church half a mile along the road — a "tin church", they called it. She set off one Sunday with the other children and found it standing back from the main road, surrounded by rough grass. She took them in. They were accepted immediately and, each according to their age, given a place in a Sunday school class.

The tin church had a small hall attached with, at one end, a platform bearing a small organ, its pipes brightly painted, and a couple of tables at which sat the people who were going to conduct the service. To the side of the platform stood two tall, anthracite stoves of roughcast metal, their chimneys poking out through the roof. With them alight, the place warmed up comfortably. The stoker was a Mrs Pavitt — small, thin, wispy grey hair, toothless, pale blue eyes, a sort of smile from time to time. She seldom spoke, but worked very hard to keep this place warm and clean even though the odd shilling or two would be all that this poor community could afford to pay her.

At the organ for a rousing hymn, a tall, young man called Cyril Smith perched on a stool, his rather lank hair flopping down over his forehead — but a nice face with a good smile. The preacher would read aloud a verse of Rally Round The Banner or some similar lively, lilting, marching sort of hymn, then off Cyril would swing and the congregation heartily followed, singing various parts to the best of their ability. Turning the pages of the sheet music for him, if necessary, and keeping close to him, was his girlfriend... I suppose you would call her. Marjorie Peters had blue eyes, bulging somewhat, a broad nose, very prominent, front top teeth, a healthy colour in her cheeks and as tall as Cyril. A well-matched pair. She too played the organ and socked out those bracing hymns.

Two men took charge of the service for the whole congregation. Two very different types. Mr Reardon, rather flat of foot, average height, a good head of hair and a droopy moustache, much given to smiling. When he preached a sermon or composed a prayer there was gaiety to it, happiness, and he played a very sweet euphonium when they went out to sing their hymns in the street. Mr Reardon worked as an insurance agent, collecting local people's pennies and halfpennies door to door.

His opposite number, Gillette, had a deep bass voice, splendidly underpinning the hymns. They may never have consulted the music, but some of the congregation had a fair ear for an alto, treble or tenor line and the whole thing didn't sound too bad. When they sang, Gillette's face was white, but his eyes burned. Young, with a blue chin and a big Adam's apple, when he preached it was with all the depths of sincerity he could muster. His strong speaking voice was just the vehicle to transport the brimstone and fire which would be slopped over the people should they stray from the narrow, straight path. Yet, while he stood on that small platform, his eyes would stray to follow Marjorie Peters's every movement, and when he sang solos to her organ accompaniment his loud voice became harsh with emotion, his face more lugubrious every time he looked her way.

The children in the choir and congregation noticed every detail. "Cor, look at his dial now!" they'd mutter. They felt that his unrequited love for her as a little local tragedy in which they were all, to some extent, concerned — and that the fiery words he used in his addresses would become soft entreaties were there any possibility that Marjorie might gaze smilingly upon him. All this lent a little colour to those parts of the service, which might otherwise have seemed dull.

On Sunday afternoons the children went to Sunday school and sat at benches arranged in groups around the teacher's chair. Tommy's group had a Mr Blackhead, a little man, ashen of face, a bluish, shaved-but-still-visible beard, black, wavy hair, small, dark eyes, 45 perhaps. Certainly he wasn't an open-air type and one could assume that he worked in a foundry.

What made such a working man become a Sunday-school teacher Tommy didn't know, but every Sunday he took charge of 10 or 12 children, read a passage or two from the Bible, then talked to them. One couldn't like him, one couldn't dislike him — the children just listened. If you happened to sit near him his sourish breath would come floating over. That was bearable. But his message was not a very clear one. His class was useful in that it helped to pass the time.

These sessions did occasionally become a little more pleasurable, though, when the children were encouraged to present a small entertainment for their parents. Tommy always remembered a girl called Bessie reciting a poem; he couldn't recall the title or what it was about, but he liked something about the way she spoke — not surprising as his mother told him later that Bessie had taken elocution lessons. (Coincidentally, through the chapel, Tommy became friendly with Bessie's brother, Reggie, although for some time he didn't realise they were related.)

Mr Blackhead turned up one Sunday and showed them a card headed "The Anti-Smoking League". Below followed some description of the horrors and dangers of smoking and he invited the children to join, on payment of a small fee per year. Shortly after that, Tommy did use one of his dung-collecting pennies to become a fully paid-up member.

One sunny Sunday evening, the smiling and happy Reardon stood on the platform, euphonium under arm, and called upon the brothers to sally forth into the streets and take the message to the people. With Cyril and Marjorie carrying a small harmonium between them, the whole congregation set off. In a side street they formed a circle, the harmonium in the middle. All had their hymn books with them and, led by the two instruments, they sang heartily. "Happy day, happy day, when Jesus washed my sins away/He taught me how to watch and pray." If the little bag passed around at one of these street meetings realised two or three shillings, that would be a very good evening.

Over the year or so during which the children attended that chapel, they put the odd ha'pennies and pennies they'd saved into the annual outing fund — a trip to the sea, the crowning day of the year for the children. When it arrived, their excitement was intense. The Sunday-school teachers took them to the nearest railway station where they boarded a specially chartered train. The cost per head must have been very small.

Tommy paid no attention to the name of their destination, but the thing he did remember was the tea. Lots of women bustling about ushered them into a big hall, hustling them towards trestle tables. Enamel mugs full of lovely tea. Bread and butter. Butter! What a treat. And cake. Plenty of cake. The cake did smell lovely, it really thrilled Tommy.

And after all that, mother suddenly discovered they had gone to the wrong church! Had sister taken them just a little further along and to the right side of the main road they would have found a Church of England. Another tin church — corrugated iron, that is.

As mother reminded them, they had been christened into the C of E[12] shortly after their arrival in London. At that time a lady had called and given them some little silvery sweets which they had relished. She chatted with mother, told her she was a visitor from a nearby church, and learned of the family's circumstances. So she sent along some very useful things: a sack of coal and a few items of food.

Mother could do no less than take the children along to that church and have them christened. Previously, this wasn't considered necessary. Up north, it was probably assumed that they would follow the religion of their father and grandfather. But they had joined the C of E fold and now the discovery of the correct tin church began a better and very interesting phase in the life of the family.

This was a mission church.[13] A large church in the wealthy part of the West End of London had set aside a fund to establish a mission among the poor people living in these semi-developed outer-London suburbs. There was no real hint of snobbery or class in this. The clergyman received a very small salary.

He turned out to be a very likeable man. Glanfield Rowe was his name. He, his wife and child lived in a small dwelling close to the church. As was the custom, soon after the children joined his congregation, he visited their home. He met mother and later father also. Mr Rowe being a reasonably well educated man, father felt that here was somebody to whom he could talk freely.

The two met on several occasions, on one of which father was persuaded to change his faith and be baptised into the Church of England. He was well on in years, but it presented no difficulty. The collapse of the family business in Manchester had dealt a severe blow to father. Ever since, he had become rather timid and fearful. But his association with the rector in this small church seemed to stiffen his morale a bit. He got a slightly better job as an under-manager in the shipping firm for which he was working and this meant a small rise in salary.

The strict allowance of five half-slices of bread and marge at breakfast and tea-time was abandoned. The children were allowed to eat their fill. They still never had any butter, and jam only occasionally. But meals improved and, reasonably warm too in that home-made suit, Tommy felt he started paying a little more attention to what went on around him.

So did his brother. Quite a tough, resourceful chap, said, "We must do something about our garden", and thereafter took a great interest in it. As a first step, he led Tommy and big sister over to The Rookery where he selected two small trees which had grown from seed. He dug them up carefully, damaging the roots as little as possible, and together they carried them home. He dug a hole at each end of the garden, filled them with water, stood the saplings in them and packed earth round them, poured more water on, then mixed some more earth with water and stirred it into a sludge which he piled in cones around the narrow trunks. They took and grew. Some years later they were beauties, lime trees.

But home life remained variable. Despite recent slight improvements, the trial of all the years since the family's tile company in Manchester collapsed had sharpened the mother's temper. Her hand would whip out with a smack at very slight provocation. She frequently recounted the quality and style of their life as it used to be and had ceased to be and the blame for all this, of course, she laid at father's door. Perhaps he *was* an easy-going, soft type of chap. She classed him as such. He was working hard doing the best he could in all the circumstances, but got not much credit for anything as far as Tommy could hear.

Even so, about this time the Sunday walks started. The parents would sit back after dinner. Father would look at the paper and have a little doze. But round about 4 he would say, "Well, now we'll go for a walk". The children were pleased. Tommy began to learn more and more about the area.

In the winter as they walked the neighbouring streets, father would talk about any interesting building they passed. In the summertime, they'd set out across the fields. One day, father pointed out a house built at the time of Elizabeth 1 and then another large house standing well back from the fence surrounding it, the garden full of trees. He said it was the So-and-so Hall where Judge Jeffreys used to put up, and told them who he was — "the hanging judge" of "the Bloody Assizes" back in the 17th century.

Walking through the outskirts of town, sometimes they had to pass a very smelly sewage farm. In those days sewage was often disposed of by the simple means of letting it flow into some low-lying open space and dry off in the sun. If you have a township of, say, 40,000 people, and all this waste is allowed to just seep out over the countryside, then there is a hell of a stench.

There it all depended on the direction of the wind. If it blew towards the town then from morning to night the air would be heavy with this stench. But people were used to this. It must have dated back to the days when all drains were open and life was lived in the perpetual stink of sewage and rotting rubbish... Past that a canal, a busy one with barges pulled by horses constantly passing through the lock. Over the bridge and on to a large area formerly marshes, but now well drained with a natural river on the far side of it, plenty of good fish in it.[14]

To cross the river you had to use a footbridge and, at an adjacent cottage, pay the penny toll demanded. Well, adults would pay. Boys seldom did. There was an art in approaching this bridge without being seen. No gates barred entry, so small boys — thinking they were getting away with it — crept up, then made a mad dash across to the other side... Although, actually, the owners didn't bother too much about small boys.

So across more fields, then a fairly steep hill till they reached the start of a country lane and, alongside it, a beautiful old church. Turning left along this lane, first one inn, unchanged in hundreds of years, then a crossroads with another inn and a huge oak tree outside it — hollow, so it joined the claims of many others to have been the hiding place of King Charles when he was on the run.

Father planned a longer jaunt for them. On one of his own long walks, when he was saving every penny he might have spent on a bus or a train fare, he saw a gap in a fence, went through and found himself in a forest[15]. Next summer, perhaps they'd go there, he told them. And they did. No public transport in that direction — and they still could not have afforded it anyway — so the excursion was thoroughly prepared. Blessed with a fine, hot day, they set off. Mother pushed the pram, carrying sandwiches and bottles of water as well as the baby. Father walked alongside her and the three children milled about together, a bit ahead or behind.

To reach the forest they had to walk about four miles, the last stretch across marshland and a river. They were stopped twice on this stretch of road, first by a dark, swarthy man; he stood beside a gate, which he held shut. He had only one arm. The other terminated at the elbow with a metal hook. He wanted to collect a toll. We had no money to spare and told him so and he let us through. A mile or so further on, the same thing happened. Another gate. A sort of blackmail but, again, nothing to be squeezed out of this family. Father suggested a genuine tollgate may have restricted access to the path at some earlier time and that these men had just taken them over when they ceased to be "official".

That day, most of the people of the town seemed to be headed in this direction. A cheery sight. At the end of the walk, at the top of a steep hill with tall, shady trees, the children ran about and gradually ventured further and further away. As he roamed, Tommy suddenly became conscious of the silence in the forest. The rustling of leaves high overhead. A slight breeze. A sensation of loneliness, which he had not experienced before… So he went back to the family. They had settled by some brambles — blackberry bushes, said father. He promised that towards the end of summer they would come again and collect them and have stewed blackberries, perhaps with apple.

The sun was going down. They packed the remains of the picnic in the pram and moved off downhill until, through the bushes beside the path, one of them saw a small cottage in a clearing. Mother said, "We've used up all the water. Let's go and ask if they will let us fill our bottles."

The children ran ahead, feeling safe together, and tapped on the door. An old lady in black answered, looking rough, but kind enough for the children to make their request. She said, "I'll come and speak to your parents". The two women had a chat and she said, "For 3d I could make you a nice pot of tea. A nice drink for all of you. Could you spare 3d for that?" Mother and father discussed it. It was a lot of money, bearing in mind that tuppence ha'penny would buy a pound of the cheapest breast of mutton. They agreed and the old lady brought them a large pot, which she placed, on a wooden bench. They gathered round and the children thoroughly enjoyed their first bought cup of tea. Somehow the smoke from the wood fire in the cottage had penetrated the water. A new flavour, a new taste. They felt adventurous. They were drinking a cup of tea which father had paid for.

The long journey home began. They paused at one point on the opposite side of the road to a country inn where a large party of costermongers had gathered. By chance, Tommy had gradually come to know quite a lot about the costermongers because Mr Phillips, the brickmaker next door, was one of them, although he didn't seem to mix with his fellows very much and he could be friendly enough as a neighbour.

While not separated from the populace by blood like, say, gypsies, costermongers made themselves a race apart in those days, identifiable by how they dressed when wearing their best. The women had large feathers in their hats, their dresses long, wide, ankle-length, and all black, except possibly a touch of white lace round the neck. The men favoured black as well for the most part: bright-coloured mufflers, but black caps and suits — which they customarily had made to measure when they married — of heavy, good-quality cloth with long jackets not stopping much short of the knee, and trousers narrow at the waist but bell-bottomed, not quite so full as a sailor's. These suits had to last a lifetime of Sunday walks to the pub, weddings and, particularly, funerals — elaborate affairs for which they would stretch all their resources.

Although formally clad, they really let themselves go, dancing and singing out in the open air in front of the inn. Looking on as they rested Tommy's family felt very aware of being outsiders. Had they attempted to join in or even talk to the costermongers they would probably have been laughed at, insulted you might say. Costermongers looked down on poor clerks and the like and their pretensions to correct speech, behaviour and dress and would mock them on the street without any direct provocation. That barrier — which seemed to be of distrust on the costers' side — could never be broken.

In public, between themselves, they talked incomprehensible backslang — turning words back to front and still speaking at great speed[16].

Naturally, when working, they didn't wear their finery, just a jacket with corduroy trousers and a bright neckerchief. Again typically, they would carry cooked meals to work in a basin with a red and white-spotted handkerchief over the top of it. And, when selling their fruit and vegetables from barrows in the street, they could still cajole and charm and persuade the very people they scorned into believing they offered the best bargains available.

One afternoon, after quickly eating his lunch at home, Tommy set off for school, taking the route he could rely on to provide something of interest every day. He walked to the end of his street — itself almost made up now — to the main road where the navvies swung their picks, shovelled great lumps of earth aside, and manhandled tram rails and wooden blocks into place. To make their way towards the town square, pedestrians had to jump over various trenches which, for Tommy, only added to the excitement of what was going on.

A little way along, a row of small cottages had been converted into shops. You could buy all your requirements in one or other of them: a laundry, a fish shop, a confectioner, a barber, a cycle maker, general stores. Then you passed a large church, very big for that area, and a row of houses obviously occupied by middle-class families — who, only a few decades earlier, would have lived on the other side of the road, in The Crescent, a terrace of houses built early in the 19th century and adorned with ornamental stonework. Each house has its basement, two floors, and attics above. The servants of earlier days did their work in the basement and slept in the attics. Now families of comparatively poor people occupied The Crescent, but a shared garden laid out as part of this estate remained in front of the bowed terrace. It still bore some appearance of dignity.

After the middle-class houses, Tommy passed a blacksmith's forge, horses coming in and out constantly. Children spent many happy hours watching the procedures there. The horse would be lead in, the blacksmith would examine its hooves, and then start removing the shoe. He heated pieces of roughly shaped, thick metal. Holding the glowing, new shoe with tongs, he would try it out on the horse, then adjust it by reheating and hammering away. Sometimes the horn of the hoof had to be pared away a little. When the blacksmith had achieved a perfect fit, he heated the shoe again and nailed it to the hoof amid a cloud of tangy smoke. Tommy's greatest thrill came from watching the blacksmith work the bellows until the fire roared while the black coals turned red, then bright orange and even white.

Re-crossing the road, another blacksmith's place, more bellows, and then the piercing shriek of the circular saw in the wood mill next door assailed his ears as it cut trees into planks and planks into squares. He could only stand just so much of that noise.

A little further on he came to a huge pub. He always wondered at the size of this place. Why had it been built there? Behind it were fields and then Tommy's school. A large square building, the pub had four floors, tall windows and ornamental stonework at the front. It must have been intended as a hotel, but in a small town with little wealth on the edge of London, who would use it? Probably another product of the short-lived speculation boom which left those abandoned and overgrown roads out in the fields. It must have shocked the people who built the hotel when they realised their customers were the rough-and-ready working classes.

Tommy often looked in and saw men sitting on the benches in there, smoking clay pipes and spitting on the floor. He'd inhaled the foul smell of stale tobacco, stale beer, and smelly humanity and it didn't attract him in any way. But the pubs never seemed to shut — at least, when there was work around — serving from 4 or 6 in the morning until midnight. It was quite common to see men staggering drunk along the street at all hours[17].

Once, as Tommy walked to school, he encountered a large crowd gathered outside the pub. Tommy squeezed his way in among them and saw a policeman down on the ground; a big man knelt over him, punching at him and then clamping his teeth onto the policeman's ear — a feature of brawls in those days. Soon some bobbies who'd heard what was going on came running up, grabbed the big man, and arrested him, while a couple of them took their colleague off to hospital. Tommy heard later that the policeman died of the wound he sustained, no doubt from an infection. His assailant served a long term of imprisonment.

When the uproar faded, Tommy turned into a road made of railway sleepers which ran along one side of the pub and something else caught his eye. A dirty, unshaven man sat on the ground with his back against the rear wall of the pub yard, filling an old, clay pipe. Tommy paused to watch and realised he was packing it with horse dung. When the man looked at him, he ran off away past the brickfield and reached the school gates in safety.

Sometimes, on his way home from school in the late afternoon, when he came to the main road and the huge pub he would turn the other way, towards the general market area. He'd smell it long before he saw it; strong odours of meat, fruit, stale beer, piss... every dark corner had its deposit of human excreta, no public lavatories at that time. If it happened to be a Thursday afternoon, you could see the sheep coming up the busy road in the care of just one man and his dog, driving them to meet their fate in the butcher's yard. Butchers in those days killed their own animals and the meat was really fresh and good. However, this particular butcher would buy his beef "on the horn", as it was called, at Greenwich — slaughtered there. He ferried the carcasses back to his shop on a horse-drawn wagon.

This market area was triangular: on the left side, from Tommy's direction, a row of shops selling foodstuffs and every household requirement — fishmongers, bakers, grocers, greengrocers, a pawnbroker. Facing them, across a wide paved footpath, a group of stalls also selling food, mainly cabbages and other greens from the market gardens nearby.

At the base of the triangle ran a single-track railway with level-crossing gates. This railway bisected many living areas, an heirloom of early bad planning. Oddly, a short stretch of track in the market place had been built on tiles and underneath them flowed a wide stream. Obviously, before they built the railway, this place had been a ford. The engineers had driven in piles to set the railway and a small station[18] above the water — not always very sweet water either. Some people seemed to regard any stream near a town as the natural dumping ground for dead cats and other items for which they had no further use.

On the remaining side of the triangle (should you be getting lost: to Tommy's right, that is, but in the far corner near the railway) stood an old coaching inn, untouched over several hundred years, with a cobbled yard at the side and, in the rear, an extensive stable. The innkeeper himself kept several horses, a few local people had one or two, and visiting circuses also made frequent use of the premises. In fact, the proprietor almost always wore riding breeches, red waistcoat, hacking coat and a bowler and did all his journeying around the neighbourhood on horseback. A very popular man.

A couple of doors along, father, sons and daughters ran an old-time family pharmacy — the shelves arrayed with bright blue and orange decanter-shaped containers. The premises served also as a large post office. Two of the sons had trained in dispensing medicines and their father oversaw everything, a venerable figure with his long, lean face, pointed beard and, invariably, a smoking cap (a sort of fez with a tassel on top).

While the pharmacy portrayed the respectable face of medicine, every market worthy of the name would have its resident quack, generally known as Doctor Brown. That name might cover a multitude of sins. Our Dr Brown was a fine figure of a man clad in a cutaway black coat, striped trousers, patent leather shoes and a tall silk hat on his head — proper morning dress — his fair moustache waxed to two long points. He looked clean, every inch a doctor, and the tale he told about the pills he sold, that was part of the weekend entertainment and a huge crowd would gather around him. According to their number, so the length of his story grew and, proportionately, the sales at the end of it. He gave value for money in pills, potions, and perorations and did very well indeed.

In the middle of the triangle was the old village green, as it had been before this small town became a botched urban district. Marked out by a low iron railing, it comprised a pond, a patch of grass, and a couple of may trees. On warm summer days the out-of-work and assorted idlers would sun themselves there, six or a dozen of them lying on their backs while, around them, the activity of the market went on.

This was a market of long standing and not just weekly, like many in the country. Most of the stallholders worked every day of the week except Sunday (a few on the coaching-inn side operated on Saturdays only). Although they held regular pitches, they had no licenses, no permits. Rather, they occupied their places by right of conquest. If you went along there at 4 in the morning you would see that a board or a trestle had been thrown on the ground at the site and a man or men guarded it. Later in life Tommy became quite deeply concerned with these people, but more of that later[19].

As darkness fell, the shops around the marketplace lit up incandescent gas lamps, reasonably bright, none of the brilliance of electric lighting. The stallholders used paraffin flares — a can with a metal tube hanging from it and a burner at the bottom producing a flame about 18 inches high. It would have been very dangerous in an enclosed space. According to his wealth, each stallholder had one, two or three of these flares burning. This always attracted crowds on dark nights — the greatest numbers guaranteed on Friday nights when, as Tommy sometimes observed, the market's character changed to a degree.

That was the night the workers drew their wages and a little more money than usual flowed into the tills of shopkeepers and stallholders who shouted their wares ever more vigorously to make themselves heard above the hubbub. Everybody with a few pennies to spend felt the pleasure and excitement of it. The publicans did well too, of course. Diagonally opposite the coaching inn, stood the market triangle's second, less grand pub and on Fridays a throng would gather on the pavement outside both establishments, holding pint pots and talking until late into the evening.

This played a part in generating another of the market's thriving businesses, operated by gentlemen offering funds to those who, during a hectic weekend, got through their wages, perhaps leaving no money to buy even food for the family until the next week's pay arrived. On the Monday morning the procession from the sidestreets would begin, a ragged band making for the pawnbroker's shop (adjacent to that second pub). Father's best Sunday suit, mother's best Sunday costume, even the children's boots and shoes would go over the counter. The pawnbroker advanced a shilling or two on them. The hope was — and, generally, it did happen — that these goods would be redeemed the following Friday night, ready to be worn at the weekend.

Some women carried huge bundles to the pawnbroker's shop, undoubtedly including sheets and blankets, which would be missing from the family's beds for the week — if ill fortune befell them in the meanwhile, how were the children to be kept warm? How were the old people to be kept warm? Short of clothing, short of bedding, short of food during the worst part of the week until the man's wages, to some extent, redeemed them...

Even so, many did survive on the tiniest of incomes, like Tommy's family, keeping at least an outward appearance of what was called respectability. They frequently suffered deprivations in their home. But even in those circumstances they could still find energy and time to do a little to help others, as with church work. But the toll on nerves, the irritation, the bitterness, the feeling of instability and fear of even worse overtaking them often blighted the lives of people who were doing their best to keep things going under difficult circumstances. And of course the children often suffered the lash of the tongue or the slap of the hand, not always deserved.

Chapter Six

The school was experimenting. It had been decided that Tommy and some others would spend two years in the same class with one teacher. They had a "standards" system numbered 1 to 7 and Tommy's group would be going through standards 4 and 5. After two years they would move on, depending on the teacher's assessment of their abilities as displayed by general work and termly exams. Luckily, Tommy liked the teacher, whom he observed closely. He liked his white teeth, his silky moustache and his grand nose with its high bridge marked at the top by the spectacles he wore in class. But all the boys appreciated him because they felt he treated them fairly. In turn, they were willing to do their best.

Tommy learned the essentials. The world, its continents, its countries, the people who inhabited them. What they grew or mined in the way of fruit, grains, metals, minerals, and what they did with those things. Whether they treated them before selling them. Also what they bought in, treated, and sold again. Then history… a plodding progress from the time of the Romans onwards. Learning the kings and queens who ruled our country and whether they were good, bad or indifferent. Something of the laws promulgated during their reigns. The children had to memorise the year in which each monarch came to the throne. Most could remember these dates for a brief period, but recollection was apt to lapse quickly except when, perhaps, some big event or some battle occurred, or some important law was passed during that reign. Of course, they did arithmetic — the quicker means of adding and division and subtraction.

The teachers worked to a syllabus. At each hour of each day they commenced a given subject. A short pause between each lesson and then straight on, teaching interrupted only by a break in the morning and the midday meal.

No marvel, Tommy did come somewhere near the top, third to fifth generally. If he fell below that it would be because of illness — all the usual ones.

At about this time, on one of the very rare occasions when he stayed out after dark, he saw something that thrilled him: simply a boy standing under a lamp-post, with the gas light shining down on him, looking at a book — but wearing a uniform Tommy had never seen before. A hat with three dents in it and a wide brim; a bright-coloured scarf tied around his neck and hanging down the front of his shirt; short trousers held up by a belt; long socks and short boots; and in one hand he carried a staff, a pole. Tommy had to find out who he was, what he belonged to, and why he dressed like that. He couldn't bring himself to approach the boy and ask him, but he soon found out that he must have been an early member of the Boy Scouts.

With family fortunes gradually improving, shortly after Tommy had seen his first Scout, his brother joined them, got rigged out in that uniform, and was soon acquiring many skills and the badges that went with them. Tommy looked forward to the day when his parents could afford to buy a uniform for him — and it wasn't too long in coming.

He enjoyed everything about it. The pleasure of going to the outfitter's shop. The smell of the clothing. The khaki shirt, red scarf, blue trousers, black hose with scarlet tops. In addition, he had to buy a lanyard with a whistle, a belt to which he attached a clasp knife, and a staff with three dents in it, like the hat — to remind him of the three main promises he would make on becoming enrolled as a Scout[20]. Each patrol had its own flag; Tommy's bore the head of a buffalo in red. But even when he got used to the uniform, Tommy never felt he looked so eye-catching as that boy standing under the street gas lamp...

Baden Powell, the movement's founder, had carefully considered the significance of every detail and set out the principles and rules in a book called *Scouting For Boys*[21]. He had organised the first experiment in camp living on Brownsea Island[22] and formed the first Scout Troops shortly after that.

Becoming a member of this movement opened a new phase of living for Tommy. Life had been hard and grim. Now very pleasant pastimes came to occupy many is his out-of-school hours and he began to enjoy the company of other boys under happy conditions, free from the pressures of schoolwork and the overseeing of the form teacher. He experienced more tolerance and kindness from the Scoutmaster and his assistants, this being a voluntary organisation. The object was to give the boys the greatest possible amount of good.

Troop members had a complete gym available to them for one hour every Thursday night, and several hours on Saturday afternoons. Vaulting horses, parallel bars, and rings stood or hung eight feet apart in rows the length of the hall. They could stand on a platform at one end, grasp a ring one-handed and jump and swing through the air and grasp the next ring with the other hand, then work themselves backwards and forwards to gather momentum before swinging on to the next ring and so on. A refinement, known as a half-dislocation, was to swing your body right around clockwise, heels over head, while holding on to a ring one-handed ready to reach out to the next row.

They worked on climbing ropes too. Up to the top and down again with legs crossed in the approved manner. Tommy's brother wanted to demonstrate his skill and climbed up faster than anyone else could. Then, to descend, he almost let go and just slid down. The boys thought this was fine. But then they saw the friction had burnt the insides of both legs. He had to have dressings on these abrasions and they took some weeks to heal. Tommy did not try to emulate that trick.

At the Easter and Whitsun holidays — and sometimes on ordinary Saturdays, as an alternative to gym — the Troop would assemble outside their hut and put together what they called their trek cart. They fitted the wheels on the shaft and loaded up with tents, containers of water, packed lunches, and anything else the leaders thought useful. They formed up and marched off — usually in the direction of that large forest, four or five miles distant. The boys hauled the cart along by means of long ropes attached to the wheel hubs on each side, three boys on each rope — and a couple behind, pushing.

At the selected place, they set up their tents and a day of fun and games and sports would commence. They practiced running, vaulting with the pole over brooks and other obstacles, tracking in woodland areas — and tying knots, of course. The leaders imparted some knowledge of wildlife and they collected wild flowers to dry and place in a book with its name and details underneath. They fenced, not with swords, but stout sticks. They tried cock-fighting, as it was called, with the pole passed behind the bent knees, the arms underneath the pole, each boy edging up to the other and trying to upset him by swinging the pole round to get him off balance. The older boys took boxing lessons — Tommy did, in due course. And yet they still seemed to have plenty of leisure time when they could wander through the forest by themselves or in groups.

Even from those early days, the Scouts would also take care to show the parents what their sons could do, given the opportunity. Every three months the Troop presented an entertainment in the hall where they held their gym sessions. Some of the mothers volunteered to serve a light meal beforehand with tea, orange drinks and so forth all arranged on a long, trestle table covered with white, cotton cloths. Then, the older boys and the Scoutmasters entertained to the best of their abilities, and a happy afternoon would be had by all.

The Scouts' training in how to handle certain emergencies did find an application to reality on one of these trekking days. A few minutes after they set off for the forest, Tommy noticed a man who had been walking beside them on the pavement start to stagger and lurch about. Then he fell down with his back against a shop front, rent with paroxysms of tension, clenching of the jaws and hands. The Scouts' nursing sessions had taught them enough to recognise that this was an epileptic fit, so they did what they had been trained to do in these circumstances — they formed a semi-circle around the man to keep back any people who might be curious, holding their Scout poles between them to make a barrier.

They could have done one or two other things for him, such as putting pads between fingernails and palms and teeth and lips, if possible, to prevent damage. But, before they could do anything more, a man climbed over one of their poles into the middle of their semi-circle and took charge. His notion of treatment was rather curious, the boys thought. He took an old handkerchief out of his pocket and put a lighted match to it until it smouldered. Then he held it under the poor man's nose — the idea being, I suppose, that the smoke would irritate his nostrils and bring him round.

Nothing the lads could do about this. The intruder persisted until suddenly the epileptic's paroxysm stopped. He lay quiet for a few moments, then stood up and walked straight ahead into the middle of the road where a tram had stopped. He boarded it and vanished… leaving behind the semi-circle of boys with their poles and the pseudo-doctor with the smoking handkerchief in his hand.

The Scouts demanded discipline –particularly self-discipline — of all. Any who rebelled against it, especially more senior boys, found themselves quickly turned out of the Troop. The Scoutmaster, Mr Frusher, believed that an older boy who elected to rebel against accepted rules of conduct would contaminate younger members and must be got rid of.

It must have been about this time that newspapers began to warn that a comet[23], apparently heading for the Earth, would soon become visible to the naked eye — something of a scare, a spice of danger. Eventually, when it appeared, people in their thousands would gather in open spaces to gaze at this large star, its long tail illuminated, glowing.

On a clear night it provided quite a spectacle and, combined with the remote prospect of it hitting the earth and knocking it sideways, it created a feeling of national excitement — although, in schools, teachers reassured children that astronomers knew quite well that the comet would miss the Earth by a colossal distance.

To watch it, Tommy and his friends and neighbours would repair to a field bordered by a row of houses and the brickfields. Soon, the more observant members of the crowd began to discern curious white objects in the distance moving across the field. Imagination or not, Tommy and others did spot something in white running and leaping. That provided a very spicy note of terror and, each night, the size of the crowd increased so conspicuously that the local press made mention of the mysterious apparitions.

So, one night, a party of bold fellows set out across the field to find out what was going on and, when they returned, they said they had nearly caught a couple of men covered in white sheets who had been springing from one brick kiln to another to provide this ghastly spectacle which had made many people believe in ghosts after all.

The children still went every Sunday to the Church of England, and the occasional treats there would run along much the same lines as Tommy's Scouting adventures. For instance, the annual outing invariably comprised a walk to that same forest which father had introduced the family to and the Scouts visited regularly. The minister would lead them. Tommy thought him an unusual chap. An Irishman, tall, fat, with a powerful head. A character. He governed by rule of whistle. When the hundred or so children gathered outside the church, he explained that, when he blew his whistle, they had to stop and listen to what he said.

The children brought their own food — sandwiches, cakes if they were lucky. But, knowing that on any substantial walk with children thirst was the major enemy, the minister would provide the drink: lime juice. He had large containers of it set on a wagon pulled by several boys. Sometimes they sang as they walked. If anybody straggled the whistle would blow, the minister would order them to close up and off they would go again.

Fortunately, he took them to a part of the forest new to Tommy and the other Scouts in the group. Its main feature was a farm, quite large. Had any trouble occurred, any child fallen ill, the minister had made an arrangement with the farmer that they should be looked after. Most of the time the children played games. But they were allowed to wander for an hour provided they didn't go beyond certain boundaries he pointed out to them.

At home, mother announced suddenly that the front room, which still contained very little other than a pair of steps, was to be let to a small family. Somebody had approached her and asked if she could accommodate a man, his wife, and their small boy for a short time. They were moving into the area and had nowhere to live. The man had been promised a job and they would be glad to bring their few sticks of furniture along and share the use of the scullery, the outside lavatory and other amenities. And the arrangement benefitted both parties. Tommy's mother, no doubt, had two or three shillings rent for the room, a valuable addition to the family income.

For the children it opened up a new outlook. The man worked as a navvy. Well set up, he wore a long black jacket and corduroy trousers with a strap below the knee. He had a tanned face, light-blue eyes, and always a smile. His wife was a strange-looking woman really, bulging eyes, bulging teeth, a ruddy face, but she smiled constantly too. They came for "a week or two", but stayed for a month or two.

The fascinating thing about this change in circumstances was that on a Saturday night this man would play some music on a phonograph — the forerunner of the gramophone and only a stage forward from the original machine made by Edison[24]. Cylinders slid on to the machine gave forth, in a rather tinny way, the latest songs of the day.

Each Saturday night, when not otherwise engaged, Tommy would seek an invitation to go and hear this machine play, perhaps, When Father Painted The Parlour[25] which was very popular then, along with other more sentimental numbers. They all had much the same thin sound on the phonograph, but there was the little group sitting round listening, the comfort and companionship of the room, and above all the father sitting or standing, smoking his clay pipe, bending down to operate his machine, proud of it, this lovely navvy. Tommy enjoyed an hour or so in that company.

This good man, Mr Williams, suggested that the light in the passage — just a gas jet –would be better if replaced by an oil lamp, which he provided along with its glass chimney. The evening he put it up, it certainly did brighten the passage.

But, after Tommy had gone to bed, something went wrong. Tommy heard a bit of a scuffle, so he went out onto the landing. Looking down to the hallway below him, he saw a flame rising up from the lamp all the way to the ceiling. He had thoughts of the whole place burning down. Just then, though, the door of the front room flew open, out strode Mr Williams, grabbed this flaring oil lamp, dashed through the house — throwing three doors open as he went — out into the garden where he threw the flaming lamp as far as he could. When it hit the ground at the bottom of the garden, for a moment there was quite a conflagration. But the house didn't burn down, nobody was hurt. Mr Williams had saved the place and the people living in it.

His job did come through, but it entailed travelling some distance. The Williamses needed to move nearer his place of work, so they found a cheap house for rent and the two families parted, losing contact for many years.

Not long after this, with family circumstances further improved, mother felt justified in ordering a suite of furniture to put in that once more empty front room. She bought some floor covering and a suite, which consisted of two armchairs and five straight-backed chairs, a couch too, quite nicely upholstered. The whole thing cost £5, to be paid at one shilling a week, including some interest — but the room tolerably well furnished at last, a change from the bare boards.

At the same time, a friend up in the North who had stored a few items for father when he had to leave Manchester quickly, now sent some of them down. Nothing of great use really. Old newspapers, song sheets — in better days, father had fancied himself a singer, at least in the drawing room with the family.

One thing that interested the children was a long, blue box. They lifted the lid and found it was full of fishing tackle. Every style of float and artificial bait for everything from tiddlers to salmon. So it appeared that father had been quite a fisherman in his time. One or two of the children got fish-hooks entangled in their clothing and it entailed some careful work on mother's part to remove them.

They opened another curious oddment, a leather hatbox, beautifully made, lined with white silk; inside, a black silk hat, a topper. So there was a topper in the family… How ludicrous, though, a silk top hat in their condition. But it probably gave the parents some pleasure, thinking of days gone by.

Father's family in Manchester, those who still remained there — aunts, uncles, in-laws — kept in touch and the children were guaranteed to see a few shillings on their birthdays. One aunt would send a postal order for half a crown[26] to each child with a nice little letter. But that half a crown was a big sum of money so mother had to take it. She would buy some small thing for the child, but the rest had to find its way into the family kitty for food or clothing. Another aunt would send sweets — often Edinburgh rock because she visited that city once or twice a year. She was the one who had become an artist, painting and drawing. One of her efforts came down with the other items from the North: a picture of a matchgirl[27] sitting on the kerb, legs crossed, feet bare, a very sad, wistful look on her face. Not really a cheerful subject, but it hung in one of the bedrooms for a number of years. Other little presents that aunt sent perhaps helped the children to view the dispiriting picture with more toleration than they might otherwise have found.

Father continued to get on well with Glanfield Rowe, the clergyman in charge of the C Of E tin church. They enjoyed a chat about the times, current affairs. In due course, Mr Rowe persuaded father and, to some extent, mother to play a more active part in church events. Father became secretary of the men's club — its purpose to provide an hour or two's friendly entertainment to the members of the congregation.

The parson's ambitions soared and he organised a committee to draw up the plans for a garden fete. One of the more wealthy local residents was persuaded to permit the use of his fairly extensive grounds. Of course, the committee took several months to organise the day. Various people were voted into taking care of specific tasks. Father was voted treasurer. Mother undertook to be in charge of the food and drink side. From its original small concept onwards, it had begun to grow into quite a large affair. When the day dawned, even the children were involved to some extent.

Tommy and his brother were to take their turn selling ice cream — made by a local shopkeeper — in cornets and wafers. With no bulk manufacturer then, each trader made his own in a small machine and supplied it in cylinders, which Tommy and several friends collected on the morning of the fete. They set them up on a stand constructed by a carpenter member of the congregation.

The aim was to raise as much money as possible for a fund dedicated to building a new church hall. Since this was a mission church, for every £100 raised the mother church would certainly contribute at least another £100. Everybody worked to that end. The parishioners were poor, but it looked as though the women had been working very hard to make clothes to wear on the day, sewing their own dresses and decorating hats — bulky affairs with rims of trimming around the crown, often flowers. Their appearance on the day did them credit. The men couldn't afford new suits, but those they had were clean, the trousers pressed, and they all looked fine. A feeling of brotherhood and endeavour prevailed.

Almost without exception, these events provoke heavy rain, but on this occasion the sun shone on the sports events — for the children and the adults — and the stalls which dotted the grounds, attracting those out to get all they could for as little as possible.

You see here the beginnings of a change in the life of the family. Formerly prosperous and then down to the depths of poverty and despair, they were now getting integrated into a community at times. The parents became known by the people in that district and, although very poor, seemed the better for it — especially father, through his part in the church men's club.

Soon after the fete, the new church hall was built and the club had the good fortune to be given the use of a large room with a full-size billiard table and equipment for other games. The wives provided light refreshments and Tommy remembered his mother sewing the heavy leather cloth together for the cover to spread over the billiard table at close of play. A nice, social atmosphere developed and when the boy was allowed into the club room for a few moments, he noticed the difference in his father. That normally quiet, sometimes morose man became quite affable among other men, smiling, chatting away in a manner which Tommy had thought impossible.

The church had to raise more money for maintenance and to pay off the borrowings which had allowed an early start on the hall. So mother and father took part in more social events there. They organised dances — the music, the catering. They would plague the local shopkeepers for assistance, donations in kind. Tea, sugar, anything of that sort, lemonade, ice cream — generally members of the congregation, of course, the shopkeepers must have suffered a sort of sweet blackmail at times to get them to part with stock they could hardly afford to give away. But commerce and religion were closely linked; the tradesmen did tend to join the church they thought would bring them the most customers.

The dances gave amateur musicians the chance to show their skill. At first, the band consisted of violins, mandolins, a cello, a bass, kettle and bass drums. They gave a swing to it. Old-time dances. Valetas and other waltzes. Humble though the company, a mantle of great decorum, restraint and respectability descended on them when they took to the floor, partly because they had a professional MC. As was the custom, dressed in tails, with a large buttonhole and white gloves, he occupied the centre of the dance floor and took strict control. During each dance, he would take a lady round and demonstrate the steps, beating time, and talking to each couple in turn, ensuring that they followed his instruction.

The price of admission included the purchase of a dance card for each lady, a booklet really, printed on stiff board with a pencil attached on a silky cord. When approached for a dance, the lady would note the name of the applicant against the numbered dance of her choice.

You couldn't be glum on such occasions, each helping as much as he could. They were all learning to conduct themselves in a nice, happy way with their fellows, the ordinary poor people and those few with a little more money joining together.

The ones who remained at home, what could they do there? Read. Or otherwise go to the public bar with the sawdust on the floor to absorb the spit.

Tommy could detect things in the company of the church people that didn't attract him either, but he understood them better than the pub-goers, I suppose, and so preferred them.

Chapter Seven

Suddenly a change occurred for Tommy. In charge of the Scout Troop was a cultured man, whose name I've mentioned in passing — Mr Frusher, who was also the vicar, the organist and choirmaster at the parish church. He had private means, being a member of the family which owned and controlled the three local newspapers (he took no active part in the business, concerning himself with the church and the Scout movement). He approached Tommy at one of the Scout gatherings and said, "I'd like you to join the church choir. Ask your parents if they will be agreeable. It will mean you changing your church." The full C of E church — as opposed to their familiar "tin" mission — was a mile and a half further away from Tommy's house. But the parents agreed to the move.

Tommy joined the choir having only just passed the vocal test, which proved pretty strict. The assistant organist played the tune and he stood up there in the choir stall while the choirmaster moved around the church, judging his voice from close to and at a distance. The boy didn't think he was good enough and Mr Frusher's eventual approval surprised him — as did the small payments to be had from singing with the choir. Four times a year the Sunday collection would be shared among the members — a fair amount, for the congregation filled the building.

Tommy would walk to choir practice after school. The route took him through the marketplace where, beyond Dr Brown's pitch, he passed a stall belonging to an Italian who had a big oven wherein, during winter, he baked large potatoes. The customers stepped up and handed him their halfpenny or penny according to the size of the potato — the Italian's assistant plunged his heavily gloved hand into the oven, brought out a spud, laid it on a piece of newspaper, crushed it, sprinkled it with salt and vinegar, and handed it over. Having no halfpennies, Tommy could only watch, sniff the delicious smell of the hot potato and make his way onwards.

This brought him to the railway crossing, the gates usually open, so he walked straight across over the cobbles and the railway lines, then bore right to the church. The footpath ran alongside that stinking brook running under the railway — on the other side of it a row of the tiniest, meanest cottages one could imagine. They could be reached only via a small footbridge.

From the brook side, he turned into quite a select road where the business people of the area lived. Then a row of terraced houses and a bakery whence the smell of hot bread and cakes constantly drifted out. A horse and delivery van stood outside; no matter how small the order you could always have it delivered to your home if you preferred. After that, Tommy came to what was known as the charity school. Some 200 years old it was. I don't know who built it but it was used by various youth organisations[28]. Next, a few more shops, including Granny Winterbottom's tuck shop, much favoured by the choirboys when in funds, and another old coaching inn with the yard in front where wagons would draw up in the old days.

Then came the entrance to the vicarage, large grounds surrounding it, quite a big house this — and beside it the old churchyard and the church, mostly Norman. A path to the left of the church led to the grave of a well-known poet and his sister[29].

The vicar, an MA, was a Cambridge graduate and a fellow of Trinity College, the Royal Academy of Music, and the Royal College of Organists too. He served as an examiner for these bodies at the annual tests for piano pupils held in each London district. In addition to all this, the vicar had attained the rank of Past Master in the Order of Freemasons, undertaking all the study and learning of set speeches required at each stage of advancement from initiation to the Master's chair.

Through his contacts, musical and otherwise, he often persuaded men who would really merit parishes of their own to act as curates in Edmonton — some of them parsons serving overseas in the colonies who would come home on long leave or for good and, before re-settling properly, needed temporary appointments.

When Tommy joined the church, the vicar had three of these over-qualified curates assisting him. St. John Law, stout, a rather dark countenance, had spent many years as a missionary in India. He wore a monocle always. His sermons flowed, he made lavish use of words and gestures and always held the interest of the congregation — although perhaps they didn't always get his message. Another curate came from Canada. He had tales to tell and frequently illustrated his sermons with descriptions of incidents from logging-camp life. Then a chap from Africa — a glum, dour man, this — apt to fill people with dread of the afterlife, rather than anticipation. Even so he had his interesting aspects.

The vicar himself, Mr Frusher, with his dome of a head, his powerful voice and perfect diction, had the gift of making people believe that all was well in this best of all worlds; after his sermons, they would leave the church feeling secure, strong, fortified, ready to meet the trials of the coming week.

The vicar had further support from two church wardens and a bevy of sidesmen — all local businessmen, some more prominent than others. Their motives for doing the work — entirely voluntary, of course — were probably above reproach. No doubt, as tradesmen, certain little perks came their way. But who could deny them when they were willing to give a lot of their time in a good cause?

A very striking figure, one of these sidesmen; about six foot six, broad of shoulder, and he dressed according to his station as a businessman in a fairly big way. At church, in winter, he would wear ordinary morning dress — the black cutaway coat, striped trousers and topper. But as soon as the flowers began to come out he would don a light grey suit and cutaway coat and a grey silk hat. With his big cigar, which he puffed immediately he stepped outside after the service, and his gold-mounted walking stick, he made a striking figure as he strode away and out into the open country at the far end of the road.

The choir too had its businessmen and professional men. The one who stood right behind Tommy, up there in the stalls, owned quite a large factory. His bass voice was loud, it was hard, and it constantly assailed Tommy's ears during the service. This man never smiled, as far as Tommy could see. Also in morning dress, of course, he dashed into church, and then at the end of the service he dashed out and dashed off down the road, with a quick, mincing sort of step. Neither Tommy nor anyone else seemed to get within friendly talking distance of this man.

Among the choir members in the facing stalls stood the tenor soloist, a leather merchant, a quiet man in all aspects other than vocally. He chose to be the tenor soloist. He sang well but his was the type of voice Tommy hated then and throughout life. That hard sound which seems to come out of a little chamber down in the throat, half-closed and just allowing this voice to escape.

And nearby, Tommy's schoolteacher. Curiously enough, in this place he never acknowledged the boy. A couple of faint smiles outside the church but inside, no, Tommy didn't seem to exist at all. Well, probably correct in the circumstances.

At the very large organ, controlling all the musical proceedings from the height of his stool, sat Mr Frusher, whom Tommy liked and respected so well. A mirror above the keyboards gave him a complete view of the choir and the younger members were well aware of that so no misbehaviour ever occurred during the service.

The usual Sunday evening saw this grand church, almost a cathedral, completely filled with people and everybody enjoying the singing. None more heartily, I fear, than Figgy Avverdate — extremely tall, ragged clothes, a pot hat on the back of his head, a face of extreme ugliness with bloodshot, bulging eyes, beetling brows and a high forehead, a fattened nose, his mouth surly when closed and displaying blackened fangs when open, a dirty rag round his long, scrawny neck, a discarded long, black gent's morning coat worn and torn, trousers of indescribable filth, and on his feet big, club-soled boots, the toes cut away to reveal corny toes and bunions. On the street, he would usually stand leaning against a wall, a figure of dread to all children.

So a new world opened up: music. Tommy's training was strict and very detailed and he felt his life becoming quite full. In addition to schoolwork, on Tuesday night he had choir practice, Thursday Scouts, Friday choir again and Saturday afternoon Scouts. The Sunday morning service could last all day when they sang the full litany. If not, Sunday afternoon remained free until Mr Frusher, in his vicar role, asked him to join the private religious instruction course he held at his home.

He had a big house, much too big you might say for one man and his housekeeper — she and her family occupied the basement. But the whole place was well used. He had two music rooms, one at the front on the ground floor, the other on the first floor, and each contained a Bechstein piano. He used the breakfast room, at the rear on the ground floor, for choir or Scouts meetings and a large back room on the second floor for church committee meetings and the Sunday afternoon class. On the lines of Sunday school, it also involved wider discussions, Tommy discovered.

Picture Mr Frusher of medium height, well-built, wearing a beard, pointed, and the then fashionable pince-nez. Most days he wore a frock coat with a silk hat and striped, trousers. Tommy used to love looking at the boots he wore; without toecaps, of fine soft leather, kept in good condition by his housekeeper. He was one of those cold-bath-in-the-morning men. He would sometimes describe with relish how he had broken the ice. The water was poured out the night before into his hip bath in his bedroom where there was no heating (it was not customary except in case of sickness). His working day, training people to play the piano, started at 9.30am and went through to maybe 6pm. Comfortably off, he varied his terms according to each pupil's financial position.

Around that time, Tommy heard how this good man had been engaged to be married some years previously, but the girl died of consumption. He had been very broken up and went to live in Switzerland. Some regarded this as a selfish thing. But there was the possibility of him having contracted this highly contagious disease and Switzerland was the recognised place for curing, or at least alleviating, the condition. He came back to this life and devoted all his waking hours to church, music and the Scouts. Many boys were the better for these activities and the older ones maintained contact with him even if they went abroad.

All that left two evenings vacant for Tommy, but before long he joined the vicar's class to learn music. The children could afford to buy only one type of instrument, the flageolet, big brother of the tin whistle. The vicar gave them sheets of music in staff notation and Tommy had no difficulty in playing the tunes as soon as he mastered the simple technique of covering half the hole to play the half-note. The two- and three-part arrangements provided by Mr Frusher sounded very good — rather like the recorders children play nowadays.

Some months passed. On the main road the navvies had finished their work: tramlines put down and rather high standards erected with light fittings on the top of them. Arc lamps. The night they were switched on was the first time street lighting by electricity in that area had been attempted.

These lamps rely on two sticks of carbon fitted with a slight gap between them so that when a current passes through them it leaps the gap — the arc — and creates a bright light. Sometimes they work well and sometimes not at all. Sometimes they give a steady light and sometimes a flickering light. But the effect excited many people to take an evening stroll just for the sheer joy of seeing the lights and their road illuminated at night.

Tommy too felt something romantic, quite thrilling, about it all as he made his way to the marketplace and up the street to Mr Frusher's house or the church. Very old, dingy buildings became interesting in this mauvish, pinkish light. So did people on the street. Their clothes could not be seen in detail, their faces took on an unusual colour, and they looked different — not the rough-and-ready folks he was used to seeing about.

Up this newly lit road on the right he immediately passed a big house, probably the residence some years ago of quite a wealthy family — many in this area had owned houses and even estates, now broken up, built over or left derelict. Then a number of others of fair size. After that, just before the choirmaster's home, a real old pub, the Jolly Farmer. A jolly, boozy old place it was too[30].

Tommy had become aware of two other notable houses quite close by. One, lying well back from the road, used to be occupied by a renowned essayist[31], and the other by a doctor and his young son — with whom, Tommy heard and believed, the poet John Keats, an apothecary's assistant, had worked for a short time[32].

Tommy would walk through the churchyard gates and turn left for the vestry. One day, the first to arrive for choir practice, he found that somebody had left a besom in there. He picked it up... and neither then nor at any later date did he know why he did what he next did. He placed himself on guard at the vestry door with the sharp twigs pointing outwards and awaited the arrival of the enemy. Not a particularly fierce enemy, of course. But when the next boy entered the vestry, Tommy lunged at him with the besom and drove him back. Soon quite a crowd of choirboys built up outside the narrow door until, finally, Mr Frusher appeared behind them... and I leave to your imagination what followed. It nearly cost Tommy his place in the choir, but not quite. He was forgiven.

But that lunatic idea. What made him do it? He didn't know. But it caused a bit of a laugh, of course. When all the other lads had taken their places in the choir stalls Tommy had to endure a walking lecture — walking round the aisles with the boss telling him what sort of behaviour was permissible, what was nice, what was decent. And what was reprehensible.

Choir practice over, the joyful dash through the marketplace to Dr Brown's lecture and sale of cure-all medicaments. Silk hat shining by the light of the market flares. Tommy's Friday night treat, inexpensive but good.

Chapter Eight

The family remained poor, but things improved gradually and mother decided she could buy Tommy a suit... yes, a real suit. Only 30 shillings, but it was a jacket in the Norfolk style and britches, which buttoned below the knee, worn with black stockings and short ankle boots. Even better, a piece of waterproof cloth, grey, had come mother's way and, clever woman that she was, using a pattern, she turned it into an overcoat. He was feeling quite wealthy.

During that period, he didn't see a great deal of his elder brother, George[33], who continued to forge ahead at school, automatically picking up every prize going. He seemed to take it all in his stride. By contrast, Tommy saw himself as struggling, though doing well with his limited gifts.

Nothing scholarly about George's appearance, mind you. A capable, self-contained lad, self-assertive, of course, while perhaps short for his age, he was sturdily built and his young fists as apt to go into action as his brain. He didn't persecute anybody, but nor did he stand any nonsense. If, at times, Tommy sensed that George was favoured at home because of his prowess — and that may have been the case — he never felt envious. He loved him as a brother, at that time and throughout his later life.

Although George, in his early teens, had many interests he didn't share with Tommy, they did walk along to Scout meetings together — George had already become a Patrol Leader, his arms and his breast pocket covered with proficiency badges — and sometimes Tommy could take a part in one of his older brother's more temporary enthusiasms. In fact, one of them provided him with a fruitful hobby.

George decided to build a chicken run — a wired-in stretch of the garden for feeding and scratching — with a shed for the birds' sleeping quarters and a nest box too. When George and father procured the chickens, Tommy found he enjoyed feeding them, replacing the straw in the nest box, and looking after them generally. He did his fair share and they produced some quite nice eggs. Soon they'd given each chicken a pet name — their favourite, a Plymouth Rock they called Speckles, a splendid bird, very perky, laid a large white egg every day of the week. A real treasure was Speckles.

On one occasion, George bought some very cheap eggs, foreign ones, and, more for fun than anything, they placed them under a broody hen. Fourteen of them had cost only a shilling, so not much was expected of them, you can imagine. After three weeks, several did hatch out. Curious things the chicks were, though. Smallish, mainly black, in time they grew, but never to the normal size of the average English chicken — and one stayed more or less the same size as the day it was born. This runt got into the habit of coming into the house, where it would sit on the stairs and go to sleep. During its brief life, it never attempted to lay eggs. It became a household pet really.

The brothers put that chicken shed to rather illicit use once. There was always the moment when a lad would be introduced to a cigarette. For Tommy, this came about through curiosity and the wish to copy George and his friends. For the outlay of one penny Tommy's brother got hold of a cardboard packet of five, each one with its own little, paper holder. George gave Tommy one.

They dare not be seen smoking, of course, or both of them would have been in real trouble. So the brothers sat in the shed — on the perch the chickens used at night — and lit their cigarettes. But as Tommy puffed on he felt ill, more and more ill. He wanted to vomit. His head went round and round — until he fell off the perch and retched. It was many a long day before he tried to smoke a cigarette again (although he did eventually succeed and became a habitual smoker).

Tommy's friends, in the main, came from the Scouts or the choir. One was Reg Curtis. In his family it was the custom to wear your hair long. Reg's Dad and three brothers had thick, wavy hair; I doubt if the father would have let a barber lay his hands on any of them. When Tommy got to know them he realised what a close-knit group they were — the father a deeply religious man with a generous nature, rather dark of countenance, jet-black hair, a cobbler by trade, running a fairly large shop. As soon as the children grew capable of picking up a hammer or a knife, he taught them this craft. But he didn't overwork them. Nothing of slavery about it. When Tommy went in there he knew at once this was a happy place and a happy home.

One Christmas, they invited Tommy into the family celebration. Reg's father had a phonograph and he'd bought one of those early records — mainly of a religious, sacred character the tunes were, Jerusalem and similar things. They all made free with the Christmas fare and the happiness there was a revelation to Tommy. Reg shared with him the affection which permeated the family, the brothers and Dad. I don't mention Mum because, curiously, she remained in the background and Tommy seldom saw her. He and Reg were to maintain their affection into manhood. They didn't see each other for long periods, but when they did they would always walk along talking, swapping hopes and ambitions.

Another little chap, Fred, a reasonably happy fellow with a very fine voice, an asset to the choir, Tommy heard mentioned frequently in later life. A few years on, in his teens, this boy was walking along the road when a car struck him. The driver stopped, got out, took him to hospital, followed his progress to recovery and afterwards gave him a good job in the local music hall, which he owned. The same man also ran another music hall down on the Southeast coast. Eventually, a big man in the entertainment world took them over and converted them into cinemas. He promoted Fred to manager and, from there, Tommy's childhood friend went on to become a well-known figure in show business.

Higgins, another splendid singer, had a far less pleasant manner; surly, never a smile out of him, cocky about that good voice. Then there was Hewlett, who behaved quite like Higgins and yet something about him fascinated Tommy. He never laughed, but he always had a superior sort of half-smiling smirk on his face, which Tommy didn't find agreeable. Years on, he read in the newspaper that some notoriety came Hewlett's way; he stabbed some member of his family, and that was the last Tommy heard of him.

More agreeable was Tully, short, dark, broad of shoulder, always a cheery grin on his face. At choir practice Tommy spent some time with him. A lovely, happy-making companion to have. And Willie Atter — he smelt like attar of roses too! Hair beautifully groomed and oiled, clothes of fine quality, a cheery chap.

Tommy, with his rather humble garb, found his place among many such, notably better dressed than he, and suffered no bullying because of his poverty — although, beyond the choir and Scouts, he did experience it once, for no other reasons than that he was small and alone at the time.

In the winter, boys who had no gloves would sometimes make what they called hand-warmers. They would get an opened tin, knock several holes into it, stuff a rag inside, and set fire to it. Holding it by a piece of string, they would swing it round and round until the rag blazed, then hold the tin in their hands. One day, when Tommy was getting on nicely, swinging the tin around and warming his hands, a chap who was actually known as Jack the Bully grabbed him. Jack stole his hand-warmer and threatened him with a clip round the ear if he didn't hop it.

Fortunately, Tommy didn't see much of Jack, but the following summer he did get the chance to watch him in action from a safer distance. Tommy was paddling in a stream when Jack turned up with his sycophants, that horrible type of boy who sucks up to a bully and basks in his glory. Jack was showing off. His followers captured tiny frogs from the stream and passed them to him. One by one, he held them by their hind legs high above his opened mouth and dropped them in. Tommy, unnoticed on this occasion, watched him swallow quite a number and wondered what would happen — perhaps the bully would meet his Waterloo.

At home, Tommy's parents made an important addition to the furniture in the front room — the parlour, as they called it. A friend of Tommy's sister told her that, her father having died and her mother being compelled to let half of the house, an old piano had to go. It was completely out of tune and very old, but when it was mentioned to mother she agreed to have it. She paid only a few shillings, just for carriage. The piano looked extraordinary; very tall — almost three times the height of modern pianos — with ornamental woodwork, candlesticks and red silk curtains covering the front part of it above the old, yellowed keys.

Tommy, already much interested in music, made a wild promise to tune it. He felt sure he could do it by ear. He'd seen a man in the local piano shop doing it: the tool, the "key", he used on the screw at the top of each string, turning it this way and that until it sounded right. Tommy discussed it with his friends and one young man said that, if Tommy took an impression of the shape of the screw at the top of each string, at his place of work, he could make a tool to fit.

Tommy mentioned his intention to Mr Frusher. A rather derisive smile greeted the proposition, but he gave Tommy a tuning fork for A. With this to guide him, he used the key to get the middle note right and the rest followed from that. The complete job took a long time. Day after day, in his spare moments he'd be sitting there tapping away on the keys and turning the screws until his ear told him it was as near as he would get. The deep bass remained questionable, the ear alone could not get that correct. But he had the beginnings of a piano. Good enough to play with one finger.

When he told Mr Frusher he'd about finished the job, curiosity overcame the choirmaster and he had to call round and see it. Although, when he played a few bars on this thing, his face betrayed a degree of pain, still he complimented the lad on what he'd done and said, "If you like, I'll give you a few lessons. You already know something of music. I'll teach you the scales and arpeggios and so forth and we'll see how you get on."

Thereafter, Tommy took a half hour's lesson every week — free, for Tommy's parents couldn't afford to pay, of course — all scales as promised, apart from the odd small practice piece. Scales of every key and major harmonic or melodic minor. Mr Frusher's lessons concentrated on getting the fingers supple, in the correct position, covering the correct notes. Tommy would faithfully carry out the practice as directed by the master and then, at the end of each session, he would treat himself to a little informal tinkering about on the keys, perhaps working out a few bars of a popular tune, a music-hall ditty.

At school, generally he was quite happy. But soon his piano studies gave him a chance for more enjoyment and to enhance his standing among his classmates — all because of the scholarly teacher's willingness to encourage any special talent he might find among the boys. When he heard about Tommy taking lessons from Mr Frusher, he had the school piano wheeled right through from the hall into the classroom, sat Tommy down, fixed his music up on the rest, and said, "Right, well, play". And he did. A popular piece of the day called Blake's March and, after that, one of the simple songs he had learnt. For his age he played very well. The class felt somehow relaxed, a relief from pressure, and Tommy's performance became a regular feature of Friday afternoons for several weeks in succession.

He found that time simply rushed by, every waking moment occupied — the pattern for the following three or four years. In due course, he moved up to his final classroom. The clever master there — A.E. Page, known as "AEP" — managed to handle a syllabus which covered three groups of pupils at different stages in their education. A huge man, over six feet tall, athletic in build although getting quite old now, he had played for quite a well-known football team, the boys believed.

AEP was a Cambridge man and proud of it, whereas the headmaster had studied at Oxford... and when he made his rounds and came into their class, the slight — not antagonism — but that little thing rubbing between them became obvious to the boys. The head would pause for a while for AEP to complete what he was saying, then start on a talk on some subject he deemed important. He would ramble on rather and the boys got a bit of fun out of this by watching their class teacher's gorge gradually rise. He had rather prominent eyes and they began to stare, and his face coloured up as his blood rose. The boys quite welcomed these little interludes, especially if AEP's lesson concerned a subject they didn't know too much about. Perhaps sometimes they even hoped the head would step in when he didn't.

The class was called standard 6 — above it only standard 7 and X7, the cream. In Tommy's classroom, the majority of the boys were triers. Some didn't bother and they would come in for a good deal of deserved abuse from the teacher, but he would concentrate on those putting in effort to get the best out of the education offered. AEP could even distinguish ability in the quality of nervousness which can prevent a lad appearing successful in a class. To the right teacher it was obvious that these boys would come through and do well. In many classes such pupils received scant attention — they would be dubbed dunces come to think of themselves that way.

These last three years[34] became the most important and informative in his school career. They had to cover a lot of ground in a short time and one doesn't pretend that any education in depth was achieved. But they acquired a sound grounding in English and that included a study of grammar until they really understood it. A boy had to take a sentence apart, give the grammatical name to each word or group of words in a sentence — noun, verb, subject, object, and so on. "Parsing" it was called. If you could do that successfully you had learnt a very important part of elementary grammar.

Latin couldn't be taken in any depth and it was doubtful that AEP had the ability anyway. But he did lay down that prefixes, roots, derivations and suffixes of Latin had to be memorised, for he quite rightly considered them to be the basis for understanding many English words. Frequently in later life, a chap would be able to deduce for himself the meaning of a word by looking at its Latin elements.

However, AEP didn't devote his English-teaching solely to grammar. He put much energy into bringing literature to life too. He even suggested a project to take the class to a good theatre. But first he prepared them thoroughly in advance, undertaking a study of Shakespeare's *The Merchant Of Venice*. The class read through it in silence — often puzzled by the language — then he gave various boys their speaking parts and so they learnt a great deal about the play.

Meanwhile, they saved up penny by penny for the great day when they would journey into the West End. Finally, one evening, they set off for the Royal Court Theatre in Sloane Square[35] where this great play came to life before their eyes, a memorable evening (as Tommy soon proved via a dramatic venture of his own).

Each subject had its allotted half-hour, hour or two hours a week, although some, such as arithmetic, they took daily. Anatomy and physiology they covered in an elementary way, but enough to give knowledge of the human body and what it was composed of. The skeleton on a huge chart would be hung up, the bones named and memorised, and the types of joints. Another brightly coloured chart showed muscles and organs. The chap in the picture, it was noticed, had no bladder and no privates. And they were never mentioned in instruction. One assumes it was similar for the girls in their class.

Under AEP, Tommy had the great pleasure of being in the same class as his brother, who sat on the far side with the select group. Those chaps more or less worked in a freelance way. The things they wanted to do they were encouraged in. They read books not in the syllabus. If they were particularly good at writing or painting, AEP permitted them to spend long periods on these subjects. The rest of the classwork went on under the master's direction, but the select group could ignore what was going on and persevere with their own special interests.

On one occasion, when they discussed the "topic of the day" and AEP gave his view of current affairs, Tommy was thrilled to see his brother espousing the cause of the Conservative Party, well knowing the teacher to be a Liberal-radical type. And the two went at it hammer and tongs for a while. Then it finished with obviously no ill will felt. The boy had stated his point of view and he had not been shouted down. His opinion had been considered, listened to. Tommy's brother would shortly go out into the world to make his way and already he was being treated like a man. This was noted by the younger lads.

However, in answer to a discreet enquiry Tommy's parents made of AEP, they learnt that neither boy would be able to take advantage of an examination that could secure them a place in the local grammar school. They couldn't afford the fees.

Good teachers are born not made and AEP, Tommy's last and best teacher, was a shining example. Let's take the matter of music. The ordinary elements Tommy learnt from Mr Frusher, but AEP particularly loved to teach the class four-part chorus tunes — full songs with all verses and a proper accompaniment –such as Sweet Lass Of Richmond Hill, Who Will O'er The Downs Go Free, and on the sacred side, that old anthem How Beautiful On The Mountains.

So he when a singing lesson was timetabled, AEP made preparations. On the black slate which lined the wall above the cupboards he wrote out the words and four-part tonic sol-fa music for the songs. Long before this, Tommy had discovered he had a natural gift for singing tunes in tonic sol-fa (if anybody whistled a tune or picked it out on the piano, Tommy could spiel it off — doh, me, soh etc — without any effort at all, so he found this method of learning very agreeable).

AEP was in no hurry, the time each song took immaterial. For him, the point was that the class should learn to sing properly. So he would test the boys' voices. He soon discovered who should sing the alto, treble and even a few tenors. Some voices in X7 were on the verge of breaking. When the class had learnt the whole thing, he would sing the bass line. He had a marvellous voice like a lusty old corncrake, but he carried the tune and, anyway, the full blast of the class drowned out his rasping efforts. It was one of the more pleasurable lessons.

About then, with some regret, George left school and got a job in the wholesale paper trade — we shall hear more about that.

Still with a year or so to go, Tommy was doing reasonably well in his exams despite always feeling he could never rise to the same heights as his brother. The thing was to get on and do the best possible. At English, in composition and dictation he was good. In arithmetic and everything that came under that heading including a smattering of algebra, percentages, rates of interest and what were generally called problems — things that made you scratch your head and think — well, you could call Tommy's performance moderate to poor. Sometimes, though, he would feel inspired and shine briefly.

One of AEP's more dubious methods of inspiring those who were a bit backward entailed what he called "Questions" where he would point to a boy and ask him a question, then, if he couldn't answer, move on to the next and the next. When he had established that nobody knew the answer, AEP would turn to one of his high-fliers and say, "Well then, Jones?"; on the whole, this chap would come up with the answer quickly. Once or twice, AEP must have forgotten that Tommy's brother had departed and suddenly swing this question on to him. Often, Tommy could do it, but he remembered one occasion when he couldn't and he wished the floor would open up and let him through.

Meanwhile, to raise money for the Scout movement, Mr Frusher began to train the lads to sing choruses from the Gilbert and Sullivan light operas — *The Mikado, HMS Pinafore,* and one or two others. It was work Mr Frusher loved. The time came when the parts had been fairly well mastered and they took to the stage of the local institute opposite the church[36]. He had no difficulty in persuading quite good professionals and semi-professionals to come along for one rehearsal and then three productions of the show. Full houses provided useful money to hire tents for the annual Scout camp.

Now old enough to be appointed a Patrol Leader, Tommy had his own group of lads to look after and a certain responsibility at these beautifully organised camps. The lads had the assistance of four or five young men in their late teens or early twenties who would go ahead and set up the tents and make arrangements for the supply of food in quantity. By the time the Troops arrived with their kit bags, everything was prepared.

The site comprised a hill at the edge of a large farming estate, with the tents set up in a row at the top, their water supply a spring at the bottom. A line of youngsters took it in turns to lower their buckets into the small pool around the spring — very carefully, so as not to disturb the silt at the bottom. The water looked clean and unadulterated, but for safety's sake they boiled it anyway.

At 6.30 each morning, a bugle call, reveille! Up and out of those beds and, given fine weather, the Scoutmaster, assistant Scoutmasters, and all of the boys in their pants and vests rushed down to the river and in they went. The water came up to their waists or shoulders. They took their soap, so a cold bath and a quick towelling on the riverbank, then back up the hill to breakfast; large containers of hard-boiled eggs or saveloys[37] — very popular with the lads — and bacon with plenty of bread and butter and boiling tea. Done over campfires, it all went off with the precision of a military camp.

On the first morning, just after breakfast, the senior assistant dashed into his tent, reappeared with a sports gun and fired at a few ducks flying overhead. No duck for dinner, but it brought a shocked Mr Frusher hurrying from his tent. Shooting was not on the agenda and he didn't approve. But the same young man took them running across the fields, after which they formed into a square and some exercises did them a power of good.

Nearby lived a family who, from the old, bearded, grandfather down, worked on this huge farm. Tommy learned that the old man earned the princely sum of 18/- a week. Other family members got proportionate sums, the boys probably 4/- or 5/-. But they had certain perquisites which helped them along; for instance, at the back of the barn behind their house, free-running poultry nested — they ranged over the fields to feed themselves, but the majority came to this row of nest boxes to lay their eggs. The family could take as many as they wished and, no doubt, a cockerel whenever they felt like it.

They had enough ground to grow all the vegetables they needed too — all this far more valuable than their wages. Lots of rabbits to be trapped, milk from the dairy a mile or so across the field — a gallon for a few coppers. They seemed a remarkably happy family. Full of jokes. They gave the lads a good impression of life on the land. The farmer seldom came round the place. As head of the family, the grandfather took responsibility for organising the work and employing any extra labourers.

One of the farm girls was a merry lass, 20 or so, considerably older than the boys and her name was Mary Anne. A popular song of the time went, "Mary Anne she's after me/Full of love she seems to be/My mother says that Mary Anne/Wants me for her young man". Once or twice groups of the young lads got under Mary Anne's bedroom window late at night and serenaded her with this beautiful song[38]. Mr Frusher was inclined to frown on these efforts, but Mary Anne appeared to be flattered and very well pleased.

One wet night, rain leaked into some of the tents. The boys were quickly moved into the barn. They threw their camp mattresses down on the floor — covered with hay, fresh and sweet-smelling — wrapped themselves up in their blankets, snug and warm, and spent what was, to them, quite a thrilling night — for the barn had other occupants, owls and bats, who flew in and out, a busy traffic.

On one occasion in camp, when Tommy got a rather nasty cold he was given a bed in the tent with the four assistant Scoutmasters. He enjoyed that. Waking in the morning he looked at them as they lay there.

The senior one attracted his attention. His face still, absolutely immobile. Tommy thought, "How different, how young he looks, compared to when I've seen him going to the station for work". Employed by a firm of stockbrokers, on some occasions the Scoutmaster had to wear the uniform of tall, silk hat, cutaway morning coat and striped trousers. Tommy had seen him with his coat tails flying and tightly rolled umbrella, the picture of health and activity. Yet here he slept, almost boyish.

How could Tommy possibly have known that, soon, this splendid young chap, with many others, would be lying at the bottom of the North Sea after the Battle Of Jutland...

Near him lay a younger man, the soul of kindness. He could not be faulted in his treatment of the lads. He was liked and Tommy admired him. He was shattered on the Somme battlefield...

Chapter Nine

It was decided, for the first time, to hold a special "school day". The plan included a bazaar, several small plays, some singing, and a long afternoon during which parents and friends could visit, listen, do what they wished, and make quite friendly contact with the teachers. Tommy and a friend were allotted the task of going to the bigger houses in the area, whose occupants might be willing to give old items such as trays, candlesticks, any sort of metalware or jewellery — anything they could clean, burnish, and offer for sale.

The two boys sacrificed much school time to hike miles, always collecting something useful. A pair of heavy solid-silver, engraved candlesticks, he remembered — black they were, from being stowed away in a lumber-room. Tommy polished them up.

One of the shows the pupils put on they called Mrs Varley's Waxworks[39]. Tommy's pal, Charlie — the one who lived in a small drapery shop — had developed the gift of the gab with a vengeance, so he took the part of the showman who strutted around, spoke about each of the dozen "waxwork" characters on the stage, and told them when they should step forward and jerkily perform the actions he described.

Drawing inspiration from his trip to the Royal Court, Tommy played Shylock. His father procured a false nose — hooked, of course. His mother cut up a bright red, silk skirt and turned it into a cloak. Then, with an old smoking cap on his head and his face made up swarthily, he jerked forward with a large curved knife and went through the motions of removing his pound of flesh from the victim.

Another boy took the role of a Red Indian; he did what he thought the correct dance and performed a wee bit of scalping.

The audience took to it so well that a tour of the church halls and the schools in the area was suggested. Quite a professional troupe they became — and this led to the first party ever at Tommy's home. His mother thought she would like to entertain all the waxworks. Quite an undertaking, with their furniture and accommodation so limited, but it went off well, a jolly party, and Tommy's friends spoke of it for some time afterwards.

Even in these later years at school, no homework was given so, in the evenings, the boys' time remained their own. Apart from Scouts and choir, Tommy sometimes earned a few coppers by working as a ball boy several hours at the local tennis club. And when George left school and started work, Tommy took over his Friday spare-time job: collecting the registers for a number of schools and taking them to the home of the attendance officer. So, a little pocket money, and, generally, life continued to lose that keen edge of hardness and want which had characterised it ever since the family moved to London.

People watched with interest the construction of a new building a mile along the main road from where Tommy lived. The Alcazar. A German named Romberg conceived and built it[40]. He brought new ideas. The front part had a distinctly foreign appearance with a large balcony above, fronted by a wooden railing in ornamental style and decorative woodwork around it.

Beneath it, you entered a spacious vestibule, swing doors at the back of it — an entrance to a cinema — while another door admitted you to open tree- and shrub-filled gardens enlivened by various fairground games and amusements, including an American soda fountain. Placing an order for one of these ice-cold drinks, which cost a penny, would start a very devious process of manufacture before your eyes as this machine of many glass tubes and bulbs filled with coloured fluids sprang to life. Eventually, the attendant poured the finished product into a glass and handed it to you.

Well, Tommy couldn't go into this place, of course, because he still didn't have the money. But he watched fascinated as people milled about on their way in or out. He listened to their comments when they emerged and sometimes heard a little of the music floating out when the doors opened.

However, on one occasion, his mother was very keen that the children should see one particular item at the cinema and she gave him enough to buy a ticket. The enterprising German had actually had a cinecameraman attend one of those church fetes Tommy's parents helped to organise. This time his mother had run a baby competition — babies decked out in their finery and exhibited to a couple of judges — and the Alcazar showed the film. So, briefly, the children saw their own mother walking across the screen…

Romberg charged only 6d to stroll around the grounds, and another 3d for the cinema, so on warm summer evenings the Alcazar drew large crowds. It seemed the high life had moved into this somewhat backward suburban area.

Another German conducted the orchestra, which accompanied the dancers or roller-skaters, depending on the season. A very stout man with cropped hair and a rubicund face, he had quite a catholic taste in music. He would, of course, play the popular German and Viennese waltzes and also one or two by the English composers gaining a bit of renown then, most notably Charles Ancliffe, whose best known piece was called Nights Of Gladness[41].

But the orchestra quickly learned the American syncopated music which was coming in with such tunes as Everybody's Doing It and Alexander's Ragtime Band[42]. This in turn demanded that the dancers pick up the accompanying dance, the Turkey Trot, a sort of rocking from side to side.

A new look for the more avant-garde men came in too: suits with high, padded shoulders, long coats down to the thighs, and trousers full at the top, but tight down to the ankles; shoes with a high toe — like a mound — and a deep cowboy heel. A right ugly outfit it was.

The Alcazar's glory proved short-lived. A simple, pleasure-giving place it was at first, but the proprietors introduced boxing, then all-in wrestling and its reputation became a bit lurid. After a good many years, the dances ended and the grounds were closed after the lads from the East End had moved in and one or two girls were found naked and raped in the bushes. So it went on until the Second World War when Hitler marked his disapproval by dropping on it one of the first bombs to hit London[43]. Up went the old building, just a mass of rubble.

That summer[44], Tommy sometimes joined a group headed by an Irish lad called Joe Sheahan who was a couple of years older than him and a very enthusiastic outdoors man.

Several of the lads followed Joe on one of his enterprises which was to get up early two or three mornings a week — before breakfast, around 6 o'clock — and run the three or four miles to a nearby town and a lake where swimming was allowed. Although it had an irregular shape, with islands and trees, chains fixed around the outer banks ensured you could always get hold of something to help you out of the water. They would run back home in time to eat and go to school.

As the summer sun continued until autumn, Joe proposed they go and camp in the forest for a night or two. Tommy's parents were difficult to persuade, but they agreed and furnished him with a little tea and something to eat. Joe provided two methylated water heaters. Each could boil a pint of water.

They spent the day in and around the forest and, when it began to get dark, they brewed up. As night came on, the birds ceased their singing and new noises took over: the rustling of the trees, the leaves, odd branches cracking. Unexpected movements around them... in the end, without too much discussion, they grabbed up all their equipment and ran for it to the nearest road. They arrived home about 9 or 10, but in no mind to admit what had made them forsake their intended adventure.

When he wasn't off with Joe Sheahan's group, Tommy often joined his schoolfriends, all aged 13 or so by then, to stage mock battles on the old brickfields. Each kiln had an open space in the middle, so they made good forts. But came the day when a rival gang, led by a boy called Wayland, started a quite vicious and serious attack — because, it seemed, they had a grudge against Tommy.

This was hard for him to understand. No particular incident had provoked it. But he sensed it may have arisen from his close friendship with Charlie Bolton, the brainiest lad in the school (once Tommy's brother George had left to go out to work). Within their own group, Charlie insisted on Tommy taking the lead in any activity such as the brickfield battles. Maybe he saw himself as the organiser of strategy and Tommy as the chief when it came to fighting (albeit play-fighting, usually). People did tend to cast Tommy in that role in his later life, for reasons he could never fathom; he always shed the ill-fitting cloak at the earliest possible moment.

But Tommy had become aware that Wayland's crowd referred to his group of quieter types who tried their best in class and did quite well as

"The Good Boys". When Tommy considered this, he realised that, while he and his friends pitched into school activities like the bazaar and the waxworks show, Wayland and company did not. Even though Wayland always appeared assured and competent, he spent his time criticising and complaining about teachers or anyone else in authority over the children. After the waxworks show, particularly, he started to behave towards Tommy as if he hated his guts. He insulted and persecuted him, as children can.

Then came the battle at the brickfield. Tommy and his friends took shelter in the middle of a kiln and returned the shower of bricks and pieces of brick coming their way. It went on for some time quite evenly until Tommy, standing up to look for a possible target, caught a brick on the top of his head. Then the battle stopped. A great deal of blood poured from the wound. The aggressors departed in a hurry and Tommy's friends saw him home.

Over the following weeks, the one-sided feud took a strange turn. A boy called Hoy, normally a bad-tempered lone wolf who snapped at anybody who dared to disagree with him, seemed to appoint himself Wayland's deputy. At school, he picked a quarrel with Tommy and a fight started. Tommy's pals stopped it, but all agreed that the matter needed settling. Between them, they fixed a time and venue: lunch break the following day in the neglected field in front of the school (in a spot concealed from the main road by tall hoardings which Tommy remembered carrying huge pictures of the great John Philip Sousa[45] and his Military Band).

They didn't make the arrangements in any casual way. Both boys appointed seconds — Tommy, naturally, had Charlie — and they asked another boy, Arthur Fowler, to referee because he had nothing to do with the conflict and both sides rated him a "good sport". Son of a carpenter and joiner, Arthur was considered very affluent because he had a halfpenny a day pocket money compared to Tommy's penny a week, but he'd often share his sweets with other boys, including Tommy.

So, at midday, a crowd gathered, the two gangs among them, but keeping well apart as they filed through a gate into the field; fighting on school premises was forbidden but they understood this pre-arranged affair outside the grounds had the approval of AEP himself. The two sides had agreed that each round should last only a minute, Arthur blowing his Scout whistle to signify start and end, as they didn't have a bell. Between rounds they rested for two minutes and the bout was to continue for as long as they could keep going. All the "officials" saw that everything went according to the book[46].

Tommy fell into the boxer's stance he'd learnt during Boy Scout training and shuffled about. Bigger and stronger, Hoy lashed out frequently, but somewhat blindly. His face evinced murderous malice throughout. Tommy himself found real hatred rising in him as soon as the bout got going. He was being hurt. Yet a certain coolness, fruit of those boxing lessons, kept his emotions in check and helped to compensate for Hoy's physical superiority.

While resigned to a beating, Tommy got in the occasional whack. Round after round, the battle raged. Tommy's mouth and face began to feel like a huge, puffed-up thing, ten times their actual size and, although, clearly, both boys were becoming exhausted, neither capable of landing a knockout blow, Tommy felt sure he was going to lose. How much longer could he hold out?, he wondered. When should they finish? When they sank to their knees? It seemed endless.

With Hoy's friends yelling at him to finish his foe off, by an indescribable piece of luck Tommy swung his arm over, missed his target and struck Hoy on the upper right arm. It dropped to his side and he yelled at Arthur, "I can't hold it up! It's paralysed! It's paralysed!" That finished it. Arthur awarded the win to Tommy, despite the opposition's protests. Fearing a general attack, Tommy's friends hurried him away, shouting congratulations and slapping him on the back — Tommy pretended to be unimpressed and said nothing about the sheer good fortune of the punch hitting a nerve to end the fight.

While the others withdrew to the playground, Tommy ran off home, joyful yet scarcely aware of what he was doing, so great had been the strain of the punishment he had taken. When he got there he dashed to the sink, turned on the tap, and ran icy cold water over his face and neck time after time until the pain eased somewhat. Looking around, he saw a large basin full of Benger's Food his mother had prepared for the baby[47]. Without thought, he snatched this up and drank the lot.

Then he went upstairs and lay down on his bed, hoping to gain strength to face his mother, and then make his way back to school for the afternoon session. He made it, but went about as in a dream for several hours.

Tommy neared the end of his school days. He knew that he just had to leave, start work, and earn a few shillings. He would have welcomed some sort of further training, but clearly the family's finances would not allow that. He felt particularly aware of this because his greatest friend, Charlie, the draper's son, was able to continue his education at a commercial college. Their friendship lasted until later years in life. But, for the time being, the break had to come.

During his final months at school, Tommy found himself in the top group of class 7X. Not only that — his teachers, including AEP, began to give him what they called the "top-boy treatment". He didn't believe he was top boy and thought perhaps the glory of his brother was shining on him a little.

But, along with some of his fellows — as had happened to George when he reached this level — he took certain fixed lessons with the class and then worked independently on any subject in which he was especially interested. For Tommy, that meant the history period he had reached; the end of the 19th century, the wars in Africa.

He read several books about it, fiction mostly, and conceived the idea of writing a book on the subject himself. He set to work, spending an hour or two on it each day. That continued until the end of his time at the school. Unfortunately, it grew very long and he could not complete it before he had to leave.

Aside from this freedom of study, AEP gave him responsible, practical jobs too, such as making a stock list of the school book store to help the teachers draw up their syllabuses for the new year beginning in September — a task AEP would normally have undertaken himself, but he thought it would give Tommy useful experience.

The settled life he'd enjoyed — school and then all those regular evening activities — was about to be fractured. Even his voice began to break, ending his participation in the church choir. That made a great change; Sundays and two nights of the week free. He had time on his hands. Too much even.

Finally, a month's holiday, a brief return to school in the summer until his birthday in July[48], a farewell chat with his teacher, AEP, the big, admirable man, another with the head, who handed him an excellent testimonial. And goodbye to all that.

PART TWO

1912-1914

RECRUIT:

OUT TO WORK

AND OFF TO BE A SOLDIER

Chapter Ten

Suddenly, what had been a school day was a working day. But nothing to do. A sense of urgency soon built up and the necessity for finding work and earning money became quite oppressive. Tommy felt he was not doing his bit.

His father procured interviews with two firms, the first a terrifying experience for the lad, at a famous glovemaker's, Dents[49]. The idea was that be might start as a boy in the counting house. A man of very severe appearance and manner interviewed Tommy and he thought it didn't go at all well. For one thing, even though his father accompanied him, he felt far too nervous.

From there, straight across the middle of London to its Eastern outskirts for an interview with a firm called John Howell, who manufactured walking sticks, a huge variety, their name known throughout the world[50]. The idea was that Tommy should train to be an invoice clerk and packer. The head of the department, E. J. Moss, an ordinary sort of man, interviewed him, then said he could start the following Monday if he wished. He and his father forgot about the glove business at once. The department boss introduced Tommy to the man under whom he would work and, the following week, he began to accustom himself to the routine there.

Apart from Mr Moss, only one man and one boy — himself — occupied his workplace, a huge room arrayed with benches or counters, each about 12 feet long. Every morning, the man's first call would be at the counter nearest the door, where Mr Moss sat. He handed out a sheaf of customer orders, then man and boy went to the stockroom to fetch the required types of stick and pack them in a particular way — to avoid damage in transit (even the common ash walking stick they produced) — which took quite a bit of learning. Then they made out an invoice in triplicate.

This entailed a great deal of running about to the different storerooms and climbing ladders to the higher racks. Quite an active job, then.

But some sticks in the more expensive grades of wood had to be made to order. In that case, the man wrote a specification in accordance with the customer's wishes. This the boy took through the works to the bench of the craftsman who would shape that stick. Tommy noted the tools of the trade: a heated tank of water, usually boiling, a flame of the Bunsen burner type, clamps — the craftsman would have to know all the various types of cane and wood and be able to select them and bend them into the required shape, perhaps having first turned them in a lathe. A skilful job.

In short order, Tommy too had to learn about the materials used, high and low grade, their colour, graining and finish — and the correct names for them: natural canes such as Nilgiri and Malacca, whose names indicated their countries of origin[51]; others with a manufactured colour and finish. In addition, either the craftsman or the production line might ornament them with genuine silver and gold bands, or complete handles finely chased, or with cheap imitations of the precious metals. So Tommy learned how to polish the gold and silver parts using a fine rouge powder with a buffing stick — a piece of wood with leather wound round it.

Howell's made swordsticks too — still popular in those days. Tommy never heard of anybody drawing his sword from his stick and jabbing it into anyone, but perhaps it did occur in some remote part of the British Empire.

One thing the boy couldn't get used to was the supervisor, Mr Moss. His right eye looked to the right and his left eye to the left. He had a harsh voice and he considered it his duty from time to time to yell at the boy, who, he thought, didn't work hard enough. He could put the fear of God into Tommy. So the lad rushed around doing his best.

The job and its location made for a longish day. Tommy left home at about 6 in the morning, caught the train at 6.20 and hung about near the works until 8 when they opened, then he worked through to 12, an hour for lunch, and on till 6 with the train journey of about an hour to come.

Even so, he carried on with his Scouting activities, two meetings a week, Thursdays and Saturdays, and he now attended evening classes twice weekly too. It had been decided he should learn commercial book-keeping and typewriting, two useful skills whatever job he chose or had to do. So most of his weekdays concluded at about 9.30pm.

You can imagine how delighted he was when he found that his old pal from choirboy days, Reg Curtis, worked near him. They could meet at lunchtimes and Reggie knew of one or two places to sit and listen to music and singing for half an hour. He also knew the places where, for a penny, you could get a large cup of tea — one, part of a chain called Lockharts (bless the promoter of them), where just buying a mug of tea entitled you to sit there and eat the sandwich lunch mother had prepared for you. Rest and refreshment for a penny...

Another place Reg introduced Tommy to was known as the Alexandra Trust, where hundreds of people went for cheap food. And it was cheap too — apart from the tea, a large, toasted teacake cost a penny too.[52]

Tommy reckoned he was getting down to his life. But one day he had to climb some very high steps to the top rack in one of the storerooms. As he reached out to the shelf the steps fell away. He felt as though, for the moment, he was suspended in the air. Then he crashed on to his backside. A terrible jolt to his system and that put him off work for a couple of weeks.

At the end of that time, he didn't want to go back to that job. He wasn't even sure the firm would take him back, because there was always somebody to fill a vacancy left for no matter what reason.

But, to his relief, he got another job, in the City of London, at a company quite near the place where his brother worked. Even better, his work didn't start until 9am so he could take a later train, 7.15 rather than 6.20 — although that meant he still ended up in the City almost an hour before he had to start. Still, often he could travel in with both his brother and his father; Liverpool Street happened to be the nearest station to all of their workplaces. So, arriving early, together they would go to one of the little squares in the area and, if it was a light morning, look at the paper or just sit and talk if it was dark. Tommy could meet George at lunchtime too, another advantage.

A job of a different nature — only the office boy this time — but he quickly realised he had much to learn. It would be up to him as to how he progressed. The firm, Lake & Currie, had large interests centred on the tin mining and smelting industry and scattered around the world: in various parts of Nigeria, in Penang[53], New Zealand and, at home, in Cornwall at Helston and Redruth.

Promptly at 9, Tommy's routine commenced under the supervision of the commissionaire, whom everyone called "Sergeant" — the day's first task the opening of all incoming mail and sorting it into piles, department by department, except that addressed personally to one of the partners, or to the Secretary Of Companies, which Tommy would place in their individual in-trays. He dealt with mail deliveries throughout the day too. And once the directors, the Company Secretary, and the rest of the staff entered their offices, the product of their thought and labours would soon start emerging. A very varied correspondence it made too, Tommy discovered — by reading most of it because, as office boy, he had to make copies of every letter that came in or went out.

Sergeant taught him their old-fashioned method of copying letters and signatures into a large book: place each letter on a blank page of its very fine, soft paper; cover it with a damp cloth and a waterproof oilboard (to prevent the moisture spoiling the previous copy); then put the book in a heavy, iron press. A clear facsimile resulted, complete with signature. Tommy completed the job by filing the typed carbon duplicate supplied by the typist in the book alongside this copy.

The junior boy, the last one in, Tommy had to take the mail to the post office too, before he started his lunch break — making sure he stamped each letter or package with the correct rate, especially for foreign destinations. In addition, he delivered some items by hand, to banks and so on in, so he learned many of the backstreets and alleys. Tiring work, padding around.

He quickly realised that, had he been not quite the junior, he would have been able to undertake slightly longer trips to deliver the more urgent messages and these would have entailed spending cash on bus fares up to the limits of the City, or a taxi for more distant destinations. Apart from the comfort and pleasure of such journeys, in some cases the senior lads would charge for a taxi when they had actually used a quick bus route and thereby gain a little pocket money from the cash they'd been advanced. Naughty, but an opportunity any poor boy might consider taking.

Merely buying stamps Tommy had to apply for petty cash, of course, and, each time, a clerk entered a ticket showing the details of the transaction in a ledger — the biggest book Tommy had ever seen, ruled in vertical columns, one for each type of item the company purchased. Every penny spent had to be accounted for in this book. When I say the petty cash was dealt out in amounts not exceeding £5, this may seem very small money, but five gold sovereigns from that era would probably now amount to £50 or £60[54].

The Sergeant taught Tommy how to keep this record, likewise how to operate the company's small telephone switchboard, which directed calls to every department in the building. In fact, Sergeant told the boys under his supervision they would have to learn to do all the jobs he did, because he didn't intend to remain there. He was perfectly sure a big war was coming up shortly and, in the natural order of things, he would go to the War Office to take a job which had been waiting for him in that event.

In one of many lunchtime discussions, Sergeant told Tommy he had been a Warrant Officer — a Sergeant Major — in the Army, having joined as a boy[55]. Back straight as a ramrod, legs slightly bowed, clipped moustache iron-grey and hair about two inches long, oiled, parted in the middle, his eyes dark, sharp, penetrating — almost black — with bushy, grey eyebrows above them, and complexion sallow, parchment-like from service in India; he could cause trepidation with a look. He wore a black uniform of quality cloth with some gold-braid trimming and three gold stripes on each arm, lacquered buttons, and several medal ribbons on the left breast. His shoes shone.

Tommy found him a most interesting chap and admired the way that, when he took his lunch, he always stayed in the office. He probably thought his job important because he was in charge of greeting everybody, from the big businessmen directors of other firms in the City down to the girl hoping to solicit an order for carbon paper. With all these people, he had to be tactful and informative.

However, Tommy did come to realise that, in practice, Sergeant fulfilled his role very well in regard to callers of higher status, but often gave short shrift to those, in his view, beneath his own social level. Even so, he made an exception for one of the carbon-paper sellers, a dark, attractive girl. When she arrived, she would lift the outer desk flap and come through into Sergeant's inner office where she sat on one of the stools — Sergeant's or Tommy's — to display her wares and her charms. Sergeant had to be careful — people about — but he got in his touches and caresses and perhaps the girl netted a small order.

Tommy felt he must emulate Sergeant and learn the geography of the building, the whereabouts and types of people in each department.

Through swing doors first on the left the board met — around a large table, green-baize-covered, seated in large, comfortable chairs, they would discuss the affairs of the many companies they controlled. Facing the boardroom on the opposite side of the corridor were the men's toilets. Black marble predominated, washbasins and other fixtures, beautifully clean.

From there out into the corridor again, up a passage and into a room filled with typewriters — Miss Binney in charge, a woman in her late forties; under her four typists of various ages.

Out and along a short corridor, the Company Secretary, F.C. Bull, FCB as he was known, a truly important man, possessing vast knowledge of company law and of his own company's subsidiaries around the world. He stood about 5 foot 4, slim, balding, dark, some grey hair, quick in movement, with rather a harsh voice and a middle-class accent, very different from that of the partners; sharp distinctions existed in those days between working-, middle- and upper-class accents.

Then, to the right of FCB's office, the accountants; the chief accountant and his assistants all busy at their books. And, further along, one company director, Mr Currie, a huge Scotsman with a large estate out in Buckinghamshire. On the same side, next door along, the office of the other director, Mr Lake. A big man indeed. The squire of quite a large village up in Norfolk and the possessor of a dwelling in the fashionable Boltons area of Kensington[56] and a flat in one of those small streets at the back of Trafalgar Square.

Over the corridor again, the drawing office where men who understood mines drafted plans and designs for their digging, construction and operation.

Tommy soon realised that F.C. Bull occupied a particular and peculiar place in Sergeant's view of social class and status. Because, despite his eminence within the company, he didn't come from what the Sergeant called "the upper crust", Sergeant treated him with respect to his face, then derided him behind his back. Tommy would snigger at these jibes.

After a while, when Tommy felt more comfortable with the job, a mad mood seized him; a six-verse limerick about FCB resulted. It was libellous and it was untrue, but Tommy asked his brother to get it typed — his wholesale paper firm had offices nearby in Upper Thames Street — and Miss Violet Turner, prim, young secretary to George's boss, presented it very tastefully on mauve-tinted paper. What a strange thing to do. But George persuaded her, and with some trepidation Tommy showed this script to Sergeant. He laughed heartily and evilly at Tommy's vile, cheap sarcasm, then furtively passed it around other departments, accounting, shipping, the draftsmen.

Some members of staff stopped to congratulate Tommy and he progressed through fear of dismissal at perpetrating this crime to a swelled head because of the kudos he had gained. Only later did he realise, guiltily, how far he had let himself become Sergeant's lickspittle. F.C. Bull was a man who deserved better of his underlings.

While any of the boys could take care of lesser visitors to Lake & Currie, Sergeant always stepped forward when anybody important showed up. Perhaps a mining engineer would call to see one or both of the directors to discuss a written report he'd submitted on work abroad or to seal a new contract — their agreements usually lasted three years with a break of two or three months in the middle because of the wearing climates encountered in, for example, Nigeria[57] or Malaya. Before they passed through the green doors to the inner sanctum, a quiet few words with the Sergeant on the way in would prepare them for any changes in staff and, perhaps, the prevailing temper of the directors.

When abroad working, an engineer may have sent back samples of ore to be assayed and, although he would receive an acknowledgment, perhaps he didn't hear the results before beginning his journey home. If any information of that sort came the Sergeant's way he would give it. Tommy would sometimes learn that such a meeting with the directors had reached a happy conclusion via an instruction to take a new contract round to the Government office in Moorgate Street where an official stamp would confirm it as a legal document, at the cost of half a crown.

These mining engineers bore great responsibility and Tommy viewed them as men of independence, skill, and authority who did difficult jobs in faraway places; he liked the look of them, a touch of hero-worship in his gaze, no doubt. When they were prospecting for new mines, the samples they sent back to England for assay could have quite an effect on the market; if the yield looked good and word got round the City, then the company's shares might rise rapidly. If this proved over-optimistic and the actual yield from the mine proved poor, then a good deal of money could be lost.

The firm retained the services of a top assayist and his staff at a laboratory south of the Thames. Beautifully spoken and dressed in the height of fashion, yet popular with all ranks, this man paid regular visits to the office and his well-defined officer-and-gentleman status permitted a special relationship with Sergeant, the non-commissioned officer. Sergeant called him Mister or Sir without any reserve. Each respected the other's qualities and privileges. A few words, an understanding look, conveyed much. No condescension on one side, no taking of liberties on the other.

Gradually, Tommy became aware of the complications in these relationships Sergeant fostered. He learned that, to obtain this uniformed but civilian job, Sergeant had deposited a sum of money with the Corps Of Commissionaires[58], by way of security — in case of exactly what eventualities Tommy wasn't entirely clear.

More valuable than the deposit was his apparent integrity. Men like him knew and maintained an expected code of conduct — although, curiously, they had, and they showed, contempt for anyone of their own class who attempted to improve their status by study and hard work. Yet these old and trusted servants also felt they were themselves aping the gentry and becoming traitors to their kind thereby — if one can follow that line of thought.

Many a tirade on these matters assaulted Tommy's ears. Sergeant in his lunchtime strode the office floor: a bite of his sandwich, a champing of the jaw muscles, a long swig from a tankard of beer, and out flowed the bitter words. FCB, and Sampson, head of accounts, and Otley, the top draftsman, all came in for it, the last classed as a "homo" as well as an upstart.

But the upper classes, equally, could bring on a rant. The very men with whom Sergeant shared a number of confidences on a servant-and-master basis, who trusted him — rightly so — were, apart from business considerations, enemies of his class. Wont to growl, "God bless the Squire and his relations/Long may they keep us in our stations"[59] — probably the only couplet of verse he knew — he repeated it endlessly in the course of his lunchtimes orations. The boy listened, but kept his own council.

Daily at a quarter to six, the Sergeant would remove his braided and bemedalled tunic, place them on a hanger, polish his shoes, and take from the locker his bowler hat, coat and umbrella. At five to six Tommy did likewise. They locked up everything lockable and, having wished everybody else goodnight, waited for the last member of staff to depart, accountant, draftsman or typist (though, if Miss Binnie permitted them to go, they had been drifting out since 5pm). The Company Secretary often stayed on later than all others. Directors came and went or stayed away as they pleased.

Let's have a look at Sergeant and Tommy for a moment. The old boy's train home went from Liverpool Street too so Tommy, the most junior boy in the office at that stage, was permitted to walk with him. Probably 5 foot 2 then, at 14, to Sergeant's 5 foot 9, he strode out to keep step. Comical he must have looked in his skintight trousers and short, bum-freezer jacket, topped off with the square, bowler hard hat. The gentry favoured a different bowler with the brim curled up at the sides and a half-spherical crown. Thus one could easily distinguish the officers from the other ranks — though a closer look would further reveal jackets of fine-quality cloth, more fully cut too, and trousers more fully shaped from the top to the narrow bottom (permanent turn-ups had not been heard of; a man turned up the bottoms of his working trousers only if they were too long for him).

The walk stationwards took them through several of the City's narrower streets. With his recent history lessons in mind, Tommy concluded that these deep gulleys between tall buildings must have been laid out before the Great Fire Of London — Wren's contemporaries would surely never have planned so foolishly after the lessons of so great a disaster[60]. As soon as their route crossed in front of the Royal Exchange they became members of a huge, walking army. Across into Broad Street and past the Stock Exchange, the solid, advancing mass filled the pavements and the whole roadway — useless for vehicles to try to move during this great exodus. Vehicles using the City moved around from early morning to early afternoon and slowly made their way through the streets, the majority still horse-drawn so the cracking of whips and urgent cries of drivers added to the continuous hubbub. To cross a road one just threaded one's way through the tangle, developing some skill in avoiding contact with wagons and horses.

Some taxicabs, powered by small petrol engines despite design still based on horse-drawn carriages, did represent the beginnings of automation. A shilling would pay for more than a mile and include the driver's tip. The internal combustion engine had become just about dependable and most bus companies had already replaced their horses. However, one company preferred steam engines and their buses ran almost silently, a pleasant hiss their only contribution to the hellish clatter around them. A large, low bonnet concealed these engines and Tommy often wondered what fuel they used. But apart from seeing something glowing in a metal tray when he looked down from the upper deck, he never found out. He guessed it might have been a gas[61].

When it rained, the solid rubber, rather narrow bus tyres provided a thrilling skidding on greasy roads with a steep camber for drainage purposes. The awkward vehicles often slid sideways and hit the kerb.

Chapter Eleven

After a while, a new boy with black hair, a ruddy face, and sparkling eyes, called Norman Praeter started work — as Tommy's helper. Thereafter, deliveries of letters and messages fell to Norman, relieving Tommy of much walking and sore feet.

Tommy got a pay increase too, which he thought would buy a 4d seat in the local music hall[62] and a French pastry and a glass of hot cordial in winter or an iced drink in summer or a bag of broken biscuits. Or he could buy a piece of cold fried fish and, say three large cups of tea all for a bob. His chops slobbered at the glorious prospect. But his parents allowed him to keep only 3d of it which brought his legitimate pocket money up to 1s 3d.

However, given his small promotion, he could take over the journeys further afield by taxi for urgent deliveries of mail and other documents which offered opportunities for a little profit on the fares as, surprisingly, the company's accounting procedures did not require him to supply tickets or receipts. Nor did he feel compelled to tell his parents about this mite of extra income.

So, often, he was able to join his brother in a lunchtime visit to a local Italian shop. They became known as regulars and, if the shop was full, they were ushered downstairs to a disused basement room. There a voluptuous maiden served them.

Sometimes an older fellow joined them — always well dressed in a City suit, hair well cut and a white face, very pale indeed, with rather small eyes. Neither Tommy nor his brother really liked him, but he fascinated them because of the tales he told. He was engaged to a beautiful girl and one gathered they hadn't waited on the formalities of marriage for consummation. He described how, if her parents were out when he visited her, she would undress completely, and he would lay her out on the dining-room table and "have" her. The brothers concluded that he was a bit of a bird-hound and, no doubt, his wishes were father to his thoughts with regard to many of his stories, if not all of them.

Living where they did, neither brother could be ignorant of what went on around them in the world, some of it not entirely beautiful or creditable. And yet the thoughts and conduct inculcated in them by dear old Frusher still governed them. Well, they governed Tommy at any rate — he realised he couldn't speak for his older brother with complete certainty.

On occasions, the two would take walks out into the country, only a matter of a few minutes away, of course. On one of these trips they crossed a long, low field and reached a river. They were walking alongside it, watching for the occasional fish, when two rough-and-ready, young, labouring types, with two women in tow, came hurrying by.

Later, Tommy and his brother crossed a footbridge and started to ascend the hills opposite, climbing through fields bordered by hedges. Glancing up towards one of the higher fields, they caught sight of the two couples lying down and indulging in a very natural enjoyment. Suddenly, to the boys' surprise, the men jumped up and ran to the nearest hedge where they apparently relieved themselves.

They were returning to the girls when another man caught the brothers' attention; he was snaking up the hill between the hedges and bushes in the direction of the two couples. By his suspicious movements, the boys concluded he was a Peeping Tom. This they could not endure, so they let out a terrific yell, "Look out, there's somebody coming!" The Peeping Tom saw the boys and came towards them, but they ran up the hill and avoided him.

Just the matter of a couple of years separating the brothers could feel like quite a gap at that age; George had friends of his own and so did Tommy. The same applied to girls. Up at the old church Tommy had got to know one or two girls, mainly sisters of the choirboys. He would walk with them and talk a short while perhaps.

But one day, his brother introduced him to two girls, cousins, and they got chatting. One of them was the daughter of a greengrocer and she liked talking about the family trade. The other worked in an office somewhere. The four of them were just sitting at the edge of a field, watching the people go by, when an old woman dressed in black walked deliberately in amongst them making noises of disgust and disapproval. They had done nothing of which they should be ashamed, but apparently even that amount of closeness between the sexes met with her disapproval. Probably mad, at first she provided a little perplexity and then some amusement.

They met the girls on several other occasions, but at that time Tommy had no interest at all in the greengrocer's daughter, so he didn't see any more of them until a Sunday afternoon just after dinner when mother, who'd apparently heard some sound, hurried to the front door, opened it and, after a moment, started shouting. The boys slipped over to the window and saw the two girls standing in the road. They had called to ask if George and Tommy would be coming out and mother was ranting away saying that her sons wanted nothing to do with them and she'd see that they didn't have. "You shameless hussies, throwing yourselves at young lads like my sons!" she yelled — "hoossies" in her Manchester accent, Tommy always remembered the sound of it. "Clear off, before I give you something to help you on your way!"

It was embarrassing. Well, George was more incensed than embarrassed and, thereafter, he took care to keep his friends, both male and female, away from their home. Out of such things are the seeds of dissension and dislike sometimes sown in families. A growing chap like that getting treated as a child... But I'm afraid that no protests on his part would have deterred the mother from acting in that way[63].

After that, Tommy rarely saw George with a girl, though he never knew whether this resulted from the secrecy inspired by their mother's rage or simply from feeling too preoccupied with boyish-cum-manly pursuits. Apart from his Scouting activities, George would spend time at weekends with various pals, occasionally inviting Tommy along on one of their lengthy Sunday morning walks in the nearby forest — these walks usually eased by a pause for a game of cards if they, by chance or design, found themselves in the vicinity of their favourite, little pub tucked away beside a quiet lane and amid ancient, massive trees. An old lady, the only person they ever saw serving in that pub, carefully filled glasses from the wooden taps on the barrels lined up behind the counter — just one penny for a glass of mild ale, tuppence sufficient to obtain half a pint of really strong beer.

A boy must have his heroes and Tommy very much admired a junior in
the accounts office. Breeman his name was, slim with well-styled clothes,
fair hair brushed back, dark blue and usually twinkling eyes, a face which
any girl would have been glad to possess, but nothing girlish about him.
His way of walking most engaged Tommy's attention and admiration —
long, confident strides. Tommy thought, "I can admire him, but never
begin to look like him".

On one occasion, Breeman paused to chat and he told Tommy he
usually walked to the office from his home in the Minories. His family
ran and lived at an inn. Nothing of the publican about him, though, he
seemed too delicate, too fine a type for that kind of upbringing... But
Tommy recalled that, when his own family had come down from the
north, they'd put up at an inn in the Minories; he wondered if that was
the Breeman family's place.

Tommy has lasting memories of many people with whom he worked
at that time.

Even a boy could see that Corker, the chap in charge of the shipping
office, was a man who knew his job; for example, how to move a piece
of machinery from the foundry to the docks for use abroad in the mines.
Goods of varying types had to be removed to remote places, distant
countries, and Corker would make all arrangements to that end. He knew
all about the packaging demanded by the shippers, the invoicing, the bills
of lading and insurance matters, bulk measurements, special markings of
the containers — every detail. Corker conducted his work with a look of
careful concentration on his sallow face and nothing ever appeared to go
wrong. His black suit, which always looked as though it had been slept
in, seemed to indicate that here was a devoted worker worthy of higher
reward than came his way.

Unforgettable too, the appearance, manner and behaviour of the senior
partner, Mr Lake; he had this tough, grey hair with a military cut, fairly short
back, sides and on top, no parting — a style that became generally popular
some years later — and a wide forehead above bushy black eyebrows above
small eyes set unusually close, and yet between them stood the very high
bridge of a thin, pointed nose; below that, the then fashionable, clipped,
grey moustache, and small, petulant lips; the jawbones narrowed to a small,
pointed chin; bright red cheeks blazed out from an otherwise pale skin.

On the rare occasions when Tommy thought his presence had passed unnoticed, he furtively — perhaps one should say fearfully — studied this unfriendly face. A high-pitched, domineering voice issued from that small mouth and it could provoke near-panic in some employees. He stood over six feet tall too and his well-cut suits somehow proclaimed that inside them operated a powerfully muscular body. Trousers closely embraced hefty calves and straps under the soles of the shoes kept them tightly bound at all times. The leg, in stepping forward, bent to an unusual extent at the knee, then sole and heel struck the ground simultaneously and the leg straightened as the other began its forward movement.

A typical cavalry officer was Sergeant's verdict. Sometimes, when work or pleasure prevented Lake travelling to his estates for the weekend, he would dictate a letter to his agent or head gardener giving instructions about work to be carried out in his absence. The agent he addressed as "Mister... ", the gardener simply as "Grey". The letter had to be typed on fine-quality blue paper and completed by the boss's large, child-like signature.

A totally different type, the other, "junior" partner, Mr Currie. Tall, very broad of shoulder, he would wear dark suits, generally blue or black, with white, chalk stripes. A florid countenance, you would say, a big, red face, and a hearty manner, but always on the ball, a financier as well as a practical mining engineer. This partner had a little estate in Bernard Beeches[64], Buckinghamshire. As a rule, people outside of his office seldom made contact with him — the Company Secretary the frequent exception.

The company regularly held meetings with business associates and others, and when the partners considered those attending worth entertaining fairly well, a lunch would be laid on, bought in from nearby caterers. If a small, intimate group were invited, they would gather in the senior partner's office. A day or so beforehand, Tommy had to visit the supplier to hand over the order — often at a famous restaurant and bar over in Cheapside called Sweetings[65], where he observed really prosperous City businessmen, bosses all, who wouldn't even spare the time to sit down to have their lunch. These toffs, as Cockneys called them, clad in fine morning suits, lined the long counter, munching and drinking their ale or whatever they favoured. The smell of all these delicious foods pleased Tommy; he loved to stand there and look and breathe it in. White-hatted waiters dressed up as chefs carved succulent slices of beef or ham.

When the customers finished eating, they would just throw down some silver on the counter and walk out — no question of bills or talking about the cost. As Tommy came to understand, much company business was based on trust, confidence. A word, perhaps a handshake, even a nod, would seal a bargain. City men expected all their associates to deal with them in this way. And all the people who served them, who wined and beered them you might say, came out very well from that sort of arrangement. They were never let down.

In addition to the special drinks and foods the restaurant supplied, Tommy had to buy certain cheeses and a special type of coffee. This task took him to a shop of the old style where soft cream cheeses hung from the ceiling in muslin bags... Fortunately, in due course, Tommy would get the chance to do more than look at all this enticing provender.

When one of these feasts had concluded, the bosses would take their guests to a club, maybe to continue the discussion or just enjoy good company. Often, when they left Mr Lake's office — the temporary dining room — Tommy went in to clear up before the caterers came to collect any utensils and crockery they had provided. But he'd pause to inhale the fumes of cigars and cigarettes, the aroma of all this good food — and of an appetising cocktail they regularly took called gin cup[66] which they drank from small, silver tankards, a sprig of a small mauve flower with a yellow centre floating in each one.

And, until the men from Sweetings arrived, Tommy could eat and drink anything left over — often quite a lot. Quickly as he could, he'd run through the menu. The lovely cream cheese, the crisp little rolls, some meat, ham or tongue or beef, a little salad, and then, of course, the gin cups had not always been emptied so he sampled them as well. It was very good. And one further pleasure he would save for later; some of the senior partner's Turkish cigarettes — made for him by a chap in Burlington Arcade[67] — would be left lying on the table and Tommy, who sometimes collected parcels of them from the tobacconist, felt free to take some of them if he wished. For a brief while, the boy would think of himself as a man. And fare like a lord.

Because of long hours taken up by work, travel, evening classes, and Scout meetings, after leaving school Tommy's reading tended to comprise an occasional glance at the family newspaper and a brief browse through one of the many weekly magazines, which cost only a penny or two, such as *Yes Or No*. It contained some quite good short stories — early Edgar Wallace[68], for instance, and efforts by others who later became well-known.

The infamous "Dr Fu Manchu" was first heard of in a monthly magazine, quite bulky and costing only fourpence halfpenny, called *The Story-Teller*[69].

Meanwhile, *Pearson's Weekly*[70] was running a series called "While England Slept". Week after week, it described the invasion of Great Britain by German Forces, detailing the Channel crossing, landings on the beaches, battles through Kent and Sussex villages and their eventual approach to London.

Ordinary people had for some while generally accepted that war with Germany was inevitable and they read this carefully constructed story of a surprise attack with excitement and, perhaps, concealed fear. Tommy and others of his generation could not see what would prevent the Germans from achieving their objective if they landed along the low-lying coasts. No great mountain ranges between there and the capital...[71]

Tommy no longer had the benefit of free piano lessons from Mr Frusher. Certain advantages available to a schoolboy were not on offer to the worker, however small his wage packet. But, as Scout- and choirmaster, the governor — as the boys called Mr Frusher, though only in his absence — did provide compensations relative to Tommy's age and new standing.

He introduced new subjects to the Troop's training schemes: so Tommy learnt signalling, semaphore and Morse code (the last, he particularly liked). Using flags — one for Morse, two for semaphore — and, at night, signal lamps, they sent messages across fair distances. Furthermore, after training at the church hall on Saturday afternoons, Tommy and other seniors could go to a rifle club where, for half an hour, they practised shooting on a covered range about 300 yards long, using old Army rifles (surplus from the Boer War, fitted with Morris tubes which allowed them to fire .22 ammunition). Supervisors checked their scores and entered them on competition cards. They paid a nominal sum for bullets used, but some kind person unknown had paid for their club membership. Dear old Frusher, they guessed.

He also undertook courses in first aid. Adapting his instruction from the Red Cross manual, he paid a good deal of attention to treating wounds.

A subtle change occurred in Mr Frusher's treatment of these seniors, both as Scouts and members of his church. Consultation with them about the organisation of events and outings became his new approach where, previously, he had taken charge. Those who had, before their voices broke, served as choirboys under him and attended Sunday school, he now invited to separate meetings. Like the first-aid classes, these took place at his house. Usually, they took the form of a discussion, on Biblical subjects mostly, chaired by the governor. He did not repeat Sunday school's childish views of the book's teaching and stories, instead suggesting more earthy explanations.

On these occasions, Mr Frusher even led discussions of men-women relationships. Discouraging romantic notions without deriding them, the elderly, bachelor teacher continued where the school lessons in anatomy and physiology left off. "Frankness in these matters kills morbid curiosity," he would say. He explained the sex organs — particularly the female genital parts always omitted from the school's anatomical charts.

In a sensible way, he described the feelings contact between the sexes could arouse, the actions and the results that would follow: the girls in trouble, the unwanted babies; the worry, regret, fear; the difficulties which beset a young man who has fathered a bastard. He drew this picture so impressively the lads were never likely to forget. In fact, he constantly impressed upon them that sexual intercourse before marriage was wrong, a crime, it must never even be considered, let alone indulged in.

He instructed them about another aspect of sexual development too: masturbation. He told them what a habit it could develop into, assumed they had never done it — correctly in most cases, thought Tommy — and assured them that if they never started they would never be bothered by the habit. What he used to call "night losses" — about which most young men know something — would, he believed, have an ill effect on a lad. But they could be averted, he said, if you didn't sleep on your back. This could be achieved, he recommended, by tying a cotton reel or bobbin round your waist and placing the uncomfortable object against the spine.

But, beyond such practical matters, he wished the lads to grow up as what he called "gentlemen". The girl being so constituted that marriage and child-bearing were the most important things in her life, she would generally submit to a man's desires — after a certain amount of caressing had taken place — in spite of any advice she may have received. Mr

Frusher's conclusion: the man — stronger, physically and mentally — had a bounden duty to accept responsibility and ensure that nothing occurred, when the girl was in his care, which he could not freely reveal to her parents. The final word had a memorable simplicity to it: chivalry.

Coupled with lessons in physiology and home nursing, both part of advanced training for all Boy Scouts, this early debunking of the sham romanticism so prevalent in those days did help the boys. Furthermore, the Scout Code they had sworn to included the words "To be pure in thought and word and deed"[72]; sticking to it became a settled part of their life and conduct. Tommy remembered all these things in the company of the girls with whom he occasionally formed friendships. Some may have thought him reticent or slow, but all realised that, at any rate, he was safe — except on one occasion when, unfortunately, Sergeant interfered with the natural course of events.

This arose when, one evening, as he got on the train to go home as usual, a voice called out his name. It was Bessie Dibbs, the girl whose recitations Tommy had so admired at the tin church he and his brothers mistakenly attended for some months when they first moved into the family's present home.

He hadn't seen her for several years since, as children of eight or nine, they'd played postman's knock at a Christmas party her brother Reggie had invited him to. The game involved a boy choosing a girl, or vice versa — Tommy seemed to recall that Bessie had picked him, he couldn't imagine why — then the two would leave the room to kiss and cuddle (if agreeable) while those left behind giggled and then, on the couple's return, made saucy comments on what they might have got up to out in the hallway. Now here they were, 15 and meeting again.

She sat beside him and they talked as much as they could in a crowded compartment full of people smoking. They alighted at the same stop, of course, and walked together until their ways parted. But when they said their good evenings, Bessie suggested Tommy might let her have his firm's telephone number so she could ring him up for a chat. Rather weakly, Tommy agreed. A day or so later, she called and he was very glad he happened to be on the switchboard to pick it up.

The next time, though, Sergeant answered, and when Bessie said she was a friend of Tommy's, he somehow changed his voice to produce an imitation of Tommy which Bessie found credible and he chatted away calling her "darling" and "sweetheart", while Tommy sat on a stool beside him, blushing and unable to do anything about it — although, from what he heard, Bessie didn't sound too displeased. Well, Sergeant loved to embarrass the boy.

On his next homeward train journey sitting with Bessie, Tommy noted the appearance she had of being well-fed, well-clothed — everything right in her world. Then he appraised himself: his home-made grey mac, the cheap suit beneath it, the cheap shoes. Comparing the obvious difference in circumstances between himself and the girl, he knew he would have to break away before he got in too deep. That wasn't easy for a naturally shy lad who wasn't too good at expressing his feelings. But he did tell her he hadn't called her sweetheart, darling and so forth, it was all that Sergeant up to his games — and that they'd have to discontinue their walking home and talking on the phone. Although they did see each other from time to time after that, it must have been quite apparent to Bessie he was not the lad she'd thought him to be.

George was already earning good pay. He had shown exceptional ability at school, winning every worthwhile prize. But, after the family's finances forced him, like Tommy a year later, to leave when he was 14, lack of extended education never hindered his progress[73].

Starting in the wholesale paper trade, he set out to learn everything about it, partly through talking to more experienced people, partly through evening classes where he studied the manufacturing processes involved in production, home and abroad. In short order, he knew the type of paper used for every purpose one could think of from boards to greaseproofs, which firms were agents for which mills, what kind of paper each of the main London dealers held (this for quick delivery of stocks his own firm didn't have to hand).

To this end, he sent out a constant stream of enquiries to paper mills and warehouses. A trade custom, this procedure, but few employees showed George's persistence in pursuing the matter. As a result, he could satisfy potential buyers much quicker than many others in the trade. The required quantity of paper or board could be delivered to his firm's warehouse, then re-packed, labeled and dispatched rapidly. Alternatively, some stockists would attach George's firm's label to the goods and dispatch them direct to the buyer, often with minimum expenditure of money and labour by

George's firm while a handsome profit accrued — a profit bearing no relation to his humble salary. He well understood this and often explained all these matters to Tommy, vowing that one day he would secure the sort of pay he knew he was worth.

Despite all that activity, George decided to try his hand at some manual work at home. He bought a few tools and soon erected a small garden house with boards and trellis — seats along each side, and ornamental wooden borders for flower beds which he filled with annuals, mainly, so they were soon colourful and gay. He quickly turned that half of the garden into a very attractive area.

Although proud of his brother's handiwork, Tommy did feel a bit regretful of his own inability to do something practical. He could not have afforded it, though, and also feared that his mother would have ridiculed any such attempts. Perhaps he did her an injustice, but she had always expected and accepted top results from the older lad and not much from Tommy. So Tommy settled for being second best, for the most part admiring his brother, seldom envious. As a result, the brothers — the young man and the boy — rarely argued.

On Saturdays, for his half-day's work Tommy had to get up just as early as on weekdays and hurry to catch the 7.18 train. On those days he often felt stale and played out. Leaving the office around 1pm, it seemed that he, his clothes, the big station, and the crowds rushing away from the City, were all dingy, condemned to a life of hopelessness and frustration. But after a dinner at home, a wash down, and a change into his Scouts uniform — then he felt clean and free again.

Meanwhile, August of 1914 was not far off and a holiday with his Scout Troop an often anticipated treat to come.

However, he soon discovered that Scouts were not alone in camping out on the edge of London. Walking by himself one Sunday, Tommy came to a wide open space beside one of the main routes from London to the North[74] and he saw with great excitement that this usually uninspiring area had become a town of tents; soldiers with rifles on their shoulders, men filling bowls with water from tanks on wheels, then holding the bowls for one another to help with shaving and washing. They emptied the used water into a large hole dug for waste disposal.

Tommy watched it all, for an hour or more. In another area, men were cooking a meal in large containers heated by open fires in shallow trenches. They fried bacon, boiled water for tea. When the bugle sounded, the soldiers lined up in orderly fashion until the cooks forked and ladled good helpings of bacon and tea into their mess tins (the lid, with a folding handle, held solid foods or acted as a frying pan, the larger bottom part contained all liquids). Soon afterwards, the clatter of eating changed to the noises of an Army striking camp, taking down tents and packing them and generally getting ready for departure, their work accompanied by much banter and laughter…

Scouting, Tommy realised, had taught him a good deal that would be useful to a soldier. He could help erect a tent, use a rifle, and communicate efficiently by semaphore or Morse code or a simple field telegraph. As a Patrol Leader, he had acquired the ability to stand up in front of a group of lads and give brief orders.

If any of these things might appear to have been intended to prepare youngsters for military service this was certainly not the intention behind Mr Frusher's work. As a practising Christian, at heart a pacifist, he never said anything to Scout meetings about the war scare and the training had nothing of a military character to it — no yelling of orders or foot-stamping drill. Saluting, with three fingers raised and thumb and little finger touching, served as a frequent reminder of the three promises a Scout made when joining the movement.

Tommy, while savouring the excitement and deep interest he felt when observing the soldiers' encampment, felt no desire to join them. As far as he knew, drummer boy was the only Army job he might be eligible for.

Chapter Twelve

Although the routine of living continued for Tommy, his family, and all around him, excitement mounted daily as events abroad, culminating in the assassination of a royal person, led many to believe that a war in which Britain would be involved was imminent[75].

The morning paper, which Pa bought on his way to the station with two of his sons, was eagerly read by their mother and the other children in the evening.

On the train to work men loudly and strongly expressed opinions about events and prospects and Tommy listened. At the office, the Sergeant really let himself go on this one; he believed the prospective enemy, the Germans, had always intended to attack England, but that our well-trained Army would soon finish them off once the two forces were face to face. Too old for active service himself, he would be doing his bit for Britain through that job at the War Office he had told the boys about.

Meanwhile, brother George, sunburnt and lusty after a fortnight at a camp for assistant Scoutmasters, frequently talked about England going to war and what part he might play in it. He encouraged Tommy to join him and two friends of his own age, Len Winns and Harold Mellow, in long walks at the weekends. Then, when they stopped to rest and eat their sandwiches, a pack of cards would be produced and they'd play their favourite game, solo whist. But discussions of war always cropped up. Exciting speculations on how long it would last might vary between a few months and several years.

Len Winns stood 5ft 10 inches, broad-shouldered with a habitual stoop; he favoured a plain, dark suit and white shirt, always immaculate. He had thick, black hair, bushy eyebrows, kindly, hazel eyes and, more often than not, a briar pipe between his large, white teeth. Tommy loved to observe Len filling his pipe. The good tobacco he used smelled fragrant and later, when he cleaned it, a sweet, manly tang hung in the air. The bowl all reamed out, he laid the pipe in its case and tucked that in his pocket.

A clerk on the Stock Exchange, Len earned a good salary for those days and had an assured future. Yet he could be a purveyor of gloom. With Tommy as very willing audience, he would think aloud about the stars, planets, the universe, and his own insignificance by comparison. Plaintively, he would suddenly sing a few lines from a concert favourite of that time, White Wings[76]. A sad sort of bloke, at times, Len. But a reluctant grin on that strange face would feel as good to Tommy as sudden sunshine on a dull day.

Harold Mellow, no taller than Tommy, was excitable, quick-witted, quick to anger and quick to subside, self-opinionated, moody at times. In irascible form, capable of passing friends in the street without a glance of acknowledgment, he earned toleration from the others by his sudden acts of generosity. To earn a living, he pushed a pen at Imperial Tobacco's City offices[77].

Battalions of marching soldiers became a common sight in the City — largely civilian volunteers given time off from their places of employment to undergo extra training in case they should be mobilised to replace regular soldiers who might be sent overseas. Most of them had already received considerable training at their Territorial establishments and in camps where regular-Army instructors supervised their activities.

The frequent conflicts in that region, then described as the Balkans, had been of merely passing interest to the British people, but this war, now looming, affected all, rich and poor. Fears and anticipations coloured all their thinking.

In particular, hope burgeoned among many small businessmen. War creates shortages and speculation can yield enormous profits. But among employed people too flourished a fine flush of patriotic fervour. For instance, a common boast — notably among older men quite sure they would not be called up — claimed that one trained British soldier was worth any five foreigners.

Without thinking too deeply, one could become part of this emotion and go about one's daily activities lightened and illumined by a self-righteous glow. Probably the nation had smarted under the German threat hanging over their heads for some years. Tommy and his like caught the infection. To the enthusiastic, people who behaved and talked rationally or, at least, just as they had always done, seemed selfish, perhaps even scared.

This national surge flowed through the millions of men who were more emotional than thoughtful. They pulsated, they were invigorated, and sustained. For many, this overexcitement would later be replaced by grim determination, perhaps directed towards helping one's country while trying to preserve one's life — or towards making money out of it and having a good time wherever possible. But Tommy's generation was experiencing the last of the great patriotic upsurges in this country. Wonderful while it lasted.

Normally, Len and Harold took later trains to their work in the City, but that summer they decided to rise earlier and travel in with Tommy and Ted[78]. "Ted", by the way, was a nickname. As a baby, someone had called him "Tiddle" and later, for dignity's sake presumably, that changed to "Tid" and then Ted.

Now, on the train, father would join his contemporaries to discuss the threatened Armageddon — the word applied by a journalist and taken up everywhere[79]. Imaginings of war with Germany centred on the imposing figure of Kaiser Wilhelm, as portrayed in photographs and cartoons — that waxed moustache the ends of which were screwed into points and pointed upwards, a spiked helmet on his head, mounted on his horse, a fierce warrior. But people began to call up images of the huge German Army too; the infantry, they thought, would comprise rather big men wearing long, blue-grey overcoats, who travelled at great speeds too with their mechanical transport. The new thing was the lorry; one looked in vain on the roads of this country for great convoys transporting large numbers of soldiers, a sight quite commonplace in the Kaiser's country,[80] we gathered.

Soon, historic events overtook speculation. On August 4, 1914, Germany attacked Belgium, at which an old treaty impelled the British Prime Minister to declare war on Germany[81].

Despite expectation and possibilities conjured up, the actual declaration of war caused tension to most, and much worry and speculation about the future. Older people with family and commitments entered a period of worry with regard to their loved ones — it was to last a long time. Youngsters, though, soon threw off doubts and unpleasant thoughts.

But the war declaration did bring about immediate and visible changes which touched the lives of many. In the City, at Ted's paper firm, a German mill owner's young son, who'd been working for the firm and perfecting his English, failed to appear on the morning of the 5th of August — the day after Britain's declaration of war on Germany — and was never seen in that office again.

Similarly, many German families lived in working-class areas of London and, from that day or soon afterwards, they just vanished... English children began to miss their German pals[82].

Workers went on with their jobs, but it was obvious their thoughts were on other things. Each day, the younger men either moved nearer to volunteering for military service or worried about the possibility of being conscripted as soon as a law to make service compulsory passed through Parliament. However, that did not, as one might have expected, happen immediately[83].

Company Secretary F.C. Bull, with knowledge to back his forecast, made no attempt to conceal his pessimism with regard to those companies owning property in Africa and Asia whose affairs he handled. German submarines would cripple our sea transportation, said he, sagely.

Most people thought it would be a short war, "all over by Christmas". The minority, like F.C. Bull, who read and listened to those with some real knowledge of the situation, knew the struggle would probably be long and difficult. Pessimists even gave reasons why, if we weren't careful, we might *lose* this war. They reminded one that the royal family bore the German name Guelph, their origins Hanoverian[84]. And they would argue sarcastically that the Army was all ready to fight... the Boer War again! Such opinions, of course, offended the loquacious patriots — "Treasonable," said some.

Meanwhile, the newspapers talked bogeyman stories — suspicious characters, spies and so on. The propaganda had its effect; Tommy saw with regret one day that someone had completely smashed the windows of Mr Schultz's butcher's shop. No more luscious faggots and pease pudden, thought the lad. Mr Schultz left for Wales, Tommy heard, as did another branch of his family who lived in the neighbourhood.

A schoolmate called Charlie Schmidt whom Tommy talked with occasionally also disappeared. A round, ruddy face he had, but serious, with an incomplete smile — it never quite made it. His family left with no farewells, no fuss and no destination that anybody local knew of.

Another three or four German men often provided street music, playing merry Viennese waltzes on cornets, euphoniums and basses. But they all went, never to reappear. Spies, said folks. Didn't you notice how they use to play beside the gates of the gasworks and listen to what the workers were saying?

A local family of house decorators, including several young men in their teens and early twenties also departed without a word — they'd offered low prices for their low-paid customers, useful members of the community and much liked. Napper their name was. Surely not Germans. Or were they?[85]

Minor riots arose in some areas, starting with attacks on German nationals and their places of business.

One weekly magazine, *John Bull*, edited by Horatio Bottomley, a man able to discern what line of thought would arouse millions of partially educated people, used the war to excite the masses to do things which always had the ultimate result of putting money into his pocket. At meetings advertised in his publication and where he was the chief speaker, he would advocate donating money to the John Bull Victory Bond Club.

Tommy often read this weekly paper when his father had finished with it. The fiery patriotism impressed him, the condemnation of the foul enemy with whom we were at war, the constant watchfulness the editor and his staff maintained to discover and expose traitors in high places. He, and thousands of others, began to believe that this man could be the leader and saviour of Britain and the Empire. Men in large or small groups and organisations always search for and hope to find the ideal leader, the good man, the honest man, who combines these virtues with vast knowledge and statesmanlike skill. Men will follow such a person to the death... And they do and they die and the superman proves ultimately to be a lying rogue.

This popular editor and public speaker, who could persuade large, glassy-eyed audiences to part with money supposedly for various causes but undoubtedly for his own benefit, was exposed some years later and tried and jailed. But by that time Tommy's experience had made him sceptical of all orators and he contemplated this villain's fate with farty derision[86].

Meetings such as those organised by Bottomley encouraged men to join the Forces and large numbers made up their minds on the spot. At this, they would be marched away to some depot where a cursory medical examination preceded the signing of an Attestation Paper swearing the oath of allegiance — and, thus, sudden severance from their normal life and their usual associations. Others who had served in the Forces before, perhaps in the Boer War, and then joined the reserve list, would suddenly appear in their communities wearing the khaki uniform of war. But they too soon vanished, gone to their Regimental depots, it was assumed.

Schools now had to teach children the anthems of Britain's allies — in English, except that, in grammar schools, they sang The Marseillaise in French. The Belgian national anthem became familiar to all. So did the Russian. Gradually a feeling grew that we were one of a group of nations and this gave a sense of confidence. Rumours of large numbers of Russian soldiers seen on trains travelling through the English countryside spread and reinforced this optimism — the joke was that Russia had dispatched these soldiers so quickly they still had snow on their boots.

On the train each morning, the four lads discussed the latest news, telling each other about chaps who had either been recalled to their units or had volunteered to go. They talked with both excitement and unease. Confused emotions pervaded them and everybody around them. One morning when Tommy got to work he heard that young Breeman had joined up — the chap in the accounts office he admired so much. Tommy thought what a splendid officer he would make, a good physical specimen, mentally alert at all times. But the gap in the ranks at the office only increased that sense of unease, that something was wrong somewhere.

Not all the war news was good. The sudden advance of the British Army across France, sweeping the Germans back into their own country, hadn't occurred yet. And the General in charge inspired no faith. Inevitably, because seniority and maybe a little influence decided who should be at the top, he was an elderly man[87]. Nor did the Government, Liberal at the time, reassure ordinary people who generally thought the Prime Minister an adequate man, but nothing more[88].

Chapter Thirteen

As frequently as they could, Tommy and his brother met during their lunch breaks. A few coppers being available, they would go to the Italian café, joining others there to exchange opinions on the latest developments. All felt the same — that life as they had known it was finished, big things looming. What was going to happen? Being young, their view of the future tended to optimism. Adventure would soon come their way — of that they were sure.

If they had no money spare, the brothers would go down to their favourite wharf on the River Thames and sit on the wall with their legs dangling while they ate their sandwiches and watched the seagulls. From time to time they'd throw these birds lumps of rather hardcore cake — their mother's speciality, nourishing one assumes, but not too appetising… Threw the cake *at* them more than to them, in truth. They never registered a hit as far as they could see, but they felt sure that, if they had done, the effect would have been pretty deadly.

On one occasion, Tommy tried to introduce a little fun into the now gloomy life at the office. On the street outside the company building a newspaper deliverer stopped him — they dashed about the City on bikes with high handlebars and low saddles. The chap said, "Like to buy one of these for a penny?" He held out what appeared to be a small booklet. Tommy opened it to find it comprised just two pages. The first thing he saw was a piece of sandpaper glued to the inside of the back cover. Then he noticed a rhyme printed on the inside of the front cover. Somebody had cudgelled his brains to work this thing out and come up with the following: "As times are hard/Please buy this card/Dame Fortune I can't make her/ But let that pass/Just wipe your XXXX/Upon this piece of paper". The painful consequences… poor humour, coarse humour. Tommy laughed heartily. But he had to tell the man, "I've got no money, I can't buy it".

However, at home that evening, he found a piece of sandpaper and a piece of card, pinned them together, wrote this elegant rhyme inside, and took it to the office next morning.

He showed it to Sergeant who roared and, in his usual way, passed it round the various parts of the office. Under cover. Later though, crestfallen, he reported scarcely a grin, scarcely a chuckle, everyone apparently so borne down by the weight of the war they didn't have a laugh left in them.

Summer slipped into September, good weather still, a beautiful autumn. But it was not being enjoyed at home. Mother began to worry about the possibility of food shortages. Already some of the cheap items she bought had become scarce or completely unavailable.

Meanwhile, an enthusiasm built up among ordinary men. "Stand by your country," "Be prepared to defend it," and similar remarks abounded. Accordingly, more and more were actually joining up. Often fearing their civilian jobs would peter out, they felt, even so, they had done the right thing by their families, their country and, of course, themselves.

Around September 8, Tommy recalls, the four pals — although their junior by several years, he tried to think himself into being one of them — went off on their usual train. But when they reached Liverpool Street, the elder three were talking quietly, leaving Tommy on the outside of the conversation. In the end, brother Ted said to him: "We're not going to our offices today. We three are going to join up."

Perhaps you can imagine the sinking feeling in Tommy when he heard this. Was he going to be left on his own with the diminishing number on the train journey to an office where all was gloom? Was he going to do that? No thinking required. "I'm coming with you," he said.

Thus they wended their way from the station, heading north along City Road where they came across a depot of the Royal Field Artillery and went inside. The spaciousness and height of the hall surprised Tommy. A balcony ran around it. The lads were scrutinised by a dozen or so men grouped around a soldier who wore a parti-coloured tunic, riding britches, well-polished boots, and puttees (Tommy knew what they were because Scoutmasters wore them).

Conversation ceased while the soldier scanned the fresh arrivals and greeted them, "Good morning, men". "Good morning, Sergeant," replied their senior, Len Winns. The others followed suit, Tommy hopeful he was included in the greeting despite his size and years[89]. "I was telling these chaps this depot is unmanned at the moment," said the Sergeant. "We are a unit of the Royal Field Artillery. We operate 18-pounder field guns. And we are Territorials. Since the regular Army went to France, our men have already been called to a large training camp and followed them there. They won't return to civilian life until the war is over. They're part of what we call 'the first line'. We shall raise a second line. Here, so far, we have no authority to enlist recruits, but we expect to get permission at any moment so if you fellows are ready I can prepare the forms as regards your height, weight and so on. Of course, it's not official yet, but it will save time if you're willing to wait for a short while."

The men all followed the Sergeant upstairs to the balcony and into an office. He sat down at a table, a pile of pale blue forms in front of him, took the top copy, picked up a pen, thought for a moment and then asked, "Any clerks among you chaps?" Almost every would-be recruit raised hand and voice. "I am, Sergeant," they chorused. "Well, we can get these Attestation Papers done with preliminary details if two of you will act as my clerks."

He selected two men and they sat on chairs at either end of the table, furnished with pen, inkwell, blotter and a supply of forms. The Sergeant divided the volunteers into two groups, one to each clerk, then left the room, but soon returned with a combined height-and-weight measuring machine.

At about this point fear entered Tommy's mind. Could he get away with the deception he planned to attempt? There would be penalties for giving false information. But he must try to stay with the other three. They hadn't encouraged him much, but they did say if Tommy must enlist then perhaps he had better try to join the same crowd.

Tommy was almost the last to face the Sergeant's machine — he'd calculated that, if he stood at the very end of the line, he would be more noticeable and the Sergeant would refuse to let him join up. Searching for reasons to feel a bit more confident, Tommy reminded himself there was nothing official about the formation of the Company at the moment. The Sergeant had not yet any written authority to proceed with enlistment.

The volunteer clerk who took down some of the details required — name, address, occupation —scarcely looked at Tommy, concerned only with writing carefully and then listening to the Sergeant call out his information to be sure he'd got it right. The Sergeant had stipulated that the lowest age of enlistment was 19[90], so hereafter Tommy tried to look as though he had reached that advanced status. Now the clerk had written the lie into a statement which Tommy must eventually sign as being true to the best of his knowledge and belief.

By the time the two clerks had dealt with all the men and the Sergeant gathered the completed forms, midday had passed. The Sergeant told them that nothing further could be done, so all could leave and return at around 4.30pm when he would be able to give them some definite information.

Time had passed almost unnoticed and everyone agreed on the necessity of something to eat and drink. In seconds, that drill hall emptied. Len, Harold, Ted and Tommy walked side by side out of the red doorway, all trying to talk at the same time: "Hard to believe it, but we're almost soldiers already," "There'll be a medical exam to get through next no doubt," "I'm glad we're going into a mounted Regiment and not the infantry. Long marching would kill me."

"Hey, Ted," said Tommy quietly, nudging his brother. "Where shall we go to eat our sandwiches?" "Wait and see what the others suggest," proposed Ted. "Don't worry, I've got a few coppers, we'll manage."

When, without comment, Len pushed open the swing doors of a Lyon's Corner House[91], perforce they followed. The place provided brisk and friendly waitress service, cleanliness, good food, and comfort at low prices — almost unbelievable. Clerks who had 6d to spare could have a tasty snack and a large cup of excellent tea for their tanner. And when the four had finished eating, with time on their hands still, they played drafts with board and pieces supplied free by the restaurant. Then they took a stroll around this unfamiliar district.

Talk naturally dwelt on what life would be like in the Army. The idea of living among horses, looking after them and riding them, appealed greatly. Tommy, Ted and Harold, it was agreed, could well become riders of the leading horses. They already knew that, usually, four horses pulled a gun carriage and a man rode one of the leading pair.

Optimism and growing excitement finally carried them happily back towards the Royal Field Artillery depot, all ready to undergo the medical and other tests. But there a deflated Sergeant told them he had gone farther than he should have, that no authority to proceed had arrived, and there was nothing he could do about it.

The small gathering dispersed. Men who had become acquainted and, for a short time, expected to become comrades, parted. Our four found themselves in some trouble, they reckoned. Their employers had a right to an explanation. But, after much discussion, they agreed to persist in their intention to enlist. They would return home by the trains they normally used, say nothing to their families about their actions during this unlucky day, and set off to the usual train tomorrow morning.

That evening as he prepared to leave them at his road end, the almost paternal Len, for whom Tommy had begun to feel an affectionate regard, looked closely into the faces of the other three. He said, "We catch the usual train around 7.15 tomorrow morning, right?" "Right, Sergeant," said Ted, echoed by the other two. It was good to suddenly discover that they had a leader. It gave them a feeling of purpose and security at a time when doubts assailed them about what they had been up to.

"White wings, they never grow weary/They carry me cheery over the sea" — sung in tune, but with a rather creaky sort of voice — drifted diminishingly back to them from Len's retreating figure. And so to home and the evening meal.

With all the usual family natter going on around him, Tommy found no difficulty in concealing what had gone on. Tomorrow's events would decide where his future lay. If the Army would not have him then a humdrum life lay ahead. His job, humble though it was, would surely end soon. Necessity would force him to try something different. In wartime, who could say what would turn up?Meanwhile, he meant to stick with his brother and the others if possible — although a glance in the mirror convinced him that he looked almost childish compared to them. Far removed from chaps who needed to wield cutthroat razors in order to look presentable. "I'm going to be left behind. They'll be off and away without me," he feared.

Without giving the subject really deep thought, he became obsessed with the need to go where Len, Harold and Ted went. There's safety in numbers was what he really felt no doubt. Before he had been allowed to join the three, he had gone his own way, unattached to any specific group, just keeping company with one or two friends. But suddenly those schoolmates had drifted into the background, unconnected with the present.

Later, the brothers went out to spend a couple of hours together. At least it removed the risk of saying something which might give rise to questions from their parents. They talked over the day's misfortune and the morrow's prospects. Already they had one day's absence from work to explain, should they not be able to enlist the following day. Despite youthful optimism, the original thoughts behind the proposition — adventure and perhaps a touch of the popular patriotism — were submerging beneath anxiety and disappointment.

Still, next morning they set off to join the other two in fairly cheerful mood, Tommy less happy than his brother because he had greater doubts. Len and Harold met them at the station and immediately said they had heard of a depot where recruitment had been in progress for several days. Although it entailed a lengthy walk from Liverpool Street to Bloomsbury, they had no reason to hurry because their early train landed them in the City before 8 o'clock and they reckoned 9am would be quite early enough to present themselves at the depot.

They wandered the length of Newgate Street — the Old Bailey down a side street to their left — then straight on into Holborn before turning right into Grays Inn Road. Unfamiliar territory to Tommy, but Harold knew these parts well; he had them turn left into Guildford Street then left and right and so on till all but he were lost. They stopped beside a large building which occupied the whole of one side of a short street[92]. They approached a pair of very large, closed, green doors to one side of which stood a noticeboard headed by a badge, rather intricate in design and roughly triangular in shape. With mounting excitement they noted the words "Battery" and "Field Artillery".

Nobody was about, so they pushed at a swing door set in one of the large ones and stepped through into an open, paved area. Further along a substantial group of men shuffled about, waiting it seemed. So the four decided to join them at what they concluded must surely be the Artillery's recruiting entrance — marked, apparently, by a smallish soldier in khaki uniform, a crown over three stripes on each arm, who stood a few feet from the men with his back to an open door into the building.

Tommy looked at him intently, standing on his toes to see over the heads in front of him. The man had a clean, spruce appearance, a moustache with long, waxed points, an unattractive face — small eyes, the mouth downturned at the corners. No colour at all in the cheeks. A short cane held by the left hand was tucked under the armpit.

Somebody inside called out a message to him. This caused some excited movement among the waiting men, who bumped into one another and stumbled forward. "Keep back there, keep well back!" shouted the Company Quartermaster Sergeant — for such was his rank, according to one of the would-be recruits. He pointed with his cane at man after man, "You, you, you", and the selected ones hastened through the door, about six of them. This procedure he repeated time after time during the next three hours, then the Sergeant called out, "We now break for lunch, back at two!"

So off into a small, nearby park went the lads and ate sandwiches and talked. "We were getting near the front before we broke up"; "We must get back there in good time, soon after one o'clock?"; "That Sergeant has a mean look — pity we have to smirk and try to catch his eye"; "I don't give a damn what he looks like — get past him and we may never see him again"; "I've got a feeling he'll rumble my age — anyway he looks the type who would enjoy making a kid look foolish." Tommy now felt really up against it and he had already determined what he would do if only he could get into about the third row of the crowd.

One of the others stood him a cup of tea in the Italian café around the corner. Another bought him one of those lovely cheese cakes which have no cheese in them at all, but thick icing under shredded coconut and a fruitcake filling.

By one o'clock they got back to the depot — Len, Ted and Harold in the front row and Tommy, intentionally, in the fourth row. The Sergeant resumed his routine, looking as though he'd had a couple, as one man suggested, but still far from jovial.

His first after-lunch selections took in Len, Harold, and Ted, but as they moved forward Tommy bent double till his right shoulder was level with the backside of the man in front of him. Annoyed, the man behind Tommy yelled at him and shoved hard against him. With that unexpected extra push to boost his own violent surge forward, Tommy's ruse succeeded. The men in front of him staggered and one of them collided with the Sergeant who shouted at him while the man apologised

— and Tommy squeezed round this little melee, behind the Sergeant and on through the door in the wake of his pals. "Down those stairs," directed a uniformed man inside. Tommy descended and joined a queue.

"You cheeky bleeder," said a voice behind him. "Why? What have I done?" asked Tommy. "You shoved me and slid around that old goat. I banged smack into him — and while he yelled I edged around him and shouted 'Righto, Sarge!' and ducked through the door behind you." "Good for you," said Tommy.

Thereafter, he kept strictly in line, his head down, hoping that, if anybody searched for the chap who'd broken through, he would not be recognised. But nobody troubled him and the line of men slowly inched forward until Tommy, in his turn, came face to face with the doctor. An elderly man, thin and not far from unkempt, he worked under great pressure and at speed. "Open your mouth." He looked in. He pulled down the lower lids of Tommy's eyes. Glanced into his ears. Put a stethoscope to his chest. He held Tommy's scrotum in one hand and said "Cough". Again he applied the stethoscope to his chest, then said "You'll do".

Tommy moved across to where a two-stripe man weighed him and measured him — 5 feet 7½ inches. Onwards to a long table where several uniformed clerks were filling in Attestation forms, asking for all the usual details, including age. "19," said Tommy. Here came the catch. "Date of birth?" Tommy had that worked out. "July 6, 1895." "Any birth marks?" Then the clerk read to him a declaration that all these things were true and said, "Sign here!" All that completed, he was told to go upstairs and wait.

He found himself in a large hall where, amid the crowd, he felt reasonably safe. Rightly or wrongly, he thought some men looked surprised when they noticed him. The serious face he wore — or tried to — would, he hoped, conceal his inward wavering. Useless to show uncertainty. From now on he was a man among men and would have to march long distances and carry heavy equipment and a rifle and ammunition. All this, he knew for sure, would tax his boyish strength, but he remained determined to go ahead. Pleasure at seeing the other three in the hall rid him immediately of forebodings and he listened to their accounts of the medicals and so on and shared their joy in having at last achieved their intention of becoming soldiers.

"Artillerymen you mean," said Tommy.

"No, just infantrymen," Len told him. "The footsloggers. No riding lovely horses for us. We made a right mess of things in that respect. Didn't you read the top part of your form when you signed it? We're in the Royal Fusiliers — the Royal Field Artillery where we were yesterday is next door, apparently. RFA, RF, we didn't notice the difference."

"I was too tense and windy to read anything," Tommy said. "Where the finger pointed I signed. I feel everything depends on how I cope today as to whether I'm allowed to stay with you. It's all right for you lot, you're old enough or near enough, but the three-year difference makes it difficult for me. I had to wangle to get through that door without being stopped by old wax whiskers and, since then, they've all been too busy to look at me. But there'll be difficult times ahead I'm sure."

For an hour or two, the new recruits were free to sit and talk or explore the building. Most doors were locked, but one led upstairs and as Tommy approached it a richly complex aroma came his way. Ascending, he found a large bar and canteen and looked around, calculating that the smell which had attracted him comprised beer, spirits, ginger beer (the best, served from large earthenware jars and poured through a wooden tap), hot meat pies, apple turnovers, and a generous variety of other good things. Tommy had no money to spare, but still he savoured the atmosphere, the roar of conversation and the sight of many glasses being raised, sipped from, or in the case of some reckless fellows, emptied in one long swallow. He later learned to avoid men who drank in this fashion since they were generally show-offs, frequently broke, and therefore often on the mump — Cockney for cadging.

After a final, appreciative look at all the animated faces, the pleasantly loaded counter and the busy couple in charge of it all, Tommy made his way back down the stairs into the hall. He couldn't see Ted and the others. The milling crowd must have concealed them.

Time passed until some sort of fuss around the street entrance announced the appearance of the first commissioned officer Tommy had seen — a man immaculate in a new uniform obviously tailored to his trim figure. He wore his stiff-peaked military cap straight, no tilt to sides or back; each epaulette bore three bright stars (designating a Captain, as Tommy soon learnt); his leather belt and the strap worn over the right shoulder, which joined the belt at the left hip, were glossily polished, as were his brown boots; at the hip hung a sword in its scabbard.

Tommy never forgot his first impression of an officer and a gentleman

— the popular perception of a man holding the King's Commission. He certainly never saw a more handsome and correct representative of that class. The Captain's face did credit to his rank. Firm chin, small, neat moustache, quite kindly eyes.

A group of soldiers followed the officer and the new recruits immediately made way for them as they marched through the hall and halted halfway along. A three-stripe man, a Sergeant, stepped forward to bellow at the new boys: "Now men, form up in lines along the far side of the hall!" Untrained, of course, they did so as speedily as possible. That left about half the hall clear with the group headed by the officer standing facing the recruits. Said the Sergeant: "Captain King will now address you!"

The smiling Captain stepped forward and made a brief speech in an easy, flowing style, putting them at their ease. "I am assured," he concluded, "that everything entailed by joining me in His Majesty's forces has been fully explained to you. You have completed and signed your Attestation Papers and you have passed your medicals. All that remains to be done today is to have you take the Oath of Allegiance to our King and country and, thereafter, draw your first Army pay, the King's shilling plus one shilling for a partial day's subsistence. Afterwards, instructions will be given to you by the Sergeant in charge. That is all. Thank you."

The Sergeant then gave the order, "Attention!", to his group of uniformed soldiers. Smartly their feet came together, their faces became expressionless. The Sergeant ordered the recruits to raise their right hands and to repeat after him the Oath of Allegiance[93]. Throughout this little ceremony, Captain King and the other soldiers saluted.

Then the soldiers quickly set up tables and chairs at equal distances along the clear side of the hall, and guided the recruits into single lines, one to each table. Each recruit gave his name which was entered on a sheet together with the amount paid under the two separate headings — King's shilling, part-day subsistence. In due course, all the recruits had received their first soldier's pay. Then the Sergeant called for silence before instructing them, "Report at the depot tomorrow morning at 8 o'clock! That's all for today. You may now go home."

Crowds of them gathered outside, discussing the day's events, telling each other they were now soldiers, little as some of them looked the part.

Young Tommy had watched and listened with rapt attention to all that had gone on.

A fateful day for him, he knew. He needed reassurance now and, having left the building, he looked anxiously along the street for his brother, Len and Harold. With relief he spotted them and they set off for home, each probably thinking very different thoughts regarding the immediate future. Harold and Len, at least, would have no explaining to do when they reached home, while Ted might be in some slight difficulty and Tommy could face grave trouble.

But, by way of a change, Tommy did have money in his pocket to pay his way. So, instead of taking the long walk to Liverpool Street, they spent 4d of their pay on the tram fare back to Edmonton[94]. They went on top and chatted away about their personal experiences that afternoon. Quite sure of themselves, the three elders felt confident they would be able to explain to their firms that they had done the right thing, being prepared to fight for their country — the popular phrase of the time.

Tommy would have to tell his firm as well, but being such a junior he didn't imagine that losing him would mean anything to them. The first thing, though, he knew, was to get home and tell Ma what he had done. Even so, he probably didn't appreciate the shock his news would cause her.

Back in Edmonton, the lads parted to the sound of Len's supplication not to be late in the morning. "We must allow an hour for the tram plus a few minutes to make sure we're not late for our first parade." They went their ways and, as they walked, Tommy spoke to Ted about his fear of what might happen when they told their mother and, later, father that their older sons were now soldiers. Well, the brothers would stand firm and support each other it was agreed. "You do realise," said Ted, "we have signed a solemn declaration that the information about ourselves we gave was all true?" "Yes," said Tommy eagerly, "and I can tell Ma that if anyone informs the Army that I've lied I shall probably be sent to prison."

When they went indoors she commented that they were home earlier than usual. Then out poured their news and not, to Tommy's surprise, in any apologetic way but with something like pride. Watching mother's face the boys saw various emotions aroused. She and father being politically of a Conservative persuasion and quite firmly patriotic people, she did not immediately protest or reprimand. She did point out that Tommy was much too young to think of being a soldier. That concluded it, though; before any decision was made, she would have to talk with father.

Later that evening, when father returned from work and mother told him the news, the brothers awaited the outcome of their discussion. Eventually, their parents called them together and told them they could agree to Ted staying in the Army, but they would have to get Tommy out. At this, Tommy played his trump card. He said he knew, strictly speaking, he'd done a very dishonest thing, but pointed out that his motives weren't bad — and, finally, that he didn't know *what* prison sentence would be inflicted on him for making a false declaration regarding his age... In conclusion, he pleaded with his parents for permission to carry on as a soldier for a time, at any rate, and prove he could do the job for which he had volunteered.

Father talked of the physical strain a boy could suffer in trying to do the tasks expected of full-grown men. Still Tommy begged to be allowed to try. Then, perhaps, he won the day by explaining that in all, while living at home, he would be paid 21/- a week, a guinea. That is, 1/- a day soldier's pay, plus 2/- a day subsistence money. That rate, though temporary, matched what many full-grown men earned — a very good wage, in fact, for unskilled work. Eventually, they agreed that Tommy should, for the moment, carry on soldiering.

Chapter Fourteen

Next morning the lads were up in good time, met as arranged, and took the tram back to Bloomsbury, near the depot. When they arrived they were amazed to see the road in front of the adjacent (as we now knew) RF and RFA depots packed tight with men and hundreds more queuing along another road behind them — all enlisted men like themselves, they learned, and ordered to parade that morning. Harold observed that it would take a mastermind to sort this lot out. But he was soon proven too skeptical.

Presently, a uniformed man, extremely stout and ruddy-faced with several chins, mounted a box or chair, they couldn't see what. In an extremely powerful voice, he called for quiet, then issued instructions. With surprising, almost professional, speed, men on the outskirts of the crowd formed into lines of four across, and the mass became a somewhat ragged column.

The rotund Regimental Sergeant Major took his place at the head of it and, with no attempt at ceremony, started marching. Stragglers at the back attached themselves in new lines of four and followed in his wake. Within a few hundred yards, the whole of the leading formation had fallen in step to a man. That almost spherical RSM necessarily set a steady, almost slow, pace. But two streets crammed with men had to be cleared and he'd achieved that very quickly.

Had he been dealing with conscripted men, he would undoubtedly have had a problem on his hands. These were volunteers, though. A small, but sufficient, proportion of them had seen service previously and, of the remainder, many had come through various youth organisations, Scouts, Boys Brigades, and others, Companies of which trained and marched in every town throughout the land.

No new experience for Tommy, of course, this marching in step, but the pace, the stride, felt different — longer, slower, heavier, and somehow more exhilarating.

On this, their first rhythmic progression as an Army unit, each member carried himself as he believed a real soldier would and kept in step with the man in front of him. No one shouted, "Keep in step there, left, right, left!" None of that. Crunch, crunch, rrrp, rrrp, a steady pace with arms a-swing.

Tommy liked the rhythm — and the thrill as he saw the column of men ahead, bearing left round the far side of a London residential square. "We're all in step then," he thought. "Marvellous." He did notice the odd one lose the step and touch the heel of the man in front or trip the man behind — no natural sense of rhythm or perhaps over-eager or anxious. But correction soon followed. Such culprits would later endure the wrath of newly appointed non-commissioned and commissioned officers who had to justify their existence. But today not a word.

Every man wished that he should do well and that his comrades should do well… and that perhaps some famous General might be watching unseen, later to issue a full report full of praise for the volunteer soldiers… who reminded him of the Guards…

If Tommy dreamed thus, we may assume others did too. But he did notice, at first with incredulity, that some men on the pavement — invariably smart well-dressed types — raised their hats on sighting the column. One such, coming down the steps of a large house, reached the pavement as Tommy drew level. He raised his bowler hat, and as his eyes rested momentarily on Tommy's the boy felt himself blushing. "Ridiculous," he told himself. "The gentleman was saluting the volunteers, not a lad who had lied to get in. There'll never be another march like this one."

The houses they passed interested him, and he resolved to take walks in this district, so redolent of London life from bygone days with which he felt he had ties somehow, he didn't understand why — until, that evening, he concluded that gazing year after year at a picture hung in his parents' bedroom may have caused his sense of familiarity with the area. It showed a woman, a shopping basket on one arm, descending the several steps from her front door to the street; her young daughter, with a tiny Pekingese dog on a lead, waited on the pavement. Both wore bonnets and the full-skirted costume of the Victorian era. And both, Tommy used to think, looked far too prim and prissy. Their house could have been almost any one of the hundreds lining these Bloomsbury streets and squares, their aspect solid and enduring. Much stone had been used in the arches that topped front doors and windows and to face ground floors. Stout iron railings prevented people from falling into the small paved areas outside the basement rooms 10 or 12 feet below street level. While many basement windows were barred, during the day the residents often left open their porch doors, adorned with brass knockers and letter boxes. Tommy reckoned such houses would all have been built with servants' quarters and he wondered how many were still occupied...

These wanderings as he marched relieved him, for the moment, from his constant twinges of anxiety and nervous tautness. Would someone suddenly point the finger at him and yell "You! Out!"? Probably most of the others had their worries, especially family men. Tommy glanced at the three men along his line, then did as they were doing, stared steadily ahead and kept in step with the thrump, thrump, of all those marching feet.

The head of the column had disappeared now as they swung into a wide street ahead, then left through large, iron gates into a spacious sanded area with a substantial building facing them and high walls on either side bordered by roofed walkways supported by stone columns. Inside the gates, the column turned right, then left, until the RSM ordered a halt. The men lined two sides of the square.

A separate small group stood apart from, but close to, the head of the column, one of them obviously the senior officer, the others men of various ranks, some in officer's uniform, but several well-dressed in civilian clothes, mostly bowler-hatted and all carrying walking canes or rolled umbrellas. The RSM approached the senior officer. Halting two paces in front of him, the RSM saluted smartly, the right hand remaining over the right half of the forehead for three seconds before being briskly lowered to the side, thumb in line with the seam of the trousers... these details and many more were to occupy the hours and anxious efforts of Tommy and thousands like him for some time to come. But here was the first military occasion of which they had actually been a part. Really the beginning of their war.

One of the officer's group then stepped towards the column and counted off 25 lines of four and led them off to the far side of the ground before repeating the procedure again and again. Eventually, he assembled eight groups of 100. This left a number of recruits unassigned — and the officer's group.

Tommy admired the calm, efficient manner in which the Army men had organised a thousand strangers into easily controlled groups...

Now one officer instructed some of the unassigned men to fetch trestle tables and chairs from the building and place them under the shelters by the wall. A subaltern[95] took a seat at each of the tables in front of one of those carefully arranged columns of a hundred men. Facing Tommy's lot a tall, young man, slightly bowed shoulders, wearing a well-cut, light-grey suit and bowler hat, a tight-rolled umbrella resting against his chair. But Tommy was struck by the almost girlish beauty of his face: short, pale auburn curls showed beneath the hat brim, large, deep-blue eyes under long, auburn lashes, his complexion russet with a few freckles. Tommy felt heartened by the prospect of being commanded by a chap who looked no more than, say, six years older than himself.

A man of roughly 40 years walked smartly towards the young officer, halted and said, "West[96], sir, detailed to carry out your orders". The two talked briefly, then West, facing the men, bellowed, "Pay attention! Have any of you men served in the Army or the Territorial service before?" They all looked with special interest at the four who raised their hands. West ordered them forward.

Then West approached the column, counted off six lines, and ordered them to stand firm. The remainder he ordered to turn around, then take two paces forward. He counted off six more rows of four and told them to turn around and face the table. In this way, he eventually had the column divided into four sections of 24 spaced equally apart. He then called for one man to act as clerk for the time being. Several hands shot up, but one volunteer speedily stepped forward, Mitchell his name — he wanted that pen-pushing job and the young, rather shy subaltern was not the man to deny him.

West, rank yet unspecified, told the men that each one in turn, starting from the front, would step up to the table and give required particulars to the clerk. This business would take time and, meanwhile, the officer would give an explanatory talk.

The young chap in the grey suit blushed as he took up a position facing the men, but soon shed all self-consciousness as he explained that, of the, roughly, 1,000 men assembled there, 800 had been divided into eight Companies of 100, named alphabetically, A to H. The remaining 200 included officers, non-commissioned officers, and a reserve who would fill vacancies in the ranks of the Companies as they occurred — through men being selected to become NCOs and specialists, he explained, lest any darker thought occur to them. "Specialists" included Signallers, cooks, transport men, stores and equipment workers.

They would see many changes in the following weeks, he said — for instance, promotions to the ranks of warrant and non-commissioned officers, temporary or permanent, might be offered to men with previous military experience. But the objective at all times would be to create a Battalion[97] able to take its place on the battlefield and operate with credit to all concerned. For the first few weeks they would be taught the rudiments of drill by Regimental Sergeant Major Cole — finally, they learned the name of the spherical RSM whose voice could reach a thousand men's ears simultaneously.

"You must all bear in mind that the movement and formations taught in military drill form the basis of control of troop movements on the battlefield," said the officer. "At a later stage, hand signals from the men in charge will take the place of spoken words — which, in certain circumstances, cannot be heard. Remembering that drill has uses which are not always obvious, we may not get too bored by repetition I trust."

Now came Tommy's turn to step up to the table. Again, no awkward questions about his age. He finished dealing with the forms just before the young officer gave orders for those yet to be registered to return in two hours, after lunch. Those already registered were free until the following morning when they should return to begin training.

After some searching, the four friends got together again. Brother Ted and Harold had managed to get into the same Company, G. Len found himself in C and young Tommy in H. They ate their sandwiches as they walked and talked, then they stopped for a cup of tea in a small shop. Len and Harold had not yet registered and must return to the parade ground after lunch, so Ted and Tommy decided to face their employers and confess what they had done. They made their way to the City. Not knowing how long each would be detained, they agreed to make their separate ways home afterwards.

Having parted with his brother by Garlick Hill in Queen Victoria Street, Tommy strolled into Cannon Street. Already this familiar area seemed to have finished with him. From belonging there — he really had come to like the old City — he now felt rejected. Not working there, he had no business to be there.

He turned off by the pub on the corner and walked downhill, towards the river, glancing left and right at the familiar brass nameplates of the firms occupying the old buildings. And so into the small square and the building where he had so recently worked. "Had worked", past tense already. Up the old stairs and into the office, carried along speedily by excitement born of fear about what might happen and a desire to face it all and have done with it. Just a few words from the Company Secretary to the Battalion commander about Tommy's true age and he'd be in sore trouble...

"Ah, there you are. Don't tell me — you've got another job. Well, so have I. Do you remember I told you about the War Office work I'd been booked for if war was declared. Well, I start on that next Monday. What's your news?" So spake the Sergeant, full of his coming change of work, but pausing just long enough for Tommy to tell of his enlistment in the Army. "What as? Drummer boy or something?" "No, ordinary Private." "But..."

Here Tommy interrupted to tell of his sudden increase in years and to beg the Sergeant not to speak of this to others in the firm. Whatever his view of such a deception in ordinary times, the Sergeant entirely reassured him now, perhaps because he simply had no interest in anything but his own preparations for leaving. "Go and see F.C. Bull," he said. "Tell him what you're up to. I'm sure he won't mind. Big changes are coming here. Most of us will be shoving off before the year is out. War breaks up most peacetime arrangements."

So, along to the Secretary's office. The customary tap on the door and the call to come in. The bustling little businessman, always signing something, phoning somebody, or hurrying from one office to another, sat quietly and listened to the boy's story. He said something like, "Well, I hope you've done the right thing. Strange times these. Who knows what we'll be doing in a month or a year hence? If the war ends soon, all will be well. If not, this business for one will be finished. I wish you all the luck in the world."

He gave Tommy a gold half-sovereign. A little overcome, Tommy had difficulty thanking him, but when that surprisingly friendly man said, "Now you must come along and tell our Scottish director about this", he felt scared. That man was huge and powerful. "He will make me look silly," thought Tommy. He was very relieved when the big man listened gravely to the Secretary's account of Tommy's enlistment. The boisterousness which Tommy feared did break through briefly as the six foot odd of tough, engineer manhood sprang from his chair, raised a mighty hand and brought it down on Tommy's back in hearty congratulation.

Then, when FCB shook his hand, the Secretary insisted that he should visit the office again before leaving London. Previously, Tommy had felt that few at Lake & Currie knew of his existence, yet now he encountered this great kindness from the top. Saying his goodbyes to the old Sergeant and others, he began to feel regretful that this part of his young life was over. As he walked up the hill again towards the station, the smells drifting up from warehouses and factories along the Thames below seemed almost sweet, homely — qualities they had lacked when working among them was compulsory.

When he got home, he handed his mother the gold coin, worth 10 shillings. Very pleasantly surprised by this, she returned him three shillings for fares and so on. "There'll be more money soon I understand," Tommy told her. She looked happier than she had done for many a day.

Much later brother Ted got home, well satisfied with his visit to his firm's office and warehouse. Violet, the senior typist who had typed out Tommy's horrible poem some time previously, welcomed him and told him they'd all guessed what he'd been doing.

Ted's employer thought he had acted unreasonably, without warning or consultation. However, he valued Ted's services and committed to paper a letter stating that he would re-employ him when released by the Army authorities. To this generosity he added the gift of several pounds, expressing his personal view that the war would be over by Christmas or soon afterwards. Ted then dealt with outstanding letters and handed over to the boss some private records he had kept, the result of his ever-diligent enquiries regarding certain stocks and lines held by mills and dealers throughout the country.

All this made Tommy reflect again on the differences in their situations. Clever, persevering and full of self-confidence, Ted had a guaranteed future should he survive the war. Tommy had only the near certainty, as related by F.C. Bull, that his employer's business would soon disintegrate because of the war.

The four recruits travelled in by tram again the next morning, sitting on the open upper deck and enjoying the September sunshine. Ted still looked sunburnt from his camping with senior Scouts on the east coast in late July and early August. Dour Len, frisky Harold, and the brothers each had plenty to talk about regarding the previous day. Harold, lucky devil, had not only secured a guarantee of employment after the war, but his firm, Imperial Tobacco, had undertaken to pay all their employees half-salary during their wartime service in the armed forces. Len had merely been "promised an opportunity" to rejoin the stockbrokers he worked for "after hostilities ceased" — a favourite and somewhat optimistic expression frequently heard at that time.

Assembly of the troop Companies took place at 9am as arranged. A realisation that they had indeed become soldiers permeated the ranks when the young officer appeared and West, now wearing three stripes on each arm, called out: "Pay attention! Stand with your feet apart. Hands clasped behind your backs. I am about to give you your first ever command. 'Attention!' You will bring your left foot smartly up to your right foot and your hands to your sides, thumbs in line with the seam of your trousers. Proper training will follow, but for now do your best. Company at ease. Company, atten... *shun!*"

For the motley mob, the resulting crash of heels together was commendable no doubt. Irregularly clad in ordinary office or shop suits or work jackets and trousers, a few with white or bright-coloured wrappings around their necks and maybe black and white check caps on their heads, these volunteers really wanted to pull together and do this new job to the best of their abilities.

In front of them, Sergeant West turned right, took several paces towards the officer, brought his heels smartly together and saluted. "Thank you, Sergeant. Call the roll." Their next instruction was, "When your name is called out, answer 'Sir!'" The Sergeant called the names alphabetically, a ritual to be repeated hundreds of times in years to come. Some chaps missed their cue first time, but as Sergeant West approached the Ns, Tommy was ready for him. Hearing "Norcliffe!"[98] he promptly yelled "Sir!" in the deepest tone he could manage.

During the morning, they learned to march in step and how to respond to one or two simple words of command while on the move: turn left, right, and about. These movements looked easy but, at this stage, Sergeant West needed all his reserves of patience and understanding. After a 15-minute mid-morning break, Lieutenant Swickenham, the young officer, whose name Sergeant West had announced, addressed the Company — again initially shy, then speaking well. He explained that the men accepted as prospective NCOs were receiving intensive training under RSM Cole and that they would be able to commence some elementary duties with their Companies the following Monday.

At lunchtime, while Tommy waited for the other three near the gates, he took a good look at the old and imposing building way back at the far side of the large sanded area, their parade ground. Tommy had learnt little about it so far, although he'd heard it was called the Foundling Hospital. In the distance he once caught sight of several boys all dressed up, but otherwise never came in contact with any of the occupants[99].

Reconvened, the four City Of London Royal Fusiliers, well-fixed financially, repaired to a nearby workmen's dining room. They sat at a marble-topped table for four, unusual privacy secured by wooden seats with backs easily five feet high. "What's it to be?" all made into one word, asked a spruce man wearing a large white apron. Having read the menu, white-chalked on a blackboard outside the shop, they gave him their orders, which he shouted through a serving hatch. Soon he placed in front of each of them a large plateful of meat and two vegetables well doused with tasty gravy — soon followed by a sweet consisting of individual college puddings with custard sauce and a large cup of tea. This meal cost one shilling plus the then acceptable tip of one penny. This sum — one and a penny — loomed significantly in other transactions in some soldiers' lives Tommy later discovered[100].

That Friday afternoon provided Tommy with an experience that really thrilled him: learning how to conduct himself on Pay Parade. He hadn't thought much about this perhaps mercenary aspect of a soldier's life, but it felt like a step away from his fear of being exposed as a liar and a mere boy, and towards emulating his brother, Len and Harold, and them regarding him as an equal.

Sergeant West, not yet giving orders in the formal military fashion, told H Company to line up in twos and face him. While he explained that he would call out the men's names in alphabetical order and they should form a single line in that order, Tommy studied him and noted details of his appearance: probably 5 foot 10, dark hair, kindly eyes, large moustache with waxed ends, a roundish face, serious but probably given to the occasional smile, rather high-coloured cheeks, a good figure for a man aged about 40... That age seemed ancient to the lad, placing the Sergeant in the fatherly category in his estimation.

For this still informal Pay Parade, as before, they placed the tables and chairs in the shelter. Lieutenant Swickenham, the clerk, and another man sat there. As each recruit stepped forward, the unknown new man counted out coins from the piles on the table and placed them before the officer who pushed them towards the recipient who said "Thank you, sir", and rejoined the ranks.

Tommy pocketed 15 shillings. Five days at a bob a day and 2/- daily subsistence pay. Wealth indeed, but only for a short time, he knew. As soon as the Army started to feed him, the bare 1/- a day would have to suffice. Clothing and other items would be supplied without charge so it could be all right for a single lad; the bargain was a good one, and thereafter he gave it little thought.

Later, the men were lined up and addressed by the Lieutenant who explained that, while the trainee NCOs would continue their intensive training over the weekend, everyone else was free until Monday at 9am. They would all, from that time onwards, be subject to strict military discipline and must pay attention to all instructions given. The fact that, for some time to come, they had to remain dressed as civilians would not excuse any slackness. They had undertaken to do hard, trying work, and from now on they would cease to regard themselves as civilians.

"From Monday onwards," he emphasised, "you will be soldiers, members of His Majesty's Armed Forces. Do remember that. Dismiss the Company, Sergeant!"

Having lots of time on their hands, the four lads strolled around the area between Tottenham Court Road and Grey's Inn Road, finding much to observe and to talk about. Streets, squares and buildings, all of considerable age. Much of what they gazed on had been old in Charles Dickens's time[101].

Through their jobs, they had become familiar with the ancient City of London — the "Old Square Mile", as it was called by those who liked it — so they quite expected to be constantly discovering ancient buildings, quaint little streets and alleys, all very different from Edmonton or the densely built-up areas they glimpsed from trains and trams on their daily return journeys. But, in Bloomsbury, was richness to be glimpsed and smelt — as well as genteel poverty to be viewed with a side-glance one hoped would avoid giving offence. Here they noticed many people who would have attracted some attention among the unsophisticated folk of their half-developed suburb because of unusual headgear, clothing of some individuality, even a way of walking — perhaps swaggering — which suggested freedom from care as to what people might think about them.

Suburban folk at that time felt constraint on their behavior when walking in parts where they were known. Tommy felt as conscious of this as anybody else, and discovered quite young that, to liberate oneself from this sensation that critical eyes lurked behind lace curtains, one had only to make for the Central London area. There the milling thousands gave one anonymity and consequent confidence.

But then a surfeit of such crowds could sometimes bring on loneliness and send one scuttling back to Edmonton's quiet main road, the mean market place, the side streets of small, terraced houses, and, of course, those lace curtains. Out there on the extreme edge of the metropolis there was cool, fresh air to be inhaled with appreciation — unless a hot day and an unlucky breeze brought the local miasma, the stench from the fields on which evaporated the fluid part of the district's sewage.

At times in that awful war, recollections even of those aromas would evoke nostalgia, a weeping longing but, in Tommy's case, just momentarily.

The pals parted that Friday afternoon, after agreeing to meet at 8 o'clock on Monday morning.

Tommy felt very pleased to be able to give his mother some more money. A good week financially: the almost unheard of sum of 25/- the total received from Mr Bull and the Army. An exciting future was opening up, although forecasting could go no further than the immediate weeks in and around London learning the rudiments of soldiery.

Tommy gave some thought to the officers and others working over the weekend, teaching the men who wished to become Lance Corporals and Corporals and Platoon Sergeants to understand commands themselves, and then how to give the required orders to their men with appropriate explanations so that the Battalion of untrained men could be organised into something resembling a military unit as soon as possible. A difficult task.

Most of these would-be NCOs had no experience of soldiering, no knowledge of how to perform Army drill, yet they would be trying to instruct recruits very soon. "It's possible that I'm the youngest in the whole Battalion," Tommy reflected. "But in two or three subjects it's likely I'm more proficient than many of them: things like shooting, simple drill using semaphore signals with flags, and the Morse Code with flags, lamps and buzzers or tappers — all thanks to old Frusher and the Scouts."

Tommy never mentioned these matters to his comrades because he knew what their reaction would be: remarks expressing all shades of feeling from amusement to outright derision, depending on the former occupation of the commentator. The "workers" would jeer and the "white-collar boys" would register amusement or toleration for an I-intend-to-improve-myself boy. If of a radical liberal persuasion, they might even express abhorrence for the regimentation of children. One seldom heard outright approval of Scouting expressed, except perhaps by some members of the religious organisations to which the Scout troops were loosely attached.

These thoughts reminded him that, in all the excitement, he had overlooked Thursday evening's meeting of his troop. In fact, having become a soldier, the thought of putting on the uniform of a Boy Scout suddenly seemed incongruous — more so when he briefly imagined appearing in front of the mass of men among whom he had spent recent days wearing the dented frontiersman's hat, khaki shirt adorned with various badges and shoulder ribbons, short, blue knickers and bare knees, with, final touch, in his hand a stout five-foot staff. Yes, what sort of greeting would this apparition receive from that mixed crowd? Horrible thought.

That Saturday afternoon, Ted and Tommy went along to the hall where the troop assembled. They intended to tell Mr Frusher they were now soldiers and would therefore have to give up membership of the troop. They arrived purposely a little late, perhaps 20 minutes after the usual time, assuming the programme for the afternoon would by then have commenced without help from them. They would have a few words with the governor, then walk out, severing the association of several years just like that.

"There you are, at last, and not in uniform. Is something wrong, Mr Norcliffe?" This to Ted, now a qualified assistant Scoutmaster, therefore addressed as a man. "Do please tell me about it." Ted explained and Mr. Frusher's usually pale face flushed. This may have been due to relief that nothing awful had occurred in the Norcliffe family, but Tommy, studying the governor's bearded face, suspected that annoyance really caused the blush, which was accompanied by three rapid blinks and a long stare — signs of his inner struggle to subdue anger.

When Ted ventured to speak of leaving the Scouts, back came the assertion, "Once a Scout, always a Scout!" and the brothers found themselves assigned to their respective duties for that afternoon and getting on with them –after having exchanged glances which conveyed the advisability of tolerance and co-operation at this juncture.

Tommy's feelings were strangely mixed. Facing his patrol he felt it was good to be back among familiar faces and subjects and where his falsehood regarding his age was of no consequence. No exciting, unknown future. Here, he would always be allowed to play his small part. This thought helped to soften his sadness at the coming separation from familiar faces and places. He knew the new life to which he was committed would have some awful periods, but youthful optimism kept him from dwelling on such possibilities.

The meeting over, Mr Frusher called his seniors together, told them of the brothers' enlistment and expressed the hope that all the others would not desert him. Those able to give assurances did so, but the senior assistant Scoutmaster had to tell him that, as an officer in the Royal Navy Voluntary Reserve, he would have to report for duty shortly. The brothers promised they would give what help they could in future, but they said their goodbyes just in case military duties prevented their return.

The farewells might have been said with deeper regret had those present been able to foresee that years would pass before the few who survived would be able to get together again.

Chapter Fifteen

Came Monday morning and their first training parade, with Company Sergeant Major West, promoted to that rank over the weekend, one of the few present wearing khaki uniform. Above his three stripes on each arm now gleamed a small brass crown identifying him as H Company's senior NCO, above two new Sergeants, products of the weekend's intensive training.

Lieutenant Swickenham had abandoned his sober civilian garb and looked quite resplendent in an outfit of obvious good quality. Cap, jacket, cream, cord breeches, light faun puttees and highly polished brown shoes; all bespoke wealth and good taste. Just right for the job, in Tommy's eyes.

CSM West gave the order "Company fall in!" and the men took up the positions facing him they had held on the Friday, Tommy in the front rank of the two lines. On Tommy's left stood a man of 36, probably, wearing a cap at an unusual angle — the soft cloth pulled back and the hard peak pulled forward as far as they could possibly go. Tommy wondered if the two sections would part under the strain. Under the peak, dark inquisitive eyes moved constantly, taking in everything with keen interest; a cheerful, though pale, face with a sharp, red nose and black moustache; a soiled black jacket, dark grey trousers shiny with what appeared to be grease, and heavy, black boots completed Tommy's sidelong view of Joe Parker.

Had Joe cut his eyes to the right, he would have seen that Tommy too wore a black jacket with tight grey trousers but, instead of a cap, he wore the City office boy's hard, flat bowler. A boy in men's clothing?

A rather elderly fellow of scholarly appearance called Ewart Walker stood to Tommy's right. He looked stern, or somewhat benign, or quizzical, all dependent on what the brainy bloke was observing at any given moment. He wore grey flannel trousers, a Norfolk jacket[102], brown, brogue shoes and, unusually at that period, no hat to cover his cropped grey hair.

The inculcating of elementary drill details occupied them throughout that morning with one ten-minute break for a smoke and a rest. Tommy set himself to do the necessary movements as neatly as possible — marching forward, turning left, right, and about. He watched each demonstration and listened attentively to every word said, mainly because he felt that, if he could avoid drawing attention to himself, then one more day might pass without someone noticing his extreme youthfulness and calling for his dismissal from what was reckoned to be an Army of men.

During the break he chatted with old Joe Parker, as he thought of him, and learnt that he worked at Billingsgate fish market as a casual porter. Tommy told Joe, "I was working not far from here in a lane off Cannon Street". "At what?" asked Joe. "Oh, just a penpusher," Tommy told him. Junior clerk or glorified office boy would not have done at all. He hoped Joe would assume he'd been at it for years.

Joe asked no more questions, but added that he'd spent much of his life at sea, mainly on coastal vessels. He proceeded to describe nights ashore in small seaports, winding up with his choicest experience — his face glowed, his eyes sparkled, as he told how he put up at a lodging house once, ate a lovely meal, and shared his beer with the buxom landlady, her husband presently away at sea it turned out. Then he turned in. The bed had lovely, clean, white sheets and pillows, but to all this luxury the landlady later added the pleasure of her curvaceous body. Joe relived the delights of having her meaty legs wrapped round him until the order to fall in saved Tommy from making the expected noises of approval.

CSM West resumed his lessons. The troops learned to set off with the left foot at the order to march. They marched, they halted. Left, right, left, and on it went. Came noon and, before being dismissed, the men were told that a sharp, short route march (pronounced "rout", apparently according to Army custom), would provide their exercise that afternoon, "Promptly at 2pm and, bear this in mind, be ready at 1.50. Company, dismiss! Stop! Listen, don't just walk away in future when I give the order and no officer is present. You will turn smartly to the right, pause, then steadily walk away. I'll show you all later how to dismiss when an officer is present. Company, dismiss!".

The men standing in two lines facing the CSM then swivelled, each on the heel of his right foot, brought up the left alongside the right with a satisfactory crash, paused, then walked quietly away. They were learning. CSM West's face showed the pleasure he felt at their willingness and ability to comply with an order. With almost two hours on their hands, our four gathered again by the gateway to the Foundling Hospital. Then, strolling in pairs, they swapped experiences of that morning's work.

Ted and Harold from G Company had formed an unflattering opinion of their CSM, named Johnson. His words of command were not sharp and clear. His face reddened and he muffed his words a bit when describing the meaning of an order. But their Company officer was great. He'd shot on to the parade ground on a big Harley Davidson motorbike[103].

CSM Johnson called the men to attention, saluted, and their Lieutenant, Bigginford by name, gave a very smart salute in return. He then stood and looked steadily at the men, his gaze moving slowly along the lines from right to left. This gave them a chance to size him up too. They liked what they saw. His clear eyes, a Charlie Chaplin moustache (as it was then called), very white teeth, a full-cut, large peaked cap worn at a jaunty angle, dark khaki jacket with two breast pockets and two full-cut side pockets, well polished Sam Brown belt, light faun breeches and puttees and glossy footwear, brown — the whole 6-foot, broad-shouldered look of him guaranteed the hero-worship which such men inspire. Not all of them justify this regard in times of stress, but G Company's first impression could be summed up as "Bigginford's the boy".

Len in C Company had no very clear opinion to offer regarding those in charge of his lot. The CSM, he said, was very short, stocky, red-faced, abrupt in manner, a former Territorial but... "Decent bloke, we'll be all right in C Company".

They entered a Joe Lyons and ate Welsh rarebit or poached eggs on toast and drank several cups of tea. Three of them smoked fags while Len brought out one of his beloved pipes. The three of them watched Len's careful routine of scraping out the bowl, taking a slice of hard-packed tobacco from its silver-paper covering, rolling the baccy thoroughly in his palm before packing it into the pipe and placing the flat, wide end of the stem between those large, front teeth. He struck a match and, as the flame over the tobacco rose and subsided with each breath drawn through the pipe, he emitted a puff of blue smoke from the side of his mouth. The drawing in and puffing out continued a while, accompanied by a look of intense satisfaction on Len's face. "You can close your mouth now," said facetious Harold to Tommy, who suddenly realised how engrossed he had been in Len's pipe drill.

Returning, they stood around waiting to rejoin their Companies a full half-hour before assembly time. Idly gazing around they fell into discussing what they knew of the Foundling Hospital. Old Ewart Walker, standing nearby, caught Tommy's eye and joined the four. Tommy introduced him and asked him about the building and its occupants.

"I do know just a little of its history," he said. "In the early 1700s, a Captain Coram retired from seafaring and became interested in trying to help some of the very poor children he saw haunting dingy streets, often parentless. The Captain had the idea of erecting a large building where these waifs and strays could be housed and educated. He put it to influential people and they raised a fund to that purpose. Much financial support was derived from performances of Handel's Messiah, sometimes conducted by that good composer." Ewart Walker added that rumours he could not confirm suggested that certain wealthy gents gave financial support in return for the accommodation of their unacknowledged offspring.

They returned to the parade ground, welcomed by the order to "Fall in!" Before CSM West reported to Lieutenant Swickenham, he divided H Company into two platoons of 50 men, led by Sergeants Blake and Eon. Blake stood facing Tommy's platoon. "Teach them quickly how to form fours," ordered CSM West. So they learned how to number from the right. Blake explained: "On the command 'Form fours!' men with even numbers will take one pace to the rear with the left foot, one pace to the right with the right foot, and bring the left foot smartly up to the right foot. You will then be in fours."

With the best will in the world, some men had difficulty at first in performing this simple move. Now that their Company officer could be seen approaching, rehearsal had ceased. All hoped for the best when the order "Form fours!" was given. Called to attention, all the men stood silent. The salute and report by CSM West to Lieutenant Swickenham followed. Then Swickenham told the men about the march to follow. He asked them, in spite of their varied civilian garb, to bear themselves like soldiers. The eyes of many London citizens would regard them and a good impression must be aimed at.

Thus began one of many foot-slogging ventures in the course of their elementary training. This one took them along Tottenham Court Road, New Oxford Street, and Oxford Street, to Marble Arch and into Hyde Park, where they rested and did some drill before returning via a different route. They marched at attention and in complete silence for the most part, with a deal of conversation breaking out when the CSMs ordered "March at ease!" — but all of it subdued by the unaccustomed public performance they felt they were staging.

However, the column was long, not much short of a thousand men, and probably at quite an early stage the officers began to realise that an error of judgment had occurred.

People crossing the road could not possibly wait while this long procession passed so they would try to hurry through any gap they espied. This caused pauses and broke the marching rhythm. Elderly folk would be helped by the men, pretty girls too — as the occasional shriek or squeal would attest. Policemen controlling busy crossings could not help causing gaps in the long column. So did congested traffic, especially in Oxford Street, where a bus or a lorry frequently became interposed between Companies, even though drivers of all sorts of vehicles, motor or horse-drawn, tried to let the Battalion through.

Cart and dray drivers, perched in high seats, some of them no doubt old soldiers, shouted words of sarcastic encouragement to the self-conscious recruits: "Keep them 'eads up!" or "Swing them arms there!" along with one or two unfavourable comparisons to another Army apparently commanded by a certain Fred Karno[104]. But it was just cheerful banter and, provided you didn't take yourself too seriously, no offence was taken.

All the same, the officers ensured that future route marches avoided Central London and were undertaken Company by Company rather than the whole Battalion together.

But familiarity with the new routine of living soon encouraged those men who had subdued noisy and garrulous natures on that first march to commence raising their voices in joke and jibe. Some of the Cockneys' humour was amusing, some of it downright rude and embarrassing. When the Battalion marched at ease, singing would break out — and not discouraged by the CSMs because it helped to maintain a marching rhythm and to overcome boredom.

They started with innocent numbers like Clementine, Boys Of The Old

Brigade, John Brown's Body and so forth, but a sort of vocal degeneration gradually set in. John Brown's Body became John Brown's Cow — it went peepee against the wall. The music hall song which went "Our lodger is a nice young man, such a nice young man is he" lent itself to suggestions about his lewd practices[105]. The Company officer had to lead his men and Tommy, anonymously tucked away, felt sorry for the young man who marched alone in front of this sometimes blasphemous company.

On the gritty area in front of the Foundling Hospital, a playground now became a parade ground, the crunch of hundreds of feet continued throughout that sunny autumn. The recruits ceaselessly marched short distances, turned about and re-traversed the ground, turned left and proceeded that way briefly, turned right and after a few paces halted and listened to a brief, loud oration delivered by an instructor.

Pupils and teachers all learned from these antics, but Tommy surmised that residents, and others, passing by the railings and big iron gates might speculate as to how all this was helping the troops already fighting and being wounded or killed[106]. How about giving each man a rifle and showing him how to fire it, how to use a bayonet? Many people were saying that would have been better preparation for war. Tommy agreed. But we hadn't the uniforms or the arms apparently... And Tommy and many thousands of other early volunteers may have owed their survival to that lack of war materials.

Two Companies each day had the use of the Battalion headquarters, the comfortable building where they had originally signed up. But the two lucky Companies paid for this privilege by providing a night guard of ten men from 6pm to 8am. Two men would stand at the entrance for two hours, then be relieved by a fresh pair. The Battalion provided mattresses and blankets so some sleep could be had — essential, as ordinary duty would have to be carried out next day. But, needless to say, some men on guard duty got so involved in card games that they got no rest at all.

When Tommy's Company took their turn at HQ, they assembled in the street outside the depot at 9am. Tommy noticed that several poor-looking girls stood on the pavement opposite, watching the recruits, although they made no move to attract attention. Tarts or toms hoping to get bookings for the evening, bold Joe Parker told Tommy.

When volunteers for night guard duty were called for, the somewhat older and mostly noisier chaps were quickest to offer themselves, filling the required number in a matter of seconds. But Tommy kept quiet. Although he would not have demurred had he been called, he hoped to be allowed more time to become accustomed to the company of so many adult men. He'd had no difficulties during working hours, but he feared he might feel awkward among older strangers when off-duty.

For the time being, Tommy's daily routine had a marked similarity to that dictated by his civilian appointment. He rose about 7am and journeyed to London to arrive at parade ground or depot by 8.20; later, the day's duties done, he returned home, though sometimes earlier than had been usual for his office work. Meals, though, whether taken at home or in a café, were now of better quality and greater quantity. That 2/- a day subsistence pay made a great difference to Tommy. Ted, being older, had earned higher wages than his brother, but their combined extra shillings raised the family income to a more comfortable figure.

All realised this was only a temporary bonus and, around this time, mother and sons held a little family council. They discussed the war. Victory for the Allies, as our lot were already being called, did not appear imminent with news from the Front anything but cheerful. Fears of shortages had grown. So they decided to buy extra food of a sort which would keep well: certain tinned goods, flour, dried beans, even some potatoes for the medium term.

To this end, the brothers contributed all their money apart from what they needed for fares and light meals around midday. Over a few weeks, the family built up a food store which the brothers hoped would help sustain their parents and the younger children for a period after the Battalion moved from London (as they knew it must).

For lack of equipment, including weapons, their training still had to be limited to drill marching, though not just on the parade ground and the city streets. Hampstead Heath began to see much of them. There they learned how to advance across country in open formation, their movements being controlled by hand signals from officers and NCOs. The previous war in South Africa had provided useful lessons: it was now realised that columns of marching men in view of enemy troops made easy targets for riflemen and artillery[107]. So, where frontline soldiers had to go forward, single lines of men with two or three paces between them were considered to be more difficult targets and economical of casualties.

Marching to and from the Heath provided useful marching practice — vocal exercise too, as they sang lewd, or perhaps merely rude, adaptations of various songs of the day in march time. Onlookers must have felt the war had indeed come very close to them, if in an unexpected form. The famous Spaniards Inn at Hampstead found itself swamped with customers on days when Army trainees were in the vicinity. Tommy enjoyed the cheap, satisfying lunches there. He felt good beer replenishing his strength, chunks of bread and cheese satisfying his hunger, the crunchy crusts adding to the meal a rhythmic percussion. Afterwards, on that Indian summer's remaining fine days, they could sometimes take a restful hour reclining on the sloping meadow at the rear of the inn — times to remember for Tommy.

War, according to the school history books he'd read, had never been this pleasant. But, while good weather lasted, the men naturally enjoyed this period of playing at soldiers, as some described it.

So passed that strange, rather beautiful September. With October came cooler weather and rain — a difficulty, for no officer cared to keep his men tramping around in rain-soaked clothing. Some chaps had good suits and overcoats and sound footwear, but what of the poor devils in flimsy suits and shoes?

Generally, unmarried fellows had been able to buy strong boots and waterproof coats, but family men in hard times could not afford the outlay. Tommy had bought the necessary garments but, even so, found it difficult to remain comfortably dry after marching for an hour or so in steady rain.

The officers considered what sort of training could be done under cover but, newly appointed, they had only limited knowledge of the subjects to be taught. Much time was wasted; according to the recruit's degree of conscientiousness, these sessions might seem agreeable, boring, or downright maddening. The worse the weather the less brightly burned the flame of that patriotism which had induced some of them to quit their jobs suddenly and volunteer to become fighters for their country. Even those who had joined for some imagined advantage had, for the most part, also believed the cause was a good one and so had tackled the new life with zest and good intentions. The temporary stagnation was depressing, but any sharp, bright day would enliven the men as their limited training got lively and meaningful once again.

However, came the day when all doubt and disappointment vanished: an announcement that, from the last Monday in October, the two Companies who, each day, took their turn to occupy the Battalion Headquarters would be solely occupied with the long-anticipated distribution of uniforms: greatcoats[108], tunics, trousers, socks, boots, puttees, undervests, shirts, pants, all crowned by a military cap with a Regimental badge. Much mirth ensued from the announcement that each man would be issued with a housewife, but this turned out to be nothing more sexy than a roll-up cloth pouch holding needles, cotton, buttons and so on.

The recruits were expected to buy tins of a paste called Soldier's Friend, also a small brush and a peculiar six-inch piece of metal with a lengthwise slot — called a button stick, for reasons soon revealed. An instructor demonstrated the art of accurately directing a shot of spittle to the centre of the paste, scooping some buttons into the slot on the stick, dabbing the brush into the paste, scrubbing the buttons, and finally polishing them.

Then the NCOs showed them how to convert their great coats into long slim rolls, the ends of the rolls to be brought together and secured with a cord or strap, the loop then passed over the head to rest on the right shoulder diagonally across the body. In fine weather, the welcome order to listen out for was "Great coats will be worn en banderole". Was this expression borrowed from Napoleon's Army, Tommy wondered. Nobody enlightened him and he never heard the phrase used by officers of any other Army unit. He assumed the Foreign Legion and his Royal Fusiliers had at least those two words in common.

On receiving his kit he couldn't get home fast enough.

Later in the war he sometimes recalled that day. He didn't realise its importance at the time, none of them did as far as he knew. Quite light-heartedly, he wished to throw off the clothes of a mere civilian and be seen as a soldier — after weeks of trying to be one while still dressed in his boyish suit and bowler. But, in truth, he was shedding the garb of freedom, doing so eagerly, divesting himself of clothing which entitled him to go almost anywhere in Great Britain without let or hindrance and putting on the uniform of service or maybe of serfdom. From then on, if called upon to do so by Military Police or gentlemen holding His

Majesty's Commission, he would have to account for his presence in any location.

His family showed great interest in the quality of the clothing, touching the uniform and rubbing it between thumbs and forefingers like so many tailors. All good stuff, they agreed: vest and long pants of wool, warm, heavy garments; socks too would obviously stand much hard wear and ensure warm feet in he coldest weather. The name Schneider in the cap struck them all as being rather strange. "What," asked Dad, "is the British Army doing with headgear of apparently German manufacture?"

Hastily, Tommy changed into the uniform. He found all the garments fitted him well, except that the boots were too big, albeit the smallest in stock as the Quartermaster had explained when issuing them. So, for his early months in the Army, Tommy had to wear two pairs of grey socks to fill out the heavy boots. He would have to buy two pairs of socks as near to the official ones in colour and weight as possible so he could rotate two pairs on and two in the wash.

He'd put on everything but the puttees. He began his first attempt to wind these bandages round his calves, starting with a turns around the ankle… spacing each turn evenly a requirement not easy to satisfy. However, after a few awkward failures, he came close to achieving the correct outcome. Then he stood up straight and still, eyes looking straight ahead at their own level, chin in, shoulders back, chest out, stomach in, knees back, heels together, toes apart at an angle of 90 degrees — all as per instructions, the very figure of a soldier, he hoped.

Mother studied him, tears in her eyes… and she laughed and laughed and laughed. This puzzled and disappointed the self-conscious lad. He searched her face to discover if the mirth was a derisory reaction. As he watched her, understanding came to him and he also laughed and laughed. "That's it," she said. "You can see it all as I do. I'm not sneering at the boy soldier, but to see one of my children dressed as a fighting man for the first time, standing stiff as a ramrod and so serious with it. Well, it's just too much." The laughter petered out with some quickly concealed tears.

Tommy ventured into the street to avoid further embarrassment and perchance to see if neighbours had any comment to make. Looking up the street towards the main road he thrilled to see brother Ted already wearing his Army gear, striding briskly towards him.

His keen scrutiny turned to pleasurable surprise and pride when the boy saw how neatly the clothes fitted Ted's small, but well-proportioned body. He would have valued a pair of legs of that shape himself — slightly bowed, the calves flattered by his carefully rolled puttees. A flicker of the heartache he felt throughout life, whenever it seemed that someone he loved was drifting away, assailed him briefly at that moment. Faulty reasoning, sentimentality, a soft streak, these he always feared were at the root of these feminine lapses which must be concealed if he was ever to become a real man. Other people didn't appear bothered by them. In any case, people's feelings were only of interest to themselves, not to be indecently exposed.

The present emotions stirred because of Tommy's realisation that each member of his group of four had already begun to act independently. No longer did they wait for each other at the end of the day's training, for their Companies often used different parade grounds or might be dismissed at some distant place away from the depot or the Foundling Hospital. Tommy hoped he and his brother would try to spend time together as often as possible, but he would not make a nuisance of himself by hanging on, as he put it to himself.

The evening meal over, the brothers agreed to spend an hour or two walking around familiar streets to meet acquaintances — and, perhaps, impress them. Ted walked confidently as always, very able in most things he tackled, used to dealing with local problems in his own definite way — to whom should he defer, whom should he fear? In these streets where he was well-known, he could walk along with an easy grace. No need to swagger defiantly, no need to cringe. Anyway, that was how Tommy saw him and he gained confidence as he walked alongside Ted.

The first familiar face they met was a girl coming home from the station, Alice Goodman. Tommy had been aware of her in school days as a very forceful character. Roughly of Ted's age, she had made no secret of her liking for his company. But, even before he joined up, he'd shown no wish to confine his spare moments to any particular girl, given his duties as assistant Scoutmaster, his enjoyment of twice-weekly sessions at a gymnasium, and all the walking and suchlike he did with Len, Harold and other friends. Still, Alice would snatch the odd chat in the street or on the train.

As far as Tommy could see, Ted had genuine respect for Alice's educational and, later, business abilities, but he resented and skilfully avoided her completely obvious design to take him over, to have him and shape him to her requirements. Tall, her hair all but black, keen, dark eyes in a very attractive face, she could be the very devil if thwarted. Tommy had seen the eyes flare, the face blanch, the corners of the mouth turn down. There she was. Bitterness, hatred, personified — but only temporarily...

And now, confronted with Ted the soldier, Alice looked amazed and a trifle confused. In fact, Tommy gathered she would have preferred to be consulted about Ted's enlistment. Ted implied, not quite truthfully, that the Battalion might be leaving the country shortly, so Alice insisted that he should write to her regularly, no matter where he might be and promised she would respond. He promised to do this.

Tommy placed himself so that he might face Ted and convey his willingness to walk away if that were necessary. While still conversing with Alice, Ted caught his eye and shook his head, so Tommy stayed. Meanwhile, vivacious Alice at no time noticed or commented on his presence as she pursued her purpose relentlessly. Anyway, had she actually spoken to him, he would have found difficulty in disposing of the extra hands he'd suddenly sprouted and his legs would have shortened so that his backside rested on the ground, while paralysis of the lower jaw prevented him from replying.

But now Tommy observed her with growing admiration, noted the dark eyes, the clear rapid speech, the perfectly-fitting costume of a quality rarely seen in these parts enhancing her slim figure. He knew that, for her, a spell at a commercial college had followed ordinary school, and a typewriter had replaced her pen for all correspondence. What a gem of a secretary some fortunate businessman had in her — though, probably, he would find in due course that she had taken over his job...

On several occasions during the war years, when the brothers had the good fortune to meet, Ted let him read the long news reports about local and family happenings typed by Alice on foolscap sheets of fine paper, true to her self-imposed undertaking.

Many years later, Tommy chanced to meet her — the dark hair greying, her face a little lined, all else immaculate and charming as ever. But there was no Ted, had not been for some years. Tommy raised his hat, as was the custom, and told her who he was. They talked for a while of their distant days. She lived elsewhere, was just visiting. She had married her one-time boss. The brief meeting took them away for a short while from present concerns. Back to youthful times and through some trying periods. Finally back to now, but with no Ted, no Ted. So goodbye, Alice, and all good wishes…

The brothers' first promenade in the King's uniform proceeded. People glanced at them as they passed, but the lads heard no comments. Had they, in civilian dress, ventured to wear any unusual garment, some critics would most certainly have commented quite loudly — perhaps the driver of a passing tram shouting an enquiry such as, "'Ave you broke the bank of bloody Monte Carlo, mate?" Those passing nearer to a fellow who they thought was putting on the style might sneer loudly and even prevent him from walking on for a while, especially if he was of small stature. But Tommy and Ted were not subjected to any unpleasantness, only an occasional approving smile — allaying Tommy's continuing fears that his obvious lack of years might be noticed.

He marched on alongside Ted, his confidence growing — until they met Madge Rocks, Harold Mellow's (sort of) half-sister. Their family structure has its mysteries: a sister of Harold's mother lived with the family and, when she too produced her contribution in the form of a bonnie baby girl, some arrangement agreeable to all must have been evolved, for later on she added a son to the growing population in the small house. The father, a quiet man, spent his days providing for all these healthy eaters. It was not disclosed how he spent his nights.

Nevertheless, Harold had done quite well and Madge became a competent shorthand typist and a solid church worker. She was wide. Wide, that is, of shoulder and hips, not in the worldly, knowledgeable sense. A little over five feet tall and wide, her face wide and attractive, her fine hazel eyes wide apart, her wide mouth usually further widened by a smile. As to the rest of her, the long skirts of the period meant that no one really knew what allowed Madge to perambulate except that, of course, the wide shoes she wore doubtless covered a pair of wide feet. But those who knew her valued her good will, so when she cheerily answered Ted's greeting, then looked at Tommy and laughed, she mangled the boy's pride. He really took offence and, red of face, walked away and went home.

Chapter Sixteen

Next morning's parade of Tommy's H Company at the Foundlings Hospital parade ground took on a purposeful efficiency never previously seen. Why? Because every man present dressed as a soldier, therefore he *was* a soldier. All the work and instruction of recent weeks had already implanted habits of thought and movement which could be used to their fullest now that a military force was seen to exist.

A mixture of types such as one would have seen in any street of Central London at that time, now suddenly all alike, or nearly. No more Joe Parker in his threadbare jacket and almost worn-out shoes. No more Ewart Walker in his country-style sportswear. No more Sticky Pryke in his Soho wide-boy outfit, a black jacket with lapels ending only inches above the waist, pink shirt, spotted bow tie, his thick, black hair cut and shaved high at the back in a straight line.

In uniform, they all looked the same — except for commissioned officers. These gentlemen yet preserved certain individual features, although one could see that the older generations presented a more standardised appearance than the young bloods. The latter tended to have lighter, almost cream-coloured breeches and puttees and their caps had longer peaks and were worn at more rakish angles. Immediately, many men in the ranks mentally credited these youngsters with more daring courage than their colleagues –creating expectations in many cases far from justified later, on the battlefield.

H Company lined up and obeyed orders shouted by NCOs. They did everything smartly and made satisfactory noises with their heavy boots. When the roll was called each man replied with a staccato "Sir!" when he heard his name. On the order "Number!", "One!" "Two!" "Three!" and so on down the line rapped out short and sharp.

Awaiting his turn to take over command, young Lieutenant Swickenham must have noticed with pleasure the authority of his NCOs and the transition overnight of his collection of civilian volunteers into a fairly well-drilled Company of soldiers. Meanwhile, Tommy enjoyed the feeling of anonymity which the uniform conferred on him. Though smaller than most of the men, he now felt he really belonged with them and his fears of being rejected began to fade.

Presently, they set off on one of their familiar route marches to the Heath. Now the crunch-crunch of the heavy boots really did sound businesslike. Part of the Army was on the move; people's ears told them so long before their eyes confirmed it. When the Lieutenant ordered "March at ease!" — repeated down the line by NCOs — comments from the witty ones about the new soldiery raised many a laugh and the men started singing some of their good-humoured, rude parodies. All to the steady tramp of well-shod feet. As these days passed, a routine of living appeared to establish itself. Not quite what they'd expected of wartime, but at least everybody could see they were doing their bit, as the saying went.

Then, one morning late in October when H Company assembled, Tommy walked into a hubbub of excitement and speculation. "We're going," he heard one Sergeant tell another. His further enquiries yielded no more detail except the certainty that they would soon leave London. Only then did he realise that he had become a little ashamed of the almost-peacetime way of life which had continued since he and the other three quit their office jobs.

This thought reminded him he had promised Mr F.C. Bull a farewell visit. Feeling that things were now moving apace, during a lunch break, he hurried by underground[109] to Cannon Street and on to the Lake & Currie building. There the kindly FCB greeted him warmly and gave him another of those lovely, gold half-sovereigns. Then everybody he knew at the firm showered him with congratulations on his smart uniform and good wishes for his safety when he reached the fighting front. A quick glance round the familiar place — with regret that old Sergeant had already left — and he hurried back to his new life, finished forever, had he but known it, with the old City.

His inner excitement increased by the day, but the question was, "What next? What next?"

An immediate answer came: nothing more dramatic than the issuing of missing items in the kit. Once they had been received and signed for, any pieces not displayed at a periodic inspection had to be paid for out of the soldier's meager bob a day. CSM West explained this most carefully, removing the grins from the faces of some who had assumed that the Army presented these useful things, including a cutthroat razor, in the way of gifts from a grateful nation.

On a Friday morning the whole Battalion was ordered to assemble at the Foundlings. Sergeants from each Company took positions as markers and the men fell in beside them until the parade formed a large square with a space in the middle where officers stood chatting, although the rotund RSM Cole remained apart, short cane under his arm.

A clatter of hooves, then an officer riding a black horse came through the wide gateway. An astute Sergeant in charge of the nearest platoon quickly assessed the situation. The Colonel — this officer's rank, undoubtedly — would have to be given access to that inner space which all the men were facing. Clearly, the Colonel might find breaking into a gallop and essaying a leap over the heads of four lines of men beyond even his equestrian skills.

So the Sergeant ordered one man to about-turn, counted off eight men from him and told the ninth to about turn. Then he yelled at all the men between those two to about-turn and promptly ordered "Quick march!" — forward and outward went that group, then "Right turn!" and onwards, and "Halt!" when they moved clear of the gap and, again, "About turn!"... so they faced the Colonel as he made his quite magnificent entrance. After which, by the reverse procedure, the astute Sergeant returned his men to their original positions and completed the square.

Tommy admired him — Sergeant Emon — for his quick response to a sticky situation. He had seen confusion overtake Lieutenant Swickenham and, possibly, CSM West, and acted — perhaps inspired, thought Tommy, by The Galloping Major, a popular song of the period, with its rousing chorus, "Hi, hi, clear the way/Here comes the galloping Major"[110].

Sergeant Emon could probably have been in all sorts of trouble for acting without instruction, but the young officer knew little about correct procedure and Tommy heard him quickly and quietly congratulate the Sergeant, concluding, "The CSM and I approve of what you did in this very unusual situation". So even if CSM West felt aggrieved, the deviation from what were termed "the proper channels" must be overlooked. Tommy keenly savoured the nuances in the officer's remark and hoped that some day, if difficulties arose when they were on the battlefield, he might be under Sergeant Emon's command.

When the required formalities had been carried out, in a voice which carried well, Colonel Gunaway addressed the thousand or so men of all ranks present, reviewing progress from the early days of forming this Battalion to the present time. Now he was able to tell them that the following morning, a Saturday, the Battalion would assemble at 8am, ready to march to London Bridge station, there to entrain for a destination near which an important job awaited them.

Action commencing at last. Tommy thought about his family, about to be reduced by two, its income much reduced too.

That evening, when he and Ted explained the day's developments, their parents said they were pleased there was no immediate risk of their sons going to the battlefront. They had read the casualty lists the daily newspapers published — lists headed by the names of commissioned officers and their Battalions, followed by the numbers of "other ranks" killed or wounded. This practice must have been customary in previous wars, but this time the numbers of dead and wounded soon grew far too large to catalogue daily — secrecy, too, concerning the whereabouts and movements of troops, came to take precedence over the honourable mention of casualties among officers and gentlemen.

They all assumed that, initially, they would not travel far away and they would be able to come home fairly frequently, so they said their farewells that Saturday morning at home without any suggestion that father, or anyone else, should go to London Bridge to see them off. Kitbags slung over shoulders, the brothers hurried away, pausing on the corner at the top of the street to wave to the family standing outside the house.

His usual phlegmatic self in a family not given to demonstrations of affection, Ted didn't tell Tommy that he had any particular pleasure or regret at the coming change in their lives. So Tommy imitated this almost casual treatment of what was surely a very important occasion. As far as he could judge, he might be the only one who did feel sad about the parting — if so, he too would also show no sorrow.

Of course, Tommy may have been wrong about this. Perhaps mother would miss Ted; she had always been proud of his achievements. But little about himself appeared to have pleased her, Tommy thought. He lacked the push and drive and confidence she frequently preached about. He always tried to behave as if he had no doubt about his own abilities and, among strangers, he usually did feel able to cope with most situations. But at home with his family, a sense of inadequacy assailed him often. A psychiatrist would have a convincing explanation ready, but Tommy found no good reason for it, much as he regretted it...

However, before he left the house, Tommy's father had shaken hands with him, wished him well and looked directly at him while doing so, which made Tommy feel that, probably, here was one who had some affection for him. Mother let him kiss her cheek, which was something — he could not remember when such a thing had last occurred. His young brother had his own special interests. His elder sister had always been good to him except when he annoyed her, as brothers will do at times. These thoughts nagged at him when he and Ted turned the corner and walked away from home.

Even so, anticipation of where they were going, where they might sleep that night and under what conditions, soon put a spring in his stride.

PART THREE

1914-1915

PREPARING FOR BATTLE:

KENT, MALTA, EGYPT

Chapter Seventeen

His imagination wove a tapestry designed by vanity, coloured by optimism. Its title could have been "Me, Wonderful Me".

Following instructions, Tommy had written his Regimental number 2969, his name, Company and Battalion in bold capitals on his kit bag. Carrying it balanced on a shoulder, he felt little discomfort, its weight not great, even with all the items issued so far. Companies marched separately to Greys Inn Road, where they joined up in a long column heading south towards Holborn.

They kept well into the side near the kerb to cause vehicles no undue obstruction. Accordingly, drivers waved and called out good wishes or cheery banter. Later, as recruitment stepped up, people became more used to seeing these columns of marching men but, still in the early stages of war, onlookers knew these recruits had volunteered and had their own pleasant ways of acknowledging them[111]. Tommy felt this infectious friendliness made the troops, as the recipients of kindness, more considerate of each other.

He could see his comrades to the left and right and some of those ahead of him... several familiar faces from their first parade as untutored recruits. Sticky, the Soho wide-boy, outgiving with his rich Cockney humour, but quick to take offence, marched in the row of four immediately in front of Tommy. Alongside him, Ewart Walker — nice to watch the steady, kindly, old chap plodding along on his sturdy legs, a slight roll to his body as he marched. "Wonder why he didn't go for a commission. Money problem I guess," thought Tommy[112].

Looking left along his own row, Tommy might receive a nod and grin from old Joe Parker, from his right, perhaps, a snappy quip from Frank Lawler. About 33 years old, Tommy surmised, slim, sporting a trim, narrow moustache, outspoken and, when they marched at ease, Frank chap showed himself a loud singer of popular songs — and home-made parodies thereof. His comments could be rather personal, but he took the rough replies and studied insults with the good humour he expected of others and successfully pricked the bubbles of conceit which made some men sullen when their pride was assaulted. Tommy had been an early victim of Lawler's sallies, but by now the blush of self-consciousness no longer suffused his face at every jibe and he could sometimes manage a retort or otherwise grin and appear to enjoy what he couldn't avoid.

The garrulous Goodbody, his broad shoulders visible over rows of those in front of Tommy, was one of several men he tried to keep clear of. Goodbody had a bright, penetrating eye. Tommy knew the fellow guessed he was too young to be a soldier. Always, if Tommy met his gaze, he seemed about to say something.

"I always found something to be doing elsewhere when it appeared that Goodbody intended to talk to me," Tommy later recalled[113]. "Fear of the man, or of what he might say in the hearing of others, made me keep a wary eye on him. But I always felt that once we were out of England there would be no risk of him forcing a showdown."

Much more comforting to have in view on the march was Price, a six-footer with a sort of baby face, soon dubbed "High" Price. When pleased — which meant most of the time — he had this girlish sort of smile. A pronounced dimple showed in each cheek. Nothing girlish, though, about that strong physique nor his challenging mien if he suspected anyone of getting at him.

No danger of that from High Price's neighbour on the march, Nick Thompson, about 28, a purposeful family man, a believer in all the decencies, who never deviated from his obvious lifelong habit of giving and expecting fair dealing. He marched carefully, steadily, and yet joined in the sociability around him, their comradeship already developing.

A couple of rows further on, Jack Pawson, tall, thin, but just the figure to show off a uniform, along with a face and neat moustache one would expect of a real soldier — yet his head looked rather small, giving a suggestion of frailty, as did his thinnish, putteed calves. Tommy had found him to be kindly and serious; probably most of the slick, Cockney humour, which flew back and forth, had no meaning for him. Jack marched with a Harker at either shoulder, brothers Percy and Reg; Percy of medium height, slight build, black hair, blue shaven chin, a sort of non-stop seeker after knowledge, always delving away and questioning; brother Reg quieter, diffident, very likeable.

Heavens, thought Tommy, there's the Old Bailey already. Thinking about his comrades — these men becoming a real part of his life — had made him oblivious to the distance covered. If he was only a lad, at least a fine, protective screen of older men was forming around him…

The crunching tramp, tramp of all those heavy boots proceeded… sometimes sounding above them, the din of clattering horses' hooves, merry or cursing wagon drivers, noisy petrol engines and hooting motor horns. Now a disappointment for Tommy: they would miss Cannon Street, so no chance of a quiet look down the narrow hill, no chance of someone from the office glimpsing him in his new situation. Instead, south from Cheapside along King William Street and across the Thames via London Bridge.

Came the order "Break step!", cheerfully obeyed by many who indulged momentarily in some fancy footwork for a laugh; Battalions of troops always walked out of step over bridges to avoid setting up a swinging motion which might cause damage, perhaps even to this stolid structure.

At London Bridge station, the Battalion, together with a great deal of equipment, filled a fairly long train of the old London, South Eastern and Chatham Railway, LSE and C for short, a line saddled with various nicknames including "Lazy, Slow, Easy and Cold". But Tommy considered the seating to be roomy and well-upholstered compared to, say, the Great Eastern Railway[114].

His travels on railways, none of them very long — with the ladies of the chapel to Walton-on-Thames or with the Scout troop to Bishop's Stortford — had always brought inner excitement. Whenever a train stopped, he would look out and speculate about the lives of people he saw working or just walking by. He hoped that one day he would be able to live in the country.

Chapter Eighteen

Well, now here was Bunbridge[115] and Tommy's feet were among the first to touch down on the station platform.

The troops left the station as quickly as the exit allowed and gathered into their various Companies on the road outside. Thereafter, things moved at a speed which gave Tommy very little chance to take stock of his surroundings. Lieutenant Swickenham announced that men should go to their allotted lodgings as soon as they were handed their billeting slips. They would reassemble at 3pm in this same place outside the station. A large map hung on a nearby fence and NCOs, who had visited the town previously to plan the operation, helped their men to locate their new addresses. Tommy's slip of paper read: Mr and Mrs Fluter, 12, Leigh Drive.

To avoid delay, instead of joining the scrimmage around the map, he approached a lady on the street, saluted her — which appeared to please her — and asked for directions. Along the main road, turn left, then third on the right… He soon found the house and rang the doorbell. He looked around. How pleasant was the street, the houses with their large front gardens, even though the trees lining the footpath had lost most of their leaves. A maid leant out of an upstairs window some little way up the hill, her occupation revealed by her white head cover and apron.

Number 12 and its neighbours were rather smaller dwellings than that one, but also detached. Tommy faced the front door again, considering whether he should ring the bell once more but, just then, from behind him a soft voice said, "I hope you haven't been waiting long". He turned and a middle-aged woman stood smiling at him. She went on, "I've been gardening and, being a little deaf, I didn't hear the bell ring. My friend next door told me she'd seen a soldier standing in the porch. I'm Mrs Fluter."

Tommy stated his name and that he felt very lucky to have been given such a nice billet. "You'll have a pal here," she told him. "The billeting officer asked if we would help by putting up two lads. My husband and I are pleased to be able to assist."

She had come around the side of the house, so the front door was not opened to him then — nor ever afterwards. Mrs F led him through a side gate and along a gravel path. Outside the kitchen door, she indicated a boot scraper, just inside it a large doormat which should always be used. Tommy saw the need if the kitchen was to remain in its current spotless condition. He removed his heavy boots, which had nails in their soles, and tugged a pair of far from new slippers out of his kitbag — which move met with Mrs F's instant approval.

While she made preparations for lunch she said, "We shall have dinner each evening at about 7 with Mr Fluter. On Saturdays and Sundays we shall dine at 2 o'clock." She looked at Tommy frequently, trying to decide what sort of stranger had come to live under her roof. She encouraged him to talk about himself and his family. He tried to give a truthful account, although he did describe himself as "a clerk", hopefully omitting the word "junior" which should have preceded that vague term.

Meanwhile, he felt increasingly comfortable in this almost all-white kitchen. He admired the several copper saucepans and utensils, cabinet, plates and dishes, a large, deep sink with two brass taps. Hot water would flow from one of them, he thought, a luxury not available at home. Why he had been allotted such a good billet he could not imagine, but he resolved he would not lose the privilege through carelessness.

Mrs Fluter led him out of the kitchen into a wide passage, then a roomy hallway with doors on either side opening on to various rooms and the stairway, which they ascended. Mrs F showed him into a room containing two single beds, a small wardrobe, two chairs, a chest of drawers and a large cupboard. Luxurious compared to his room at home.

Now he gave all his attention to Mrs Fluter, her serious but kindly face beneath greying hair. She said she hoped they would all get along together. Her husband managed a printing works belonging to a well-known London firm, she explained. He left the house before 8 each morning, usually came home about 6pm and spent the evenings quietly reading. Sometimes chapel affairs took him out to evening meetings. Would Tommy please pass these things on to the other soldier when he arrived, including the requests for quietness and care of furniture and bed linen? Churniston, whom Tommy recognised as a member of H Company, soon appeared and, after they'd talked for a while, Tommy decided he was a good sort. He repeated Mrs F's requests and asked his roommate to call him Tommy. Came the reply, "I'm Bob and I used to work in a London hospital. Strange job. I had to look after human remains which had been pickled. If a teaching surgeon required one of these specimens I'd extract them from the tank and deliver them." It seemed to Tommy that familiarity with the gruesome had conquered Bob's fear of it.

So here was Tommy's roommate, about 20, fairly tall and, he noticed, rather pigeon-toed. He wondered how Bob had managed to get into the Army with that deformity. Then came recollection of the perfunctory examination by the harassed old medico, which preceded his own admission. In truth, Churniston and he, either or both, might crack under the strain of military training and the work which would, undoubtedly, start soon.

Mrs F showed them the bathroom at the far end of the landing and pointed out the shelf for their toilet things. On it Tommy placed his cutthroat razor, soap, toothbrush and paste, and hairbrush, but he kept the Army-issued comb in his pocket. "I've never handled a cutthroat razor, but I guess I'll have to get used to it," said Bob. Tommy nodded and might have added that he'd never used any sort of razor at all. But he didn't say it. Any fine down which close examination might reveal on his face would be matched by that on the face of most maidens. Here, he thought, was another giveaway he'd better be careful about.

Mrs Fluter called them to the kitchen where she sat at the end of a small table and offered them cups of tea and bread and cheese. As they enjoyed this she told them the Government would pay her an allowance for supplying meals, but it wasn't much and she proposed to ignore it and give them as much good food as they could tuck away: "We have no children. I'm so glad they sent us you two youngsters. I shall enjoy looking after you. Are you members of a Christian church?" Tommy told her of his baptism, life as a choirboy, and confirmation too. This all pleased the good lady who spoke of the work she and Mr Fluter did at their Baptist chapel.

Churniston said he had lived in a block of flats off Tottenham Court Road in the middle of London and attended services in a famous Whitfield Street chapel nearby. But he had dropped out of it two years earlier, always finding somewhere new to go on a Sunday — a film, a cheap seat at the theatre or music hall, not to mention all the parks, displays, meetings and concerts. Living where he did had obviously given him many advantages over Tommy, who hoped to learn more when they chatted in the bedroom at night.

As was his habit, Tommy carefully observed the lady whom he was already thinking of as his temporary mum. Black eyebrows and lashes. Fine, grey hair. Strange that her complexion had that redness which Tommy always associated with an outdoor life — or possibly a liking for strong drink, as chapel people called it. She's a very good woman, he decided, and renewed his resolve to interfere as little as possible with the life of the couple at number 12.

After their snack, the two lads made their way to the station where the Company formed up and, with young Lieutenant Swickenham at their head, marched off to a road by the railway allotted to them as a temporary parade ground, where they joined three other Companies. Their Lieutenant told them that, although there would be no training or work of any sort until Monday, the following day, Sunday, the men would fall in at 9.30am, the roll would be called and then all Companies would join in a march to the parish church for morning service. Any wishing to be excused church parade should state their reasons to their platoon Sergeant and he would decide whether they were valid.

Later, when they had been dismissed and fallen out, Tommy searched for his brother. Soldiers stood around in groups discussing their billets and general impressions of the town. He soon found Ted and Harold's G Company. They were billeted together, they said. It turned out Tommy's "home" in Leigh Drive was quite near theirs and Harold said, "Come along to our place. There's quite a family: Mr and Mrs Prout and two daughters, 18 and 12. Very friendly people — told us to come and go as we pleased."However, it being early for an evening meal — they certainly didn't expect their hosts to supply tea and supper — the three walked to the main street to find the town's pleasure spots. Apart from some pubs, they found two places where, it appeared, the locals threw inhibitions to the winds and really let themselves go — a small cinema[116] and a roller-skating rink. They also discovered an old castle standing in lovely grounds[117], and two fairly large hotels near the cattle market. As they wandered along the high street towards the town centre, the size and style of the shops became bigger and better. But they went on until they passed only the occasional shop among houses of varying size and finally the town became countryside, the road bounded by hedges, or a cluster of cottages, or the grounds of a large house with a sanded drive.

Tommy savoured an air of prosperity, the sweet smell of late flowers and shrubs, and noted the absence of the uncouth and depressing sights and odours which go with poverty or insufficiency of life's requirements. The friends discussed these differences from some London parts they knew and agreed it was unexpected that becoming soldiers should, at first, plant them in a cosy, country town rather than in a war-blasted battlefield. They told one another even Bunbridge must have its poor people; but they supposed that, perhaps, living in uncomfortable conditions was more easily bearable in an environment like this...

Presently, they separated agreeing to get together after church parade. Tommy found his way back to his lodgings, finally turning into Leigh Drive and climbing the steep hill to number 12.

A new cause for speculation now occupied him: what would *Mr* Fluter be like? Large or small, cold or kind, so far he had no clue. It transpired that Mr F perhaps exceeded five feet in height by one inch; he had a sharp sort of face, scant hair, a rather penetrating stare, tired eyes, thin lips, many wrinkles across his forehead and a high bridge to his nose. If ever a lad felt foreboding, Tommy did on first sight of his host. If ever a lad felt reassured, Tommy did when Mr Fluter smiled, which he did when smiling Mrs Fluter introduced them. He bade Tommy welcome and said he and his wife would do their very best to give both lads a happy time while under their roof.

Churniston came in shortly and the four enjoyed a very good evening meal. Mr Fluter explained that he tried to keep himself fit, that he lived quietly and enjoyed fairly long walks. There were many nice places to be explored quite close to the town. "I have an idea," he said, when the table had been cleared. He vanished momentarily, reappearing with what he called a bagatelle board. Tommy had not seen this game before.

An excellent breakfast on Sunday morning prepared Tommy for the preliminaries to the church parade, which included much standing around before the Battalion's approximate one thousand officers and men lined up in an apparently endless chain of rows of four.

To the rear, in the distance, the Colonel's white horse could just be seen. That important man had placed himself so that, having given the orders to set the column in motion, he could make a spectacular dash on his flying gee-gee to the head of the column and take up his position as the leader of this huge threat to Kaiser Bill. Fortunately, the soldiery knew all the noises the Colonel would make in order to get the column moving churchwards. When they heard "Batt-alion-a!" they came to attention; "Ayon on er raye!" and they all turned to the right; "Ee aa!" obviously meant "Quick march!" so they all stepped off with the left foot, as they had been taught.

Once again, Tommy enjoyed the steady rrrp, rrrp of hundreds of heavy boots striking the road. Heading along the high street he noticed a photographer's tripod standing on the pavement. He decided then and there to order a print, provided he could find one where he was well in the picture.[118]

Soon, caps in hand, they all filed into the fine, old, parish church. As he walked up an aisle, Tommy looked around and felt compelled to admit this church looked richer than the one he attended — the carvings more ornate and numerous. This being a military service, it was taken by the vicar himself. He had a clear, tenor voice but, thought Tommy, we score over him because our old man in Edmonton is a Prebendary and a Surrogate and other impressive things which the Bunbridge vicar wasn't — and our vicar had a deep, old-port, very rich sort of voice while Bunbridge's was bell-like, and not so grand that it could even charm the choirboys and induce them to stop fiddling and listen.

Considering that many soldiers present had only the vaguest notions about the order of events, the service proceeded well and smoothly — although, during the singing of one well-known hymn, the vicar had to call a halt in order to insist that the words as printed should be used. For instance, after the third repetition of "Glory, glory, hallelujah" the final line wasn't "Then we all went rolling home", at least not on his hymn sheet.

The return march to the station completed, the men were free until 8.30am the following morning. Ted, Harold and Tommy walked slowly in the general direction of their billets, discussing such things as what to do with themselves when not on duty. Pubs perhaps? But that cost money. Each suggestion encountered this same limiting factor, so they settled on an occasional drink, pictures once a week, and roller-skating as often as possible. They had, of course, all done some roller-skating in their boyhood, mainly in the street, and felt sure they would polish their skills pretty quickly.

Entering the Fluters' house by the back door, Tommy removed his heavy boots and put on his house slippers with the pleasant certainty that he would not soil or damage any of the very nice floor coverings. The Fluters noticed and appreciated this thoughtfulness. Churniston did likewise when he arrived, and Mrs Fluter led the two lads along to the dining room.

"Everything's ready," she said. "I thought we'd start off with good old English fare. Roast beef with Yorkshire pudding and apple pudding to follow." Grace was said at the beginning, briefly, and at the end. The lads could add their amens with genuine feeling, for it was a splendid meal. In conversation, the Fluters again mentioned that they would take no notice of the Army allowance for feeding the boys. "Yes," said the kindly Mr Fluter, "we have no need to rely on that, and we hope you will enjoy what we are able to give you and realise that we shall get quite a lot of pleasure out of doing what we can to make your stay comfortable and happy." That night, just before they all retired Mr Fluter said, "I'm an early riser. Have to be. As manager I feel I should be first on the scene. So I keep the entry keys. Nobody can work till I open the doors so I must never be late. To give my day a bright and fresh start I step into a cold bath at precisely 6.30am on every working day. I'm shaved, dressed and ready for breakfast at 7 and away before 7.30. So you lads can consider the bathroom yours from 7 o'clock onwards."

Tommy remembered that other early-morning, cold-water enthusiast Mr Frusher. So he asked if he might indulge in this discipline and received permission. He associated the habit with good living, good clothes, and success. Churniston did not ask this favour for himself, but expressed his admiration for Tommy's pluck.

At 7 the next morning, there was a noticeable nip in the air. The cork bath mat had a nice sloppy surface on which Tommy stood while running his four inches or so straight from the chilly, mains, water pipes. His previous cold, morning dips had been those enjoyed by all at Scout camps — a preliminary gallop down the hill before plunging into the stream, fun pushing or pulling in the slackers, marvelling at the mystery of Frusher's floating soap[119], and other diversions.

But, here, nothing to distract him from that white, chilly bath, and its icy water. He climbed in, sat down, breathless. Soaked his flannel and got to work, quickly rinsed off the suds, stood up and dried himself furiously. Soon feeling clean — and elated by his own bravery — glowing now with warmth, he went down to the small breakfast room and devoured everything dear Mrs F offered him: porridge, egg and bacon, toast and marmalade. She expressed her surprise at his opting for the cold dip and suggested he gave it up if he didn't really enjoy it. But he resolved to endure this little ritual about which Mr Fluter made no fuss at all.

That first week away from home flew by for Tommy. Route marches through the lovely countryside in late autumn — pausing sometimes in a small town or village for a break –alternated with exercises over commons and large, open or wooded spaces, and map-reading classes held on high ground from which features could be visually identified.

Although they still lacked rifles and some other equipment, they could learn useful skills. On the first Friday night, they had instruction in marking out and digging trenches. Then Saturday morning saw the troops at the railway sidings. A long line of carriages and several goods wagons had been allocated to the Battalion. The windows already displayed Company signs, A, B, C and so on, and they practised entraining in correct order. They loaded quantities of picks, shovels and spades into the wagons, along with large boilers, and sacks full of sufficient unbreakable enamel mugs and plates for all the men.

At the last moment before dispersal each Company officer told his men what was afoot. As a precaution, lines of trenches were to be dug around Outer London. Their Battalion, responsible for a small part of these defences, would entrain at 8am and travel to their section where they would dig from 9 to 4. Time for cleaning tools and loading them would allow departure at 5 and they would be back in Bunbridge by 6. This work would occupy several weeks and the good people at their billets should be told that their guests would be out between 8am and 6pm. It was hoped that their hosts would provide some sort of packed lunch for the men. Tea would be brewed at the site. So Saturday mornings should be spent thoroughly cleaning clothes, footwear and themselves — at the town's public baths if their billets lacked the facilities. Thus, their temporary pattern of living became established. This helped the host families because it gave them a chance to organise their own work and leisure.

Tommy had seen a mass of men changed from civilians into a working Battalion of soldiers, moved away from their homes, placed in other people's houses, and all arrangements for their maintenance and training planned and carried out with reasonable efficiency — all this executed and supervised by men who had, until recently, been engaged in other professions and businesses. For example, one Major had been a barrister, another officer a junior partner in a Covent Garden firm, while the Colonel came from an old country family with wide interests. All were caught up in this rapidly developing war machine, determined to get it won and finished with as quickly as possible. Tommy wondered whether there had ever been another time when a young soldier could have been part of forming a new Battalion like this.

But still they had no guns. The trenching work would eventually make good or bad navvies of them. However, had they been given weapons, trained to use them and then gone off to France, they could have made a useful contribution at a critical point in the Allied effort to hold the German attack. Their confidence high, their knowledge of war abysmal, they would have gone into their first and, perhaps, second battles full of zest and patriotism.

They talked freely of their wish to "have a go" and "get over there" to see the damn thing off. Even Tommy occasionally ventured a few words along those lines — while guardedly watching for the sneers about his youth and lack of size which he feared such boldness might evoke. But his worries proved groundless. The others took it for granted that he felt as they did, sharing this desire to risk life and limb in defence of their country and people — ignorant, at that stage, that a minority existed who moved heaven and earth to ensure that they never ever became involved in actual warfare and remained free to take every advantage while the mugs were away at the Front. In due course, riches and honours rewarded some of those types, testament to their understanding of certain facts of life.

Came the Monday morning, the air clear and pleasantly chilly. Tommy and Churniston expressed their surprise and delight when Mrs F laid out the food she had prepared for their first day's digging. She had wrapped fine, white, table napkins round large, meat pasties, marmalade turnovers and lots of sandwiches. Wonderful food, lovingly prepared and packed. Each of the boys had sufficient for four men and, although they thanked her sincerely, Tommy certainly felt he had not done justice to the kindness shown to him — at that age, boys are often tongue-tied if there is emotion present. He hoped Mrs F would make allowances.

But, at the station, when the troops opened the carriage doors, laughs and curses filled the air. Cattle trucks, pigsties, travelling chicken sheds, were among the popular names for the compartments. Very old, small in all dimensions, they had bare boards for seats and partitions. The question arose, who had used them before? Hop-pickers came the answer — seasonal migrants, mostly from the city, who worked hard during the few weeks of the harvest. Because they were poor people the railway company had gone to the trouble of constructing this shabby transport for them. No doubt the workers paid special low fares to travel to their low-paid work, therefore their bottoms were not to be cushioned nor their heads to rest on upholstery. Similarly, as the railway company would no doubt be paid a low contract rate for moving troops, they were to be treated as paupers, even though the citizenry in general treated them as men worth a smile and a wave of the hand…

Still, good humour prevailed and the loaded train clattered off to the small town outside which they were to dig the trenches.

Given fair weather most days, the work moved ahead at a good rate. Tommy found that, because they had more men than tools, they got generous rest periods between spells of digging and shovelling. Although his hands became tender and his arms tired towards the end of the morning, he felt sure he would be able to cope.

When the lunch break arrived, he soon realised he would not be able to eat all the fine food Mrs F had packed, so he put about a third of each pasty to one side, wrapped them in newspaper, and hurried along to find his brother in G Company. Ted gladly accepted this addition to his smallish packet of sandwiches. "If my landlady keeps up this level of grub supply I'll be able to pass on some tasty bits most days," Tommy told him. "If she ever asks me about the quantity I'll assure her not a crumb is wasted."

Ted's landlady was a good sort, he said, and his lunch about the size that most of the troops' hosts could afford to give them: "Mrs Prout tells me that your Mr Fluter is the boss where her husband works. Naturally, there's no surplus money at our house. You struck it rich at your billet. But Harold and I are OK with the Prouts. We're treated just like family. In fact, Mrs Prout has to go to London shortly and she says she's going to call on Harold's family." Tommy wondered about that — whether the situation up there, with one husband and two wives and mothers, might not cause embarrassment to somebody.

On days when steady rain set in, mud soon made trench-digging difficult. A halt would be called and everyone stood around until, perhaps, the officers decided to cease work for the day. Regardless, Army caps had waterproof linings, the greatcoats made of strong, thick cloth, and the boots stout, so nobody suffered. But when they finished early, since the train would not arrive until the appointed time, the station had to shelter this great crowd of soldiers; some enjoyed a crafty game of cards, others just chatted, dozed or read (many, like Tommy, always carried some sort of reading matter with them). Gambling was forbidden, so card schools made sure they concealed their bets and had a man looking out for approaching NCOs too.

As Christmas 1914 approached, and it appeared likely the Battalion would remain in England during the holiday, the chaps began to speculate about whether they would be allowed home. "They're sure to grant two or three days leave," was the general opinion. So warming anticipation of reunions with families gave rise to a happiness which permeated all the men. Officers must have noticed the prevailing joyfulness but, perhaps, did not realise what caused it.

An announcement that Christmas Eve would be free of parades and work contained no reference to leave of absence. Puzzlement and doubt replaced anticipatory elation. Then, as groups of men discussed the strange silence about Christmas plans, anger caused some men to threaten to go home without permission. "But that would be a crime, either desertion with trial by court martial or else a charge of being absent without leave" — so cautious men told the impatient ones.

It developed into a serious situation; on the morning of Christmas Eve, no guidance having come from above, a large number of men gathered on the London platform at the railway station. They had bought their tickets and were now committing their threatened breach of military discipline. But somebody had informed the RSM about the looming exodus and his powerful voice could be heard ordering all men to return to their billets.

Most anxious not to provide authority with any excuse for questioning his stated age and discharging him, Tommy had not made a decision about joining this rebellion. He had found a position outside the station from which he observed the following scene, and even heard much of what was said.

He saw no general movement by the, shall we say, insurgents to leave the platform and, quite suddenly, the booming voice of the RSM fell silent. All faces turned towards the station entrance. The Colonel marched in with a substantial group of officers, followed by porters carrying a large number of bags. The party stopped abruptly at the sight of the assembled troops.

The Colonel's face expressed great surprise, as Tommy could clearly see. Then he turned to confer with Captain Blunt, his adjutant. Other officers moved in closer and there was much quiet discussion.

Some Privates standing nearby were called forward and, like good soldiers, all saluted correctly together, straight and upright, eyes looking straight ahead and not at the officers asking the questions. They may have contemplated doing a bunk, thought Tommy, but they had remembered their training. Soon the men saluted, turned about and rejoined their comrades. Then the Colonel came forward and addressed the men.

A terrific cheer followed his speech so Tommy readily guessed its import. He climbed down from his perch, passed through an open gate on into the station coal depot and crossed several railway lines till he came to iron railings and called to men on the platform, asking for information.

He learnt that the amateur officers had made their first major blunder. They had taken no thought of what was to happen to their men during the Christmas festivities. Vaguely, they had assumed that the rank and file would remain mostly in their billets and take meals with the families. For a start, this rather haughtily assumed that those families would or could supply Christmas fare for comparative strangers and also took for granted that the soldiers would wish to remain in billets in such awkward circumstances. Yet the officers themselves had no doubt as to where they were going to spend the holiday.

Of course, not all the men had gathered at the railway station, so volunteers offered to go to each CSM and pass on the good news: two-day leave had been granted to all. Thus, the remainder of the men would travel to town by the next train — as Tommy resolved to do.

Hurrying back to Leigh Drive, he yelled the good news about Christmas leave to the few men he passed. Mrs Fluter, kindliest of women, said she could have managed easily had the lads been staying over the holiday and she thought her husband might even be disappointed that they were not to share the good times together. Tommy had not seen Churniston since breakfast, but assumed he also would travel to London. No worry on that score, said Mrs F; she would tell him about the unexpected two days off.

A few hours later, Tommy received cheerful greetings at home and found Ted already there, as he'd expected. "Bet your life I got on that first train," he said. "We knew there would be nothing to do during Christmas, and no order had been given to *forbid* us leaving Bunbridge, so we were on our way regardless. The officers must have felt foolish when they realised they hadn't given any instructions as to what we should do during the next two days. Still, who's grumbling, eh?"

With money in their pockets, the brothers bought a turkey in the market place along with fruit, sweets… and Turkish cigarettes, probably costing 4d for ten instead of the usual 2d for English — their rich aroma seemed to lend an air of opulence to that small home.

So they all settled down to spend a really happy Christmas together. This might be the last family gathering for several years and, for once, all of them did their utmost to make the occasion memorable — starting that night with the collective manufacture of decorative chains from strips of coloured paper and flour paste. A gay touch in the living room.

Mother spent much time at the coal-fired, cooking range. It took skill to stoke it and arrange the dampers so that pots of vegetables on top kept boiling while the bird and stuffing in the oven roasted without burning.

Pa had bought a bottle of cheap claret, a favourite of mother's though, to put it mildly, a bit sharp for the tastes of the youngsters. But all protested that they liked it. Drinking some fizzy mineral water, of which they'd bought several large bottles — "penny monsters" — soon softened its harshness. What with playing games, telling yarns about Army experiences, and resting between unusually large meals, the hours passed quickly.

They all praised Ma's cooking and even Dad put aside the load of worry which always appeared to be crushing him… and smiled occasionally. The war was hardly mentioned, although this Christmas should have marked the end of hostilities according to many forecasters. Everyone knew it was not going well, and flickers of fear disturbed even reasonably optimistic people.

But, just for the moment, self-indulgence quite rightly ousted serious thinking and all felt the happier for trying to encourage forgetfulness and joyfulness among others.

Chapter Nineteen

Too soon, even Boxing Day had passed, farewells had been said and the brothers, with Harold, were on their way back to Bunbridge. And so into January, 1915.

That part of the London trench defence Tommy's crowd were responsible for had reached an average depth of about five feet. People tend to visualise a trench system as one long, straight line but the British Army at that time used a different design. A trench would run straight for perhaps ten yards, then take a 90-degree turn to the right for three yards, becoming narrower too, then a similar left for three yards, then right again and thereafter resume the original direction and width.

Most of the excavated soil would be thrown over the back of the trench, forming the parados[120]. Having dug down five feet — and four feet in width — the troops would further deepen it to around seven feet (depending on the nature of the ground), but leaving an 18-inch-wide step at the front which soldiers on lookout duty would stand on to observe the enemy or to fire from. The top foot of earth at that front side would be removed and moved forward somewhat, and unevenly, to form the parapet.

From time to time in that war, well-constructed trench systems, properly reinforced with wood, wire net or expanded metal, and, at the bottom, drainage sumps covered by slatted boards — duck boards — served as home to hundreds of thousands of men. But at any point where a major attack developed, the structure which looked so strong could soon be reduced to a useless shallow rut, its only occupants mutilated corpses; yesterday's bright boys, today's cadavers.

With short, wintry days and muddy trenches to work in, Tommy fully appreciated the warmth and comfort always awaiting him at Leigh Drive.

Before entering the house, he scraped the thick mud from his boots; then his next care demanded using old newspaper to further clean boots and puttees. He hung his damp, outer clothing in a corner of the large kitchen and put on a pair of civilian trousers. This broke no regulations provided he stayed indoors. He knew good luck had set him up in a very special billet, so he tried to make the Fluters feel that housing and feeding a strange lad was not one of life's greatest trials.

The question of how to pass the winter nights did not arise after all. Lingering over the wonderful evening meals, listening to Mr Fluter's reminiscences or thoughts on current affairs or, on occasions, Churniston's chilly experiences among the cadavers at the teaching hospital, saw him through easily to about 10 o'clock when preparations for going to bed usually commenced.

Ever one to survey the past and compare the present, Tommy concluded he could count this Bunbridge sojourn among his best times. He felt almost guilty when he read about the misfortunes and sufferings of soldiers on active service. True, the men at the Front in those early months of the war were almost all regular soldiers carrying the kind of work for which they had long trained and, by all accounts, doing it well — but they lacked numbers, as well as sufficient machine guns and artillery.

For years, ordinary people — even Tommy — had known that war with Germany was probable, but apparently the message had not reached the Liberal government and the War Office. "Nobody thought to tell *them*, poor souls," Tommy would reflect. So fear of a long war grew and the patriotic bloom began to fade from the eager defenders' faces. This gradually changed many a cheerful patriot into a thoughtful schemer. For them, the mad rush to the Front turned into a careful study of the Rear, and a search for some niche there wherein their talents could be utilised.

Early in February[121], 1915, the whole Battalion was granted one week's leave on a vague understanding that they would leave England shortly. At this, something like an electric shock jarred Tommy's nervous system –which proceeded to maintain a level of tension previously unknown to him.

This routine of life at Bunbridge had lulled him into accepting its pleasures as his lot for quite some time to come. Tommy lacked much in knowledge, little in imagination. As each new experience loomed, inward excitement — of various kinds — had to be concealed from his fellows by the assumed appearance of calm. He hoped no one ever detected the state of high nervousness in which he now existed. He aimed to appear interested, but not bothered, by what went on around him; keen enough, yet always willing to let a better man shine while he stepped aside.

He felt this method would make him no enemies, might even generate a spark of good will — and perhaps assist self-preservation under certain conditions.

Let us have a word-for-word statement from Tommy, about that momentous period in his young life[122]: "That week passed like a dream. Playing at soldiers was over. If we were to cross to France we could be right up there at the Front within a day. Our wounded could be on their way back to hospital in England in less than a week, our dead comrades buried if lucky or, if not, lying smashed and cold under a sun or moon they couldn't see.

"The first day back at Bunbridge after leave, we did not receive orders to pack our kitbags. We still lacked rifles, belts, ammunition, straps and pouches, haversacks, packs and several other things. The only move we made at that moment was to go for a nice route march of about eight to ten miles. That took much of the steam and most of the tension out of me.

"Once again I found myself being more concerned about young Lieutenant Swickenham. Recently some of the men, notably the older, coarser types, had begun to gain confidence in their ability to cope with soldiering and now asserted their thoughts and opinions loudly, as they had probably been used to doing in their former lives as civilians. So with the February weather chilly and young Swickenham, who marched at the head of the column of course, suffering a head cold, one humourist commenced bellowing 'Our Lieutenant's got a dewdrop on his nose' — to the tune of John Brown's Body. Others joined in, inventing punchlines according to taste. The NCOs did nothing about it — apparently then, when the order to march at ease was given, license to insult an officer went with it. I felt this was all wrong and did not join in the singing, but made no comment on the subject.

"The Lieutenant was a very serious young man, somewhat at a disadvantage with his apparent self-consciousness. But, one afternoon, he proved how much thought he had for the men's welfare in spite of the mockery. He marched the Company to a local hall; a white screen faced the audience and a machine for projecting pictures rested on a table halfway along the middle gangway. Lieutenant Swickenham stood beside it, waiting till all sat quietly as they had done in childhood for a 'magic-lantern show'[123] to begin.

"Then his rather thin, but clear voice related how, some time previously, he had been a Midshipman in the British Navy. For health and other reasons he had to leave that service, but while abroad he had taken many photographs on plates. These pictures had now been coloured and he intended to show us a series he took when based, for a short time, on the island of Malta. As each picture appeared, he named and described buildings and places, including several beautiful beaches, colourful plantations and much attractive scenery.

"Finally, he admitted he'd really given this little picture show to capture the men's interest before talking to them about the dangers and evils with which men travelling abroad for the first time must cope. In particular, soldiers just looking for entertainment would be tempted to visit places where cheap liquor and loose women might inflict sickness and diseases on them. Details of some of these diseases and magic-lantern illustrations of the effects they had on human bodies were received in complete silence, chilling men previously basking in the Lieutenant's alluring images of a land of sunshine, luscious fruits, blue skies and cool seas.

"Finally, the CSM offered thanks on behalf of all present to Lieutenant Swickenham who had, he explained, hired the hall at his own expense in order to help men who would shortly be leaving England.

"Opinions afterwards differed about the show — and the sermon, as some called it. Some older men thought the officer had a nerve to preach to them about these matters, but all admitted surprise that the apparently shy youngster had carried out the self-imposed task so efficiently. For my part, Swickenham confirmed my regard and respect for him and I looked forward to serving under him abroad.

"'But why,' many asked, 'did he show us pictures of Malta of all places? There's no war going on there.' Well, soon the affair was almost forgotten.

"One morning, as soon as the roll had been called, the CSM read out an order that 50 men from each Company should be volunteered, marched off and placed at the disposal of the Lieutenant Quartermaster. I felt somewhat joyful about dodging this chore — until the CSM warned me and others to rest until 9pm when, with all our belongings packed in kitbags, we would report for duty at the railway station. We should say goodbye to our hosts before leaving, having told them that they would be called on during the day by an officer who would settle outstanding debts.

"So this was it. News spread that we should go to a London terminus where our train would remain for several hours before being re-routed. At the station, I quickly found brother Ted at work loading stores on to the train, having volunteered for the Quartermaster's detail. He would spend that night in his comfy bed whereas I would remain on guard duty at a railway siding…

"Not many civilians had telephones in those days, but we managed to persuade a sympathetic chap to let us into his home to use his and we got a message to our father in his office. We told him it seemed certain we were finally leaving England, but that our train would stop at Waterloo for some time before we set off. He promised to hurry home as early as possible and collect mother and then they would try to get to us at the railway station.

"There suddenly welled up in me an unsuspected affection for our homeland. 'Homeland'? The first time we had thought of calling it that. And the family always rather taken for granted — their value rocketed suddenly. Uncertainty as to when, if ever, we would see them again made this coming, improvised farewell terribly important.

"Back at the billet, during the course of the morning, Churniston startled me when he came in and announced that when our train reached London he was to leave us and go to Battalion headquarters. He had acted rather cleverly, having discovered unbearable discomfort in those unsightly feet of his. The doctor had looked at them and pronounced him unfit for active service.

"That last, rather sad day with the kindly Fluters passed with the dear lady feeding us far too liberally. When I regretfully left them that night, I took with me several of her gorgeous pasties. Lovely people. I would never forget them and intended, as I promised, to see them again as soon as possible.

"During that dark night in the railway sidings, I had to make periodic inspections along one side of the several coaches placed in my care, a comrade doing a similar job on the other side. When resting, I could have one carriage door open and sit in the doorway on the step. The Sergeant visited us from time to time and, when you heard him approaching, it was important to be on your feet and keen. Nothing happened and, when daylight began to cheer up the scene, most of us were allowed to take our ease in the station waiting rooms and drink some of the strong tea brewed on the coal fires there. I ate some of Mrs Fluter's tasty food and had a couple of hours sleep on a long seat.

"As the hours passed, I began to doubt the necessity of all the hurry to leave our billets and spend the night guarding an empty train. I felt unhappy at leaving the Fluters almost a day before I need have done. Others had their grievances too. So we grumbled and swore to relieve our feelings. A stranger might have thought he was witnessing the start of a mutiny. He might also have noticed that the approach of an officer effected a sudden reduction in the vocal noise, so perhaps rebellion was not exactly imminent.

"But we had fallen victim to one of many blunders at the top which, throughout the war, made us call into question the parentage of officers from Field Marshals downwards. With a whole day to get through, our superiors had made no provision for feeding those of us who guarded the train all night and who now, for lack of orders, hung about the station and sidings. With no information about time of departure, we didn't dare risk wandering off to look for somewhere to eat. No better informed, NCOs could not permit absence...

"We had to devise an unofficial catering system. Four men would swiftly vanish over a fence and eat a hurried meal in a café a hundred yards or so along the road; one of our chaps lingered near the fence, ready to climb over and warn them should a quick return be necessary. Thus, we all in turn were supplied, but at our own expense, whereas the Army should have fed us without charge.

"Later, I talked with one of the men who had been ordered to report to the Lieutenant Quartermaster and load the stores on to the train. I wanted to know who and what was a Lieutenant Quartermaster. It transpired that this man controlled all food supplies, all cooking and distribution of meals, all clothing and equipment. He would be assisted by Quartermaster Sergeants, clerks and some storemen. A Sergeant Cook attached to each Company would also work under him.

"'Thanks for the info,' I said. 'But do we know him? Who is he?' 'Oh, average height, slightly bandy, large splayed feet, a uniform like an officer's, but he doesn't look right in it. Pale parchment sort of face, small wicked-looking eyes. A fair moustache with long, waxed points. Just one expression on that horrible face — it said, "I hate you".'

"This, I realised, described the man who had stood between me and the doors of the depot at the beginning of this Army lark. The Sergeant who had separated me from Ted and the others when it seemed of supreme importance that I should be with them. Where other people's eyes were white, his were yellow. How did it ever come about that sane officers selected such a horrible specimen to do this important job? I was to ask this question quite often in regard to other appointments and promotions, but a mere young Private had to be careful with whom he discussed such things.

"The short journey to London took a long time. The railway controllers could have done without our long train running among the scheduled commuter traffic at peak hours so, where a line ran behind station buildings avoiding the platforms, they diverted us and left us standing there for long periods. It was evening before we reached Waterloo.

"Within a moment of the train stopping, we had all piled out on to the platform, stretching ourselves and stamping our feet. The next order: 'Men wishing to pump ship will be taken in groups to the lavatories by NCOs'. The train had no corridors, no sanitation, so groups quickly on the move were encouraged to hurry by shouts from those who had to wait for relief.

"Men who hoped that family or friends might be trying to get to them for a last farewell gathered as close as possible to the platform gates. I spotted my parents, but at first we could only exchange a few shouted words. The crowd waiting outside the guarded gates looked surprisingly small, considering the hundreds of men involved — but most of us had had little time or opportunity to communicate with our families. Ted and I simply struck lucky in talking to a helpful man who had a telephone in his house.

"As time passed, the majority of the troops made themselves comfortable and returned to their seats on the train. Now, as the platform cleared, officers and NCOs could see that, were a brief reunion of soldiers and their relatives permitted, it would not increase the risk of some demented soldier making off. Anyway, the watch on platform entrance and exits made that almost impossible. As I wandered about, waiting, I heard several discussions on the subject and noticed a general movement of officers towards the first-class coach in the middle of the train. Shortly, they called the NCOs to that coach and, in turn, the CSMs and Sergeants soon hurried back to their respective Companies to loudly announce that civilians would be allowed on the platform for the remaining half-hour or so till departure time.

"I found Ted, then Harold joined us and so, unexpectedly, did dear old Len. With our mother and father, and Harold's mum and dad, and his broad and beaming half-sister, Madge, we all relaxed.

"Our family became far more talkative and forthcoming with each other than we had ever been before. No reticence — it no longer mattered that we should try to be witty, sarcastic, grudging in praise, proud of or ashamed of each other. Here were a few precious moments we could spend together before being parted for a long time. Or perhaps only a short time. But maybe forever.

"We youngsters might possibly feel ashamed of this blatant display of affection at some later date, but at that moment natural feelings dominated. Even Dad smiled and chatted all the time and to each and every one of the party in turn. He noticed that quiet Len had no parent or friend to wish him farewell and so gave him special attention. Both families had brought gifts of food — sandwiches, cakes and fruit — and these they shared out equally between the four soldiers whose last minutes in London they were making so sweetly memorable."

Chapter Twenty

Despite the unusual emotions of the family farewells, once the train moved off, Tommy found himself wholly forward-looking — until sleep overtook him. He'd had little of that for 36 hours and even the natural excitement caused by the journey to an unknown destination — which might be a battlefield in France — could not prevent his eyelids drooping.

For him, then, a journey of hazy impressions, because nervous tension demanded some awareness of what was going on: the sudden hissing snarl of a train passing in the opposite direction; the change of sound from clickety-clack to echoey racket as they sped through a station; raised voices attempting to win an argument against the roar of the train as it raced through a tunnel. Eventually, he emerged from yet one more doze to comparative silence. No roaring, no smoke swirling past windows. Just quiet conversations and a distant hiss of steam.

"Fall in, H Company!" bellowed the CSM and they quickly lined up on a station platform. Southampton. There it was in large letters — the first port he'd ever seen. And not overmuch of it visible on a darkish night. The same men who had loaded stores on to the train, set to work offloading them.

"The rest of us," says Tommy, "set off on foot through large areas covered with corrugated-iron roofing on a framework of girders. Lighting was dim but sufficient, the air chilly and damp."

Suddenly, here on their right, the sea… They moved along with many stops and starts, gradually able to discern dark shapes of ships and smaller craft on a large area of apparently calm water. And now, quite some distance ahead, Tommy could distinguish the shape of a huge steamship. Huge to him, anyway. Its tall funnel loomed against the night sky almost like a factory chimney.

During these last moments with his feet still on English ground, he was cheered by the realisation that he would be one of the last to leave it, a member of the last section in the last Company of the Battalion to board that great ship. That was the good thing about being last, oh yes, very nice. But what about being last into the accommodation on board? "We'll finish up in a cargo hold way down below," lamented Joe Parker — soldier today, Billingsgate porter recently, and ordinary seaman before that. Joe was right.

The CSM led H Company "for'ard" (Tommy had read many a sea story including *Treasure Island* and *Masterman Ready*[124]) — and, not far from a low structure right at the front of the ship which Tommy knew must be the forecastle, he had to follow the others down steep steps. He clutched a hand rail with one hand and his kitbag with the other. There, below, a combination of many smells assailed him. Tar he thought the most powerful.

Hammocks hung from the whole ceiling area of the space allocated to the Company. A merciless rush to grab one of them ensued — an early experience of man's inhumanity to man, Tommy reckoned. Pushed and shoved in that dimly lit, smelly place below, he felt lost and fearful at first, the contrast between this and his lovely billet with the Fluters almost too much for a lad to cope with. But when he saw a hammock in the dark corner to which the impetus of the crowd had carried him, he pulled down one side of it, chucked in his kitbag and stood there ready to assert his right of possession.

For Tommy, the war to stop the Kaiser and his crowd from taking over the world had really started — and he clearly saw that another, smaller, but, to him, equally important struggle to preserve the life of a boy among a crowd of older, stronger men would also have to be fought.

Camaraderie existed among members of groups which had formed within the Company. These men would help their own, particular mates in certain ways: information which had come their way would be passed on; if a particular job might yield an advantage, they would contrive ploys which might secure that job for a pal — soldiers called all such jobs "fatigues", but they weren't all demanding or disadvantageous in any way. And then a group of men closely and firmly holding positions round an NCO who was doling out, say, tea from a large container, could ensure they got served first (an advantage if, say, the NCO began to fear he didn't have enough tea to go round and started to reduce the quantity, in which case the first in line came off best).

Some of Tommy's fellows were strictly loners, probably from choice, but he fell into that role because he was too young and, so far, unused to mixing with men.

Looking round he saw tables and forms along each side of the hold, all secured to the floor. "So we sleep tied to the ceiling and eat screwed to the floor," he thought. Realising the air down below would soon become foul, he looked around for some arrangement which would allow them to breathe, apart from the stairway they'd descended. What was that expression from sea stories he had read? "Batten down the hatches!" A panic-making thought.

Spotting one of the more elderly men with whom he had ventured to chat several times, he resolved to ask him about this Black Hole Of Calcutta prospect. The man, Bill Jones, had formerly worked as a butler, and possessed that sallow, yellow-tinged complexion which Tommy associated with life in hot countries. He showed real interest in Tommy's concerns and described the ventilation systems used on most large ships of the period: "They have large pipes topped on the open deck by cowls which can be turned to face the wind if necessary. They'll ventilate every deck, even way down in the ship." Looking around, they spotted four large openings in the ceiling, which allayed Tommy's anxiety. The ex-butler added that on some ships he'd seen big, canvas air conductors used to give additional ventilation.

A Sergeant, a stranger from another Company, came part way down the stairway and called for four volunteers to get tea for everyone. He explained he had been told to look after this section of the living quarters and the men in it. A little man with a loud voice, he was; Tommy thought it strange that such a small chap should receive Sergeant's rank; later, as the voyage proceeded, he concluded that the man had been imposed on to do the job, for it proved to be an unpleasant one.

Shortly, the volunteers returned with two large containers of hot, strong tea, some packages of biscuits and tins of jam. The men set out their enamel plates and mugs upon the tables, seated themselves on the benches, and the volunteers ladled out tea and gave each man two of the biscuits — thick, brick-hard, about two and half inches square — and a dollop of jam. A testing time for teeth. Tommy dipped a corner of the biscuit into the jam and managed to bite off a piece; no pleasure to be had in the eating, but natural caution made him persevere in case things got worse and even biscuits became scarce.

Hard tack and hammocks had suddenly replaced the Bunbridge style of living, to which Tommy had only too gladly become accustomed. The bareness all around engendered pessimism: bare, wood floor, tables and forms, hammocks suspended from deck joists above. Nothing else whatsoever. A cargo hold in peacetime, surely, and here they were using it as a home.

And yet another cause for anxiety about living in this confined space began to bother Tommy; he started thinking about the German submarines already taking a toll of Allied shipping...

He hoped his face betrayed nothing of his thoughts... and just then a queasy feeling under his belt, plus a revulsion against the tarry, painty, stuffy smell of the place begat doubts as to his ability to retain possession of the food he'd eaten. But the fuggy atmosphere wasn't all. He became aware of a feeling of uncertainty, of instability... In other words, without announcement or ceremony, they had set sail, they were at sea[125]. As far as Tommy could tell, this new motion did not affect the men around him, although surely they must have felt the hard seats alternately pressing against their backsides and then apparently slipping away.

Trying to look as though he had serious business up above, Tommy briskly climbed the stairway up on to a cold, dark deck and searched for latrines.

So far he had formed an impression that the standard of food and accommodation on this troopship probably equalled that of the cheapest transports on the North American run from Britain. Hundreds of emigrants left the homeland every week; they could pack very little and feared the rigours and discomforts of the long, sea journey, but faced them rather than endure near-starvation in Britain. One such family had been acquaintances of the Norcliffes so, around 4 o'clock on a cold, dark morning, they had all gone with them to a North London railway terminus[126] to wave goodbye and wish them good fortune when they travelled to Liverpool before sailing for New York. Classed as "steerage" passengers, they knew they would have to fend for themselves on the ship.

Tommy had that family in mind as he gripped a handrail at the side of the ship. Behind him a gangway led up to a higher deck, in front of him the bows, forecastle, and a mast with rope ladders on each side and a small enclosed structure on top, the crow's nest lookout shelter. At the far side of the ship he saw a sort of long, low shed. Using a steadying hand here and there, he crossed the deck to inspect it. Half its width rested on the deck and the other half jutted out over the sea. He entered through a doorway at one end. A hurricane lamp gave dim illumination to the narrow enclosure on the seaward side of which, at regular intervals, he saw seating — with holes of convenient size. Sea noises and surges of air from below informed Tommy that here was a system of instant natural disposal.

Sitting there, the seat's thin boards seeming to cut a circle into his freezing backside, splashed by spray when that side of the ship dipped towards the waves, he tried to imagine the scene when men rushed in there of a morning in really rough weather. How, for instance, to dry the sea-washed bottom? Who the hell thought up this rotten idea? Obviously, someone who believed that donning Army uniform reduced one to a status worthy of the treatment he meted out to his black workers in Africa — the continent this old ship travelled to in peacetime.

Once is enough of that sort of thing was the lad's resolve — to which he pretty well kept, as we shall see.

Back below again, he found that a blanket had been issued to each man. Removing his boots, he folded his greatcoat to form a pillow and arranged the blanket with a quarter of it hanging over the side to tuck around himself as he made himself comfortable. After several ungainly attempts, he succeeded in mounting the hammock and lay suspended perhaps 24 inches from the ceiling.

One advantage to sleeping in a swinging net soon became obvious. When the ship did a sideways roll the hammock did not, it just hung there. However, when the ship's nose dipped into a trough one could feel that all right. Head up, feet down... then vice versa, of course. A strange night, that first night at sea; half-awake for the most part, fully awake several times when the forepart of the ship seemed to receive a terrific blow. No alarm call followed... she hadn't struck a rock... so one dozed off for a while.

Large, two-handled urine tubs had been placed in an area where no hammocks hung and, as the night wore on and the ship's wallowing increased, the homely sound of men pissing gradually gave way to the horrible noises of men vomiting into it.

In wakeful moments, Tommy felt vaguely, but increasingly, uncomfortable, so when the hatch above the gangway was noisily shoved aside to announce the morning he felt relieved. Heavy footsteps clattered down and the diminutive Sergeant yelled "Git aht of them 'ammicks!" and "Show a leg!" time after time until all the men complied. Tommy again marvelled that such a little man with such a crude way of using the King's English should have the audacity to offer himself for NCO rank. Ignorance and self-confidence frequently went hand in hand, he already knew. But speculation ceased as he realised he must "Git up them stairs!" at speed or risk facing a personal disaster.

So, boots on, laces roughly tied and up to the cold and windy, dark deck. Once the keen, fresh air had helped his stomach settle, at least temporarily, he hurried below to don his greatcoat and cap, then climbed back up on to the deck.

He clung to a rail, amazed to see and feel the fore part of the ship rise high, then plunge... at which his side of the ship would sink down, then rise up, up, while the far side almost vanished beneath the waves. These plunge-and-wallow movements increased in depth and height as the weather grew worse. And so the thing he had been fighting for several hours took possession of him and his loss was the fishes' gain.

All the same, when he saw men tottering towards the hatch bearing large dixies and bags of food he followed them down below. Hot tea got rid of the chill and, that morning, there were loaves of warm bread and tins of Irish butter. But the butter proved to be very rancid, so Tommy helped his mouthfuls of dry bread down with swigs of tea.

A few men already far gone in seasickness appeared to let themselves subside into misery and mess just wherever they happened to sprawl. So, once more Tommy climbed out on deck where the air was sweet, even though it came in great cold gusts and the waves were now unbelievably big — he felt so ill that fear vanished and even the fact that the troughs between the waves were long enough to accommodate the whole length of the ship caused him no concern.

When the ship wallowed in a trough, various sideways rolls occurred, but fore and aft movements were only slight. Then, when the peak of the next huge wave rushed at the ship and looked to be about to fall on and bury her... at the last moment her bow rose about 50 degrees until, as she started to level out on top of the wave, a big bang for'ard preceded a horrible vibration shaking the whole ship as the propeller, now out of the water, raced madly before... the slide down the other side of the water mountain began and a foot or two of water scurried across the deck. Seeing this coming, Tommy raced towards the stairway leading to a higher level and just beat this on-board wave. Happily, there he found that only an occasional fine spray wafted his way.

Teetering along, he noticed that the small windows of the cabins on his right had drawn blinds. Soon he turned a corner and found protection from the head-on gale.

There he squatted for several hours — save for an occasional dash to the side. No companion and none required. Ruefully, he reflected that he might still have been doing the daily trip to the City; and he alone must take responsibility for his present plight. People had warned him about what could follow his foolish actions...

Sea, very rough sea, in every direction. If only there could be land. Say a nice seafront from which he could observe the glories of the gale-swept ocean. Vain thoughts. Not wishing to be reported missing, he decided to return to the hellhole up front, but by a different route.

He descended by a gangway to the lower deck astern and made his way back along the side of the ship at that level. Against the head-on wind, he had to grip the rail with both hands, proceeding slowly, hand over hand. Halfway along he saw a narrow door, managed to open it slightly, squeezed through it and let it bang to after him.

Heavenly calm. He walked — lurched — along a passage, noticed a door on the seaward side, opened it, and entered a small room containing a washbasin and a lavatory with hinged seat and flush tank above. Faint light came through a small fixed porthole. He bolted the door and dealt with a wave of sickness which assailed him. The weakness caused by this regular vomiting made him appreciate the warmth and privacy of this little room. He sat and dozed at first, while endeavouring to keep wakeful in case someone really entitled to use the place should come along. However, no one disturbed him and, in due course, deep sleep for an hour or two did him a lot of good.

There was a homely touch about this little room and he had no wish to leave it. Hoping to come back, he slipped out, closing the door carefully. Out on deck and heading into the gale-force wind again, he hauled himself forward. He saw men crouching on every spot which afforded any shelter, some soiled by their own vomit but, seemingly, unable to force themselves to move.

Down below he found comrades in varying states, some quite fit and cheerful, some hopeless and listless. Odd groups wearing greatcoats and caps sat at tables, sometimes talking, the rest lay in hammocks or on the floor, seldom speaking, though sometimes moaning to give vent to their suffering. Removing the lid from a large pot standing on the floor, Tommy found it still half full of stewed meat and vegetables. He conquered his sickly aversion to food and ate some of it with as much dry bread as he could swallow.

Tommy rested there as long as he could stand the stench, then continued his exploration of the ship, taking refuge from the wind and rain, clinging to the handrail when he needed to throw up over the side.

Eventually, the need for rest drove him to that little room. He approached it warily, listened outside and, on hearing nothing, slipped inside and bolted the door. Still no one came. Wondering why, he reckoned that the Battalion officers had cabins above with sanitation in or near them. Maybe this lavatory on a lower level was intended for a ship's officer? He told no one of his discovery and it remained a boon to the lad throughout seven awful days[127].

"Git aht of them 'ammicks!" — the following morning, the little Sergeant's morning cry, failed to arouse any response, submissive or derisive, with most of the men far gone in sick suffering. Some still fit appeared to have quit the stinking hole. "We've got to clean this place up and somebody's got to draw the rations," yelled the little man. Approaching one reclining figure after another with his demands, he encountered total lack of interest. No one exactly refused to obey an order, but no one moved, not even to look at him. They had lost interest in living, let alone working.

Tommy too had spent a terrible night getting in and out of his hammock with increasing difficulty to slide about on the slimy floor and throw up in the piss tubs. The weather only worsened and the ship pitched and rolled horribly. Tommy thought even experienced sailors must have worried that the ship would, at some time, either fail to come out of a sideways roll and capsize or continue one of those mad slides down the distal side of a huge wave and maintain that stern-up 50-degree plunge straight down to the ocean's bottom.

He lay motionless in his hammock until the Sergeant departed in search of the help he needed to restore discipline and cleanliness. To whom was he to appeal, Tommy wondered. Not a sign of a commissioned officer had he seen since coming aboard. Probably they were all suffering, but in considerably better circumstances than those in the ship's holds. And, Tommy reasoned, with a cosy room available only a fool would leave it for the wind and sea spray outside.

Through the second day and third night, Tommy endured sickness, and then retching on an empty stomach, which caused pain and increasing weakness. But he still tried to move about the ship, while spending long periods in his hidey-hole.

As darkness fell, he left the ghostly deck for the odorous quarters below and, finding a quantity of hard biscuits and cheese on a table, ate his fill. Although he had no appetite and found the food almost repulsive, he chewed and swallowed with determination for seasickness seemed harder to endure if the stomach was empty. The dixie stood on the floor at the end of the table; it was half-full of lukewarm tea, so he dipped in his mug and drank some.

At night, he resolved to spend the wakeful hours stretched out on a form, hard though it was, rather than struggle to climb in and out of the hammock all night. With kitbag for a pillow and hands gripping the form on either side, he dozed. Not once did he fall off, nor did he have to get up and repair to the tubs. And when the funny little Sergeant descended the gangway once more with his Cockney cry, Tommy stood up, albeit unsteadily, convinced that his bad time was over. Of course, the Sergeant immediately grabbed him for ration-drawing duty. But, already, restored youthful optimism lent cheer to this drab scene.

Rendered bold by returning vitality, Tommy ventured up a stairway to the higher deck he'd visited before finding his exclusive sanctuary — the one with cabins, preserved for officers he assumed, although he'd heard of no prohibition on other ranks venturing there.

He struggled along one side — occasionally trying to stand upright without holding on to the rail, placing his feet well apart, one leg extended while the other gave way at the knee to compensate for the roll of the ship, feeling no end of an old salt. Tottering onward once more, actually pushed onward from time to time by gusts of wind on his back, he turned right where the cabins ended, found an area of comparative calm — and also found his brother.

A reunion more demonstrative than ever before ensued. Normally, they greeted one another with the studiedly casualness befitting men of the world. But pleasure and relief at each discovering the other safe and well compelled them in that unguarded moment to throw their arms around each other and behave as humans should.

Typically, Ted appeared to have remained well throughout. Tommy told him of the awful conditions in the hold for'ard and of his personal sufferings, but gave his assurance that henceforth he would be enjoying the seafaring life. He said he would like to spend as much time as possible with Ted. They descended to the afterdeck where Ted showed Tommy the entrance to the hold where his G Company slept, or tried to. Things were still very bad down there and Ted asked where else could they go to escape the perpetual wind and rain. Tommy, of course, had an answer to that one. He showed Ted around to the side of the ship where the small door and corridor led to the handsome little lavatory and told him of the restful spells he had enjoyed in there.

"I have the feeling that, as more and more people recover from seasickness, those who have the right to use the bog will turf you out of there," was Ted's opinion. But Tommy secured his promise to keep the matter secret and they arranged to meet there each morning at about nine for a chat — not for a smoke, however, as both had found that sea air way out on the ocean completely ruined the flavour of cigarettes.

"Come down with me for so-called dinner," invited Ted. "There are still chaps who can't eat much and I'll make it all right with my Corporal." The cleaner condition of their hold impressed Tommy by comparison with that of his Company's quarters and he guessed that discipline was better in G Company. The place stank all right, but the floor had been mopped and the urine tubs washed out. The tables too had been scrubbed and one had no hesitation about eating there.

Tommy made the acquaintance of several G Company chaps gathered around the table. They told him what he'd occasionally wondered about, between bouts of nausea; according to their Sergeant, their destination was the rock of Gibraltar. Not the Front then, thought Tommy, not the battlefield. Not for a while, at least.

With many men still very ill, plenty of grub remained for those who could face the stew of tough meat and undercooked potatoes. Each of them had devised their own methods to eat their food before the ship's violent motions spread it over table, trousers and floor, but usually this involved filling their enamelled, iron plates then, with both hands, raising them to lip level, tilting carefully, and swiftly drinking off the liquor. Solids could then be forked up with ease, though not much enjoyment.

The brothers, with memories of simple, tasty meals enjoyed at home, realised the difficulty of cooking for hundreds of men. But they compared this meal with dinners at Scout camps prepared over open, trench fires; Ted expressed the opinion that the rotten cooking on their ship was all that could be expected if it was superintended by that evil-faced curmudgeon appointed Lieutenant Quartermaster. "Satan with a waxed moustache," said Ted. Indeed, later events proved that to be a not ungenerous description.

Later, Ted, Tommy, and several others set off on a purposeful walk around the deck to start restoring their fitness. There were knocks and a few bruises to be garnered as well — with accompanying laughs or curses — according to prowess or failure in the struggle to cope with the antics of this curious ship. Sometimes they caught sight of a two-funnelled liner in the distance, obviously going their way. She was bigger than their vessel and yet she completely vanished from view as she and they slid down into troughs between huge waves.

At Tommy's suggestion, the party halted one of their laps near the stern. "Now," he said, "stand with feet apart and look for'ard. You can see how she dives. Down we go, up goes the bow; let your body lean forward with it. Now up we go, the propeller is free of the water and shaking you to bits…" It was awful really how these lads, now free of the sickness which had claimed so many, now began to laugh and play at being old salts. Their efforts to stay on their feet without holding on to anything amused them all, freed them of the depression which illness and foul quarters had imposed and enabled them to glimpse the first signs of return to normal living.

At dusk, though, someone shouted orders for all to get below and H

Company's Sergeant West told them no lights must be shown, no matches struck. A submarine which, in darkness, could only locate them precisely if lights were exposed, was following them. So, down below with hatches covered, portholes shielded. Terrible, just terrible. And the fear that, if a torpedo struck the ship, the imprisoned crowds of men would not stand a chance of surviving. Only the really sick showed no sign of concern.

Some men had thoughtfully brought packs of cards to while away idle hours — and perhaps gain a few shillings too. Small groups passed the time in partial forgetfulness of their wretched condition by pitting their skill and luck against the wiles and strategies of gambling opponents.

Tommy regretted having brought along nothing to read. Somehow, when making his meagre preparations for departure, he had never thought there would be time to spare. A few cheap magazines or weeklies would have saved him much pessimistic, undirected thinking. The roll and pitch of the ungainly ship constantly reminded him that they were at the mercy of very stormy weather far out on the Atlantic Ocean, as well as in some danger from enemy submarines.

"Surely," he reasoned sometimes, "it would have been better to take the shortest route to Gibraltar and reduce time at sea. Or perhaps the people in charge had reason to believe that the Germans would lurk along the coast of France, Spain and Portugal... " Whatever their ideas, they never explained anything to the troops. As the fourth day at sea dawned, Tommy had still not had sight of a commissioned officer.

During the hours of daylight he continued to spend quiet hours in the unused khazi, sometimes alone, occasionally with Ted. They also spent short periods watching the great waves advance on them and the way the ship rode them to the crest and slipped down the other side, no harm done. But every so often something interrupted this rhythm and there was a resounding smack, a pause and then one of the huge waves would cascade across the deck, briefly surrounding the forecastle — the crew's quarters — the hatches, cowls, donkey engine, winch and all. Momentarily these all became little islands. Then the ship did her sideways roll and the water vanished.

Other groups ventured out briefly, had their breath of fresh air, and vanished below again, but Ted and Tommy's spent as little time down there as possible. The thick Army clothing kept them reasonably warm when they hid from the raging wind. They were getting more than their rations and walking exercises provided all sorts of competitive fun and opportunities for showing off and getting laughs. Harold joined the brothers occasionally, having got over the worst of his sickness. Around the fifth day, they located dear solemn Len too and, now and then, persuaded him to take part in their rambles and scrambles.

Together, they began to explore the highest regions of the ship, on the same level as the bridge (which they instinctively kept clear of). Up there, they came across a small gathering of Corporals and a Sergeant, all squeezed into a quiet, wind- and spray-free hollow — and actually singing Clementine, tunefully and harmoniously.

"None of us knew any of them," recalls Tommy. "But it was a sort of tonic to our spirits to hear them singing. Even a bad effort would have been helpful in that ship of debilitated soldiers, but these fellows were good, so we crawled in near them and listened."

He noticed certain points of appearance common to all of them: the well-shaved, clear skin of their faces, bright eyes, white teeth, and a general neatness of uniform. Tommy, his friends, and the Company H men in the hold had never undressed since they embarked, so illness and soiling of clothes had given most of them a bedraggled appearance. How did this group of harmonious warblers contrive to look so good? Given his secret wash place, Tommy hoped he looked something like these NCOs, but he doubted it.

At last, on the sixth day, conditions improved. A grey, lowering sky still, but now they had a following wind, so no more racing propeller to cause those unnerving vibrations. Old sailor turned soldier Bill Jones stated that the ship's course had changed from heading south almost due east, though how he knew that was a mystery to Tommy, given they'd had no sight of sun, moon or stars.

Far more men now moved about ship. Officers, several of them strangers, appeared on deck, and NCOs who had been invisible until this day, visited the holds, saw their awful conditions and commenced organising a general clean-up.

When Tommy sighted two or three civilians — ship's crew members — going in and out of the forecastle he made his way forward and managed to get a few words out of one of them, a pale-faced youngster on his first voyage, it turned out, who said he'd been sick most of the time. His mates had told him that this rolling old tub, the *Galena*, with her factory chimney, was noted for her wallow.

From that forward position, Tommy looked back at the superstructure, all of it now a dirty white colour. "What colour is the chimney supposed to be," he asked. "Red and black really, but everything is covered with brine," the lad explained. "I suppose we'll be busy hosing down and scrubbing as soon as the weather eases up. It's easier already, now we're riding with it. Like to come into our place? We've got some tea brewing."

In the forecastle, an anthracite stove, wide and squat, gave out cheery warmth. A rim about two inches deep encircled its top to prevent the large metal teapot or anything else falling off. The young crewman placed a thick mug full of the darkest tea Tommy had ever seen on the deal table beside him. "Help yourself to sugar, and milk from that tin; take as much as you like." Tommy took his word for it and spooned in lots of sugar, trickled in condensed milk without stint and left his new pal, and the several men who lounged in bunks, in no doubt that he really enjoyed the hot, sweet liquor.

A new, little adventure this and Tommy knew he was grinning like a Cheshire cat and rubbing his hands together with pleasure. To make friends with civilians, already regarded as a separate race, gave Tommy happiness, even a feeling of achievement as though he had surmounted some great, racial barrier. Queer. That gap grew wider as the war grew older and bridging it demanded ever greater effort.

On the morning of the seventh day at sea, Tommy saw something indistinct ahead, something big. Between whatever it was and the *Galena*, the two-funnelled ship struggled on, but not disappearing behind the waves as she had done previously.

The land mass now assumed a recognisable shape, presenting a picture which had faced Tommy every time he walked out of the classroom into the corridor during his last years at school. "That's the rock of Gibraltar," he yelled to all within hearing.

Soon the regular throbbing of the engines changed to a slower beat and the shape of the rock altered as the Galena's course changed, barely moving now, just veering slightly to the left. Excited soldiers packed the formerly unused, lonely decks.

"There goes the Marook[128]," shouted someone as a massive chain roared across the foredeck and vanished through an aperture. The chain stopped moving and slackened. A noisy week of raging winds and crashing waves and vibrating engines ended with a calm… in which men could converse without shouting and once more regard one another with interest, to see what degree of suffering had been endured by their comrades.

An elderly H Company man looked at Tommy almost with amazement. He had obviously never been deceived about the boy's age for he said: "I can't believe it — a kid like you and you've grown a moustache".

Tommy borrowed a pocket mirror and saw that the beginnings, fine and fair, had indeed emerged since he last saw his face over a week ago. Elated, and knowing that repeated shaving resulted in stiff whiskers, he scraped it off as soon as possible — but without the desired effect as, next day, no further sign of a moustache appeared, nor did this herald of approaching manhood darken his upper lip for many a day to come. Had it grown, it would have helped; so far he believed he had performed everything asked as well as any of his comrades, yet for peace of mind he needed to feel accepted as an equal.

Chapter Twenty-One

As the morning passed, the depressing greyness vanished; hot sunshine warmed them and dried out clothing which had remained damp day and night.

Numerous craft of various shapes and sizes moved about in the sheltered harbour and the bustle of activity lifted the weight of boredom from those — and they were the majority — who had wilted under it for a week. Bumboatmen rowed and bumped and jockeyed to secure positions near the ship's sides, displaying their wares, holding up articles and deploying limited English to declaim their merits: "Very good, very nice, very cheap!" The soldiers called "How much?", a question asked and understood in most parts of the world.

Haggling about prices, with much use of fingers as counters, sometimes brought agreement. Then the seller would sling up a thin, coiled rope which the soldier endeavoured to catch. Eventually succeeding, the soldier coiled a couple of turns around his hand and let fall the rest of it, so that the seller could secure it to the handle of a basket.

In most cases, this was the moment for fresh argument to commence. Naturally the boatman wished the buyer to haul up the basket, place in it the purchase money and lower it back down, whereas the buyer thought the goods should be sent up first — and used more gestures than words to make this point. Somebody had to give way, but the great reluctance down below to trust the doubtless honest man above suggested that some unscrupulous cads in uniform had passed that way before. Could there be a man so wicked as to empty a basket of its contents and then vanish among the men swarming over the decks without paying? Apparently so. Nonetheless, some small deals did reach completion.

Tommy ventured a sixpenny purchase comprising four packets of ten cigarettes. He tried to smoke one, but it tasted awful. Blaming the strong sea air, he put them away for later use.

The ship with two funnels had anchored closer inshore. How very superior to the *Galena* she looked at close quarters, Tommy thought. So it was with a feeling of smug superiority that he learned of three men being sent ashore from the grand ship because prolonged seasickness had affected their hearts and they required hospital treatment. After all, we had it much worse, he reasoned, and comrades he chatted with agreed they had endured far greater hardship in their scruffy, old, cattle boat than the pampered soldiery in the liner over there. Must have done. They've got two upper decks with cabins all round. Likely enough, a huge restaurant. And, someone said, a ballroom full of bunks for the men, installed during the conversion to troopship.

After some hours at Gibraltar, the *Galena* moved quietly onwards. With changed weather, all began to feel cheerful, even energetic. On the calm, warm Mediterranean a renewed feeling of purpose and comradeship prevailed. Smiles replaced the bleak, hopeless, solemn expressions seen on most faces during the week of low, grey skies, heaving seas and roaring winds which had reduced many averagely good men to neglecting all the usual habits of self-care.

Their NCOs outlined a vigorous programme: cleansing of quarters, polishing of boots and buttons, and daily exercise in small groups. This was received with enthusiasm. There followed three days during which all on board improved both appearance and spirits. Only the six or so hours after midnight turned cool enough to make one seek shelter below in the overpopulated hold. During the day, when no work or exercise was required, one could manage a nap in a quiet corner, so a shorter night's sleep might suffice.

Tommy enjoyed the role of traveller, particularly leaning over the rail at the ship's stern, watching the churned-up water, its apparent phosphorescence and the always widening wake — he felt a sense of urgency, a scurrying away of water humiliated, thrashed by the propellers... Back there too a small engine enclosed in a cabin of its own remained motionless for long periods then, suddenly, without apparent human aid, started up... and just as suddenly stopped. Tommy allowed himself to be pleasantly mystified and never asked anyone about it, although common sense insisted that it operated the rudder.

The present, happier way of life put him in a state of optimism and appreciation of the moment's blessings — able, for instance, to largely ignore the unappetising, badly cooked and underdone food still served to them, regardless of calmer seas. Strong tea, often taken with hunks of bread and watery jam, usually passed for breakfast. That jam wouldn't have fetched tuppence a pound in a grocer's shop; issued in tins and made by a firm seldom heard of before or since that war, it needed no spoon, it ran like water.

Even the boy could guess at the sort of profits the villains made and, in idle moments, soldiers discussed what they would like to do to the manufacturer *and* the people in authority who placed the orders and, no doubt, shared his gains and guilt.

For some reason, the same low standards did not apply to Army biscuits, as they were called. Tommy believed that just one firm supplied the square, white, easily chewed biscuits — very different to the brick-hard squares referred to earlier. Proud of its product, the company baked its name, Jacob's, into each biscuit — and men rejoiced when they were given them. For the rest, as far as Tommy could see, anonymity concealed the shame of their victuallers. If soldiers' hopes have been realised they all live in a hell where the diet consists solely of their own provender.

At the end of a day of calm and deep blue sea, the sun hovered for a while, apparently, at about 30 degrees above the horizon before finally dropping towards the water. Tommy watched it descend; the whole sphere rested on the sea's surface for a moment, then it quickly sank to three-quarters, a half, a quarter, then nothing remained save a bright glow, and that only briefly. Darkness came and, with a small amount of lighting permitted at that time, Tommy had flickering reflections to watch and accompany romantic, boyish thoughts.

Leaning on the rail, he was joined by Jimmy Green, a nice fellow with whom he had chatted occasionally — probably four years older than Tommy, he belonged to G Company, Ted's lot.

Several months in the Army had not hardened or toughened Jimmy. His blond hair and pale face had that fresh, cared-for look Tommy already associated with the upper middle classes. One wondered how these types achieved it. Ordinary blokes well washed and scrubbed looked fine, but still ordinary. The Jimmy Greens of that period had quit their usually pleasant occupations and homes, generally on patriotic impulses. Their parents must have been terribly shocked but, in many instances, ensured their sons would at least have the King's commission to cushion them against the worst buffetings of war... well, to some degree. Jimmy's gentleness and trustfulness, his gay, white-toothed smiles, induced in Tommy a feeling of untaught inferiority, which he hoped to goodness, didn't show.

Some sort of counterbalance seemed to be required, so he said, almost casually, "Ah, there it is, straight ahead". "What is?" said Jimmy, peering through the night. "Algiers, brightly lit up. You can actually trace the layout of the streets by the lines of the lights. That wide one in the middle comes straight from the back of the town down to the harbour. Now, taking the ones which branch right from the main street, can you see the second one up from the sea? That's where we used to live."

Green responded with immense interest to this lie and begged for more details. Tommy promised to return to the subject later, but pleaded the urgency of a visit to the Ohang, as the bog had become known. Leaving Jimmy, he actually entered the place convulsed with laughter, but also feeling somewhat uneasy about the silly untruth. Anybody but Jimmy would have jeered jovially and perhaps called him something chummy like "You lying little sod!" and the boy might have had to duck a sideswipe, but no harm would have been done.

Now, for the moment, he relegated the matter to his mental storeroom as he looked along the spotless seating with its circular holes evenly spaced — how many could it accommodate at a sitting? How many had suffered frozen bums while attending to natural requirements in that novel latrine? Indeed how many had almost drowned when the raging sea thrust upward through the holes, rushed along the deck and away through the scuppers? He could grin now as he thought about this formerly filthy, wet, and slippery contraption and recalled the hymn, For Those In Peril On The Sea.

On the third day after Gibraltar, a blur on the horizon rapidly took shape as an island and the ship approached it at what appeared to be almost indecent speed for the old tub. Tommy was so enjoying his first Mediterranean cruise that the sight of land ahead failed to excite him.

For an hour or two, the ship lay off the island, just outside a bay with rocky headlands at each extremity, a lookout tower on each. Beyond the shore, the land rose gradually in levels defined by walls, with some houses visible of a type which pleased Tommy's eye. In England most houses had roofs of blue-grey slates sloping from a ridge — frequently seen against a grey sky, often in chilly, wet weather... the lad's mind associated them with feelings of depressing discomfort. But here the houses — some in groups, others isolated — all had flat roofs, their walls white or cream or pastel shades of yellow or green. At that distance, under a blue sky, the bay appeared to be the home of wealthy, fortunate people, living in abodes of luxury and romance.

Tommy concluded that the possibility of being put ashore in this heavenly place must be remote, but he enjoyed the experience of gazing at its beauty. Regret, he felt, when the ship moved off... then renewed excitement when she sailed into a large and wonderful harbour, busy with several freighters and other troopships — naval vessels anchored on the far side in front of a cluster of dockland cranes. As at Gibraltar, many small boats quickly surrounded the *Galena*, each with a man standing in its stern skilfully manoeuvring among the swarm by wiggling an oar from side to side. Looking back to the harbour entrance, Tommy saw stone buildings everywhere, not a brick in sight. Occasional horse-drawn carriages passed along a road on the side nearest the *Galena*.

Soon NCOs moved around advising any who hadn't heard that the island was Malta and telling their men to pack kitbags and prepare to gather in Companies. H Company grouped around the forecastle area and, for the first time since they left England, CSM West addressed them, announcing, "Your new Company officer will take charge".

Even as he spoke, a tall, rather elderly officer appeared and they were called to attention. That was when they learnt that the kindly, but rather ineffectual Lieutenant Swickenham — who had shown them his magic-lantern pictures of Malta for reasons not understood at the time — had not embarked with them. Whatever they might find to sing about in future, thought Tommy, the subject would not be the dewdrop on the end of that young Lieutenant's nose.

"I am Captain Boden," said the new man. "I shall expect H Company to be as good as any other Company in the Battalion and I'm sure you will all do your best to make that possible."

These words were followed by the news that the Battalion would be going ashore shortly[129]. Tea, bread, butter and cheese would now be issued and consumed as quickly as possible. Kitbags should be packed. NCOs must see that quarters were left in good condition and all should be ready to assemble in an hour's time.

Tommy procured his rations and chewed busily while trying to take in the great harbour scene: the naval ships, sailing craft, one of those fishing boats with a funnel and a sail at the stern, and lots of small boats being rowed or paddled busily between shore and ships.

On the *Galena*'s foredeck, three horses, presumably officers' mounts, were being released from the small containers in which they had spent the entire voyage, poor devils. Tommy could see these containers had sides and tops of padded leather, but the horses' legs and bodies bore awful lacerations and discolourations. Tommy wondered if they could ever be restored to a decent condition. What a hell they had endured, confined thus and, for the first week, thrown about day and night.

Tommy met up with Ted and Harold briefly and enjoyed pleasant speculation about the island, where they would live, and for how long they would remain there. One thing they knew for certain already — the temperature was higher than they had ever experienced, except on the very hottest days at home. They shared a particular happiness because they and the *Galena* would shortly part company. That ship was a bad'un and they'd had enough of her.

Even while the men gathered in Companies, the ship eased towards a quay where the crew made it fast and placed two gangways in position. Captain Boden announced that six men would be needed from each Company to offload stores. CSM West asked H Company for volunteers… who would later travel on the transport wagons, he shrewdly added, whereas everyone else would march to their destination carrying their kitbags. Since the whole Company suddenly became volunteers, the CSM selected the biggest and beefiest.

The Captain led his men ashore past an enterprising member of the ship's crew who positioned himself at the head of the gangway and sold pictures of the *Galena* to those who wanted to treasure a memory of that floating palace. Tommy bought one, and never regretted the financial outlay of 2d — shown to friends, it provided many a laugh in later years[130].

On reaching the road, Captain Boden turned left and, followed by his men in no particular formation, continued walking for some distance.

Then he stopped and, loudly, requested the CSM to carry on. After ten days of confinement in the old ship, the smartness in drill which had become customary in England could not be regained immediately. All had recovered from their sickness, but lack of exercise and indifferent food had taken their toll. However, the novelty of being in a strange country — first steps on foreign soil for nearly all of them — and the certainty of release from their hammocks in the cargo holds made them anxious for a fresh start under their new officer.

The Company soon lined up in correct sections and platoons with their Corporals and Sergeants; the roll was called and the CSM reported, "All present and correct, sir!"

During the long wait which followed, Tommy, thrilling to every new sensation, scanned the long waterfront: buildings all of the light-coloured stone he found so pleasing, among them one or two shops, the names above their windows emphasising the exciting foreignness of the place — "*Mateoti*," [131] for instance, what did that mean?; next door to that a homely touch, The Seamen's Mission; a cab with curtained windows clattered by, drawn by a skinny horse, its bones too prominent, the sallow-faced driver wearing a floppy hat, a dark red shirt and very old trousers, his feet bare...

On this occasion, the Battalion had lined up behind H Company, the last in alphabetical order, so Tommy could see A Company way back in the far distance; what an anonymous mass of men it was compared to, say, the troop of Boy Scouts of which he had been a fairly important member a few months earlier. Even in his London office, as an insignificant junior, he felt like a recognised member of a sort of staff family... "I suppose all goes on there as usual," he surmised — though perhaps not, bearing in mind the Company Secretary's forecast... And the family at home? They would manage, perhaps even do well if Pa could find some work connected with the war effort...

Eventually the Colonel and his white horse took their place at the head of the column and the Battalion moved off. Although the month was February, the thick wool underwear and sturdy uniform, plus a full kitbag carried over one shoulder, soon demonstrated the difference between marching conditions in far-away England and those now to be experienced on this Mediterranean island. The men relieved their feelings with many a "Phew!" and "Oh gawd!" — by "having a moan" or "effing and blinding".

And, while thus occupied, their feet transported their protesting bodies onwards at a steady four miles an hour. Authority required no more than that of them.

At least, Tommy felt reassured to see he wasn't the only one becoming increasingly sweaty. But, here again, the recollection that he had lied about his age and shouldn't really be there at all gave him the determination to endure without complaint. So he just plodded on... And savoured the air, its flavour exciting to him simply because it was foreign. On the waterfront, smoke from coal-burning ships drifted over them at times... but something stronger, probably from the drains though not too objectionable, had also been noticeable. Now as they marched, variety of aroma supplied almost as much interest to his questing nose as did the people, the buildings, and narrow side streets, to his appreciative eyes.

All this he regarded as a great bonus. By now he had expected to be under fire and subjected to the ordeals of the Front where, the newspapers reported (with extensive casualty lists), Allied advances occurred so rarely we had to persuade ourselves retreats counted as moral victories — some of them therefore worthy of a special medal. That was not the kind of war that patriotic Englishmen had hoped to take part in. Our wonderful Army with its 15-rounds-per-minute rifle fire should have scared the Germans. As it transpired, the enemy had lots of machine guns, any one of which could lay a hundred men low in a minute. Now why hadn't we thought of that? Of course, we had some, but they had many...

Well, instead of being quickly involved in all the roaring of guns, holding of positions till forced to move back, woundings, deaths, mud and filth of the battlefields, Tommy and the others had been put ashore on this charming island. Should he have felt shame about this? He did think about these matters at the time, he remembers... but he only felt thrilled, even joyful.

Common sense urged him to enjoy the sweets while available, there would be plenty of bitters later without doubt.

Across the town of Valletta, before, alongside, and behind him marched his comrades, but inside Tommy was this very personal thing which looked, sniffed and listened to people and places...

No pretty girls. The women he saw walking the pavements mostly dressed in dark or black velvet. They had sallow complexions, though a minority added a touch of rouge to their cheeks. So many of them looked alike to him that way back, he surmised, they must have had a common ancestor... The older chaps made noises which bore witness to their interest in areas of the ladies' bodies remote from their faces and Joe Parker once again proclaimed that, with sacks over their heads, all women looked alike.

The lad, with no real, personal interest in the subject, nevertheless fully understood that married men used to regular companionship in bed would have physical problems which demanded solutions; from the discussions with the senior Scouts group chaired by old Frusher, he knew that confirmed habits become men's masters. He could grin at the witticisms men used to conceal or excuse their interest in subjects of this sort. He was not expected to do as they did — something he had already discovered with some relief.

Their route followed what was obviously the most important street in the town — the Strada Reale a road sign announced. Impressive buildings and churches to the right, Tommy noted, fine shops, restaurants, cafés... But they soon turned left, and then right, into a thoroughfare across which hung many lines of washing. Families evidently shared accommodation in these fairly tall blocks, and the articles of clothing and bedding overhead added gaiety, like bunting at a carnival.

The clatter of soldiers' heavy boots on ancient cobbles brought heads peering out of windows. Some of the British lads sang, others shouted greetings and waved, but no response or encouragement came from above — the town clearly too long associated with garrison troops to get excited about marching men.

But soon they reached open country. The occasional women walking by wore black headdresses draped over their shoulders. A wire frame concealed in the fabric enabled them to swing them across their faces for concealment from foreigners. This had a historical significance, Tommy learned later, but considering the unattractiveness to himself of these females, he thought the cover-up quite a good idea. In any case, the headdress business had that quaint, exotic touch he hoped to find in foreign parts.

The road became dusty and bordered by walls built with the rock which was in evidence everywhere. They passed through a village, but saw no inhabitants, except that some young men sat around a table in what appeared to be a drinking shop. They just stared at the passing troops; imaginative Tommy thought he sensed their hostility. So along a coast road and on their right a beautiful bay bounded by long headlands, with a residential area — few signs of business there, just an occasional shop or café.

They now traversed firm road and tramping boots supplied a steady beat for the singing troops. Between choruses, one of the witty chaps would be sure to raise a laugh or two — especially in H Company, at the front of the column when, not infrequently, the Colonel's horse farted and they took it full blast as it hung in the still air. So, with some good humour, they bore the heat, their awkward kitbags, and the sluggishness caused by both the privations and inertia of their voyage.

Finally, the way ahead lay through a barren, rocky area but, at the end of it, they saw buildings, some single-storey, others two-storey, all flat-roofed and extending over a wide area. Had the setting been the African desert, Tommy would have expected to see French Foreign Legionnaires manning the ramparts — but a closer view revealed no ramparts, camels or *képis*.

Still, these were barracks, he realised, and he was about to experience the sort of life he'd read quite a lot about in the penny weeklies. Nobby Clark, Spud Murphy, and other tough soldiers had enjoyed wonderful times in such accommodations and, surely, great times lay ahead for the new adventurers about to move in[132].

Chapter Twenty-Two

H Company swung right and entered a huge barrack square with covered pavements on either side on to which their dormitories opened; the design offered Tommy hope that these rooms would be cool in high temperatures, since the sun could never shine into them[133].

Plans of the barracks must have been previously supplied to the officers for, after a brief halt in the square, each Company was soon marched off to its allotted quarters. H Company finished up on the upper floor of a two-storey block behind the main square, somewhat to Tommy's disappointment. He'd hoped for a room by the shady sidewalks and pictured himself lounging there enjoying a long, cold drink.

However, his platoon's room had a covered balcony, a good view of the whole barrack area from the front, and a fine outlook seawards from the rear windows. Tommy liked it at first sight: wide and long, the ceiling and stone walls whitewashed, the stone floor scrubbed and, as they discovered, easily kept clean to a standard which satisfied the officer doing the daily inspections. Six iron-frame beds with mattresses stood along the sea side, five along the opposite wall, with ample space in the middle for wooden tables and forms for seating — these they also had to scrub, using stiff brushes and sand. One of the tables bore a tall, polished-steel bucket and a large, steel bowl with two ladles. Two blankets and a pillow for each man rested on wide shelves fixed to the wall above each bedhead; that left enough space to store clothing and equipment on them too.

Home of 11 men for some time to come.

Ginger-haired Corporal Ash — 5 foot 8, becoming quite an efficient NCO — had charge of them. He explained he would appoint two room orderlies immediately, but all would take their turn and would do this work in addition to all "parades" — which word covered all compulsory attendances for drill or general training. Later, he despatched two men to the cookhouse carrying the shiny bucket and bowl, and their return brought cheers from the happy men even though their burden consisted of the usual potatoes with tough, stewed meat. On this occasion, they required only quantity to fill the aching void and, indeed, there was plenty for all. They enjoyed that first meal in the barrack room in a happy mood of banter and speculation about the future.

"Get that lot down you," said Corporal Ash. "Then the orderlies will take the pans down to the cookhouse and, when they've scrubbed them out, they'll be issued with tea and hard biscuits and that will be all the grub for today." The tea was good but the biscuits presented a problem again, although they definitely came from a different source to those provided aboard the *Galena*. About three inches by three and a half inches, thick, dark brown and very hard; the strongest teeth could make no impression on them. Soaking in tea failed to soften them.

Ewart Walker, ex-journalist and very knowledgeable, spoke of a huge reserve food store maintained underground in Valletta. It lay under a stone-paved square, he said, each of many entrances covered by a large circular stone[134]. Over many years the food store had been maintained at a level sufficient to feed the population of Malta for the duration of a six-month siege. Walker reckoned that older provisions must be taken out and replaced by new ones periodically, and he estimated that these stony biscuits could well have been placed below during the Napoleonic Wars. Their hardness and their repulsive dark appearance lent weight to his theory.

All attempts to eat them had to be abandoned, although an enterprising chap with a hammer and small chisel did chip carefully away at some of them to make what he sold as frames for photographs.

With no further duties that day, Tommy wandered around the barracks to get a general idea of the layout; outside one of the rooms he came across dour, old Len, squatting on the covered pavement — strangely enough, its roof also appeared to be made out of little paving stones. Len the silent was really as much of a romantic as the younger Tommy, whose pleasure at being allowed to live in such exciting quarters he shared. He said, "It's funny to think that, if we'd been put into such bare buildings in chilly old England, we'd have thought it was worse than a prison. Yet here, with sunshine and warmth around us, we're thrilled!"

Tommy told Len where he was living and soon discovered his brother and Harold lodging in the same block, on the ground floor. He chatted with them in their room and, glancing around at their companions, he began to feel that his brother might be a little out of place. Marlow for instance: about 22, nose flattened (where else than in a boxing ring), but in a way that made him look handsome with his very white teeth and wide smile; he was a natural intimidator who, having selected his victim, would shift his weight constantly from one foot to another while talking, and suddenly flash a right to the eye, a left to the jaw and a right to the solar plexus... none of them actually landed, but they were so close. Although his equals would have returned the treatment and no harm done, he didn't appear to select equals.

He and several others spoke a garble, parts it difficult to understand. Hard men, they supported each other's boasts about bits of trickery and ponces and fights in the King's Cross area. But Ted didn't appear bothered about them and Tommy guessed that, as he had always done in the past, his brother would fight his way through any trouble which cropped up.

Before darkness fell, the orderlies fetched four candle-lamps and a large, iron, piss tub, which they placed, on the balcony outside the door. At 10 the Sergeant came round banging on doors and shouting "Lights out!" Someone doused the candles... and Tommy was awakened after what seemed a very short night by cries of "Show a leg! Hup, hup!" So hup he got, grabbed soap and towel, and followed others to a large covered area with rows of metal bowls and cold-water taps.

A good wash made him feel fine and awoke him to the fact that he hadn't put on his trousers, unlike the others. But men around him busy with brush, soap, lather and cutthroat razors hadn't time to notice him. He resolved to go through that shaving routine from time to time, for he saw that, once he'd covered his face with lather no one could observe that he had no whiskers to remove. Today he washed his feet by way of a treat, but soiled them somewhat walking back to his room because he hadn't put his boots on either. So started his first full day on foreign soil.

The routines of parades and meals soon became established and, at last, they were given rifles, bayonets and other items of equipment. The rifles looked pretty old, but that sort of weapon never really wore out. Lance Corporal X[135], wearer of a South African War ribbon, said he'd used the long Lee-Enfield rifles with the short bayonets back then[136]. He taught the rudiments of their use and care — most of the officers, and many NCOs, had little knowledge of these matters and groups of them were sent off for training from which they returned very brisk and well-informed.

The Army forbade swimming in the nearby sea at that time of year; there was a theory that some sort of organism proliferated in the water during the early months of the year and it caused Mediterranean Fever, whatever that was. An old wives' tale left over from the Victorian era, many men asserted. But orders had to be obeyed.

In any case, the coast near the barracks was difficult to approach: large areas covered with rocks surrounded by what looked like hardened lava, its burst bubbles creating sharp points, painful to walk over barefoot. If the origin of those formations was indeed volcanic, they must have survived just like that for many thousands of years. But Tommy heard no opinions expressed as, apparently, nobody knew or cared. Still, on good days, it was pleasant to strip off for a while and dangle your feet in the water — although, looking down, Tommy could see rocks beneath the surface so jagged and spiky that a wave pushing you against them might cause injury.

Apart from such brief diversions, daily programmes kept the troops active from 6.30am to around noon and from 2 to 6pm. Beyond those fairly strict morning and afternoon work sessions, the rotaed extra duties as orderlies and guards rarely came Tommy's way; he never discovered why. Perhaps perks and privileges about which he knew nothing attached to those jobs. He was quite satisfied anyway; constant marching and stamping around the barrack square, hoisting and lowering the heavy rifle, and learning the peculiar style of bayonet fighting they practised hour after hour in constantly increasing temperatures amounted to just about as much as he could manage.

The food remained the one faulty part of the organisation. Whenever the men discussed the subject, they cursed that beady-eyed rascal so much in evidence on Tommy's enlistment day. He was seldom seen around the barracks and general opinion held that his job had scared him. Such an unprepossessing person would be fair game for more experienced supply officers. But dozens of men in the ranks at that time possessed more ability than that reptile to do the job of quartermaster in a responsible manner.

"Imagine," thought Tommy, "what strange sort of caterer would so bungle his ordering that men's breakfasts in a hot climate would consist of strong cheese and onions boiled together?" This occurred on two or three days of each week for a period. It appeared a vast amount of cheese had been stored so carelessly it partially melted. And obviously some bright lad had bought a large consignment of Spanish onions. So someone induced Quartermaster Muggins to take quantities of both. Hence, the repulsive breakfasts.

Corned beef might have proved an easy solution, but it bore no resemblance to that on sale in shops: delivered in large cans, dry and almost tasteless. Soldiers on the battlefield expected indifferent food, but a good quartermaster could surely do better than this for a Battalion in barracks.

Mostly, the weather stayed warm and fine, but Tommy learned that the Mediterranean could occasionally cut up rough. Perhaps for three days on end heavy rain showers would prevent them training in the open. Then instruction, limited by space available, continued in barrack rooms or along the covered sidewalks.

These occasions provided opportunities to give tired muscles and overworked sweat glands a rest — and if, sometimes, flies or mosquitoes became a problem, for sixpence they could buy a little bird, similar to an English wagtail but yellow, which busied itself devouring insects all day long. The Maltese vendor clipped its wings so that it couldn't fly away.

So the first few weeks on Malta passed and familiarity with daily complicated drills and exercises achieved the desired result of making the men feel confident and, collectively, a creditable organisation. Although the individual valued his personal standing, in each Company a real feeling of comradeship grew as they endeavoured to at least equal their rivals.

In the barrack room one saw groupings develop — two, three, or four men would spend much of their spare time together, playing cards, going to the canteen or outside the camp in their groups. But, overriding these alliances and friendships, all sharing the room showed a common consideration for each other and Tommy felt comfortable among them despite being so much younger.

Only one of them could and did shake his composure: George Goodbody, mentioned during the Battalion's training days in London. He still had the capability and habit of downgrading Tommy's ego with a snide remark accompanied by a white-toothed smile which, to match his words and tone, should have been a scowl. Thus, while never saying anything to the authorities, he wielded the bit of power he held by knowing Tommy's real age.

Still Tommy felt fortunate in having roommates who could not be described as coarse in any sense. When so moved or inspired, they would use adjectives which would not have shamed a Billingsgate fish porter, but all was free of malice to anyone present.

Furthermore, every soldier really wanted his Company's officers to be something special, maybe even asserting that theirs were better than the others. Although some disappointed, of course. Many eyes watched the officers while they did their work; the men could easily identify the most efficient. Those not too fortunate in their leaders showed impatience and near-resentment. But, hopefully, they still gave of their best. Although, by nature, some NCOs and officers were more tolerant than others, most grew used to demanding a reasonable standard of discipline. The average was satisfactory, at least, and most men disregarded the grumblers.

Tommy saw, heard and felt what went on around him and often feared he might be something of a liability in his Company. However, nobody told him so and his boyish efforts to please gained him a little good will. In fact, when a phase of playing boyish pranks hit the barrack room, he actually felt glad to be one of the first selected for the role of victim.

It happened one night, after lights out. Some talking went on for a while, followed by comparative silence with the occasional bump, grunt, or snore. Tired Tommy slept... until something he could not identify woke him with pulse racing and a sense of shock, eyes wide open, but the room black dark. He did not yell or speak, just lay there trying to decide what had disturbed him. Smack! Something struck him in the face and he shouted in protest. Responses varied from "What's up, mate?" to "Go to sleep!" and "Shut up!" So he told them something or someone had hit him. Accused of having bad dreams, he said no more. But when another light blow landed on him, someone laughed.

Wide enough awake to judge from which part of the room it came, Tommy said nothing, feigned sleep, and for some time all was well. Then the joker struck once more, but the lad grabbed at the offending object and found himself holding what, from the feel of it, he guessed was a boxing glove... attached to a thread. Tommy snapped it a smart jerk and flung the glove in the direction from which the laughter had come. As this elicited a loud curse and some threats, he lay doggo, feeling he had not come out of the lark too badly.

Daylight revealed a strong, black thread passing over a bracket supporting the shelf above him and stretching over other brackets to a bed at the end of the row. Private Willis had been the joker, raising and releasing the glove.

Interested blokes wracked their brains in devising further funny tortures with which to enliven the first hour or so after lights out each night. Grown men these, but in many cases sharing a large dormitory with other males for the first time; they perhaps felt impelled to behave like boys they had read about in *The Magnet* and *The Gem* weeklies[137].

One man discovered that the beds could be taken to pieces; so if the legs were detached and re-placed in position so that it looked normal, of course, it collapsed as soon as the occupant sat down on it too forcefully or rolled over in his sleep. One evening, while others lingered in the canteen or perhaps, having avoided detection, sampled the wines in some drink shop down the road, our funny men faked about half the beds. Those who came home first had their crashes and either laughed or cursed as they considered appropriate, Tommy among them. But two or three who returned after lights-out were landed with wrecked beds in pitch darkness, and their boozy efforts to reconstruct them kept the other men amused for some time, until the victims settled for sleeping at floor level.

No harm done, but the less ebullient of the roommates complained about this childish conduct. A conference next day decided that they'd all had sufficient of these larks and bed-wrecking was out. All settled down quietly that night… until, around midnight, a crash broke their slumbers. Striking of matches revealed three beds with front legs collapsed. Because the back legs hadn't been tampered with, the beds stood for some time then, a little after lights-out, someone crept about passing a rope round each unsecured leg, then pulled hard. Real anger erupted, and nobody admitted responsibility.

That was almost the end of comedy japes and men once more became as adults. With one exception, that is. The orderly Sergeant doing his rounds, rousing men at 6.30 one morning realised just how unpopular he was when someone (well, there must have been two of them) tipped the piss-tub over him from the balcony high above.

No one confessed so the innocent suffered with the guilty when Captain Boden ordered H Company confined to barracks for several days and had them march up and down the square during the mid-day hours when they would have been resting. Thereafter, Tommy's comrades lived the high life, if any, outside the barrack room. Within, they just rested or ate their meals. Happy day.

Out of the blue, tropical kits consisting of lightweight, cotton-twill tunic trousers and a sun helmet were handed out. What a relief to get out of the heavy uniforms. Now they could begin to enjoy the Mediterranean climate.

Some men looked good in the new clobber, others had unluckily drawn clothes that fitted badly. Tommy regarded his baggy, overlong trousers with some dismay. Their length could be concealed by turning up about four inches at the end of each leg — this would not show when he wore puttees. The baggy backside was the problem and it really worried him so he searched for his brother, thinking he might have learned something from his particularly artful associates.

Ted, whom he found wearing the old trousers, told Tommy to go and get his heavy ones too. Then he led him to a building within the barracks area. Inside, there four Maltese men, two of them busy on sewing machines, one cutting pieces out of tunics and trousers, while the fourth drew white chalk marks on the uniform of a soldier standing before him. "Take your place in the queue," said Ted. Soon after complying, Tommy was getting chalked. "Pay one shilling, come tomorrow," said the tailor. Tommy left the twill trousers and put on the heavy ones. So, for a bob, the necessary alterations were made — though next day the lad worried anew, because now the trousers were almost skin-tight, the tunic shaped and close-fitting too, and all this done without official permission. Also, was this tight outfit really suitable for a hot climate?

Too late now, anyway. He regained some degree of comfort by ceasing to wear vest and pants. Many sinners besides himself used the tailors' services, and perhaps the officers approved the slick effect, for no action was taken about the matter.

Hours of work now changed. What the Army called the "gunfire ration" — a mug of tea and large dry biscuits — was taken at 6.30am, followed immediately by 30 minutes physical training, wearing only the twill slacks. Then "ablutions", breakfast — whatever that might turn out to be — and on parade at 8am. Three hours non-stop training next, then dinner at noon, after which those who had no "jankers" or special jobs were free till 5pm.

Most of them easily acquired the siesta habit, waking for tea at 4pm and all set for three more hours of stiff evening training which left most men fagged out at 8pm.

Not many ventured far after that hour, Monday to Friday — especially at the end of one of those occasional days when, despite the high temperatures, they'd undertaken a long march lasting some hours (albeit with a 10-minute break every 4 miles, and an hour's break and a meal after the first three hours). Each man carried a water bottle and a haversack and the contents had to last until evening.

The heat made these marches very severe tests. Most of the men dispensed with underclothing as soon as they knew what was coming up. Sweat soon darkened their uniforms. Tunics could be taken off during the hour's rest and they dried off quickly, leaving white patches of salt in strange patterns on the cloth (despite this, Tommy never once entered the barracks laundry for, like many others, each week he gave his soiled clothes to a Maltese woman who washed and pressed everything, no matter what the quantity, for sixpence). Back then no one in authority thought of giving the men salt to replace what they sweated out. Tommy suffered fatigue intensely, but his resolve to do no worse than the older men around him prevented him from admitting anything.

Troubled as he was, he yet felt sorrow for the oldest man among them, dear old ex-journalist Ewart Walker. Never a groan nor a word of complaint from the gallant old man, but the sweat streaming down his face and eyes bloodshot and strained behind those pince-nez, the legs that wouldn't straighten up, all told their tale.

Thankfully, Saturdays were different with most of the men free from any duties after 11am. With Friday's weekly pay in their pockets, they felt they could really go to town in every sense. "I didn't wish to explore the village or town areas alone," Tommy recalls. "Already one of our young chaps had been chased by a gang of Maltese youngsters who, according to him, set upon him for no apparent reason. He merely put his head inside the doorway of a village drink shop where the local lads were playing cards. As one man, they came for him. He ran, but they eventually outpaced him and pressed around him. With his back to the wall, he was spotted by a party of our men who charged forward, and the village lads ran away. At least one of the attackers was seen flourishing a knife, so I was glad when a chap called Hayson, who was probably three years older than me, suggested a Saturday afternoon outing together.

"By then the Maltese tailors had rendered my sun helmet ready for wear too. Issued with it had been a pugaree, a length of fine gauze material which you had to arrange in layers just above the helmet brim. To do the job correctly required many pins and more skill than I possessed. But one of my scarce sixpences crossing a Maltese palm put me among the really well-turned-out soldiery. Although we still had to wind those puttees round our ankles and calves. Why, in that hot climate? And it was compulsory for rankers, but officers could wear neatly creased trousers with turn-ups.

"Anyway, I felt eager to see everything on this island. Hayson and I walked along a road flanked by low, loose-stone walls into a village with several nondescript shops and a saloon called Old Joe. In the fug I could see some of our men. But we passed that dingy place, and soon the road joined one by the sea and we found ourselves in the substantial village of St Paul's[138].

"Now we strolled among pleasant houses and people walking around in a good-class district, which gave me a thrill after a period spent exclusively among men. Women, girls, children — so, still such human beings to be seen and heard from. One could not understand what they said as they passed, but their voices were as sweet music to me. I liked the occasional whiff of perfume too, though all the women seemed to use the same heavy brand. Having grown up with the range of hair colourings between blonde and brunette at home, I found the uniform black hair and dark complexion somewhat unattractive.

"But it was good to be clear of the military environment for a few hours. Always, in those days, I had the feeling of something quite marvellous awaiting me at the end of each new road. New to *me*, that is; the older in years, the better the prospect of an interesting discovery."

After that first long walk, their Saturday excursions became a regular treat. Tommy accumulated a few shillings out of his meagre 7/- a week pay — even though he had acquired the regular smoking habit and spent a few pence a week on it (he got little pleasure out of it, but he felt that being able to offer or accept a fag made him one of the crowd). If two more men joined him and Hayson, they could share a *karozzin*[139] and could travel to Sliema at a cost of thruppence farthing each (a shilling fare and the customary penny tip for the cabby). One could stay in Sliema, but more went on in Valletta on the opposite side of Marsamuscetto[140] harbour, so usually they took a penny trip across on a little, steam ferry.

After disembarking, Tommy's usual first purchase was a tall glass of a *limonada* — heavenly flavoured, price 1d, dispensed by a man who occupied an unusually solid, nicely ornamented, old kiosk. Tommy wondered for what purpose it had originally been built.

His friend Hayson preferred beer as a thirst-quencher and Tommy had no objection to joining him, especially when he found that half a pint, could also be had for a penny; light or dark, it had a fair strength, must have, for he felt slightly tipsy after only two glasses.

They rarely made any plans when visiting Valletta, but one time Hayson said, "Why don't we look for the Strada Fontana[141]? They say it's the official brothel road. Some of the older men go there for a shag, or say they do. I could never touch a bag of that sort, but no doubt the older, married men miss their regulars. It might be a bit of a lark to walk through the street."

Tommy too felt something adventurous about the idea. Perhaps seeing how the business was conducted without apparently looking at the whores. When they found the Strada, they saw that the houses — small and terraced — were all to their right. "We'll keep to the left side of the street along by the wall," suggested Hayson.

This they did, talking as they walked, hoping that their guarded glances to the right passed unnoticed by women whom they could see standing on the pavement by their front doors. Rather old most of them looked to the boy. He'd seen mothers of chaps like himself standing chatting to neighbours at their front doors back home who looked no older than most of these women — and they certainly didn't shout coarse invitations such as "Come on, darky ginger" and "Very nice, very cheap" in loud, harsh voices. After which, when the lads took no notice of their offers, came the insults: "English soldier no good, no money," "Territorials plenty beeg preek and no money," "Give him bottle of milk — call yourself a man!" and so on.

So the adventure lost its savour. The youngsters' uselessness was so obvious that women way ahead of them took up the shouting. Although they continued to the end of the street, their walk almost became a run and they felt lucky to escape without injury. Probably the women could tell from long experience when they were being inspected as curiosities.

Tommy learned later — through a visit where he actually did wait for a friend without using the establishment's services himself — that each house was controlled by an old woman who performed certain necessary duties beyond her nominal job title of "cook". First she took out the customer's penis and cleansed it with a swab dipped in water and then in Condy's Fluid[142] which she kept in a bucket in the corner of the room. Then, in full view of the customer — by way of guarantee, up to a point — she performed a cleansing of the whore with the same fluid. The "cook" also attended to payment: one shilling for the use of the woman and a penny for herself.

Another place in which Tommy and Hayson spent an hour or so probably had a depressing effect on some visitors, but amazement was a better word to describe Tommy's reaction. Known in those days as the Chapel Of Bones[143], it was just that. A smallish man in a black cassock admitted them and, unbidden, pointed out features of the decoration on ceiling and walls, which appeared to have been lined with a black fabric. Set against this sombre background were intricate designs, all composed of human bones. Consider the possibilities. The bigger part of some motifs would be made of femurs, the small intricate patterns composed of finger bones. Ribs used generously suggested ripples on water. Sternums portrayed daggers (with small bones arranged as hilts), while a scapula with a tibia for a handle made a fair axe.

The main effort had been directed towards achieving very ingenious geometric patterns. The whole gained a gruesome dignity from four complete human skeletons, one in each corner of the chapel, guardians of the treasure which filled deep bins the length of each wall — namely, the thousands of bones remaining surplus to artistic requirements. "All," intoned the cheerless guide, "are the remains of hundreds of French soldiers."

Malta had suffered many attacks by invaders who tended to remain on the pleasant island after rape and debauchery had ceased to amuse them. The French, however, had proved just that much too repressive and the populace slaughtered their garrison to a man. Mass burial had been quickly followed by disinterment lest the wicked dead'uns should sleep quietly when they did not deserve any sort of peace. The Maltese decided the invaders' remains should be set to work again, their bones earning some small remuneration for the church by attracting visitors to see the pretty patterns they made — and hear the tale of French misdeeds. Thus, at any rate, said the priest. As luck would have it, Tommy had little money on him and, with some embarrassment, he handed the priest threepence farthing, all he could find in his pockets.

On that visit to town, having still some time on his hands but no money in his pocket, Tommy urged his pal Hayson to go his own way and enjoy himself. Strolling alone in a paved area, quite spacious, between dwellings, he stopped to watch some women making lace. Each thread, attached to a pencil-shaped weight, hung down over a cylinder which the lacemaker turned occasionally as she plaited and shaped the threads into delicate and beautiful designs. The lad knew that well-off ladies in England valued Maltese lace and wondered how it found its way from quiet squares and side streets in Valletta to the shops and stores of London.

Glimpses into the lives of these dark-skinned strangers excited in him a feeling of participation in things which escaped the interest of most of his fellow soldiers — so far as he could judge from the accounts of their outings he heard whenever one of his louder comrades held forth to him or, more likely, a group of mates. Bars, booze and women were the subjects on which they vied with each other to arouse envy of their frolics.

In the brothel tales, their skill in gaining a price-cut from the madame by means of threat or persuasion must be admired by him, their manly performance with the prostitute duly purchased must merit applause. And when it came to drinking, three pennies bought a glass of fiery wine and two bob's worth of the stuff might turn a normally mild fellow into a raving fighter — by their own account, certainly. This was, indeed, the stuff of wild, reckless living about which Tommy had only read stories, never daring to hope that he would one day live with men who really did these things.

Nonetheless, he found their tales could not inspire him to emulate their swashbuckling conduct. The one occasion when he wandered into a situation involving alcohol and sex led only to an embarrassing contretemps.

On a hot Saturday afternoon, after the *karozzin* arrived in Sliema, he bade farewell to his travelling companions at the Valletta ferry quay. The boat moved off and he stood alone, the dockside soundless, nothing and nobody moving. Siesta time for the Maltese, of course.

He strolled, then entered a drink shop. The very dark-skinned, moustachioed barkeeper asked him to sit and, having the place to himself, Tommy selected an old armchair and felt like Lord Muck himself when a pleasant girl appeared, collected his beer from the proprietor — obviously her father — and brought it to him. She sat in another armchair beside him, they chatted and he probably bought another beer.

Later, Papa suggested that they move into a room at the back — just an ordinary living room it was. Tommy spent some time with the girl and what seemed unbelievable in later years occurred, namely nothing of note. But a certain awkwardness gradually overpowered him; conversation became impossible and no help came from the girl, kindly and patient though she was. What role was he supposed to fill? A stolen kiss, a cuddle, a hand on her knee then further exploration? This and more would have cost money, he suspected, and he had little. Or was it supposed to be the start of an orthodox romance followed by marriage? He never found out. Given no other customers entered the bar during the whole time Tommy spent there, perhaps Pop was just desperate, business being so bad...

Still, his awkward agonising over that uneasy encounter faded after a few days, and he could always find his own kind of romance in just lying on his mattress at 10pm each night when a bugler played the long and beautiful Last Post — until the orderly Sergeant spoiled the moment with a raucous shout of "Put them bloody lights out!"

Chapter Twenty-Three

What were termed "Company orders" would be posted on a board outside the Company office, and the men expected to familiarise themselves with the contents. One such notice I[144] read with great joy: it announced that, now all ranks had completed basic training, a Signals Section would be formed. It invited men having some knowledge of semaphore and Morse Code to volunteer for transfer to the new section. Tests would precede acceptance.

My name went in pronto, I passed the fairly simple general knowledge and signalling exams, and in no time — though with some regret at leaving my pals and roommates of several weeks — there I was with a new group of lads sharing one of those pleasantly cool barrack rooms fronting on to the roofed and shady sidewalk alongside the Barrack Square.

Inevitably, we had much in common; most of us owed our special knowledge to recent or long-past membership of the Boy Scout movement. The Corporal in charge of the new section, was probably 22 years old, the rest of the chaps between 18 and 20 (not counting me, still 16 until July). He told us we would be spared most of the square-bashing and repetitive drilling which had so far been our lot. On exercises and manoeuvres we would take responsibility for maintaining communications between Company and Battalion Headquarters and, on Brigade exercises, between Battalion and Brigade as well. We thought we were on a soft number at first but, as organisation progressed, demands on us increased.

Our Corporal Catland had the appearance and manner of a dedicated peacetime soldier; the peak of the cap perseveringly bent downwards and moulded till the eyes were only just visible, the trimmed moustache, the unsmiling face, the smart military gait at all times, on or off duty. We had to find out what brought him among us; no suggestion of the Boy Scout about him. So where had he learnt his signalling? Answer: as a GPO[145] telegraphist among other things. But the Guardsman-like bearing? From the Boys Brigade[146], the very antithesis of Baden Powell's lot. None of us could even begin to look like Corporal Glossyboots, so no warm co-operation twixt us and him ever. Above him was Sergeant Cullen, also, it transpired, a GPO man, but from a higher stratum; he usually remained aloof, relaxed occasionally, and proved himself a damn good teacher.

The remaining 16 chaps, all Privates, entered into the training with enthusiasm, never begrudging time, spending more hours each day on the job than they had ever done in Company ranks, and often working while the other troops rested. I remember some of them clearly:

— Mossgrove, about 20, tall, slightly pigeon-toed, fair, wavy hair compulsorily short at sides and back where it showed below the cap, unruly otherwise; he would overcome ill humour or garrulous chumminess with his never-failing courtesy and friendly smile. Before he spoke one knew what to expect — the speech of a well-educated fellow. He never patronised people, not even the occasional fawning type.

— Nicholas, short, Inner-London resident, 18 unofficially, he'd been on some extended-education scheme until that age, very bright, impatient and unkind to dullards.

— "Fatty" Mills, big and fat and plodding and pleasant.

— Dickie Dixon, five-nine, dark, a smiler, but nobody's fool.

— little Hamilton, small, perky, always busy.

— Stanley Drake, also something in the GPO with the speech and manners of the then popular conception of a Lord, though no one could imagine how he came by these qualities — a good sport.

— Loehr, dark with bright, blue eyes, schoolgirl complexion and mannerisms, but only slightly — a kindly bloke.

— Benning, five-ten, earnest, honest, diligent, with no time for easy-going chaps.

— Peter Miter, of Swiss birth but English upbringing, must be mentioned; his father managed a famous London hotel. Dad had taken Peter into the trade very young, starting him right at the bottom as kitchen boy. He progressed through many stages by the time the war started, rising to the role of receptionist.

About five-two but, as far as appearance goes, conjure up what you believe to be the perfect manly figure and that would be Peter. Just turned

20, he already had what novelists then called a blue chin, requiring a second shave if going out for the night. He was justifiably vain about his physical assets and probably truthful about the trail of deflowerings illuminating his experience of life so far. Before leaving barracks for an assignation with a dame whom none of us ever met or saw, he would relate what occurred during his last visit; by then he may have worked up an anticipatory horn, as it was then termed, and would perhaps show to admiring comrades a penetratory organ which looked much too big to belong to a little man.

Thereafter, a really well-groomed soldier of that shabbily dressed period, he would swagger off to do his stint in amatory battle. A foreigner in looks and by birth, he yet was the most consistently patriotic Britisher I have known. He enlisted to prove that, and always performed his military duties with liberal determination. On active service later, always in very trying circumstances, he retained his manliness and faith in the cause long after others had said to hell with it all. Usually, his type could only be found doing jobs so important that they were compelled to be separated from the actual battlefield by a hundred or more miles, poor chaps — their belief in a man doing his bit for his country often stronger than that of a soldier up to his knees in mud and shit, say near Ypres or the French funeral factory, Verdun.

Those men were all superior to me in most respects, if only because of their three or four years more experience of life.

The variety of work kept us youngsters fully interested. Because it concerned maintaining communications over distances, we frequently had to take light rations and full water bottles with us and spend whole days away from barracks. Generally, we were divided into four groups of four per station, either running out light cables for field telephones working between them, or perhaps using heliographs and flags.

The old routine of drills and marches soon became almost a memory, and probably we began to regard ourselves as signallers rather than soldiers — specialists, in fact. A jolt to our boyish fancies was delivered once in a while when an order went out that all specialists, cooks, officers' servants, clerks and so on would have to rejoin their Companies for a day's refresher training. Rather out of practice, we performed badly sometimes, feeling not quite so cocky about our status afterwards.

The Saturday trips to town became less frequent, being subject to the exigencies of our special training. But, when free, I sometimes had the company of one of our young chaps with similar, limited requirements to myself. Usually, instead of spending hours in a bar listening to musicians and singers, we would look at the sights, buildings, or views, and sometimes have tea in a gem of a place we discovered in the main street of Valletta. After a surfeit of Army grub, a tea with waitress service, your own teapot and lovely, fancy pastries taken among pleasant civilians, mostly women, was well worth one of our scarce shillings. English people ran the teashop and, if you managed to get a table near a window, you could survey the gay scene below as people and horse-drawn traffic moved along the Strada Reale.

By way of a change, we might have coffee and sweet cakes in a place mostly used by Maltese businessmen. One seldom saw a soldier in there, but the regulars appeared to have no objection to our presence. On several occasions, local men sat with us and talked about civilian life on the island and sometimes of their own visits to Britain. I enjoyed these brief spells in a world so different to the Army in which I now seemed to have dwelt for so long.

In town by myself one particularly hot day, I walked down to the Grand Harbour. A large battleship stood at anchor and a boatman offered to take me out to her for thruppence. Coming alongside I realised that, her name being *Jean Bart*[147], she was a French Navy ship. But when a *matelot*, seeing my uniform, gave me a sign of welcome, I had no hesitation in stepping across on to the gangway.

The friendly sailor became my guide on a long tour of that huge battleship and my eyes made up for his paucity of English words and mine of French. It may surprise you that the memory of her kitchens, with their large ovens, remained with me after much else was forgotten; even at sea, Frenchmen respected their tummies and catered for their needs on a grand scale.

Ashore again, I found the waterside area where our Battalion first landed and spotted the Seamen's Mission which had caught my attention while we waited for orders. Curiosity took me into the building and, there being no one around, I settled into a large leather armchair. On that hot, drowsy, late afternoon I soon dozed, contented, comfortable, unworried by thoughts of NCOs in search of victims.

I awoke some time later, well rested, and looked around expecting to see perhaps a seafaring gent or some official, but all remained silent, nobody appeared. It reminded me of that small office in a street off Haymarket in distant London, next to a flat which one of my bosses owned or rented, on the door of which a brass plate announced the registered office of a fund for needy seamen. Never, in my visits there, had I seen any sign of life in the seafarers' office. I wondered why. Would a needy seaman in London's dockland ever find his way to the West End for a sub? Likewise, in that Maltese seamen's home-from-home I found no one to thank, so left the place much refreshed and somewhat puzzled.

Life as a member of the Signals Section felt far more fulfilling than that of an ordinary "squaddie", but now came our turn to learn something of armed combat. This brought our group under instruction from men who regarded soldiering as something much tougher and harsher than did our own Sergeant, to whom ohms and amps, dots and dashes, and field telephones were the tools which would actually win the war.

A major part of the basic training concerned the ranker's weapon, the rifle. Once issued to him, that rifle's number was entered against his name. It became his main responsibility, a court martial for him if he mislaid it, and the "rookie" must learn the name, position and function of every part of his gun.

The bolt was an intricate piece of mechanism, a moving and removable part containing within it a strong spring and a striking pin. Consider then what happened when you squeezed the trigger — the bolt spring was released, the striker pin pierced a small explosive cap, this ignited tightly packed strands of cordite in the cartridge case creating enormous pressure in that small space which propelled the metal cone blocking the outlet at express speed through the rifle barrel to the destruction or mutilation of some unfortunate person... or as the instructor would say, "It'll put paid to some poor bastard". If your aim was good...

When you raised the bolt's lever it came backwards, engaging, withdrawing, and expelling the cartridge case of a fired bullet. When you then pushed the bolt forward it shoved a fresh cartridge into position ready for firing. Speed must be developed in doing this, so that you could kill more enemies in a given time. The instructor pointed out a brass plate on the wide butt where a hinged, small tongue protected a hole out of which one could extract a small oil container and a pull-through — a cord with a slim metal weight at one end and a loop to hold a piece of cloth at the other. Lubricating and cleaning the rifle and its barrel was quite an important part of a soldier's job.

Now, dear reader, you are almost as proficient as I was in the mechanics of a lethal weapon and probably hoping, as I was, that you may never have to shoot a fellow human. You may say so freely, but I kept my trap shut, perforce. I continued adding to my knowledge thus… at the tip of the barrel is the foresight and, closer to the rifleman's eye, the backsight, adjustable. Cut into the latter is a U or a V and so, holding the rifle tightly to your right shoulder, left hand supporting the barrel, you look with your right eye along the gun and bring the foresight's tip into line with the shoulders of the backsight and both in line with the bottom of the object to be shot at. Pressing the butt hard into your right shoulder, now squeeze the trigger between the right thumb and forefinger…

But, before actually firing a live round, we need more training. "Lie down," says the instructor. "Take aim as taught." He lies down too, a few yards in front of you, facing your rifle, brave man. The target, which he holds, has a tiny hole in the centre of its bull's-eye through which he peers to see if your gun is correctly sighted. At his command you fire… fortunately, you are using wooden bullets, so when the trigger is pressed only a sharp click follows, but the instructor can see if, in the firing process, there is too much movement of the rifle barrel. By the way, the instructor examines these wooden bullets before and after each practice because, he says, a live round got among the dummies once and the Army lost a good teacher.

For several weeks, we dedicated day after day to this sort of repetition, longer than necessary in all likelihood, because the policy was that, in any given five days, only one Company at a time could be accommodated on the range where we were all introduced to firing live ammunition. But finally H Company signallers got their chance, all of us thrilled and nervous as, clearly, this would be a crucial time of testing for these would-be soldiers. As ever at such moments, I was in a state of tension, but determined to show no sign of it while we marched the two miles to the range along the seashore in the morning sunshine with prickly lava underfoot.

Waiting for your turn to fire your first live rounds felt like pretending to read in a dentist's waiting room. When, finally, I stepped forward the instructor showed me once more how to position myself, lying beside him, facing the sea. Then he reminded me of two important things about firing a rifle with real bullets rather than wooden fakes. Having taken aim, I must press the butt of the rifle into the hollow of my shoulder as hard as I could, he cautioned, or risk having my jaw broken by the recoil. And then the trigger must be squeezed, not pulled. The latter would spoil my aim.

He told me that, lying beside me now, he would take notes and every shot would be assessed — the man at the butts who controlled the targets would signal by how much I'd missed the bull's-eye and at what angle. I knew from others that even my behaviour would be marked too.

No need to hurry for the first exercise, he stressed, just concentrate on every detail of what you have practised. Although the gun is stronger than you, you be the master... I took aim — the target, at 400 yards initially, represented the appearance of a man's head and shoulders, grey with no white background to help the marksman's focus... tip of the foresight in line with the shoulders of the backsight, both in line with the bottom of the bull's-eye. I pressed the butt back hard and, with thumb against trigger guard, forefinger on trigger, I squeezed. Nothing happened.

"What about the safety catch?" my trainer asked quietly. My right hand fumbled about and pressed the catch forward. Back to firing position, trigger squeezed... and for a fraction of a second the gun came alive with awful power. The jolt almost detached my head from my shoulders, the explosion deafened me, the shock shot through my whole body.

Firing .22s with the Scouts had not remotely prepared me and I had to repeat that shattering experience between 50 and 60 times that day. The old long Lee-Enfield was the very devil, a hellish shoulder-bruiser.

Every few shots, the instructors increased the range by 100 yards until we were trying to take good aim at the unheard-of distance of 900 yards, over half a mile. This has to be tried to be appreciated; at that distance, although the target was now on a white background and greatly increased in size — they were mounted on "butts", iron frames raised and lowered by chains and pulleys — the whole business seemed detached from reality. I thought, how can any action of mine affect a man so far away from me? Perhaps the weapon's designers had outstripped practicality.

As each man finished his first morning stint, he was allowed to make his own way back to barracks. When I neared my quarters, an awful pain drew down my right shoulder and I walked into our barrack room in that contorted attitude. Enquiries as to my trouble I answered with my self-diagnosis that I'd got indigestion, hoping that was correct. I looked around for a cure. On the table stood a bottle of Worcester sauce. I promptly unstoppered it and took a long swig of the stuff. It burnt mouth and throat and probably worked as a counter-irritant, so gradually I was able to straighten up. Indigestion or battered nerves, I never found out.

After that first day, we had to take our noon break for dinner, then return to the range for repeated drills on various different ways of firing a rifle — in the course of which I got over the shoulder-bashing ache. Snapshooting at 200 yards proved an exciting session, but sailing vessels passing close behind the butts distracted my attention. Then a phone message from local police complaining that fishing boats were being shot at brought a temporary halt to the work. In truth, some of the lads, aiming high, had deliberately sent a few whizzing among the masts.

The trickiest lesson of all demanded that we try to emulate the renowned 15 rounds a minute fired by the soldiers of our standing Army — already proven no match for German machine guns on the frontline in Belgium and France. Each shot must still be carefully aimed, our instructors insisted. Normally you loaded five bullets in the magazine, but for rapid fire you inserted 10 — wooden ones at first as we tried to master the mechanics of just getting the shots off so quickly — and fired them, then dealt with five more, all in the space of 60 seconds. I failed time after time, as did many others, even using dummies. How the heck would we cope with live ammunition, its explosions, recoils, smoke and fumes?

One day, as we Signallers struggled with rapid fire, what with the sun blazing down on our frustrations and the general strain on nerves, we began to express our feelings of discomfort freely, till the officer in charge, Captain Bicknell, yelled, "You are the most foul-mouthed gang of louts it has ever been my misfortune to command!"

While regarded as a good sort, something of a showman and a dandy, sporting a Charlie Chaplin moustache, the Captain did not know that the Signals chaps rather prided themselves on being decently behaved and had only recently begun to emulate and perhaps even improve on the swearing abilities of some real "old soldiers" they swapped drinks with in the canteen. Thus, they felt they were becoming old-timers themselves, but the officer's rebuke stung, and shame brought on milder forms of self-expression, the bs and fs fewer, damns and blasts more frequent.

And, eventually, they did complete their rifle-range programme — the 15 rounds a minute all blazed away... On my card, with the final five bullets fired at 900 yards, hitting anywhere on the target seemed tolerable, I thought. But, surprisingly, when the instructor totted up the figures, they showed I was a "first-class" shot, only a few points below the top level of marksmen qualified to work as snipers when on active service.

However, between those weeks when we got our turn on the range, the Signallers endured training in another combat function of their rifles. An effective infantryman, it was then believed, must be able to shoot accurately when at a distance from the enemy and then, with bayonet fixed, fight fiercely hand to hand.

But the style of bayonet fighting then taught caused much merriment among the troops when off parade. It all started from a comical semi-crouching position, an unheroic stance suggesting, some averred, a man who'd soiled his pants. To simulate combat, little, hopping, forward movements were followed by similar retreats. Thrusts and parries alike had to be executed from that preposterous semi-crouch.

We did our best with it, and put up the pretence required to satisfy the instructors' test of proficiency in this murderous occupation. The performance might have been more convincing had we been allowed to leave the scabbards on our bayonets. But, ordered to wield these short, sharp steel daggers unsheathed, we knew that an over-enthusiastic movement could cause a comrade injury or even death so we kept to our stilted, hopping about, more concerned with preserving life than taking it. Anyway, given my lively imagination, I decided there and then that I could never face goring a man and that I would always keep a round in the chamber when face-to-face fighting threatened.

Suddenly it was time, they said, for all good soldiers to pack their kitbags, move out of barracks and, a mile or two up the road, pitch their tents on rising ground alongside a military cemetery[148]. We Signallers had our line of tents alongside the road. One of them we equipped as an office complete with field telephones and we wired up a system connecting the Headquarters of each Company and Battalion and handled all communications.

Two things furnished me with permanent memories of that camp. One of them was the frequency with which a band playing The Dead March In Saul[149] distracted my attention. This would occur once or twice a day because, as I learned, Malta had become the medical base for all the British Services in the Mediterranean area and, inevitably, many men brought to the hospital died of their wounds. Those who died on the battlefield, I gathered, could receive no such military honours — perhaps the Malta garrison authorities were clinging to a kindly peacetime ritual for as long as possible.

So you heard the slow beat of the big drum away in the distance, then a few notes of music from the brass would gradually swell in volume as the cortege advanced with stately tread — the blasts from the trombones dominated because they occupied the front row to make room for their slides.

If I could persuade someone to take over the headphones, I would hurry from the tent, slither on my backside the few feet down the embankment to the road and await the arrival, the slow approach of my hero, the big, bass drummer: wearing a real leopardskin between his torso and the drum, and given lots of space around him to allow his skilful whirlings of the flying drumsticks with their white, furry tips, "Daa da dada bang! Daa dada dada da bang!" — he supplied the hefty thuds at the end of each phrase.

Nearing the cemetery, the band drew to the side of the road. The pallbearers carrying the flag-covered coffin passed through the gates with the firing party. And then I could approach the drummer, show him my admiration of his skill and perhaps persuade him to demonstrate how, amid all the drumsticks' twirling, he could give the stretched skin a light touch or a hefty wallop just as he wished.

The farewell chorus of musketry fire would soon be followed by the reappearance of the troops. Then the really excellent band led the homeward march to a cheery tune so different to the funeral dirge which had marked their arrival. We envied the Battalion which could afford to set up and train that morale-raising band. Apparently, some of their officers — wealthy men — paid for all the instruments before the war. I, at any rate, felt that by providing music for gay or sad occasions, the bandsmen did a good job, even in wartime. If their musical skill made it possible for them to be spared the horrors of frontline warfare, it also enabled them to provide enjoyment to those resting from battlefield tensions.

Our officers, generous as their own personal circumstances allowed, had supplied the makings of a drum-and-fife band: a big drum, four side drums, and a dozen or so assorted flutes. Our band volunteers were learning to play them, some doubling with bugles. Soon, we too would have our flagging spirits uplifted and be inspired to march smartly, instead of slouching through the last mile or two of a trying route — it was customary to transport a band to some point where, fresh as paint, they could join the Battalion and render this restorative service to the sorely tried soldiery.

We already had a Corporal who played all the calls on a very melodious bugle; he roused us with the Reveille most mornings, and his repertoire covered Cookhouse, Fall In, Sick Parade, Post Corporal, Officers' Mess, and, at the day's end, the full Last Post. So, at his musical behest, men ran or halted, put out lights and relaxed into sleep, spirits soothed.

When he sounded the dreaded Jankers, though, naughty boys hurried to the barrack square to toil back and forth, heavily loaded, while good, honest souls like me took their well-deserved ease. Meanwhile, the Corporal's pupils blew their bugles better every day and we heard calls the like of which we'd never heard before[150]. Soon they would play tunes which meant something to us, for already a few could tongue their mouthpieces well enough to produce a couple of true notes.

At the camp, the food issued to us got progressively worse. At meal times, the orderly officer and a Sergeant visited the messes and the Sergeant called "Any complaints?" to which, normally, no one responded. It was assumed that a complainant would be marked as a grumbler and might suffer for his temerity.

But, finally, one day several did complain — all greeted with a stony silence and a hostile look from the Sergeant. No improvement followed and, soon after that, around midday, from my raised situation in my Signals tent, I witnessed a couple of hundred men marching round and round the footpaths bordering the camp, led by a man carrying a leafy branch torn from one of the few trees in the area. They shouted slogans such as "Poor food, no work!"

Roused and, understandably, incensed by hunger, more men joined the protest. Little as I knew of military law, I felt certain the ringleaders risked court martial and severe punishment, whereas complaints forcefully but properly made would have brought improvement; the difficulty was finding someone bold enough to stand alone and state the case. As it was, the leader, a chap with wild, staring eyes, pursued his rabble-rouser role with infinite zeal and no apparent idea as to what the next move should be.

A young officer made the decision for him. He appeared suddenly in front of them and gave a clear, sharp order, "Halt!" Without quibble, all the marchers obeyed. "Follow me!" he said, and turned and started marching — making himself the head of the column. And follow him they did, on to the road and out of my sight.

Later, I heard he had taken them all to a nearby large marquee in which a famous firm of brewers and caterers, official concessionaires, retailed food and drink. That place was the nearest thing to a canteen we had at the time. By cheque, the officer — Lieutenant Booth[151] — bought a large quantity of canned sausages, bread and biscuits and organised their fair distribution to those present. He also undertook to put the mess complaints to the Colonel and told the men to disperse quietly.

Thus, a situation, which could have resulted in imprisonment and punishment for decent, but desperate soldiers, was settled quietly by a good man who had some regard for human feelings and failings and not so much regard for the book of rules.

Some good did come of the mutiny-that-wasn't. Lieutenant Booth, who had a flair for organisation, accepted a job which would often intrude on his off-duty periods; he was given authority to inspect food stores, to check cooked meals before they were issued to the men and generally to look after the men's interests regarding quantity and quality of foods. Perfection was not achieved, but sufficient improvement elicited praise from some former complainers.

The young officer was of that type which bases opinions and judgements on a conception of honesty, which is all too rare in the world. "Scrounging" or "winning", he described as cover-up words used by thieves to convince themselves they really were decent men. The few who persisted in making frivolous complaints got short shrift from him, as did careless Quartermasters and cooks. Lieutenant Booth, admired by most, scorned by cynics, remained incorruptible and steadfast in his pursuit and practice of honesty and fairness to all. A rare bird indeed.

Chapter Twenty-Four

Most of our training completed and, in our case, much of the specialist knowledge mastered, we were about to become a nomadic tribe, it appeared. The camp site suddenly swarmed with busy men directed by skilled NCOs.

Up tent pegs! We reduced that town of tents to tidily stacked canvas bales of uniform size in a remarkably short space of time. Pack kitbags — tubular, about 2ft 3 ins long and 14 inches in diameter — don the ingenious arrangements of straps and buckles which made it possible to carry the pack containing overcoat, mess tin, boot brushes, housewife (remember?), towel and toilet items, socks, vest, shirt — and a knitted wool tube called a cap comforter, which could be worn as a scarf or to cover head and ears high on the back — as well as ten ammunition pouches each holding ten bullets across the upper abdomen, a trenching tool handle and shovel-cum-pick head (attached to the belt at the back), the musty-smelling water bottle at your left hip (I never saw the like of that bottle after we left Malta, of Crimean War vintage we estimated and made of wood of all substances…) — and your heavy Lee Enfield slung over your right shoulder.

But then, we Signallers — after rewinding our telephone lines and packing our instruments into carrier cases — had to hang our specialist equipment over the basic infantryman gear: a field telephone/telegraph, a message case the size of a briefcase full of message forms and copies, and probably a mile spool of fine enamelled wire for temporary communications… and a couple of signal flags. Without the signalling gear, the infantryman of that period carried about 91 pounds of equipment if his ammunition pouches were full, so with the thermometer at about 80°F and soaring and that load suspended around or resting upon my meagre body... I had little difficulty in restraining myself from breaking into a gallop. In fact, I was sweaty and exhausted quite early in the march.

Thereafter, my will alone conquered the wish to allow knees to sag and collapse underneath this hellish load, and crash on to the dusty, stony road. But had that happened, I feared, my game would have been up, my true age discovered. Wounding protests about cruelty to children would have been heard, I imagined... Although, actually, I need not have worried for, later, many men around me admitted they had felt pretty distressed — soaked with sweat, the salt of it stinging their eyes, the load on their shoulders seeming to double in weight with every mile.

Well, the march didn't kill us and we reached our new campsite — at a place called Ghajn Tuffieha[152]. Some hutments there housed ablutions, cookhouse, officers' mess, and offices. And, mercifully, we were welcomed with pints of tea and hunks of bread with melted butter — our cooks had moved in earlier and made this ready for us, further proof of Lieutenant Booth's good influence over the formerly slack (or worse) Quartermaster's department.

On arrival, the officers granted us an hour's rest. As one man we made for the sea where we found the first sandy beach we'd seen on the island; off came every stitch of clothing and we were into that lovely water quicker than our hands shot forward on pay day. Previously barred to us, because of those dubious concerns about "Mediterranean Fever", the water was warm and salty enough for us to appreciate its buoyancy.

After we erected our tents, a silence settled over all, darkness came, and sleep began its healing work — until, at midnight, a storm broke with a violence most of us had never experienced before. The majority of the Battalion were housed in large, pointed bell tents, hastily and perhaps carelessly erected given the day's weather. We Signallers had smaller bivouac tents, three and a half feet high with rubber ground sheets secured to the tent all round; thus, our weight — four of us per tent — and that of our equipment helped to hold it down. So we dozed and sometimes chatted through the stormy hours, and by dawn the thunder and lightning ceased.

When we opened the tent flaps and crawled out, we were amazed. Everywhere, among dozens of fallen tents, men wearing next to nothing struggled to put things right. Others sheltered in the wash house. Those who had anticipated the swimming ban being lifted were wearing the trunks they had shrewdly procured. But as the sun rose so did everybody's spirits and the vast drying-out operation commenced.

That first night was a bad start at the new camp, but several happy weeks followed. Work hours were now strictly observed so we performed only the lightest duties during the hottest part of the day. The officers' apparent policy of exhausting the men for the sake of, supposedly, toughening them up had ended and everyone had now come to recognise that the hours of darkness were not necessarily best dedicated to sleep alone. If we trained during the evening and the early part of the night we could, with clear consciences, sleep, doze, float in the sea or loll about in the sun during the day — which we often did for hours on end.

We Signallers did further training, often with Maori pals from the New Zealand (Maori) Pioneer Battalion, who had lately arrived in Malta[153]. Parties of four or six of us were sent away to defence points around the island for periods of one or two weeks.

Typical of such observation posts was one on a headland by Salina Bay[154]. A group of Signallers, Maoris and Maltese Army engineers lodged there in a stone tower[155]. We maintained contact with a section of soldiers camped somewhat inland. If we saw anything suspicious at sea or ashore, we could signal to them, or to Naval Headquarters near Valletta, for search or arrest of the suspects.

At all times, day and night, a Signaller was on duty on top of that tower. One evening, when doing my stint, I relieved the boredom by watching an old man and a young girl working in their very small plantation not far off. A small building — one room or at most two — was their home. It must have been uncomfortably hot inside for, as twilight briefly warned of night's approach, the girl came out, placed an old pillow on a heap of dried straw just outside the door of the hovel, and lay down.

Earlier, in full daylight, I had observed the poor, old, shapeless, black dress she wore; now it functioned as her nightdress. Our family had known severe hardship but here, on this lovely island, poverty seemed more out of place. Yet I perceived advantages which were hers: she would not have to endure periods of bitterly cold weather and occasional days with no fuel to provide any warmth; if, at times, she and granddad had no money to buy food, they could always find something to eat on their own land — a sugar melon, a few grapes, or a hunk from one of the huge pumpkins growing in the plantation — and, withal, they had the blessed warmth of the sun most days of the year.

If the possibility of sharing her natural couch occurred to me, it must have been immediately rejected. The soiled, probably smelly, old dress, the dirty, bare, horny-soled feet and the easily imagined, unwashed body must have been powerful deterrents, but in any case the principles regarding correct human relationships instilled by dear old Frusher still held strong magic for me… And there was the old man to reckon with, even if one's advances were coupled with the purest motives…

As darkness took over from the bright sun, which sustained the day's heat until the last moment, I gave my attention to the job in hand. We were told of German submarines being refuelled somewhere in that area of the Mediterranean and communicating with someone ashore on Malta. So we had to spot all signals at sea or on land, read them if possible, and alert the troops waiting to take any necessary action.

We had a phone line to a section of our men now camped back in the bay and, when I saw a flashing light coming from a place not far from their small camp, I quickly got in touch with the Sergeant in charge. Watching from my tower at the tip of a seaward finger of land, I concluded that the recipient of the signals must have been offshore beyond me. My mate wrote down the letters as I called them out, but the message, if such it was, had been encoded.

The military operation to deal with the matter had its funny side. Sergeant Watson and his merry men hurried to the position I had indicated on the phone. They spotted a flashing at the top of a high stone wall by the road. A born leader and a man of action, the Sergeant sprang and heaved himself upwards — as I learned later for, having sent the message alerting him, I wished to participate in any excitement which might follow, so I asked a pal to take over the lookout job on top of the tower and commenced the fairly short walk from the tip of the headland back to the bay.

In case the suspected collaborator with the enemy had helpers in the vicinity, I decided against taking a well-used track which ran along the high ground and, instead, made a rather tortuous progress among rocks low down by the sea. I soon realised the dark, moonless night was quite unsuitable for this silly choice of a route. I pressed on, but knew for certain I could not join the Sergeant's party in time to help them.

And when someone fairly close by let fly with a gun of some sort I was shaken to the very marrow. It had been a lark of sorts up to that point, but that terrific bang spoilt everything. The picture I'd had of the mettlesome young soldier voluntarily facing danger to help his comrades was phoney; the scared boy crouching low among rocks, scarcely daring to breathe in case he was spotted was real.

I waited some considerable time before moving, and then used great care to avoid making any noise. So, when I reached the coast road and approached the place where I guessed the light had been flashed, I found no one. The scary silence made me hurry to Sergeant Watson's small camp, where my story of being fired on was received with some scepticism.

There was no glory for anybody to be had out of the entire incident. Certainly, somebody had been on the wall, but after Sergeant Watson sprang upwards and straddled the top of it, apart from hearing the noise of a hasty departure he made no contact with the possible enemy. The Sergeant acted quickly, though. He jumped down on the far side — and his yell of pain brought others to the wall top, intent on saving his life if possible. But "Stay up there!" was his whispered command so they waited. They could hear him quietly moaning and cursing until he told them to move along and climb down at a point two or three yards away, whence he led his men on a search of the area. Still they caught no spies.

However, the Sergeant was sorely wounded. Sorely being the appropriate word since his brave jump had brought his backside down on the hairy spikes of a huge cactus and he needed careful search and extraction treatment before relief from pain enabled him to write his report.

On my return to the lookout tower, my friend who had so kindly taken on my job up top immediately asked about a shot he'd heard soon after my departure. I told him how close to me the explosion had been and how ear-shattering. We guessed that, if it had no connection with the flashing light, then the owner of one of the small plantations in the vicinity must have mistaken me for a thief in the night.

Soon our small party returned to the Battalion base close to the beautiful beach. The work routine of early morning start, long afternoon break, then evening and night training resumed. We spent long, afternoon periods in the calm, warm sea, with immense benefit to health and morale.

Some of the combined signals training and practice with our Maori comrades provided my happiest experiences; those fellows were so mature, so calmly balanced. Worries which could afflict British town-dwellers appeared unknown to them... Either that, or maybe they possessed an ability to extract all the joy from the situation prevailing at any given moment. Their relations with an officer who sometimes helped with their training were unusually good, I thought; combining friendship and respect for his rank called for real self-discipline on each man's part.

Next, half the Signallers were packed off to an Army school in Valletta which had the most up-to-date field telegraph instruments available. Hour upon hour of sending and receiving messages, using the forms we would handle on active service, and learning approved abbreviations and message codings and everything timed by the 24-hour clock. Gradually we developed speed in translating the dots and dashes into letters and words and writing them legibly regardless of noise, talk and movement going on around us — of which the instructors created a lot.

In Valletta, I liked to rise even earlier than necessary for the pleasure of breathing the cool morning air and gazing over the mostly flat rooftops of the neighbouring village, but particularly to watch an elderly but remarkably agile Navy seaman perform a nerve-twisting ritual walk on top of the narrow wall bordering the tall Navy Headquarters building opposite our place. At a given moment every morning, followed by his pal, he completed a circuit of the entire wall. His pal by the way was a monkey.

Later, back in the camp I loved, I found myself with three other Signallers mentioned in Battalion Orders being required to report to Lieutenant Wickinson at a certain hour. I didn't like that at all, because this camp in its pleasant situation had given me happiness and a feeling of security. Any threat to the continuity of this beautiful mode of life chilled my blood. Although such interesting work, performed in almost idyllic surroundings, had not figured as a possibility for me when I enlisted, I felt we had indeed struck it rich. I had envisaged frontline service with all its risks and horrors. So this present respite whetted my appetite for more of the same treatment... Even though I'd concluded that, the longer this sheltered-from-reality existence lasted, the greater degree of repugnance and fear would I feel when I had to face doing real active service close to the enemy.

The young Lieutenant told the four of us to sit and informed us that we had been selected for promotion to the rank of Lance Corporal. Though well aware that this was the worst possible rank to have, that a lance jack was the lackey of all the NCOs and the butt of many Privates' ill humour, we yet could not refuse this pestilential promotion. Dolefully, I assumed it meant separation from my Signals pals, a return to H Company and the accursed drill and guard duty routine. Imagine me having to give orders to those older men with whom I had first soldiered. They would just sneer and dare me to report any lack of discipline...

Fortunately, Lieutenant Wickinson said we should remain in the Signals section, each being responsible for a quarter of its men under the Sergeant's surveillance. On active service the Signallers would be posted to various Companies and Headquarters offices in small groups, each of them in the charge of a Lance Corporal.

Then followed our inquest on why we had been selected. The Sergeant said it was because we were best at the work, and I was eager to believe him, but couldn't. I feared it was because those in charge calculated that we four would lack the nerve to say nay to our young officer.

When the Signals lads learnt that we had been placed in some sort of authority over them, reactions were very varied but never complimentary. One thing entirely lacking in their response was envy. Too well they knew what a thankless number we were on. When you live and sleep in a tent or barrack room with men, any discipline you might attempt to uphold is undermined by familiarity. Sergeants, for instance, had their separate quarters and messes and must not fraternise with rankers, only coming among them as an urge and a scourge when duty required them to.

The only practical advantage of this most minor of promotions proved to be monetary. A Lance Corporal's stripe should shortly bring a small increase in pay, I'd heard, albeit for administratively tortuous reasons. Normally, it was an unpaid rank. However, it appeared that our qualification as Signallers entitled us all to a small rise as specialists. There again, the paymaster had been unable to secure this increase for us — we didn't know why. But the four of us who had been awarded the petty promotion then received a bonus of threepence a day for performing "extra duties". Today that sum would not induce you to hold out your hand to receive it, but the 1/9 a week addition bought many good things back then.

Despite this, in the following weeks I had little spending money. This had not mattered to me because I was too young to have any substantial addictions, such as to alcohol or tobacco — although I'd enjoyed smoking now and then, and certainly found renewed strength and wellbeing in drinking a glass or two of beer after a hot, heavy day. But my sudden relative poverty came about after brother Ted and I had betaken ourselves to a quiet spot for one of our periodic chats and he had called my attention to an item on the Battalion noticeboard.

It stated that if any soldier wished to allot part of his pay to a next-of-kin relative, the Government would add to that sum. In our case, if we allotted 2/6 a week each to our family out of our seven-shillings basic wages, 3/6 would be added making a weekly payment of 6/- each, to be collected from a local Post Office. So our mother could be 12/- a week better off. This we arranged to do, leaving ourselves with the derisory — as it appears nowadays — weekly wage of 4/6 each (plus that extra 1/9 in my case).

Most of this I spent on eatables to supplement the filling, but unattractive rations. I had also been able to afford a few cigars at a penny each and cigarettes — small Virginia — at 7d a hundred, tall glasses of lemonade at a penny a time, or half a pint of good beer for a penny halfpenny. Whiskey was available at 1/6 a bottle, but I never touched it though wine at 2d a good glass was an occasional indulgence.

A flutter of excitement arose in our section when our young Lieutenant sent for Mossgrove, who, like me, had suffered "promotion". He was missing for some time and then only rejoined us for long enough to pack his kitbag, ask us to return his equipment to the Quartermaster's store, and briefly explain to his fellow Lance Corporals what his future job might be.

You may recall he had obviously been educated to a higher standard than most of us, had lived well, and must surely have enlisted under the influence of patriotic impulses of great depth. Why else had he done so? One didn't ask such a question of a mate and, among soldiers, patriotism was never mentioned so we never knew the answer to that one. He extracted promises of secrecy from the three of us, then told us he was being temporarily attached to the Navy. They would give him training in those aspects of signalling work which differed from Army practice. After that, he would join a ship. So, goodbye Mossy.

Chapter Twenty-Five

Subsequently, blows to my hopes of spending the rest of the war by that heavenly beach at Ghajn Tuffieha fell thick and fast.

One day, I spent much time lining up outside the Medical Officer's hut with hundreds of others, being dismissed when meal-times came, then resuming my place in the long line until I eventually got inside. "Shirt off!" said somebody. Right. A medical orderly wiped my left upper arm with spirit, and a Corporal held a very thin sort of blade in the flame of a Bunsen burner, withdrew it and made scratches on my arm. Then, the Medical Officer painted the scratches with fluid from a bottle. Those three men did that hour after hour, to hundreds of men.

Next morning, I knew that I had been well and truly vaccinated and was glad to rest whenever possible. Urgent activity everywhere now, though, much packing of stores and, finally, down came the little homes we had become so used to. Headed by our now very proficient drum and fife band, our long procession headed for Valletta where we spent a couple of days confined in a children's school — no passes to leave the building were issued. Medics examined our vaccinations and applied new dressings. The old, long rifles were withdrawn and, once more, we became weaponless warriors. We Signallers had to hand in all our instruments and, thank goodness, those weird, clumsy, oil signal lamps — surely the Quartermaster placed them back in the museum from which they had been borrowed...

A short march from the school, there we were again at the Grand Harbour and I was one of a line of men moving up a gangway to embark on, this time, a fine, big liner turned troopship, the *Ivernia*[156] — spacious enough to accommodate our thousand or so men without looking crowded.

Excitement concerning future events did not smother my sadness at leaving an island which, though small, still had many features I had not been able to view. I recalled that, oddly, my natural boy's homesickness had shown itself only during sleep, in the form of dreams wherein I once again lived my daily routine from the time before I enlisted. This occurred frequently and, discussing the subject with young pals, I summed it up by saying that, by day, I lived in Malta and by night in dear old England, all quite happily.

Looking across the water at the familiar scene as the *Ivernia* moved slowly away from the quay, I felt reluctant to take my eyes off the place I loved; while I could still gaze shoreward, I wanted to remember everything...

Bunches of oval green grapes, sugar melons whose dark-green skins contrasted with the sweet, pink flesh inside...

Lying on the quayside at St Paul's all afternoon, watching baby swordfishes swimming about, then walking back through the village and people on their steps saying "*Buona sera*" and me saying it back to them — I felt a different person, a man, when I got away from the Army like that, not a number any more...

That poor man who stood in an upended barrel and let people throw heavy sticks of wood at him, three goes a penny, in beautiful San Antonio Gardens, near Valletta; not as terrible as it sounds, because he just ducked down into the barrel to the accompaniment of much laughter and I never saw him hit, nor did I even see a nasty type with a strong arm really trying to catch him out and hurt him...

Night hours of training, during a break, resting in a plantation, back against a cool, dry stone wall, sometimes reaching up to pull a green fig from the tree above...

The pleasure of sitting shaded inside a stone structure over a well from which water was constantly drawn by means of a bucket-chain contrivance; inside, beautiful coolth enhanced by the sound of dripping water, outside, in a temperature of about 90 degrees Fahrenheit, a mule trudged round and round to work the gadget which brought up the water — resting in there was one of my ideas of heaven...

And the battered roller-skating rink I'd come across on one of my outings with Hayson... Beside the sea, on a headland just off the coast road near the barracks the Battalion occupied for our first few weeks in

Malta; nobody in attendance, it seemed. We opened a gate by the ticket kiosk and walked in. The floor of the rink was in poor condition, patched and filled by someone who obviously didn't know how to do the job. After a while, a smallish man approached and told us that, since the war started, hardly a soul used the rink, but for sixpence we could hire skates and stay as long as we wished. Although we had little money, this bargain was too tempting to turn down. As we inexpertly teetered, laughing and joking, or, when fortune favoured, glided between those lumpy patches — paying for our carelessness if we didn't — a recurring thought entered my mind and wouldn't go away: "There's a war on"... A scruffy old roller-skating rink it might be, deserted by all except for two boys larking about, but what a setting. A blue, cloudless sky, sea on this side, sea on that, all to be enjoyed indefinitely, whereas a year ago a cheap, Sunday excursion by rail would have yielded perhaps three hours on some English beach or promenade, the weather would have been uncertain, likely as not wet, grey, chilly...

But perish memories like that and above all appreciate this present loveliness. And I did, I really did. Every moment of every day men are being mutilated, shot to the point of collapse, killed, buried when found. I joined the Army to join them. But wise men have decided that a reprieve shall be mine for a while, so be grateful. I did not share these thoughts with others, perhaps fearing ridicule. On the other hand, of course, I never knew what the other chaps were thinking, did I? Hayson and I skated on...

Brought back to earth by a pal asking me if I'd fixed up my kip (somewhere to sleep), I followed his directions to the small area allocated to our section and was surprised to find I had a small bed, of sorts, to myself. Much of the first deck below had been ingeniously fitted up with a maze of metal frames providing hundreds of single beds, each with a mattress and two white blankets.

This showed how differently shipping companies honoured their transport agreements with the Government. This company, the Anchor Line if memory serves[157], treated soldiers well. Every morning, we had hot bread or rolls with first-rate coffee, boiled eggs distributed in large string bags, or bacon served from large, hot dishes with lots of lovely bacon fat to soak our bread in. They served daily two other good meals, each equal to our usual dinners on land. Fine-flavoured yellow apples, kept in a barrel, could be bought at one penny each.

The pity of it was that we stayed aboard so briefly. Rumour, put about with some confidence, had us bound for India, but that order must have been cancelled, for we disembarked at Alexandria in Egypt.

I was amazed to witness scenes of great cruelty on the quayside, where huge, black men supervised gangs of workers, lashing them frequently with long cane swishes. If this wasn't slavery — which we had been assured at school was long ago abolished — then what could it be called?[158] Nevertheless, the men chanted as they heaved and hauled and I supposed the small wages they received might ensure sustenance for their families.

Catering for the feeding and general wellbeing of troops in transit was well organised at this busy port. They had been doing the job for years and their efficiency showed in marked contrast to places where temporary wartime officials controlled organisation. So we had a good meal, an hour or so of rest, then found ourselves climbing into open railway wagons.

Someone could no doubt have explained why trucks, not carriages, were chosen for a journey through mostly sandy country under a scorching Egyptian sun; if wagons it had to be, then why not covered ones? It was all accepted at that time as part of the soldier's lot, so we sat on the hard boards or occasionally stood up to give our backsides a rest. When the track ran through a cutting, fine sand swirled around us and caused discomfort. No singing to be heard: a sure sign that Tommy Atkins — as soldiers were fondly, or patronisingly, known — was not amused.

Cairo proved to be the destination. After climbing out of the trucks, we were allowed to fill our water bottles and eat hard biscuits and melting cheese. Then we started marching through busy Cairo streets till we reached a quieter district, mainly residential and, I guessed, favoured by fairly wealthy people. After that, the road became more of a track, the open-sided electric trams no longer clattered by, and soon the only buildings in sight were Army barracks.

I hoped we could anticipate another spell of life in solid buildings with shaded walkways and roofs. I was wrong. We followed a track by the outer wall of the barracks and soon moved clear of all buildings while, to left, right, and before us, stretched a vast area of sand. However, we came to apparently chaotic heaps of items dumped at intervals and in orderly lines. These we duly assembled into tents, each the home of ten or more men — in fact, at a pinch, 20 men could lay down in a bell tent, but not comfortably, nor healthily.

A tent town soon appeared, a rough board named each "street" from First onwards, a number was stuck on each tent, and a list of occupants hung on the pole at the front. So we had addresses, purely for administrative purposes, of course. Meanwhile, nearby, men of the Royal Engineers erected the frames of several large huts, in due course adding roofs and walls composed of what looked like rush or raffia mats. They left large openings in place of doors or windows and, while not intended to be sun-proof, the huts provided cool, shady areas where we could take our meals and recreation.

We discovered that other engineers were busily connecting up systems of water pipes, the provision including showers in cubicles made of that same matting. When, later, I heard that we were temporarily under the command of the Indian Army, I appreciated that they specialised in efficient housing and sanitation for troops frequently on the move in hot, dry climates.

The intense interest I had always felt in new sights, sounds, and smells once more dominated all my waking hours. Thoughts and vague fears regarding future assignments I pushed to the background — and here, on the edge of the desert, the romantic ideas of life in the Middle East culled from short stories in cheap magazines appeared to be based on fact.

At that time, some agreement between the British and Egyptian Governments, a pal told me, demanded that each of our soldiers be supplied with two new blankets. True or not, we were each given two wonderful, bright-red blankets, with stripes of brilliant hues at each end. At night, it turned cool, and wrapped in these fine-quality wool blankets we hoped, some of us, that we looked like the sheiks about whom we had heard love-lorn ladies singing in church-hall concerts back in England. Their new smell pleased me tremendously; I made a hollow in the ground for my hips and laid down my groundsheet, placed my kitbag as a pillow, wrapped one of the gorgeous rugs around me and laid the other loosely over the top of it... luxurious soldiering indeed.

Early on our first morning in this camp at Abbasieh, just outside Heliopolis[159], two Arabs with a cart drawn by a donkey passed through our lines selling large baked-clay jugs capable of holding about a gallon of liquid. The jugs were cheap and the sellers told their customers how to make best use of them. So we dug a hole inside our tent, filled the jug with cold water, covered the open top, and buried it. Next day we had only to scrape away the sand, remove the cover and dip in to enjoy an almost ice-cold drink.

Then, with what joy did we learn that old wax-whiskers, the villainous Battalion Quartermaster, had remained in Malta, his department now placed in the care of the young Lieutenant Booth who had guarded our interests since the rather comical mutiny some time back. He made his rounds in the straw-mat hut at dinner-time to inspect the food and told us that — in addition to their blanket-supply commitment — the Egyptian authorities were obliged to provide money for additional food for our troops. As he said, the meat we had just eaten — or not — was very tough, but nothing better could be bought for love nor money. The sweet potatoes that went with it were strange to us, but there were no ordinary spuds to be had. So he proposed to spend the additional funds on canned goods, meats if available, otherwise fruits from a big importing company.

A sound businessman, he looked after our interests carefully. Most men would have helped themselves to something to repay them for the extra work and still believed themselves to be honest, though quite mistakenly. But we knew instinctively that he would not take the kitty, for he was a rare, honest man; he would not deviate even by a hair's breadth from the straight and narrow path, no margin of doubt, just honest or dishonest. Those who believe that a little scrounging is excusable merely give support to the "criminal fraternity". I learnt in that war that "lifting", "borrowing", "finding" or "scrounging" became a habit with many men, one which made them bad comrades in difficult times.

With no training schemes nor other compulsory activities to occupy us during the first few days at Abbasieh, I was able to explore a great sandy hill at the rear of the camp. The story spread that a big battle had been fought there some years earlier and, since then, sandstorms had buried the buildings which stood there. How, during a war already claiming thousands of lives, I could possibly feel excited while prowling over a former battlefield I cannot explain. I seriously hoped to stumble on some wonderful trophy. I didn't, though odd bones I came across were possibly of human origin and I did identify one as a thighbone.

Climbing to the top of the hill, though, I had a fine view across part of Cairo to a group of pyramids. I decided a trip to see them was essential and, on returning to camp, applied for a chit for 24 hours leave.

I spent a piastre — then worth tuppence ha'penny — on a donkey ride to the main road in Heliopolis, and there boarded an open tram. You took your place on a seat which spanned the width of the tram and the conductor made his way to you, standing on the footboards which ran the length of each side. Somehow he clung on, took money and issued tickets, occasionally beating off small boys who tried to secure a free ride.

On alighting, one of these boys halted my progress by placing a shoeshine block in front of me and endeavouring to lift one of my very heavy-booted feet on to it. I resisted, shouting, "No money, empshi!" — a handy word I had already learnt. Force was necessary to remove the obstacle. Then, for a piastre, I bought a book of useful phrases expressed in French, English (sort of) and Arabic spelt out phonetically in English characters. I remember from it "*tala-hena*" (come here), "*saeeda*" (good-day), "*empshi allah*" (go away), "*mush quois*" (no good), and a funny one, "*ruk shooh*" (translated as "up to shit") — I never knew when to use that last one.

I wandered, shop-gazing and trying to decide why these places with their attractive displays interested me far more than those in London suburban streets — until I bumped into Tim Thane from my old H Company. Assuming that all Englishmen would prefer to stick together in foreign parts, he joined me. I was pleased in one way, almost annoyed in another. He wasn't interested in meandering and looking around, and I hoped he would soon push off, but he was convinced that we should spend the day together. I had little money and that little came under threat when, inevitably, he needed a drink. I should be a churl if I didn't pay my whack.

That's how it went. Within a few minutes of our entering the drink-shop, I had four glasses of some very potent brew under my belt, and less money in my pocket. You notice I don't call the place a "pub" — it bore no resemblance to one. Comfortable chairs, small, marble-topped tables, waiters wearing white jackets, fezzes on their heads. Customers probably all Egyptian, apart from us. Most of them wore European-style suits with, again, fezzes; a few had robe-like garments, but none of them wore the white nightshirts, as I regarded them, of the manual workers. So Tim had probably landed us in a pricey joint and I was living it up in a style far beyond the limits of my small income.

Those four glasses of the strong stuff had made me drunk. I thought I was concealing that fact as I essayed to rise from my chair. It must indeed have been a high-class place for I had hardly fallen back into my seat when a waiter placed a small dish of radishes in front of me, indicating with a couple of words and several expressive actions that if I ate them my head would clear and my gait would be steady. He asked for no money and appeared happy and satisfied, so I concluded he had helped himself to tips when changing my five-piastre pieces.

Poorer, but wiser as to the medicinal properties of radishes, we resumed our stroll, and were soon joined by a native who wore a gown of pleasing colour, with fez and sandals for trimmings. No conversation with him took place for some while. Tim and I chatted and we glanced at the fellow from time to time. Neither of us ventured to state what we feared, but the man smiled when he caught us looking his way. Our mistake had been in not telling him to go away immediately he started to walk near us.

Later, he insisted that we go, with him as guide, to the Pyramids, the Sphinx, and other wonderful sights. I told him that we had no money, but he just smiled and said "You come" and "My name is Abdul". We both made it clear we could not afford a guide.

Nevertheless, we found ourselves gazing at the Pyramids and then at the Sphinx[160], before walking along a sort of road below ground level where there were many carvings, and an outstanding figure — I seem to remember being told it represented Rameses. I just couldn't take an interest in these marvellous things, because this man's job was obviously to guide tourists around and impart his knowledge to them for a monetary consideration and I had no money to spare and I wasn't a tourist. Both of us had tried to convince the chap about our poverty, but he just smiled and continued his spiel.

Come the time when nature demanded relief, and who could I turn to but him? At breakneck speed we followed him along crowded streets, presently left the busy part of town and in a narrow passageway climbed stone steps in a poor sort of dwelling and finished up in a small room with a stone floor in the centre of which was a circular hole, nothing else. That had to do, but the self-conscious performing over that hole with an audience added one more humiliation to the day.

Tim Thane didn't appear to be worried. "I'll put my boot up his arse if he doesn't *empshi* soon," he once whispered to me. But he didn't do it. It occurred to me that we were in an Eastern city, had no idea of its geography, and knew only five or six words of the language, so we had better play Abdul's game for the time being.

We three strolled along narrow streets where Arabs of all ages jostled each other and us and no Europeans were to be seen, civilian or military. Thane still looked untroubled. But perhaps he hadn't read such hair-raising tales as I had about trusting English people being set upon, robbed, and left to die in just such murky passages as these.

My faith in our man's good intentions revived considerably when we unexpectedly found ourselves in a bazaar, the stalls displaying metal objects of many kinds. Such a hammering and tapping was going on around us, such beating of brass and copper with mallets and hammers, such chasing of fine patterns on trays and bowls and shapely vessels as made me wonder where this vast output of ornamental metal might be disposed of. To moneyed travellers, I presumed, if any still came by in wartime. Those informative short stories in weekly magazines had left me with the conviction that much of the stuff sold to tourists in marketplaces Middle-Eastern and beyond had first seen the light of day in Birmingham, but the goings-on in this market persuaded me otherwise.

Still, a boy soldier with few piastres in his pocket could neither do justice to the genuine nor spot the fakes. Since I couldn't buy, I tried to give the busy craftsmen the idea that I couldn't see either; a white stick might have helped, but that idea hadn't even been thought of in those distant days (I think they came into common use during the '30s).

Soon we passed along a narrow path on either side of which men displayed carpets and rugs, all presumably of local manufacture. Fortunately, most of the merchants were away out at the mosque or dinner or otherwise engaged. The occasional exception squatted either behind a hookah, the loading and lighting of which was a home industry by itself, or on a sample of stock, propped up by piles of rugs, and so deep in thought their eyes had closed, their chins resting on their chests. So we were able to admire some of their lovely, colourful rugs and carpets, but without any knowledge of their true worth.

The presence of our unwanted guide had relieved us of the shoeshine boys' attention, so perhaps we owed him something. Having now returned to the street where the electric trams ran, we assumed that Abdul felt the time had come to part. Thane still felt free of obligation, but I thought that life must be very difficult for such men since war had put an end to the Cairo tourist business. We talked about the matter for a while. When I pointed out that we had, at least, the certainty of being fed, clothed, and some sort of roof over our heads, while the poor blighter still keeping pace with us probably had a family to look after, Thane said I was a fool to bother about such things.

He eventually agreed to add two piastres to the three I had decided to give, and when an open-sided tram stopped beside us, I put the money into Abdul's hand, we slid into a seat, and that wretched situation came to an end.

On arriving at Abbasieh, we had worked so hard to set up our camp I had not noticed another, very large camp quite nearby — many tents and marquees, bigger than ours and of different shapes, but they lacked the matting huts where we rested and ate.

We were not allowed to go into their tent lines and they never came into ours, but I learned they were a contingent of the Australian Army, the first to come over to help with the war; fine physical types most of them, equal to the best we had, superior to the majority of our chaps in physique, and with an independence of spirit which made our strict military discipline look suspiciously like oppression. An officer gave orders, but in a manner which permitted a strong, healthy man to retain what he regarded as his self-respect. Yet what had to be done was done, as far as I could judge.

Gambling was forbidden to us and, officially, it may have been to them, but a mighty sight worth seeing was the Australian Crown And Anchor school. Soon after dusk, quite some distance from their camp, a line of little lights would commence to twinkle. Curiosity lured me over there, spiced by the knowledge that, if our Military Police caught me near those wicked Aussies, I'd be in real trouble. I believe I planned to vanish into the dark desert if trouble threatened, and make my merry way back to our camp later.

I found a long line of improvised desks, a space of several yards between each of them. A couple of candles on each desk illuminated the Crown And Anchor board — actually a leatherette sheet, easily folded up and pocketed in an emergency, with the six symbols of the game printed on it. The operator sat on a box and called out his line of persuasion or temptation, such as "Come on, me lucky lads! The more you put down the more you pick up. Who'll have a bet on the old mudhook[161]?"

Some operators always had a group of punters around them, others did less business. Why should some be more successful than others, even there at the edge of the desert? All had the same to set-up, although they did vary the odds. The lowest offer made was to double your money if the symbol you'd backed turned up when the dice was thrown. Perhaps the variations which could be introduced by ingenious operators attracted men who applied careful thought to their gambling. Watching from my respectful distance, I was very impressed, at times amazed, at the quantity of money which changed hands.

Looking along the line against the blackness of the desert night, down-turned faces of operators and punters registered complete concentration on the business of money-making, oblivious to any possible interference — or police raid. I did hear that, several times, groups of disgruntled losers had assembled way out of sight, then charged, grabbing such cash as they could, knocking desks over, dousing lights and vanishing, hopefully unrecognised.

Each morning the most hideous cacophony imaginable assailed our ears. A crowd of Egyptian Army musicians came out of their barracks some distance away from camp — but not far enough — and, standing about two yards apart from each other, filled a big square bounded by posts and ropes. Their instruments varied, brass and woodwind of types unknown to me.

People today speak of "doing your own thing". Those Egyptians did just that with fine enthusiasm; each man blew and blasted his own thing for an hour and a half to two hours each morning. No bandmaster could have coped with the volume of noise. Who needed band parts anyway, when untutored men could create such a musical pandemonium? I have only heard its equal when, on radio or television, an orchestra has tackled a piece by one of the ultra-modern composers.

I was able to approach fairly close to the melodious military one morning and, contrary to my suspicions, the hoots and yowls were not created by bandsmen being flogged or tortured; no, the lads were enjoying themselves. Each stood on the spot on which he had been placed and blew into his flute or squawker or trumpet until told to desist. The result was hellish, the purpose of the exercise incomprehensible.

After the next payday, I again secured a pass to spend some time in Cairo, and set off, this time joyfully — having for company my brother Ted whom I liked above all men.

I knew his Company included some tough, Cockney characters and I admired the confident way in which he lived among them. Never on the defensive, always able to convince them of his equality, even with the most belligerent; at that very moment he was short of three front, top teeth, knocked out in the good cause of supporting his self-assertiveness. So, good to be out on the town with him for a few hours; I had made one or two pals, good fellows, in our Signals Section, but my brother... I revelled in his yarns and confidences, would have gone anywhere with him. We walked around that strange town until we stood at the entrance of a great mosque — was it the Blue Mosque[162]? We assumed we should not enter.

I told Ted of prickly-heat spots which, in addition to causing irritation between my fingers, also adorned my belly. We found a chemist's shop, but the French proprietor spoke no English. Who needed speech anyway? I showed him my hands, briefly exposed my tum, and he soon mixed up a potful of ointment which, in the two or three days following, completely cured the rash.

The remainder of a very happy afternoon and evening we spent in a beautiful park or gardens. We used the intense heat to great advantage, I would claim, since we were able to lounge in large, comfortable chairs under big trees, and enjoy ice-cold beer or lager or soft drinks of unknown, but delicious flavours. Yet my boyish palate best appreciated the Egyptian version of ice cream. It came in two-inch squares, half an inch thick, and in two colours; it was hard, firm, smooth, with lovely flavours. How did they achieve its fine texture, its hardness which prolonged the pleasure of placing small pieces of it in the mouth and enjoying the tasty, melting process?

At dusk, the place gradually came to life. We had paid a small sum to enter the park, and now we perceived that some free entertainments would be our reward. We saw an open-air cinema with the screen set well back in a recess, making the pictures visible even in daylight. Chairs and tables were set up and waiters available. Elsewhere, we found a stage on which acrobats and other performers displayed their skills.

A smaller show gave me my first view of genuine belly dancing. Accompanied by the kind of noise to which I had become inured back at the camp, but enhanced by rhythmic percussion, we saw dark-skinned females circle the stage, gyrate, or gradually sink to their knees, the while their bellies kept up spasmodic circular movements to the time of the music. Ted said the dances were designed to get a man going, but I thought he might do himself an irreparable injury if he attempted anything while those violent abdominal movements were occurring. Happy days.

We heard one day that some Australians had gone to the Wasser where the whores did their business. Because men had caught disease from the women there, the Aussies had smashed up several houses; soldiers told tales of furniture thrown out on to the street, pianos chucked from upper storeys, fires started[163].

The Australians continued to make a lively impression on the less flamboyant British. One morning so much noise, so much shouting and banging came from the Australian camp that, despite our rules, many of our lads went over to investigate. Along one side of their camp, traders had been allowed to set up temporary stores and stands. There, I heard, an Aussie could buy almost anything he might require, and you could think it significant that no trader wished to do similar business near our encampment. "English soldier no good. No money!" — I'd heard that one before! The Aussies were paid on more generous lines so their custom was worth courting.

In view of what now followed, it's possible that those traders wished they had been content with the minuscule profit which would have been theirs had they dealt with us.

I believe I'm right in saying the British Mediterranean Expeditionary Force canteens had set up a marquee with the colonial boys where some of the local traders could supply smoking requisites, groceries and beers in a more official setting. When I joined the dense crowd milling around the trading area, I found that the dinkum Aussies had taken over. The long counter of the nearest store was exposed to the mob and a man stood on it, comically conducting some sort of auction. Men rifling through the stock handed him articles for which he pretended, with coarse humour, to accept bids from the crowd. The highest bidder never secured the goods because the man up above always threw them in another direction and the recipient paid nothing.

All sorts of horseplay was going on around me, and soon groups of men appeared carrying large, metal cooking pots filled with beer. They had raided the official canteen and ladled out the liquor to any man who had his mess-tin handy. With strong beer inside them even the timid became bold. When stocks of merchandise to loot ran out, smashing up the various stalls and shelters became a competitive occupation.

Finally, when all appeared to have been demolished, a simple fellow who hoped to sell ice-cream from a tub on a small donkey-drawn barrow was foolish enough to cross behind the shattered trading area. I heard his pleas and protests; he and his donkey survived unharmed, but barrel and contents vanished. And that was that.

Next day, the lads from Down Under departed — men who had any of the pilfered goods were told to hand them in…

I was sorry about it all, feeling that a crop of hatred had been sown that day, quite unnecessarily.

A period of general unease now set in. No more trips to Cairo town, no rooting about up my hill of mystery. We were ordered to wear our heavy uniforms and return the cotton drills and our lightweight sun helmets to the Quartermaster — but the sun didn't vanish in sympathy.

We were given new short rifles with long bayonets to replace the ancient long rifles with short bayonets turned in on Malta. The brains of Britain had been busy. There must have been some significant advantage in this change of arms, though what it was eluded me.

Next, brand new signalling equipment came our way; a clash of interests resulted because, at the same time, we Signals men were ordered to rejoin our Companies for training in the use of the new rifles, while the officers on the communications side wanted us to spend every moment available learning about the new telephone, telegraph, and electric signal lamps. The latter involved making our way in darkness over fair distances from one point to another using only illuminated compasses, meanwhile improving our speed at sending and receiving messages. So, with neither set of trainers relenting, they kept our section busy all day and half the night.

A sharpness and impatience was abroad. Officers told us we lacked diligence and application and had fallen well behind other Battalions in our Brigade. Our Brigade? Where *were* the other three Battalions which comprised it? Where was that marvellous band and my hero, the big-drum wizard with the leopardskin? Come to think of it, where was our Colonel? Our corpulent RSM Cole? And the dashing Major who mysteriously appeared among us one day in Malta? — his appearance, his bearing, the very epitome of an officer of that rank, his blatant uselessness to a wartime Army balanced by his ornamental qualities.

Have I told you about how, on practice manoeuvres in Malta, that handsome gent plucked me from my humble job as a Lance Corporal in charge of a line of signals communications and handed me the reins of his horse and his fly-whisk and told me to keep in sight of him as he wandered along? That took some explaining to my officer later, but I dared not have disobey or argue with the Major. Probably nobody knew or cared what the old boy was doing; probably Headquarters had attached him temporarily to us to keep him out of mischief. He looked as though he belonged in the upper-bracket, and his horse had peculiar hind legs — if he made it trot, the hind legs moved stiffly as though made of wood, most weird.

Anyway, he had stayed behind in Malta and so, I gradually concluded, had a number of others. It was ominous.

Paybooks for use on active service were issued to each of us — columns for amounts paid, date, and signature of the officer who made the payment. The last page was printed in the form of a will. It was not obligatory to use this, but it would be useful in the event of a soldier's death.

Death? A certain tension built up inwardly at the possibility thus openly presented. In the excitement of the early days of the war, the remote prospect of being killed or wounded had appeared an acceptable risk which all Britons must face, and an early dispatch to the front line would probably have settled the issue before one had very much time for contemplation of all the possibilities.

However, my Mediterranean sojourn, with all its pleasant experiences, had conditioned me for an indefinite period of such unwarlike soldiering, with no bangs bigger than those made by the bass drummer, no sounds more distressing to the ear than those produced by those Egyptian bandsmen.

An inner resistance to all forthcoming horrors would be necessary to conceal the truth about me from my comrades — I was actually scared windy, as it was termed, but I must remain the only one aware of this. While behaving as normally as possible, I would maintain this preparedness for any dire possibility, always be one step ahead of the enemy who happened to have the bullet or shell with my name on it.

Thereafter, although I joined in fun and games and general conversation with those around me, I never fully relaxed. The perpetual awareness of danger, which wild creatures display at all times, became part of my way of life — my defence against the risks which would soon beset me. Having settled into this new animal-instinctive preparedness, I could do my work and, when necessary, exercise the petty authority of my one stripe with ease, realising that at least some of my mates must be feeling a bit of tension, a twinge of anxiety.

Soon, we were on the move once more, with not a word of explanation, nor hint of destination. We spent two days beside a railway, at a place called Sidi Bishr, then off to Alexandria…[164]

And there I was, high up on the deck of a ship, chatting happily with brother Ted and looking downwards at men still climbing up the steep gangway, loaded with full equipment. Ted sat on the deck, his back against a cabin wall, obviously somewhat uneasy. This actually pleased me, I recall, because if my strong, assertive older brother could feel like that, I could be excused for worrying a bit.

At long last, only five or six of our men remained on the Quayside and now I felt quite confident about the future, doubtless encouraged by Ted's presence with me on a ship about to take us — where?

He remained seated, taking no interest in what was happening around us. I observed that a Company Quartermaster had lined up the few men still on the quay to "call the roll". He looked around and spoke to the men, then commenced climbing the gangway, calling loudly. It was someone's name he shouted, other voices on the ship repeated it and a shock, a wave of grief, shook me: "Private Norcliffe, G Company!"

Those near us urged my brother to show himself and get the thing finished. "It's my missing teeth," he told me. "The doctor refused to pass me till I have some replacements, false ones. They told me I couldn't go with the boys, but I thought I might swing it by keeping out of sight." With barely time to shake hands, he was hustled off and down the gangway. I kept him in sight. We waved goodbye during all the time we could still see each other.

Gone was the happiness which had returned to me when we so fortunately got together on that ship. Now I felt only the grim prospect of a very difficult and doubtful existence for an unknown length of time in some strange land. I felt very sad until a chap who had witnessed Ted's departure revealed a good side of the affair. "He'll be all right whatever happens to you, the lucky devil," he said. And I thought, that *was* how *I* felt about it, and I hoped Ted would remain in Egypt for the duration of the war.

PART FOUR

1915-1916

WAR:

GALLIPOLI

Chapter Twenty-Six

We slipped out of Alex very quietly. Back over the stern of the ship lay the town, already too distant for buildings to be identifiable. To the left — the east — I could see a sandy area from which, I guessed, lucky soldiers would be able to swim; to the right, buildings gradually became fewer in number — an oil storage depot, a lighthouse, a long sandbank, nothing beyond that but desert... At Sidi Bishr we had all enjoyed an excellent bath in square tanks, each accommodating several men. I was to recall that bath on many occasions during the coming months.

I laid my equipment on the floor of the hold in a small area allotted to our Signals Section — in addition to all the standard infantry and specialist Signaller impedimenta I listed when we left Malta, alongside the water bottle on the right hip we now bore a haversack with its very important contents: a can containing a block of solidified methylated spirit and could be made into a burner, and "iron rations" comprising a bag of small, hard biscuits, single packets of beef cubes, tea and sugar, and a can of Maconochie's stewed beef[165] — this last, one of that war's great successes. To broach these rations without the permission of an officer was a serious crime; they were to be used in grave extremity only.

The whole of this weighty collection could be easily shed by unfastening the belt buckle and slipping out of the shoulder straps. But I had become very aware that I could not cast my rifle aside so carelessly. On active service, it must never leave a soldier's side. Headquarters had a record of its number and, if it was found on the battlefield unaccompanied by a fit, wounded, or dead owner, that man would face trial by court martial.

Having dumped our loads, several of us explored the ship. Rather old, long and narrow, she'd plied the North Atlantic route, usually as a cattle-boat, someone told us. Apart from a few cabins, she lacked sleeping accommodation so, as a troopship, she could be used for comparatively short journeys only. That pretty well settled our minds as to our destination: it would be north of Alex, just a day or two, according to speed and interference, if any, by enemy submarines.

Our machine gunners busied themselves lashing their weapons to the ship's rails at suitable points. As far as we could see, the ship's own armament consisted of a length of telegraph pole mounted on blocks, apparently to mimic a naval gun — a contraption which might mislead and scare an enemy lookout man, provided he had faulty eyesight or a dirty telescope. A thousand men at risk because some daft idiot at the Admiralty didn't prepare for a war which all but he knew was coming...

We had plenty of tea, bread and stew on that trip, and what more could hungry soldiers have asked for? Instinct, more than knowledge of what was to come, made me load myself with all I could manage to swallow — the taut, nervous condition, brought on by anticipation of what I feared, had me scheming about any steps I could take to improve my survival prospects.

What bread I, and others around me, couldn't eat, I stored in any space in haversack or pack. Stew couldn't be so readily saved; surplus remained in the big dixies for return to the cooks and probable dumping overboard. But I picked out leftover pieces of meat, dried them off, wrapped them up tightly in an oilskin cap cover, and crammed this little package into my haversack.

Excited speculation about our destination, a lot of rather forced, hopefully humorous remarks about it, and eagerness to listen to anyone who claimed to have heard something official — these things, along with meal times, walks around the limited areas available, and frequent catnaps on the hard decks, all provided distraction during this period of inertia and ignorance.

Many took their turns at lookout duty, searching the sea's surface for any kind of vessel, but in particular for that slim, upright stick which might be the periscope of a submarine. Signallers had been warned to note any flashing lights that proved readable. In addition, I was told that, should the ship be at anchor in the darkness, I must take one man with me and report to the officer on the bridge. I would send or receive lamp signals as required and my mate would write down the responses.

Around dawn on an overcast morning, we passed an island which may have been inhabited or merely just a large rock. Soon another appeared and vanished behind us. Several others followed... and I hadn't entirely wasted my recent schoolboy geography lessons, I felt: these must be islands of the group our teacher had called the Grecian Archipelago. I didn't hear the lads on the ship call them that — "Greek islands" was, of course, good enough.

Still no information about our future movements. In fact, as had been the case on our previous voyages, our officers mainly confined themselves to the upper deck, probably resting in the cabins most of the time. Well, their privilege, for when the action — whatever it was — started, they would be responsible for giving instructions to their men and must show themselves to be steady and capable of carrying out whatever part of the general plan we had been allotted.

Even a humble Patrol Leader in the Boy Scouts had felt the weight of responsibility which bears down on one who must make decisions affecting others. Praise for good leadership, criticism for bad, could enhance or diminish personal pride during peacetime but, on active service, men's futures were at stake and a junior officer might blunder and wreck major strategy at the cost of many lives. Our men always felt happiest when commanded by men from that class which traditionally produced fine officers. But, obviously, there were not many of that calibre around — fewer and fewer in a war which consumed men daily by the thousand. Still, the Army tried to come up with and train new top-notchers. Good substitutes. There had to be.

Our ship entered a perfect natural harbour[166] with several large ships at anchor — among them liners and smaller passenger vessels, no doubt acting as troopships, and a big hospital ship, cream with green lines along her sides and large red crosses prominently displayed. Many small craft moved around them, including a lot of lighters similar to those I had seen on the Thames — metal vessels with steel decks, all cargo carried below.

As it grew dark, I reported to our Sergeant and told him whom I proposed to take to the bridge for night duty. Up there we found a fairly junior officer of the watch and I saluted him and stated why I had come. This puzzled him. He told me he could read any Morse messages that came by signal lamp. He seemed disposed to dispense with our help. I offered to act as his writer if that would be helpful, and he admitted he would need one. Then we two landlubbers posted ourselves so each of us could scan 180 degrees and the ship's officer probably had several longish rests in whatever shelter was available.

During the evening, a nearby ship signalled an invitation to our Captain to visit. Later, we received a longer message completely in cypher. One could not even tell to whom or from whom it had come, but we got the sender to repeat every detail because we feared the slightest error would bring down bad trouble on our heads and disgrace to our Signals section. I found myself trembling as I handed the completed message to the officer. It all seemed so much more important than any previous job I'd done, no doubt because I was working with a different service and felt I had to do well and earn a good opinion.

Dawn came and we rejoined our lads, had some food and settled down for a good long sleep.

Perhaps we did have a few hours before being roused to consume as much stew, chunks of bread and mugs of tea as we could manage. Then we got our first sight of "on active service" postcards and green envelopes. The cards had messages printed on them and all we were allowed to do was strike out the lines which were not applicable: "I am well/I have been wounded" etc. I filled one in immediately, addressed it to my family, and handed it in.

Told to prepare to leave the ship, we strapped on all our gear again. This set the tension mechanism really racing — although I flattered myself no one knew about that. If a boy like me tried to assume the cool, steady demeanour of a man in full control of his emotions, then an older chap might behave with gaiety, perhaps sing a few lines of a bawdy song, or take the micky out of a mate who was the usual butt of his jokes. The thing not to do was stay silent and look gloomy — that way you would be labelled "windy" and lose all your pals. You had to consider that others might be feeling worse than you, but they didn't let it show. So it may be that battles fought inwardly to preserve the good opinion of one's fellows made possible some of the bigger victories on the battlefield...

One man who simply had to win the personal inward struggle was the commissioned officer in charge of men in the front line. This subject I'd heard debated many a time; I don't recall discussions about the deeper feelings of fellow rankers, but officers being a class apart, loved or hated, we expected them to act as the leaders they had set themselves up to be. If they had their men's good will, they carried all our hopes that, in action, we would acquit ourselves well together.

I wondered about those field postcards; anybody else I should tell I was going into action? The dear old Fluters, of course, who had been so good to me in Bunbridge. With appropriate deletions, I addressed a field-card to them. It told them I was going to a battlefront, but didn't say which one. My address consisted of my Regimental number, Battalion and "British Mediterranean Expeditionary Force". So just a little guesswork would lead them to the spot or near enough.

One of those smaller ships came alongside and, in the calm water of that natural harbour, it was easy for two of our Companies to go down our gangway and, from the platform at the foot of it, step across and climb the shorter gangway of the smaller ship.

Transfers to other small ships followed and, with three other Signallers I found myself assigned to my old H Company. As our ship moved off, a pal told me that a really big boat we were heading for housed Army Headquarters. The Fluters' card, I thought — could I speed its delivery with a bit of luck? We sailed close enough for me to risk it; a fortunate flick had it spinning nicely and I saw it land on the deck of the *Aragon*[167].

Much too soon for my liking, we were ploughing through a choppy sea. One minute it seemed safe and quiet in harbour, the next out here in a small ship on a grey, cheerless day, bound for God knows what. Tired out, I slipped out of my heavy equipment and, with pack for a pillow, soon stretched out on the deck and forgot fears and fancies in deep sleep. That must have lasted for an hour or two, because when a cold shock woke me I got to my feet in fading daylight with the ship heading into a strong wind — a wave had lapped over the side, splashed around me and made me jump.

Little harm resulted and I found a more sheltered place near the stern on the other side where I joined a chap leaning on the rail there. It was too dark for me to identify him. General chat became more detailed after a while, when I remarked that I'd be happier, perhaps, if somebody had told me what we were up to.

This man did tell me — and thus whipped up inner tension to its highest level so far: "We are going ashore at a place where landings commenced some time ago. Unfortunately, that lot haven't done as well as hoped for. There are big hills quite a short distance from the beach and our chaps should by now be on the far side of them, but they're not. We go ashore tonight, advance through their lines and try to get to what was their objective. I don't like it, but we can only do our best."[168]

By then, I realised he was an officer, and I remember surmising to myself that he must have felt deep anxiety and, perhaps, loneliness to have been moved to confide in a young ranker.

He drifted off; I had no idea who he was, nor did I wish to find out. Now I knew what we were to attempt. Still leaning on the rail, I tried to envisage the probable course of events during the hours of darkness now commencing. On past sea journeys, the dark, grey waters and the lighter lines of the ship's wake would have evoked thoughts about their beauty, but now they looked cold, even threatening...

That this small ship's course ran surprisingly close to the shore was revealed only too clearly when a burst of rifle fire had me scurrying to the sea side of the ship. I believed I could see, darker than the general darkness, the top of a cliff mass. Yes, and the sounds of desultory rifle fire came from up there. No bullets zinged past, though, so we were not the target.

Word passed around for all to be ready to disembark and I donned my load, message case, field transmitter, rifle and all — in one hand I gripped a bunch of four signal flags. Whether excitement or fear brought it on I don't know, but I suddenly felt terribly hungry. Then I recalled that I had not eaten since early morning. Nor, as far as I know, had any of our men. Someone had blundered. Or was it usual to land troops on a battlefield with empty bellies?

The sound of the ship's engines changed. We four H Company Signallers stood shoulder to shoulder with the others awaiting the next move.

As Lance Corporal in charge of our small group, I knew that our job would be to supply communication between our Company commander and Battalion headquarters, and perhaps between us and Companies on our right and left. Runners would carry messages between platoons and Company HQ. So I located our Captain and resolved to keep close to him and to have my mates close to me. Ever since our Signals Section had been formed back there in Malta, I had not had much to do with H Company, and the good Captain had not been really aware of my existence. He had his intimates — usually two junior officers and his batman; he called on his Company Sergeant Major in respect of drills and training and procedure when on parade, but as to Signallers he knew nothing, nor did he seem to wish to.

"I can send messages by word of mouth," he told me when jammed together, as we all were on that small ship. We four appeared to be crowding him in that darkness. Proximity to the scent of power boosted my confidence sufficiently for me to disregard any intended rebuff. I'd had my training, I felt that I knew my job, and perhaps felt sorry that the Captain did not appreciate our role. By signals of whatever sort, vital information could be transmitted immediately, even in darkness, whereas messengers might be delayed, get lost, wounded or killed, even over a short distance.

The next part of the military operation was simple. Our small ship carried G and H Companies, and each assembled without fuss on its appointed side of the boat. Where the dark cliff had towered above us, I now saw the lighter colour of the sky. Across a wider stretch of water than earlier, on land rifles fired continuously and artillery lit up the blackness, each flash followed by a bang, a shriek or a strange whine which often increased in volume then ended up in a big explosion. Guns were being fired with intent to kill and here was my first experience of warfare.

I heard the engine of another vessel chugging nearby for several minutes until it bumped against our ship's side. It had no superstructure, a lighter of some sort. With the decks of the two vessels roughly level, although the sea was choppy, part of our rail was removed, and a voice from the lighter quietly instructed us to "Move across carefully when your turn comes. Watch the rise and fall, then step across."

Those nearest to the gap in the rail started to do as he said. Occasional pauses brought requests to be quick — but careful — and I soon found myself at the edge trying earnestly to estimate the right moment to step across. One foot on the lighter deck, then it rose 12 inches or so, and in the moment while it sank again I forced myself across the slight gap and the weight of my body and all my equipment carried me forward. It was difficult to avoid crashing into men ahead of me, but this I managed somehow and then braced myself to steady the next oncoming bloke. By lucky chance, I hadn't pushed anyone overboard and I certainly didn't intend to be shoved off the lighter by anyone else.

Its deck, I found, was metal — as were the tips and heels of our Army boots, so retaining a good foothold presented difficulties. The chaps around me did afford some support, but they were not to be leant against or grabbed, as their remarks quickly made clear. Certainly, the men on the seaward edge must have had a very dicey trip towards the shore.

A howl became a shriek, then a shattering explosion — and a short silence was followed by numerous thuds as what had gone up came down on the nearby beach. While still at sea I heard for the first time that sad, though urgent call, "Stretcher-bearers!" A tightening of the gut and clamping together of the jaws accompanied an inner alarm which then and many times afterwards seemed to produce an acid-like smell on hands and other parts of the body.

The lighter moved in closer and our Sergeant Major's voice came clear above all other sounds, "Take your turn! Go quickly down the ramp, then form two ranks and follow your leader!" As we faced the shore it seemed that rifle fire came mainly from half-left and a fair distance away. But from a wider range of positions came artillery fire.

With some relief I formed the opinion that the troops who made the first landing had done a good job in clearing the Turks from the beach, but I soon discovered that the occasional sniper had stayed behind to harass and scare by the uncertainty he created. As I took my turn down the ramp, I heard a quiet chat going on between our Company officer and someone ashore. Without pause, in pairs, we followed our leader on to the beach — the while he continued his conversation with the stranger.

We moved uphill for a while, veered right just before reaching the top of a ridge, and shuffled along on this fairly steep slope, left leg bent, t'other extended, an awkward progress, overloaded as I was. When our leader stopped and squatted, we all did likewise along the line. "Stay well below the ridge top and await orders," was the next instruction passed along.

I was in a full tizzy of excitement having been primed by my confiding officer on the ship to expect immediate and violent action. However, when we stayed there for some while, pangs of hunger became pressing — we had not eaten since early morning. In a fairly loud voice, which I hoped would reach our officer's ears, I said I was starving. "Quiet!" came a reproof, but muttering spread along the line, confirming that others also felt empty. A word of mouth message passed from man to man brought a junior officer over and he explained that no rations had been issued since we left the island harbour. Rightly or wrongly, he agreed that we should start on our iron rations.

Fortunate the ridge concealed us, for we were soon lighting our little methylated stoves to heat water in our mess tins. Into this we dropped beef cubes and some of the small, hard biscuits. With this below our belts we felt stronger. I set about chewing dry biscuits as well. A swig from my water bottle, and I felt twice the man.

Soon we arose, advanced over the ridge, and moved on across fairly level country, rather barren, though supporting the occasional clump of trees. We stopped several times, lying prone on the ground, as ordered, while quiet discussions just ahead of me took place. Too dark to see much, but a fair number of bullets whizzed our way. Sometimes they struck the earth nearby with a ffft; once one hit the trunk of a tree near me with a surprisingly loud crack.

We hugged the ground, of course, to let the bullets pass harmlessly above us, but one of those wretched things broke that rule. When one move forward started, young Nibs, more of a boy even than I was, didn't get up. The Captain was told, all paused again, and the shocking news came along that he was dead, shot through the head. Had he been standing up, that bullet would presumably have damaged a foot or ankle. Stretcher-bearers carried him to the beach.

Our first casualty, I thought, young Nibs, the cheerful Cockney; a victim of random firing, not an aimed shot... Later, though, I learned that Nibs was not, after all, the first member of the Battalion killed; old Ewart Walker, the erudite ex-journalist, had died within moments of reaching the beach — a time-fused shell exploded above his head, relieving him of any requirement to further tax his ageing body, and depriving us of a very good comrade.

Heads down now, shoulders bent, we advanced as though we thought this posture offered some protection. I wondered how soon we would reach the position from which our attack would be launched and felt horribly shocked when an order was given to spread out and, in pairs, start digging holes to give us cover from enemy fire. We had to do this before dawn came with only our small trenching tools to help us.

I paired with Bacon, who'd very recently joined the Signallers Section; I didn't know him well and had found him rather taciturn except when something that really concerned him turned up... A few blows with our light tools revealed little ordinary soil — instead, it was hard and broke away in flakes and pieces. In my hand it felt like a soft sort of rock. "This is marvellous," I grumbled. "I suppose we must try, but we shan't make much of a hole in the time we've got."

We slogged away at it, took turns trying to make a hole just long enough for we two to crouch in. As we penetrated a few inches we could hear the sides shedding bits and pieces, which had to be shovelled out. By dawn our hard, non-stop work had excavated a shallow trench about four feet long, two feet wide and two deep, providing very little cover for two now exhausted, shaky, and rather scared youngsters.

We rested in the half-light, tired and hungry. I had that unknown officer's forecast about our future movements constantly in my mind. If Bacon, or any of the others nearby, had been similarly informed, none mentioned it.

Surveying the scene around me, I had doubts about our fitness, at that moment, to advance and capture the heights which loomed above. Facing the hills which, apparently, would be our objective, I saw that someone appeared to have selected a base for our Battalion's attack which was completely exposed to enemy observation and fire. The terrain to our left and half-left rose gradually at first, thereafter steeply. Before us, ridges and several lowish hills. Beyond those, steadily rising country ascending at some distance from us to a considerable height — black hills of daunting aspect, enough to make me despair of reaching their peaks, even without an enemy's presence.

Some of the men had made holes much deeper than ours — having, I gathered, secured picks and shovels from a dump they had discovered. Older and wiser men than I, they had not just blindly obeyed orders to commence digging with puny, trenching tools, but had put brains, eyes and instincts to work and benefited accordingly. In the early days of my military life, I felt inadequate in matters of that sort. The fly men could always secure the extra bit of bread or bully beef, cadge, beg, borrow or steal things to improve their condition or perhaps increase their chance of surviving. Beginning their war with deeper holes than most wasn't bad for a start.

That first morning we had cause to bless Lieutenant Booth, the enthusiastic young officer who had replaced Quartermaster wax whiskers. He did his job of feeding and clothing us with complete dedication and, during the hours of darkness, had applied his energy to bringing forward from the beach some of the stores unloaded from the lighters. A certain sense of security, because enemy artillery had not yet fired on our "advanced" position, encouraged volunteers to distribute food. They gave each of us four rashers of bacon and half a loaf of bread, small paper bags of tea and sugar, and a tin of condensed milk.

One volunteer from each group of four holes was allowed to hang the occupants' eight water bottles over his shoulders and make his way back to a clump of trees and bushes behind which sheltered a mule-drawn water cart. I began to appreciate the varied uses to which those all-metal lighters could be put; men on the deck, food, water and other requirements of war inside them — though I wondered whether their journeys from ships some distance offshore would remain feasible in rougher weather.

Still we huddled there unmolested. We could hardly believe our luck. The mess-tin lid with its fold-over handle made an efficient frying pan and most of us still had the methylated-spirit heaters. I fried the rashers, soaked up the fat with bread and ate that up, then boiled about half a pint of water and dropped some tea, sugar and milk into it. It was good, I felt very much better and happier after that meal.

Some men either had no heaters or found them unsatisfactory so, regardless of their own safety or ours, they lit small fires in the open beside their holes. Our luck gave out at that point. The Turks had either not been looking our way or else observing us with disbelief that we could be so foolhardy, but the smoke offered a perfect target for their range-finders.

Shrapnel shells shrieked our way, burst at a height of 20 to 30 feet and sprayed the area. Howls of pain, calls for help, and the disappearance into their holes of the thoughtless fools who had brought the rain of hurtling metal bullets down on us, all occupied but a few seconds. We had wounded and possibly dead men to care for, but we required a few minutes at least to allow for the shock of this unexpected attack to subside.

And then, almost as unwelcome as the shellfire, came the behaviour of one man, our RSM, who — with his batman — happened to occupy the next hole to the one Bacon and I shared. He briefly showed himself, brandishing a pistol, and shouted: "Keep down! Stay under cover! I'll shoot the first man who shows himself above ground without permission!"

I had not seen much of this gentleman previously, but for a while, in Malta, he had enjoyed immense popularity with the rank and file. He was a Sergeant of Marines, lent to our Battalion to raise the standard of our training, particularly with regard to physical fitness. An exponent of a new style of physical training and drill involving non-stop movement, he would issue rapid, staccato commands which had the trainees bending, stretching, turning this way and that, marching running, flinging their arms about, doing knees-ups (as in Mother Brown), and obeying his exhortations to raise them ever higher.

At the time, we all felt he was the man to make real soldiers out of us amateurs, God's gift to a mob of willing, but unskilled volunteers. So we willingly sweated our guts out in high Mediterranean temperatures, unbelievably anxious to merit the approval of this military Messiah. Even the fact that, during training, he dressed so differently to anyone else, enhanced his attractiveness. He wore navy-blue slacks and a white sweater at the start of a session; as he warmed up, off came the sweater, revealing a smart, white singlet to match his white, canvas shoes — whereas we wore grey shirts and khaki trousers and heavy boots.

Shortly before we left Malta he surprised us all by appearing in a uniform remarkably like that worn by commissioned officers — an arrow on each arm just above the cuff — and there he was, our new RSM, no less. Why was it we felt there was something wrong with his appointment?

Now, in addition to this artillery attack, we faced the threat of bullets from our own RSM's pistol… Realisation of the awful position in which someone's error had placed us, had a bad effect on morale. And the RSM's queer behaviour deepened the gloom. What, I wondered, had he done about helping to get the Battalion into a condition ready to meet the demands which would be made on it? Our officers had no previous experience of active service, but this expert soldier from the famous Marines should surely have consulted with them, adding his experience to their enthusiasm. This we had expected of him, but he failed us on our first night in the front line.

Apparently, when the order to dig in was issued, he and his batman secured pick and shovel and spent the hours of darkness getting his hidey-hole down to a really useful depth. Indeed, over the following days, their excavations became so elaborate that, by design I think, though to what end I could not deduce, they tunnelled through to our hole. It introduced an unwelcome intimacy. My feelings must have shown for this RSM never loved me.

I still expected a sudden instruction would set us hurrying towards those hills in the "extended order"[169] we had been trained to use in attack. But that did not happen.

Instead, we were told to make our holes deeper; hard work indeed for those of us with trenching tools only. Those fortunate enough to have secured picks and shovels improved their holes fairly quickly. Had we been digging in good earth, all of us would have done better, but this curious, flaky rock — grey in colour, layer upon layer of it, each about half an inch thick or less — was difficult to handle. Frustrating, irritating, productive of little but despair.

The men who moved around collecting and filling water bottles, and others who, during the day, returned to the beach for supplies and brought them up to us, did so at great personal risk from Turk shells and bullets. Others routinely in danger because of the nature of their work were our Pioneers; back in Egypt, the Regiment had formed this section composed of men prepared to take care of sanitation. In places without water-flushed WCs, even on the front line, these men erected shelters, emptied and cleansed the waste buckets and seats housed in them, and sprinkled chloride of lime about the place.

Now, in the battlefield, their work was of great importance. Canvas screens surrounded the bucket areas. With bullets and shells wreaking their havoc, these men exercised great self-discipline in servicing the latrines. Men needing to use them sat in real peril, their excretory movements probably accelerated by bursting shells and whining bullets. Holes appearing in the canvas screens added urgency to these operations.

In fact, the Turks fired ever more frequently as that first day wore on. They took a steady toll on our men, in ones and twos, woundings and killings. Meanwhile, we attempted nothing, achieved nothing as far as we could see, our landing and presence apparently a sad, military waste.

But our second night ashore brought the relief of movement: digging trenches well in advance of our initial position. When darkness fell, large parties stepped forward, armed with picks and shovels. As soon as they started digging, the noise brought shot and shell their way, and stretcher-bearers were kept busy.

Still, they persisted, and soon established a trench system substantial enough for full occupation by half our Companies — the rest of the men and Battalion Headquarters remained in our original position which, despite further efforts to deepen our holes, remained lamentably exposed. Nevertheless, a tendency for some to regard that place as home became evident, although wise men realised the better organised forward trench system offered more protection.

I had to move around constantly; as a Signaller I had no choice. When our comrades built and occupied new trenchworks, we had to run out lines and man the instruments to maintain communications from Battalion HQ to Company and from Company to Company.

Fifty yards or so from one end of that original collection of holes — where I still lodged from time to time — was a clump of trees and bushes... and one morning I was amazed to hear a voice coming from it. It said, "Devine! Devine!" The bearer of that name I knew to be an officer's servant and the voice belonged to Lieutenant Chalk, the Battalion dandy. Crawling that way, I came upon this gent sitting naked in a hip bath and, fortunately, unaware of my presence.

Apparently, not war nor any other damn nuisance was going to deprive this P.G. Wodehouse character of his morning cold tub. As requested, Devine took him a towel. And presumably John Turk had the Lieutenant's permission to resume fighting soon thereafter.

That pale pink figure squatting in that round shallow extra-large frying pan — what in heaven's name had it got to do with war? A few slender trees and straggling bushes screened him from the eyes and rifles of an enemy who gave no quarter and was reputed to castrate and hang by his feet from a tree any infidel foolish enough to allow himself to be captured... An enemy who split lead bullets before firing so that they would spread out when striking bone and cause massive laceration.

Reflecting on this strange apparition, my thoughts moved on from farce and risk to... water supply. We were always restricted to one pint daily per man. So where did the dear Lieutenant's Devine procure more, much more, than this meagre ration for his master's bath? Somebody told me several old wells had been uncovered, but they contained poison. In one, he said, they found a dead Turk. Still acceptable as bath water, I guess; perhaps the batman used that.

I never saw Lieutenant Chalk again, nor did I learn whether he survived the war. Somehow I doubt it.

Chapter Twenty-Seven

We settled in. No more advances. And no more bacon. Most days there were only two items of "solid" food available, namely, hard biscuits and apricot jam. How come? It appeared that, for some weeks, a ship stuffed with these two eatables plus tea, sugar, and canned milk, served as our sole source of supplies. We of the PBI (Poor Bloody Infantry) accepted these rations without question, believing what we were told without doubt or quibble...

At first, the weather stayed hot, very hot. Some troops, not compelled to English standards of hygiene on account of their easy-going colonial habits, unwittingly fed and caused to multiply millions of dirty, fat flies and any foodstuff, or even hot tea, exposed however briefly to their attention instantly turned black with swarms of these filth carriers.

Dysentery plagued the Army and many men existed in a weakened, dazed condition with only moderate chances of survival because they had no opportunity to replace the large loss of body fluid caused by the disease. When they finally collapsed, they had to be carried off to the beach, there to await transport to the Greek island hospital or to Egypt. This scourge spread alarmingly and one missed comrades only to learn that they had succumbed to it.

For a very specific reason, I remained one of the few who steered clear of dysentery throughout that campaign (although I did experience its horrible effects rather later in the war). Around that time, some parcels from home were brought ashore and one of them was for me, the only parcel I received during that campaign. Beautiful goodies delighted and uplifted me from the prevailing gloom. But the package was small, of necessity, and the contents soon vanished, so intense were my hunger and their sweet appeal.

However, there remained two medicine bottles, each containing 200 tablets. Knowing something of the front line's risks of disease, my parents spent some hard-to-spare money on water-purifying tablets, surely one of the most useful purchases they ever made. I dropped one tablet into my daily water ration. I kept the tablets in my tunic pockets and, since one could never undress, this meant I had these life-savers on my person day and night.

We ordinary soldiers, in our trenches and holes in the ground, had no protection from the weather. Time passed, but for me and those among whom I worked, no opportunity for stripping down and washing occurred. Mostly, I would sit on the floor of a trench, headphones over ears, sending or receiving the occasional message. If the trench was narrow, passers-by would step over my legs, exchanging curses if they tripped over them.

I could work more easily in the front-line trench where those on duty stood on a firing step, a ledge about 30 inches above floor level from which they could observe enemy positions — and, on a bad day, stop the occasional sniper's bullet; the step provided a seat for me.

The Battalion had built a recognisable, if roughly constructed, trench system. A front line of bays and traverses, if skilfully used, offered some protection from frontal or flank enemy fire or attack. Some distance behind this and parallel ran a support trench and, a long way further back, a reserve trench. One Company would man the front trench for a spell, then exchange places with the support Company, and finally swap with the reserve.

Front-line duty allowed for very little rest; in support, regular spells of duty and sleep could be arranged; in reserve one might be able to sleep through much of the day, but then you moved forward to do work which could only be done in darkness.

While the trench system suggested permanence, we had some small indication that progress had not been ruled out — we were building up a series of advance posts in "No Man's Land", that horrible space between the combatants' front lines. These "posts" amounted to walls of sandbags. A shell dropping inside one of them would kill or wound all present, more than likely; but this seldom happened, as the target was a small one from the artillery point of view. Shrapnel from airbursts caused casualties but, until the advance posts' walls could be thickened — to at least two sandbags wide — the rifle bullet remained the main threat to the occupants' safety.

All of us had to beware of a constant danger from some Turk marksmen's practice of making careful observations to find places where British troops frequently passed, and setting their rifles on small tripods with their aim fixed on those spots. During hours of darkness, one man could move around, fire each rifle and replace the used bullet. This caused many casualties. Even when sighted on a sandbag wall, each gun's repeated shots had the sand draining away unnoticed in the dark until the next bullet cut through freely and, perhaps, fatally.

Once, in ridiculous circumstances, I garnered the contemptuous dislike of an officer. I had run out a telephone link to an advance post still under construction. After I returned to the front line, bursts of rifle fire from the post brought our Captain out of his hidey-hole; in quite a rage this normally kindly man yelled at me, "What the hell are they up to out there?" Elderly, quite as old as my father, he must have suffered cruelly under the wretched conditions obtaining there. "Get hold of the officer in charge, then give me the phone!"

Easier said than done. To operate the microphone — a small, round thing, containing carbon granules — one pressed its small button, shook it until the granules vibrated against a disc and, with luck, reproduced your voice in the distant receiver. I eventually had Lieutenant XXXX[170] at the other end, so I handed the whole headphones-and-microphone paraphernalia to the Captain. His struggles to fit the phones to his head, then to manipulate the mike were productive of more expletives until he finally gave up the effort and thrust them back at me.

"Take the damn things and repeat exactly what I say," said he. I obeyed his instruction. "Who is speaking up there?" the Captain/I asked. "Lieutenant XXXX," came the reply from the advance post. "This is Captain YYYY." "Yes, sir." "Now, what the devil are your men doing all that firing for?" I repeated the Captain's words exactly, you understand. "Because there's a Turk patrol… (pause)… You're not Captain YYYY, who the devil *are* you?" "Signaller Norcliffe."

A terrific thump landed in the middle of my back. "You bloody fool, you *are* Captain XXXX if I say you are. Chuck it! Give it up if you can't do better than that with your bloody sinecure of a job."

He vanished, but in my ear there snarled the Lieutenant's voice, "Right, Norcliffe, I shan't forget this!" So I had to add one more worry to all the others caused by lack of food, exposure, fatigue, and the constant tension caused by flying shrapnel and bullets.

All hope of quick action and outcome gave way to pessimism engendered by the prospect of enduring a long period of this wretched life with an Army which had no effective leadership. We all felt it and cursed it.

News filtered through that the General in charge of the whole operation, Hamilton[171], lived in a battleship some miles out to sea and sent home wordy reports of our progress — progress of which we, in the front line, were quite unaware. Poetry was his speciality, they said, and he wrote as if for the school history books in flowery language, the sort of bilge which had persuaded children that mass murderers like Napoleon were somehow brave and wonderful men.

From towering hills the Turks looked down on us continually; we lived in their sights from dawn to dusk, and the fact that we sustained some sort of existence in that situation proves how difficult it is to destroy an Army except by physically and individually killing every soldier. But attrition continued every day.

Rough seas meant poor rations, slack organisation of supplies back at the bases resulted in monotonous repetition of the same food items, as with the already mentioned apricot jam and hard biscuits — the oft-abused corned beef became, at times, a welcome luxury. If some bully beef came our way we felt stronger, the nourishment taking effect rapidly in our debilitated bodies. If a piece of bread and a chunk of cheese filtered down through the hands of all those who organised supplies to the ranker, the lowest level of Army life, then there was much slow, careful chewing and such pleasure evinced as would warm the heart of whoever had consigned the delicious grub to such humble men. Unfortunately, long gaps lingered between such treats.

With the best will in the world, our officers could not attain efficient feeding and welfare of their men under active-service conditions. They had not received the necessary training and it was easy to let things slide, to let the willing workers overtax themselves while slackers lurked in places they believed safe spots. A good officer would see that every man had his share of what's available; not many of ours took so much trouble, probably because they themselves were overcome by discomforts and lack of rest and sleep.

Anxious though I was to prove myself a man who could stick it out, I became aware of a slowing down of my movements. But I need not have worried that this might make some suspect I was still too young to be wearing a uniform; everybody knew that disease was just as likely as enemy action to put paid to a man.

So, for reasons obscure to themselves, British troops continued to man outposts and trenches while always aware that a mere three or four miles lay between their front line and the sea.

I did sometimes wonder where our top officers were. One of them, at least — our adjutant[172] — had what it takes I knew, although I saw him once only in our front line… As I sat in a trench with my headphones on, sending or receiving a message, he appeared above me. He stood up there, on the rim of the trench, in a very exposed position, one arm in a sling, his face showing the pain and tiredness he was suffering. Why he was there in that awful condition I did not know. Had a ranker exposed himself thus to enemy fire without good reason, he would have been put on a charge. Obviously wounded, he should have been sent away from the line by the Medical Officer; but then we all knew of that peculiar medico's terrible reputation — I soon gained personal experience of his utter ineptitude.

I recall too that I saw our Colonel[173] only once, and that in the early days, not long after we had come ashore and dug in.

We had gone forward and occupied a series of holes in the ground just vacated by the members of a famous Battalion, by then much reduced in numbers. They had dug these holes into both sides of a gully; somebody appropriately labelled it "Borderers' Gully"[174]. At dusk, just after our arrival there, a party of officers entered the lower end of the gully, walked rapidly through the middle of it and disappeared — among them our Colonel, almost bent double.

"He'll get a medal for this," said somebody, and we concluded he may have come ashore for that specific purpose, for we never saw him again.

I suffered a sad loss in that gully, when we had to leave it and move forward in a hurry. Through all our travels I had carried in my haversack the flageolet I used in the Scouts' band. When I got the chance, I would quietly play some of the choruses then popular, particularly ragtime songs — Everybody's Doing It, You Made Me Love You, and Alexander's Ragtime Band. It seemed to make a link with home for a brief moment.

After having a blow in that gully, I must have laid it down beside me instead of shoving it into my haversack. Then, when we got the sudden order to advance, I forgot it. The loss saddened me, made me feel completely cut off from the old life...

I wanted to talk to somebody like Harold or Len, the intimates of pre-war days. Back in our front line, I moved around the trenches as much as I dared without permission — and got shot at once or twice by the apparently tireless Turk snipers. When I found a hole which sheltered some G Company men, I asked if they could direct me to Harold and their replies shocked me: "He's away on a hospital ship, wounded in a foot. Trouble is, the bullet came from his own rifle. A self-inflicted wound, which means court martial. He has to convince them it was accidental. It happened in the dark in one of these holes in the ground. But how did the rifle muzzle come to be resting on his foot?"

If fear and desperation had driven Harold to do it, I didn't blame him, but I said, "I believe what Harold said and good luck to him". It was a very serious matter, depressing to contemplate, and I tried to find Len, but he had vanished too, wounded or ill.

The Medical Officer mentioned above — he was tall, thin, stooping, and sallow and mournful of countenance — must have escaped from a civilian practice which, because of his ignorant incompetence, had yielded barely enough money to keep him supplied with watery soup and a few crusts. Some of his diagnoses and treatments were so ridiculous as to be unbelievable by all except his victims.

Early on, I developed a very painful toothache and, when I eventually traced him to the hole in the ground wherein he lurked, his advice to me came in the following words — do believe me, this is true — "I have no instruments with which to extract teeth. Take this Number 9 pill[175] for your bowels. Perhaps the artillery can help you by attaching a string from your bad tooth to a shell. When the gun is fired, your tooth will be pulled out!"

Well, I had seen what I assumed to be centipedes moving around in the holes and trenches we occupied — perhaps an eighth of an inch thick and five inches long. Sometimes, I would find one curled up in the blanket I wrapped round me when resting. And one day my left hand swelled painfully. Between my little and third fingers I found a yellow spot.

For over 24 hours I stood the pain, but by then the hand and the forearm had swollen to twice their normal size and, under my left armpit, a swelling throbbed. I knew this poison was spreading rapidly and could be fatal. I had to visit that wretched medico. What do you think he said? "You have had a poisonous bite, but I can't do anything about it. Take a Number 9 pill. It might help to clear the blood." That too is absolutely true.

I walked away, the pain reducing me to moans and tears. I wandered off towards the beach, deserting my Company, but not caring any more. To be shot would have been a relief. At some point along the track I found a small, marquee tent with a Red Cross flag flying above it. I entered and received a kindly welcome from a Sergeant member of the Royal Army Medical Corps[176], who listened to my story while I removed my tunic. The shirt also had to come off, the arm so swollen that the Sergeant helped me by pulling the garment over my head and peeling the left sleeve off last of all.

An officer made an examination; his speech suggested American origin, especially when he, with a penetrating gaze right into my eyes, asked, "Can you stand some?" Of course, I assured him I could stand anything but the current pain. Whereupon he told the Sergeant to hold my swollen hand — which looked remarkably like some sort of puffed-up frog — over a large basin, keeping apart the little finger and its neighbour. The Sergeant took a firm grip and the Yankee doctor inserted his small blade into the palm side of my hand first, then cut upwards between the fingers and a little way across the back of the hand.

Normally, I would have let out a howl but, as the pressure eased, I experienced only relief. Then the surgeon, using both hands, commenced squeezing, starting at the top near the shoulder...

Amazed at the quantity of red and yellow muck which had almost filled the basin, overjoyed by the pain receding, I told the doctor about our strange MO. Etiquette, I suppose, prevented him pursuing the subject, but his sympathetic eyes and his care during the following fortnight dispersed all my bitterness. That was my first experience of American kindness and efficiency; more such generous aid from our future allies came my way before that war concluded.

The Sergeant led me up a hillside to a small encampment consisting of a marquee and half a dozen bell tents. For beds, the patients had stretchers, the sort that folded up when not in use; each of us had a pillow and two blankets. At regular hours, the only nursing staff I saw — the Sergeant and a Corporal — brought us food, drink and medicines. If not serious, wounds were dressed. Mine they kept open by more squeezing, but the swelling subsided rapidly, while whatever medicine they administered improved my general condition.

Most of all, within a few days, the kindness of those men, the generous helpings of good, plain food, and lots of restful sleep, turned a doleful kid into something once more resembling a soldier.

I began to take a real interest in everything. Looking around, I saw that this little Field Dressing Station stood on a hilltop in full view of the enemy, its only protection the large Red Cross flag at the top of the flagpole. Occasionally, Turk shells would howl past us, but none would hit us, of that we were sure. Could one rely on that today?

From the part of the Front my pals occupied, sounds of the usual sort drifted up to us; frequent rifle shots, bursts of machine-gun fire, the bang-howl-crash of shells from smallish field guns.

Turning to my right, I faced a difficult sort of battlefield; in the background, a range of harsh-looking hills called, I believe, the Anafarta Heights (I did know the names of the main, geographical features at that time, but this is the only one I remember, probably because, with my low-level type of imagination, this name suggested the possible condition and emissions of this girl Ana after she had eaten one of the tall tins of baked beans and fat pork which all too rarely came my way). Ranges of lesser hills ran roughly parallel to them.

On my extreme right was the sea and, rather nearer to me, a strip of land jutted out into it. On its tip I could see an Australian gun battery… for Anzac Cove, of beloved memory, was nearby. The acoustics were such that, when they fired a shell from that position, it set up a terrific roar like all hell let loose.

Chocolate Hill[177] was inland from that point and when, one afternoon, the Aussies mounted an attack, in that huge panorama it looked like a play staged by midgets: puffs of smoke, flashes, then tiny figures running forward, pausing, dropping down prone, then mingling with the terrain, becoming invisible. I could do no more than wish them success in their raid.

I saw a monitor — really a floating gun platform — supporting the action by, from time to time, sending a huge shell into the Turkish rear positions. Anchored some distance out to sea, the monitor had, I was told, just one big gun and a stock of shells.

Another day, a huge battleship, which I believe was the *Queen Elizabeth*[178], bombarded Turkish roads miles behind the firing line. I heard that one of her shells killed 62 Turks, but could not imagine who counted them or how.

My fitness for return to my Battalion became obvious. On the very day when the good American doc decided I could depart, I was shocked to hear a battery of our own guns open fire from a position directly behind our little hospital. This was all wrong, absolutely wicked, and I walked away from that little bit of heaven feeling that it had been befouled by some brainless British officer. Now you wouldn't blame the Turks for strafing the Red Cross tents — and that is what happened. I heard that bad news a few days later, and just hoped the good American and all staff survived intact.

As I walked down the hill, the awkwardness of my present position began to worry me. I had the vest, pants, socks, boots, and tunic trousers I was wearing when I left my post to seek medical help. Nothing else. No rifle. No pack… and it had contained all my personal belongings including a towel and soap, an unwashed set of underwear and socks, and my two bottles of water-purifying tablets.

I had wandered off a fortnight earlier, suffering so badly from the poison that I hardly knew or cared what I was doing or where I was going. I had departed without authority to do so; that might be adjudged desertion from my unit — on active service, one of the most serious crimes a soldier could commit.

I was convinced I had at least told my mates I was going to see the Medical Officer and perhaps one of them had told our Sergeant or an officer. Would old Number 9, our long, miserable streak of an MO, recollect my appealing for his help or was his memory as bad as his knowledge of medical matters?

I hurried across the open country between the little Field Hospital and the beginning of the trench system without stopping a bullet or anything equally lethal. When I slipped down into a communication trench leading towards the front line, I soon encountered a chap I knew and liked, named Whiting. He gave me all the news as he'd heard it. The part of it concerning myself proved both reassuring and disappointing.

The pals I'd left behind had more awareness of my trouble than I'd suspected. They had given the appropriate NCO lurid details of my condition — the throbbing, twice-its-normal-size hand and arm — and he formed the opinion that, even if I did not die, I would be put aboard a hospital ship and would not return to my unit. It happened that, because of a lack of senior NCOs, this Sergeant suddenly found himself in charge of supplies for our Company. So he decided that my tablets should he distributed among our chaps in the front line to help keep them free of the dysentery that was knocking out so many men.

This Sergeant's surprise at my reappearance matched his dismay when I demanded those precious water purifiers. Nevertheless, he ordered the return of all those not used and, eventually, I recovered a fair quantity of them.

However, I didn't actually rejoin my Company, because a request had come through from Brigade Headquarters for a Signaller to be sent to a hill with a commanding view of Turkish positions. There, to provide some protection for our men in forward positions, they had decided to bring together all the machine gunners from the four Battalions constituting the 88th Brigade. This Brigade, part of the famous 29th Division, was composed of regulars, the good old soldiers who made a career of serving their country in peacetime as well as in war. I felt proud to be allowed to join them, for I had seen how much better their organisation was than ours.

I found my way to the machine gunners on the hill. Below us, in places, I could see the trenches of our forward positions; quite a network had been constructed by now and I ruefully admitted to myself that the steam had gone out of the whole operation, the purpose bogged down in holes and trenches.

The machine gunners could give useful fire cover to our chaps down there should they be attacked. But why should the Turk bother to attack? He must have concluded by now that the British had failed in their original objective and that, if he came forward to drive us into the sea, he would suffer many casualties and gain only a useless strip of land. Leaving us where we were to face a winter in terrible conditions was the better strategy; we would have the awful burden of trying to get supplies ashore in bad weather to troops who had, in many cases, fallen victim to sickness and depression. Meanwhile, the Turks could withdraw some of their men to reinforce their other fronts.

As a Lance Corporal, with one man to assist me, my job was to maintain communications with 88th Brigade Headquarters. Clearly, that meant one man resting, one on duty. I talked over the possibilities with my helper, and we decided to try doing four hours on and four off, night and day. We occupied a square hole, about six feet each way, with no roof. A short trench joined it to the main trench along the top of the hill. This was to be my home. Although on a hilltop, these trenches had been dug into the same soft, layered rock as those first holes we'd worked so hard to excavate down near the beach, so their unstable walls constantly flaked away.

My first Signaller mate there was a pleasant chap, quite a philosopher in his way, probably my senior by four or five years. He showed me photographs of his parents and a sister, and I warmed myself in the glow of love emanating from him as he talked about them and their life together before the war. A good worker too, meticulous in his time-keeping, he woke quickly during the night when the luminous dial on my watch told me four hours had passed and I nudged him to take over.

At that point, you placed the headphones and microphone in the other man's hands, briefly switched on the torch to show him that the combined phone/Morse signal instrument with its buzzer key, earth pin and single landline, and the message pad and pencil were all handy. Then you swapped positions in the hole.

On duty or resting, at night you arranged your thick, rubberised groundsheet so that you rested on half of it and pulled the other half over your legs for protection from the cold or rain. When writing down any messages coming in, the groundsheet also came in handy to screen the heavy-duty torch beam.

But it was all very difficult and uncomfortable.

Even though the autumn weather in that little strip of Turkey remained dry — pleasant, really — we learned that four hours on, four off, meant we never had a satisfactory sleep. So we experimented with two on, two off, eight on, eight off, every arithmetical combination we could think of to cover the 24 hours. Nothing really worked.

When you took over after whatever interval, your mate, released from that crampy corner of the hole we lived and worked in, should have felt free for some hours of beautiful sleep — but was he? On duty, you must want to go to the bog some time, so your mate had to wake up and take over. During the day, you would need nourishment, so your mate had to procure it, and very often cook it on our small meths heaters. Actually, we catnapped day and night and just made the best of a terrible existence.

The resulting fatigue, along with poor diet, was reducing us to shadows of ourselves. They sent our rations up to us every two or three days. As before, our staples remained plain, hard biscuits, apricot jam, and tea boiled on our methylated-spirit heaters, corned beef the only meat supplied with any regularity, though occasionally a few rashers of bacon came our way. Look again at that food list and imagine yourself trying to live under such conditions and maintain your intelligence or even your sanity.

Add to this the occasional shell-burst, the sniper's bullet if he spotted you moving around, the bucket in a short trench into which all men on the hill shed their waste products amid an odour of chloride of lime and shit...

Barely a week had passed on the hill when my friend turned a nasty shade of yellow and I had to phone HQ for a replacement. Before he was taken away, he confided that he'd been smoking cigarettes he'd made out of pipe tobacco and brown paper; he surmised that these had caused his jaundice.

His replacement was a jolly fellow, always cheerful, named Bill Jackson. He wore thick lenses in wire frames — I saw his presence in Gallipoli as one more tribute to the doctor who had examined us volunteers at the time of our enlistment. The daft, old medico shouldn't have approved him for active service. The truth was, if Jackson lost or damaged his glasses he'd be almost blind. He had a lovely wife and three children of whom he talked often. Such a loving family as he described must be missing dad terribly...

For a week or two, as winter crept in, we managed doing our spells on duty and resting between stints, but suffering pangs of hunger some days and showing signs of debility all the time. One night, as we sat in chilly darkness and thoughts once more turned homewards, the futility of what we were doing became very apparent to me. "Bill," I said. "Why are you here? A wife and kids thousands of miles away, you stuck here in a hole in the ground. What's the use?" He had no sensible answer to that one, so I told him I had a plan aimed at getting him away from this rotten country.

It was simple, his part being to remove his spectacles when next taking his rest. Should he happen to lay them on the groundsheet anywhere near me I would not be able to see them. If I happened to kneel on them they would be crushed on that hard ground and he would be unable to see where he was going, let alone write down messages.

He demurred about all this. But later, in complete darkness, just such an accident did occur, and when daylight came I had to give Brigade HQ a detailed account of the strange occurrence and they sent up two men, one to replace Bill, the other to guide him down to the beach and a hospital ship, no doubt.

To replace Bill, they sent me up a sad, little man called Harry Green. His arrival coincided with a brief period of wonderful luck with our food. The machine gunners nearest to my hole in the ground belonged to a regular Battalion of the Essex Regiment; country lads, very shrewd — and tired, as we all were, of the poor and monotonous diet, they secured an officer's permission for two of them to make a foraging trip to the beach. A lighter had unloaded a cargo of fresh meat, we'd heard — very likely this had happened many times previously, yet our lot had never had a mouthful of it, not the rankers anyway.

These two resourceful men returned with — would you believe it? — a whole leg of beef. Whether they stated that they represented a large group of men I don't know, but they got hold of it, and they carried it, each taking turns, a long way across open country, risking shells from field guns and bullets from snipers until they got down into a communication trench leading uphill to our position. When I saw this huge piece of meat I marvelled that two men could have hauled it such a distance.

Generosity to comrades was part of the faith of these Essex farm men, so they included me and my dour helper in their feastings. They gathered old planks and anything that grew nearby. At dusk, they partially covered over a disused trench with sawn-off branches and started burning small quantities of our scavenged wood, restricting the flames carefully to avoid inviting a shell. Gradually, they built up a big heap of glowing embers whereon we laid our mess-tin lids with their folding handles to cook thin slices of the beef. The smoke filtered away through the branches and the night air grew rich with the smell of meat roasting.

Then, during daylight hours, we filled our bellies with beef stewed in a couple of large dixies left overnight on the smouldering mound — small additions to it being made at intervals by those whose duties kept them up and about. Large tins of dried potato shreds had been issued and we all added our shares to the cook pots to thicken the liquor. Into one dixie, went a quantity of curry powder for those who liked their stew really hot — and had no fear of possible consequences.

This feasting continued for several days and I felt my strength building up and youth's natural cheerfulness returning. We could smile again; such a change from the dejected hangdog expressions with which we had all been depressing each other.

Even my fellow Signaller, Green, a gloomster to the depths of his nature, permitted himself to speak of his home life and his girl. She I pitied though, for the prospect of sad, little Private Green for a husband, even in his happier moods, was daunting. I knew I was a mug to put up with his moanings instead of telling him what a miserable devil he really was.

One quite pleasant day around the end of October, I had planned to walk some distance across country to make a request to the Quartermaster of our Battalion. But, that morning, the Turks commenced a huge bombardment.

While all the familiar field guns flung their shrapnel at us, additional bigger reports high up in the hills were followed by large explosions among our positions. This provoked the general belief that a great enemy attack would follow — the attempt to drive us into the sea would take place that day. The bombardment continued for hours… eventually to our puzzlement. We had expected it would stop suddenly, signalling the start of the Turk infantry advance.

Eventually, I decided to set off on my errand and safely reached one end of Essex Ravine, where our Headquarters sheltered, and dropped down into a communication trench which would take me in the right direction. But just before I reached the end of the trench, a huge shell exploded above me. It baffled me because, although it exploded in the air, it produced black smoke and all the shrapnel shells I'd so far seen gave white smoke.

I never did learn what the difference signified, but I wondered and waited, feeling another of these big, black bangers must be on its way — and, while I paused, I thought with some dread about how shells of many shapes and sizes were booming and crashing over the whole countryside, and about the large number of casualties our Army and the Anzac boys must be suffering... Getting them all down to the beaches, on to lighters, and then transferring them all to hospital ships, would be almost as difficult as the original landings...

The next black shell exploded above and I commenced counting. When I reached 60 I almost decided to stop, but then a third one went off and I started running, counting still, and, well before 60, I had jumped out of that trench, turned sharp left and joined our chaps in the shelter of Essex Ravine.

This being our Battalion HQ, the lucky people there had covers over their holes. I had come to ask the Quartermaster[179] if we two, stationed on the hill with the machine gunners, could be attached to the men of the Second Essex Regiment for rations, to save men having to bring the stuff up to us two Royal Fusiliers separately. But, while we talked, an unusual thing happened.

High above us, shells exploded and I saw that, near the white puffs of smoke, were two flying machines, their wings somewhat swept backwards like a large bird's. Although I had never seen a warplane in action before, I was able to recognise them as German Taubes[180].

Only a year or two earlier, I had seen my first aeroplanes taking part in a race from London to Manchester and back — now the things had already been adapted to combat uses. Moments later, various oddments from the shells buzzed down among us and went phut as they hit the ground. I told a man nearby that I'd recently heard a nose cap from one of those high shells had struck a man in the back of his chest and come out through his belly, but this cheery piece of information only provoked a disbelieving laugh.

My little bit of business at HQ being finished satisfactorily, I paid attention once more to the near end of the communication trench into which I must run and jump. Sure enough, the black devil was still bursting above that point periodically, but my counting again enabled me to get in and away without injury. I did my open-country run, using whatever shelter I could find along the way, then slipped back into the long communication trench which led, eventually, to our hilltop with the machine gunners.

This time that communication trench yielded a strange experience; on my right, at a spot I hadn't previously noticed, an opening caught my eye. I peered in and it revealed a sight almost unbelievable to me: a rather wide, roofed trench, with a long, narrow table, on each side of it a plank seat occupied by men who looked remarkably clean and spruce; on the table, their enamel mugs and plates, knives and forks, symbols of civilisation and decency. They did not appear to see me, perhaps because the light from the candles placed at intervals restricted vision to things close by. I recall standing there, tears, for some emotional reason, streaming down my face... although I was now 17 years old. The difference in the way of life of those trained, experienced soldiers, and that of myself and most of my Territorial comrades was never so apparent to me as at that moment.

Of course, it all started at the top. Their officers were all career, military men, capable of assessing the usefulness of every single thing, place or circumstance within their purview. The very disciplines to which the best of them submitted and which they practised in peacetime too made them admirable leaders when war surrounded their lives with discomforts and dangers. The amateur officer would try to carry out basic standing orders to the very letter, regardless of the health and comfort of his men and the fact that wounds and sickness were daily reducing the numbers of those he commanded; so his surviving men would have to do longer and harder stints and themselves become gradually reduced to mindless, humourless automatons.

Much of the routine stuff wasted energy at a time when all signs indicated a position of stalemate, be it only temporary. The good officer would use such periods by allowing — or ordering — men otherwise unoccupied to give attention to personal hygiene, improvement of habitation, sanitation and the procurement of maximum rations.

Memory may play me false here, but I seem to remember that those fine men I glimpsed in that side-trench, who conspicuously insisted on preserving some of the decencies amid conditions which defeated less efficient soldiers, were members of the Royal Scots Regiment[181]. I learned that the small number seated in their improvised dining hall were all that remained of a full Battalion who did marvellous work in the earliest landing on that Turkish peninsula.

I left the long communication trench when it neared the earlier-mentioned Borderers' Gully and took the opportunity to search the hole I had shared some time back in hope of finding my sadly missed flageolet. But no luck.

Moving up the gully there, you had to pass through two points exposed to snipers on a higher hill ahead. But that day they appeared to be looking elsewhere, perhaps watching the shell bursts going off all over our area. I rejoined my unsmiling assistant on the hill among our Brigade's machine gunners. No casualties there, but much speculation as to the reason for the massive bombardment...

At dusk, the hideous noise suddenly ceased.

On duty that evening, I received a message directed to all units by Army Command HQ. It stated that every available piece of Turkish artillery fired continuously during that day and that our casualties resulting from it were not too heavy; in fact, it said, only one man was injured and he damaged an ankle when jumping into a trench for shelter. All that firing, that huge waste of ammunition, had been in celebration of the last day of the Feast of Ramadan[182].

Chapter Twenty-Eight

Late in November, a sudden change of weather made our Army's already depressing situation almost unbearable. The heat, and consequent plague of filthy flies carrying germs of disease, began to abate, and then came freezing winds with sleet and ice-cold rain.

After several days, some trenches were deep in water. Still heavier rain fell non-stop throughout one day and night, snow followed on, then the whole wretched lot froze solid[183]. Our Essex Regiment friends had no food to spare for us and, having no protection from the terrible cold, Green and I looked like dying quite soon[184] — even though, fortunately, our trench on the hilltop remained dry. I decided to attempt the journey down to Battalion Headquarters to beg for food and tea — no shortage of water now, surrounded as we were by ice and snow. Do you remember the woollen tube with sewn-up ends, described as a "cap comforter" in Army equipment lists? If you stuffed one half of it into the other half, you had a sort of pixie hat. Being unable to face the blast unprotected, I made small openings for eyes and mouth and pulled the thing down over my face, so heaven only knows what I looked like to the few men who saw me.

Descending the hill, I had to risk being sniped and proceed on top, for most of the trench system lay deep in ice and snow. I assumed the enemy would be similarly afflicted and uninterested in slaughtering infidels, but at one point a couple of bullets came very close and I dropped into a trench and tried slithering on the ice, but soon had to climb out again.

A dreadful sight confronted me when I reached low-lying Essex Ravine. Rising water had forced our men to quit their trenches and, already very chilled and wet, stand exposed to the biting cold wind and sleet with nowhere to rest. Their resourceful officer told them to form circles and bend forwards with arms around each other's shoulders. He and others then covered each circular group with their rubberised groundsheets tucked in here and there to prevent them being blown away. Thus they stood all night, pressed close for warmth, and most of them were still in that situation when I arrived.

I eventually met a Sergeant who had assumed responsibility for acting as Quartermaster to our much diminished Battalion — not many more than 200 of us remained on active duty by then, the rest sick, wounded or dead from illness or enemy action. I told him of our predicament, our lack of food. At first he disowned us, saying the machine gunners whose communications we maintained ought to feed us. But, relenting, he gave me a handful of tea and two hard square biscuits, this to feed two men for an indefinite period.

On my journey back, the going was tough, especially when I slid down into a trench with ice at the bottom. Each step forward broke the ice and I was continually delayed by struggles to free my boots. Exhausted and in despair I had a great piece of luck, for I discovered an entrance to another of those short, covered trenches. This was on higher ground, so not flooded. I went in, I was greeted by a tall man, who treated me with Christian kindness; he let me warm myself by some sort of stove, and gave me a large mug of hot cocoa and a chunk of buttered bread. I suppose I was too overcome by this luxurious fare and lovely treatment to ask questions, but thanked him sincerely. I could see he was a chaplain, but to whom I did not know.

One chap I questioned later reckoned my benefactor was the Bishop Of Croydon, but I'd never heard of such a Bishop[185]. I guess I never will know, but the memory of the good man who revived my strength and enabled me to continue remains always.

I found Green, my mate on the hilltop, in no condition to be interested in the biscuit I offered him for, in my absence, the thoughtless man had removed his boots because his feet were so painful. Now, swollen considerably, they could not be forced back into the boots, so he was in a right mess. Cold, wet, without footwear, and exposed to weather which, I suspect, was coming to us direct from Siberia.

To make tea, I had to find clean ice, put it in my mess tin, and melt it over the small methylated spirit heater. This Harry could drink and, meanwhile, I phoned Brigade HQ for a man to replace him. Throughout that night he moaned and groaned and sobbed, being in awful pain. I wore the headphones continuously, cat-napping at intervals.

Next day, I spotted a disused trench more than half-full of ice and snow on the hillside facing the Turks. So I risked becoming a sniper's target, got out into the open, dashed across, filled my can and hurried back. Using tea repeatedly and carefully, I was able to supply Green and myself with warm fluid.

Moving around, I maintained some bodily warmth too. Harry was now delirious and I hoped past feeling much pain, but one more day passed before men from HQ were able to reach us, lay Harry in a blanket, and carry him, groaning and shouting, away to the beach.

My feet felt uncomfortable, but I didn't remove my boots then, nor for a week or more afterwards. Later, back in Egypt, my already brown toenails turned gradually darker and at intervals fell out, but sound new ones grew in their place.

A gradual thaw set in and, as moving around became easier, I learnt more of the tragedy the smaller number of us now remaining in that benighted place had survived. Many men had drowned in flooded trenches from which they could not escape quickly enough or had fallen into when they took a step in the wrong direction in the dark. Others died of the cold — a few had laid hands on jars of rum sent up for distribution as tots for all, then drunk themselves insensible and perished in the freezing winds.

The sun shone briefly most days, growing warmth dried out our heavy coats, and life became far more bearable to me. Especially because my new companion on the hill turned out to be that shortish man of Swiss origin I have previously described[186], he who was more patriotic than most British-born soldiers — and after all our tribulations, he still felt the same about his dad's adopted country. He even made excuses for the failed author/poet who had, by some accident, become the Commander-in-Chief of that unfortunate Army and composed lyrical dispatches for home consumption in his comfortable cabin way out at sea.

After that wasteful Ramadan bombardment I had no further fears that the enemy would ever launch a big attack on us, and now I felt convinced that our depleted force would never have a go at him... so all one had to do was be careful to stay alive, until someone told us to get the hell out of the wretched place.

Attached once more to the regular Essex boys for rations, we fared well. And I had my disused trench for water — it remained several feet deep for some time. However, fetching it became risky because a sniper had spotted my movements as I darted hither and thither to fox his aim.

I carried a can to which I had tied a length of string to lower it into the trench. I would climb out of our trench and dash several yards, freeze there for a moment while I pictured John Turk taking aim at me, then make another short dash while the bullet smacked somewhere behind me. One more pause, then run to the trench, lower and raise the can, and return via another pause or two before a final, fearful charge back to and into our trench, having retained as much water in the can as possible. The bullets always seemed to arrive at the spot near where I had last paused. But I was careful to operate in poor light, morning and evening, because I had rightly assumed that the sniper was a good shot…

So you can imagine my sorrow when two Essex men laid a boy on a firing step just opposite my hole, pointed to a wound in his chest, and told me the lad had attempted to copy my water-getting dash in broad daylight. Probably he didn't bother about foxing the sniper either. He belonged to the Hampshire Regiment, but an Essex man had watched his progress, seen him wounded, and with a pal had risked death to drag him in.

I phoned Brigade HQ for stretcher-bearers, but doubted if the lad would live — the bullet had pierced a lung. We fixed his field dressing over the entry wound, but I dared not move him to search for the exit, which may well have been a gaping hole. As I tried to keep him warm and give him support such as I could in response to those frightened eyes, I felt quite old in spite of my mere 17 years. He — the first wounded man I'd had to deal with — was even younger than I.

The stretcher-bearers were gentle with him; I knew only too well they would have to climb out of trenches in several places where a stretcher could not be accommodated; in full view of the Turk, they would have to rely on his clemency.

Thereafter, I stayed away from the watery trench and made do with such water as the machine gunners could spare for me.

Returning confidence due to better feeding, certainty that the campaign was fizzling out, and the buoyant nature of my newly arrived mate, resulted in moments I could only describe as merry.

When the Navy suddenly opened up a noisy bombardment of Turk positions one day, Nieter and I actually cheered and sang A Life On The Ocean Waves. Another time, we two idiots decided to serenade the enemy by tum-te-tumming a tune favoured by brass bands at that time entitled The Turkish Patrol. The barmy thing about this effort was our pretended assumption that the Turks would recognise the tune because of its title.

I had been feeling that the small number of people of my Battalion who still remained after the blizzard must have forgotten my existence, but a week or so after Nieter's arrival I had pleasant proof that this was not so. A replacement for me suddenly appeared at our hole on the hilltop and I received instructions to join the Signals Section at 88th Brigade Headquarters until further orders.

Sorry to leave Nieter, but flattered and excited, I made my way to the ravine which sheltered HQ. There, they had built small but comfortable offices for administration and communication. Low, wooden buildings with earth-covered roofs on which the local weeds and grasses grew. Hopes that I would live in one of them quickly died the death when I was conducted to a nearby hole covered by a groundsheet roof, and told I could set up house there.

Thankfully, it was dry, but it was sited beside the junction of two footpaths, and I quickly discovered that the position had been honoured by an enemy sniper. He had one of those tripod-rifles fixed on the point where the paths met; at intervals, a bullet smacked into the ground about a foot from one end of my hole. As the new boy, the privilege of avoiding sudden death by a sniper's bullet automatically became mine. But the pleasure of working in a warm, covered structure, properly seated, with cooked food and big helpings of hot tea, more than compensated for the sniper targeting my sleeping quarters.

Some days we had steak and onions for dinner; it seemed incredible after the hard tack and occasional bully beef which had usually been my lot. Bacon for breakfast was not unknown, cheese and bread in the evening common. If the pecking order worked that way, the lucky devils at Divisional HQ probably got breakfast, a meat lunch, afternoon tea, and dinner in the evening. It all passed through too many hands before the ranker's turn came, God help him.

Meanwhile, I felt the benefit of this luxury, my spirits rose again, I smiled, even laughed occasionally. Fully occupied on duty, when not working I hung about in one or other of the small HQ buildings as long as possible. Then, in my hole, I could sometimes remove my tunic, shirt and vest and destroy all the body lice I could find, replace these garments then take off my trousers. With candle ends scrounged from the office, I could burn off the filthy things infesting the inside seams of my trousers, crush the devils in my long pants and have a couple of days free of the continual biting.

Well into December, the weather generally remained pleasant. That awful blizzard now seemed like a sad dream although I had my funny-feeling feet and brown toenails to remind me — as did the stories recounted by survivors who had fared much worse than I.

A sight I'd missed in my rather isolated position on the machine-gun hill was large numbers of men in various stages of illness, many with layers of socks and rags over their frost-bitten feet, heading hopefully for the beach. How could such a suffering multitude be dealt with properly?

The beach people must also have been rained on, then snowed on, then frozen and tortured by that Siberian blast if they dared to venture into the open. Then the sorry throng, with their frostbitten feet and hands, some already gangrenous, all of them short of food, descended on them and they just had to cope. What a commandeering of lighters and small steamboats there must have been. I with my two biscuits and a handful of tea had seen almost nothing of these larger events.

Suddenly, my brief, beautiful life at HQ ended with an order to rejoin Nieter on the hill; his helper — my substitute — had gone down with a high temperature and no one else could be found to replace him. Before I left the kindly men at 88th Brigade Signals, they gave me bread, some cold meat, bacon and a useful bag of tea.

This eased my return to the more Spartan existence up above and ensured a warm welcome from my sturdy Swiss Cockney. I found anyway that he had not fared too badly, having been authorised to draw rations from the resourceful regulars of the 2nd Battalion Essex Regiment.

I also took back to Nieter a rumour, whispered to me as I left Brigade

HQ, suggesting that our days on that foreign shore were numbered. The promise of release from our deprivation and danger, so useless, so purposeless, cheered us up considerably.

Messages of instruction to various Companies around us passed through our hands and these confirmed our opinion that the end of the failed campaign drew near. Groups of men quietly withdrew, and those remaining had instructions to appear busy and show themselves more — but with reasonable care — to enemy observers. I heard that members of the Engineers Corps were working in the forward trenches, fixing fuses connected to detonators along the parapets.

The Turks still lobbed over the occasional shell, their lazy snipers with their apparently fixed rifles still squeezed their triggers, perhaps from force of habit, but the earlier war-like spirit had departed.

So, I assumed, had our seaborne Army commander because one day, as I squatted in a trench and chatted with one of the Essex men, a sort of apparition appeared; it was a large man, somewhat florid of countenance, wearing much red braid on collar, epaulettes and around his cap.

As he approached we stood up — not wishing to be trodden on — and our action unexpectedly put the cat among the pigeons. "Why the devil are these men standing to attention?" he roared. "If this happens again I'll have everybody put on fatigue duty out on top collecting cans and rubbish in broad daylight!" He squeezed past us, quite a beefy gentleman, followed by a retinue, the first few of whom also carried much red tape on their uniforms. Several ordinary officers followed, looking almost shabby compared with the top brass.

An Essex Sergeant brought up the rear and, in answer to my questioning look, he said, "General De Lisle[187], General Officer Commanding this Army".

I considered the incident and the strange logic it suggested. The General bellowed at us for standing to attention — although that was what we were supposed to do when an officer approached — because it might expose our heads to enemy snipers. His loud voice was calculated to scare all within earshot, including, I guessed, his escorting officers. Yet he must have known that his own head, with its red-braided cap, would regularly bob up above the lip of the trench as he proceeded with his inspection. And apparently that didn't matter. A fine bravado perhaps. Except that he was the General Officer Commanding wilfully risking death...

Thereafter, I assumed that General Ian Hamilton had at last packed it in[188]. When I told witty Nieter of my assumption, he pointed out that this change at the top would not necessarily mean rapid promotion for me.

Chapter Twenty-Nine

Christmas Day coming up... All we were missing was the Christmas tree, the holly, the oranges, Christmas puddings, iced cakes and booze. We did have ample bully beef, hard biscuits, tea, tinned milk, sugar and, because of our Army's reduced numbers, two or three pints of water each day.

But one could feel how appropriate it was that, as the season of good will to all men drew near, the tension which had been spoiling one's life, waking or sleeping, had vanished. With luck we'd be up and away from this depressing place before John Turk had time to miss us.

No one talked about the fuses and detonators so carefully installed by the engineers all along the front trench, but we hoped they would bang off at regular intervals and kid the Turks that our positions were still manned for a long while after the last soldier had put to sea on a lighter. That was one of our really fervent hopes — another, that perhaps the Turks knew we were lighting out and would be up on their hill laughing fit to bust.

At the same time, we did know that, when the time came for us to slip away and leave John Turk once again in possession of his strip of territory, halfway through the operation hordes of screaming enemy soldiery might suddenly descend from the high hills which formed a sort of semi-circle around the area held by the British, Australian and New Zealand armies.

Nieter and I discussed more than once what extremely hard luck it would be if one of our few remaining chaps was killed before we got away — and, of course, it happened.

Impatient and excited, under a partial moon, I waited one night for a code word over the headphones. When it came I passed the word "Now" along the line and machine guns were dismantled, our signal lines disconnected, container satchels hung over our shoulders, and rifles and all equipment taken with us, as we all very quietly moved beachwards in a single line. By then, all troops in forward positions had already departed[189].

Sufficient light glimmered down from the slice of moon, and perhaps from the Milky Way, always brighter there on clear nights than it appeared to be in England. As we approached the point where I'd watched those big, black Ramadan shells burst at an earlier date, Nieter and I took whispered farewells of our kindly Essex pals, left the file, and joined the remnant of our own Battalion assembled there, awaiting the order to move beachwards.

This was when we heard about an unfortunate young man who had just been killed, a member of H Company from when we first enlisted — I mentioned him quite early on in this narrative because, when he heard me singing along with the others while marching, he remarked, "You've got a voice like a man's — I hadn't expected to hear that noise coming out of you"[190]. Or words to that effect.

Most unexpectedly on this quiet night, a bullet had struck him in the upper arm. The man with him applied the first field dressing, which every soldier carried in a special pocket. But, in the dark, nobody saw the blood welling from a severed artery, or perhaps something better could have been done to control the bleeding. By the time they were able to get him into skilled hands he had bled to death.

Whatever other skills we lacked, organising evacuations was not among them — not then, nor many years later. Red Indians had nothing on us regarding silent getaways. As we passed a huge store dump, I could see that oil drums had been placed at intervals around it. Thick wires connected them. Fuse wires perhaps…

With no undue hurry, we got aboard those all-metal lighters once more and chug-chugged out to sea. On a calm sea we transferred without any real accident to a smallish steamboat — it accommodated all who were left of our big Battalion; many had died, but more had gone away sick, some wounded[191].

The Navy was lobbing shells at the Turks, probably to keep them busy while the very last of our men got away. I noticed positions to the left of our old lines receiving particular attention, but couldn't imagine why.

Soon, out of sight of the explosions, some singing started up, our first for many a day. And then we really gave vent to the joy and relief we felt. A youngster who had obliged at concerts back in Malta climbed to a position by the bridge and sang a quickly improvised parody of that popular song, Moonlight Bay: "We were sailing away from Suvla Bay/ We can hear the Turks a-singing/'Please don't go away/You are breaking our hearts/So please do stay'/'Not bloody likely, boys/Goodbye to Suvla Bay'". All joined in, inventing their own versions as we sang along time after time.

Our destination was unknown to us, as was the situation on another part of the Gallipoli Peninsula where our men had landed. Had they evacuated too? To leave them would have seemed risky, for all the Turks from the Suvla Front would now be available to turn on them.

While we "sailed away", as the boys put it, on the trim little coasting steamer named *Robin Redbreast*[192], I felt pleased to be back with my original lot, the men and boys who had been so enthusiastic about "doing their bit" less than 18 months previously; I'd lost touch with them recently, and felt that perhaps their views might have changed after recent experiences. I would soon learn about that.

Recalling recent happenings, I wondered what finally became of two Germans whom I have not previously mentioned. One afternoon, I had received a message for the information of all ranks warning everyone to keep a lookout for two men wearing British officers' uniforms; unfamiliar officers were to be questioned and detained if unable to supply proofs of identity. But the brave pair covered quite a lot of ground unimpeded because, in reality, Privates and junior NCOs did not dare to question commissioned officers; instead, they dutifully answered any questions the two gentlemen asked. Those spies must have had a field day. They probably gathered, at least, general information about our evacuation, and I never heard that they were caught.

As dawn broke we came to an island — called Imbros[193], someone said — and paused briefly in its small anchorage. From the sea we saw signs of military occupation, but only one hostile action — a big bang followed by some smoke. A gun belonging to us firing at Turkey, or a shell from a distant Turkish gun exploding, or someone blowing up stores before evacuating? Nobody knew and, the mystery unsolved, we soon moved away again.

We steamed merrily on; travelling in the opposite direction at an earlier date I had felt sleepy, had a kip on the deck, and been swamped by a wave. Not so this time for, soiled and unbathed, skinny almost to the point of emaciation, I was yet full of hope and joy because life once more offered prospects, changes of scene, sound and smell, and the luxury of sleeping with a roof of some sort over one's head — a happy spell of rest and re-adjustment.

So optimism and smiles all round were the order of the day. It would take time to build us up to general fitness and the Battalion to its full numerical strength, time in which we hoped to live a better sort of life than had been our lot recently.

We reached Lemnos, the harbour from which we'd sailed, it seemed a very long time ago. Without delay we were put ashore and, as we lined up, I was shocked to see clearly how few of us remained. No Colonel in the distance on his white horse. Actually, no Colonel. Perhaps a couple of hundred men in all, a few Company Officers and Sergeants, one or two Corporals and a smattering of puny Lance Corporals, myself included. In charge of this small contingent now was young Major Booth[194], who had received rapid promotion from the rank of Lieutenant. While all the senior men had vanished from the scene of action for whatever reason they may have had, this young man proved himself capable of withstanding all hardships and caring for his men as well as circumstances permitted.

Back in Malta, he'd demonstrated his ability to act wisely, rather than in accordance with Army regulations, when he encountered the soldiers' revolt against the lack of quality and quantity of food issued to them. As you may recall, he quelled a potential mutiny at some financial cost to himself rather than allow impulsive men to face courts martial and harsh punishments.

At Suvla Bay, "Keep your head up, Sergeant Major!", an outspoken reproof he'd issued to one of our top non-commissioned officers — the ex-Marine I mentioned, whose behaviour on active service had lost him all the popularity he had previously gained — had become a favourite quotation for all of us. Its ironic use inspired many a hearty laugh. The new Major had become our man of strength, the leader greatly needed by men who felt they had participated in a failure. Under his guidance we all felt the future would give us opportunities to shine just a little bit brighter in the military firmament than we had done in the past.

But, ashore now on Lemnos... suddenly I felt weak and utterly wretched as I stood there with all that equipment weighing me down. Not in any particular formation, we began walking from the shore along a track towards an encampment ahead. Many obviously shared my dejection. It must have been a reaction to all we had recently endured[195].

However, when we approached the camp, we saw several men coming towards us — and, among them, one who looked remarkably like my brother Ted. Impossible, I thought, for he'd been taken off that ship at Alexandria and I could think of no reason why he should be on this Greek island. But it was Ted, and a very happy reunion we had.

While we talked he quietly relieved me of everything I was carrying. He slipped into the straps to which were attached my pack and haversack and took my signalling equipment and my rifle — which, as a Signaller, I had still not fired in action — and left me feeling almost naked. He had a word with one or two men nearby, then set off for the camp which, he said, he and others had been cleaning up in readiness for our arrival. Sick and wounded men had previously occupied the bell tents, but new large tents had recently been provided for the Field Hospital and Ted said that other men who had quit the peninsula would soon arrive. Old, but large marquees could be used by our people for meals and recreation and only four or five men need occupy each bell tent — luxury indeed since, in crowded camps, ten and even 20 men might be packed in.

A great start. But now we all hopefully awaited news of some sort of food — only to be told that, in fact, very little was available that day, only hot tea, more of the detested hard biscuits and a little cheese. Ted had nothing to offer at that point, but he promised that, after dark, he would scrounge around the Field Hospital nearby and might manage something.

It was so good to be with him again; I felt like an old campaigner suddenly returned to the days of boyhood. As night fell, he vanished and later I heard his voice calling me outside. He expressed regret that he had been able to procure only a few slices of beef. "*Only*", said I. *Only* some beef, indeed. As good or better than slices of gold, I told him.

Then he took me to the outskirts of a big camp, to a place where the embers of several large fires glowed, great heat still rising, and we laid our meat on the hot ashes. Sticks were our cooking implements. We sat there, warm, safe and very soon — after quite easily scraping ash off the meat — happily eating.

Back at our camp we drank tea, and told each other of our experiences since parting. Because I had been on active service and Ted hadn't, he felt inclined to treat me as more important than himself, and this I did not like. He'd always been the clever, strong, elder brother; I'd had pride in his achievements and I knew that, had he been allowed to remain on that ship way back and go to Gallipoli, he would have done far better than I had.

Without mentioning these things, I told him of the real interest I had in his experiences back in Egypt and encouraged him to talk. It was a tale about horses. He had become skilled in caring for them. From the Alexandria docks, he had been sent to Qantara[196]. There were assembled hundreds of horses, tethered in lines, belonging to officers mostly, men who had to leave their mounts behind for various reasons. They needed careful feeding, grooming and riding to give them the necessary exercise. So Ted had become a horseman; he liked nothing better than taking them for gallops across the surrounding desert sands. That sort of work seemed to me far more attractive than humping heavy equipment around on long marches.

In return, I gave him some details of the recent hopeless campaign. From our reduced numbers, he appreciated how difficult the effort had been and, perhaps, how the undue physical strain had broken the health of many men.

Next morning, Drake, a fellow Signals Lance-Jack, and I were told to go searching for missing communications, so to speak. In fact, we were to board a steam pinnace — lent by the commander of a battleship — go round to the east side of the island and search for mail dumped there; it had been allowed to accumulate while we were on active service because transport to deliver it had not been available. In charge of the trim, little vessel was a midshipman, a lad of about my age, quite pretty with his pink cheeks, his immaculate uniform, but a fine young officer. He had a rating for crew.

Off we puffed round the coast after leaving the big harbour. East Mudros had a useful jetty and, going ashore, Drake and I found piles of full, canvas mailbags — a quantity commensurate to the full Battalion of a few months back. We began carrying them back to the pinnace and stacking them on the deck. By the time we'd loaded up there was little to be seen of the boat but her funnel. Not a word of complaint came from the young officer, though. The cherubic smile, the acceptance of things as they were, inspired me, given that almost all my companions of late had been depressed by the pervading feeling of material poverty and defeat.

Happy in the knowledge that we were accomplishing a really useful mission, to avoid rolling overboard Drake and I crawled over the sacks, seeking places with handholds. I spotted a sort of handle near the top of the funnel, clambered up and held on there. Drake jammed himself close to the small superstructure which housed the steering wheel, the rating, and the midshipman. I had my doubts that they could see where they were going, but of course they managed fine.

Just as we cast off, someone came running towards the landing stage, waving. It was Jackson, the man whose spectacles had been damaged one dark night on machine-gun hill. Before we passed out of hearing, he yelled that he had temporary glasses he could just about see with, and he was awaiting shipment to Egypt. His rosy face was all smiles and his wife and children could surely hope to see Daddy before long.

Back in Mudros, Drake and I did no unloading, for an eager party of helpers awaited delivery of the first mail many of them had seen for some months. We two got down to eating a meal thoughtfully saved for the two heroes of the moment.

By candlelight, we all read late into the night, each concerned with his own news and feelings. Ted and I had a couple of parcels each from our parents, letters too. He also had some small packages from girlfriends. Among many nice things, our parents had sent photographs of our family taken in the back garden. Our baby sister was standing there, now able to do so without help[197]. Our young brother looked bonny, the older sister all smiles, the ever solemn dad still solemn, while mother wore her usual rather stern expression.

It was good to have this reassuring picture, visible proof that life at home had not greatly changed. Father's letters, written in his impeccable hand, gave us a clear picture of the national scene as he understood it, and Ma's gave us news of family and local happenings. All was well there, and that was great.

I also received several long, interesting letters from my school friend Charlie, the draper's son, telling me about his life in the newly formed Royal Naval Air service, first at Howden in Yorkshire, and later at Cardington in Berkshire.

Late that night, a message circulated that after careful thought and discussion it had been decided that all parcels intended for men no longer with us — in one sense or another — should be opened and the contents fairly divided among us. The absent men's letters would be cared for pending final disposal.

Christmas nearly upon us and, next morning, our generous Major had our crowd assemble and announced that arrangements had been made for a supply of beer, lots of it, to be collected from the Forces' Canteen. Volunteers, genuine on this occasion, set off, carrying the large dixies in which the cooks normally prepared stews or tea. When they returned, noticeably more talkative and cheerful than before, they carried far more beer than it appeared likely we could cope with. The distribution of cakes, biscuits, Christmas puddings and sweets from the parcels of absent comrades followed — such a plenitude of good eatables compared with the scarcity during recent months.

Ted spent as much time with me that day as his odd-job duties at the nearby Field Hospital allowed. To work off the heaviness from over-eating and drinking, we two took a walk — nostalgia and the effects of strong beer rendering us untypically sentimental about the dear dead days beyond recall as we strolled, perhaps a little unsteadily, in no particular direction. The day was dull, the sky grey, the wind very chilly, but divil a bit cared we... until we came to the hole.

Yes, yet another hole after all those others I'd lived in recently. This, however, was a big one, circular and possibly 15 feet deep. When, why or by whom it had been excavated we had no idea, but now it provided shelter from the winter for a number of Arabs. Dressed in the usual poor man's gowns and hood-like headgear, they crouched in circles well below the rim. They looked ill and miserable. Dotted all around, above and below them was their excreta, all noticeably coloured by the blood which escapes from dysentery sufferers.

Of course, I stated my belief that it was wrong to bring these people from a very poor sort of life in Egypt to an even worse one in this cheerless island, but Ted informed me they had competed for the opportunity to come and earn some cash, a chance seldom available to them at home. Things had not been all that good for me in recent months, but I still had pity to spare for these poor devils. Even more so when Ted told me how they, and others, had travelled from Egypt; he knew because he had been ordered to escort some of them on to a ship, to send them below and close the hatches. During the voyage, the labourers had to be kept down there at all times, their guards armed with trenching tool handles to quell any revolt that might occur.

It all seemed wrong to me. We walked away discussing the wisdom of the officials concerned in deciding that these poor, debilitated souls should be sent across the sea to finish up shivering in a hole in the ground surrounded by shit…

We came upon a village with several small shops and a number of our fellow soldiers, British and ANZAC, wandering about. We had no money, but out of curiosity we entered one shop and were surprised to see the Greek man and woman who ran it, and all their stock, sat behind iron bars. We had seen something similar in post offices and banks back home, but usually those bars were made of brass, whereas this black, iron enclosure had the aspect of a prison.

However, justification for the bars appeared almost instantly when an altercation between a Scot and an Australian flared up. The Scot wanted a loaf of bread similar to one he'd purchased previously at about eightpence. The shopkeeper told him today's price was two shillings. The colonies were paying this without demur, while the Scot knew that, at home, a bigger loaf than this could be bought for threepence or less. So the eightpence he offered appeared more than generous to him out of about seven shillings weekly Army pay. He upbraided the Aussies for spoiling the market just because their Government treated them far more generously than ours did British soldiers.

We left them still pursuing their argument and returned to our camp where Christmas parcel goodies, lashings of beer or tea, Christmas puddings, and all things nice, were there for the picking-up and guzzling. What a reversal of fortune — we looked forward to some days of ease and over-indulgence. Late that night, Ted left me to return to his tent and we, the very happy brothers, promised ourselves another lovely day tomorrow.

Chapter Thirty

I had slept for possibly five hours when the unwelcome roar of a Sergeant roused us all. We had to pack up as quickly as possible, he bellowed, and be ready to move.

Into every available space in pack, haversack and mess tin, I crammed as much food as possible. Cooks handed out fresh-baked loaves — enough to last a few days — and fried bacon in quantity. They had opened a long, wooden case containing two large sides of bacon packed in salt, so we ate our fill, stored the remaining rashers in our tubular cap comforters, and tied these to our belts. Hanging all the usual pieces of equipment about our persons we picked up our rifles, slogged down to the landing stage and boarded a small ship, similar to the *Robin Redbreast*, which had evacuated us from Suvla Bay.

Whither away we knew not, nor cared overmuch, for disappointment at the interruption of our Christmas celebrations was deep and our mood doleful. To hell with everything and everybody; wasn't that war over? So what were *They* up to? Many hours later we heard the unwelcome sounds of occasional gunfire and now, in darkness, when we could just make out land ahead, a shell screamed overhead and burst somewhere ashore. Our ship crept slowly forward, far too slowly for my liking, because, added to the likelihood of injury, was the unpleasant one of drowning as well; and we should by rights have been feasting and lounging on that Greek island[198].

Now we could make out the black shape of a big ship, berthed in the shallows head-on to the shore. Moving closer, we saw a large, square opening in her side and, the tide being just right, our shallower ship could tie up to her and we could step across into her innards and eventually emerge on to a sort of landing stage. We hurried along it before gathering, briefly, on the beach beneath towering cliffs... But no enemy fire came our way.

Excitement and interest now replaced resentment, as we filed some way up a gully and waited. I saw someone approach our Major, who then led us further upwards into this rising gully. A great flash some miles distant seawards gave short illumination to the scene; we saw we were passing a strange, wooden tower... and at that moment, almost unbelievably, from the top of it a hunting horn sounded.

"Lie down!" yelled an unidentified voice and, being no strangers to this life-saving precaution, we were probably flat on the ground before he was. We heard the usual tearing scream, the crash, and below us — about the spot where we had first paused — we saw a brilliant flash and a large cloud of smoke, followed by the whinings of many flying pieces of shrapnel, the phuts as some of them landed nearby.

Said the voice who had given us the warning, "That shell was from Asiatic Annie[199], a real big gun across the sea there in Asia Minor. When the lookout up above sees her fire, he blows his horn and we have about 30 seconds to take cover. The shells don't always land here, of course, but we assume they will." The informative bloke added that we had landed at V Beach and that the ship we had come through was the *River Clyde*[200], beached there in the first Gallipoli landings months earlier.

So at last we knew that a complete evacuation of Gallipoli had not taken place, that we were once more stuck on that ill-starred Turkish peninsula. I recall wondering what brother Ted would think of my second disappearance; he would be mad about not travelling with us, that was certain. Still, although he really belonged to us, he was attached to the Field Hospital for duty; what a surprise he must have had when he found our tents empty.

We moved steadily upwards along a track which eventually brought us to flat ground at the top of the cliff. Now, away in the distance, we recognised all the audible and visible indications that over there was a battlefront; personally, I felt once more the growing nervous tension, the alertness generated by the desire for self-preservation.

Even so, through a few days good living and the contact with normal people provided by the letters from home and those lovely parcels, I felt changed and strengthened; I knew this tautness was not, at present, allied to fear, as it sometimes had been when lack of food and sleep had caused debility. I'd had proof the normal world still carried on, albeit with certain difficulties, and that we had not been forgotten or given up for lost.

We few remaining Signallers stood together talking quietly. Short, sturdy Nieter recalled our days and nights together on that hill; I hope I told him how much his faith in the cause and his cheery optimism had helped me when the physical after-effects of the blizzard got me down.

Consultations continued between our officers and a group of strangers until, finally, orders for our disposal emerged, and a guide took Nieter, two others and myself to the strangest Signals post I ever saw. Located on the cliff top, high above V Beach, it comprised a nice, square hole with a good earth-covered roof, entry being through a "door" dug through on the landward side — this last a necessity because the hole had only three sides: the seaward side didn't exist, if you understand me. So if, in your sleep, you rolled in that direction just a little too far, you must, eventually and too late, realise that your next stop was the beach way down below.

On that open side, curtains made of sacking concealed our candle lights. We had blankets and a rough table or bench with boxes for seats; we worked on instruments far superior to those we carried, and a small, simple exchange or commutator enabled us to link certain Signal posts.

Evidently, here the Army conducted the war on a more civilised level than had been the case at Suvla Bay, largely because the April landings had driven the front line much farther inland from the beaches. No cooking in mess tins over methylated heaters — we four would take our meals in rotation at a small Royal Army Medical Corps camp nearby.

We took over from complete strangers, men of a unit whose name I forget. They, with others, would soon be leaving the place for good, they told us. Evacuation under way then, it appeared. A puzzle therefore: why the heck had we been sent to the place?

In fact, we spent a few pleasant days on that job. From our clifftop, the activities around the beach provided interest in idle moments.

But one day, as I watched a party of civilians moving along down below, without any warning blast on the hunting horn, a big one from Annie burst among them. Some ran, too late, in search of shelter; some would never move again. Watching them, those little figures seemed to exist in a separate world from mine...

Not in any way separate, the RAMC men quickly appeared and bustled among the casualties quietly doing their good work.

The lookout on the tower must have been missing. One of our chaps said they were Greeks brought in to do construction work. That seemed strange to me, civilians working close to a battlefront.

Soon, an order came through for us Signallers to disconnect everything, take all the equipment down to a store on the beach, then rejoin our Battalion. A guide took us to where they were living in a series of square holes not far from the beach all connected by a long trench. At last, we learned the reason for our return to Gallipoli; we were to work every night at dismantling and loading stores on to lighters and small ships. Night work only, in order to conceal evacuation preparations. We could take some rest during the day — but, should enemy planes appear, like the occasional small groups of Taubes we'd seen high above Suvla, we must expose ourselves, move around as though busy upon routine matters, and generally try to convince the observers that our numbers were as great as at any previous time.

Shortly after dawn that first morning back with our crowd, a lone plane did fly back and forth over our area, so we put on our busy act for the pilot's amusement and information. Quite rightly, acting on instructions, some of our men fired their rifles upwards — imagine our surprise, though, when the pilot dropped a bomb. It exploded much too close for our liking and caused a brief interruption to our "busy bee" programme.

That was the first time I'd thought about the possibility of planes carrying bombs. Probably the pilot hurled it out of his cockpit. Although it could only have been a small one, it made quite an impressive bang. Still, no harm done, so nobody worried too much about air-bomb possibilities.

However, soon after that incident, one of our chaps approached our position, a message in his hand, when another low-flying plane appeared. Our friend more or less disintegrated before our eyes. Sheer bad luck placed him in the spot where bomb Number 2 exploded, poor fellow. So, very early in that distant war, did I see death from the air strike a man down.

Still we continued with our task of deceiving the enemy, so much so that aerial visits became quite a regular feature. The Germans must have spared those planes from the Western Front — a small formation, but capable of causing some harassment...

One day, we were watching a water cart coming our way — no shortage of water there, unlike at Suvla; the cart consisted of a tank on an axle and two wheels pulled by a mule and driven by an elderly member of our transport section who we knew to be rather deaf. We heard a plane coming and yelled a warning, but he obviously heard nothing. The plane appeared, flew low, and a strange swishing sort of sound followed — but no explosion. Some of us dashed out to the rather puzzled old chap to tell him what had happened and persuade him to shelter for a while. That he scornfully refused to do and he went on about his business.

Then one lad let out a shout. We ran over to him and he pointed to a six-inch-long metal dart protruding from the earth. That set us all searching and acquiring further specimens, some lying on rocks, others dug out where small holes indicated their presence. A shower of darts had scattered around mule, water cart and the lucky old driver, but all was well.

The one I found was heavy, thick at the head, then slim, and the tail had enough flukes to cause rotation when falling. The inventor presumably thought this might aid penetration of the victim's head — bearing in mind that steel helmets for soldiers had not yet been introduced. I thought about the method of delivery employed and guessed at a box with apertures at the bottom and a sliding grid operated by the pilot. I kept my dart as a prize souvenir, until it vanished in a kitbag I lost some time later.

At V Beach — in fact, during the entire Gallipoli campaign — I saw only one British aircraft, though it appeared several times. The pilot, I gathered, was the famous Wing-Commander Samson[201]. His forays were probably of a "showing the flag" nature rather than attacks on the enemy, although the Turks did fire a few shells at him.

No Signals work was required at that time, for the Battalion's numbers had dwindled to about Company strength and our work concerned simply helping to prepare for evacuation. Our Signals group landed a lovely job which consisted of going to a large dump near the beach and gradually dispersing its contents: canned and bottled food and drink intended as extras for officers — anything that would keep well in cans, boxes, cartons, with smoked items in cotton wraps, also biscuits, some cakes and sweets, wines, beers, but not much in the way of spirits. We loaded these good things on to small mule carts.

A very fair way had been devised to consign them to the troops in equal quantities. Those up at the Front got the first deliveries, naturally. The officer in charge at the dump had records of all the units in benefit. We could only work at night, but during breaks for rest, or while awaiting transports, we were allowed to eat and drink. Chicken, asparagus, Irish bitter from round brass-coloured tins, Schweppes lemon squash or Seltzer water, thin lunch biscuits and other luxuries… for a brief period our small, but fortunate group guzzled these lush items.

Quite fairly, we were not allowed to take anything away from the dump for our own use; but we would be entitled to a share of what was delivered to our Battalion. In fact, we Signallers hadn't the gall to accept our share when it was offered since we stuffed ourselves to capacity during the night and, in daytime, only wanted to sleep. But we did work with a will on the job — and so shortened its duration, unfortunately.

A few days[202] after our disembarkation at V Beach, around midnight someone called out "It's New Year's Eve!" and a special search produced several bottles of what may have been cider, although some called it champagne. We didn't know which, but heartily toasted each other and anyone else we fancied, before renewing our onslaught on that marvellous giveaway job.

We had still not completed the task when, a few nights later, our little group was detailed to join other men and trail off behind a guide in the general direction of the front line. In faint light from a clear sky we could see the nature of the terrain: sometimes fairly level, sometimes hillocks, ridges, low areas. Halting at the entrance to a gully, the leader said, "We now enter Krithea Nullah, which leads to our front line. It gives good cover against rifle and machine-gun fire, but the odd shell can be dangerous; the Turks have got it taped as a route we use regularly, so flop if you hear one coming."

We reached what I assumed was the support-line trench where all the men, except lookouts, were dozing. Forward again and the front line was our next stop. There, we were each handed a pick or a shovel and our guide led the way up over the firing step and parapet into No Man's Land, the space between us and the enemy. He spaced us out in groups of four and told us to start digging holes. The picks made more than enough noise on that hard, peculiar ground and we were sitting ducks for any Turk who cared to take a pot shot. I wished I was still way back helping with the charitable work at the officers' food dump...

When several Turk light field guns let fly, their nearness surprised me; a strange feature was the thin, red line visible as each shell left its gun, making me wonder if they used rather antique pieces. Their trajectory was high, its zenith roughly above us, yet the shells — not trench mortar bombs, their whine confirmed — burst only a couple of hundred yards behind us.

No one told us why, at this stage of the campaign, we poor mugs were digging holes in front of the Turk trenches at great risk to ourselves and our underpants, but even we of the lower orders could guess that we played a part in the great game of bluff. Our top brass hoped John Turk would reason, "They can't be leaving yet or they wouldn't be digging works in advanced positions". I wonder if they were right — if the enemy even cared what we were up to? Perhaps he too had seen enough of the farce. We suffered no casualties.

Orders to prepare for a move[203] gave rise to excitement — which I suppressed because I didn't wish anyone to see my intensely joyful feelings when I felt sure we would soon be on the high seas and well clear of the threat, ever present, of wounding or death.

I must say, however, that there in the Cape Helles sector I had suffered little of the tension, the anxiety, and sheepish desire to seek a safe spot which, combined with hunger and dirt, had always made me feel a rather sub-standard specimen at Suvla. The only consolation I could offer myself regarding my soldiering there was that I had remained till the very end whereas many had departed who might have carried on after receiving field hospital treatment — or so I heard it said.

Once again the quiet line-up in the darkness, the very quiet roll-call, but then the strong, firm voice of our idolised Major saying "Forward!" Little artillery activity as, in two lines, we followed him...

After we had walked for some time, I saw the dark shape of a large building on our left-hand side. We stopped 30 yards away and I could see that light escaped from several slits in doors or windows. Apart from slight indications of habitation behind enemy lines up Krithea way, this was the first real building I'd seen near V Beach, so I was interested when the voice of one of our best officers informed us that there stood the fort of Sedd el Bahr, possibly dating from Crusade times.

Cautious no longer, the Major's voice boomed out, "Corporal Bebb! Corporal Bebb!" It appeared that this popular chap, friend of my brother's, well known to and admired by me, had taken a small party on an assignment to the front line with orders to return to us in time for our move off, but they were still missing.

I felt an atmosphere of mystery just then... standing near the ancient fort, Bebb and his little party missing, our contingent now so small that some months before had been nigh a thousand strong, all our senior officers missing, apart from Major Booth; we had successfully crawled away from one battlefront and now we were at it again. Would the Turks let us do it twice?

Only a few hundred yards to go and our ears told us that the enemy guns were dropping more shells around the beaches than they had done for many a day. Why?

Hope of Bebb's party abandoned because we had to follow a precise timetable, our Major said we must now move. As we reached the cutting at the landward end of the beach area Asiatic Annie flashed and one of her huge shells crashed down a couple of hundred yards away, but we walked steadily forward, hoping to be spared. A sad thing it would be if she wiped most of us out when we'd got this far...

The men organising embarkations had shown a stroke of genius by covering the flat area of the approach to the beached ship *River Clyde* with sawdust or something similar. Thus a number of large shell-holes showed up clearly, even in the dark, and no one fell into them.

Safely on to and down into the ship... Arriving at the hole in her side through which we had landed a couple of weeks earlier, the lighter alongside again ready for the return journey, we were warned that there was a swell and each pair of men, as their turn came, must wait until the lighter rose to their level and then jump across. Loaded as were Nieter and I, this was not easy, but we sprang without hesitation, having everything to gain by so doing. Willing hands steadied us as we hit the lighter's all-metal deck.

This time, we were sent below, told to move forward and stand very close together. Dim light from a candle lantern, the air already foetid, and the horrible feeling of being imprisoned in a dark, stuffy hold frightened me more than anything ashore had done.

With all aboard, we stood too closely packed for anyone's peace of mind. We heard the engine start, felt the motion, up, down, and somewhat sideways. We stood silent, prey to individual fears and hopes. Time passed. A distant gun, the shriek of a shell overhead followed by the familiar explosion heightened the claustrophobic threat of our situation.

I forced myself then, as I have done many times since, to take stock painstakingly of every factor relevant to our position.

On the credit side of the account one could enter: the excellent protection provided by the stout metal hull and deck of our lighter — nothing but a direct hit could hurt us; the proven steadiness and, in many cases, the courage of my companions — they had fulfilled their contract, signed when they had enlisted, to be loyal at all times to their king and country, good chaps to live and toil with when difficulties and dangers had to be dealt with; we had shelter from the weather — it wasn't at all bad outside, but it could change and showers of rain, shot or shavings couldn't touch you down there.

But, debit: it was getting hot and stuffy, we were jammed very close, the tiny light might blow out... supposing one was taken short, what could you do about that? No room to get across to the steps and the cover over the opening would be closed and your pants would be holding an unwelcome load before you could do anything about it.

For what seemed hours, a voice up above had been shouting "*Partridge* ahoy!" time after time so, although that told us the name of our next transport, it didn't guarantee we would ever set foot on it. In the dark and heat down there, I was on the point of feeling scared again, when a bump shook our craft and I knew that all was well.

In an orderly manner with no suggestion of haste we took our turns at the ladder and all quite quickly transferred to the small, but very sturdy passenger ship *Partridge*[204]. What a blessing that fears and doubts don't make a noise as they move back and forth inside your head; companions might hear them and then you'd never convince them you are unafraid, a brave fellow and all that sort of thing. They'd know the truth about you, the last thing you'd wish for.

Because of the job we had done on the Helles Front, we assumed we were among the last troops to leave. We had worked with a will at the job of sharing out the officers' food stores to the troops, but there was still a lot of stuff to be shifted when they told us to do that bluffing stunt in No Man's Land. So if we had filled our packs with some of that luvly grub, no harm would have been done... We had been good, little boys, though, as far as I knew and scrounged nothing. Mind you, a tinned tongue or some chicken or both with a swig of wine would have gone down well after that "Black Hole" experience.

Partridge, probably related to the *Robin Redbreast* that lifted us from Suvla, chugged off into the night, taking us away from all the nasty bangs and flashes and wounds and deaths which make life on active service so unpleasant for us who would much prefer life in an equable clime with a full belly under a tree with a glass of wine and thou and that sort of thing.

Enjoying myself, I recall, leaning on the ship's rail, looking at the dark sea with its occasional streaks and flurries of white foam, I heard a conversation in which one speaker was a nice chap and very good worker named Harry Greengrass, a member of our Pioneer section. Harry and his mates did most of the unpopular jobs. He said to someone unknown to me, "The Padre insisted on doing a short burial service over Lewis's body. You remember, don't you? The man who copped that bomb from the plane. We collected as many pieces as we could find and sewed them up in a sack, but as we went to lower it slowly into the grave his legs fell out. That scared me because I was sure I had stitched up the bag properly."

I moved away. Poor Lewis. A year earlier, who would have imagined it — in pieces in a sack in a bleak strip of Turkey.

The good ship *Partridge* slipped quietly into Mudros harbour, edged up to a liner-cum-troopship called the *Minneapolis*[205] and an improvised gangway made our transfer to her quick and easy.

In the decks below, ingenious use of metal tubes and wire mesh provided rows of comfortable, connected sleeping bunks. Clean pillows and warm, cream blankets encouraged us to proceed quickly to the ablutions area where we enjoyed showers. In a few minutes, I got rid of the dirt of months, but unfortunately had to put my mucky clothes on again. Still, I felt grand and would not feel ashamed when I wrapped those clean blankets around myself. Hot coffee, warm bread from the ship's

ovens, tins of butter, cheese. Ye gods, what luxury, enough to make me
sob for joy.

As dawn improved visibility I went up on deck, watching numerous
small craft move among the several big ships anchored around us.
Probably the very last remnants of our Army were arriving, completing
the evacuation safely. I saw a destroyer gliding slowly past, soldiers packed
close on her deck. She sat low in the water and, looking down from quite
a height, I recognised Corporal Bebb and several of our men standing near
him. Of course, I yelled "Mick!" loud and often, and others joined in till
we had quite a Bebb chorus.

He saw us and waved, but the destroyer moved on and out of sight.
Probably the officers in charge of her had to report to their flagship and get
instructions regarding disposal of their human cargo. No doubt soldiers
jammed every space down below as well as the deck. I was impatient to
hear from Mick Bebb how he and the rest had been rescued. My guess was
the destroyer had gone close inshore, at great risk, and hauled our men
out of the water — this at some time after all the official evacuation craft
had departed.

We actually remained on-board the *Minneapolis* for three days while
more and more men boarded her as well as other waiting ships. Brother
Ted did not appear, so I guessed he had already gone to Egypt.

We few remaining Signallers did two-hour spells on the bridge each
night, in pairs, and I became familiar with the names of several ships in
the vicinity including, I remember, the *Nestor* and the *Minnewaska*[206] (the
latter belonging to the same line as our ship). The ships' officers probably
did their business during daylight for most of the messages we handled
came before midnight and concerned inter-ship visiting.

Because the ship's third officer proved extremely kind and friendly, I
didn't always bother to go below and wake up the next pair for duty when
my stint ended. A steward supplied him with large helpings of coffee and
sandwiches which, he pointed out, had been warmed "to take the chill out
of them" — and he shared everything with us. Talking of his home, wife,
children, friends, gave him and us great pleasure; he lived in a well-known
Surrey town and spoke in pleasant English country accents.

Such a lovable bloke; I learnt later that after we left the ship at Alex,
she put to sea again, but half an hour out of port she was torpedoed[207].
The odds were that the happy family he'd talked about lost their very fine

daddy. A warm heart had shared those warm sandwiches with two scruffy Tommies.

Shortly before we left Lemnos our ship's Captain, complete with gold braid on a smashing uniform, was rowed out to join us. The last man aboard, he stood on the platform at the bottom of the gangway for a moment, chatting with the two men in the boat. And, while I watched, something puzzling happened: a fairly big flag escaped from under his jacket, landed at his feet and opened up as he retrieved it — revealing the Stars And Stripes! As you can imagine, seeing this early in 1916 my mind got busy searching for the significance of the incident. The States were not at war at that time[208]...

Finally, we set sail[209] and the *Minneapolis* gave us a comfortable run at first. But then that violent weather which starts suddenly in the Med brought rough seas and torrential rain. There being no signalling work at sea, I'd copped a guard duty — down below, fortunately, so I kept warm and dry. While not too clear what I was supposed to be guarding, I had to patrol a long corridor. The ship reared and rolled, but no one came my way, so perhaps they all slept deeply.

We maintained a southerly course and the rough weather came from the west for we frequently rolled sideways — further over each time. I gripped a large, door handle to help keep my footing, but at one moment I was horribly scared because the great ship lay over on her side and stayed there. "Next she'll capsize," I thought — nothing I could do except hang on with my feet just about able to touch the facing wall which had now become my floor, if you understand me. A few more degrees over and we would all drown, no doubt about that.

What all the sleepy devils did during those awful minutes I never found out; probably rolled to one side of their bunks and continued snoring... But to lonely me the danger of flooding and capsize felt very real and frightening.

It was good to see the chanting dockworkers haul two gangways into position on the quay at Alexandria and to join the queue of men slowly making their way ashore. Our contingent grouped alongside a railway track. Then we were directed into goods wagons and travelled a comparatively short distance to that dreary place called Sidi Bishr where we had spent a short time just before sailing for Gallipoli.

There we had to remove all our apparel, wrap our overcoats round the lot, secure the bundles with several big safety pins, and print our names on cotton labels to identify them. Orderlies of some sort packed these bundles into goods vans connected by flexible pipes to each other and, finally — ingeniously — to the railway engine. Hot steam was thereby forced into the vans and so into the clothing. One visualised blood-gorged fat lice bursting under the pressure and derived quiet satisfaction from that hopeful justice.

Meanwhile, we naked, skinny specimens entered a large shed with a concrete floor; facing us, several men sat on boxes, each of them with a paintbrush in hand. We formed up in single lines and, as each of us reached the painter, he dipped his brush into a bucket of dark liquid and slapped it under our armpits and around our dickies. "Creosote!" yelled somebody, and how right he was. We needed no urging to jump into the tanks of water which lay ahead of us, the first consideration being to get rid of that blasted burning fluid. After that, the coarse, yellow soap provided helped us to get clean again. We dried ourselves on linen towels and our bundles of de-loused clothes awaited us outside.

"Shake each garment thoroughly!" yelled a Sergeant and his promise that all dampness would vanish if we did this proved correct. Not exactly mother's washday routine, but we felt good. The ravenous lice were dead and this we really did appreciate.

At about this point the New Year is just getting under way, so I'll pause here as 1916 begins to offer a new set of experiences. I must decide if there is justification for recording some of them.

PART FIVE

1916

WAR:

THE SOMME

Chapter Thirty-One

February, 1916, found us in camp somewhere near Alexandria — "us" being the rag-and-tag fag end of what had been a Battalion of volunteer soldiers, close on a thousand, less than a year ago. Over the next 14 weeks, a few men rejoined us, fellows who had recovered from wounds or sickness. They brought our strength up to around 250.

Many had died, of course. But, when talking of such matters, we who had soldiered on to the end of the Gallipoli campaign preferred to hope that some of those absent still lurked in pleasant places, enjoying a good living and soft jobs in the land of the Pharaohs. "Good luck to'em," was our wish, if indeed they did still exist. We had no means of finding out what had happened to them. We merely hoped they had been transferred to other units for various reasons, or were still receiving medical treatment.

During our first weeks free of the battlefield's constant threat and danger, some of us could not shake off the habit of being constantly alert, ready to run, fall, take a dive, or make any swift move to ensure continuity of our so-valuable-to-us lives. Natural-born survivors, we few, I suppose, and, whatever people like Sergeant Majors and such may have thought of our several contributions to the whole war effort, we fortified our consciences by recalling the creditable or, sometimes, comical actions and situations in which we had participated, while conveniently concealing, by silence, events we suspected might not qualify us for honourable mention.

We took stock of our belongings and discovered we lacked many items which, in more orderly circumstances, we used to lay out for kit inspection. When preparing for active service, we had been told to pack certain necessaries into our packs and haversacks. The remainder we left in our kitbags stacked in some out-of-the-way place and, to my knowledge, never saw again. Ordinarily, we would have had to bear the considerable cost of their replacement but, the loss being no fault of ours, we were promised free replacements.

I had no clothing but what I was wearing and that in poor condition, so I put in for a complete new kit. We secured nothing at that time, but had established our need of new gear without charge.

Military paupers indeed, and we looked and felt the part. We'd had no pay for months and still got none, so, when a pal called Miller suggested a visit to Alexandria, we two got there by walking and cadging the occasional lift in an Army vehicle — horse-drawn, they were.

From our previous visit to Egypt, I still had a few coins left totalling two and a half piastres, worth about sixpence at that time. As we wandered, this hoard of cash procured for me three small eggs and two sweet cakes in a market and a glass of beer in a bar.

In this latter place, we two sat among Arabs of various types, some prosperous and well-dressed in robes and fezzes. Several of them hired hookahs, with their glass water containers standing on the floor. The long, flexible tube leading up to the mouthpiece gripped between their teeth, each smoker, with much solemn care, conducted the elaborate routine of igniting the tobacco leaf in its hollow, surrounded by a small quantity of glowing charcoal. An air of content and much wisdom settled on their faces as soon as their miniature smoke factories became operative.

Other customers talked loudly and animatedly, while a few once more intrigued me by counting circular strings of beads the while they muttered prayers — before Gallipoli, I had seen men do this in Cairo. Perhaps they had converted to the Roman Catholic faith? Or do followers of the Prophet Mohammed also practice this ritual, known as "telling the beads" among Catholic youngsters I knew in childhood.

Thereafter, penniless, we two swells wandered around the town, which we rated less interesting than Cairo. As we strolled aimlessly, a boy joined us. Probably nine or ten years old, he wore a dark-grey Norfolk jacket — popular casual wear for males of all ages at that time — shorts and, below the knees, hose with turned-down coloured tops and short-sided boots; a white shirt with a knitted, striped tie completed his neat outfit. He spoke good English, though with a strange accent — soon explained when he said he was Russian. At that tender age, he was already tri-lingual, French being his favourite, he explained.

When he invited us to visit his home, we felt pleased and excited. The prospect of spending an hour or two in civilian surroundings fulfilled a longing — a desire to return, however briefly, to the old life at home — about which we seldom spoke for fear of being dubbed soft. Absence had illuminated our memories of life in peacetime, attractive glowing pink edges coloured our mental visions of people and places we used to know in that far-distant past.

The boy led us to a flat on the first floor of a fairly large block. He introduced us to his three sisters, small girls, probably aged between 12 and 15. Their fairly large room was furnished with one or two chairs and three small beds. Uncertain, but not embarrassed, I sat down. Miller did likewise and we attempted polite conversation, but were completely defeated because the girls spoke only French.

In England the old teapot would by now have been brought into service to ease developments, but I knew French folk favoured coffee. None was offered, though, and the girls sat around, smiling and sharing remarks and giggles between themselves. I had felt real pleasure on entering this plainly furnished yet clean flat, but now the boy had vanished and, without him as interpreter, we were sunk, no valid reason to remain. Standing up and looking at each girl preparatory to leaving, I decided they were plain as to looks and, though tiny, may perhaps have been a little older than I had at first supposed.

Out on the gallery, from which a staircase led downwards, I glanced at the wall behind me and noticed a brass plate beside another front door. Doctor So-and-So, it said. Seeing one of the girls still standing outside the flat we'd just quit, I called out *"Pourquoi* 'Doctor'?" Her reply supplied the answer to several questions I'd been asking myself. The baby voice shouted "Doctor Cunt!" So then I realised that these children were prostitutes, the Russian boy their tout, and some fat, filthy swine using them to enable him or her to live comfortably during a war which brought death and disease to millions of people.

We commenced our return journey, passing a street famous for its brothels, Miller had heard. Its nameplate proclaimed it to be Rue Des Soeurs[210] — I often heard it mentioned afterwards as "Sisters Street".

Still without money or new clothing, one day we filthy few marched to a railhead where we loaded on to trucks a great many heavy, canvas bags containing tents, along with several marquees, quantities of shovels and picks, and provisions including packages of tinned bully beef, large tins of "julien" (a shredded potato and vegetable preparation), and boxes of hard biscuits — far from appetising fare, but precluders of starvation. We were ordered to fill our water bottles in readiness for a long, dry rail journey. Some lucky devils travelled in roofed wagons, most of us in open trucks, while a coach with proper seating housed the officers and senior NCOs.

At times the sun irked those of us in trucks, but our troubles eased when we took a long break in the vicinity of Cairo. With biscuits, bully beef and unlimited drinking water available there, we had little cause for complaint.

Offering us frequent views of the Nile, at times the railway passed through large plantations. The workers in these places usually paused in their labours to look at us and, if they were males, generally honoured us by raising their gowns and displaying their genitals. Although the exact significance of these gestures remained obscure to us, as soldiers we doubted that they intended respectful salutes, and suspected the Egyptians were not exactly swooning with love at the sight of us.

After some hours, we detrained at a railway halt with several small buildings and a short wooden platform. Immediately, the work of unloading commenced — much easier than heaving the stuff on-board and a couple more hours saw the end of that chore. Then, hard biscuits and individual tins of corned beef were handed out, large dixies full of strong tea appeared and we took stock of our surroundings.

There was the river, reeds and greenery along its banks, and on its far side a cultivated area — irrigated by a piece of machinery which could well have been hundreds of years old. An ox turned a large, wooden wheel by walking in interminable circles; wooden cogs on the wheel's underside rotated a shaft (a smoothed tree trunk) which dragged a chain of leather buckets into and out of the river; these buckets spilled their contents into a large, earthenware container whose overflow poured into a wooden duct and supplied the irrigation system of channels throughout the plantation.

Nearby, we could see a village called Beni Salama[211] — or at least that was the name of the railway halt. It mainly comprised small mud huts, the homes of poor folk who worked the plantations. The flat roofs of these hovels bore piles of ox dung, the round cakes used as fuel to heat the workers' cook pots, we guessed.

On our side of the river lay the desert — sand and more sand, on and on forever, it appeared. We hauled the tent bags some distance away from the railway; officers measured out spaces and minions laid out ropes to mark the lines where the tents were to stand. We had earlier learnt the drill for erecting tents without wasting a single move and a camp sprang up quickly. The marquees proved tricky, but we managed and, before nightfall, we had settled into our own allotted canvas homes. With two blankets apiece, being really tired, we soon slept — all except the poor devils who had to mount guard and scare off intruders if any, or, more likely, the jackals which scrounged around desert habitations.

We spent the next couple of weeks toiling for long periods each day on a diet of hard biscuits, corned beef and dried, shredded veg, with a little jam and a small amount of cheese once or twice a week. The corned beef, basis of the main meal, would be served cold one day and warm the next, as a hash with the shredded vegetables. An unusual addition to this diet was a daily measure of lime juice, compulsory drinking. The official reason for this latter treat never reached my ears — men who professed to know said it was to cool the blood and subdue men's natural lusts (though they used less churchy words). Like a clever little ex-Boy Scout, I preferred the anti-scurvy theory.

Each day a train brought in a fresh load of tents. These we loaded on to some splendid horse-drawn wagons manned by really fine Australians, big, powerful fellows. They had brought in their own equipment and set up a camp where, looking on from the outskirts, I could see that everything worked on a better and more generous scale than ours ever had. I believe they were the Australian Light Horse[212], probably some of the first volunteers from Down Under.

The camp grew, each day's work providing accommodation for one more Battalion.

My brother Ted reappeared one day, to my joy and my amazement, for he was riding high on a camel led by an Arab. An arrangement of rope netting slung over the beast's back provided, on each flank, a container, one filled with loaves, the other with large clumps of dates. A sort of cavalcade followed Ted, some animals carrying similar loads, others with tins of bully beef or special provisions for the officers. "We're what's left of the old Transport Section and eventually we shall be with the Battalion permanently," he told me. Good news indeed.

Once we got talking, I told brother Ted — himself, unpaid for weeks — how I longed for something luxurious to eat after the long period of small, poor rations which had been my lot. I knew complete replacement of all apparel and equipment lost in the recent campaign would soon occur, and we decided that my heavy, wool, long pants might yield a harvest of a few piastres if offered to the local fellaheen.

We didn't know how to go about it but, a few evenings later, in brilliant moonlight we went strolling, both of us enjoying the opportunity to chat without interruption about our affairs past and present. Three Arabs interrupted our pleasant interlude when they approached and asked if we had anything to sell.

We had wandered some distance from camp and I might have been a wee bit anxious about our safety, unarmed as we were, if Ted had not assured me with complete confidence that he understood these people and could handle anything they might start.

Well, when I mentioned my pants — and exposed the tops of them because these men spoke no English — much interest was shown. So I stepped aside, removed them, replaced my trousers, and asked "How much you give?" Their English could cope with that, or the obvious implication, and up went two fingers. Two pieces of five piastres I signalled, but they wilfully misunderstood and proffered two pieces each of one piastre.

The pantomime dragged on and I didn't like the way they crowded us and made grabs at the pants. Their final offer appeared to be three piastres and, at that, Ted's patience ran out and he yelled, "Empshi, empshi allah". When they still lingered, he swung at one of them, hit him on the side of the jaw, and he sank down. He caught number two the same way, took another swing at the last one and just connected, but by then all three were up and running away.

It all happened quickly, I found it hardly believable. I didn't like it for, scurrying away in their gowns, they looked like whipped children. The short, wiry Ted assured me it was the only way to act in these circumstances; soon they would have thought they had scared us and that might have turned out badly. It demonstrated the power a quick decision and quick action gives, rightly or wrongly, to the man who reacts swiftly. (I didn't say that to Ted, I just thought of it while recalling this episode.)

As we walked back to the camp, looking behind us I glimpsed one of the Arabs still hovering dimly some way off and, after I said goodnight to dear old Ted at the horse-lines, I walked in the direction of my tent and waved to the fellow to join me. He must have been expecting this for he came at the trot. I dickered with him briefly and eventually got about four piastres, worth tenpence, for my pants. Next day, I bought a large can of pears at the Nile Storage Co. depot, which had opened near the railway stop.

In due course, we completed our Pioneer task of founding a large camp, which fresh Battalions from other Regiments moved into as fast as we erected new rows of tents. Any additional structures they required, they created themselves.

Now the Royal Engineers arrived, obviously regular Army men, trained for construction work in hot countries. Their main stock-in-trade, apart from a lot of tools, was a huge quantity of sectional piping and standard-sized rectangles of the framed matting we'd often seen used to build reed or cane huts. In no time, they put up showers, ablutions and cooking shelters of uniform size in endless lines between camp and river. I never saw their pumping and purifying plant way over by the river, but blessed them for their good works. Now we could have a cool shower quite often, a boon in that sweltering heat.

Still no money and a very limited diet — though now including dates, from which we often had to scrape annoying grains of sand. We remembered, however, the trying conditions recently endured, and there were few grumbles.

To sleep, I used to make a hollow in the sand into which a hip could sink, then fold one blanket double and, clad in just a vest, lie down with the other blanket wrapped around me. Using my pack for a pillow, I slept in real comfort most nights. So different, almost luxurious, compared with the Peninsula... I would recall one trench in the reserve area where one could never stand upright during hours of darkness because a number of Turkish fixed rifles targeted that position and bullets thudded into the back of the trench at regular intervals... So a tent on the edge of a desert was much to be preferred.

However, one night a double tooth[213] gave me hell and I walked around the camp in awful agony. At dawn, I dressed, told my mates what ailed me, and made my way to a distant tent over which flew a Red Cross flag. There I found a Medical Corporal who, without comment, sat me on a box. He got a grip on the bad tooth with his extractor pliers and, with a knee in my back and a firm grip on my head, he pulled. Without benefit of anaesthetic, the brief agony while he heaved proved memorable, but the relief when he'd finished made it worthwhile.

My brother and his Transport mates finally rejoined us — tough types mostly, who had never taken kindly to drill and only tentatively to military discipline. They cared well for the animals entrusted to them: at that time, a few wagon horses and ten or 12 officers' mounts. Ted had sole charge of a fine, black stallion, which — out of respect for a former lawless horseman, or perhaps in sheer ignorance, and anyway quite bizarrely — had been dubbed Black Bess. He groomed and rode this handsome animal with a skill he'd acquired during those months working in the Qantara horse lines.

Under the surface, Ted and I remained as close as ever brothers could be, but now my one measly stripe marked me as a conformer, I felt, where he and his merry mates were freebooters. In other circumstances, perhaps, they would not have got away with it, but they managed to prove that parades and such were not for the likes of them. On the other hand, if heavy lifting or transporting jobs required doing, they had the know-how and strength when others didn't.

If an officer had the authority — which probably depended on the cash — to acquire a mount, then one of them would readily find time to act as the groom.

We began to see a tall, burly officer around our camp, a Lieutenant Colonel[214], very stern as to facial appearance, and a complete stranger to all of us, officers and rankers. We didn't wish to know him, but secretly feared that, at some not very distant moment, he would force us to acknowledge his existence. Because, since coming to this place on the edge of a desert, we had done practically no formal training or drill. Months of living in holes or trenches on a poor diet and with insufficient water — until the flood and freeze came — had reduced the vitality of even the strongest men.

Anyway, we had been busy during most of our waking hours, erecting tents to create this huge camp. I considered our masterpiece a latrine which in shape and size resembled a large bandstand, but without a roof.

First, we'd dug out a large hole, say 15 foot deep. Into it we threw layers of quicklime, shingle, straw and coarse sand. This arrangement, said the

Royal Engineers officer who designed the contraption, would assist in speedy dispersal of the deposits which, he anticipated, large numbers of visitors would be eager to contribute. The seating — good, stout wood with plank back-rests — ran around the perimeter of this vast hole, facing outward.

Each morning all seats were occupied, while a circle of waiting clients kept keen watch for imminent vacancies. All this took place in full view of our camp and must have excited some interest among passengers on the nearby railway.

Chapter Thirty-Two

A previously unsuspected tide of comradely feeling had recently manifested itself among all ranks; a sort of reaction to recent experiences, a feeling that we had all endured many risks and hardships together, that we had been true to the volunteer spirit and stuck it out when so many others had managed to get away from it all.

All men differ in the degree of sincerity with which they express themselves. The human animal is, perforce, selfish because the instinct to survive, under test, masters all beliefs, hopes and emotions. So this feeling that we had become a band of brothers — that we 250 comprised the valuable essence squeezed by harsh experiences out of the former one thousand — while warming and heartening, was subscribed to tacitly en masse and never individually declared.

A hub around which, or whom, the consequent accumulation of loyalty could revolve had to be agreed upon; without discussion, dissent — or, indeed, any actual voting — we elected the Major, pride of all ranks. And Major Booth, a junior officer a year ago, was indeed now officially in charge of us, since all of more senior rank had vanished, in most cases for reasons unknown to me and probably to all of us.

In the early days back home and on Malta, his ability to learn, to practice what he'd learnt, and to lead men stood out above that of all others and quick promotion to Captain's rank followed. Whereat, being now in charge of a Company, he imposed on its members a discipline sterner than that applied in any other — and for this, men worshipped him, because he tempered power with justice.

An average officer would not investigate a charge brought by an NCO against a Private, but would listen to the charge, then listen to and, usually, disregard the accused sinner's reasons or excuses, find the case proven, and pass sentence. In our hero's case, though, clear enquiry would be made. The NCO would have to prove his case, or not. But if the charged man were then found guilty, he'd get it right in the neck. In the nick as well.

The good officer's fame spread throughout all Companies and most men wished they belonged to his superior cohort. His men's buttons and the brass on their equipment shone more brightly than theirs, their deportment on parade, even the horse the Major rode on long marches, made the rest of us look rather lacking and down-at-heel.

Later, in action, his fearless way of walking upright while surveying and inspecting the front line in full view of the enemy was very impressive — some said foolhardy, but in the men's eyes it was great and it did wonderful things to our morale. And then the Major had brought us safely out of two evacuations and had supervised the setting up of our new camp home.

But, rightly or wrongly, the rank-and-file chaps felt that the officers in the upper bracket generally, and perhaps class-consciously, despised this man now in command of our small Battalion (as we still liked to call it). He was a Jew and a year or more in the hotter climate had darkened his complexion so that, had he donned the robes popular in Egypt, his appearance would have matched that of any other Semite[215].

He had, and deserved, the loyalty of all of us. Now though, on to this scene strode the tall, burly Colonel, from whence or for why none of us knew, but most of us fearfully guessed. He marched everywhere, he looked healthy, fit and sternly purposeful, with his stout, leather leggings around his hefty calves. The unfairness of what we saw developing became the subject of discussion during most of our waking hours.

We drew our first pay for a long time, followed shortly by our first ration of fresh meat (tough, probably camel, but a step in the right direction). In fact, we had started to achieve something towards becoming cleaner and healthier... when along comes this Colonel to take over and humiliate our guvnor.

A parade — us, mind you, ordered to fall in, stand to attention, at ease, and all that stuff! — was ordered. Groups representing former Companies lined up, an officer standing in front of each. We Signallers stood together and found, for the first time, that we too had an officer, a slick, young man in light breeches, soft cap tilted a little to one side, a cane under his arm. Our gallant Major did indeed stand before us all, called us to attention and then turned and waited as, on the lovely Black Bess, the new, unwanted Colonel rode forward.

The final degradation came when our Major saluted the Colonel, then strode away out of our sight. All this seemed unreal… taking place on a flat, sandy waste under a hot, African sun, like a scene from a Foreign Legion yarn in one of the weeklies I'd read before I enlisted.

Formalities over, astride the big, black horse, the Colonel addressed us. The Battalion had acquitted itself well on active service, he knew, but now the time had come for reorganisation, for training in up-to-date skills of warfare. He had been deputed to originate and carry out the new programme and felt sure that all would co-operate… And so on and on while the resentment boiling up among those glaring at him must have been almost visible like a green cloud ascending from the tops of our heads.

He crowned his unpopularity and poisoned the minds of all except us, the Signals Section, when he turned in our direction and proclaimed, "And I expect special attention to the details of your work from you, the Signals Section. You are the cream of the Battalion and will be expected to set the pace in this new effort."

That blackballed our little group to the rest of the men — ensured that our name stank among them for good and always. Had the Major made such a statement we could have strutted around with haloes illuminating our bonces but, coming from the unwanted Colonel, it infected us like some dirty plague and separated us from all but the most generous among our former good friends.

And, of course, down there in the Transport lines was my brother Ted who groomed, polished and trained the horse between the new man's beefy thighs. Wouldn't Ted be the popular one now it had been revealed for whom he was labouring!

The haphazard way in which we had fixed ourselves up to share living quarters with compatible mates was scrubbed right away. The new regime re-allocated tents away in the rear of the camp to officers, with separate marquees for Officers' Mess and Sergeants' Mess now dividing them from "other ranks". Each diminutive Company had its own tents. We unfortunate Signallers in two tents of our own stood out like sore thumbs, being fairly close — much too close — to a tent called Battalion Headquarters in which lived the Regimental Sergeant Major.

Do you remember him? The man seconded earlier, on Malta, from the Royal Marines, briefly a hero with our men, but later, on the Peninsula, disliked for several good reasons and held in some contempt by the Major on account of incorrect behaviour on the front line, such as brandishing a revolver and threatening to shoot men who were already having enough trouble from Turkish guns.

The RSM seemed to positively hate Signallers, probably because the new Colonel had praised us, and he decided to humiliate us at every opportunity — in fact, he picked on me in particular, having viewed me with disfavour since our days in two adjacent holes at Suvla Bay.

We had laid out a system of field telephones from each Company HQ to Battalion HQ, and one of our men was on duty at each point. The work, of course, was a piece of cake so it caused some further resentment among the rest of the Battalion, doing hours of training, drill and various jobs of hard work around the growing camp.

But their resentment was as nothing compared to that of the RSM; he pledged himself vocally, loudly, to have the Cream Of The Battalion off the jammy jobs and on to something which would make the sods sweat — he may even have had some support among our comrades, given that the usurper Colonel's high opinion of Signallers (along with some skilful wangling on our part, I should admit) meant that we were excused certain unpopular tasks, especially "Lion Patrol", the humourous title for a chore which took a party of men prowling about at night in the desert darkness looking for Gawd knows what. Sometimes, when I heard the jackals howling in the distance, I thought of our brave lads out there and then thanked Heaven I was part of the Cream Of The Battalion.

One of us, of course, had to take his turn at manning the phone in the RSM's Battalion HQ tent and that was an unpopular number, you bet. One of our lines ran from Battalion to Brigade HQ, whence all the big, dirty jobs were dished out. When one of those requests landed on the RSM's table he would jump up and yell one name, joyfully it seemed to me: "Corporal Norcliffe!" He knew I would then have the painful duty of detailing a man or men to do whatever scruffy chore had come along.

Not even by detailing myself to telephone duty in his Headquarters tent could I get him off my back. He would hand me the order or, if I'd written down the message myself from a verbal instruction over the phone, he would still have me supply the required men from my small group of Signallers. Well, if available…

Something had to be done to end this victimisation, so when a gap appeared in the brailing[216] of our tent at the back, we enlarged it. The fabric was old and tender and the hole we'd improved on sometimes let in a draught, but we deemed occasional discomfort preferable to satisfying the unending demands of the unjust RSM.

Thereafter, when we decided we'd done our share of the odd jobs for the day, we simply went missing. Before the man had completed his shouting the lads would be through that hole, racing through the lines of tents and on the far side of a ridge at the back of camp, where they would continue their siestas or meditations in peace and quiet. This would force the RSM to call on another junior lance jack for the required labour; although, on parade, the RSM was great at yelling orders, stamping about noisily, and saluting ostentatiously, he appeared to be almost afraid to give orders to older men.

Our Signals Sergeant at that time lived strangely. What enabled him to arrange his personal comings and goings without reference to us and our work remained a mystery. Believe it or not, he had taken up oil painting, scenic and portraits.

His pictures looked good to me. I'd never been able to achieve any kind of understanding with him, perhaps because he considered me too young. So I had the pleasure of his company only on rare occasions, moments when he perhaps felt that the war should sometimes be permitted to interfere with his hobby. All this sounds daft, so shall we assume that this quite brainy Sergeant performed duties about which nothing was known by his associates?

Meanwhile, our new, young officer in charge of Signals, Lieutenant Wickinson, began to organise training schedules which soon occupied most of our waking hours and would eventually bring us up to a level of efficiency justifying, to some extent, the Colonel's inclusion of the word "cream" in a sentence which also contained reference to ourselves.

As opportunity offered, I had washed my uniform and underwear piece by piece. In the warm weather everything dried quickly so, although one spare pair of socks was my only item of clothing beyond what I wore, I never had to go about partly undressed for long. Whatever my appearance, at least I was clean.

And soon, new kit and uniforms did finally arrive, thanks, we understood, to the Colonel's influence in high places. With weekly pay parades restored — the basic enhanced by the refunding of "credit accumulated" — we now had money, almost wealth it seemed for a moment, and, with Lieutenant Wickinson keeping us fully occupied, our Signallers group no longer loitered at the RSM's beck and call.

The further we penetrated into the desert in the course of our exercises, the more hilly it became — ideal for visual signalling practice. Some days we would set up a chain of hilltop stations using heliographs, well-made instruments mounted on tripods. The simple, yet exact process of using them involved flashing Morse messages to a distant station by observing and controlling the positions relative to one another of two mirrors — often while you noted incoming messages at the same time. By means of a graded sight, your sending mirror had to be kept in a position yielding clear signals to the man at the receiving end. This work kept two men quite busy.

I did find it difficult to assess the heliograph's place in modern warfare, except perhaps in dealing with dissident tribes in desert areas. Flags might also have a role in those circumstances, and, at night, possibly the electric lamps. But, in the recent campaign, the only communications media we used were field telegraphs and phones — except that, sea to shore during the landings, flags and signal still proved very quick (though even then, ship-to-ship wireless Morse signalling had come into its own).

These activities once again restored interest to our lives after a period of heavy, manual labour, or equally exhausting efforts to avoid same. The Colonel with the hefty leather-clad calves did effect substantial changes in the lives of all ranks so, although our loyalty and sympathies remained firmly with the Major, we nonetheless found ourselves feeling and looking somewhat the better for the new regime.

Occasionally, leave of absence for a whole day was granted, so we could spend a few hours in Cairo. Travelling took up much of the time, but on the French-run trains the journey was comfortable — the upholstery rich, floor space ample, and stewards served good cool drinks at low charges — and, at times, enriched by entertainment.

I had received a parcel from home. In it I found a large, home-made fruit loaf, one of the good things my mother made (you may recall the hard cake with which, as young office workers lunching by the Thames, Ted and I would attempt to down seagulls). A couple of pals I gave some to praised it lyrically.

The more unexpected items included two light, cotton, faun shirts; I knew I must not be seen wearing them around camp, but I risked it on days off, even accompanied by a pair of light, cotton trousers which I bought off a local for a few piastres. In this garb, I felt like a real dandy and the spice of danger in sporting forbidden gear added to my pleasure. I wore them several times on Cairo visits and got away with it, though surely I must have puzzled one or two Military Policemen.

A card manipulator and conjuror provided part of the entertainment on the Cairo-bound train. His sleight of hand made cards do all sorts of seemingly impossible things. Standing at one end of the coach, he held all the passengers' attention — in fact, he eventually discovered playing cards in many of their pockets. Perhaps a confederate had placed them there, but it was all enjoyably mystifying.

"Before last wonderful trick, you give money, please," he said and, at a remarkable speed, made the rounds with his little velvet bag. The cash collected must have satisfied him, for he produced a pigeon from beneath his robe. The poor thing struggled as he bit into its neck. Then, with a flourish he held the bird out away from his face and some of its flesh appeared to tear off, a string of it, dripping blood, stretched from the man's mouth the length of his arm to the bird's neck. A sickening sight and, of course, his audience recoiled. But, with a loud cry, the man waved a hand and, presto, now the bird looked quite unharmed, restored, and the bloody string had vanished. At which the magician did likewise, probably to give a performance in the next coach.

Lieutenant Wickinson liked to have a programme of work ready for each day and, presumably because our Sergeant was able to avoid working with us, he occasionally asked me to go to his tent of an evening. We would sit and discuss progress and make plans. I enjoyed this unusual procedure, smoked his very nice cigarettes, and got to know this shy, young officer fairly well. I needed no telling that this relaxed relationship began as I entered his tent and ended when I left it. I can't recall ever having discussed it with my mates and was probably more punctilious than they in behaving correctly when on parade.

My heart almost bled for the young Lieutenant on one occasion when we had set up a chain of signal stations at half-mile intervals.

Suddenly, gunfire broke the silence and shells shrieked overhead. Fear did things to my stomach. I had by now achieved freedom from the day-and-night tension one endured in Gallipoli, and this sudden artillery outburst shocked me and temporarily I thought war had spread to this part of Egypt.

Then, as the explosions and shell-shrieks ceased, I saw a party of mounted officers heading towards us. Closer view of them revealed that several of them wore red bands round their caps and bits of red on epaulettes and tunic collars. A grey-moustached, red-faced senior officer yelled "Who's in charge here?" and, as our Lieutenant stepped forward, the old boy yelled at him, "You bloody young fool, you've placed your men in line across an artillery range. You are endangering their lives and interfering with our Brigade training. I am Major General [So-And-So] and I'll have you disciplined for this. Now clear off and take all your men with you."

Still, for the most part, our training went rather better than that. Our energetic Colonel quite rightly said we must be terribly out of touch with shooting. I think I can say that we all thoroughly approved of arrangements made for our firing practice.

The desert was anything but flat, and the range comprised a fairly extensive hillside dotted with clearly numbered, empty, petrol cans. The instructors allotted each man a can. We followed load and fire orders which varied from taking careful, single shots to ten rounds rapid fire. Using then-new Mark VII ammo and the short rifle, I didn't suffer so much from the kick as I had done with the old, long rifle. At conclusion, we each handed in our empty cartridge cases, plus the remaining live ammunition and the total had to be equal to the number of bullets first issued.

It was good sport, for who wouldn't enjoy taking pot shots at a petrol can, even with stones, let alone a powerful rifle. We ended with a walk out to our cans to count the holes in them. Results were pretty good.

Meanwhile, the camp kept on growing. A large contingent of Welsh troops settled close by us. If memory serves, they were the 53rd Welsh Division and, of course, the thing most of us feared did prove true. They had a large choir. So they had to build a stage, didn't they?

The men stood up there on various levels and their Major Choirmaster waved his arms and implored with his hands as, time after time, they sang that stirring anthem Comrades In Arms[217] till I knew every note of it and hated it like hell. Nonetheless, as soon as they had perfected a few male-voice-choir favourites, we had to attend their concert — by order, although we had done nothing to merit such punishment.

Apart from that, time passed fairly pleasantly and we were inclined to assume we should spend the rest of the war in the Middle East, perhaps seeing action again in lands east of the Suez Canal.

But that modest imagining vanished when the Colonel made one of his impressive pronouncements, mounted on the beautiful Black Bess. Only a faint hope remained, he said, of our staying together as a Battalion. The powers-that-be were in favour of scattering us among other units. Even so, if we could perform exceptionally well, we might yet be treated as a cadre into which reinforcements could be introduced until we eventually constituted a modern Battalion of four Companies — eight hundred men in all.

We immediately put all we'd got into training to reach that high standard. I never again had the experience of working with such dedicated men and the results must surely have impressed the men at the top. Even leisure we devoted to games aimed at improving fitness, and the Quartermaster's department seemed to enter into the spirit of the thing, providing even better food and more of it.

However, one successful innovation in no way concerned with enhancing our military skills does deserve mention. Horse racing it was, the riders being officers who had mounts.

Several painted posters placed in prominent positions advertised what some bright spark had dubbed the Desert Derby. These named and described the horses and the events in which they would run. The riders would be listed on the day, they said — and, since neither my brother nor I could imagine the hefty Colonel participating, we hoped the ride on Black Bess would be given to him, since he was so used to handling the misnomered stallion.

Much grooming and trial racing went on until the great day arrived. We were amazed to see men streaming in their hundreds towards the course our Battalion had marked out. Using a natural ridge and lines of sandbags to mark the boundary, we had made an oval track about one and a half miles in length for the longer races, with short sprints to measure the length of the ridge.

A festive air prevailed. Last-minute acceptances of entries from outsiders were arranged and an enterprising clerk assembled the final list and ran off copies on one of those gelatine slabs, and sold them at a piastre a time. I saw a Yeomanry Sergeant, brandishing one of these "programmes", shouting the odds and taking bets, writing slips for betting cards while his assistant made up the book.

The excitement of the occasion must have gone to the Colonel's head, for he insisted on riding the black and denying me the pleasure of seeing Ted win a race which I was certain he would and the Colonel wouldn't — and, indeed, he didn't. But the meeting's terrific success made us all feel, for the moment, that we were human beings once more and not just anonymous pieces in a game of kill or be killed.

A day or so later, even while the festive light still shone in our eyes, came the order to break camp and entrain once more for Alexandria. We embarked on a large liner-troopship and in no time I was watching the familiar coastline of Egypt recede, and feeling deep regret about leaving a country I should have liked to know better[218].

On this voyage, to me the only event of note was passing close to a huge ship with four funnels. I had thought that our boat, the *Transylvania*, was a big'un, but this was colossal and chock-a-block with troops, thousands of them. Several years later when I was buying a pair of shoes, the chap serving me said, as we discussed the late war, that he was on the *Transylvania* when, just south of Italy, a U-boat torpedoed her; he survived because a Japanese cruiser rescued him and many others and put them ashore in Italy — in that war, Italy and Japan were among our allies[219].

How lovely France looked when we anchored off Marseilles, the shore lined with the white, usually flat-roofed buildings I'd found so attractive when viewing other Mediterranean towns from the sea. Close up they usually didn't look quite so white, nor did the air around them always carry aromas as pure as sea breezes, but I preferred the illusion to the reality until proved wrong.

A three-day rail journey followed. I found it delightful. No hurry about it, evidently. We would be shunted into a siding for food and natural relief and, if the streets of a village or town were adjacent, we'd take a stroll. A wave or shout would fetch us back to the train in a moment — we were good boys, still chasing that soldierly perfection which would win for us reinstatement as a Battalion.

The beautiful greenness... I couldn't describe the pleasure it gave me. Grass, green acres of it. Trees — copses, woods, forests of the lovely things. Until I saw all this beauty I didn't know I'd been missing it. And another kind of vision on show to us could stir a young man's pulse to extra activity — the sight of a European girl with white and pink complexion, brunette and blonde, as opposed to sallow or dark tan with near-black hair.

At the time all these differences aroused thrills of appreciation in me. So when, on one occasion, I inadvertently stepped from the train almost into the arms of a girl, words failed me. When she indicated she would like a tunic button for a souvenir (one of the few words we both understood) I cut one off with my jackknife pronto — in exchange for a kiss.

During the night, when our train paused in a big, well-lit station, local people brought along big jugs of red wine from which they filled our mess tins. No charge! Living it up, indeed, and we quickly became a joyful crowd. Although we had to sleep sitting up in crowded compartments, no one complained; who knew what pleasures the morrow might yield?

And so to Rouen[220], where the British Army had a huge base camp. Perhaps we hoped that a small unit like ours would be lost sight of among so many; but no, our training was taken out of the hands of our officers and NCOs.

Each day we were marched off to an intensive training ground where we had our first experience of a battle course. With fixed bayonets we would charge forward, jump a ditch, climb a wall, then see ahead a line of hanging sacks which represented men. We had to stab them with our bayonets, the while we emitted blood-curdling yells calculated to scare the enemy stiff before we skewered him. Instructors lined the course, swearing at us, urging us lazy bastards to scream and stab. The whole thing was like some horrible, mad orgy and they soon had us behaving like the lunatics they appeared to have become.

Our frantic performance did have a purpose, of course, however daft it looked. One day, the Sergeant who put us through our paces marched us into some lovely woods, had us sit down, and made a pretty little speech — it almost brought maidenly blushes to our cheeks. We had, he said, passed the battle course with distinction and he was sorry he had only just been told, before the morning session, we weren't "rookies" straight out from Britain, but veterans of the Gallipoli campaign. He appeared concerned that we had been put to this trouble and assured us we would not be bothered by that sort of thing any more.

Personally, I had no wish to be regarded as an old hand at the shoot-and-stab lark and reckoned that, if we were to be sent to the Front in France, then the more I knew about tactics up there the better.

Thereafter, we trained once more under our own officers, our efforts directed towards drilling and marching in preparation for a passing-out inspection. The General in charge of the Rouen base would decide our fate.

You can imagine how hard we tried, repeating all the drill movements hour after hour, concluding with a fixed-bayonets march-past. Came the day and, watched by the General who stood throughout on a rostrum, we executed our routines — very well, we felt. Then we marched off home and, full of hope, awaited the big man's verdict.

The parade at which the verdict would be announced found us tense but confident. The message read out by the Major spoke of devotion to duty, splendid efficiency, and a march-past which would have done credit to the Grenadier Guards. Delighted, and certain we would soon be made up to Battalion strength and soldier on together, we celebrated in our various ways.

A man called Haines, who belonged to my original H Company, surprised me by asking me to go with him into the town of Rouen. From the camp, we could cover much of the distance by electric tram — the single-deck type popular on the Continent. I looked forward to sight of the Seine because my father had told me long ago about an incident during a holiday in France; bathing with schoolmates near the bridge in Rouen, he got into difficulties and was rescued only just in time. I leant over the bridge and looked for a likely spot from which boys might dive. But buildings occupied the banks for as far as I could see. Many years had passed since my dad was a boy, and what had I hoped to see, anyway, to mark the spot where the near-tragedy had occurred? A hole in the river maybe? But I did feel a sentimental sort of connection. A bit of homesickness.

After that, I wanted to see the cathedral, again on my dad's account, because he had described a large and wonderful stained-glass window he'd admired in that fine building. Haines told me he had not come to town to look at that sort of place, but still we sought information about it, crossed to the town side of the bridge, took a turning to the left and walked towards it up a narrow, uphill street.

Two items I recall: a bucketful of slops tipped from a window high above narrowly missed us, and then we were passed by a very short, bearded man dressed in a suit of green velvet, comprising a longish jacket with white, lace frills, along with breeches, hose and buckled shoes. His appearance, the narrow street and consequent dim light suggested to me a connection with evil in the little man, and caused a feeling of foreboding.

The cathedral was splendid, with several quite wonderful windows, but Haines remained anxious to move on. He suggested having a drink and we entered a place which, from its appearance, I took to be the kind of *estaminet* where a glass of wine or beer could be had cheaply.

Inside, though, I saw no bar, only some marble-topped tables and chairs. Then, unprompted, an electric bell rang loudly — it shook me, being so unexpected — a door opened and in marched a line of eight or so women dressed in gowns of various colours. Facing us, they threw open these gowns and stood there, obviously inviting inspection and selection. None of them was young, some as old, I judged, as my mother. I hope I didn't show the revulsion I felt. I expected my companion to get out with me right away, but instead he pointed to one woman. She stepped forward and he departed with her.

I was in a dilemma, but made it clear by my actions that I wasn't interested and the women marched out — all except one. By now I felt scared and ordered wine to propitiate whichever invisible person ran the establishment. It meant spending a couple of scarce francs, but provided time in which to think. I remember pouring myself a glass from the bottle, pushing it towards the woman and making signs that she should help herself... and when she had drunk that, insisting she had another glass. Some time passed, the awkward situation becoming ever more distressing for me. Relief came with the reappearance of Haines. I stood up, waved farewell, and was outside the place in a second.

Naturally, I protested about being let in for a rotten experience, but Haines laughed that off. He'd assumed I'd known what it was all about, whereas I would have expected a chap who wanted that sort of thing to choose a man with similar tastes to his own for a visit to the town. I recall asking him if he was married. He was, of course, so that accounted for his need of a woman to fill a wartime lack in his life.

From cathedral to brothel, from beauty to horror, from procreation to recreation... And from prostitution, commercial copulation, battle, murder, and sudden death, Good Lord deliver us.

Days passed, and our enthusiastic hopes for the old Battalion sagged; no news came of the new men who were to fill out our shrunken ranks and make up the full-strength unit we could help to train and improve.

Came a day when everybody — without exception! — was ordered to parade. With all present, we were surprised not to see our popular Major out in front[221]. Instead, his adjutant stood there. I had not seen him since the occasion of his appearance at Gallipoli, walking out in the open when we were all in holes or trenches — when one of his arms was bandaged and supported by a sling and he looked ill. Today, he looked fit physically, but his face was pale.

He quickly told us that, in spite of all our endeavours and successes, it had been decided that our numbers were too small for making up with reinforcements. Groups of us would be sent to various Battalions in the two Territorial Divisions on the Front in France. He said much more. One could see tears on his face. But no comment came from the ranks, no response whatsoever. Had the Major done the execution job, some men would have said a few words, heartfelt if not exactly polite. However, the adjutant's emotion was wasted on us; when we dispersed we were quite a different set of men to those hearty mugs who had, for weeks, tried so hard to please.

I had one desire now and that was to somehow get a leave pass. To spend a few days in England before going into action. I, and many others, went around voicing this desire and also letting it be known that, because of the scurvy treatment we had received, the Army could get stuffed. Dangerous conduct this, but our outraged feelings needed some outlet, the more so since it became known that a new Battalion bearing our title[222] was already in existence in England.

One of our men, Brotherton, did get compassionate leave for family reasons. But, before he'd left France, he ended up in hospital with serious injuries; travelling on the cheap to the Channel coast, he boarded a goods train and climbed into a small cabin on the roof of the wagon. But the train took the wrong line, one where a tunnel wasn't high enough, and the wagon was smashed, Brotherton with it. He survived, but it seemed odd that the only ranker I'd known to be granted leave failed to reach home.

This is no tale of a God-fearing patriotic boy facing death and achieving glory for beloved king and country. After Gallipoli, the survivor members of our Battalion had felt some kind of joy-in-comradeship bond, but we'd backed a loser and that was that. Henceforth, we owed allegiance to no one, every man for himself and devil take the hindmost.

I spent much of my spare time in a Church Army hut, where the mother and daughter who ran the concern provided home-made wads (buns, rock-cakes, and the like) and cups of good tea cheap, and always had time for a chat. They never rushed about trying to work up more business, that was not the object of the venture; wisely, the organisers of the overseas church missions to the troops realised many men would value a quiet place where letters could be read and written, or books borrowed and read, without interruption from hale and hearty religious fellows, who meant no harm, but could be nuisances. Mum protected her daughter from physical contact with the licentious soldiery, but permitted friendly conversation across the counter as part of the service.

In camp, though, where were the smiles and cheery greetings which had become customary during our recent combined effort to impress the top brass? Gone missing, replaced by faces registering all the wrong emotions, such as scorn, sadness and defiance.

Family men must have felt additional anxiety at times, after having survived some risky situations and come now so near to home, yet apparently still to be denied a short period with their loved ones before going into battle alongside strange comrades, men about whom they knew nothing. They did understand that no definite undertaking had been given as to permission to visit home being granted after a specified period abroad, but this did appear to be an opportune moment for a kindly gesture from above… Our Battalion disbanded, no training programme to be interrupted, still some days to be passed in idleness while our individual fates were decided.

These matters occupied almost all our thoughts and conversations. We became monomaniacs on this subject of leave. Battles, logistics, advances, retreats — those things concerned others; we were single-track thinkers who just wished to go home for a while.

At least, during our period of uncertainty, the opportunity had been taken to ensure we were fully equipped, so when our transfers to new Battalions came through we would make no demands upon them, beyond normal requirements of food and ammunition.

I was foolish enough to allow today to be fouled up by speculations as to what tomorrow might bring forth, but I ought to have enjoyed that spell at the huge Army base near Rouen. The weather compared unfavourably with Egypt, but we did have a sort of roof over our heads — albeit canvas — a luxury after the Gallipoli experience. In addition, our circular bell tents had strong, sectional wooden floors.

We took our meals in large huts, the food plentiful, nourishing, and of a higher standard than our Battalion caterers had ever produced. So I could appreciate the camp organisation was in the hands of men skilled in providing for the needs of large numbers. Conscientious men maintained efficient sanitation — on the buckets and night-soil-carts basis — using the unskilled labour freely available to the best advantage. A large incinerator dealt with all combustible waste. If many rounds of live ammunition found their way into the furnace, the consequent explosive cracks served to remind us all that, not far away, there was a war going on.

But the impending dispersal of the old crowd soured most of my waking moments at the time. Even though, in my estimation, the dispositions of these men ranged from more than decent to anonymous to detestable, they had been my companions for the last 20 months. That most of them felt similarly afflicted showed clearly in their faces. A generally held opinion developed that the sooner the chop came the better — since, apparently, none of us in the ranks were going to see our homes and families before they dispatched us to join some strange Battalion up in the front-line trenches.

For me, the parting proved quick and rendered almost painless because, without warning, three or so of us were assembled, our kits and rifles inspected, and off we marched to a railway station. I had no time to seek out my brother to say goodbye, so once again I was on my way into action without benefit of his company. Reflecting sadly on this, I felt consoled when I realised that, if we had lived together in constant danger, we would have feared for each other's safety and, if one had been injured or killed while we were together, the other would have suffered deeply. For some months thereafter, we had no news of each other, since he didn't know my destination and we had no means of corresponding.

My little group travelled some distance on the French railway, then transferred to open trucks on a narrow-gauge line run by British engineers and drawn by diesel engines. After detraining, we marched until we reached a quite pleasant-looking village, the first I had been able to see at close quarters. Far in the distance, I could hear the rumble and thud so familiar a few months earlier. Once more, the belly-tightening tension resumed its grip and I was all set to face and deal with personal risks to the limit of my physical ability.

In that state, I could play a role apparently a shade more light-hearted and carefree than my normal one. The paramount necessity: to appear free of anxiety, as unruffled as possible by nasty things which might be happening in the vicinity. And thus would one exist during the coming months or years until relief came in the form of wounds or death — but preferably, as optimistic youth would have it, in the form of a piece of paper authorising one to depart from the scenes and stenches of trench warfare and travel to a land where all was sweetness and kindness and about which, to some extent, real memories had been replaced by fantasies.

In this village, soldiers occupied most of the buildings. A brief stroll along the main road and one or two along short side lanes revealed barns and out-houses serving as quarters for the hoi-polloi, while commissioned ranks luxuriated in farmhouses and cottages. I viewed one splendid establishment through big, wrought-iron gates; the buildings surrounded a large courtyard. One of our lads stood outside on sentry duty. So, I wondered, what exalted rank dignified the occupant of that fine residence?

I found considerable wreckage at one end of the village, but also some small farmhouses there still in the care of civilians, mostly women and old men. It was great, I felt, as I often did during such interludes, to be in fairly close proximity to non-military folk.

Just the sight of females, from time to time, made the place seem homely. Not that any attractive girls lived there, though many must have graced the place before filthy war and rape, or the risk of it, drove them elsewhere... I still retain a mental picture of a youngish woman behind whom I walked a while as she drove three cows along a lane: her hair coarse and matted, she wore a man's cap, an old, dark-blue, military tunic much too big for her, a knee-length skirt of mud-coated, dark cloth — below which her thick calves were clothed in British Army long pants, with grey Army socks and heavy, Army boots on her feet. A boy such as I was then could feel sympathy not untinged with amusement, but I imagined she would remain totally safe from the lustful cravings of even the most sex-deprived old soldiers. That apart, she was a good'un just to be in that place so near to the front line, at risk from long-range enemy guns, trying to keep the little farm going while her men were away.

Chapter Thirty-Four

They'd transferred my small contingent to one of the Territorial mobs which had its Headquarters in the London area. Our lot, as you know, were based in Bloomsbury — this crowd came from the richest and most royal borough, whose name you have correctly guessed, though I won't confirm it[223]. I encouraged any chap who cared to talk about the Regiment to do so, but they knew little about it because they turned out to be the first conscripted soldiers I had met.

It seemed that, during our sojourn in the Mediterranean Expeditionary Force, changes had taken place in England. The original voluntary-service fervour had quickly expired and heavy casualties on the Western Front had to be made up by the only means now available, namely, compulsory service.

These men, my new comrades, proved more than willing to shed a new light on the behaviour of some civilians in the dear old homeland. Setbacks on land and sea had brought realism to the fore. In the early days of the war, natural optimism, faith in the unbeatable British Navy and our world-beating Army, plus much official propaganda, had encouraged those who intended to keep clear of personal involvement in the nasty business to believe that Britain would surely smash the Kaiser's forces.

Many at home already earned more money than they had in peacetime, and they intended hanging on to their jobs come what may. Should call-up papers pop through their letter boxes they could appeal to tribunals. Deferment of their conscription to armed service might be arranged if, perhaps, their employers could prove their work important to the national effort. Who, would you guess, comprised the membership of those tribunals? Local bigwigs. If an appellant was by way of being acquainted with a member, 'twas said he might secure deferment almost forever.

So the next best ploy was to change jobs and get work in one of the new armaments or ammunition factories being built at a great rate. These places paid well, perhaps two or three times more than in peacetime factories, because of the urgent need to speed up production. They employed many women too and one conscript told me bullets and shells were not the only products of some folks' work on the night shift.

Moreover, some prominent people concerned with improving the status of working-class people had promoted the idea that, if a man had religious convictions strong enough to forbid him taking part in warfare, he should be allowed to state them before a special tribunal, the members of which might decide that he should do "national work" other than join the armed services[224].

As World War I progressed the numbers of men who held or adopted these strong pacifist beliefs increased, and some men thus avoided all the risks and sufferings to which most were exposed. I heard that if the tribunal disbelieved the heart-rending yarn you spun, if you still refused to take up arms you would be imprisoned, or put to work in agriculture, or something of that sort. In any case, you avoided all the pains and hazards of the battlefield — that had its attractions. Some of these "conchies", as the "conscientious objectors" were contemptuously called, were politicians, and some later achieved high positions, after the prejudice against "war dodger" types had subsided.

And yet... here too was a concession which appeared to indicate that one fence separating The Workers from the rest had been demolished — in part, the "conscience clause" entailed an admission from on high that the dwellers in the terraced side streets were capable of thought, able to form, maintain and explain a conviction reached after study and evaluation.

Naturally, we volunteers, enduring hellish conditions, would think on these matters and wish that, in 1914, we had conducted ourselves more artfully, had possessed sufficient courage and foresight to know where proper self-interest lay — and act on it. I could have remained at home and then, when my "call-up papers" arrived, I could have claimed exemption on one ground or another and perhaps sidestepped active participation altogether.

The conscripts' up-to-date description of life among some working people in the changed conditions of wartime made me feel that I, and many others, had been foolish to cut ourselves off so completely from our occupations much sooner than necessary. Of the four of us who enlisted together, the elder three would have been conscripted more than a year after they'd actually volunteered, and I was still under-age and, allowing for the usual period of training, would probably not have been sent on active service for a further two years…

Probably, I would have thought little about these matters had our original Battalion been reinforced after our tremendous efforts to prove ourselves worthy of special treatment — and even then, that scheme having failed, had we been allowed visits to England before once more going to the front line.

The tales I heard about goings-on in England — the good times many enjoyed while thousands of their fellows were maimed and killed in France — gave rise to some pretty bitter thoughts and made me decide to take advantage of any opportunity which might arise to bring about an improvement in my condition. Living among strangers, one felt free of any loyalty or obligation, except to the extent imposed by military regulations.

None of the men who had come from the old Battalion in Rouen with me ended up in my new platoon. I even felt glad about that; a feeling of comradeship would have existed had any of them been with me, and I wanted no more of such attachments.

But I soon recognised that this Battalion was run by men more skilled in caring for and providing for their rankers than any I had encountered earlier. A Quartermaster Sergeant, a Sergeant Cook, and some well-trained men worked miracles with the rations to produce meals of a quality I'd seldom experienced in front-line soldiering. They had several mobile field kitchens, comprising large boilers, food store boxes, fuel containers, fire boxes under boilers with tubular chimneys and so on, along with two-wheeled vehicles, usually pulled by mules, which allowed cooking to proceed while on the march. According to circumstances, they either stayed behind to work and caught up with us later, or moved with us in the column, or went ahead to our destination if our progress was slower than their wagons could achieve.

Always, a substantial hot meal and good steaming tea arrived when needed — well, except when "enemy action" occasionally disrupted their praiseworthy efforts. The Quarter-bloke, a tall, strong, purposeful man, a tower of strength and efficiency, often achieved near-miracles under terrible difficulties. For men who, for hours, had endured exposure to rain, cold, shot and shell to unexpectedly be given a mess-tin full of hot stew or tea with bread was to restore our faith and hope and courage — the very knowledge that others thought about our discomfort, even misery, and had been kind enough to do something about it heartened us.

None of the messing about with bits of rations here, no cooking puny portions in a mess-tin over a small spirit burner — often producing nothing worth eating. No going for days with nothing but hard biscuits, jam and a small allowance of water...

Observing this, and other matters of organisation, I came to understand that, here in France, with the war obviously going to be a long one, the British Army conducted it rather on the lines of a business.

The Medical Officer, strong and thorough — unlike old Number Nine, that long streak of misery from my old Battalion in Gallipoli — frequently talked to the men about both sanitation and medication. He inspected our quarters, checked up on latrines. Furthermore, I learned that he and his like had given much thought to addressing the health hazards of the Western Front's static combat. For instance, until recently many men had become casualties with a complaint called "trench foot"[225], caused by wet, cold feet receiving no care over long periods. Regular washing, careful drying, massage with mild oil and putting on clean, dry socks prevented this foot trouble and, when no major affray was in progress, men were sent to the rear in rota for this simple treatment, proven to be so effective that the Army had declared it a punishable breach of discipline to have trench feet (except in circumstances where the remedy could not possibly be applied, the authorities allowed).

My new Company occupied a barn, a big one. Strong bunks — wire netting over wood frames — filled all floor space, apart from a central area where tables and benches were set out. Imagine this, near the front line, such luxury! At Suvla Bay I never even had a cover over my hole-in-the-ground — except briefly when I worked with 88th Brigade HQ. And here... blankets two per man (dark, not laundry-fresh admittedly, but cosy). Plenty of water for all ranks; so different from the small, daily ration out East which had to suffice for drinking and all else... and I drank mine, so "all else" was a non-starter.

Here I could remove boots, tunic and trousers at night, instead of wearing them continually except for brief louse-hunts. Up in the firing line, men told me, you might have to remain fully clothed for 10- to 14-day periods — but never for weeks on end.

Most of the men in my new mob wore steel helmets, an item I had never seen before. All I had was an old cap from which I had removed the shape wire so that I could still wear it while sleeping. Stylish headgear — the soft top could be pulled to one side quite rakishly, suggesting I was no end of a devil — yet ineffective protection if a bullet or a piece of shrapnel came your way.

Some of my new comrades had what were called gas masks too; in the previous year, since kindly German scientists had devised portable storage tanks deployable on the battlefield, poisonous gas had fearfully damaged many men. At the front, should the wind be blowing towards our men, the Germans would release clouds of the stuff. We knew nothing about it in the early days, I heard. Our men would be asphyxiated, *hors de combat* immediately, and often permanently afflicted. But these efficient gas masks worked well, if you got them on in time.

At Gallipoli[226] our hopeful protection had been a pad of cotton you had to piss on and then clamp over our nose and mouth. I never had to use it, thank goodness.

Because this new lot's Signals Section was at full strength when I joined, I became a humble Lance Corporal on ordinary duties. So I sought an interview with the Captain in charge of our Company and asked to be allowed to revert to the rank of Private, but he refused.

I wanted no rank, no responsibility except to myself. Rank entailed being careful, steady, a good example, even though a Lance Corporal was everybody's lackey, often jeered at by the Privates and ordered around by Corporals and Sergeants. I longed to lose that stripe and be a carefree nothing.

But, with pleasant fellows in my platoon, on the whole, and a new mood now upon me — occasioned by living among strangers — I could behave in a relaxed manner, laugh without restraint at even the corniest joke, and make a few cheeky comments about people around me (usually taken in good part). The underlying bitterness remained in me, though, and stoked up the fire of reckless humour which ruled out thoughts of a serious nature and ensured that nobody would wish to attempt serious conversation with me — while roughly the opposite of my style in the old Battalion, this resulted in a sort of coarse popularity which pleased me. Consequently, I quickly earned for myself a soubriquet I liked, to wit, The Pisstaker.

Came the day for us to pack up and move forward... and now my gut-gripping tension increased, although I believed, or hoped, I remained outwardly the flippant ass they liked. For some kilometres our drum-and-fife band led us on with tunes which had probably cheered up our soldiery in the days of Good Queen Bess. Anyway, the rhythm of the drums kept our feet moving in unison — most useful in that it saved us from tripping each other up.

When the band stepped aside we marched on awhile in silence, save for the crunch of boots on gravel road. Soon we entered the ghost of a village and halted. Each Company remained cohesive, but the general idea, with enemy onlookers in mind, was to get lost visually.

Far away, we could see active "sausage" balloons, with baskets housing observers[227] suspended beneath them. I learnt that both sides now commonly used aeroplanes for observation purposes too, so we had to take great care to avoid being spotted, because artillery might open up and polish us off before we even reached the front line.

We spread out in small groups among the village's remaining walls, or parts of same, all remaining within hailing distance of our officers. Our Company cooks demonstrated their efficiency as usual, for within half an hour we were enjoying a rich, tasty stew, a generous helping for each man. Obviously, they had prepared our meal on the road as we marched. Then, when we had our meal, they quietly cleaned the boilers, filled them with water and brewed tea, for they soon gave us a welcome drink of that morale-improver. In addition, most of us had little extras we'd bought earlier — chocolate, biscuits and the like.

The rumble, roar, and occasional extra-loud crump of a shell exploding nearby, offered constant reminders that some of us would have to pay for this present indulgence in blood and pain ere long. With the sun sinking, we were warned to pump ship, attend to all nature's wants, and rest, in preparation for some trying hours of movement in darkness across open country, and then in strange trenches.

The enemy maintained fairly steady bombardment of places where he knew transports and troops must pass during the hours of darkness. Horse-drawn and motor vehicles usually had to stay on the roads, so crossroads became favourite targets for German gunners. Soldiers on foot could avoid these deathtraps, but the necessary diversions added mileage to their journeys and often took them through messy, muddy areas, slowing progress.

As we set off "across the plain" — a Sergeant's words — there was no moon. His remark aroused little interest among the troops; they'd done this trip before, and I refused to remind them that I was a stranger among them by asking, "What plain?" Our Company, walking in twos, must have formed a considerable crocodile as we weaved around shell-holes and various vaguely visible humps which mystified me until ear-splitting explosions and skyward-leaping flame flashes, changing to brief red streaks and short-lived shrieks issued from one of them — British gun batteries, of course. Someone could have tipped me off — we were stumbling through such a concentration of guns as I had never imagined.

And I had no idea about the extent of this "plain", but if these batteries were lodged to left and right of us, not to mention fore and aft, for distances which one could guess at as more and more guns opened up, then this was war on a scale to which I was a complete stranger. Sometimes we had to walk in front of and quite close to these artillery clusters and a fear assailed me that they might let fly at one of these moments. If they were sighted on distant targets we would be at little risk because the guns would point upwards, but if they were aiming to hit enemy positions only a mile or so distant the barrels would be lowered and the shells pass through *us* before exploding among the Germans...

By the light of muzzle flashes, I saw that gun-pits had been dug to house these guns, placing them below ground level and giving their crews some protection. Their mound-like appearance in the dark came from the nets slung over frames to camouflage them in daylight.

"Into single file now." This order passed quietly from man to man as we moved down a slight incline... and there I was once more in the confinement of a trench. I could perhaps move to left or right if self-preservation seemed to require it, but not far. After several months of freedom from this wretched situation the whole, hateful, trapped feeling returned. Bursts of machine-gun fire, the crashes of bursting shells, sometimes singly, often in numbers, the whining of bits and pieces — fragments of metal. This was to be my life, night and day, for several weeks to come, or for longer if anything in the nature of attack and counter-attack developed.

But then came a shaft of hope, almost of joy, for I remembered that here no sea lay behind us, that in periods of rest from front-line trench life we would withdraw some miles away from all noise, wounding, or sudden death, and enjoy relief from our fears and these unnatural living conditions.

We steadily made our way along the winding communications trench, seeing little, hearing much. When I sensed, rather than saw, a cross-trench going to left and right, from past experience I identified it as the reserve trench. Somewhere along it would be located our Battalion Headquarters and various ancillary services. In the next cross-trench, the support trench, probably two Companies were stationed. But we moved on… and into the front line, the trench that faced the enemy. He might be close, 20 or 30 yards distant, in which case we would have some advanced holes and short trenches in between the front lines — probably manned only during hours of darkness. If there were a wide gap, it would be scouted by patrols from both sides during the night.

As we approached the front, a stream of men passed us, going back the way we had come — happy, because we were relieving their burden of tense preparedness with no let-up, night or day. Always some part of the trench system was being damaged or destroyed, some danger threatened. Mates maimed, blown apart. So, as they threaded their way through our advancing line, they made quiet, little jests, wished us good luck, gave useful hints occasionally about special features of the terrain. Nice chaps going for a well-earned rest, bless'em.

I felt I was a stranger here while the others had done all this before. In my previous spell of front-line service, as a Signaller, to maintain communications between points A and B I had been compelled to make my own decisions, once I had received orders. Now, I was a member of a Company and must decide nothing until my immediate superior told me what to do. This situation, which reduced me to just a soldier with a number, and a damned long one at that, added further to my suppressed anger about the way things had gone of late.

In this regard, with some cynicism, I noticed a ploy the authorities put into operation. Now that masses of men were being "called up", as the expression went, those in command — military or political, I didn't know — abhorred the idea that chaps who had volunteered when war started should have anything to distinguish them from conscripts. My first number, for instance, was 2969, but on joining the hordes rolling off the Kitchener production line, I and all the other "old-timers" must be branded as one of them. So 2969 became 302337... Well, may I remind you once more that this yarn has no connection with the story of World War I; it's a record of what happened to just one very insignificant member of HM military forces in that scrap.

We now halted and took over a small stretch of the front-line trench lately vacated. Nobody told me anything about procedure, no doubt because they had all done this routine on other occasions. I asked no questions, but chatted to an older man who sat on the firing step beside me. He had the unusual name of Smith, worked in a coal mine, he said, though his speech didn't smack of Yorkshire or Wales or any northern area. On my other side sat a youngster who said little.

Soon a man whom I couldn't see in the darkness detailed us off in pairs for lookout duty. This meant that the first pair would get up on the firing step and keep watch on the area between us and the German trenches for two hours and would rouse the next two when it was time to change over. Meanwhile, the rest of us could sit and doze if we wished. But, the enemy artillery being lively — salvos of shells roared over and burst nearby — we knew some of them might land among us at any moment. Sleep didn't come easy.

The Germans also sprayed the area with machine-gun bullets from time to time, frequently making our lookout men duck down.

Smith said, "Come with me if that stuff starts to get too close," and this I did when necessary, but with increasing misgivings; I perceived that if I repeatedly moved along to the traverse — a deep trench section to our right — we would get no rest at all and be quite unfit for duty when daylight came. In that traverse, when a shell came near us Smith would say "Down!" and we crouched as low as possible. We bobbed up and down constantly...

I thought about the wretched life I'd often endured on that Turkish peninsula. But I was coming to understand that warfare here could, at any moment, be more intense and dangerous than at Gallipoli. However, I felt certain that this bobbing up and down business would, in itself, soon be the death of me.

I had no idea whether personal movement was restricted, so I presumed not and wandered along the traverses and bays, the former unoccupied, each of the latter crowded with its complement of soldiers. None of them knew me, but no one questioned me, until I came to a bay — think of a bay window and you'll get the idea — where, as I could see by the gun flashes and the occasional flickering glare of a falling Verey light[228], the men were taking their war in a more relaxed manner than my new comrade Smith.

In particular, one man stretched full length on his back along the parapet above his comrades — twixt him and the Jerries just a mound of earth perhaps 18 inches deep. When he spoke, I joyfully identified him as a happy former member of our old Battalion and I congratulated him on the obvious comfort of his chosen bed. We exchanged wisecracks and, amid the resulting laughs and chatter with others present, I recognised two more of our "old boys". Conversation roamed over our Mediterranean experiences and, naturally, favoured our former close comradeship and our sorely missed Major. But we laughed and joked a good deal, and forgot present dangers in the brief, but mutually affectionate spirit of reunion.

Of course, I had strayed from my Company and, after a while, it dawned on me that two chaps standing near me wore different uniforms to the rest of us and must be officers. I'd heard them join in the giggles at times, but still thought I'd better express a hope that I had not offended by barging into their Company. They told me not to worry, they were just out from England and our bit of fun had relieved the nervousness felt by every newcomer to the battlefield. Nice chaps, but I just hoped they would not recognise me should we meet in daylight, for I had deserted my own section for rather a long while.

On returning, I avoided Smithy as far as possible, did my stint of lookout duty, and dozed at every available opportunity — I wanted to be of some use at "Stand-to" dawn alert, when with fixed bayonets and loaded rifles we had to be keenly ready to repel any enemy move. That uncertain light of early morning gave advantage to an attacker provided he moved cautiously. Every man must remain intently watchful, speech forbidden, save if an order must be given. When full daylight arrived, came the order to "Stand down" and fags could be lit and the rum ration issued to "warm the cockles" after a chilly night.

It was then I heard for the first time the regular morning performance of a short, swarthy Sergeant who had come, someone told me, from South America, just to win this war for us. He would yell his "Stand down, men!", then call out a greeting to "You German bastards — I'll be over after you in a minute and I'll knock seven different kinds of shit out of you!" This he repeated as he strolled along the line, getting many a hollow laugh from men who'd heard it all before, but still hoped he meant it.

Chapter Thirty-Five

I was already becoming accustomed, once more, to shells exploding, singly or in groups, near or far, and to bursts of machine-gun fire. These noises went on without cease. Some of them would be shattering the eardrums of those nearby even as they shattered the bodies of the unlucky ones caught by a direct hit. Death or injury could afflict any one of us at any time of day or night, and we had to learn to live with this risk and outwardly to ignore it. The tension inside... nobody's business and never mentioned.

The men standing on each firing step in the bays had to be extremely careful; snipers looked out for such targets. But, armed with the knowledge that, after spotting you, a sniper still had to take aim, you could quickly raise your eye level to just above your earth parapet, then — if you had not attracted a bullet already — keep still and rely on movement of your eyes to complete your observations, then duck, stay ducked, and never bob up in the same place twice. Of course, an unlucky machine-gun bullet might get you, but the odds were against that.

A dead soldier was of no use to his mates and most of us understood that the careful man probably outlived the careless, even though a well-placed shell could upset all calculations.

Whereas periods of relaxation in some safety occurred on old-time battlefields and also arise in more modern mobile warfare, on the Western Front risks had to be lived with through the whole 24 hours of every day. Furthermore, while I was in the front line with that Battalion, at no time did anyone senior to me say I was free to rest, to sleep.

Meanwhile, we knew our opposite numbers in the German trenches usually had deep shelters available, so that, in the intervals between significant actions, only a skeleton force manned their firing steps. Indeed, my new comrades told me that it seemed the majority of the Jerries remained down below whenever we started an artillery bombardment intended to prepare the way for our infantry to launch an attack by dashing forward across No Man's Land. This spared them many casualties and, at the opportune moment, comparatively fresh and unshaken, they could emerge and offer a telling defence.

At that time and place — the Somme Front — our officers did have below-ground shelters, but it wasn't until a later stage of the war that I served in an area where the common soldier could rest in dugouts furnished with bunks.

As days and nights passed, I gradually got to know some of my fellows and to like several of them. A young Sergeant I thought particularly admirable. Like his name, Heather, he had something of the outdoors about his looks and manner. He performed his duties with fairness and honesty and, since none could fault him, all the best people liked him. When things got noisy and threatening, a sight of his purposeful face could still a quivering tummy.

Somewhere in trenches to the rear of the system, or perhaps in a hollow free from enemy observation, toiled our Sergeant Cook and his crew. Their labours were expected to produce 1) in the first hour or so of daylight, sufficient large containers of hot tea to give everybody a good helping, usually something over half a pint 2) a hot meal, usually stewed, roughly around the middle of the day — sometimes with a slab of plum duff to follow 3) another issue of hot tea towards evening.

With morning and evening tea, they also portered the usual solids, such as bread or biscuits, jam or cheese. They carried the tea through the trenches in deep, rectangular, iron containers supported on wood bars resting on the shoulders of two men, one fore, one aft. Only the bigger outbursts of fighting would disturb these excellent services, delaying or preventing them according to severity.

And our MO, efficient and caring, attended to our toilet needs in the front line as diligently as he did in the less hazardous areas further back. Each latrine up there was of the seat-and-bucket type and housed in a deep, square hole approached through a short trench. The Pioneer Section treated them all with liberal quantities of chloride of lime and quickly repaired or replaced any damaged by shells. You could always locate one by the disinfectant's pungent smell, but normally unaccompanied by the foul odours resulting from careless sanitation.

This competent man also took responsibility for the advanced first aid Station at Battalion HQ in, I think, the third line of the trench system. His trained stretcher-bearers worked like beavers to collect wounded comrades and hurry them back to him and his small staff of Red Cross male medics. His diagnosis decided what treatment would be advisable on the spot and his sound, quick decisions must have saved many a man's life before further transportation rearwards to the Advanced Casualty Station.

I give these and other details so that you may know something of the organisation which maintained a huge Army in the field for years under often terrible conditions without its members becoming victims of some awful plague. Major battles would disrupt these systems, allowing water-filled trenches, mud, and dead and decaying bodies awaiting disposal to spread discomfort and despair, while a flood of damaged men choked the channels rearwards — but the will to restore order and decency would eventually, sometimes ever so slowly, always perseveringly, overcome the worst of difficulties.

Of course, self-discipline has to be maintained before mass discipline can be attempted, but not all members of even a generally well-disciplined nation subscribe to this principle.

In my early days with my new lot I had no responsibilities for other men as I managed to keep busy doing ordinary duties. I still had no wish to retain my humble one stripe. I never gave an order to a Private; I did a job myself rather than tell anyone else to do it. In fact, I behaved in a manner which, I thought, would soon have me relieved of the fishbone on my arm.

One night, another Company relieved us and we moved back into the support line of trenches. Here, when not working, we could sleep at last, probably wrapped under and over in our rubberised groundsheets to keep rain and the dampness of the ground out. This felt like a wonderful boon, even though it was during daytime only — because our busy periods came overnight, when the enemy, though at times he heard us, could not usually see us.

A meal with hot tea would warm and cheer us before, when darkness fell, we each took a pick or a shovel and set off. It had been decided that the space between our front trench and that of the Germans was too wide, so we must construct a new front line.

To our knowledge, there were two ways to do this job. The first involved digging one or more trenches beginning at your own front line: two men swinging picks loosened some earth, then stood back while two others shovelled that into sandbags held open by another two who passed them back through further pairs of hands which in due course dumped the loose earth and passed emptied sacks forward again. Then the pick-men resumed, and so the work proceeded. The front pair, perforce, worked in short, sharp bursts, before being relieved and taking their places further down the line.

Of course, we knew the growing trench could not remain unobserved and we often did this work amid shell bursts and bullets whining — knowing too that our labours might be undone the next night if a German patrol got close enough to throw their stick bombs[229] into our would-be new front line.

The other method of establishing an advanced front line, quicker but costly in casualties, was to send a large party of men forward at night and have them dig like hell on previously marked sites. A covering party provided protection, lying in a long line between the diggers and the German trenches, ready to fight with bayonet and bullet. To construct a usable trench, this operation would have to be repeated several times. More about such an undertaking later...

Either way, as dawn approached we all felt tired, and glad to plod back to our support trench, back among the boys, almost like returning home from furrin parts. We'd quaff hot tea and chew bread or biscuits and anything else the cooks had sent up, then fall asleep in sitting, lying or crouching position according to circumstances.

I really enjoyed life in that support trench for several reasons, the main one simply that I was getting rest and sleep, but also it ran through what remained of an orchard. The occasional tree, the fruit bushes, and wild brambles seemed to cut us off from the war — just because we couldn't see much of it...

I found a strand of steel wire and, with music nostalgically in mind, fastened it to the butt of my rifle, carried it over my adjustable back-site and tied it off on the fore-site. Now by raising the back-site I put tension on the wire — and plucking it produced an almost musical note. Using the wood covering the barrel as a fretboard I could play a tune of sorts.

Always ambitious, I pictured myself playing the thing cello-wise. So I procured a supple, thin branch from a fruit tree growing by the trench-top and, using some cottons from my "housewife" (the cloth mendings holder), I made a bow. I drew it across the wire cello-wise, but without result. Then I recollected that one must treat a violin bow with resin to make it grip on the string and vibrate it. I again looked to the tree for help and, sure enough, I spotted some gummy exudations on the trunk. Gathering a couple of pieces, I tried rubbing one against my cotton bow strands. Some stickiness resulted, but the faint noise emitted by my rifle-cello could not be called music. I decided I would have to play it banjo-wise and, using a tooth from a comb as a plectrum, I could just manage a few recognisable notes.

One day, prowling along a nearby disused and partly demolished trench, I saw a big man lying quite still out on top among the trees and shelled stumps. He held a rifle with a telescopic sight which he peered through, although, beside his head, stood a separate small telescope on a tripod. I crawled out and asked him what was going on (of course, I wouldn't have done this on the front line). He told me to move slowly and carefully, keeping well down.

"I'm a Canadian," he said. "A sniper. That's my job and I work alone. I report to Headquarters way back." He described his work: watching enemy country, reporting anything noteworthy, taking the occasional pot-shot when doing so might serve some useful purpose. The enemy also had snipers — whose attention he preferred to avoid. He pointed out, high up among nearby trees, a small platform approached by a frail, metal ladder which he sometimes used.

"Some job," I thought, and wished I had the confidence to apply for such work… but even more that I should have the courage necessary to fight this lone battle with the enemy.

Earlier in the war, I knew, the French Army had manned this sector of the Front and, making a further foray along the disused trench one rainy day, I found that, unlike the British, they had provided themselves with covered accommodation — recesses dug at intervals along their trench, roofed with heavy, waterproof sheets, the half-rotted remains of which still hung over them.

When the rain got heavier, I sheltered in one of these places. Inside, unfortunately, about six inches of water had gathered, but I rolled a sandbag into it and kept my feet dry while I waited for the weather to improve. A dank smell of death hung about this shelter, but in the semi-darkness I couldn't see what caused it.

The rain continued and I realised I'd better get back, regardless. Nobody knew where I was, I might be wounded and never found, I thought, letting imagination run away with me for a moment... Then, near the junction of this old trench with our own communication trench, I was startled to see protruding from the earth the bright, red cloth of a trouser leg — still shaped to some extent by the bones inside it. I knew some French soldiers wore baggy, red uniform trousers, but I was amazed the cloth had endured exposure for a long time without rotting, and even retained most of its colour.

So the days and nights passed and soon came our turn to move back to our Reserve line. It ran through the outer, westward side of a small country town, much of it wrecked. My section occupied the ground floor of what remained of a small, detached house.

After I settled in, having nothing special to do, I bethought me of my musical rifle. Sitting beside a stairway leading down to the cellar, I attached my length of wire to butt and fore-sight and plucked it to produce the best semblance of a tune I could achieve. A scuffle on the steps was followed by a shout: "What the hell's going on up there?" An officer emerged from below and I had to confess that I was torturing my rifle as well as the ears of my neighbours. Quite truthfully, I assured the officer I had been unaware the cellar was occupied.

More amused than irritated, he asked me to demonstrate my method of using the gun as a one-string guitar. Probably The Last Rose Of Summer[230] had never sounded quite like that before, but he returned to his colleagues below without putting me on a charge.

With us now quartered in the comparative luxury of part of a house with part of a roof, our night work became more difficult and dangerous — to mark our gratitude for favours received, perhaps.

Wearing light equipment consisting of belt, shoulder straps, ammunition pouches and haversack — worn on the back instead of at the side — with rifle carried in the right hand and a pick or shovel in the left, we moved up the long communication trench to the front, then straight "over the top" in a long line. Guides stationed out there already led groups of us to positions where a short length of advanced trench had to be dug as soon as possible.

Soon, all of us were hard at work — and the noise we made was frightening. Only too well aware that we must soon be heard and seen by Jerry, we picked and shovelled like madmen, hoping that German observers sending reports of our activities back to their HQ, and then senior officers deciding how to dispose of us... would all take a long time.

Fortunately for us, enemy reaction did prove slow and when, eventually, their wrath descended, we squeezed down into the hollows we'd dug and found we did have a few protective inches of earth above our precious bodies.

Machine-gun bullets spattered around me and I marvelled that I should lie there, hear and see them striking, yet remain untouched. But our semi-trenches afforded little protection when light field guns joined in and their shattering whizz-bangs[231] filled the air with noise and flying metal. One could only hug Mother Earth and wait for an order to retire, which didn't come.

I heard the occasional muttered request for "Stretcher-bearers!" — brave fellows indeed, themselves not immunised from injury or death by their labours of mercy. Brilliant flickering Verey lights fired by the Germans revealed all movements; when one hovered near you, you froze no matter in what posture. I always looked down to conceal the whiteness of my face, though more in hope than conviction.

Later, after the firing had died down, the order "Dig like hell!" was passed along. We complied until, after a while, we reaped a further rich harvest of bullets and shell which compelled our officer to order a retreat. We stood not upon the order of our going, and one still had to find a gap in the barbed wire to reach our frontline trench. But, having done that, one savoured the rich pleasure of having survived a risky piece of work.

Via such skirmishes and the general attrition of low-key fighting, the odd few casualties took toll of our men. But no major battle had yet taken place during my few weeks around the Front in France, and our Company next moved yet further back. Even so, we still had to provide the occasional nocturnal working party.

One night, with six men I think it was, I was sent to meet a Sergeant of the Royal Engineers at a certain point in a communication trench. A very different job, this one. Thankful I was that my task only involved ensuring the men reached the rendezvous, and obeyed the Engineers' instructions, then returned with me to our Company.

So, not trench-digging, but proper excavation this time: first, a tunnel sloping downward at a steep angle; then, when we got deep enough, we dug out a large hole and shored it up with pit-props — accommodation for a Brigadier and his staff, we heard.

While one man worked at the "face", the rest of us formed a chain, passing buckets of "spoil" back up to the surface. Every couple of feet, we could all pause while the Engineers hammered a new wooden frame into position to support the tunnel roof and walls around us. We quickly reached a depth sufficient to require the use of a manual pump up above to drive fresh air through a tube and down to us.

During a pause for rest, I made my way to the very bottom of the tunnel. The noises of war faded to nothing down there. No interference, then, with the work the Brigadier and his aides would have to conduct during some coming battle. We gathered that another tunnel was being dug to serve the same headquarters; it started from some distant point unknown to me, the idea being that, if a German shell smashed one entrance/exit, the other, hopefully, would remain and provide an escape route.

Down at the bottom of our approach tunnel, I tried to make myself feel safe. I thought of the officers and men who would spend days and nights here, poring over maps and dispatches, considering reports and making decisions. They would, of course, have ample room, whereas I had only a very confined space, and realised that the sooner I climbed out into fresh air the better I would feel. Back up top, I reflected on which situation I would prefer if the area came under intense artillery bombardment — below ground or not — but I reached no conclusion.

Then, and since, I have wondered if any conceivable consideration could justify placing millions of men under the constant nervous stress that assails them in the battle areas of a static trench war. It may not have occurred to some people that, until full voting rights were given to all men in Britain, manual and clerical workers — generally of that level of society which is referred to as "working class" — had no avenue of escape from compulsory National Service in time of war. It was probably in 1911 that an Assistant Scoutmaster, aged about 24, told me he had at last become "a real man", having just been given the "lodger's vote". Prior to that, only house owners could vote for a parliamentary candidate. Women, of course, had no vote until after that war[232].

However, regardless of my reflections in idle moments, there I was, a boy compelled to wear a stripe on each arm which gave him unwanted, albeit tiny, authority over his fellows; a boy who couldn't get even a short break at home between the Middle East campaign and the now impending Battle Of the Somme.

We soldiered on.

Next, we moved to an area in the middle of this town, further still from the front trenches. Almost peaceful. Our platoon billeted on the ground floor of a building which had suffered little damage. Completely unfurnished, the windows all gone, but otherwise weatherproof — a roof over our heads, and that was marvellous.

I had a look around. Outside, the first concrete lampposts I had ever seen lined the main street. They must have carried the then-new carbon, electric lamps which shed a pinkish light and gave faces a brownish tinge. Every lamppost I could see had been hit by one or more shells, exposing thick strands of reinforcing metal within the concrete. Twisted, bent, or knocked sideways, most of them defied total destruction. They fascinated me. So modern, so up-to-date. The French people, I thought, must be way ahead of the British in scientific matters...

Opposite stood a church, much damaged. Yet a crucifix, about eight feet tall, stood beside it, quite perfect.

Only troops inhabited this town, I discovered. With one exception: next day a dog waddled into our room and walked around without responding in any way to our calls and caresses. Finally, we decided the poor thing must be deaf and mostly blind, but still it gave us one rather ghostly link with all those people who formerly lived in this country town. Where were they all now?

We still made occasional night journeys into No Man's Land, gradually developing those forward positions, though not without casualties, of course.

I recall one disastrous night when my group had to start digging a new portion of trench between two quite well developed stretches on our side. A covering party lay between us and the Germans and we quickly excavated to a depth of about 18 inches. Suddenly we heard shouts and shots from the direction of our protectors.

Within moments, a rush of fleeing men barged among and between us. So we became the centre of attraction for enemy shells and bullets. I dropped my pick and reached for my rifle, but it was not where I had placed it. Panic froze my belly. To lose one's bandook[233] was the crime of crimes.

"Those bastards!" I thought, and dashed back towards our front trench. Luck favoured me. As I could see by the light from flashes and flares, the first man I encountered was carrying two rifles. I grabbed the one in his left hand, yelled something like "Why the hell... ?!" and "Sorry, mate," said he, and in a trice I was back out in No Man's Land with the boys in the trench-building group until somebody gave the order to retreat.

We made our way back through the wire, only to be questioned by a strange officer as to why we had returned. He happened to be a foreigner and, at that time, we didn't take kindly to seeing commissioned officers' uniforms on an outsider. Our resentment showed, but our Company Captain came along in time to stop any further trouble.

He led us away down a communication trench and when, in the early hours of a fine morning, we finally reached the main street of our deserted town, he ordered us to "Fall in!" Instead of dismissing us, he gave us some rifle drill, just as though we were on a barrack square. "That," he said, when we were done, "will steady your nerves after tonight's balls-up." We understood and, I'm sure, agreed.

May I state, sadly, that he himself later left us "under a cloud" — it was thought that a bullet wound in one of his hands had been self-inflicted. But, of course, it's doubtful if anyone thought of helping to steady *his* nerves when something shattered them.

I revert to the subject of the church on the opposite side of the road. A few days after that "balls-up", I was having a rest in "our" house when the brief shriek of a big shell preceded an explosion which shook me rigid. Bits and pieces of ceiling and walls fell around me. After the dust settled, I looked through a window-space and saw that the remainder of the church front had collapsed into the road.

Later, I walked over there. Amid the rubble, the large cross with the figure of Christ stood intact. Near it, I found a small crucifix made of brass and wood, such as a poor Roman Catholic might have on his rosary. I carried that in my tunic pocket throughout the war and kept it with other oddments for many years.

Chapter Thirty-Six

One happy day, it was announced that we had completed our stint in the forward area. We collected all our gear from our battered billets in the town, rendezvoused in a sunken road, hopefully free from enemy observation, and started marching.

Soon, all the Companies of the Battalion came together in one long column. The drum and fife band took its place at the head and gave out sweet music. Cares fell away, and we sang and whistled joyfully. Kilometre after kilometre, with occasional ten-minute breaks, we didn't worry, for this march was taking us in the one direction which pleased all of us — back!

The Cook Sergeant, as we incorrectly called him, complete with willing helpers and a field-kitchen, had been wafted way back to the pleasant place in which we were to spend a couple of relaxing weeks — no *lazy* weeks, that would have been bad for us. Many convincing excuses for slackness occurred to us, but the MO would have none of them. Strong and healthy himself, he took more interest in the men's health and hygiene than any other Army officer I ever met. Those responsible for sanitation just had to do a good job or Doc's keen eye or nose would detect their omissions.

A substantial hot meal greeted us when we reached our destination. We ate, sitting around in a field near the Nissen huts in which we were to live. But we were forbidden to enter them until we had undergone the great clean-up.

In controlled groups, we went to a building where we stripped, then ran to shower cubicles and, under the lukewarm water sprays, spent an enjoyable ten minutes, a cleansing treat after several weeks of the mucky life up front. Soon, almost before we'd dried ourselves on the clean towels provided, laundered replacements for the underwear we'd handed in were dished out: two vests, two pairs socks, two shirts, two pairs long pants, two towels — none of them new, but welcome all the same.

Our own uniforms were returned to us, hot and steaming from the pressure and heat which destroyed the fat lice infesting seams and creases. These little devils only left their hideouts to gorge themselves on our blood — and by the second day of each new stint in the trenches they had always reoccupied their deceased relatives' former lodgings. They must also have passed diseases[234] and, possibly, disfigurements such as warts from one man to another — similar pests spread the plague by way of rats to humans all around the world.

Thus, in France, the British Army continued to conduct war in a business-like, efficient manner. Somewhere someone may also have been giving thought to winning it and perhaps even ending it. But, in the forward areas, officers concerned themselves only with carrying out orders coming from somewhere way back. To do this, it was necessary to keep as many men as possible alive and fit enough to withstand the shocks and hardships which were their daily lot.

It was great to be able to sleep undisturbed between the hours of dusk and dawn under the strong elephant-iron of the semi-circular Nissen huts, two warm blankets wrapped around your vest- and long-pants-clad body. Again, they gave us substantial meals. So days spent in rigorous training didn't come too hard, although our tasks included digging trenches which — a sure antidote to complacency — furnished a replica of the battlefield we would soon be sent to; this included enemy trenches, the lay-out based on photographs supplied by our airmen (in northern France, unlike Suvla Bay, aircraft from both sides were always around).

After completing the facsimile trench system, we spent hours rehearsing the attack which should carry us through Jerry's position and, hopefully, through a densely wooded area of open country beyond. I had already seen the wood[235]. Heavy, prolonged shelling had denuded most of the trees of their branches, but the main mass of tree trunks still provided cover, we were told, for a great many underground forts the Germans had constructed. All this later proved to be only too accurate. What I never have seen mentioned is the probability that German observers took pictures of our mock battlefield — if so, it forewarned them of at least one area we intended to attack.

I was such a windy bugger that, had I been in charge of that Division, I would have insisted on the mock battlefield being camouflaged when not in use, but that only illustrates the difference between a scary little Lance Corporal and a hearty, red-face General.

Still, good food, hard work, clean bodies and clothes, plus interesting talks given by our MO about keeping ourselves and our environment in good nick, transformed grubby and weary-looking men into tolerably good soldiers. A pity they had to be sent back into hell again.

At this camp, I regularly had letters from home. All was well, they said, particularly as Pa had, through a friend, secured a fairly good job as manager of the export department in a big store — much of the exporting concerned the requirements of military officers in various parts of the world.

I still hankered after a leave pass, now due to me more than ever I felt. Because Company officers censored all our letters home, when we wrote we had constantly in mind the fact that Lieutenant So-and-So or our Captain would see every word. A rotten arrangement, I felt, but set myself to ignore it; I expressed myself freely when complaining about the wicked dispersal of the remnant of our original volunteer Battalion and about my failure to obtain a few days' leave. Meanwhile, I wrote with equal frankness, I hope, about the superiority of Army organisation in France over that of the Mediterranean Expeditionary Force as I had seen it.

Called to report to my Company Officer one morning, I received an awful jolt. With obvious pleasure, he told me that I had been promoted to the rank of Corporal. I liked and respected him, a great chap. But how could I pretend to feel the pleasure he obviously expected me to show at this news? I had tried to lie low and lose the stripe which, as I saw it, already disfigured my uniform. I can't recall how the interview went, but in some craven way I probably concealed my lack of enthusiasm.

Now I was really worried. Who had recommended me for this unwanted fishbone which could blight all my hopes of pulling some sort of smart stroke to get me a leave pass? I had this constantly in mind and resolved to grasp any opportunity which might assist in getting me off the war-front hook for a few days.

So, we returned to the front line, a different section to the one we'd previously occupied.

During my first night on duty there, away to our right I witnessed my first battle of flame-throwers. I'd heard about these brutes — and that the Germans used them first — but on this occasion our people were retaliating in kind[236]. The machines used must have been in a very early stage of development. I do know this kind of warfare was considered, like poison gas, to be inhumane and very wicked. Did this make maiming and killing by bullets and shells more acceptable?

In a lecture some time later, we were told that our specialists had assessed the flame-thrower to be ineffective and wasteful in trench warfare. Instead, they had produced a mortar which flung large containers of inflammable liquid into the trenches and ignited the stuff on delivery, thus promising rivers of fire intended to roast those who didn't scramble out of the trenches. Those who did, could, of course, be shot. Given there appeared to be no answer to this charming invention, why was it not mass-produced and used? With every German roasted or shot, we ought to have been living it up in Berlin in a few months...

On our foot-slogging journey forward, we had seen a massive concentration of guns from mighty howitzers way back, through the various calibres down to the very mobile field guns which fired 18-pounder shells — most of them well-camouflaged for concealment from aeroplanes and captive-balloon observers. Their presence in such great numbers warned us of great trouble to come.

We took over a front-line trench deeper and wider than any I'd previously seen. So very spick and span! Thereafter, pick-and-shovel parties of Engineers came in each night and worked like beavers. While we kept watch, sent out patrols, and did all the usual front-line chores, they dug drainage holes or gulleys in the floor of our trench and laid duckboards over the drains or sumps. Their labour meant that a rainy day no longer saw us standing in a sea of mud for hours on end.

For a final impressive touch, they reinforced the sides of our trenches with what the Engineers called "expanded metal" — it looked like small-mesh wire netting, but was actually made by expanding solid sheets of metal until small holes appeared. Held in place by stout, two-inch, wood squaring, this metal mesh would hopefully resist collapse under heavy shelling. Certainly, while the stuff lasted, we felt we held a kind of fort rather than a trench; a false sense of security, for what could it do for you when shells fell *into* your trench?

No additional stripes had actually been issued to me, despite the Captain's unwanted promise of promotion, and I certainly made no effort to procure them. However, I was sharply reminded of the matter when a subaltern (one pip) told me that he and I were to cross, in the open, the spaces between our trench and some lookout posts fairly close to the German trenches — our first defence against surprise attacks by the large patrol groups which sometimes raided across No Man's Land. Men in the advance posts had to stay there for several days at a time. We would visit them in turn, under cover of darkness, collect their reports and note any requirements they had.

As I had studied our trench system layout by sketch and by daytime observations, that night, once we had climbed out of our own trench, this subaltern invited me to lead the way. Waiting until no flare illuminated the area, so in complete darkness, we slowly moved in what I hoped was the right direction for Post Number 1...

Certain guidelines improved the chances of survival on such black nights when patrolling the battlefield. Large, dark patches should be avoided — being shell-holes, usually. If something resisted the forward motion of one of your feet, you stopped, moved that foot back and changed direction slightly, endeavouring to avoid being tripped. When a machine-gun opened up — unless, by bad luck, it was trained on you at the moment it commenced firing — you could hope to escape injury by quickly lying down, otherwise it might catch you as it traversed.

As we crept along, once or twice something touched my backside, but a quick backward glance provided a clue — my rather tall officer had adopted the same posture as me, advancing with head well down. His right hand, held forward, grasped a pistol and this occasionally poked my bum. Pray heaven his finger isn't on the trigger, I thought. A nice lad he was, peach-and-roses complexion, far too good-looking to be mussed up by bullet or shrapnel.

We had to do that job several nights running. Each outing took two hours or longer, including the time spent with each lookout group, who all welcomed our visits.

But came a night when this routine changed — and I was told to act as Platoon Sergeant: "You will have every man up on the firing step when the order is given. A large patrol is going out under Corporal So-and-So and, if they strike trouble, your men will give them fire cover and get them back into our line if that is possible."

Corporal So-and-So was a tall, broad, tough-looking type, rather swarthy as to complexion, somehow foreign-looking. That Sergeant I previously mentioned who shouted rude words towards the Germans at morning stand-to had the same sort of look, as did also an officer I'd recently noticed, and several other men — all this probably due to the fact that this Territorial Battalion was based in West London. I still felt like a stranger with this lot, though by this time I knew, and was known by, a fair number of men.

The order duly came through, I had the chaps on their firing steps, then I moved along the front line to the point from which the patrol would depart through a gap in our barbed wire — a spot I was familiar with, for hadn't I used it on my own nightly walkies with the young Lieutenant and his prodding pistol? Corporal So-and-So led the way up and over, his men followed quietly, and all vanished into the coal-black night. Our Company officer remained staring in the direction of the dear departed. Then he warned me that I and my men were responsible for holding our section of the front whatever happened and must on no account leave it.

I visited our bays, having a word with the lads all along my bit of front. We waited. German machine guns sprayed our section at fairly regular intervals. From time to time, the usual flurries of whizz-bangs burst... I never ceased to marvel at the speed with which they reached us, before we'd even heard the guns fire... An ordinary trench-war night, in fact, when you'd have to be dead unlucky to stop one.

Weighing up the immediate possibilities, I realised my orders were ridiculous and impossible to comply with. Between my line of men on the firing step and our patrol out there lay a mass of barbed wire we put there to prevent Jerry from overrunning us. But, of course, it would also prevent us from helping our chaps if they found trouble in No Man's Land. Corporal So-and-So would have to keep his men close together somehow, so he could lead them back through the gap in the wire — otherwise, they would end up skewered and hanging on it.

The night suddenly came to life. Shouts and screams out there. Verey lights flared, but no extra shooting broke out because no one knew just what was happening. Then, high above the other voices, I heard a shout,

"Back to the valley!" This was repeated. The Corporal's voice and it portended bad trouble.

Soon, ahead of me, as I stood listening on a fire step, I heard groans and whimpering. "What's up there?" I called. A faint reply told me the chap had a leg wound, that our lads had met a large, German patrol head-on. "Drag yourself along the wire to your right as you face me and I'll get help to you," I called. I hurried along to the patrol's departure point and reported to the Captain about the man in trouble. The little Sergeant who daily threatened to knock seven different kinds of whatsit out of the Jerries stood nearby and immediately offered to bring the man in. I suggested the need for speed because all hell would be let loose as soon as the German patrol got back to its front line. With the officer's permission and a volunteer to accompany him the nippy Sergeant was up and away.

I quickly rejoined my party. No more groans from out front and, later, we learnt that the two rescuers had done a speedy job. When they returned with the injured man, they were quickly followed through the gap in the wire by the Corporal and most of his patrol.

The "valley" he'd been shouting about was a depression about halfway between us and the enemy positions. He'd taken the patrol to it on the way out and told them it should be the rallying point before leaving for "home". Meeting a large, enemy patrol had not been a possibility allowed for in the pre-operational briefing. The unexpected encounter had, for a moment, changed a volunteer, promotion-seeking Corporal into a shouting windbag, but once the lads got together in the "valley", their leader did recover his self-control and brought them back in good order.

They had not, however, as planned, penetrated any enemy positions, nor captured prisoners for interrogation purposes. I had the feeling the Corporal had pressed to lead this adventure. Some men did strive to give forth the impression that they were braver than most. But only real action could support or confound the contention.

A Sergeant was assigned to the platoon on my right. Overly garrulous, he had the horrible habit of punctuating loudly spoken remarks with harsh laughter. What he thought or did was no skin off my nose but, from time to time, I needed to move along his section of trench to reach the Company Headquarters dugout.

After a while, one of his men stopped me for a chat and told me, among other items, that this Sergeant had, in the past, been a Military Policeman and sometimes boasted of how, in battle, he had been stationed at the rear end of a communication trench where, with drawn revolver, he stopped and drove back into action men whose nerves had broken or who, he thought, were feigning injury. Sending them back into the hell which had temporarily broken them obviously gave him pleasure.

Now here was he, up front himself for the first time, and when, on one of my walks, I saw him hacking into the earth low down on the front side of the trench I could only stare in wonderment. Thereafter, his hole grew bigger each day. With no supports it looked like a deathtrap to me, its purpose beyond my understanding.

Glancing down at it one day, I thought I saw the Sergeant lying there and bent down to confirm this was really so. He wriggled out, sprang to his feet, and his eyes had a strange, wild look in them. I said nothing, just watched him, and he started to back away. "You're going to kill me!" he shouted. "Every time you pass I see that look of dislike in your face. I've never done you any harm." And so on and on.

Never before or since have I witnessed such a strange performance. I assured him I had no feelings nor interest regarding him. Men in the vicinity looked on, and perhaps one of them reported that their Sergeant had gone doolally. He vanished from our ken soon afterwards.

Just before he went, however, he gave a final performance. That day, a heavy fog settled over the battlefield and some Germans took advantage of it by dragging forward small trench mortars and dropping their small bombs among us. The Sergeant announced that he would stop that. He climbed out of the trench and soon vanished in the fog. In vain, we waited for him to start his private war... Until he crawled back, and we guessed he'd just crept out of sight and crouched there hoping nothing would happen and that a VC or similar would reward his outstanding bravery.

For a kind of rest, we moved back to a village perhaps two miles behind the front line. Its buildings, although mostly damaged, provided ample good accommodation for all of us. The place was not attracting much shellfire, but it seemed wise to spend most of the time out of sight so as not to push our luck.

I was crossing the main street for some good purpose when a booming voice stopped me in my tracks: "Corporal Norcliffe! You are improperly dressed! Report to me in an hour's time and have that other stripe sewn on by then or else!" It was the tall, burly, Regimental Sergeant Major. So far I had seen little of him and had no idea he was aware of my existence, let alone my name. Our brief interview started in a strictly official style, but continued in a friendly, almost intimate way as these things did "up the line".

Firmly, though unwillingly, trapped in the NCO category — I wore two stripes, but often did the work of a man wearing three[237] — I still determined, albeit without visible protest, to try any ploy which might result in my getting some leave. In each letter home I harped on this subject, in the knowledge that one of my Company officers would read of the unfair treatment I felt had been my lot.

While stationed in that village, I had what was to me a heart-touching experience. I had assumed all civilians had long ago left because it was so close to the trenches. Badly strafed at various times, the parts of the village I grew familiar with had the stricken appearance I had come to associate with places that were simply doomed.

But one afternoon, free for a few hours before the nightly trek to No Man's Land where we continued the job of deepening advanced trenches, I got away from it all by slipping out through the back streets (quite unlawfully for, as an NCO, I must be available at all times).

A big stretch of open country spread before me as, clear of the village, I rested against a grassy bank, enjoying the warm sunshine. I enjoyed being completely alone and realised how seldom this happened. Then, I thought I heard children's voices... Sure enough, looking back I saw a small school and a few youngsters outside at play. It seemed unbelievable; we had walked here from the front-line trenches. The wickedness of keeping them in that situation of hourly danger worried me, yet the sweetness and homeliness of the scene and the music of children's voices almost had me weeping.

There followed a big bang and I saw a cloud of smoke floating upwards at a point much nearer to the children than I was. But the children ignored it and play continued. Then, when a second bang sounded off, I saw a heavy battery of British guns positioned below ground level, quite close to the school. The kids were used to it. If they didn't mind, why should I? And yet, one day, Jerry will have a go at the guns, I thought, and then the school may suffer.

I felt loath to leave and rejoin the men whom I really should never have left.

The forward battle area always had seemed a place apart from normal life, nothing to do with beauty, homeliness, love, children, girls, homes, furniture, gardens, flowers — no connection at all with any of those things which men and women enjoy, appreciate and lovingly care for — things, politicians told us, we were fighting to preserve. Yet, up there in the trenches, we did as ordered by our superiors, coupling with that work the really important objective — namely to preserve ourselves from injury and death.

I would have wished to continue watching those children, listening to their sweet voices. This pleasure had been so unexpected in that separate war-world.

One night, we had slunk across open country towards the front in one, long, single line — to reduce loss of men to the minimum if a machine gun or a shell found us — had re-entered the trench system, then found our work sites in No Man's Land.

Our unfinished trenches aimed to join our existing front line to manned, advanced positions. I placed my merry lads at equal intervals in pairs, each with one pick and one shovel. Work got away to a good start, but after about three hours of this exhausting labour we needed food, drink and rest. However, on this occasion, the normal rations had been issued during the day and our Quartermaster and his stores lodged way back in the village. Even the cold water in our bottles tasted mouldy and, thereafter, all the heart went out of the work. As I walked the length of the trench, I apologised to all and promised I would personally see that food and drink would be available next time.

A little later that night, a man sent from the front-line trench came to fetch me. I found the Company officer in charge of that section having a chat and a cuppa in his dugout with another officer, based in our village, who was responsible for supervising the whole trench-deepening operation. He said he would make periodical inspections of all the groups involved in this work, including mine. So I told him of the men's need of food and drink around midnight — to which his only suggestion was that, as the men were required to sleep during most hours of daylight, they should save bread, cheese and such for a meal during the night; water would have to suffice for drinking.

None of this would please our chaps — good workers if looked after, but capable of skilful toil-avoidance if displeased. I felt they were not being well treated and would be resentful. Yet, somehow, some work must be seen to be done. So I let it be known that if they did a good three hours graft, starting from our time of arrival, then the rest of the night could be taken easy, given that each man should grab a tool and be busy as soon as he heard my voice, for my coming would be a warning of the officer's presence, doing his rounds.

Each night I found it necessary to conduct two or three of these hurried scrambles, talking loudly, even giving the occasional jab or shake to a slow waker-up. This meant we shifted a reasonable amount of earth and the men's sense of grievance subsided — a satisfactory outcome, and I felt good because I had become acceptable to and even popular with a platoon of men among whom I had so far felt like an interloper (apart from also being much younger than most of them).

Our next move took us rearwards again, to the village with the ruined church and its undamaged cross, where we had previously spent a week or so. There we slept in barns and outbuildings on comfortable bunks made of wood and wire netting.

Out of the blue, the Sergeants invited me to join them in evening social drinking in the barn they occupied. Corporal's pay made me comparatively wealthy, so I could afford to put my bottles on the long table, lit by a dozen candles, around which the Sergeants gathered for an hour or two each night before "Lights out". Each contributed what he had been able to procure — at that moment, champagne was a good buy because the owners of one big house had decided they couldn't carry on living in that dangerous area, finally abandoning the hope, long shared by many in that region, that the Allies would soon drive the Germans back to the Rhine... when here we were, halfway through 1916, still bogged down in trenches nearby.

So, imagine: champagne at 2.50 francs the bottle, brandy cognac about 5 francs, curaçao about 8 francs, coarse red wine 50 centîmes[238]. The red wine I didn't favour. A few weeks previously I had drunk two whole bottles during an evening, and become tipsy in a sad, sour way; the next morning I drank water to slake a foul-tasting thirst and found myself again unsteady on my feet, with a heavy, hazy head — whereas a steady tippling session mainly on champagne yielded a night of unbroken sleep followed by an awakening to a clear head and a feeling of well-being.

The real boon of these evenings with the Sergeants was the relaxation they bestowed. I can speak only for myself, but surely the others must have felt something of it.

The expected thing was to never expose one's feelings, so I always tried to give full attention to the matter in hand, despite sometimes suffering intense apprehension about events nearby, such as shell-bursts overhead, eruptions of earth when a shell penetrated then exploded, or, in an otherwise quiet period, when I heard the wu-wu-wu of an approaching *Minen* flung high by its *Werfer*[239]. The ever-present threat of these and other devices, used by civilised people to kill each other — and yet still avoid actually seeing their victims bleeding and writhing — these threats kept me in the state of high tension which made that acid smell rise from the palms of my hands. If we had all behaved naturally we would have ducked and started to run back... ever so far back.

Occasionally, a man did just that and, if charged, would be court-martialed for showing "cowardice in the face of the enemy". Around that time, I had the unpleasant duty of being Corporal-In-Charge of a small party of men assembled to march a prisoner from the hut in which he was confined to a court martial held in a farmhouse. Having rehearsed our part in advance, we marched the poor devil in, heard the prosecution and defence, marched him out while the court deliberated, took him in to hear that he had been found guilty, the sentence to be announced in due course, and marched him out.

I assumed he would be shot — because at that time it was customary to pass from hand to hand along the front line occasional notices from Army HQ listing courts martial and their findings. So you could read that "Private So-and-So was charged with showing cowardice in the face of the enemy and sentenced to death by firing squad. The sentence was duly carried out." Those, roughly, were the words used. The list of cases would conclude with a warning to all about behaviour and discipline. Cheerful reading for men already coping with hardships and risks — often terrible trials of self-control.

These things, so very far removed from the cheerful volunteer spirit of 1914, made those early days seem like a chapter from a different war altogether. Now it was every man for himself and if Jerry doesn't get you,

General Haig's red tabs[240] will. As we often said, it was all right for those bastards at Army HQ about 50 miles back. With their maps, plans, and schemes, battle was probably no more than a game to them, to be played between 10-course meals.

Indeed, solid rations such as bread, butter, cheese etc, were distributed through "the usual channels", that is, a recognised pecking order as they passed from Division Headquarters, on to the Brigade, to the Battalion and finally to us, the Company. When, in the front-line trenches, the bread allocation they gave me to share out amounted to rather a small portion per man, I found it pretty disgusting — because I was handed my own Corporal's ration for the day separately and that was a half-loaf. I questioned this with the Sergeant controlling the distribution, but he insisted this was all correct, since those responsible for others did more work and must be maintained in a fit state to do it.

However, reverting to the one court martial in which I had to play a formal part, I should mention a couple of things. I knew the prisoner who, although in a different Regiment by that time, had previously belonged to the Battalion in which I enlisted. I never liked him — too clever by half, with small, shifty eyes — but I felt sorry that he had to die that way. Yet I never did see confirmation of the death sentence, only made that assumption… And, a couple of years after that war finished, from the top of a bus near Marble Arch I spotted Kerminger, that same prisoner, fit, well, and obviously enjoying the sunshine and life generally.

So they didn't shoot him after all. But why not? When ordered to go over the top and charge, he'd run in the wrong direction and got several kilometres rearwards before they arrested him. Perhaps courts martial did not always send men found guilty to the firing squad and the execution lists we saw on the front line were adapted to scare potential deserters?

But if the authorities thought they would improve morale by implanting fear in already frightened men, they were very much mistaken. Any man who already had doubts about the top leadership and their conduct of the war would only be discouraged from doing his best by this propaganda-through-threats.

Chapter Thirty-Seven

After a spell in that village, which appeared almost remote from the perils of war although within marching distance of the Front, we were once again to return to the trenches. Information circulated one afternoon, roughly 24 hours before we must depart. We had been training for a few hours each day but, on our last day in this comparative little heaven, we were freed of all duties except really necessary chores.

I strolled around the village noting the utter ruin of some houses and marvelling at others' apparent immunity from damage. The place was in a valley, fairly shallow, but the ridge on the western side shielded it from direct enemy observation, so only the odd plane would see anything worth reporting. Up to that time, at any rate, it had provided a very fortunate spot for troops who rested there, savouring something of its peacefulness.

As evening approached, I felt the sadness of leaving this unexpectedly cosy haven. A final sleep on the comfortable wire netting, the packing up of all our bare requirements for survival up front, and our trek westward began.

In the last three or four kilometres we slowed, for then we moved in darkness, in two files, while giving complete attention to maintaining contact with one another. The mere thought of wandering alone in that black gloom with no road or track visible, no buildings, great holes here and there usually containing a foot or two of water into which one might topple... these things kept one keenly alert, as did the knowledge that, in this new era of the conscripted soldier, trust and faith in the good intentions of one's comrades was dead or dying, and a man wandering away from his unit, no matter under what conditions, would attract suspicions of trying to "dodge the column".

We found the section of trenches we took over in fine condition. The

Engineers had installed their "revetting with expanded metal" system quite splendidly, as well as a sump under the duckboard floor of the front trench, perfect drainage, and so superior to the old, sloppy, mud floor on which we had often slithered.

The Regiment had formed a machine-gun unit by combining all the Battalions' heavy machine guns and their gunners under the control of a separate authority at, I understood, Brigade level. They had become a force to be reckoned with by the enemy. Well behind of our machine guns lay numerous batteries of field guns which fired 18-pound shells, and still further back the heavy howitzers whose shells tore great strips out of the atmosphere as they roared towards targets in Jerry rear positions — borrowed from the Navy, some of these big guns, to back up what was going to be a massive British attack.

Above us, at most hours of the day, droned one or two planes. They patrolled the length of the line, each doing a stint of observation. If our plane altered course towards Jerry's line, perhaps to take a closer look at something of interest, pops and white blobs of smoke up there in the sky around it would indicate enemy resentment.

Occasionally a group of ten or more of ours, flying really high, would head towards some enemy target way back, forging ahead despite all anti-aircraft fire. Only if the Jerries sent up deterrent planes would real action occur, and then the aerobatics claimed every man's attention. We felt great sorrow if we saw one of ours hit and descending, but cheers would ring out if one of ours shot down one of theirs. Rolling, zooming, looping — every tactic was employed and appreciated by the onlookers. Our pilots sometimes used the "falling leaf" ploy to deceive an enemy into thinking they were beaten, then a sudden recovery and upward zoom might result in a volley from below wrecking the Jerry plane.

If one of our flyers had been ordered to take a look at some development, he would make constant attempts to get the photographs he needed. I saw one such who dived repeatedly despite becoming a target for all the machine guns in the vicinity — he was flying too low for the ack-ack guns' angle. Eventually he started to wobble, but just managed to stay airborne and pass over our heads. He bumped down a few hundred yards behind us, some men climbed out of a trench near him and, while they struggled to free him and carry him off, German artillery found the range — our men barely got back under cover before a shell wrecked the plane.

Later we learned that a bullet had penetrated the floor of the plane and passed through the pilot's thigh. He lived, and that knowledge gladdened us after witnessing his display of determination.

Each day, the number of low-flying Germans increased. They just roared over our trenches and, heading towards our rear positions, vanished from sight. They never returned, which puzzled us, until we learned they used another route well beyond visibility from our positions. We got used to these forays and so, perhaps, did the people in the rear who surely should have paid close attention to these unusual tactics.

Our next spell in the rear rest sites we spent mainly in practice attacks over a model trench system resembling the one we should occupy when the Great Day arrived. This wonderful occasion we awaited with mounting apprehension, simply because we knew our people had made conspicuously massive preparations which must have shouted our intentions to the German command who would make their dispositions for the day accordingly.

If our High Command had thought on similar lines to those worrying — the infantrymen — the attack would have been postponed for a while, some diversions organised in remoter parts of the Front, followed by what would then have been a surprise attack on the Somme. A surprise, that is, to our force as well as Jerry's. We'd been talking about the damn thing for weeks and the enemy probably knew as much as we did about it.

On the day — which followed a period of massive bombardment of enemy positions to destroy their barbed wire defences etc — our Battalion was to occupy the ordinary front line, and our most advanced trenches where my platoon found itself. The support trenches behind us sheltered a kilted Regiment who would come through our line to start the infantry attack, at which our men in the front trench would advance over the German front trench — by then in the hands of the Jocks — and go on to take the German support trenches. Finally, from the advance trenches, we would pass over all those people and clean up and occupy the German rear positions.

Perhaps surprisingly, the Germans easily matched our artillery bombardment for several days before our attack. Their shells passed over us, the infantry and — not that we knew it at the time — caused massive destruction to our artillery, damaging guns, and killing or wounding their crews, thus rendering our bombardment less intense than expected. The low-flying German planes must have photographed all those so carefully camouflaged guns and calculated their distances from German batteries...

Meanwhile, enemy machine guns massed at strategic points and they stood their field artillery almost wheel to wheel, or so it seemed, and the whole area became an inferno of explosions and bullets.

When the kilted lads advanced, their numbers decreased alarmingly with every forward stride. Meanwhile, our own advanced position was being blown apart piecemeal; pockets of survivors lost touch with their leadership and the nearest NCO had to make decisions... If he could only see ahead that our first line of attack was destroyed before capturing its objective, that its members lay dead and wounded on the ground ahead or grotesquely draped over the enemy barbed wire which our bombardment should have destroyed, then when should he take his small force over the top?

Some small groups did from time to time go ahead until killed, wounded and captured. Some dedicated officers achieved marvels within limits set by the powerful enemy, but in the end this massively prepared attack failed.

Nothing was gained in our sector. Many good men were lost. Many normally strong fellows were reduced to trembling, inarticulate old-looking men.

Our beautiful front line had become an uneven shallow ditch for most of its length, the expanded metal revetments either lost under piles of blasted earth or just sunk deep down in shell holes.

The wounded men who could not walk or crawl back from No Man's Land were, in many instances, simply left there for hours following the failed attack because of the mentally and physically exhausted condition of their comrades who had survived.

I saw a Scot who, though not wounded, just sat and shook. His head nodded, his arms flailed feebly, his legs sort of throbbed, his eyes obviously saw nothing.

One of our usually most happy and physically strong men was crying non-stop while violently protesting about something. He'd been buried up to his shoulders in earth and, even in that inferno, men nearby had paused in their advance to free him, yet he had this strange grievance.

So, possibly, nervous shock afflicted everyone there to a greater or lesser degree, even though fear no longer weighed on us as earlier in the day.

Most of the survivors were stunned into near speechlessness for a time, then the strong ones initiated reorganisation with a view to resisting the enemy counter-attack which would surely follow our failure...

But Jerry must have also lost heavily in both men and morale; the German artillery gradually became less active and communication between scattered groups on our side more easy to maintain, so a front of some sort was re-established which could resist if not stop an enemy attack.

During the hours of darkness, we began to receive assistance from the rear — food and the occasional tot of rum, anything which could be transported forward in the awful conditions prevailing. A gradual return to usefulness replaced the varying degrees of stupor and inertia which for many were the invisible wounds following many hours of explosion and upheaval, shattering to eardrums and nerves... and ruinous to pre-conceived ideas of what should be occurring according to plans worked out in grandiose HQ châteaux many kilometres away in the rear.

Meanwhile, the work of holding positions with a proportion of survivors, and allowing small parties to search for and bring in wounded men was organised by the remaining officers and the unshakeable RSM, who won praises from everyone who chanced to be near him during the battle.

Our Company — such as it was now, after its brush with hell — remained in what had been the front line. By dawn, most of us were ready to stop where we stood — crouched, rather — for under cover of dark we had searched for and found many wounded men, their chances of living diminishing with every hour in which they lay exposed with wounds untended.

We felt that our work was very valuable and the joy with which injured men greeted their rescuers was reward indeed. Perhaps the failure of the massive attack had left us with a sense of guilt which the intensive rescue work relieved.

So urgent was the need for rapid recovery of the wounded, that RAMC men from hospitals and dressing stations moved forward at night, having volunteered to join the search in No Man's Land. They gave initial treatment and care during rapid removal to the appropriate medical centre further back. All this, of course, they carried out under risk from enemy guns, a new situation for hospital workers who would only have heard the odd long-range shell or a few rare bombs from aircraft explode. So shells bursting around them while they worked did cause them some excitement. They saved many lives.

In the front line — the model for all front lines until it went up in dust and smoke — our Company had some sort of cover still, but only in places, and much work would have to be done to make it suitable for occupation. That job wasn't ours, so we kept watch and rested through the day after the battle, in usable sections of the trench or in large holes.[241]

We were given two or three days rest a couple of kilometres back and then returned to continue clearing up the mess — the first few nights devoted to recovering our dead mates, the living wounded having by then all been rescued. The identity discs we wore now became very important; each dead man having this link with the living could be identified and his death notified and a train of events set in motion to inform his family, finalise his service record, accord him a proper burial in a known cemetery, and finally secure for his nearest relative some sort of pension. The real difficulty was in regard to those so badly mutilated no way of identifying them existed.

One discovery out in No Man's Land deeply affected me. While working in bright moonlight on search work, I looked down into a length of communication trench in the advanced system we had helped to construct and saw the rather large face of a very good chap I had worked with for a while in Egypt. He had gone to a different Battalion from our camp near Rouen. And here he was, long dead, eyes blank, but still the features unmistakable and formerly so familiar to me. Charlie's large face was all the more recognisable because of his large nose. The moonlight no doubt concealed the ravages of injury and exposure — perhaps the shade and coolness of the trench bottom minimised them too...

As soon as possible, I guided two of the men doing recovery work to Charlie. I recalled then, as I do now, his special qualities. He was completely honest, stubborn about things in dispute, but usually found to be right about them in the end; Cockney in speech to an extent which, on first acquaintance led one to expect illiteracy, he soon made you realise your error — he handled sending and receiving Morse Code messages better than most. In fact, before the war he'd done that kind of work on the railways, but using a machine which emitted two musical sounds, high and low, instead of dots and dashes.

Of the many men whose poor bodies we found and saw cared for that night, Charlie was the only one whom I had known well in life. He had been one of us, and thus special to us, during our first experience of Army life... Recollection of Charlie calls forth a mental picture of him walking away from me... large head, broad shoulders, sturdy trunk, strong, slightly bowed legs — more like a Frenchman than an Englishman, nothing of the Cockney about his build or his gait. Goodbye, Charlie.

Chapter Thirty-Eight

The stench of war was really beginning to get up my nose. I liked no part of it. With six of my men, I dossed in a room in part of a house just behind the trenches. Little peace to be had there, mostly because of some geographical freak. All the bits of buildings, bits of trees, humps of earth and what have you between my boudoir and some misbegotten German machine gun could not stop it repeatedly spraying bullets through our non-existent window. They buried themselves in the plaster wall in a line about two feet above our heads. Not dangerous, just horribly annoying.

Our room looked out on a large courtyard of sorts. This establishment had been the home of a prosperous farmer, I surmised. His fields would lay just outside the small town and he'd drive the cattle in and out of the quarters here as necessary. Once the proprietor, his family and stock had entered through the gateway and passage, they were secure in an area bounded on all four sides by buildings. Now, sadly, modern artillery had wrought considerable havoc among the old, but very solid structures.

Soon after I moved in, so did an anti-aircraft gun and its crew — keen to have a go with their brand new weapon, the very latest thing in artillery, they boasted. I considered this courtyard a very strange sort of site for a gun. The buildings on all sides of the yard limited the range of vision. However, when one of the crew put it to me that, from high above, with a camouflage net thrown over it the gun would be undetectable, I saw his point. Most of the day, it would throw no shadow because of the buildings so close to it and shadows were great giveaways in aerial photographs. Placed in the centre of the yard it would have ample scope for shooting at planes, perhaps up to 50 degrees from the perpendicular.

How the gunners fared later I know not but, the first time they opened up, they hit and brought down a Jerry plane. A lucky go, no doubt, but a

great morale-restorer, loudly cheered by all our blokes who saw it happen
— although we could hardly believe what we were watching. Afterwards,
we frequently talked about it, well knowing that those to whom we told
the tale tried hard to convince themselves that we were not barefaced liars,
and didn't always succeed.

The toil of trying to restore the front positions after their frightful
bashing did not inspire us. More shame, perhaps, as we felt we really
ought to have left that area far behind as we pursued a retreating enemy…
Furthermore, while we worked, the Germans blasted and machine-gunned
us wherever they saw movement. They must have been cock-a-hoop about
wrecking our carefully planned attack.

Time passed and still no leave came my way. Chatting about this one
day — grumbling to a comparative stranger — I got a hint about trying
a different approach. At first, it appeared ridiculous. The chap said he
knew a man badly in need of a break who, in desperation, got his father
to write to Lloyd George about it. Soon afterwards he was granted seven
days leave.

So, in my next letter to my father, although fully aware that the officer
acting as censor would read it, I stressed that I had been so badly treated
that I would be grateful if he would write to the Rt. Hon. David Lloyd
George[242] stating that I had not been allowed to visit my home since
Christmas, 1914, that I had served in Gallipoli and Egypt and now in the
trenches in France — when still actually below the age at which one was
allowed to be on active service.

That last item I expected to be noticed, because around that time
the authorities responsible for calling up men for military service had
discovered a gap in the supply of recruits. Thousands of youngsters to
whom papers had been sent on reaching 18 did not reply or report for
duty. This led to the discovery that these chaps had enlisted, under age,
at the beginning of the war; it was decided to bring them back, wherever
possible, and restore them to their proper position in the stream. Many
were, of course, long since dead and buried, like young Nibs, previously
mentioned, at Suvla Bay.

Having got that load off my chest, I forgot about the matter for, on
reflection, the idea of a youngster expecting his dad to write to the War
Minister or whatever his title then was, looked like madness.

As acting Sergeant, I was kept pretty busy. We moved to difficult areas fairly frequently, but the general routine of living didn't vary much: some places muddier, filthier than others, sometimes the front trenches uncomfortably close to Jerry. The red tabs way back laid on occasional raids to sample the occupants of the enemy front line. Some men were lost, one way and another.

The nervous strain always prevailing up front had its cumulative effect on me. Stripped, when we had the periodical bath and change of underwear during a rest some kilometres to the rear, I saw that insufficient flesh, let alone fat, covered my boney framework. One ate very meagrely for a growing lad, good-quality food seldom available, a really full belly a rarity. This was active service and, although our Cook Sergeant performed marvels with the food allotted to him and his men, the PBI never had a meal such as would be placed before a member of an average working-class family for Sunday dinner. There were grumbles, but seldom rebellious or very violent expressions of dissatisfaction.

Of course, the word "scrounging" had joined the vocabulary of most soldiers by that time. It was used freely by so many men, most of whom would have been ashamed two years previously to steal, thieve, or even remove without permission, things in the care of others. Not that "scrounge" gave justification for stealing a comrade's personal possessions. But the word did cover "lifting" or "borrowing" things from "them" — all those anonymous people not actually belonging to one's Company or perhaps to one's Battalion.

The man claiming to have "scrounged" something usually did so with self-forgiving humour and a grin — though sometimes with bitterness if he suffered from a sense of grievance. The proportion of previously honest men who adopted the habit of scrounging as a way of life may have been as high as 50 per cent of us.

It was also around that time I first heard someone say, "F*** you, Jack, I'm alright!" — again, something that appeared to have come into the Army via the first forcibly conscripted wave of civilians. Wrenched from their families and a settled way of living, their bitterness may have expressed itself in that harsh declaration of the rule by which they intended to live henceforth.

Still, in the forward area, we continued to "do our bit", not taking part in any notable action, but holding bits of the Front in what usually seemed to us to be quiet spots. They gradually brought our numbers up to strength, but never again to the thousand men who originally comprised an infantry Battalion. Around 800 had become the rule.

We all had our bits of luck, just to continue without being killed or seriously hurt...

There was the time when a *Minen* from one of those bloody *Werfers* burst close behind me. The shock shattered me temporarily. I wore the chinstrap of my steel helmet fairly tight, yet the blast — from below it seemed — lifted the heavy headgear off and dumped it several yards away. Eventually I appeared none the worse.

Another time as I walked along a trench a shell landed at the end I had just left. Bits and pieces whizzed in all directions and I felt a severe blow to the lower part of my back. No pain resulted, but a pal took a look and found the webbing which held the wide metal head of my trenching tool cut clean across. Without that lucky shield, the base of my spine could have been severed.

Chapter Thirty-Nine

I awoke on the piece of floor which was my bed to the sound of my name being shouted by a Sergeant. "Here's a special leave pass for you," said he, and handed me a stout piece of paper; the heading did indeed read "Special Pass"[243]. At that moment, his excitement was greater than mine for I saw at once that it was made out to someone else. Even so, the Sergeant assured me all was well, the name would be changed to mine and signed by an officer.

As I made rapid preparations to depart, puzzlement about the matter occupied my thoughts: a Special Pass granted to another man but handed to me? Soon, though, I reported to the Company officer who duly "corrected" the name — no explanation requested or given. Some bread, butter, and a tin of bully beef were handed to me, along with a note instructing me to report to the RTO (Railway Transport Office) at Salty la Bret[244], a railhead some kilometres distant. How to get to the railhead, that was up to me. I must rejoin the Battalion 10 days hence, three days being allowed for travel both ways.

With a pack of unwashed oddments, some food in my haversack, a canister gas mask in its satchel on my chest, two blue cotton anti-gas hoods in their satchel hung over one shoulder, a full water bottle, trenching-tool handle in its loop at one side and the life-saving steel digger-head covering the upper bum, also various ammunition pouches attached to their webbing belt and braces, plus my rifle, the bayonet in its sheath... this load and I were at last on our own, headed for Blighty[245].

Away from the trenches I plodded, although freedom made me want to gallop despite my heavy burden.

Now I crossed artillery-land and, when a nearby battery blasted off, I feared my Special Pass might be wasted, because most of these lighter guns sat in sunken gun-pits, their muzzles only raised above ground level when they took aim. Camouflaged into the bargain. I might well get an 18-pounder up my jumper if I didn't keep my eyes skinned.

After much tramping, I came to a village, and a kindly bloke, a British soldier billeted nearby, tipped me the wink that I might just as well wait there because a motor-lorry would be coming along. It did the trip to the railhead daily, he said, and I'd get a lift for certain. I shared my grub with him, he supplied some lovely tea. Grateful for his help, I yet had a touch of belly-tremble, fearing that the lorry might not pass that day and that the train would leave Salty la Bret without me.

The lorry stopped for me, I slipped a Bank of France five-franc note into the driver's palm — not that he asked for anything — and he dropped me and my clobber off at the railhead. I found others waiting at the little-damaged station, but I made a beeline for a handsome, blond Sergeant with a moustache waxed at the points because he wore the flaming fusil badge on top of his cap, as I had with my old Battalion. A Sergeant of the Rifle Brigade sat with him and the two were kind enough to invite me to join them for the journey to London.

Together, we went to the RTO's little office and the officer in charge there strolled two or three lengths of the platform with us to stretch his legs. Actually, I suppose he wasn't a British RTO, he was a French officer, but he spoke perfect English.

I asked about a field pitted with large shell-holes, adjacent to his station; that they were there and not in his station, amused and pleased him. He related how, throughout the previous night, big howitzer shells had arrived at intervals, but only one caused damage to the track and that only slight.

A train would come, he said, but time of arrival was uncertain — early morning the probability. That gave us time to visit a village estaminet, have a meal of wine and coffee, eggs, chips, and slightly sour French bread, and get to know each other.

The Fusilier Sergeant wore a well-fitting uniform, spotless, surely almost new. If he had come from the Front, he must have had a spare uniform stashed away somewhere. His boots shone, and — judging by face and hands — he had recently bathed. Good to see a clean soldier — sharp of wit too, a great smile; with his personal assets he could have posed as a superior type, but he didn't. The other Sergeant had greying hair, his face round and rosy, his appearance that of the trench-wallah who took great care of his gear and himself. He was a comfortable man, steady of speech and a willing listener; his kindly eyes and steady gaze kept me at ease.

I'd certainly struck gold when that pair adopted me. And we were all glowing because we were going home. They had wives and kids to love them and the reunions would be marvellous. I had family too, not quite in the same way, but I knew they would do everything possible to make my stay happy.

While the two Sergeants looked almost too good for front-line habitués — they had come via a rest camp, I believe they told me — they had kindness enough not to comment on my unhygienic condition. Having left our advanced position in a hurry, I wore an old, soiled uniform and muddy boots, for up front you had little opportunity for anything beyond a wash and a quick shave should you need one, using your steel helmet as a bowl. I had lice in my underwear no doubt, although I always kept them down to the minimum possible. I must have had something of the sour trench smell about me too, but my companions ignored it.

In the complete darkness of the early hours, the train arrived and we settled into a comfortable compartment. Lots of room, so we stretched out and began to savour the feeling of freedom from danger and anxiety. There was little talk, some attempted dozing, and, towards dawn, an eye on the passing scene — then a grabbing of gear and a rapid exit when we heard the cry of "Amyong! Amyong!"[246] The circuitous part of the journey in the little, unscheduled train was over, we heard; we would now board a mainline train through Abbeville to Boulogne.

Eventually, we three crossed a choppy Channel in a small passenger ship. She rolled a bit so I took no risk of feeling queasy, stuffing myself with dry bread. We talked little, mostly stared fixedly ahead, keeping our thoughts to ourselves... It would have been too bad to stop a torpedo at that point, within sight of the White Cliffs.

Accustomed as I had been to the hot and sandy-brown scene at the far end of the Mediterranean, and then to the shattered dwellings and blasted earth of the Front in France, the greenness and unspoilt beauty of the countryside between Dover and London surprised me... in some parts, hedges and lanes extended as far as vision permitted. My mounting excitement took a lot of concealing from my two companions, older men who had, anyhow, been in England fairly recently. But I know they too felt very pleased with life in its immediate prospects; we grinned at each other with understanding and said nothing to threaten the then fashionable (stiff) upper lip.

Only as we reached the Victoria terminus did it occur to me that I had no English money, only small denomination notes issued by a French Department — well, maybe also a couple of Bank Of France five-franc notes, but they wouldn't fetch much. I didn't discuss this with the two Sergeants since they didn't mention money. I assumed they'd had time to attend to the currency problem before leaving their units, whereas I'd been on the move constantly since our Sergeant awakened me and handed me my pass.

We reported to the Transport Officer at Victoria and he stamped our passes, told us to report to him again seven days hence, and gave each of us an information sheet which we did not pause to read at that moment, anxious as we were to hurry to our families. Before parting, we undertook to meet in a week's time — where else? — under the clock, the big one.

And there I was, outside the station, suddenly feeling strange and rather soiled among the hurrying people, all of whom looked clean and well-dressed. I saw a bus which would take me almost the whole way home, but hesitated to board it, having no money.

I walked to the front of the bus to check the destination board, saw the driver already in his seat, stopped and told him I'd just come on leave from the trenches and had no money for my fare. "How far are you going?" "All the way when I get some cash." "Then here's your fare, son." He handed me money from his own pocket.

The kind man would not tell me how to get in touch with him to repay the debt and seemed very pleased to have been of use to a lad home from the Front. But I soon discovered I need not have bothered the driver, for the conductor asked, as I handed him the exact fare, "Is that alright?" — which among us, the hoi-polloi, meant will you be OK if you part with this lolly? So I told him where I'd got the money and we both had a good laugh.

The bus took me through busy streets, free from any sort of war damage, where people hurried or just strolled as they pleased... It was good to see they felt free to do so, that the war was not oppressing everybody. People had their private griefs, surely, but that blessed Channel between Britain and the Continent protected and saved the people from fear — no column of enemy troops likely to appear at the far end of the street, nor enemy guns suddenly raining explosive shells on the town.

The almost gay scene through which I passed in London brought home to me the quietness and absence of strolling civilians in the French towns I had visited. It was great. A few days of this, I thought, would do me more good than a barrel of medicine.

As I settled into the long bus journey from city centre to suburbs, I read the sheet the officer at Victoria had given me. Of most interest was the address of the Army building in West London to which I should take my pay-book. I resolved to attend to that next day, relying on my dad to advance a few shillings to start off with. Finally, the bus reached its turning point outside a big pub about half a mile from my home and I got off with all my gear, the rifle hanging from my right shoulder, not the least bit bothered by all the weight of it, happily clumping along the pavements in my heavy, noisy boots, savouring the look and smells of the shops and houses as I passed them.

In that developing suburb, a few grand houses still remained, though no longer occupied by the bigwigs who had formerly adorned the local scene. As brass plates or notice boards announced, they had become offices or workshops. The small dwellings adjacent to them, where the servants of the great may have lived, in some cases sported shop fronts behind which small retail businesses were conducted.

Variety and interest abounded along my entire route, reviving memories, many of them connected to my brother Ted. Thoughts of him brought to mind the grim scenes I had just left behind and the sad realisation that he was still over there; he might at this very moment be at risk in some awful battle or raid. But the last thing he'd want would be me worrying on his account, so onward... and finally the walk down our street to knock on the door of Number 26.

Ma opened the door and, at first, she was unable to grasp the fact that I was her son... but soon she hugged me in welcome and in I went.

We sat facing each other, using time, of which we had plenty, to adjust to the situation. I'd known that I would be there. She had known, or thought she had, that I was somewhere in France. Now she must really believe her eyes. I'd changed in appearance, more than I was aware. She spoke of this — not quite the baby-faced lad who'd slipped away so long ago, as it seemed to both of us.

Then, when full realisation was achieved, she started laughing happily and so did I and we went at it for quite a while. Laughter was easier and more enjoyable than a lot of chat. We knew why we were laughing and why tears were flowing. You're not having a real good laugh if you're not crying too...

My baby sister didn't really know me, of course. But that would soon right itself... By the evening, the family gathering was complete, Ted excepted — my younger brother home from school, elder sister and my father back from work, and all of them so surprised by my sudden appearance among them.

I had at least as many questions to ask them as they had for me, and it was pleasant to be talked to as an adult, whereas beforehand I had not quite rated that status with brother Ted the first son — I had never seriously questioned the situation because of his obvious superior intelligence and better judgement. Rather, I had felt proud of him. But I had lived through strange events and borne some small but serious responsibilities since last we were all together, and perhaps it showed. Or they may just have been naturally glad to have me there with them for a while... Either way, happiness; nor could I have wished for a more affectionate welcome.

With less cordial relationships, I could have found difficulty in admitting that my clothing housed other creatures than myself, but fortunately tales of the crummy state of men at the front had become common knowledge and, after chatting about the lousy conditions under which we often lived on active service, Ma suggested that I strip, have a bath and dump all my clothing out back. Some items of my civvy gear good enough to wear around the house still awaited me in a drawer upstairs.

A little later, my entrance, wearing these old things, brought on a big laugh, for I had grown somewhat. If the Army clothes had not dried by morning, I would have to lie abed for a few hours until they did, a prospect which pleased me. The lovely warm bath and the new experience of being well looked after were delights I had not dared to anticipate, contrasting so greatly with my recent mode of living that I could not properly express all the gratitude I felt for the many kindnesses shown... Tomorrow I would feel more relaxed, especially after a long sleep in a soft bed, free from all necessity to be constantly strung up and ready to act quickly in the cause of self-preservation.

The single iron bedstead carried just a mattress with filling unknown, clean sheets, one pillow, a blanket, and a patchwork quilt, produced some years previously by members of the Mothers' Union at the local mission church. But that bed represented heaven to me. My younger brother was already asleep when I slipped between the cool sheets. We shared a small room, but I didn't disturb him and I enjoyed watching him, a picture of boyish innocence, before I blew out the candles.

My mother, father and I talked for quite a long time that first evening and, although we had sent each other letters at fairly regular intervals, I had to fill in many gaps because Army censorship rules meant I couldn't name places, with the exception of Malta. Meanwhile, many things had happened locally to people we knew or knew of and these matters they related to me.

But the shock that shook really hit me when Pa almost casually told me that, as I'd requested, he did write to Lloyd George about my having been denied leave after reaching France from the Mediterranean, and how unfortunate he thought that was, particularly because, having served well enough to be promoted to the rank of Corporal, I was still below the permitted age for young men to go on active service.

He had received an acknowledgment and an assurance that the matter would receive consideration. So that explained the Special Pass originally made out to another man, but hurriedly handed to me. What a rocket some big fellow must have received from the office of the fiery and very powerful LG!

The whole thing seemed unbelievable, yet it had happened; my quiet, self-effacing father involved in such an affair and myself the beneficiary of a wonderful kindness emanating from Downing Street[247].

I lay awake, marvelling at the turn of events. Elation and a resolve to make the most of every minute of every day of that holiday from the war front, starting with the easy pleasure generated by just resting in that clean, sweet bed.

Ma lent me money for the fare to the West End office where my pass, pay-book and a letter from our adjutant procured me a few pounds. Prices remained low in spite of the war and I was, temporarily, very nicely fixed. Apart from any personal outings I had in mind, I booked seats in the stalls at two music halls for my parents and myself — at one show, I took a seat for my younger brother as well.

I felt sure I should encounter no Military Police while I confined myself to the area of my suburb, so I took certain little liberties with my dress, such as wearing a pair of smart slacks I'd bought which were not the precise khaki colour of the regulation trousers; carefully creased, worn without puttees and with shoes instead of heavy boots. Out walking I carried a stick I'd bought about three years earlier at a great exhibition at Earls Court — made by natives called, I believe, Igorotti Indians, it was covered with symbols burnt into it while I waited. Puzzled glances from passing people were just what I had hoped for, and I felt the soft Army cap, pulled well down over my left ear, added the final distinctive touch. Had I met a military cop, or perhaps an officer, no doubt I would have received another sort of touch — on the shoulder.

Hours at home, walks around the old, familiar places, the two shows — everything great, freedom unlimited was mine. Until I came face to face with a girl I'd known slightly at the church. How she'd grown... in a little over two years, visibly expanded in all the approved places. She had the then fashionable method of using the eyes; you looked directly at her, but she appeared to be focussed on a point just above your head. Very effective, especially if the eyes were a brilliant blue.

We walked and talked, I self-consciously, she being the first girl I had been alone with back in London, even in the street. On a free night I took her to the pictures, to a really go-ahead place where, to add music to the silent films, you didn't have just a pianist but a small orchestra. Tea and French pastries afterwards — already well on the way to the Devil.

With another meeting arranged I felt compelled to tell my mother about the girl, the renewed acquaintance, and see the disappointed look on her face — my short remaining time at home must now be spread around more thinly. I really regretted this, although excited about having such an attractive girlfriend. Life had become quite a heady, dazzling affair. Plenty of cash, all the hours of the day and part of the night at my disposal... no one to give me orders, no Jerry to sling shells at me.

As the precious break neared its conclusion, I felt a sadness which I threw off by reminding myself that some time still remained. I took a final walk with the girl, part of it in open country... seemingly unconnected to that horrible war.

Suddenly, on that dark moonless night, criss-crossing searchlights illuminated the whole sky, wide beams terminating in big, circular blobs of light where they encountered clouds. This unwelcome display of London's air-raid defences coming into action brought my thoughts back to reality with a jerk. No enemy planes appeared and no anti-aircraft guns fired, but my feeling of security, one of the boons of this holiday, now vanished. No place, after all, completely without risk of enemy attack in some form.

We two walked to her home, lingered outside awhile, kissed and parted with promises to write to each other.

Next morning, goodbye to younger brother, sister Ciss[248] and the baby girl. My parents came with me to the railway terminus. I left them for a moment, hurried to the big clock and met the two Sergeants, who I found in a state of great excitement for reasons they cautiously told me about.

They had already checked the platform from which our train should depart. There they heard a railway official tell a soldier that it had been cancelled, that he must go to Charing Cross to board another train in about an hour's time. The Sergeants hurried away from the platform and, between them, concocted a plot which they hoped would gain us another day at home: simply, that we should hide outside Victoria until it would be too late for us to reach Charing Cross in time to catch the special train. We would then dash into Victoria Station, hurry to the Transport Officer's place, and report ready to catch the pre-arranged train. I went back to my parents and told them of the wicked plan. We said goodbye in case things went wrong.

So, after lurking outside for a while, the Sergeants and I rushed into Victoria and on upstairs to the RTO, were duly staggered when he said we ought to be at Charing Cross already, and told him we would do our damnedest to get there in time. We accepted a note from him to the RTO at Charing Cross explaining everything. Arriving at Charing Cross we manifested amazement when the rather annoyed RTO there told us the one and only train had gone. Finally, he endorsed our passes extending leave by 24 hours. And we all went home again.

Strangely, that extension of leave had an unnatural feeling around it.

All concerned had thought my departure certain, we'd said our goodbyes, yet here I was, back home again. It didn't seem right somehow.

By way of a bonus, I went off for a last look at my favourite haunts. How came it then that I finished up by a canal at a spot on the opposite bank to a factory in whose offices worked my girlfriend? No hope of contacting her during working hours, yet I wrote a note to her, wrapped it around a stone and waited. Soon I saw a girl walking from one building to another and called out to her, then threw my message across the water. She picked it up, straightened out the paper, read it, then waved reassuringly I thought. She did deliver it, I learnt at a much later date.

Chapter Forty

So there I was, making my way back to France, to the battlefield. With mixed feelings I must admit. The change, the rest at home, had certainly made me feel better. And I was leaving many things I now valued more highly than I had done before the war started. Everything so clean; life very sweet. When one thought of the conditions up at the Front — always rough, worse in some places than others, but never really comfortable...

One tried to maintain a pride in one's appearance. I anticipated that now, being louse-free, I might be able to continue in that enviable state for a few days, but the odds were against me — reinfestation inevitable. I knew from experience. I would lie down in some place previously inhabited by one of my lousy pals, bound to pick up a few of the little devils who had deserted him for reasons unknown.

When we arrived at Boulogne, the two Sergeants — such merry companions on my journeys to and from Blighty — had to leave me and right sorry I was to see them go. Before they left their respective Battalions, they had been told where they should rejoin it. I had no such instructions. You may recall in what haste I had been obliged to leave, asleep near the front line one moment, the next starting off on that most joyous journey.

From Boulogne, I was directed to make my way to our Divisional Headquarters, picking up such transport as I could find. On arrival at HQ, I was told to spend the night there and proceed next morning to the village in which my Battalion was now resting.

After a couple of lifts from Army lorries, the final kilometres I had to manage on foot. But this provided me with a most warming experience as I strolled into the town. Our lads, who had themselves arrived only a few hours earlier, were billeted in dwellings and outbuildings at various points along the main street. Groups of them lay about on the wide grass verges on either side of the roadway and, at intervals as I walked, fellows who knew me invited me to join them and each in turn insisted I took a swig from their water bottles — all charged with the same liquor, to wit, cider. I was greatly surprised, first, that so many people knew me and, second, that they should offer me a drink. Their kindness warmed and enlivened me just as much as the rather strong cider.

The insistence of one chap in particular that I should drink with him certainly startled me, though I was careful to conceal it. I'd known him from time to time since the beginning of the war — a short chap, head rather big considering his lack of height, bright blue eyes in a usually red face. He'd joined a different Royal Fusiliers Company, but circumstances occasionally brought us together.

However, I'd never felt happy or secure in his company. Sometimes, if you attempted to share a joke with him, the thing would go wrong, he'd see some personal adverse implication in it. For no reason that I could see, the red face would go redder, the eyes would glare and he'd be all set for a scrap. I hadn't chatted with him for some time, and I had not known until that moment that he, along with some others, had been transferred to my present Battalion. Maybe he felt somewhat of a stranger in this new set-up so even *my* face was welcome. He certainly insisted I should share cider with him.

From there on, my progress along the road had something of a triumphal air about it. A wave here, called to join a group there, swigs from bottles well filled with the local cider; all this camaraderie took the edge off the regret I felt about leaving family and friends to return to a life I had come to dislike, deep down inside.

But one could never remain very miserable in company with those soldiers. Every group had its natural-born comedian. Although hardship, filth, and genuine physical suffering took their toll of one's natural optimism, the fellow who showed his true feelings and really looked unhappy or just plain dejected got short shrift from his fellows. Far better, and certainly to one's advantage, to show nonchalance of spirit, best expressed in the few words "What the heck?" — borrowed from our American cousins (as we often referred to them, in those days).

On I went until, with greater pleasure than ever, I found myself back among the lads I had soldiered with before the Sergeant thrust the unexpected pass into my hand.

As I moved around, it was great to be greeted by almost all of them with words and looks of something bordering on affection. At the time I'd left them, I had been their acting Sergeant, though wearing only two stripes on my arms and those only there as a result of irresistible pressure from the big man, the Regimental Sergeant Major. But I felt no need to keep up "a position" — something usually incumbent on non-commissioned officers.

In order to maintain their authority, NCOs set themselves apart from the rankers to varying degrees. Most of them, when off-parade, would occasionally mix with Privates. But it was understood that they were the boss's deputies. Most men, given a little power and authority, however slight, succumb to the conviction that they are, well, a bit better than the ordinary fellows around them. I always found that the more ignorant — within the general meaning of that word — a promoted man was, the heavier the hand of authority he laid upon his former workmates.

Probably because of my youth, I wore my modest rank lightly and still relished the comfort given by the comradeship of the men around me. I do believe I would have been hurt more by an accusation that I was too strict than that I was behaving in too easy a manner. With some such understanding between us, I always found the essential needs of discipline easily procured or, rather, willingly granted by our men.

On active service, there could be an easy assumption that worthwhile men would do what was necessary for the good of all without any great pressure of authority being applied. Now, again, I had to fit myself into our little part of a huge organisation — the enormous business machine running the British part of the war.

Contemplate just a couple of aspects of it: feeding the mass of soldiers — what a family; and, at the other end, of course, the disposal of bodies of men killed day after day, week after week, and so on into the foreseeable future. On those rare occasions when a humble Tommy gave some brief thought to what went on nearer the top of the military operation, he quickly became convinced that the thing was getting out of hand. At quiet moments, ordinary fellows began to pose the question: "What's the object of it all?" If, with one's rather limited knowledge of history, one tried to envisage the probable sequel to the vast struggle, the outcome was far from enlivening, far from cheering.

At ground level, the very bottom of the structure, stood the Tommy, the soldier — to be wounded, maimed, or killed his most probable reward, dare one say, for his small and often ineffectual efforts to overcome the enemy.

But... leaving all that aside, I was back, my unit going into action again before long, the many hazards and the few, simple pleasures to be faced or enjoyed. In fact, as I went about my small duties and re-established my position among my particular group, I viewed our prospects with a fair amount of optimism. We had some pleasant days in that small town, with a good spirit about among the fellows. Memories of the big battle, the great losses, had begun to recede into the past, the terrific tension, the fear, the sadness, taking their proper place in the background of men's thoughts — that is, apart from the odd things one could do in one's own interests, the future, as it always had been and always would be, was outside the control of ordinary individuals.

The day came when we were ordered to pack up everything, while reducing to the required minimum those articles we must carry with us into the trenches. All the usual preparations for a move kept us fully occupied. Then off we went, marching eastwards.

At night we paused, making rough, temporary billets in outbuildings and barns on unoccupied farms. Quite exhausted with the marching, where we lay mattered not too much, provided we had some sort of cover for our heads in case it rained.

Such basics could never be guaranteed in wartime, but the good organiser made sure his men got the advantage of whatever was available. Slackness at the top could cause much discomfort lower down, whereas a good Colonel with a good team of officers around him established a reputation among the members of a Battalion which would never be lost. The men who benefited from his thoughtfulness would remember him always. It must have been a great reward, or sometimes a consolation, to a high officer who, through the exigencies of battle, lost many men for whom he had a feeling often amounting to affection.

In the next section of the front line we manned, no satisfactory or permanent settlement had been achieved following the recent battle. Away to our right we could see what we considered to be *our* front lines — occupied by Germans. Meanwhile, we had annexed the former German reserve trench, as we would have termed it; the part we held contained a number of large, deep dugouts — our chaps must have had a tricky job clearing the Jerries out of that network. Way ahead of this strong line lay shallower temporary trenches of the kind I'd often been involved in digging overnight in No Man's Land.

Of course, we now had the use of everything the Germans had established — an unaccustomed situation. But we soon took pleasure in being able to have a few hours uninterrupted sleep down there in the underground shelters which, on average days or nights, greatly muffled the sound of exploding shells. One had the feeling that the world of violence up above was distant, really remote. Reflecting that, in many parts of the Front, the Germans had the advantage of this sort of facility, one wondered if we could ever effect a real break through the enemy lines.

Never a dull moment, though, up above in the trenches. The close proximity of the front lines made it obligatory on both sides to keep the pot boiling. Short, snappy raids across the intervening, quite narrow No Man's Land occurred nightly. During daylight, a head shown for a moment above the parapet of the trenches attracted bullets — rifle fire, machine-gun fire; action far more intense than normal in periods between major battles. But we did have that consolation of the comfortable hidey-holes down below with their wooden bunks and reasonably warm temperature.

The German trench construction allowed more substantial reserves of dry rations to be stored underground, so feeding the troops from day to day did not rely on the success or otherwise of ration parties reaching the Front from supply depots in the rear.

Probably, from the senior officers' point of view, this set-up was close to the ideal. Normally, we didn't see senior officers in a real front-line position. They'd be back at Battalion Headquarters. But here HQ had moved forward to these underground complexes. Of course, this did mean more frequent and sharper supervision of the junior officers and their men. And probably the most serious crime in that situation was for a man to be discovered down below when he should have been above or out in the advanced trenches. At least, here the officers and NCOs could organise periods of duty so that we all shared the riskier tasks equally.

Certainly, time passed very rapidly there, just doing your job — or appearing to do your bit plus ensuring your own continued existence. Of necessity, it kept you constantly alert. And active. At times, very active.

Our first spell of duty up there concluded; quite a large number of casualties sustained. We withdrew some kilometres to lick our wounds, as it were, reorganise and, no doubt, fill the gaps. Rest at the rear there, some relaxation, short periods of training. A couple of lectures too.

One in particular, I recall, acquainted us with the mechanism of the Mills bomb, the British hand grenade at that time. Diagrams showed the bomb's insides: a fairly large chamber filled with high explosive, the lever on the side secured by a split pin that simply controlled a spring; when you pulled the split pin out with one hand, the lever had to be held in place by the fingers of the throwing hand; then, when you threw the bomb, that lever sprang clear releasing a sharp, pointed dart to pierce a percussion cap which ignited a very touchy explosive called amynol contained in a small copper tube — and set off the larger quantity of TNT. When the explosion occurred, the casing — moulded in small squares — split up into numerous jagged pieces of metal which could do awful damage.

That type of bomb had remained in use ever since Colonel Mills had designed it about 1914 and persuaded the War Office to manufacture them on a large scale[249]. Every man in the front line carried several of them when deployed on a patrol. In a big attack, men specially skilled in throwing the bombs carried them about in canvas buckets, chucking some themselves and handing them out to others. Using them efficiently required a pretty good knack. A loose overarm method seemed best. The further away from you it landed the better, of course. Having thrown one, it was advisable to duck or, for preference, get under cover.

Soon, again, we moved up front for minor action, patrol clashes, snatch raids, nothing yet on the grand scale although we felt, or knew, I think, that another big battle was pending...

So you may be able to appreciate my feelings when, next time out at rest, I was ordered to report to the Regimental Sergeant Major, the big man I've told you about, splendid soldier, he who ordered me to put up a second stripe when I didn't want to.

I entered the room in a half-ruined house he used as an office, stood smartly to attention, announced my name and rank, and he told me to relax. He chatted in a very friendly way — it really did amaze me that the top man of all the NCOs should have any knowledge of me, trying as I always did to play it quietly, lie low and bother nobody.

Suddenly, in the midst of our conversation he held up a piece of paper and said: "This thing's come along. Ridiculous really. Don't suppose you'll want to have anything to do with it. It seems that after all this time up here, you're still under the age at which soldiers are allowed to be on active service[250]. That's what it says here. And, moreover, it says you are to be sent back to base. You don't have to go. I think I can fix it so that you can stay here with the boys as I know you'd wish to."

I had to think very quickly. Then I recalled my letter home during the period when I was feeling, not desperate, but quite bitter about not getting a few days leave, and how my father had relayed that appeal, as his own, to Lloyd George. I realised then that this thing had not stopped with me being given special leave. The rest of it had gone through too and I was to be sent back.

No doubt, at that time, I hated to lose face with the great RSM, but I said to him: "If that order has come through, then it is the wish of my father that I should follow it and, as he's done this for me, I'll go along with whatever the order says must happen."

When the RSM saw I was set on that course, I guess he expressed his disappointment. I'm sure he'd expected me to feel honoured by his offer to wangle it for me so I could stay with my Battalion. Probably, my rank as Sergeant in charge of a platoon would then have been confirmed.

Suffice it to say I left the Battalion, gathered up my belongings, made my way to a railway station as instructed, and got on a train which didn't stop until we approached a part of the French coast I'd never seen before, near the port of Le Havre where I was to transfer to the British Army camp at Harfleur — the place has some historical significance I believe[251].

PART SIX

1916-1917

A PEACEFUL INTERLUDE:

FRANCE AND ENGLAND

Chapter Forty-One

Late in 1916, having arrived at this very large base, I had no idea what the future held for me. Truth to tell, I wasn't feeling very proud of myself. Here I was, miles and miles away from the action, and the chaps I'd known, one or two fairly intimately, were still up at the Front where they would continue to endure all the risks, physical discomfort and moments of horrible anxiety.

One thought helped to rid my mind of worry or doubt: that once I had parted from the crowd with whom I had been living, under no matter what conditions, they would forget me and, unless by chance we met at some future date, all thought of my existence or even my death would be absent from their minds. So I must look to the present.

Harfleur camp stood mainly on a hill. As I marched in with a small party who'd arrived on the same train, I saw line upon line of bell tents — like a big, bustling town really. I had to report to an officer, and he passed me to a Sergeant, who led me to a line of tents he was in charge of and pointed at one of them. "Put your kit in here," he said. "This is where you'll live. The men will show you where the dining hut is and the other places you need to know about — including that big hut down there, the ablutions, and beside that's the washing hut where we all do our laundry. Once a week our party will go down there and we'll thoroughly clean ourselves and our clothes."

I quickly acquainted myself with everything I should know about the place and went to the Sergeant's tent. A board outside announced the time at which I must parade with rifle and bayonet the following morning for training; that, I understood, was the kind of duty I would perform until I returned to the front line, presumably after my 19th birthday, July 6, 1917. This didn't hold out too bad a prospect; quite satisfactory as far as I was concerned.

Next morning, however, back in my tent after breakfast and getting ready for the morning's work, I heard my name called. I looked out and saw the Sergeant hurrying down in my direction. When he shouted my name again I called out "Sir!" and he said, "Come with me, you won't be going on that training after all. Yesterday, when you marched in with that party, an old friend of yours saw you."

This puzzled me, because I'd never been to Harfleur before. But the Sergeant continued, "He looked out of his canteen and saw you going by. He came to me and said he'd just seen a man arrive who'd make a good assistant for him. He told me you used to be a grocer, which is just what he needs." I was used to surprises by this time, but I did find it a bit unnerving to be told I'd worked as a grocer pre-war.

The Sergeant then took me to a large Army hut used for meals. In one corner I saw a well set-up shop, a counter full of sandwiches, cakes and pastries, shelves behind bearing tinned goods, cigarettes, biscuits and so on. I had to summon up a real show of pleasure and friendship on realising who stood behind the counter running this little place.

His name was Archie Barker. I'd known him in our first Battalion, though never intimately; he'd run the officers' mess. A man of some importance, then — the chap who oversaw provision of the various items an officers' club needed, wines, spirits, cigars, cigarettes, and so on. He also supervised the cooking and serving which, when circumstances permitted, had to be done in some style. Well, by some devious means, Archie had landed up here, running a small canteen.

The Sergeant left us together. We exchanged grins of understanding. I thanked him for what he had done and he admitted, of course, that he knew nothing of my pre-war life. The idea had suddenly come to him.

Said he, "It was such a pleasure to see a member of the old mob in this huge camp where I hardly know anybody that I wanted you to work with me. I knew one of the old boys would be trustworthy. Saying you were a grocer was just the inspiration of the moment. This little canteen is a more or less unofficial thing. The Expeditionary Force canteen is just down the road and they sell everything. But a Captain Quartermaster administered our section of the camp and, for reasons of his own, he felt that a small, personal sort of canteen would be of value. He let it be known and I told him about my experience of the officers' mess and running this sort of business before the war, so he gave me the job.

"Now, all the lines you see on the shelf I have to buy from the Expeditionary Force canteen and the discount is only 5 per cent, so it's a mean profit, although we don't have to pay any rent here. But the Captain and I feel that if we can get hold of lines which aren't sold in the EF canteen, we can do the troops a bit of good. Well, I can make sandwiches of many different types these chaps won't have tasted since they were civilians, and we could do French bread, confectionary, pastries, fruit, and fresh vegetables. Which are unknown on Army menus, aren't they? What do you say? Do you feel you could undertake the buying?" I must have nodded. "All right, most mornings this week you will be allocated an Army wagon which will take you into Le Havre and I'll give you the money to buy whatever you feel a Tommy will appreciate, things to surprise him when he sees them on the counter — and then on pay day we'll persuade him to spend his money here. And the margin of profit will be somewhat in excess of five per cent I promise you."

The bewilderment I felt had to be concealed. I knew nothing whatever of buying and selling, but I realised I must make this thing stand up, although it required a complete change of attitude from a member of an infantry Company used to obeying orders as they came down from the top. Still, I must have offered a show of reasonable confidence that I would at least try to do the job; the following morning, Archie told me I should make my first journey into town.

Meanwhile, I cleaned up in the canteen, scrubbing the floor behind the counter, dusting the shelves. We remained open for an hour after the mid-day meal. Then close, clean up again, and reopen in the evening. I saw the job would be one of long hours. That didn't worry me. The hours up at the Front were the full 24 hours of the day, sleeping when you could. But the conditions of life were so much better here; I could see I was going to live well, and certainly not be short of food.

I intended to do the job honestly, be loyal to Archie, and help him make a handsome profit — even though I wondered where that profit would finish up. With that Captain Quartermaster, I supposed. As the new buyer for his business undertaking I had to go along and present myself to him — a large, florid type of Scot. I didn't understand most of what he said, because of his broad accent and rapid speech. So I left not too certain he knew much about the business. Still, whatever his motives in starting the venture, in Barker and me he had two workers who would give of their best.

Up next morning, after I had breakfast, there on the road I saw a large open wagon pull up, two horses, the driver on a high seat above them. I didn't even know where Le Havre was and told the driver so, but he said he'd done the trip many times. We set off and came to a main road with tramlines running along it in both directions. As we jogged along, I was amused to see how the French travelled at that time in single-deck trams, two coupled together, the passengers packed tight inside with men hanging on to the outside and one or two standing with feet on a hand rail and clinging to the edge of the roof — on cobbled roads.

We passed through a sort of suburban area and came to one of the main shopping streets, the Rue Tière. Here I had the driver stop, and I walked along, looking for possible goods to purchase. I had a large roll of notes, mainly of five francs each. I think I'm correct in saying that the franc was then 27 to the pound[252]. It didn't matter really because the troops were paid in French money anyway.

"*Boulangerie*" said the sign over one shop. I went in — a bakery: we'd need quite a lot of bread, Archie had told me. French loaves made a nice change from hard Army biscuits — though I will say that, where the Army bakers could fix up their ovens properly, they produced very good bread too. So I had to tell the French baker, who spoke no word of English, that I wanted 70 loaves. I knew little French, but what are fingers for?

"*Demain*," he said — that I understood. Today's stock was sold. I asked him if he made apple turnovers, a special request from the troops... but that I couldn't convey and I left him at that — I'd secured the bread anyway.

Thereafter, I had tremendous good luck. We drove along the main street until I decided to take a turn to the right. Halfway down was a grocery. We went in: on our left, crates, sacks and boxes of vegetables and fruit, then the counter with shelves of groceries behind it. The smell of coffee predominated. A shady, quiet shop. On the right stood the cash desk, which almost every French shop had, no matter how small — a glass-fronted cubicle occupied by the cashier or assistant who would take your money and make an entry in the sales book. There sat my new-found friend-to-be Marie-Louise.

Marie-Louise Baudlet; I suppose I can mention her full name now as she was somewhat older than me — I can only estimate 21 or 22 — and she must have passed away long ago.

She wasn't pretty, but quite attractive, dressed in severe black with white trimmings. She probably looked older than her years, bright, smiling eyes. She made me welcome. She spoke perfect English and told me that, before the war, she had made several visits to England and stayed with relatives in Richmond, Surrey; my translator, then, ready to hand.

Her mama was probably nearer 50 than 60. She had no English, but she did me the honour of hinting that I was *très gentil* and I could only guess why and be suitably flattered. Perhaps *gentil* represented her hope more than her opinion. Perhaps soldiers in the shop previously had not been *gentil*…

I soon had a friendly working arrangement with Marie-Louise. I bought what I could — as much as possible of what they had to offer. But, as Marie said, items of which I needed a large quantity I would have to buy in the market; so, apples, other fruit and fresh vegetables, butter (selling cheaply from a counter run by a Belgian lady) — all luxuries for the soldiers.

Each morning when we took the wagon to Le Havre, before I went anywhere else I called in at Marie-Louise's place and asked her to tell me the French words for what we wanted and for the quantities — hence, no further buying difficulties at all! From her place to the central market, the Halles Centrales, was quite a few hundred yards. I had the driver stop the wagon outside. He made himself comfortable in his seat to wait for me.

One large Army Service Corps depot provided the transport for all the Allies represented at Harfleur camp, so I seldom had the same driver and wagon two days running and sometimes he would be English, sometimes a New Zealander — an Australian I remember well, with his big slouch hat and completely free-and-easy style. When I told him I was going to stay in one place for a fairly long period, he would lie down on his back in the wagon and fall fast asleep. I'd wake him when I was ready to drive around and pick up the goods I'd ordered. We exchanged little in the way of conversation. He didn't worry me and I didn't worry him, except that one day he arrived in a captured German ammunition wagon; no springs, and the greater part of the journey over cobbled streets — I had to get out a couple of times to pee that day.

In the central hall I found a greengrocery stall operated by a mother in her fifties and her two daughters, one about my age, the other a little bit older. There I could bargain, a skill I learned through doing this job, especially as I discovered how keenly the shopkeepers priced vegetables and fruit — then Archie could make his profit, for instance, by selling apples singly, which in turn made a great difference to the men because they could not get fresh fruit anywhere else on camp.

Meanwhile, mother and daughters became friendly with me and, I suppose as a reward for my custom, the mother invited me to go round to a restaurant for a very good meal, a treat she repeated several times.

I continued to buy from the first baker I'd met — the first three apple fritters (which I'd been wishing to order and did once Marie-Louise gave me the translation), were well-made with dried fruit laid out on pastry, sugared, covered with more pastry, then baked and cut into squares. We loaded them up on to our wagon still packed in the baker's trays. They proved a great favourite with the soldiers. Such perishable goods I learned to defer buying until the weekend, after pay day.

I recall one shop where I bought some chocolate. Two old maids ran it and they spoke a little English. The care, the time they took, the fuss they made of me, it was like being in a world apart from the normal Army life — it seemed almost comical, farcical, in the light of what I'd expected to be doing…

Back at the canteen, Archie taught me to make thin, very tasty sandwiches. Tinned salmon was favourite. I'd empty a can into a large bowl, beat it up adding salt, pepper and vinegar and tasting it from time to time until I got it just so, that slightly salty mouth-watering flavour to make the ideal sandwich. We sold dozens of them. He taught me to build them up in pyramids — placed out of reach of the troops, that was important, but visible and tempting. On the evenings the lads were in the money, the two of us often had difficulty coping with the great rush of trade.

More money became available to buy fresh vegetables, and I bought apples and sometimes pears on a bigger scale too.

The whole business reminded me very much of pre-war days when sometimes, to order a lunch for the partners at Lake & Currie, I'd go to Sweetings or Binns, famous restaurants, where they displayed their sandwiches stacked in pyramids and the clients ate them with a pint of beer, then threw some money down on the counter and left. Even the aroma in our canteen — the various sandwiches we served, and perhaps coffee as well as tea — could sometimes recall those grander establishments.

I did no Army work, parades or drills. Barker and I appeared to live in a world apart from the masses there. As far as I was concerned, that could go on forever.

I never failed to call in on Marie-Louise, first thing in the morning. I never saw her except in the shop, at the counter or the cash desk; I sat on a box and she on a stool — Mama occasionally somewhere in the background. Speaking no English, she couldn't join in the conversation, but she kept a maternal eye on us, so nothing else could go on. Not that it was likely to because Marie-Louise seemed the absolute soul of propriety. Moreover, she had a fiancé, a French officer who was away at the Front.

For some reason which I didn't quite understand, but didn't concern myself with, another man began to come along with me on the trips into Le Havre. A Lieutenant to the Captain Quartermaster had arranged it, and when this fellow joined me, he said he simply had nothing better to do. He could speak French, which might come in useful sometimes, and he could stay with the wagon if the driver wanted to go off somewhere. What he, a young man of maybe 20, was doing at the base I didn't know and I don't recall ever asking him. Eric Brays was his name; five feet nine, well-built and fit, his face wore a moustache and a smile. He belonged to the Honourable Artillery Company, a London Territorial Army unit with its own long traditions and barracks in the City Road; it generally recruited from the sons of City merchants and businessmen. Eric never said anything offensive nor argued about anything. He came along for the ride.

I introduced him to Marie-Louise as a chap who spoke perfect French, so they conversed in her language. Afterwards, she told me he spoke a Southern patois. He explained that, to improve the French he learned in school, his father had sent him to live with a farming family in Southern France, so he spoke as they did.

Eric was sometimes a bit of a joker, though, and one of his little amusements almost landed us in trouble. The market stood in a square with streets on all four sides. A very fine building, its roof and walls to a great extent comprised large, glass windows, so you could see in and out. One day, when I'd finished my buying, I and the two girls from the fruit and vegetable stall wandered away and stood talking in the middle of the market. Some joking was going on — slightly naughty, I expect — and Eric got into a discussion with one of the girls as to the meaning of an expression much used by Tommies, namely, "Wormwood Scrubs". Eric tried to explain about Cockney rhyming slang: so, Scrubs — bubs — breasts.

You can imagine the girl's eventual understanding and laughter; she said, "Ah, these then!" signifying with her hands, "These Wormwood Scrubs!" More laughter.

Well, would you believe that leaning out of her window on the far side of the street watching us was a licensed prostitute? Marie-Louise told me the full story later. This woman complained to the licensing authority that the greengrocer's girls were trying to take away her trade, steal her customers. Apparently, the law allowed her to make the complaint and claim some compensation. I explained to Marie-Louise the nature of the events so misinterpreted by the prostitute, and she undertook to go to the Town Hall and clear it up. She said I needn't worry about it and wouldn't have to attend court, as might have been the case. In due course, someone somewhere did put it right, or told the woman she was making a frivolous complaint.

It was around that time I had the interesting experience of watching a Frenchman buy a monocle. Barker had asked me, while in town, to call at an optician's shop in the Rue Tière. I merely had to collect some spectacles he had left there for repair.

While waiting, I noticed a French civilian searching through a box on the counter. It contained wire frames, mostly gold wire, and not for pairs of spectacles, but for single lenses. He selected one and as he tried it in his left eye, I observed that the bottom of it was distinguished by double wiring. He stood in front of the mirror. Down went the jaw as he stretched the skin on that side of his face to its limit. Into the orbit went the frame, the jaw relaxed, and the double wire gripped in a fold of flesh.

This went on for some time until he'd selected the one that suited him and handed it to the optician for the lens to be inserted. The fascination to me was this man's concentration on the job in hand, the careful selection, the serious, searching glance he gave to the reflection in the mirror — his appearance in wearing the thing obviously of the greatest importance, though perhaps it would be of aid to him in reading too. Until then, I had thought only a certain kind of Englishman wore a monocle. But the quantity of frames in that box proved the custom must have been quite common in France or, at least, in Le Havre.

Another time, back at Harfleur camp, I saw something happen to an Army wagon, which I was glad not to be a part of. Drawn by two mules, it climbed a fairly steep hill. Nearing the top, the mules apparently decided the task was too much for them, so they stopped and the weight of the wagon and its load began to pull them backwards. They either could not or would not regain control. The last I saw of them, they were gradually being dragged down the hill, swinging from one side of the road to the other. Sometimes they and the wagon got crosswise and there would be a pause. But the driver never managed to get them to resume pulling uphill. I guess finally he must have swung them round and gone back down. Knowing the obstinacy of mules, I wondered if they ever did reach the top of that hill.

A newcomer to our tent had news for me. I recognised him as a Fusilier by his badge, and I knew that, after the break-up of our old Battalion at Rouen, my brother had been sent to the original first-line Regiment, so there was just a chance that this newcomer had known or heard of him, even though thousands of men wore that badge. So I asked him about life up front, who was he with, and the long shot came off. He had belonged to the same Company as Ted.

I eagerly asked for news and he told me how, in a pretty sharp action, one of our Sergeants from the original Battalion, Billy Wale, had been severely wounded in a very much damaged advanced trench well ahead of the front line. This soldier had heard my brother say, "We can't leave old Billy Wale out there. I'm going to get him." But this soldier didn't know what happened after that, because he was already wounded himself and stretcher-bearers carried him away. So I still didn't know what had happened to dear old Ted in that very dangerous situation... How I wished I'd been there to help him. Knowing how tough and self-reliant he was, I had good reason to hope that he and the wounded Sergeant eventually came out of it alive. Probably, a letter from home would give me my next news of my brother, so I wrote to my parents telling them the details I had heard and trusted they had more recent — and positive — information.

In the canteen, I found one new development rather disquieting. After all, I had initiated this system of buying goods in the town from the French civilian dealers in hopes that it would establish itself permanently. I have mentioned those apple fritters as one great success with the troops. Well, another baker called at the canteen when I was out, offered Barker a lower price for them, and he accepted. When I sampled one of the first delivery, I didn't think it matched the taste or quality my friend in Le Havre supplied. I said so, but Barker didn't like this, he was the boss and he decided, so... nothing I could do about it.

One or two other points of friction arose, but knowing only too well the fragile nature of my job there, I didn't press my arguments. Nevertheless, the old friendly atmosphere faded. The basic reason may have been Barker's fears for his own position. A fit man, in his thirties, he should have been up at the Front. Naturally, he'd do everything possible to retain that job at the base, away from all the horror and agony.

So when, one day, it was decided I should return to England — for other duties, not on leave — I was mentally prepared for another move. No doubt I was delighted too, inwardly, although in part sorry to leave this life bearing so little resemblance to that of a soldier... the congenial relationship with Marie-Louise and her mother, the market people who knew me, the chummy drivers. In England this would be exchanged for who-knew-what?

Chapter Forty-Two

The crossing from Le Havre to Southampton took much longer than the Dover-Calais ferry, about eight hours. Then I boarded a train to London where I had to report to the HQ of our old Royal Fusiliers Battalion at the Bloomsbury depot where I had enlisted — a circle nicely completed.

In charge there, I found an officer, Lieutenant Hudson, who had been with us back then, in autumn, 1914, and a Sergeant I didn't know, an oldish chap, soldiering on in a quiet number. I gathered the Lieutenant had not left London during all that time. That's what the Sergeant implied, though it may have been wrong. Anyway, during the rest of my stay I saw little of the Lieutenant. "You'll be billeted at home and report here every morning at nine," the Sergeant told me.

Another nice change. I couldn't help constantly thinking back to the dirt, horror and squalor I was now avoiding. I just drifted with events and, for the time being, they treated me kindly.

My family was delighted to have me back once more — and a letter from Ted had just arrived, the first I'd heard of him since the worryingly uncertain story the Fusilier told me at Harfleur. It turned out he had left the infantry, gone through special training at Saint-Omer, and now operated with an obscure unit known as a Field Survey Company[253]. They constructed observation posts from which they photographed enemy artillery firing — smoke puffs by day, flashes by night — and connections through landlines automatically registered these pictures from four observer groups onto film at Brigade HQ. Calculations allowing for their respective angles, distances and so on quickly pinpointed enemy positions; orders to our artillery in the area followed at once, and thus they destroyed many a *Boche*[254] gun. War was indeed becoming something of a science, even in those far-distant days.

Financially, living at home was all right, with a good subsistence allowance drawn weekly. My days soon settled down to an almost civilian routine.

I took the bus from Edmonton every morning at about 8.15, arrived at the depot 10 or 15 minutes before the required time and did as the Sergeant requested. At first, the place was empty and all I did was dust the furniture, desk, bureau etc, in the big office upstairs, and perhaps sweep out the large drill hall once a week. Really, a matter of killing time.

Then 10 or 12 men reported for duty, passing through on their way from hospital, I gathered. They had all suffered severe wounds and required treatment in England, but recovered and convalesced to the point of near-readiness for active service. However, for no reason that I knew of, there was no unseemly haste to put them back in the front line.

The arrival of these chappies posed a problem for the old Sergeant, one he was not slow to unload. "Corporal," he said to me, "commencing next Monday morning, I want you to put these men through some drill. They've been away from their units for a considerable time, so gentle reintroduction to parade-ground disciplines will be good for them and give them something interesting to be getting on with."

Having learnt that quiet acceptance of what the person in authority said at any particular moment best suited my case, I quietly obeyed. I probably reasoned that, if I behaved in an agreeable manner, the people running the depot might even become glad to have me around... There was probably no more skilful creeper around than I designed to be. I gave good service and hoped to please...

Yet, all the time, I felt aware of an inner bewilderment. "I'm here," I would think, "safe and comfortable in dear old England, whereas a certain amount of conceit, a need to appear heroic, could have landed me in a situation where life was cheap, death and injury occurrences of every day."

And still I enjoyed this break from the wretched circumstances of a Tommy on the front line. I didn't have to grind any axe, merely obey orders — albeit I knew this would not last forever: someone in a department of the War Office called "Records" kept tabs on my movements and, on a given day, would lift my card from the file, note my age and send an order through "channels" to the man in charge of wherever I happened to be that I should return once more to where the action was.

But, meanwhile, if compliance could defer that regrettable moment I would try to be a good boy... No medals were ever struck for soldiers with ambitions as humble as mine; there again, you can't enjoy wearing pretty medals if you're kaput, *hors de combat*, disabled, call it what you will.

Back to the Sergeant's request that I should put my new comrades through a little smartening-up drill. "Well, Sarge," I asked, "where shall I give them this drill?" "Where do you think? Round at the Foundlings, of course." That big, open area in front of the Foundlings Hospital. Back to the old times with a vengeance.

On the Monday morning, I gathered my small group together and told them what was proposed, and that they would have to report to the depot until new orders came through for them. I gave them to understand that I was no pushing, ambitious Corporal, no Field Marshal's baton in my knapsack; that, in fact, I was determined to lose the stripes I had on my arm at the moment.

They understood perfectly and promised they'd give me their support in case we were watched at any time. We'd put on a smart, little drill show for a short period in the morning, take a couple of hours for lunch, then provide another small show in the afternoon, marching round and round and stamping our feet, then back to the depot, sign off, and go home.

This we did, observed or not. My suggestion that we strip off tunics and caps for half an hour and do a spot of physical training went down well too. So we established a neat, little routine. I guess the Sergeant had to resume dusting round the depot himself, for I don't think he had much else to do. In truth, I believe we took pleasure in this brief daily return to working, however lightly, on our old Foundlings pitch. People would stop by the huge wrought-iron gates and gaze through... and what were their thoughts? I trust they didn't gloomily conclude we were the last remaining members of the Great British Army.

I had several enjoyable chats with these fellows and heard with interest and sympathy of their experiences in action. Once, I mentioned to them our young Signals officer, Lieutenant Wickinson, who joined us on the edge of the desert in Egypt and took charge of our section — I'd spent several amiable off-duty hours with him, discussing what the work should be the next day... "Oh yes, I knew him," said one. "I'm sorry to have to tell you that I saw him killed. He was ahead of me walking along a road in an advanced situation — there one moment and gone the next, a direct hit by a shell, he just vanished."

Another chap gave me news of the rather elderly man, Captain Boden, who'd been my Company officer in the original Battalion from the time we landed in Malta. He'd joined another Regiment after we were disbanded in Rouen and, very shortly after reaching the front line, he too was killed. I also learned that dear old Major Booth, of whom I've said so much — a comparatively young man really, of course — had been wounded in the head; it was assumed that he too had died[255]. None of these sad items set me deeply longing to go back out there where living was really dangerous.

Our routine at the Foundlings continued, quite happily, for some time. One by one, though, members of my temporary platoon left. They received their orders and, I understood, headed back in the general direction of France. Sorry, in several respects, to see my little Army's disintegration, I still felt eager to discover what next would come my way — given I remained a few months too young for the Western Front.

When my own marching orders did come, they sent me northwards. I collected a railway warrant, said my goodbyes at home once more, hoisted the kitbag on my shoulder and caught a train from Kings Cross — having first taken the precaution of removing one of my stripes. Thus, to my own satisfaction at least, I reduced myself to the rank of Lance Corporal — than which one cannot get much lower.

Chapter Forty-Three

All change at Leeds, and onwards from there the few miles to Harrogate[256], a renowned watering place, as they were known then. When I alighted, I saw several other young Tommies strolling about on the platform. We gravitated towards each other and a short chat revealed that the six of us were all in similar situations. We had all served overseas, we had all been sent home because our age meant we should never have left the country as soldiers. And now the Army planned to give us up-to-date training to prepare us for the day when we could legally return to active service abroad.

A Corporal met us and immediately surprised us with the news that we had been allocated to a Battalion of the Essex Regiment[257].

From the beginning, I sensed among my fellows a feeling that we had been degraded. One or two had read in *John Bull*, the weekly magazine, about what its famous, later infamous editor Horatio Bottomley had branded "The Lost Division"[258]. This large number of fit men, a force formed quite early in the war, he said, had been allowed to avoid any kind of active service overseas, at the Front in France or anywhere else.

Here was something, I felt, about which I'd better think deeply, a trap into which I could easily fall. I could let myself feel aggrieved that, as a former reasonably patriotic lad, I had now been downgraded to the extent that I must soldier on in some phoney way with thousands of men who had evaded their share of the risks of the battlefield; would I be justified in objecting to being placed in this situation?

An air of comfortable prosperity emanated from the part of town we walked through to the Battalion headquarters. There, our details were duly noted, then our small group was taken to a parade of shops in the middle of which a door opened into a building of about four floors. We climbed an uncovered stairway, up and up to the top, where we found three rooms with rough and rather dusty, wooden floors and no furniture apart from a few mattresses in each. We were allowed to select whichever one we fancied. I threw my gear down in the front room.

Looking through the dirty window, I saw an extremely large area of grass common land and, beyond that, large houses set pleasingly in wooded grounds or gardens. On the right side of this common stood another line of sizeable houses, and on the left side, at a distance, hotels and other private residences. Wide footpaths crossed the grassy area in several directions. The whole place looked attractive and well-to-do. It bore no resemblance whatever to the London suburb where I had spent a good deal of my life.

So, we slept on the floor. Up in the morning early, a cold wash at a tap in a sort of washroom on a lower floor, and out on parade for the first time with this new Battalion. We, the under-age new boys, chatted away, our persistent theme that, although we were too young for the fighting line, our ambitions had never included relegation to a crowd branded nationally as dodgers, avoiders of doing their bit in the war effort. However, having considered this, I'd pretty well decided to follow my usual policy of lying low and saying nothing. There were always others around ready to do the talking, not all of it sensible.

One chap, Warley, three inches shorter even than myself (I was about 5 foot eight by then) and with one stripe on his arm too, turned out to be a bright little sparrow, always ready with a cheerful grin, but rather sharp of tongue — and he quickly decided he wanted no part of this "Lost Division" or whatever you cared to call it. The rest of us took little persuasion to go with him. When we proceeded to the common, where the rest of the troops had assembled, our little group stood to one side, waiting. We should have joined whichever Company we had been assigned to, but there we stayed, separating ourselves, plainly conducting a small mutiny. A bad start.

NCOs from various Companies came over and said we should be with them and why weren't we? Warley and others soon made it clear we wanted no part of this stay-at-home mob.

I think the height of absurdity arrived when the RSM approached us: a small man, well-proportioned, quick-moving, a swagger stick carried under his left armpit or occasionally brandished; doubtless because of his exalted rank, his small head had to bear the burden of a rather large moustache with long, thin, waxed ends. Sharp, snappy orders from this alert little Sarnt Major required us to obey orders and take up our positions in the various Companies. All to no avail.

So, believe it or not, he started to bargain, to dicker with this small group of youngsters. I'd never heard of such a thing before. My former RSM would have thrown us into the nick for this ridiculous defiance of authority, but little "Sticky" Walker, as he was known to his jolly men, made a sporting offer — take today off, he said, get used to the place, give the matter some thought, and make the right decision. Be on parade tomorrow, and the matter will be forgotten...

And that was the end of it. From then on I accepted the good life. A reasonable breakfast, a large basin of tea between us, bread, sometimes a rasher of bacon. Nothing wrong with that. My Company took dinner round one o'clock in a large church hall; generally some sort of stew — the big, white basin again — accompanied by potatoes, even some green stuff (though not often), and on Sundays, a pudding, either plum duff or spotted dick. Luxury indeed. Around teatime, that big basin full of tea re-emerged, with bread, marge, jam and, not infrequently, a chunk of cheese... These lucky men had enjoyed rations of that sort throughout the war years, while some of us led rather rougher lives and endured fare much below these standards.

No doubt the adverse publicity still appearing in the aforementioned weekly and taken up by other publications caused the top brass in "Lost Division" to rethink the system of work and training and draw up a new syllabus.

We had just started on this new programme when that previously mild winter struck hard; northern areas found themselves temporarily embarrassed by a covering of up to 18 inches of snow. Here indeed was an opportunity for the Regiment to improve its image. Out came the picks and shovels and carts and, to a well-organised plan, we set about clearing the main roads and then the side streets. It's probable Harrogate had never seen a snow clearance completed so rapidly.

I certainly saw no evidence among townspeople of dislike, let alone contempt, for the military. The local ladies organised concerts and the occasional whist drive, in fact did many things to make life a bit more pleasant for us. Not all the turns at the amateur shows reached a high standard, but we, the audience, appreciated the will to entertain, and backed up the performers with ample applause.

A character reader occupied the ground floor of my billet... the real trade description occurs to me now: "character delineator". He had, I heard, fitted up premises behind the shop window as a sort of studio. People actually paid the gentleman fees to encourage him to tell them about themselves. Did his opinion of the client exceed the client's opinion of himself? This I never discovered, but I did choose to believe a strange story I heard about this man.

The yarn had it that this character delineator wrote fiction well known among readers of popular magazines. He pursued this other line of work in order to study people's faces, general appearance and mannerisms, so that he could introduce characters resembling them into his stories. He dealt often in fictional characters of Chinese origin — the victims of these "Orientals" would, of course, be white Western people. I never met the man, but enjoyed the thought of living under the same roof as that author practising his curious trade[259].

By now I had formed a fairly close relationship with a young Scot, McIntyre. Being from Edinburgh, his quiet voice had an accent which I, and doubtless many others, have always found very attractive — even and smooth. I always enjoyed Mac's company; I estimated that his education had been superior to mine, but he had nothing of the snob about him. For me, though, he did have a touch of mystery, not unlike the alleged author. He told me that, just before the war, as a lad of 15 he'd apprenticed to a phrenologist — that is, a man whose skill consisted of "reading" the shape of bumps on the heads of, in my opinion, gullible clients. This man practiced — and trained Mac — in London, his premises on the corner where Fleet Street joins New Bridge Street.

Completely free agents almost every evening, we soon exhausted the obvious delights of the town — one cinema, the odd concert — and so Mac and I took to exploring the area. Despite the snow, we walked many of the outer streets bordering on open country, really just to kill time because the dark, still, winter evenings offered no great excitement — at least not until one moonlight night when we encountered quite a crowd of people at the top of a hill.

They laughed and chattered, passed around little bottles of reviver, even cakes — and, from time to time, parties would take off on large, home-made toboggans and sledges and race off down the hill at great speed.

Naturally, when we saw two girls standing by a rather big, but strange-looking contraption made of wood, Mac and I chatted with them and asked them about this unusual means of transport. They were friends, they told us, living in different parts of the town. The father of one of them, an employee at the local gasworks, had built this sledge some years previously.

It looked extremely strong, the wood probably three-quarters of an inch thick, but he had fashioned it in two parts. The front rider travelled astride and steered via ropes, held in each hand — these were attached to a movable section below on which his or her feet rested; to run right, they explained, press with the left foot and pull with the right rope and vice versa. One passenger could sit behind the steersman, with two others in a side-by-side seat at the back.

Unfortunately, the girls had never taken this thing out on their own before. Woe was me, then. As volunteer or pressed man, I can't remember, I sat in the steersman's position. We loaded up, Mac behind me, the girls on the back seat. We pushed off with our feet and gained a head of speed very quickly. The craft veered somewhat leftwards. Trees lined that side of the track. I tried to move the steering to the right, pressed with my left foot, pulled on the right rope, but nothing happened.

At terrific speed we hit a tree.

I came to, lying on my back, spread-eagled. I saw the moon shining above. I could only have been out for a second or two for, apart from myself, and Mac beginning to raise himself a couple of yards away, there seemed nobody else around. Then I heard sobs and groans. He and I looked around and found the two girls, both with leg injuries.

Now people appeared, having raced up from the bottom of the hill. After dressing the cuts on the girls' shins with handkerchiefs, we put them back on the sledge and the crowd helped us push the thing back to the top of the hill. Then Mac and I pressed on through the streets to one girl's home. The awful explanations. She lived with her sister. We left her, having taken the address.

Then our party shoved off to another area of town and the sad duty of explaining to the gas worker and his wife how his daughter's accident had come about. With remarkable kindness, they laid no blame on me. In fact, Mac and I arranged to visit the next day.

The crash laid the girls up for a good fortnight and, duty-bound, Mac and I visited each one in turn twice a week. The sister of the smaller girl took us up to her bedroom where we found her tucked up, professing to be quite happy. I sat on the floor on one side of the fireplace, Mac on the other, and we chatted for an hour or two. Unbelievably, the girl and her sister seemed almost grateful to us for coming. We would bring one or two little gifts of sweets or chocolates.

The other girl, bigger and stronger, showed signs of recovery first, and our visits there — the parents being present — didn't last long. But we maintained our interest and repeated our regrets. The dad reckoned his rather crude steering device had got jammed slightly out of true by ice and snow picked up as the girls dragged it along the streets and up the hill to the top of the run.

It was in the natural order of things I guess that, when the girls were once more up and about, we went for a walk with them. I recall one Sunday afternoon, striding along briskly in the cold air, they guided us out of town to some rather beautiful open country and, at one point, into a wood of wintry bare trees. There a daft episode caused much amusement.

I found myself carrying the smaller girl on my shoulders while the somewhat beefier Mac was loaded with the other quite hefty wench — and a race down a wooded slope started. My partner and I travelled some distance before we raced under a low-hanging branch and, unable to duck sufficiently, she finished up with it under her armpits and dangled there, while impetus carried me forward till I fell. There was much laughter as I lowered her from her situation of suspense.

She was an attractive little girl, very likeable, and for a while we became quite close friends, while Mac, as often as he could, called at the home of the other girl.

But then, walking in the town one afternoon, I was amazed to see my girl's sister on the arm of a soldier. I knew she was married and her husband serving in France. She saw me as quickly as I saw her. An awkward moment, awkward enough to prevent me from calling at their home any more. So that brief acquaintanceship petered out.

Now I moved from my room up above the character delineator's shop to a school the Army had taken over. In a large hall, another floor, another mattress. Along with two blankets, that was your home. Warmer than my previous billet, at least, the radiators in full working order, quite cosy.

Soon after our arrival, during the night, a youngster lying on his mattress two or three yards away from me complained of feeling very ill. Next morning he appeared even worse, so the NCO in charge suggested he saw the doctor. The rest of us went on parade but, when we returned in the evening, the sick man had not moved. He lay still on his mattress. Of course, we got him hot tea; food he couldn't take.

Then somebody did something about it. Or was supposed to do something about it. We gathered the doctors had been informed of the man's illness. But two, possibly three days passed. A couple of us took matters into our own hands; we went to the Medical Officer's quarters and demanded that the boy be seen because he was terribly ill. So the doctor did visit him and promptly expressed alarm at his appearance and the signs and symptoms the examination revealed.

The next morning, the MO reappeared, escorting a senior officer, a Royal Army Medical Corps Major, who examined the boy himself, then had him removed immediately, sent off to an isolation hospital. After that, the Major addressed the rest of us to find out who'd had contact with his patient and to take swabs from our throats.

Within 24 hours, our Company Sergeant Major was calling out the names of men whose swabs had shown positive results — including mine. We had to gather our belongings together and get into a lorry to be carted off to the isolation hospital... Though I suppose the description "hospital" flatters it somewhat. It consisted of two or three large Army huts. But they were comfortable and clean and we had small iron beds, even sheets. So we settled down into what could have been a period of relative luxury.

We were told that, although not ill, we had in our throats the germs of cerebrospinal meningitis, sometimes referred to, back then, as "spotted fever". A dangerous complaint. We harboured the germs of one sex or the other and if, while that remained with us, a germ of the opposite sex entered our system the two would get together and the trouble could start. It started at the bottom of the spinal cord and it could soon reach the brain with awful results. So we were told.

The treatment consisted of, twice a day, sitting around a large copper boiler, from the lid of which several spouts protruded. The water therein contained formaldehyde. So, heads and bodies wrapped in white sheets to keep us fairly dry, and with our eyes covered, we sat in a circle round the boiler and breathed in this very strong vapour. When that bit of treatment was over, we were free. But not to leave the hospital, of course. We were isolated from everybody. Still, they offered us books and, under the supervision of the Sister in charge, we did the cleaning, which helped to pass the time.

After spending a short time in the isolation unit I did begin to feel ill. You can imagine the lines on which my thoughts ran. But the Sister looked at my face, told me to roll up my sleeves and undo my shirt buttons — sure enough, I had a rash across my chest. "That," she said, "is nothing to do with germs in the throat. That's German measles." So I was taken to a larger hospital and installed in another isolation unit.

I saw one or two nurses outside wearing attractive bright-red capes over the usual uniforms. Very cheery. My all-white room contained five beds, I think, but the others remained empty. During the day a nurse came in frequently. When the doctor, elderly and gentle of manner, looked me over, he asked me what I'd been doing. I told him France and Gallipoli and he said that one of the things they had to do was feed me up, particularly lots of fish and scrambled eggs on toast — which wasn't bad either.

Good fortune did indeed walk along with me during those days, for out of the evil of contamination had come this period of clean, quiet living which should restore me to general fitness...

Able once again to face a front-line soldier's health-ruining existence, days and nights of nervous tension strung to the limits of human endurance, even more bedevilled by the fact that one must give no indication of what one was feeling. Ever the breezy wisecrack, the brilliant riposte, the foulest epithet, the hard laugh; it took it out of you to merely keep up with the others in maintaining these deceptive appearances while aware that, if that Jerry battery of whizz-bangs persisted in moving its aim ever nearer to your position, you and your mates would soon be surveying the site from a place way up in heaven — or shellfire might be replaced by hellfire if the judgement went against you... well, a pretty, little quip like that would have won a pale smile, even in a sticky front-line situation.

But I wasn't out there... Far from it, in my snug, little hospital ward, feeling full of gratitude to the benevolent physician who had correctly diagnosed that I had needs beyond the curing of German measles and the eradication of spotted-fever germs from my throat. Maybe some much-needed self-respect came to me because he had treated me as a man and not as a number in a vast collection of numbered robots. He smiled as he examined and prescribed, bless him.

My temperature went up and down and, at one point, I certainly became delirious. I do recall waking quite early one morning with the idea fixed in my head that I must go for a walk because I was so hot. Apparently, I found just my uniform tunic and trousers in my locker, put them on, opened the French windows — which gave on to the hospital grounds — and walked out. It had snowed fairly heavily. It seems I wandered for some time. Finally, I remember being pulled up by awful pains in my groin. I turned round and went back to bed. The cold had brought me back to sanity.

Swellings came up in each groin quite painfully. I told nobody what I'd done. Instead, being young and tough, every morning I took hot baths and managed to put up with the painful results of my silly escapade.

Shortly after that, I was moved to a single room, lucky bloke. I had all the care and attention of one very kind nurse. Dinner came from the hospital's catering department, but the nurse prepared my lighter meals with eggs — poached, scrambled and so on — in a smaller kitchen near the ward. Regarding food, the head doctor's instructions were most carefully followed and it was all excellent.

I guess a blood chill followed that ridiculous excursion into the snow-covered grounds. My arms and legs erupted into spots, boils and sores. Feeling that I'd broken faith with the dear old doctor and could have caused trouble for my little nurse, I decided to treat this new, self-inflicted scourge myself. I told nobody about it, except a ward maid. A nice, quiet girl, she cleaned my room once each day. I explained to her exactly what had happened and, remembering the French chemist in Cairo who mixed up a sulphur ointment which cured prickly heat rash on my hands and belly, I gave her some money and asked her to get some of this stuff from her chemist. This she did.

I further prescribed for myself a second hot bath daily — during the hour or two I'd be left to my own devices I could slip undetected in and out of a bathroom adjoining the ward. This I followed with a liberal application of the ointment.

Soon the spots had nearly gone and when, one morning, the night nurse caught me actually in the bath, I was able to plead I had been feeling so sticky and hot that I had taken the liberty of cooling off. Thereafter, she prepared a bath for me every morning, an hour before she was due to go off duty. She had other patients to see, but she spent as much time with me as she could without, as she said, risking a complaint from the women in the ward next door.

She liked to sit by my bed early in her shift and talk or listen — more of the latter than the former, I now suspect, since most young men think they know it all. Then when duty demanded that she move on, she would bestow a hearty "goodnight" kiss on me and depart till around 4am when, in those post-Florence Nightingale days, the round of washings and bed-makings had to begin — and, no doubt as part of her therapy, a well-delivered kiss would rouse me and have me heading for my bath while she attended to sheets and pillows.

While the thought of going beyond these little embraces never reached anything pertaining to what is today called sex, this little nurse, Flo, certainly became a very effective part of the super treatment I received; lithe, petite, and with almost tiny, rabbit teeth showing below her shapely upper lip. From the first, she was, in my book, just the type my dear old mentor Frusher would have me protect from her own generous weaknesses. I recalled anew his instruction that a gentleman would not permit a lady to do anything she would be reluctant to talk about with her mother.

His influence had to control and hold me back one morning in particular. Before any apparent activity began in the corridors outside my room, Nurse Flo came in, kissed me even more warmly than usual and stood looking down at me as I lay there. So I sat up in bed, put my feet down on the floor, and looked at her, trying to read her thoughts, fears, intentions. Her face paled, she stepped back from the bed and threw open the doors of the large cupboard behind her. She stood there concealed, she must have hoped, from observation, pale-faced and trembling. "No, no, don't," she said, as I stepped towards her. And I had no intention of taking advantage of her reaction to natural forces. Certainly, I had the feeling of a needle irresistibly drawn to her magnet. I believe I got the correct message, I believe I thought quickly around the situation, perhaps guessed what was happening to her; I returned her kiss, grabbed my bath towel and went for my morning splash.

The moment passed, I had my bath, and we were good friends. So much so that she gave me her address near Sheffield, with the hope that we might meet there sometime. With hindsight I can see that she must have thought me a dull dog, but the very fact that I was so safe in sometimes extremely intimate circumstances may have offered some compensating features for her — although, now, I suspect that repeated consummation blots out all fears during the early stages of an affair, until the pudding-club indications appear, and then you have two really scared people.

Soon I was over the measles and able to walk freely about the hospital. One day, when I passed the door of the small ward next to mine, a voice called, "Come in and have a chat!" I stood just inside the door, in case one of the staff came along. There were three beds, a girl of perhaps 20 occupied the middle one, with two women whom I guessed to be approaching 40 on either side of her.

I learned that the older women were both Army nursing Sisters who had contracted German measles. They were mad about that! They smoked most of the time — unusual for women back then. The girl said little; she seemed overwhelmed by the presence of a male in her bedroom. What she felt later when, just as I was deciding to leave, one of the old'uns invited me to join her in bed I never knew. It sounded like a serious request and had the support of the other ancient — as they both appeared to me.

Adjudged non-infectious, I was transferred to a four-bed ward and looked forward to a few days in male company as a change from the solitude of the isolation block — relieved only at intervals by nurses' visits and my own wanderings. But no one joined me there, and so the evening talks with Flo, my affectionate nurse, became the high spots of each of my remaining days in that hospital.

Came a morning when the Pickwickian, benign, round, pince-nez-adorned face of the head man looked at me across the empty ward, and I walked over and expressed my gratitude for all the care and kindness that had come my way since he had admitted me to this fine hospital.

Pleased to know I had benefitted from my treatment, while he examined me for the last time, he questioned me about conditions in those places where I had seen service. My remarks about widespread dysentery among our men on the Gallipoli Front gave rise to enquiries from him about food, hygiene, sanitation and water supplies, details of which — or, rather, of their absence — remained fresh in my mind. I told him about how superior were troop-care methods on the French Front when conditions allowed their application.

I thanked him again, particularly for treating me on a civilian footing, and he deemed me fit to return to the small Army-hut hospital and to resume treatment for the CSM contact throat trouble.

Right away, my scruffy old underwear was returned to me, I dressed, climbed into an ambulance, and within a few minutes I was back in the hut where the lads still underwent the daily ritual of the many-spouted, copper boiler emitting jets of formaldehyde-laden steam.

A real rest camp this, for we had to do no work at all. Every moment of this unbelievably cushy existence had my sincere appreciation. I never lost sight of what might have been my lot if had remained in France; my previous good luck over there must surely have deserted me by this time, so every day's blessings had to be counted.

The one female in the joint was a 40ish rubicund lady nurse of the VAD[260], a famous volunteer nursing force. A kindly soul who blushed at the slightest compliment before I left for the fever hospital, now, she walked about quite defiantly with the arm of a lad young enough to be her son about her waist. Bless'em both, they looked remarkably happy, so what had at first appeared to be ridiculous became humdrum and caused no comment. Possibly she regarded him as a son-figure but, knowing the young rascal somewhat, I doubt if he fancied himself as her pseudo-offspring, more as a potential father of such I'd say. I hope he didn't achieve his nefarious ends.

Finally, all germs killed — and a horrible end must have been theirs, surrounded by that formaldehyde vapour which was hard enough for us toughies to stomach — back to the Battalion we went. There, I made a fresh effort to really become one of them. To achieve that aim, I carried out all orders to the very best of my ability. But still I never felt "accepted". This complete Battalion which had so mysteriously remained in Britain — presumably to defend the homeland, should our great Army in France be shattered — formed a closed shop against us who had fought overseas.

None of us could please our unhappy, unjust, unattractive Company officer, Captain Tarquin. A weird type, reputedly the son of a wealthy family, he had expensive uniforms, yet he brought with him an aura of poverty — mental poverty, probably. His batman slaved away at polishing his leather strappings and shoes, this example conspicuously implying that the rest of us should do likewise. Some hope of that! We just didn't have the time to spare — and no chance of being provided with batmen. The Captain had "avoiding" eyes and no valid claims to beauty with his red nose against a background of pale skin and surly mouth whence his harsh voice barked orders none too clearly. An almost childish, short temper completes my picture of one officer, perhaps the only officer, to whom I felt superior.

What a gift he had for spreading gloom and despondency where all had been coarse gaiety before his bleary-eyed mug fouled the scene. And then why did so many men say he was too cowardly to be a Company leader? I never saw or heard of anything he undertook that could be counted a test of his strength of character, yet his subordinates despised him. It was freely forecast that when, if ever, he had to lead his men in active service conditions, he would fold up. Two hundred or more men would, in that event, fail to give of their best, perhaps die unnecessarily, or cause the deaths of others.

Many of us who thought so harshly of one Captain would possibly behave no better when surrounded by erupting earthworks, shrieking shells, whining bullets and shattered bodies. But then we had not set ourselves up to be leaders of men. Some, like me, had applied much thought, and even a little skill, to avoiding or deflecting offers of higher rank and its responsibilities.

I can't remember anything about this Captain's subalterns, but the Company Sergeant Major was tall, round-shouldered, with a pale, worry-ridden face, obviously overborne at all times by the bossy Captain. One Sergeant stands out in memory as an efficient, well-trained NCO — young, strikingly well-made, and full of good health, he contrasted greatly with those of any rank in our Company. One wondered how it came about that such a gem among so many duds remained on the home front, his qualities wasted.

However, the Battalion rank and file boasted skills of a wide variety. A few were professional entertainers. A song-and-dance man in my platoon could put over, unaccompanied, a really fine act. An opera singer had earned his living as a top chorus man, said the knowledgeable. And then we had craftsmen of many trades, including one painter of miniatures who could produce perfect little scenic pictures or portraits on demand.

Notable on the sporting side, Big Bonito, a heavyweight boxer, didn't have to defend himself against such puny amateurs as ventured to challenge him at Regimental tourneys. He let most of them punch away at his huge trunk till exhaustion defeated them, or else a swift unexpected flick of one of the otherwise lethargic Bonito's gloves persuaded them to remain where they'd finished up, on the canvas (if there was one).

I saw the Colonel several times: short, fat, red-faced, and, as far as I could tell, devoid of any of the attributes leadership required. "He's an ironmaster," someone told me. That may have been his major contribution towards victory, for we had no opportunity to see his military talents in action against the Kaiser's. His brief speeches to the soldiery on social or sporting occasions were as inspiring as my father's used to be at half-time during a church soirée and dance — and just as inaudible.

The townspeople provided social and concert evenings which I enjoyed. Of the many good turns on stages in local church halls, I recall two sisters who sang duets in sweet harmony. Very much to the taste of the troops were they, standing about six feet tall, swaying winningly to the music of a then-popular number which went, "Ooooooh (very prolonged), It's not the dance that brings the delight/But the chance of a glance from those eyes so bright"[261]. Right up your Tommy Atkins's main street, as you will agree, and an opportunity for all to join in with gusto, especially to participate in and prolong in falsetto that opening, "Oooooooooh!" Great sports, those ladies, for when they realised that burlesque, English-style, was the preferred mode, they played along, prolonged the more, swayed and pivoted ever more gracefully, and earned immense applause, encores, and, finally, lusty cheers.

Chapter Forty-Four

Pal McIntyre and I, along with three chaps formerly unknown to us — Metriam, Naylor, and Rutven — were suddenly ordered to pack our kitbags and handed rail vouchers and papers authorising us to proceed northwards from Yorkshire to a school of musketry. Why we five were chosen we knew not. Nor, so far as I could ascertain, did anyone else.

We arrived at a hut encampment adjacent to a colliery[262]. The winding gear and buildings and large slag heap formed the only noticeable features of the local landscape. We joined a hundred or so men from other Battalions living there. The huts had broad floors with beds of mattresses resting on low, board trestles with four blankets per man (twice the usual issue). Heat came from two large anthracite stoves, a zinc bath full of coal beside each of them. Unofficially, we were warned that this quantity of fuel, issued daily, comprised only half of what we needed to keep the hut warm. However, nods and winks advised us what to do about that, the pit being so handy.

We spent the few remaining hours of that first day settling in, finding the small canteen, getting to know our hutmates, and scanning the order board for information about the training programme and which group each of us had been assigned to. Each group of ten men had a Sergeant Instructor to train them, two sessions daily, 9 to midday and 2 to 5pm, Monday to Friday in the first week, Monday to Wednesday in the second. Thursday and Friday of the second week would be given over to testing the abilities of pupils as lecturers and demonstrators of what they had been taught. For a third week the whole school would move to a firing-range camp near Mansfield, Nottinghamshire, for further instruction and tests.

A cheerful assembly awaited the arrival of the Commandant in the camp hall. Despite the low temperature — snow a foot deep — good grub and curiosity kept our spirits high... Even higher when we saw a tall, burly officer of middle age walk steadily up the aisle, ascend a few steps on to a small stage, then, with a careful gaze, turn and survey his audience. In a short speech, he made it clear we should regard ourselves as responsible NCOs chosen to spread knowledge and initiate our respective Battalions' training in the use of a new rifle, designed after much research. This weapon contained all the best features of rifles used by the British, Canadian and Japanese armies.

I remember my surprise that the Army should still show so much interest in a manually loaded, single-shot gun: the heavy machine gun had been sensibly assigned its role in support of infantry, while the Lewis gun[263], lighter and carried by one man, had become the infantryman's automatic weapon and would soon be available in large numbers. Many of us thought revolvers or automatic pistols would better suit us footsloggers — lightweight, slick and confidence-giving.

Of course, officers already carried revolvers. But the Army top brass was and still is deeply class-conscious and abhors easements for people in the lower ranks. For instance, of what real use is a sentry? He stands in his box or patrols his beat, a target fully exposed to those who intend to do wrong. If he were seriously intended to guard property or persons he would be suitably armed, not with rifle and bayonet, and be either so placed that he could apprehend by surprise — or else have freedom of movement. But if this system of guarding were adopted, the ancient routine of showily saluting officers who pass the sentry's position would end, and commissioned people's vanities be wounded; rather than that, a war should be lost.

Which brings us back to this marvellous rifle, the expense of bothering with it in the middle of World War, and of training instructors to introduce it. We remained content to play our part simply because the officer commanding the school had the appearance and bearing of the soldier's ideal officer — and the useful ability to make each of us feel important. He told us that, on completion of the course, we should be capable of instructing men of all ranks about the construction, special features, and correct method of firing the new rifle. We believed all this and worked really hard to satisfy him.

Moreover, a fine system of teaching us, the embryo instructors, had been evolved. For five or six hours every day our huts became classrooms, with blackboards and charts, lectures and demonstrations. We would take notes, step forward when required to give our version of the lesson just delivered, and be criticised and corrected — and even willingly devote some spare time to further study. By the end of the course, each of us had become perfect in the form of words to be used, the actions and diagrams needed to demonstrate the purposes of the various parts, and, finally, how to use the whole rifle to the best advantage. After untiring practice and rehearsal day after day, we even mastered the occasional appropriate joke and its necessary pause for laughter.

During our training course, freezing-cold nights kept us in our huts most of the time. But, during the hours of darkness, two men from each hut had to procure coal, a zinc bathful of it, from... somewhere. Naturally, McIntyre and I worked together when our turn arrived to rob the slag heap (as we called this chore, in order to mislead any civilian who might chance to hear of our unlawful activities).

No thrills on the route described to us, until we came to a narrow path along the rim of a deep excavation, partly water-filled. Slipping on the frozen ground was a risk; we moved slowly, carefully. At the pithead, we took care to avoid being seen by the workers, and to fill our bath and get away quickly.

I saw no coal lying around, but a train of loaded wagons stood there. I climbed up on top of one and handed down large lumps to Mac. He placed them in the bath noiselessly. Nevertheless, for some reason, men carrying lanterns appeared and we feared they would search, so we left the bath on the track under the buffers, climbed up on to the wagon again and lay flat on top of the coal. A period of thumping hearts until the miners, as I suppose they were, moved on, we got away — and the really trying job commenced. The terribly heavy load necessitated frequent rests, and the narrow path along the rim of the big, dark-blue hole was nerve-wracking. But when we completed the job, elation followed, and good friends rewarded us with hot tea and listened to our hair-raising tale of near-discovery.

Of course, others had similar experiences every night. The camp's longer-term inmates had devised the system of sending out pairs of men from each hut in turn to avoid having too many of us at the pithead at once. We became thieves, no doubt, but without this extra fuel we would have endured some freezing, sleepless nights.

Probably the original intention had been that we should all spend the day training in the big assembly cum dining cum entertainment hall, then return to cold huts at night and use our ration of coal for warmth while we slept. But plans had changed and a more individual course of instruction developed, requiring the use of our huts during daytime. The resultant foraging for coal must have been known to the officers in charge and a blind eye turned to our nocturnal operations. Perhaps, if they had approached the pit owners, they would have given us the coal, but authority has its pride.

Our regular evening pastime was playing cards, but on one occasion I suggested that McIntyre might amuse us by reading our bumps — practising the "science" of phrenology in which he had been trained. As a Scot, from Edinburgh at that, he surprised me by agreeing to do it even though he knew we wouldn't pay for the privilege of being told what marvellous blokes we were. While his fingers moved slowly and carefully over a man's skull he made interesting, usually slightly flattering comments, calculated to induce those who watched to request the next go.

Finally, Mac turned to me, his pal... and spieled off a generally unpleasing report, the culmination, a charge of selfishness. Later, I asked him what it was all about; when had I acted selfishly in my dealings with him? Out came the reason for his sourness; the matter had bothered him for some weeks, and made me feel really sorry and actually ashamed of my thoughtlessness.

It concerned the two girls injured in our sledge crash. I had found the petite, brunette girl attractive and, although I had never hugged, fondled or kissed her, I showed preference for her company, leaving Mac to look after the other, more homely girl most times — unaware, because of my selfishness, of Mac's feelings of love, no less, for the little dark one. I had not seen her for quite some time anyway, because of the awkwardness I felt after seeing her sister walking arm in arm with a soldier while her husband was away at the Front. And all this time, it appeared, friend McIntyre had been grieving. He must have hated me, and so needlessly...

Phrenology, genuine science or quackery, had revealed myself to me and given me something to think about, albeit ruefully.

The three lads we'd travelled up from Harrogate with had that something which made me eager to know them more intimately than the casual friendliness of Army hutmates allowed. Their fresh-from-civvy-street appearance and tolerance of the coarse, repetitive humour, to which they were obviously strangers, proved them prepared to make the best of a situation they had been forced into, I assumed, by the exigencies of war.

Two of them were 18 or thereabouts, the third perhaps three years older — probably someone granted deferment of call-up whose time had run out. Good luck or influence, both maybe, had attached them to our home-based mob, rather than an intensive training unit in which a matter of a few weeks only separated the draft from the fighting zone. They'd all come from Cambridge where they had been students, I gathered. One seldom questioned comrades about personal matters, though information about pre-Army days, if volunteered, found a willing audience. Depending on the nature of the storyteller, it could bring a bit of the sweetness of family life into the tent, hut, or trench...

These three chaps acquired all the knowledge about the rifle in double-quick time, but when their turn came to repeat the patter, as required by the word-perfect instructors, they used their own phraseology, which certainly sounded less like the spiel of the market quack-doctor than did the Sergeants' energetic rote lesson.

Our training completed, we moved down to Clipstone Ranges[264], near Mansfield. There we commenced firing practice with the new rifle. I found it easy to handle and received a certificate stating I had qualified as a first-class shot and instructor in its use.

However, I did note the omission from the course of the usual 15-rounds-per-minute firing test. Later, I was to learn the reason why.

Mansfield, a small, friendly town, still welcomed soldiers, and a few pleasant evenings at a cinema and at concerts gave relaxation from the drabness of Army routine and living quarters. Always present in my thoughts was the knowledge that great good fortune had lately spared me from all those dangers and discomforts I endured earlier in the war and which millions of soldiers were still coping with. I was inwardly grateful for this respite, but sometimes a feeling of guilt caused passing worry about the men I had left behind to face the risks and wearing strain. Again, at such moments, I found some consolation in the probability that not one of them had noticed my absence...

A memorable experience arose from attending a Saturday afternoon garden party at Sutton-in-Ashfield, a few miles west of Mansfield. It was not obvious to me why such an event should be held so early in the year — I could recall church fetes in July which had been heavily rained on. But brisk, sunny weather favoured this occasion.

As usual, ladies did most valuable work; their enjoyment came from giving pleasure to others and it was contagious. War restrictions must have made provision of food and drink most difficult, but they offered delicacies at low prices, organised competitions and mild gambles, all accompanied by smiles, friendly persuasion, and good will. Here, though briefly, the terrors of war, the agonies and deaths, could be relegated to the back of the mind; and who should be punished for trying to forget those things briefly, or for helping others to do so?

For me, the air I breathed smelt sweeter, ordinary people seemed to have become more attractive, their kind thoughts and unselfish actions had created a temporary heaven on Earth in a small field. The affair, a modest event really, left a life-lasting impression on my memory, an inexplicable sense of temporary, very close communion with fellow humans — strangers, but real friends during the two or three hours I spent with them.

And so back to the Battalion in Harrogate, the five of us, McIntyre, Metriam, Naylor, Rutven and me, ready and willing to shake its foundations with our recently acquired expertise on the master-weapon which should hasten the end of the war — or rather, as it turned out, on the most rejectable weapon ever devised. Sad to say, the rifle was never generally issued.

The reason given for all the waste of time and money? Its magazine had a fault which caused it to jam if loaded with ten rounds of ammunition. *That* was why, at Clipstone, we had not been put through the 15-rounds-a-minute test — the damn thing couldn't do it.

So now they told us... and, after all that intensive effort, we never made use of our special training. We five had one long discussion about the matter, expressed our opinions of the brass-hatted barstewards above, then forgot all about it.

Chapter Forty-Five

The three Cambridge wallahs opened my eyes to a style of Army living superior to my crude style in all respects. They had a room in an empty house taken over by the military, whereas Mac and I pigged it on mattresses on the floor of a school hall. On rising, we folded our blankets and rolled up the straw-filled bags — that is, our mattresses. Had we added anything to this simple, if dirty, sleeping apparatus we would have been carpeted for breaking regulations. Not so our three pals, men obviously destined for greater work than the hoi-polloi.

Nonetheless, during the short period they remained with our mob I enjoyed several lush evenings with them, sprawling on their easy chairs or reclining on their camp beds, drinking their whiskey, brandy, or common wallop, and eating such luxurious titbits as they so kindly shared with me. In return, I suppose, I talked about my experiences on two Fronts, though only when they encouraged me to do so. Generally, they chatted about small everyday matters, but often, in quiet periods, they studied books or pamphlets while I read a newspaper or magazine. I had appreciated from the start that they had their roots and main interests in a world of which I knew little. But they were good fellows, generous without patronising me.

I hoped I was of some use to them with my descriptions of life under active-service conditions — chats about the types of men encountered, their reactions to the varied situations all face in front-line warfare and good leadership's importance to the maintenance of controlled behaviour. A shaky officer in charge was more demoralising than a heavy bombardment... The boss must remain firm and confident outwardly, no matter how windy he felt... Talking on these lines appeared to help these new members of the Poor Bloody Infantry, who were obviously "officer material" — horrible expression...

There followed a short period during which I spent less of my spare time with McIntyre and more with a bloke called Hackerman. Different in many ways to dear old Mac, this fellow waxed enthusiastic about quite small ventures; completely self-confident it seemed, he walked with a bit of a swagger, his feet somewhat splayed — sort of thrown upwards and smacked down as he energetically advanced. He had a true, egg-shaped head with small chin and mouth, large, bulging eyes, and wide forehead. He attracted my interest when one day he insisted on showing me a note an aunt had enclosed with her regular letter to him. It comprised an introduction to a Miss Frost, one of auntie's friends, who lived in Harrogate.

For some reason unknown to me, Hackerman thought that, if I accompanied him when he called with his letter of introduction, the preliminaries would be accomplished more easily. Much would depend, I guessed, on the age and temperament of Miss Frost — one was conditioned by romantic stories for a meeting with a ravishing beauty, owner of an immense fortune...

Reality produced an old maid with a modest job, but some remarkably convivial friends. Prepared by the aunt for Hackerman's call, Miss Frost conducted us to a basement room where a group of men and women much younger than she, though certainly no more vivacious, had gathered to bid welcome to this soldier sponsored by a London friend.

A complete stranger myself, I was invited to join in the drinks and getting-to-know-each-other routine, and found this surprisingly easy among young women bent on giving two young soldiers a good time (in the most innocent sense of the phrase). One young woman, with whom I found myself particularly at ease, told me she was married; her husband was abroad in the Forces and she found these meetings with her friends helpful and enjoyable.

This basement room, comfortably if plainly furnished, seemed to gain something in degrees of informality merely by being below ground level. A touch of the nightclubs maybe. Looking upwards through its one window, one could see part of a large building on the opposite side of the street. "That," said my new acquaintance, "belongs to Alexandrina's family. She's that lovely girl over there." She pointed to a gorgeous brunette. The building, it transpired, was a hotel, its clientele very much upper-crust, for the Tsarina of Russia[265] had stayed there and, at Alexandrina's christening, had agreed to become one of the child's godparents.

This faint link with royalty caused no reserve or restraint and Alexandrina proved to be a happy soul — and generous with the several wines and spirits obviously donated by her dad.

After circulating — as prompted and introduced by Miss Frost — I rejoined my first ladyfriend and found pleasure in her account of her life in that affable town. She required only the occasional remark of me and I studied her simple black dress and saw what good taste could achieve with little effort evident. She appeared to wear no make-up, yet the fair hair, flawless complexion, and — what was rarer in those days — perfect white teeth, all contrasting with the black dress made a lovely picture.

Comparably careless of toilet and wearing a much used khaki uniform, I behaved with a careful eye on a repeat invitation, wondering what sort of impression I was making on this cultured young wife. Completely relaxed and friendly, she gave me no cause for concern that she might be performing a be-good-to-our-soldiers service.

At one point in the evening the question arose, "What shall we have for supper?", to which all agreed there was only one sensible answer, "Fish and chips!" Then, overriding all other offers, my friend insisted that she and I would go shopping, and I found myself bustling through the dark streets arm in arm with this vivacious lady, calculating how many portions would be needed, and probably wondering how the heck I should pay for that lot.

I need not have worried, I wasn't even allowed to offer to buy the food. A wonderful evening, though later I thought of another married woman who had walked those streets arm in arm with a soldier, not her husband, and of the hasty opinion I had formed about that matter…

Like many another recollector, I seem to remember most easily and most clearly, the sweet moments of those long past days. How sincerely one hopes that all the good people who contributed to those joyous occasions continued to live for many years in perfect health and able to meet and contend with the trials which challenge all of us at certain times in our lives.

During a few spare hours one sunny afternoon, Hackerman and I wandered through the lovely Valley Gardens, sampled the healing waters from the "poor man's tap" outside the Spa buildings and walked in the pine woods, enjoying for free some of the pleasures for which wealthy invalids and self-indulgent hypochondriacs paid fat fees.

But thereafter, we walked no more across The Stray to the weekly little gatherings in Miss Frost's basement, nor could we say goodbyes and thanks to the wonderfully friendly ladies there, because that night we were told to have everything packed ready to leave next morning on a long, route march. That was all we were told, being left to draw our own conclusions — and predictably those included the unwelcome likelihood that we should make for the nearest port and proceed overseas.

We need not have worked up the consequent state of anxiety, since we spent the first night of the march in fields just outside the town housing Mr Smith's famous brewery[266].

This gave me occasion to wonder in which war did some genius devise the method by which four men, using only their own rifles and groundsheets, could construct a temporary shelter or bivouac? We had lately learned how to accomplish this, and now we had the chance to fully appreciate that care in assembling these eight items could ensure a fair night's rest after a hard day's march — although, bearing in mind that our rubber and cotton groundsheets had metal eyelets at intervals on each of their edges, and thinking I might be able to improve and strengthen our little bivouac before we settled into it, I had taken the opportunity to buy a ball of string in Tadcaster. So I was able to tie and raise the edges of the groundsheets a few inches, hoping to prevent rainwater flowing in should the fine weather break.

A couple of afternoons later, in a clearing in a wood some miles east of York, we again set up our bivouacs. The field kitchens were lined up, fuel lay all around for the cooks to gather, and they fed the great mass of men generously on a meat and veg stew with chunks of bread. Later, in the same boilers, they prepared a strong brew of tea flavoured with the oniony grease from the stew — typical Army cha, drunk from our carelessly rinsed mess tins, its rich warm flavours never to be equalled in Civvy Street. Thank goodness.

Darkness fell and each foursome squeezed into its "bivvy". Comparative quiet reigned. But only until two in the morning, when a violent storm broke over the snoring community. We four, quite dry, tightly packed in our small shelter, voted to stay put. Amid the crashes of thunder, we heard men calling, men cursing, orders and arguments mingling. All this seemed to go on for hours, but we remained safe and dry, even dozing off at times.

With the dawn, the storm passed and the rain ceased. We emerged at last to a scene of desolation and confusion; most of the bivvies had collapsed, their occupants standing about, soaked through. What a mess, what discomfort, what language! The original four-letter word was enlarged, extended, given a wealth of additional meanings, coupled for additional effect with the fatherless-child tag, all in tribute to the inventor of that so-and-so bivouac. For me and my companions, a ball of string had made all the difference between the wretched experience suffered by so many and a night in a little snuggery around which — not through — several inches of rainwater would flow.

Walking round the clearing later, I was quite amazed to see that lightning had stripped several trees of much of their bark. A terrific storm. Yet we suffered no casualties.

In fact, after my months of exposure to all sorts of weather, particularly in the Middle East, I quite enjoyed this soldiering in the homeland. I was aware that, during service on two Fronts, spells of over-exertion on poor diets had done me no good. My skinny body and limbs proved that. These months in England must build me up to better physical condition, so that when the time came, as it would, when I must once more endure the front line, I should be the better able to cope.

Some days of marching and nights of bivouacking terminated when we passed through the entrance to a huge ducal estate. There, according to a careful plan, we erected the many Army bell tents which awaited us.

Each day, supervised by trained officers, we had many jobs to do, all concerned with building a camp complete with efficient arrangements for cooking, feeding, ablutions, drainage and sanitation. Nothing must be wasted, we were told. We even installed filters to recover fat from waste water. It was required for explosives manufacture, along with all large bones — glycerine extracted became an important part of a compound which would cause havoc among our enemies (whereas I had thought of it as a sweet, sticky fluid which relieved sore throats). Whatever the nature of the work to be done, its purpose was explained.

Eventually, we'd made the large camp as nearly perfect as possible. Then, the study and practice of warlike skills filled many of our waking hours — though our activities bore little resemblance to the training for trench warfare I had done at the base camp near Rouen when we arrived there from Egypt. In France, the officers and NCOs who operated the Battle Training Schools had all served at the Front, so they confined their methods to showing the troops how best to tackle the enemy, their slogan being "Kill! Kill! Kill!" But the so far home-based Division with whom I now served set great store by well-polished equipment and boots, correct drilling and marching, and similar harmless pastimes.

They had, of course, heard that a great war had been raging for three years, but many of them must have hoped that it would not disturb the quiet, orderly existence secured for them by good luck and a little influence. One Company Captain had notices displayed summoning musicians to assemble in a marquee when the day's work was done, bringing their instruments. Soon after that we had a musical Sunday afternoon, provided by a competent orchestra and several accomplished singers, al fresco, on an improvised stage.

Our musical fame thus established, soon all ranks were invited to a Sunday afternoon concert held in the Duke's riding school, a spacious and lofty building. Rows of chairs and forms occupied most of the floor space and faced a small stage. In front of this sat our orchestra, and to one side of them, almost facing us, the party from the Duke's mansion, headed by the Duchess. I recall the pleasure I felt, sitting there in the front row and able to observe these people from a world apart from mine. The music was nice enough, most of the singing very good, and appreciative applause gave confidence to the hastily formed ensemble and their conductor.

The elite clapped heartily and beamed their smiles on the performers and on us in the audience as well, not appearing stiff-necked and haughty as some of our cheap magazine stories had led us to believe they might be.

Inevitably, the sweet elegance of the occasion gave me a pang of regret that my brother was not here to share my enjoyment. In such situations, I usually stifled reflections on how I had taken advantage of recurring opportunities to prolong this period of safety. I knew it must end ere long. One day I would be savouring these advantages, pursuing my role — encouraged by my tentmates and other acquaintances — of dry humourist and general "Pisstaker", when suddenly my name would be called and that would be the end of this peaceful existence.

"Report to Company office!" This order, sudden and unexpected, increased the heartbeats and set me thinking about my recent behaviour... But I couldn't come up with anything calling for reports or punishment.

My unfavourite Captain sat at a table in his tent, something between a smirk and a sneer on his unattractive face. Instead of the undeserved rebuke I expected, he rapidly read from a paper before him a statement that the Army required more officers than were coming forward, that promotion to commissioned rank should be offered to men considered suitable. Whether the Captain intended it or not, cynical amusement at the very idea seemed to show in his face as he spoke.

Perhaps I fell into an intended trap, but at that moment the thought of having to work with such as he appalled me; I took a snap decision. I refused the offer. And then I refused his suggestion that I take time to consider the matter. I seem to recall feeling some sort of satisfaction from being able to refuse to abandon my hoi-polloi status. I see now that such feelings were childish, though gratifying at the time.

Next surprise, an announcement that every member of the Battalion would be medically examined the following day and re-graded. This must have shaken many a conviction that this lot were reserved for better things than warfare or, perhaps, that soldiering in the homeland was a necessary guarantee of the nation's security. Everyone could think of a million reasons why "The Lost Division" should not have to board one of those wretched troopships and finish up among all the horrible bang-bangs.

A cruel streak in those few of us who had already soldiered "over there" put smug grins on our faces when we observed the grim looks of some of the hitherto gallant defenders of the homeland. In fact, we had no justification for harbouring feelings of superiority. To imply that we were not willing to spend the remainder of our military service here, rather than there, would have made liars of us.

I had no opinion for or against submitting to a medical examination and, thus, no interest in its taking place. I was, however, taken aback by an order to present myself at the medical marquee at 9am to act as clerk to the medical officer. I was scared, but asked no questions; obviously the 1914 lie about "Occupation: clerk" had caught up with me. Funny that — although now aware I had lied about my age, it appeared they still accepted the occupational tag as correct. A moment's thought by some administrator would surely have revealed that, at age 16, I could not possibly have been a full-blown clerk.

But, of course, in the earlier case at Harfleur when Archie Barker had stated that I was a grocer, the Quartermaster should have realised how unlikely that was, given I was sent down from the Front because of my youth. Mine not to reason why, better to have a try, and so forth. But I did fear making an ass of myself.

Given a seat at a small table arrayed with pen and ink, blotting paper and a pile of forms, I hope I assumed a reasonably intelligent demeanour and grasped the simple instructions given by the RAMC Corporal who assisted the two doctors. As each man entered, I wrote down his Regiment, Number and name in the appropriate space on the form. Then, on the Corporal's order, the soldier in question stripped to the buff and the doctors went to work on him. The familiar command, "Cough!", usually signalled the final test. After consultation, the Corporal pronounced the soldier's medical category, I wrote it down, and the lucky fellow departed.

The verdict meant a great deal; had a man been classed as "unfit" in peacetime when checked by a doctor acting for an insurance company, he would not have felt the elation which such a verdict evoked on this particular occasion. Most of them concealed their emotions, cheerful or otherwise, until they had left the tent, but few doubted that an A1 grade amounted to a death sentence. At that stage in the war, delusions of heroism and grandeur were strictly for the loonies.

On hearing about the medicals, a pal of mine had told me that one spell at the Front was sufficient for him; he intended to fix matters so that the medics would grade him C3, enabling him to spend the remainder of his soldiering life in Britain. Hardened and, perhaps, cynical as I had become by then, I still felt horrified by the method he proposed to use. "I've got a round of rifle ammo," he said. "I'll dig out the bullet and take out a few strands of cordite from the cartridge. A couple of minutes before I go into the medical tent I'll chew the cordite and soon my heart will be affected and beat irregularly. They'll think I've got a heart disease, mark me C3, and I'll stay in Blighty while you poor buggers go through the hoop in France."

I entered the C3 verdict on his form on the doctors' instruction, just as the man predicted. His trick may have gained him exemption from service overseas only to plague him with heart trouble[267] in later years. I never found out about that.

When we reached the names beginning with "N", as did mine[268], I left my clerkly duties and joined the strippers' queue. After that, since no one told me to resume the desk job. I stayed away from it.

I had been passed fit, but "conditionally", and was not surprised when I was told to report to our Battalion MO. I spent two days in his medical tent, during which he took my temperature at intervals. He also examined prominent veins in my left calf. Soon he sent me to a big hospital in Sheffield[269] to seek a cure for a tendency I'd had during my stint on home soil to suddenly run a high temperature with an accompanying spell of lassitude. The trouble usually lasted two or three days during which time I'd be confined to a bed in the Battalion sick bay.

After a few days' hospital treatment on a very light diet and some medication, I was moved on to a full, generous menu and allowed to walk out in the town — though, perhaps to ensure I didn't stray too far, I had to wear a suit of what was called "hospital blue". This consisted of a loose-fitting jacket and baggy trousers, neither garment in any sense tailored to the wearer's requirements. Being too long, the rather bright blue trousers had to be rolled up, exposing their white lining; a fat, white roll thus graced each ankle. Similar treatment applied to the over-long sleeves of the jacket rendered the ensemble aesthetically complete. An acceptable man-about-town look was achieved, I'm almost sure, when I placed the Army khaki cap on top of my head. I say "on top" advisedly, because I seldom secured a cap large enough for my bonce.

What girl would dare to be seen walking round her hometown with such a weird-looking companion? You'd be surprised, as I was. In a mood darkened by a momentary feeling of loneliness, I wrote to the nurse, Flo, who had mothered me during my double isolation because of CSM germs and German measles. Almost by return of post came the news that she could take a few days leave due to her and would meet me outside the hospital on such-and-such a day at so-and-so time in the afternoon.

Unacquainted, almost unaware as I then was, with female fashions, I yet felt puzzled as a little lady wearing a very wide-bottomed skirt and a snug-fitting, short, black jacket and a small hat came towards me. We shook hands and I tried to convince myself that she was the blue-and-white nurse I had previously known so well. There was the small face, the little nose and mouth and, when she smiled, the white teeth rather protruding over the lower lip. In my teens, as a soldier, I felt afraid of being noticeable when among civilians (among fellow Tommies it was different) and I recall wondering if, as a pair, we might look slightly unusual. But I realised it didn't really matter. And, anyway, Nurse Flo was kind and generous in sacrificing some of her leave to entertain me.

We walked and she told me about the town, then she got us on to a tram to Rotherham — about six miles from Sheffield. The impression remains of a long, flat road through an industrial area, then an uphill grind which severely tested the tram's capability. We alighted up there in a central area and I saw the tram set off down the hill, which seemed dangerously steep to me, but obviously caused no worry to anybody else.

A walk soon found us in pretty, open country, then on through a gate into a somewhat wooded area in which we passed occasional wooden shacks (chalets we'd call them now). Into one of these she led the way, having thoughtfully brought a door key in her handbag. This little retreat, owned by her family and convenient to the home of a sister with whom she spent free days, had a small stove and some cooking utensils which would be useful for a couple spending short holidays or weekends there.

She drew a curtain aside revealing a small double-bed and, to liven things up a bit, I pretended I was a lascivious villain and had at last got a maiden in me power and would have me way with her come what may. Laughing and giggling at this unlikely idea, we acted out the scene, then came to the part where I picked her up — thankful she was so tiny — and flung her at the bed. Probably she grabbed at the curtain but, whatever caused it, down came part of the drape, torn from the rings on the rod above. Her relatives might have arrived at wrong conclusions about our conduct, so needle and cotton had to be found and the curtain re-hung. After valuable time had been wasted on that job, we had time only to rush through the lovely strawberry tea which someone had prepared and stored in a food safe for our enjoyment. Then we had to hurry back to hospital.

Another day, we spent the few hours of freedom I was permitted at a cinema, followed by tea in Rotherham at Flo's sister's house in a quiet cul de sac. Nothing exciting happened, but again these close contacts with civilians still living normal lives found me very appreciative, though always uneasy somewhere inside.

In the hospital ward, I made two good friends — Foxon, and the other name won't come back to me — both local lads, from opposite ends of

Sheffield. Foxon invited me to accompany him to his home one afternoon. We walked uphill, to Eccleshall, a district obviously inhabited by well-off people. Foxon's family lived in a detached house standing in grounds with trees and shrubs; Dad, who shook hands and made me very welcome, wore a black morning coat — the long, cut-away type — and striped trousers, a shirt with a fairly high, white, butterfly collar, and a grey tie. Foxon, like me, wore the shapeless hospital-blue two-piece, so I felt at no disadvantage. We spent an hour or so talking, drinking milky coffee, and eating little sugary pastries.

Just as friendly was the family of my other pal. They lived in a terraced house somewhere off the Attercliffe Road and I enjoyed a happy afternoon there with his mother and sisters.

On a fine day, a concert party entertained us soldiers in the park-like grounds of the hospital. The comedian did well with a George Robey[270] song and followed that with I Ain't Never Got Nothing From Nobody, performed in a funny, forward-leaning, eyeball-rolling style which amused some and sort of scared others who weren't so sure that the man was really sane. After that, reassuringly, children from a ballet school danced prettily on the well-cut lawn.

I thought about the mates I'd left behind on the Somme staring sightless at that great big moon on the night of the final search for survivors. They would be just bones in earth now. They could have been here watching the lovely children, had they shared my good luck.

Chapter Forty-Six

I forget how it happened, but my past caught up with me. Someone noticed that although I was drawing proficiency pay as a Lance Corporal Signaller, I had not done that sort of work since I joined my present mob, before the Somme. So I was to proceed to faraway Sussex to a School Of Signallers near Crowborough — only 40 miles south of London, so I should be able to get a weekend pass now and then and visit my family.

My father had written several interesting letters to me in recent months, telling me of his better-paid and quite agreeable new job as manager of a London store's export department, supervising a team of clerks and packers. Even in my small experience of work, I had seen how, in peacetime, through agents, British firms did business in all parts of the world with undertakings needing reliable suppliers. More important than price, to many customers, was the quality of the goods, together with correct packing which took into account extremes of climate as well as possible rough cartage and handling. Assembling the goods as invoiced and seeing them right through to their delivery to the ships, perfectly packed, insured and documented, was ultimately Pa's responsibility.

Just once, I spent an hour watching him and his merry men at work. His desk stood in the middle of a large, long floor-space; three or four clerks sat on tall stools at high desks on each side of the room. Pa received orders and invoices from the incoming-mail desk and recorded and apportioned the resulting work to his staff. Occasionally, we went through sliding metal doors into a place of noisy activity where packers filled cases, some with sheet-metal linings, and nailed their lids down.

Together, we pondered how much of all this stuff would finish up at the bottom of the sea, German U-boats[271] being so active still.

The Signals School turned out to be but a small part of a large Army depot devoted to putting recently conscripted recruits through a rapid course of training prior to sending them into battle. We all lived in large, wooden huts, the food plain and plentiful, the training thorough.

None of the trainees and few of their instructors had experienced the trenches, the battlefield. Recently released from the cares of civilian life with its rents and food to be paid for, children to be clothed, the recruits seemed keen and contented with their new circumstances — their burdens now assumed by Authority. All they had to do was become good soldiers and, at some unspecified date, cross the Channel to join the gallant lads at the Front.

Looked at that way, it wasn't so bad, I guess. An insurance actuary might not have assessed their "expectation of life" possibilities very highly, but each man had his own hopes and plans for survival.

Encouraged by a competent Signals Sergeant Instructor, I regained some of my former speed at using the key, sending and receiving messages on newer, more sophisticated instruments, and laying and rigging lines — using trees where roads had to be crossed, a new skill I learned (healthy exercise with opportunities to revise map and compass practice too).

But my memories of that tall, lean Sergeant centre more around his talk of pre-war days. He loved to describe the little corner shop owned by his parents. He had helped out in spare hours. He described how farthings[272] on this line and ha'pennies on that all added up to profits which sustained the family in a fair degree of comfort. I'm sure he applied the same zeal to his studies of Army signals techniques as he had to learning how to buy and sell hundreds of household requirements. Through him, I again felt renewed contact with that civilian world in which I had dwelt briefly, such a long time ago, as it seemed.

Off-duty, in comfortable cafés within the camp — run by the YMCA, Salvation Army and other doers of good works — we could drink tea and eat cakes, play darts, dominoes or draughts, write letters or just talk. We had a soft-drinks canteen, a groceries etc canteen, and a "wet canteen" for the tipplers. A large concert hall too where, once a week, musicians, singers and entertainers came over from Forest Row, 10 miles west of Crowborough, and presented a pretty good show — for free, although they were obviously professionals. One violinist made beautiful music, sometimes playing Kreisler compositions as well as that great man himself (I heard his recordings many years later).

Most evenings during the week, they used the hall as a cinema, running a silent movie or two accompanied by a pianist who, since he could not improvise, painstakingly plodded through the score of some current musical. This he had spent most of the preceding daylight hours practicing, as I discovered when passing the building. I guessed he had hopes of retaining that job instead of being sent "over there". I know I admired his persistence and wished him luck.

Sometimes, those in charge of the camp laid on different, special events too. One night, in our concert hall, a guest lecturer gave a detailed account of the previous year's Battle Of The Somme. The speaker, fairly tall, broad and altogether imposing, was none other than the great Dr. Conan Doyle, inventor of Sherlock Holmes and his sidekick Dr Watson, whose investigations I had read about in *Strand* magazines passed on to me by dear old Mr Frusher, the Scoutmaster. The author lived, I was informed, across the valley, in a wooded estate.

Our visitor, it turned out, had mastered much information about the object of and preparation for that awful battle, and he made full use of a large map, displayed on an easel. His voice was somewhat gruff, perhaps due to a cold, but he earned the audience's close attention. Conan Doyle was doing his war work, hoping that a fuller understanding of Britain's strategy would help soldiers to better endure their part in it. I heard differing opinions about that.

At home on leave for some days, I found myself busy from morning to night helping the family move from our three-bedroom terrace house into a three-floored, semi-detached[273]. As I carried furniture and other items back and forth I got my first look at our new home, starting with several treks upstairs: on the first floor a large and a small bedroom, a really big front room which Ma intended to let furnished as a bed-sitting room, and a bathroom at the top of the first flight of stairs with a WC; above that front room another, equally large, and another room off with an adjoining large cupboard or closet quite as big as many single bedrooms.

At ground level we had a front dining room and back breakfast room, the latter with French windows through which we saw a paved yard and a long, wide garden. A passage from the hall led alongside the staircase to the kitchen with its roomy cooking range and a garden. Most of the windows, including the French windows, had strong, wooden, folding shutters which, when closed and secured by their iron-bar fastenings, looked quite burglar-proof. It all suggested that, even in those "good old days", folks had need of night-time protection against intruders.

Beyond the kitchen was what we called — perhaps because of our North-Country origins — a scullery, furnished with a gas cooker, a large sink, a coal-fired boiler (a "copper" to us) and, high above, a big water-storage tank. Another door led to a second WC and a further door opened into a large coal shed. Under cover of a glazed roof, a long passageway led to a tile-covered garage whose big, wooden doors opened on to a drive and a modest front garden protected from the busy main road by a privet hedge and iron-barred gates.

The back garden could be approached from the French windows, the scullery or from the coal shed. A well-stocked border flowerbed with a greengage tree, a large apricot tree, and several apple trees, stretched its entire length. While one would step out of the house on to a small lawn, bordered on the far side by an old wall, the grass soon gave way to an area containing more well-spaced fruit trees, mainly varieties of apple, under which grew gooseberry and currant bushes — then, further down, large flower and vegetable beds, and another grassy patch towered over by two immense trees, one a winter pear, the other a rarity indeed, a mulberry (its trunk must have been 30 inches in diameter). A railing of tall iron spikes across the far end must have deterred many a local lad from scrumping.

I give all this detailed information so that you can appreciate the impressive difference from the small terrace house we had left — and the extent of Ma's self-confidence in believing she could add to her husband's income sufficient money to cover higher rent plus the rates and some costs of upkeep.

Mine not to wonder why or how, for I was only briefly home before going overseas again. I helped where I could, and considered my top contribution laying linoleum — bright blue diamonds on a white background — in the hall and along the passage. It did sterling service for many years after the war finished.

I don't suppose it was the successful job on the linoleum that made me feel, at this point in the war, I had, at last, become an adult, and should attempt some sort of summing-up. The immediate future had to be thought about and discussed.

In late 1917, everybody knew the Germans were making obvious preparations for one final massive attack[274] which they hoped would place the French Channel coastline in their hands and compel the Allies to surrender or, eventually, contend with a German invasion of Britain.

When a few moments could be spared from all the settling-in work, I told the family what sort of future I believed I should soon face. That in the New Year, our men would have to hold back, or delay as much as possible, the masses of Germans who would follow up the concentrated artillery bombardments of our positions; that I should be just one little man among all the mess and muddle, but that, for some reason I could not explain, I felt certain I would survive, even though, for a while, I might not be able to keep in touch with the family...

Physically and mentally, during those months in England I had benefitted from the long, regular hours of sleep and rest available to me, coupled with regular meals and, most of the time, a good roof over my head. Those people who lived almost normal lives throughout that war had no real understanding of the existence endured by their men who were the actual front-line fighters. Nor did many of them wish to know about the matter.

So, feeling in better nick than I had for many a day, I took a cheerful farewell of my family, again emphasising that even if I appeared to vanish for some time, I would certainly reappear later. I had no notion of what this optimism was based on.

PART SEVEN

1917-1918

WAR:

THE SPRING OFFENSIVE

Chapter Forty-Seven

Over to Calais then — sometime in December, 1917, I can't remember exactly when. Obeying orders from I know not whom, I remained there for several weeks, enjoying life no end, partly because our huge encampment included lines of tents occupied by Commonwealth[275] troops — those nearest to me golden-faced lads from our various Pacific islands.

I spent time with them occasionally, and loved them for their happiness and their brotherliness. I would gladly have gone "up the line" with them. I imagined, though, what a massive artillery bombardment might do to them. They had led, I presumed, freer lives than we had, with fewer of the pressures which force white men to obey — threat of unemployment, eviction from one's little home, lack of money to buy sufficient food, the contempt of one's neighbours because of one's lack of success. All these things are far more punishing in a cold climate like ours than they would be in those warm island climates (I'm writing about conditions in the early part of this century, of course).

An airfield — a base for Belgian Air Force personnel — bordered one side of our canvas town, and their aerobatics entertained us daily. Flying bi-planes, they practised most of the known manoeuvres, but specialised in "The Falling Leaf": at a great height the flying man would put his machine's nose down in a deliberate stall and gyrate earthwards, delaying pull-out to the last possible moment.

With very little work or training demanded of us, we had ample entertainment of the more usual sort too, song, dance, or films at the camp, and lots of *estaminets* in Calais town, as well as brothels for the married men who needed their regulars — I actually didn't meet any young bachelors who liked to scatter their seeds on such stony ground, though there may have been such.

I can't recall names or faces of any comrades with whom I probably went around — so very different to the early war days when friendships were warm and valued. Now, with every man on his tod[276], I prowled where I fancied without need of moral support or approval.

There would have been one exception to my fondness for solitude — Ted. I'm sure my behaviour would have pleased my dear old brother more than when we'd previously served in the same unit, in London, Malta and Egypt. I'd been the great conformer most of the time, with my little stripe on my arm, my crossed flags on my cuff; Lieutenant Wickinson's good little boy, heart and soul in my work, one of "the Cream Of The Battalion" as the Colonel labelled our section.

Except on one or two boozy occasions, I'd rarely joined my brother in his relaxations. I'd been too stuffy for words — though I could plead that, in those days, I was still inhibited by fear of discovery as under age for active service. But now, in the war's fourth year[277], that dealt with, and on active service again, in some ways, I felt much less restrained.

Well, I knew that, before long, I might be wishing they'd discover I'd grown too old now and should be given another nice little canteen job back at the base... or Le Havre for preference, with Marie-Louise Baudlet as my interpreter, lovely thought. Some hopes!

I thought of Ted, up front there with his Field Survey Company, liable to be punctured, torn up, gassed, plain disintegrated, anything. Yet I would have been glad to join him. Later, I discovered that he felt the same regarding me, though he never gave a hint of that in my presence...

Next move forward took me into Arras[278], which town I first viewed from a hill across a valley. In the autumn afternoon sunshine, among streets of houses, I saw many gaps, many roofs missing, yet that warm light and shadow gave the scene an air of quietness as though the war had finished and the repairers and menders and builders would soon move in and heal the scars...

I had a Regimental cap badge, but at that stage in my progress from rear to front line, I still did not know which Battalion I would belong to. I quite liked the Regimental badge[279] depicting — only roughly, of course — a tower set in some sort of decorated scrollwork. The genuine Essex lads, I'm sure, felt proud of their county Regiment and its traditions, but I was merely a wanderer who'd come along to fill one of the many spaces in their ranks caused by enemy action.

The war had by then become a vast, impersonal machine into which human bits and pieces could be inserted as the need arose. In the course of my unhurried journey from coast to front line, evidences of efficiency in the conduct of military matters deeply impressed me. Small towns and villages, much battered, were now being repaired, albeit temporarily — roofing often consisted of corrugated-metal sheets... but homes becoming habitable once more.

Such observations induced one to seriously consider the possibility of war ending at some future date, a thought entertained by very few soldiers a year or so earlier, say after the Somme battle. Someone high up in the military organisation had faith enough to give forth instructions enabling French farmers and their few remaining workers to move back into some former battlefield areas. With the impending great German attack expected by, and freely discussed by, all those who would have to meet and endure it, such rebuilding of places which might once again suffer damage could have seemed ridiculous. But actually it did much good for the morale of the troops. Somebody up above believed that, in time, we should win the war... so optimism spread along the Front.

The consciousness of a distant rumble, a continuous underlying vibration when local noises subsided, and, by night, brilliant flashes, or even the illumination of large areas for some seconds, sharply reminded me that the days of peace and relaxation had once again passed from my life. Edgy unease and a wary eye on anything happening in my vicinity would henceforth be necessary features of my continued existence. A quick decision might preserve me from injury or even death, as it certainly had done several times previously on front-line service.

Temporarily on standby because nobody needed Signals replacements, I remained for a while as a general dogsbody at Brigade Headquarters. Anything connected in the remotest way with communications, I tackled with enthusiasm, from humble verbal messages to written ones delivered by me personally, a relief stint on phones or telegraphs, and cross-country checks of lines above or below ground. I felt glad to be back on the work I had done in the early days of the war and would have continued doing had our first dear old Battalion not been disbanded for lack of casualty replacements.

Eventually, I was sent to a Battalion to work as a Signaller, ordered to report to C Company's Sergeant Major. A reasonably pleasant and obviously efficient officer, he asked a few questions and my answers gave him a rough history of my Army life. He took my previous front-line service as a good enough recommendation and detailed a man to show me my section's quarters. Quite suitably, some may feel, we occupied a corner of a large chamber in what had been, I was told, the Prison Of Arras[280].

A mixed lot, the lads I met first, but welcoming: one chap quite clerkly, another a voluble Welshman, rapid of speech, decision and action; then Neston, only slightly older than me — he clinched an immediate friendship by shaking hands heartily, taking me to his kipping place on the floor of this spacious hall, and inviting me to chuck my clobber alongside his. He lived in Hampstead, he said, he'd been in France for several months, and so far, it appeared, he hadn't made any particular pal since he joined C Company.

I didn't tell him, of course, but never before in all my Army experience had I been welcomed to an assignment by a friendly handshake. Having one willing mate already easing my way, I could look at the chaps around me with no new-boy-asks-for-acceptance feelings, and know that acquaintances with some of them would develop to that small extent necessary for living and working in fairly close proximity.

Just once more I must hark back to my first Battalion and the brotherly regard for one another felt by most if its members, which endured long after that terrible war finished[281]. Even those one did not like among them, one disliked more with feelings of disappointment than of hatred. Why? Perhaps because we all came together in the last days of a period when, along with all the law-abiding blokes and their ladies, even the bad lads who spent occasional spells in prison and the professional harlots and their customers felt deep down that they belonged to a great nation to which they gave their loyalty — without giving the subject much thought.

But then the stress of war proved overwhelming; when conscription replaced volunteering, it quickly dissipated local, county and even national loyalties because men were sent hither and thither regardless of their origins. Well, whatever the explanation, the truth I felt and experienced was that, after several years of war, the men around one counted for little — with the odd rare exception.

Scrounging around this huge chamber with Neston, I came across an

old, iron, single bedstead. With the aid of odd pieces of string and rope, I
managed to fix the thing up and, thinking of home and its comforts I'm
sure, I persisted in sleeping on its metal straps without benefit of mattress,
wrapped in just two grey blankets. No doubt the level floor would have
given me sounder sleep, else why had no one nabbed the bed before I
found it?

Lying on it, gazing upwards and around, I took in a very casual scene
— men's kits and blankets littering the floor — illuminated by sunny
daylight, much of which came through a large, glazed dome some 30 or
40 feet above us. Despite many missing panes, no rainwater lay on the
floor... I had to stand up to confirm this, by looking down into a sunken
area under the dome; this basin, many feet in diameter, puzzled me as to its
original usage. Above it, pendant from the centre of the dome, something
in carved wood or in metal... Enquiries among the men brought no
enlightenment so, bearing in mind that we occupied the prison, and that
France carried out capital punishments via a falling blade or guillotine[282],
I decided we must be living in the execution chamber.

A narrow, railed gallery halfway between the floor and the high ceiling
ran round the four walls, presumably for the use of persons privileged to
watch some poor devil getting the chop. Who could bother about the
great war going on up the road when explorations of these weird premises
could be undertaken? I could not rest until I had ferreted around up there
and pictured in imagination a livelier crowd below: Frenchmen and their
vivacious ladies viewing the bloody goings-on in that sunken basin.

I found the stairway leading upwards and, with difficulty because
of missing steps, reached the gallery. Making my way round that much
damaged structure proved similarly risky. I had to traverse considerable
gaps by clambering along the ironwork railing or by trusting my weight
to the odd board remaining in place. Gazing at the hard floor far below
I began to realise what a daft undertaking it was, but I made the circuit
eventually, without sustaining injury.

Having recently lived in England for many months, my clothing and
equipment remained in good nick, of course, but I was surprised to see
most of my new mob's gear still well maintained too. They had done spells
in the trenches; that used to mean a general running down in appearance
among the rankers — it was considered unavoidable and seemed so to
me. The essential juice of the mud in which one frequently wallowed

so stained clothing that even the steam-pressure cleaning to which it was periodically subjected, primarily for de-lousing, failed to restore the original, gorgeous, khaki colour. So I wondered why and how my comrades maintained their passably smart looks these days whereas, in 1916 and earlier, lower standards prevailed…

Out strolling through Arras during this period at ease, I got another, greater surprise on the spit-and-polish front. When I passed the entrance to the large forecourt of a fine, old building of four or five storeys, I saw hanging from the many open windows hundreds of haversacks, gas-mask bags, large packs, and other pieces of equipment, all made of strong, cotton webbing and all dressed with Khaki Blanco — they looked posh enough to be worn by the Guards at Buckingham Palace. We ordinary soldiers had discontinued using that stuff way back in 1915. So who was clinging to peacetime standards of smartness in a place where war daily destroyed military uniforms by the thousand, not to mention the bodies they adorned?

The Guards[283], indeed. The elite in soldiery. I felt two reactions on seeing and thinking about this evidence of pride in Regiment. First, it's good for morale and surely only an Army certain of winning the war would bother to keep its accoutrements spotless in readiness for its victory celebrations. And second… what a waste of Blanco and energy when a couple of hours in the frontline could foul up everything in mud and muck!

Inevitably, one morning our Company set off eastwards, led by Captain Bailey, with a subaltern heading each platoon and the whole ensemble complete with our full complement of Company Sergeant Major, Sergeants, Corporals and Lance Corporals.

I was in fine condition, feeling none of the inferiority which had sometimes bugged me when I was still under the permitted active service age. The regular hours and nourishment I enjoyed in England had made a fairly strong and confident soldier of me; when we came within earshot of the so well remembered battlefield noise, I felt almost none of the tension which had formerly gripped me on the France Front and to some extent in Gallipoli. The certainty of survival, previously mentioned, remained strong in me.

I viewed with amazement and pleasure the sight of water pipes and taps in the rear trenches — the like of that had not even been dreamt of in earlier years. I heard that, in a support trench dugout, I would find a YMCA which could be visited occasionally, with permission. And, in the front line, further deep dugouts were available for the use of all men not on duty. Such shelters and other amenities, previously reserved for officers only in my experience, proved invaluable as morale reinforcements.

Meanwhile, foot care remained a first consideration and, in quiet times, small parties left the front line at three-day intervals for foot washing, oil dressing, and clean socks.

Neston and I, along with our excitable Welsh friend, and a calm 30-year-old from a cathedral town, comprised C Company Signals Section; four men to do work previously allocated to two. Improvement indeed, this, offering time for leisure instead of just work, sleep, and gradually increasing tiredness — as in Gallipoli, when we used to experiment with two hours on/two off, or four- or even eight-hour spells, but we never felt rested. Again, one felt that war was being organised better, perhaps with a view to it becoming a permanent condition.

In the Signallers' dugout, the men we were replacing showed us over the wiring we had responsibility for as well as a large, very modern instrument for transmitting and receiving Morse and verbal messages. We tried the new lightweight headphones and a microphone which didn't rely on its granules being shaken into suitable positions, and learnt to attend to the food and water requirements of two carrier pigeons in their basket cage. Every third day, a motorcyclist from Divisional HQ took these birds away and left two replacements. Our predecessors had attached the pigeons' special lightweight message forms to their little home ready for when all other means of communication failed. "You'll probably never have to use them," said our guide to the facilities. But he was wrong there.

Perhaps I have given the impression that we Signallers had small, individual, underground shelters? Far from it — each dugout had bunks to accommodate perhaps 20 or more men. In the front-line trench, ours had an additional room, of sorts, at one end, occupied by the Company officers. The remaining space housed messengers called "Company runners", we Signallers, the Company Sergeant Major, and off-duty Sergeants, with a few rankers to make up the number — so no place for light sleepers because something was always going on down there; messengers coming and going, officers calling out for people, our buzzers tapping out Morse signals and our phone conversations with distant stations.

I quite enjoyed it, in the circumstances — in part, because, being once again a member of that "elite" section, the Signallers, during our stints at the Front at least nobody could call upon me to take part in night patrols in No Man's Land, that ghastly, ghostly area. Death or injury could quickly overtake you on those little rambles. Many an old soldier can recall, from being stationed on the firing step to give covering fire if needs be, the noises of personal combat out front when opposing patrols encountered each other. Cries of anger or pain, hand-grenade explosions, rifle shots and later calls for help, groans, sometimes frightened cries from a wounded lad who had lost his bearings… None of that for fortunate me this time out.

However, at the time it was such a quiet sector of the Front — occasional bursts of shelling, a casualty only now and then — that a longer period in the trenches could comfortably be endured. It had developed, I reckoned, into an agreeable, reasonable sort of war. Pity they hadn't set it up on these lines at a much earlier date.

In my spare time, under guise of line-testing, I wandered here and there in our area. As always, the disused, discarded trenches, when discovered, tempted my curiosity. Tracing them — inevitably somewhat bashed in, often wet — I occasionally felt lost and lonely, which was something of a thrill. The dicey part came where an old trench had caved in so it was blocked by a mound of earth; I knew the risk if I decided to run for it over the top of the hump. So, crouch ready to climb, then dash and fall into the other side of the trench. If you were lucky, the burst of machine-gun fire would rip across just after you'd fallen in. Till that awful noise which a gun aimed at you makes, you'd have sworn there wasn't a Jerry within miles. I was lucky.

We served turns in Front, then Support, then Reserve trenches, finally in covered holes on the safe-from-the-enemy side of a ridge. After, probably, four weeks, we moved out of the forward area again and trekked back to Arras, taking our time, with generous grub and tea rations en route.

In Arras, I had one immediate disappointment. Instead of returning to the Prison, this time my Company lodged in the sound part of a badly damaged museum. I didn't feel quite so royal there, having to sleep on the hard floor instead of my somewhat restored bedstead, with those exciting scrambles round the rickety gallery replaced by climbs over masses of stone blocks and fallen masonry where I found nothing of interest or value. Too many curious soldiers had passed through earlier, I assumed. But I did discover the place still had a caretaker.

On one of my searches, hearing movement behind me, I turned to find a one-legged elderly French infantryman — tall, gaunt of feature, supported in a very soldierly, upright stance by a crutch and a stick. Using my few words of his language and he his of mine — if that's clear — I gathered that his job was to prevent anything being removed from the place, including those blocks of stone. Here again I saw proof of Allied faith in victory and of their intention to rebuild and restore.

From a canteen down the road plenty of tasty eatables could be bought, with money no longer scarce as it used to be because rates of pay had improved. A line which attracted much of my spare cash was, you'd hardly believe, Christmas pudding. Luscious, even though, perforce, eaten cold, and I got my teeth into many a slab.

It didn't seem quite fair that, on some dark nights, the Jerries should remind us there was a war on by flying over to drop noisy bombs on Arras station and thereabouts. Bad enough, surely, that we should have to put up with that sort of racket in the trenches.

I recall so clearly my carefree attitude to active service at that late stage of a most awful war… Due, no doubt, to freedom from responsibility; during my previous time in forward areas of the battlefield in France, in the trenches I had frequently been in charge of up to 50 men — up front, I'd found the officers around me very willing to delegate authority to juniors, especially during the night watches.

During the Gallipoli fiasco, the depressing conditions, the poor food, and especially the need to keep communications open between my scruffy little hole in the ground and a similar one elsewhere, had abolished all joy from living and made smiling a difficult performance hardly worth the required effort. In that wretched campaign we drew no pay and had nowhere to spend it anyway.

Whereas in France, in what turned out to be the terminal period of the war, with ample money in our pockets, we could supplement our rations and well-filled tummies and this, I found, did a lot for our self-respect and confidence. I thought the bread supplied to the troops there superior to that eaten by civilians in England, and canned foods, part of our rations, of good quality and plentiful too.

Furthermore, in the front line it was still customary to issue a useful tot of rum to soldiers. I couldn't stomach the stuff, but I traded it, usually for a can of pork and beans. I stowed these stand-by rations away along one of the supporting beams in the dugout. I enjoyed lying on my bunk and gazing up at my accumulated wealth. Thus, perhaps, were born the germs of faith in what Karl Marx abhorred, the capitalist system.

For months, one question had nagged at us, though we seldom spoke of it: "When will Jerry strike?" Well, he did strike, many kilos south of the sector we had occupied of late, but our anxiety grew because we assumed it must be the start of the enemy's Great Last Fling.

It commenced with the customary heavy bombardment day and night for nearly five days. Our most forward positions and our artillery bore the brunt. Then, during dawn stand-to on the fifth morning, the artillery fire suddenly lifted off the forward areas. Our men with bayonets and rifles and magazines full lined up on firing steps and waited for the German assault.

Many German reconnaissance planes were flying over our trench systems, which had suffered an immense amount of damage, so our senior officers hoped that, with every man standing visible in his trench, the enemy aerial photos would not reveal how severely our ranks had been thinned out by death and injury during the non-stop shelling.

All these facts we learned when our Brigade had to rush forward from Arras to the stricken area to relieve the reduced and shaken garrison. We, at full strength and fighting-fit, maintained round-the-clock readiness to prevent enemy infantry from capturing any of our positions.

However, Jerry did not pursue the attack and things went extraordinarily quiet during the remainder of our stint in that sector.

Of course, we all speculated about the reasons for this uncompleted attack. Did Jerry hope we would assume he had insufficient resources with which to complete the job? Had his planes observed large reserves in our rear positions which would, he judged, prevent deep penetration? On the whole, I think we settled for the theory favoured by older soldiers: that the enemy scheme was a bluff. It must have caused many and varied counter-moves by our strategists which German airmen could then observe and film, yielding information very useful to their Generals when they launched the real big offensive.

Our turn for a rest from the front line duly came round again and, one dark night, we filed out as another Battalion filed in. It had to be a night changeover for safety's sake — for a degree thereof, anyway — because we had been unable to repair much of the damage to our trench system. We trudged quietly for hours, pausing at regular intervals to rest and get a bite and a swig from the water bottle. The crash and scream of shells gradually softened as our distance from the Front increased — dull thuds and far-off roars our reminders that hell was only a few kilos away.

By great good fortune they quartered us once more in Arras. Unusual, perhaps, to be allotted a rest period in that delectable, war-scarred town, but we appreciated it. We even enjoyed the brief training periods, chiefly because officers and NCOs were far from heavy-handed, mellowed by close association with their men in the forced intimate proximity of trenches, holes in the ground, or the occasional luxury of a dugout.

I was delighted to find the Army canteen still had a few of those tasty Christmas puddings, my special preference. Whether they remained because of over-stocking or to meet a non-seasonal demand I knew not. Maybe I was the only customer for them, but they stored well and remained moist and luscious...

All too quickly our period of rest and ease sped by, and a careful checking of equipment began. We must take only the bare essential items which could be carried in "battle dress order" — an outfit which did not include the large pack containing the greatcoat and a few other bulky oddments. The forward trenches had reserve stores of rifle ammunition and hand-grenades and, in any but hopeless situations, food and drink would somehow be got to us. In the case of the Signals section, field telegraph and phone equipment — all the tools of our trade — would be handed to us at the time of takeover, probably quite joyfully for the chaps we relieved.

Our Company "got fell in" around 1300 hours and we marched off in good spirits, led by a short, but tough-looking Captain, with a one-pip subaltern heading each platoon except ours; we had a two-pip Lieutenant, a coarse promotion from the ranks from whom we expected much courage and wisdom in time of battle (erroneously, as it turned out).

Chapter Forty-Eight

During the early hours of the march good humour prevailed, with jokes and chummy insults exchanged. Rests by the side of the road lasted longer than usually allowed, and — with a dare-devil air — the Captain took an occasional pistol shot at a tin-can or other suitable target.

By dusk we reached the area of the big guns. No marching now. We advanced in a single file, slimy mud underfoot. We slithered, one foot higher than the other, along the steep side of a ridge. Very dark now, terribly difficult to keep going forward without sliding downhill, almost impossible for each of us to maintain contact with the man in front and...

"God help us," I silently cried. "I've lost touch with him!" Of course, a long file of men followed me and, if I went the wrong way, so would they. Inky darkness. "I'm as good as blind and scared stiff... The man in front of me will never know I'm not behind him and the man behind me can't tell that I'm leading him astray... " Field guns banging and I heard machine-gun fire way off... It felt worse than going "over the top", I thought, for later I'd have to face the derision of men I really didn't know and of officers who certainly wouldn't spare my feelings. I could be accused of attempted desertion, or showing cowardice in the face of the enemy...

I recalled being Corporal in charge of a squad escorting a prisoner to his court martial on the Somme in 1916; this time I'd be the poor bloody prisoner, though guiltless of any intention to offend. The loneliness of the lost idiot assailed me, and all my previous confidence evaporated. I, who had felt so fit, well-trained and quite the Old Soldier after my varied war experiences... reduced in my own estimation to a twitching coward. I'd never even heard of a bloke losing his way while advancing with his Company in single file or any other file.

On this very black night I could see nothing and nobody, being aware of my follower only by the sound of his footsteps and occasional curses. Then a slight noise to my half-right — some item of equipment tapping on a buckle — caused me to veer in that direction; I closed up behind that clinking sound and cunningly murmured, "Everybody happy in C Company?" in a comical query tone. "Too bloody true," came the matey reply, softly as per orders, and I knew I was back where I should be and joyful relief replaced my personal panic. Throughout all this I had said nothing to the man behind me so I guess he never knew we'd strayed from the "straight and narrow".

In the sector to be held by our Battalion, our Company took over the support line running parallel to the front-line trench and two or three hundred yards behind it. Once more we entered the rather luxurious trench system — taps available in the reserve trench behind us and so on, amazing... For our first few days there, all remained reasonably quiet.

Somewhere around the 20th day of March, being free for a couple of hours from having to sit by the transmitter wearing headphones, I took the opportunity to exercise myself and walked along the trench until it ended in an excavation some eight feet square and open to what, that day, happened to be a clear blue sky. In the middle of it stood three or four men tending a Lewis gun mounted on a tripod.

At that moment, above all the usual noise of the battle area, came the roar of approaching aircraft and then the amazing spectacle of a squadron of German biplanes, all painted red, flying lower than I had ever previously seen aircraft at the Front. They quickly vanished to our rear — we guessed, taking -field artillery positions. Wrong, for they soon reappeared behind us, not in close formation now, but each plane following the line of a different trench. So the object of their foray became obvious: they were photographing every detail of our front lines.

The complete surprise of the operation caused confusion and no orders were given, as far as I could tell, to bring rifle fire to bear on what, to me, looked like easily hit targets. For a while I watched the red machines flying back and forth with impunity, opposed only by occasional shellfire (and this seemed ridiculous) from our 18-pounder field guns, and bursts of fire from that Lewis gun in the hole on my right. But they had no success in trying to knock down the Jerry pilot covering our section of the trench system as he swept back and forth above us.

One in every five of the Lewis-gun bullets was a "marker" which left a phosphorescent trail behind it, so I could see many of their shots passing between the wings of this persistent devil. Overcome by a feeling of frustration and despair that, at this late stage of the war, our people couldn't hit such a "sitting-duck" target, I slid down into the hole, grabbed the butt of the gun from the man firing it and had a go, confident — as I shouted to him — that I'd soon shoot holes in that bloody thing.

The flyer now dived at us, firing his machine guns, and to have stayed with the Lewis gun as he zoomed towards me would have been suicidal so I threw myself towards the side of the hole nearest to him. His bullets hit the earth behind me, then I dashed back to the Lewis gun and sent a few shots after his receding tail. When he turned again, I dived for shelter as before, rushed back to the gun, and put a few more shots (hopefully) into his receding rear. Next time round he appeared to be fed up with this game and, instead of using his guns, he chucked a small bomb at us, but it blew up some yards away and hurt nobody. Then he vanished.

Now the moment of reckoning had come. A quick glance at the two gunners showed me they were strangers so, offering no explanation, I hopped it.

I think this may have been one of the last appearances of Baron Von Richthofen's lads[284] — a very different mission to their usual fights with our airmen.

That was a strange prelude to a terrible battle. One morning, shortly after my encounter with one of the "Flying Circus", enemy artillery began to take tentative pots at scattered points in our lines. The firing gradually intensified until it became a searching bombardment by every type of enemy gun. All around us, shells of every calibre were bursting and busting up the landscape. This was to continue night and day until early on March the 28th[285].

The initial shock, caused by the realisation that "This is it" as much as by the actual noise and destruction going on around me, soon settled into the state of high tension so familiar to me from earlier bombardments in times which seemed far away.

Rare direct hits on our narrow trench brought forth the old cry, "Stretcher-bearers!", and although these stalwart life-savers sometimes had to squeeze past us on their journeys of mercy, we gained no knowledge of the extent of our casualties — wounded or killed.

No let-up throughout that night. We had no deep shelters, but a series of bolt-holes — each holding six or so men — provided fair cover for those whose turn it was to "rest" after doing their spells of "stand-to" duty. A direct hit by a shell would smash everything and probably everybody in the affected trench but, doubtless because of the narrowness of the support trenches, such tragedies remained infrequent at that stage.

The perpetual roars, crashes and earth tremors became our norm, and we had to remain as alert as humanly possible in that hellish environment. Provisions arrived at long, irregular intervals, borne by very brave ration parties. All our instilled discipline was needed to enable us to stay put when every human instinct pressured one to break into a gallop in a rearward direction.

On the second day, our situation got worse; my lines being still intact, I received a message from Battalion HQ "for immediate attention of Company commander" instructing him to warn all ranks that one in five of all enemy shells now arriving contained poison gas; look-outs could identify them by the cloud of greenish-yellow vapour emitted, accompanied by only a small explosion.

One look-out man occupied a raised position quite near to my Signal-station shelter, so I had to rely on him swinging his noisy bird-scarer rattle in good time should he spot a bursting gas shell nearby. Soon enough it happened, but instead of holding his breath, rattling, and then donning his gasmask, he protected himself first then sounded the alarm — by which time I and others had lungs full of the stuff. The dreadful, choking-burning sensation set in motion our much-practised routine; we stopped breathing, withdrew respirators from satchels, strapped them to chests, breathed out, clapped masks over faces, and resumed breathing air purified in its passage through canisters containing absorbent granules.

Thereafter, for me, everything I ate or drank had about it a chemical foulness. Even the air I breathed smelled grossly tainted. We, of course, removed our respirators as soon as we deemed it safe; impossible, anyway, for those of us afflicted by the poisonous stuff to continue wearing the masks because our damaged lungs couldn't suck enough oxygen through them.

The bombardment, the awful explosions and vibrations, reduced most of us to a state of automatic action, doing those things which must be done, precisely as we had been endlessly trained to do them. At that point, for us in the support line there was no physical contact with the enemy. The front-line men would take that sort of impact in the first place. As a Signaller, I worked with my little group to maintain contact with them and with Battalion HQ.

We'd pegged our wires into the sides of trenches, visible and easily repairable. If you weren't in a shelter, such as it was, sending or receiving messages, when told that communication had broken down you moved swiftly to find and mend the damage. All this among the hellish roar, the nearly deafening crash, the cries of "Stretcher-bearers!"... Nothing to do with you so far.

That night, we had to suddenly grab all our gear and move up the communication trench, still passable-through at that stage, and take over a section of the front line. This proved to be lucky for us because, perhaps due to a bend in the direction of the front trench at that point, or to some slight error in range-finding, Jerry wasted many of his best-quality shrapnel and high-explosive shells; mostly, they fell either well in front or somewhat in the rear of our lucky old front-line trench.

Further good fortune for us Signallers: we spent most of our time in a well-constructed, deep dugout which housed Company Headquarters, so we were able to withstand the dreadful non-stop explosions going on above without undue nervous strain. Down there, our acting Company commander, Lieutenant Jewitt, occupied a curtained-off area also furnished with bunks for the three subalterns — who used it sparingly because Jewitt found many excuses for "keeping them at it".

Had I mentioned that our popular Captain Bailey vanished at about the time we entered the trench system? Men who had been with that Battalion for some considerable time said they had seen this sort of thing happen previously, a possible explanation being that HQ deemed officers who had served continuously at the battlefront for long periods too valuable to be sacrificed in risky forward positions where few were likely to survive attack and counter-attack. So a cadre of commissioned and non-commissioned officers based in rear positions maintained a Regimental skeleton on which the flesh and muscle of newly arrived personnel could be hung to replace the large number of people killed or wounded up front — the expendables, briefly on the Battalion's books but soon happily sent back through the casualty station chain or else buried quickly after their identity-discs, pay book etc had been duly removed for "records" purposes.

Moving up to the forward line from support had proved a boon to our lads, or so it seemed. We enjoyed front-line amenities such as the Germans had always provided for themselves wherever possible. Only those on lookout duty, standing on the firing step, need be exposed to the full blasts of the enemy shells. Most of them performed their dangerous duties bravely and with sound judgement — the man who used rattle or gong indiscriminately became a nuisance, unnecessarily disturbing resting comrades and upsetting carefully worked-out routines.

I continued my previous ploy of swapping my morning rum ration for eatables and built up a sizeable collection of cans of pork and beans in my store among the rafters. As I surveyed my little hoard, I felt secure against the probable non-delivery of rations which must soon occur as the bombardment intensified.

I went "up top" only when my turn came to follow a line till I found the broken cable which had cut off communications in one direction or another. Life became terribly hectic then; a real screamer would send me down flat on my belly — expertise in guessing roughly where such a big one would burst had developed with experience. Occasionally, a section of trench was blown in; there I must join spare cable to the near end of the broken line, carry it over the hump and connect my spare to the other end — all done in a rather exposed situation, usually with nobody in sight, no one to witness my skilled workmanship and brave devotion to duty… or maybe my cringing, crawling and fumbling, take your choice.

One night, the general tone of the bombardment changed; shells which whined stopped landing near us, yet colossal explosions continued all around. Curiosity took me up the dugout steps to find out what Jerry was up to, and I soon recognised an old familiar sound from way back on the Somme — woof, woof, whispering woof, woof — *Minenwerfers*, ruddy great mortars. Back to the Romans![286]

HQ experts assessed the situation and circulated the comforting news that Jerry was subjecting our area to "a box-barrage of large mortars". These often dug holes big enough to drop a house into and were doubtless intended to bring our wonderful shelters down on our heads. They might well have done so but, in our immediate vicinity, the German artillery still hadn't quite got us targeted. Creating a box-barrage required very careful range co-ordination so that, on landing, the projectiles formed the outline of a square. The director of the operation could move his square forwards, backwards or sideways, the hope being that eventually every construction and every living thing within it would be destroyed.

Still, we survived and so did our dugout until, eventually, the boxes moved off elsewhere... Unfortunately, an even more concentrated artillery bombardment took their place and now our lovely, deep shelter really did begin to shudder and tremble. One great scare came from a big shell which must have landed on our dugout's very thick "roof"; everything vibrated alarmingly and earth fell away from ceiling and walls. Two stairway tunnels led down from the trench above and these we quickly checked, but both remained sound and clear. The Engineers had done a good job of construction, bless'em.

For us four Signallers, apart from mad dashes to trace line breaks — in the dark, by touch — all was working nicely when I received a message which sealed our Company's fate. It read: "In a probable emergency the following procedures will be carried out by your Company. Should you receive the code word 'Sambo' C Company will retreat to their support line, fighting a rear-guard action. Should you receive code word 'George' C Company will stand firm and under no circumstances leave their present position."

I sent that message over to our acting Company officer — of whom we had seen little, though we knew he lurked in his screened-off end of our dugout.

Near finality here indeed... a message which presented us with two possibilities, both horrible. We four Signallers discussed our own potential courses of action and decided that if "George" came through we must smash our transmitter, attach suitable messages to our pair of carrier pigeons and send them flying, then join our comrades on the firing steps.

As well that we made our own decisions, for no instructions emanated from our leader's hidey-hole.

Chapter Forty-Nine

Someone at Battalion HQ had a sense of the dramatic for, when I received the one-word message we dreaded — viz "George" — I automatically timed it: 2400 hours. Midnight.

"George", our stay-put death sentence, was accompanied by no other words, not even "Good luck" or "Goodbye".

When we relayed the message to our Company officer, he burst out from behind his curtain yelling maledictions on all Headquarters staffs and wanting to know why we had been sacrificed. We couldn't enlighten him. In fact, his changed face told us much about his state of mind, and we knew that, as far as leadership was concerned, there would be none from him.

The monstrous roars and thumps and shudders of a great artillery bombardment continued. Regardless of normal procedures, we Signallers tried to communicate with the Battalion office, but now the line had gone quite dead. Our quiet, rather older colleague offered no suggestions, our Welsh chum talked a great deal without saying very much, so Neston and I decided to check the line down to Battalion HQ, suggesting that the other two went along the trench telling everybody about message "George" and what it meant.

At the back of my mind, I believe, was the idea that when we informed HQ staff of the front-line situation, they would tell us to stay with them, since no further signalling was required. We wasted our journey, though, because the HQ shelters were empty; having sent that awful "George" thing, they must have packed up and moved back to some pre-arranged place. That left us feeling naked and nervous, to put it mildly.

Back to the Company to break the news to our already shattered Company officer. His consequent rage about "them" having deserted us evoked in us something akin to pity for him.

Neston and I knew that we, the men of Company C, were now on our own. We left the pigeons — two beautiful white fantails — in their basket at the foot of the stairway down into the dugout, there to remain till all was hopeless.

The first glimmer of dawn lightened the day. March 28th it was. We checked our rifles, the bullets in our pouches. I grabbed two spare cotton bandoliers of bullets from a trench-side store. Up on the firing-step we could find no targets so far… Nobody claimed us as part of their platoon or any less formal group and, feeling like unwanted spare parts, Neston and I scuffled along the trench, for no particular reason other than self-preservation perhaps.

We saw dead men here and there, wounded men being helped or carried on groundsheets towards communication trenches leading rearwards. Thus for each wounded man, three left the front line, though what happened to them I never heard.

The occasional Sergeant or Corporal retained some sort of control of a cluster of men, but no cohesive command remained. We hoped to report to one of the subalterns to obtain some positive direction, but we found that Lieutenant XXXXX had just shot himself. We could see him, sitting slumped on the ground, his back against the trench wall.

Dawn proper. "Stand-to" time, so up on the firing-step we climbed. Neston on my right, an oldish man I didn't know on my left… Some mist around the uneven terrain ahead. In that dawn half-light, every feature — a bush, a heap of thrown-up earth, the occasional tree — seemed threateningly large… whereas self-destroyed Lieutenant XXXXX appeared to have shrunk a bit more each time his slumped figure caught my eye.

What leadership, what inspiration he provided for men about to engage in face-to-face battle with an enemy superior in numbers of both personnel and artillery, men with no choice but to stay put even when they had fired all their ammunition… Anyway, where was our Company commander? Still down below, apparently, since we had not seen him around the trench.

Shells of all calibres burst around us. I now felt sort of mentally stunned and a looker-on, as it were, at the heaving destruction, wounding and killing on both sides of me for as far as I could see. Still no targets for my bullets, no outlets for my pent-up fears… if this continued for much longer I guessed I'd explode from within, regardless of enemy shells.

I told Neston of this feeling, putting my mouth against his ear. He may have understood but, anyway, that much physical contact achieved something, for as we looked into each other's eyes we returned to a normal human condition in which it was possible to give some thought to the fears and wishes of someone other than oneself. The animal concentration on survival, self-preservation no matter what happened to others, was thereafter easily set aside... "Stick together no matter what happens," was the unspoken, but well understood agreement born and confirmed when we two stopped acting mechanically amid all that din and horror and probed for something worthwhile in each other while Old Man Death waited to put his clammy hand on us.

One has read of "wave upon wave of German infantry" advancing upon our depleted forces...

When, suddenly, the artillery barrage lifted from our area, the relief we felt was quickly replaced by amazement at the sight of rows of huge, grey-clad men methodically taking over No Man's Land, the space between the opposing armies' most forward positions.

Their battlefield method obviously similar to our own, they came on in lines, each numbering only 20 to 30 men, advancing in sections with first a forward-in-line movement, then swinging 90 degrees on the axis man at the end. Their officer in charge controlled movement by hand and whistle signals.

Without waiting for orders — orders from whom, anyway? — we commenced firing. Thereafter, we paused only to reload our rifles and, in the mist, our targets appeared huge and unmissable. Our training, repetitive and at times seemingly unnecessary, was at last justified. We selected our targets, aimed so that the tip of the foresight was level with the shoulders of the back-sight, and sighted low on the human target.

Germans fell, each possibly victims of more than one British marksman. Since they still came onwards, steadily, but so far not getting to close quarters, we just fired, fired, reloaded and fired again...

MURDER

I will here describe an incident the memory of which has remained with me, clear and vivid in every detail; so much so that it affected an important decision I had to make 20 years later[287].

In the desperate situation and amid the unnatural excitement, nervousness, and recurring moments of fear then being endured, one thing was proved beyond doubt — namely, that the intensive training one had undergone at various times during the past four years had achieved its purpose; when the situation required it, I became a rifle-firing automaton. Loading — transferring a bullet from its position in a clip of five in the magazine to its position in the firing chamber by working the bolt back and forth — took only a fraction of a second; a moment to sight the gun correctly on a target; squeezing, *not* pulling the trigger — well, no time really. Result: a man killed, wounded horribly maybe, and so bereavement in some family, or else sorrow over a son made an invalid or a cripple for life, all caused by one man's impersonal automatic action.

One target I dealt with was a man running not towards me but across my line of fire, about 50 yards distant.

"Snapshooting at a moving target" on the firing range; back come the instructions, "Maintain normal aim, moving with the target, then increase movement of rifle till daylight appears between target and rifle then 'Fire'".

The soldier fell… a comrade ran several yards to help him, appeared at the tip of my rifle fore-sight after I had rapidly reloaded, and I squeezed the trigger. As he too fell, the utter automatic callousness of my action registered somewhere in my brain and doubt nagged then and forever after about there being any plausible excuse for such murderous conduct.

"If you hadn't killed him he might have killed you"?

Oh yeah.

Time seemed to be suspended… My ammunition pouches now empty, I took one bandolier of 50 from around my neck, laid it out before me on the parapet, opened its snap-fasteners and reloaded from it.

Neston had no bandoliers so, when he ran out of ammo, I let him heave my other one off my shoulder.

At one point he yelled, "Duck! Jerry half-right!" and in a split second I'd seen this tall German coolly standing a few yards away with his rifle trained on me, so *down!* quickly and *phutt*, the bullet just missed my helmet. A cautious peep revealed the tall Jerry, confident and careless man, sprawled on the ground facedown.

Now I knew at last the feelings that take over when soldiers sense they have an equal chance in battle — that is, in the final face-to-face struggle. True, this feeling endured but briefly; as long, in fact, as we had a supply of bullets. But it was wonderful while it lasted — while we felt we were doing a soldier's job reasonably well.

The older man to my left died suddenly and painlessly; he was firing steadily, apparently devoid of any feelings of excitement. A strange noise near my left ear caused me to look at him; a sort of "cloink" it was. A neat hole towards the front of his right temple had appeared, but he remained standing briefly. I felt joy for him for a second, lucky man, life's problems all solved now... But my rifle bolt had become over-heated and it was jamming — his gun rested across the parapet where it had fallen from his hands, so I took it.

Men were moving along in the trench below and behind us looking for and calling for ammunition. I fired my last round. Neston had finished his lot and we could obtain no more.

We made our own decision as to our next action. With difficulty, we forced our way through the milling mob — our defenceless comrades — in the direction of our dugout, because we intended to compose that final message and attach a copy of it to each of our lovely fantail pigeons.

I collected several bruises, I guess, as one or two of our men seemed to resent our moving past them and I also suffered a couple of shocks — over and above the great prevailing shock, I mean. Looking upwards as we shoved and pushed I caught sight of one of our junior officers wandering aimlessly out in the open; half his face appeared to have been blown off and he vanished from sight and must surely have been riddled with bullets almost immediately.

Then I saw a German not far from our trench, arm raised, about to throw a stick-bomb in my direction. I turned away, hoping to avoid the murderous thing, and it exploded on the parapet above me. This, I felt, was my lot, for with the shattering explosion came a stinging blow to the back of my neck. I clapped my hand over the injured part and gripped hard, determined to hold my head on at all costs.

I raced after Neston, urging him to hurry to the shelter before I collapsed. Soon we were scuttling down the steps. Safe in the dugout, I withdrew my hand and was almost surprised that my head remained in place. Just a little blood in my palm — and a small, sharp bomb splinter lodged in the skin of my neck; I pulled it out easily.

We found our basket and the pigeons all intact. The message we two devised had to be brief. It read, I believe, as follows: "No ammunition left. Almost surrounded by the enemy. Good-bye." There followed details of our Company and Regiment.

Excited by the novelty of the situation, we took turns to hold a bird while the other inserted the quite tiny roll of fine, thin paper into the little sheath attached to the ring on its leg. Then we climbed the steps back up to the trench, flung the lucky birds upwards and watched them circle then fly to the rear of our position. Soon they would be in the Divisional loft, the message read and, one hopes, a little regret felt for the men who had been sacrificed… for, no doubt, some good military reason.

At this moment, from goodness knows where, possibly his screened-off "room" in the dugout, our Company officer suddenly appeared — his face, as before, strangely different from its usual coarse, sometimes good-humoured norm, showing signs of great nervous strain.

Pushing us aside, he scrambled out of the trench on the rear side. Welcoming what we assumed to be belated leadership, we made to follow him, but he pulled his pistol from its holster, aimed it in our direction and ordered us to stay where we were… Strange repetition this, for up to that moment I had only been threatened with a revolver once and that too by one of our own people — our Regimental Sergeant Major did it at Gallipoli, you may recall, because, he said, we were attracting fire from Turk field guns by exposing ourselves (he too was in a windy condition and never lived down the bad name he earned there).

At that, the officer disappeared and Neston and I quickly decided to attempt to follow him. But, a few yards behind our trench, we slid into the protection of a shell-hole and had a brief chat. I reminded my pal about the message with its code word "George", meaning we must not leave our position for any reason… Time passed. No one came our way. We heard only an occasional burst of machine-gun fire, usually from our support trench… We made our decisions, I to rejoin our lads, Neston to make a dash rearwards. We shook hands and parted.

Running the few yards to our frontline trench, I stopped myself from dropping into it... only just in time. I stood looking down for a moment, both fearful and fascinated by what I saw. No British soldiers in that bay, just one German.

With the utmost concentration, he was carrying out what we knew as "the mopping-up routine" — having killed, wounded or captured most of the enemy troops occupying a trench system, you then looked for stragglers or obstinate fighters. With bayonet fixed on rifle you held it at your side, but somewhat forward; you advanced quietly, cautiously; when you came to a corner you paused, then sprang round that corner ready to stab or shoot. This careful process, plus throwing a hand-grenade down each dugout entrance, was the proven method of clearing a trench system thoroughly. For the second time that day, I was surprised to see Germans doing the same as we did.

The German I watched was so taut and intent on his job he didn't see me standing there above him. I should have tackled him immediately, but I didn't. It appeared that any surviving members of our Company must already have been removed as prisoners. I heard spasmodic rifle and machine-gun fire to the rear. Probably, close fighting continued in the next trench back, the support line.

I sprang over the head of the German and that carried me a couple of yards clear of the trench.

Looking forward, I saw Germans, hundreds of them. A glance to the right made me abandon all hope of surviving. A line of Germans was charging in my direction, bayonets fixed on rifles, the job assigned to them, obviously, the destruction of any remaining opposition. They must, quite understandably, have felt bitter about the price we had extracted for their victory. A long delay like that must have interfered with their plans. I fleetingly hoped that none of them had witnessed my double slaughter... that I can recall.

As the galloping line came closer I could see their faces, their features. Most of them boys like me. All thought of bravely taking on the German Army single-handed was absent. Inaction was my response. I just stood there and waited for it to happen — the hoped-for clean bayonet thrust and goodbye. I earned no medals that day nor any other day...

At about two yards, I stared at two boys, one of whom would have to do the dirty work. Their fresh, healthy faces made veteran me feel quite old. Now. It must happen now. I concentrated on the nearest boy. All in a split second, he smiled, swung a little aside, his comrade did likewise, and they were all gone, bless the lovely lads.[288]

PART EIGHT

1918

PRISONER OF WAR

Chapter Fifty

I heard a call for help, searched a little ahead, and found a British boy lying on his back, trying to get up. "I caught a bullet through the ankle," he gasped... With the Germans having advanced in strength between us and the British Army, we were prisoners. Glad to be still alive, I suppose, but fearful of what might now happen to us.

"Help me to get to a German field hospital," he said. I got him up on to his sound foot and, obeying signs from yet more advancing German troops, with arms around each other, we struggled towards the enemy lines. Soon, a man wearing an armlet of Red Cross on yellow background relieved me of my wounded mate and directed me to proceed "that way"... That way would lead me smack into a line of field guns firing non-stop — they must have been laying a terrible bombardment on our rear positions. So, the law of self-preservation still operating, I veered to the right, slid into a shell-hole and rested a while, peering over the rim to make sure no fresh danger came my way.

As German reinforcements moved past me, up and away to support their victorious comrades, their gaze fixed straight ahead, not a glance to right or left, I learnt how we must have looked to them when we were advancing in attack. I observed in them anxiety, nervousness, ruthlessness (but rarely)... and sometimes the shifty look betokening "Not me for the chop, not if I can dodge the column", accompanied by artful sheltering behind other men.

But where were our captured soldiers? Assuming some had survived... I hadn't seen a Britisher since I handed my wounded kid over to the German Red Cross man.

The last of the German infantry vanished towards the British lines. In the following lull, I heard a few shells come over from our artillery —

which surprised me, for I felt sure most of our guns had been removed some days ago to positions far in the rear, or else destroyed by the intense enemy gunfire.

Ahead of me, I could see the German front-line trench parapet. This provided another surprise: no barbed wire lay in front of it. Both Armies usually protected their fronts with barbed-wire defences of varying density. One could only imagine the enemy command had ordered its removal to facilitate rapidity of movement for the masses of men thrown into their infantry attack.

I tensed my muscles preparatory to scrambling out of my shell-hole, dashed across to that German trench and slid on the loose earth down its steep side. As my feet touched the bottom, three Jerries sprang towards me, one thrust a pistol at my tummy and demanded "Pay-book!" I raised my arms and let them take what they would. Vultures of the battlefield, dodgers, thieves — they cleaned me out, and when they departed my worldly goods consisted of what I stood up in, underclothes, tunic, trousers, helmet, socks and boots. I'd heard of similar types in our Army — bad Military Police in Cairo who regularly robbed drunks and would-be deserters and somehow got away with it undetected…

Having grabbed what they wanted, the thugs indicated the direction in which I should go. Towards all the bangs and smoke puffs again… but I obeyed, realising I was being watched by people whose presence I had been unaware of until then.

Now, when I saw German soldiers in holes or trenches they all signalled in much the same way, their thumbs pointing to the rear. As I slowly approached the field artillery position, it shocked me to realise that, unlike our deployment of batteries at intervals across country behind our front lines, here — in a wide, deep trench like a sunken road — stood guns wheel to wheel as far as I could see to right and to left.

I had to get down into that great ditch and climb up the far side. Then I came upon 50 or so British men clustered together. Nearby, several German officers had found some concealment in a clump of trees festooned with telephones, the instruments on the ground, the headphones hanging from low tree branches.

One obviously senior officer with a blue and red face of extreme ugliness yelled an order accompanied by hand movements indicating us. This resulted in a more junior officer forcing the British soldiers nearest to him to go down on one knee, in one row, facing our own lines. The rest of us soon complied. A strange scene, shattering from our point of view — this assembly of artillery below and in front of us, stretching endlessly into the distance. How could our Army stand up to this concentration of fire power?

I assumed that, in making us kneel right behind his guns, the commander hoped that British artillerymen — if they could see us through the battlefield mist and smoke — would not wish to fire on their comrades. I could not but admire this officer's devotion to his job. In that exposed position, he calmly gave orders into one phone, hung that up, then used another, receiving and sending messages, in touch with battery commanders all along the line of guns. I could discern only one group of our guns firing in response, from way back behind the original British trench positions.

Later, a German called "Come!" and our file arose and followed him across open country much pitted with craters and cluttered with war debris.

One sight shook me: the corpse of a horse lying by the roadside, clearly not long dead, but with its ribs and upper leg bones exposed. Its hide had been slashed and all edible parts cut away. How hungry the Germans must have been, I realised, or at least how short of meat, to have butchered the animal as soon as it fell. I had never seen that sort of thing on the British side.

Soon we came to the remains of a village. On a wall, painted in large white capitals, was the word "Gavrelle"[289], which I assumed to be its name.

A hundred or so British prisoners joined us there, then we straggled on along the country road in no particular formation. I found myself walking between two fairly hefty chaps and we chatted about our recent experiences. I remember telling them about my little store of canned baked beans and pork, lost beyond recall now... perhaps being eaten by appreciative Jerries.

Although these men wore uniforms of rough, khaki cloth similar to mine, the cut struck me as unusual — larger side pockets, for instance. Looking at their epaulettes for some sign of their Regiment I saw officer's pips, and, though now wondering how protocol worked under prisoner-of-war conditions, I asked about their rank. Without reticence or demanding officer standing, they talked freely, explaining that, at the battlefront — although not in my Battalion — it had become accepted practice for officers to conceal conspicuous indications of their status because the Germans knocked off those in command as quickly as possible to create confusion among the other ranks.

We turned on to one of those absolutely straight, cobbled roads bordered by tall poplar trees which connected French country towns in those days. A signpost indicated it led to Douai. But, after a few kilometres, our guards led us into a brickworks surrounded by a high, barbed-wire fence. Kilns, rows of unfired clay-coloured bricks, stacks of finished ones — a scene familiar to me in boyhood when a similar site had been a favourite playground and setting for the mock warfare I described earlier, cowboys versus Red Indians and so on...

Not having eaten for a day or more, I felt weary and worn, and more so because of reaction to the nervous strain of the battle. So when a German officer suddenly joined a small group of us, it provided me with a kind of relief from personal suffering. His beautiful uniform looked Ruritanian when compared with the simple dress of a British officer. We, dirty and soiled from the battlefield, felt like scruffy old tramps beside this military Brummel.

His personal cleanliness, healthy complexion, friendly blue eyes behind large spectacles, perfect English speech — and enthusiasm for a little war game he proposed to play — seemed ideal distractions to help us forget our discomforts. Some chaps may even have felt that a response to his wish to complete the few details at present missing from his sketch-map of the trench system we had recently vacated might gain them some advantage, such as much-needed grub. Anyway, if their wits were still sufficiently bright, they had only to give him inaccurate information. Even if he detected a falsehood, what the heck would it matter?

I was amazed at the detail he had already, displayed on a large sheet of paper secured to a board. Built up from aerial photos and, in parts, skilful drawings, it even named some of our trenches. He just needed to identify some Regiments, he said, oddments of that sort, perhaps the number of men at some given point... I found myself in no difficulty because I just didn't know any of these things.

The only food they gave us that day was a piece of uncooked salt fish and that induced us to fill our bellies with lots of the water they did make available.

Our sleeping quarters that night? We had two choices — to lie on grass completely exposed to the March weather, or to bed down on brick dust. If you could lie on one side with your back against a brick stack you were lucky. If you found space in the open centre of a pile of bricks you had four walls around you, but no roof overhead — yet, in the circumstances, you were very fortunate. No blankets, no overcoats and March nights are chilly.

Thinking back to my relatively secure quarters in the British front line and, again, with regret, to the canned food I had stored in the niches of that dugout — and abandoned only hours earlier — I spent the first of many horribly uncomfortable nights as a prisoner of war. One slept, no doubt, but seemed, as day dawned, to remember every minute of the long night.

No food available that first morning. So, with as much water inside us as we could stomach, we shambled what felt like many, many kilometres to a town called Denain[290]. Soon, we entered the yard of a large factory; on our left a high building and on our right a row of small, single-storey structures which looked rather like stables. Perhaps they had been such in time of peace, but each of them now housed a British officer. Through barred apertures in the doors we could just discern some of them in the dark interiors.

One, a handsome flying officer, stood close to his bars and, as I slowly moved past, I asked quietly, "Why are you kept in there, sir?" "It's only temporary till I'm moved to a proper officers' prison camp," he replied. "Were you shot down?" I asked. "Yes, not far from here," he said. Then I was past his hovel and saw him no more.

A harsh voice yelled orders at the men in front of me and I saw, standing at the top of some stone steps, a swarthy chap in British uniform. In German he talked with a Jerry who stood beside him, then he shouted an English translation at the prisoners nearest to him.

"I know that man!" yelled a chap nearby. "His name's Goldberg!" Anti-Semitism was rife in Britain in those days and the man's Jewish appearance, his evident mastery of the German language, the fact that he was giving orders from a position well above us, all condemned him in our eyes. Why was he directing one man to join one column of prisoners and another man to join a different line? On what did he base his assessment?

My column headed for a huge, three-storey building some distance from the factory, but still within the same perimeter wall. We had to make our way up a formerly substantial stairway, now missing many steps and risers as well as most of the bannister rails. Each floor had numbers of large rooms, the doors gone from all of them, as were many floorboards.

I soon realised that all this destruction had occurred simply because men need warmth. Some of the occupants of the room I was ordered into had been prisoners there for a month or more. Short of nourishment and warm clothing, they had found difficulty in just keeping alive. As they were now — dirty, unshaven, stinking in some cases, rapidly sliding towards the sub-human — so might I soon become. They hung together in groups of two or three, it appeared, eyed with suspicion all those outside their little circle, and even snarled or jeered at them.

When I slipped quietly out of that shaming little shambles, nobody noticed my going. Out in the yard, I walked around watching out for the cleanest-looking men, believing that they would be the most recently captured and therefore the least debased in character.

I entered the main building, tall but one floor only and obviously a factory or foundry of some sort in peacetime, given the pieces of disused machinery, boilers and so on still lying around. One could see that the upper parts of partitions separating different sections of the works had been torn down, but they still made useful barriers against which to shelter when cold winds blew. Straw, all reasonably clean, covered the floor.

The prisoners there were newcomers, still free of that peaked, hungry look, and not yet given to constantly peering left and right, up and down, in search of something, anything, which might still the pangs in their stomachs.

That night, I tried an experiment in bed-making. Before lying down in the straw, I removed my tunic, bunched up straw for a pillow, placed a none-too-clean hanky on top of it, laid down and pulled the tunic over my top half and thereafter dozed and wakened through the night.

Nourishment for that second day as a prisoner had consisted of a litre of coffee substitute (mainly roasted and crushed acorns) and a piece of sour, dark-brown rye bread, which yielded two slices. I was to become familiar with these items during the coming months. The only daily addition to this, now that we had entered some kind of makeshift war prisoner camp, was a litre of stewed root vegetables — swedes, turnips and mangold wurzels — doled out every evening. Some old horsemeat may have been cooked with them, but none came our way; the under-fed Germans saw to that.

This diet just kept me alive. Now, even in these earliest days, I too started to become hollow-eyed, emaciated.

First priority was to acquire an empty tin can in which to collect your liquid rations. I managed that quite soon and, with a penknife which had eluded the Germans who robbed me on the battlefield, I began shaping a spoon out of a piece of wood.

Finding some potato peelings one day, I washed them at a stand-pipe in the ex-factory building, put them in my can and filled it with water, gathered wood shavings, straw and odd bits of floorboard for a fire, cadged a light and cooked them. Without any seasoning they tasted awful, but down they went.

Prisoners had no work to do there in Denain and laying about in that unsavoury, crowded place took its toll of morale as well as of physical fitness. I soon formed an opinion that death in the battlefield would have been preferable to this sub-human existence... But, meanwhile, I must somehow manage to survive, difficult though this was looking. Small possibility now of my dying of "gunshot wounds" (a favourite military description of damage caused to a soldier's body by shot, shell or aerial bomb), but we faced new enemies: starvation, chronic diarrhoea, and weakness resulting from diet deficiency.

Of the hundreds of men around me, no single one now looked worth an attempt on my part to form a friendship. Of course, I don't know what *I* looked like, having no mirror, but my uniform had become soiled, my boots mud-encrusted; I seldom washed, never shaved. I guess I looked like the rest of them with their sunken cheeks, and purposeless shuffling hither and thither.

Hope revived, though, when a Sergeant of the Essex Regiment, miraculously clean and robust compared to the rest of us, came along and quietly told those of us who wore the Essex shoulder badge — including me, although I had not known him before — to make our way to the entrance gates. Goldberg had told him the Jerries were moving a certain number of men to another town and that the Sergeant could select them and go with them. Naturally, he gave preference to his own chaps; when we lined up, the count revealed a small deficiency in numbers and volunteers scrambled for the chance to join us.

A small bunch of Liverpool men and a few from Brum, pushing types, made up the quota and so, after a nourishing meal — a slice of bread and a can of so-called coffee — we shambled off.

Armed Germans, about six of them, walked on either side of us. By then we had passed from the hands of fighting soldiers and into the care of the more elderly *Landsturm*[291] — mostly sour, stern old codgers, steeped in anti-British dislike, and with a determination to make us suffer. These guards prevented any attempt to walk on the footpath in search of scraps of food such as discarded cabbage leaves or stumps, potatoes, or indeed anything at all which could be eaten.

Even so, if a prisoner spotted any such trifle, and risked a beating by breaking ranks to pick it up, half a dozen starving blokes would pounce on him, hoping to grab it first, until one or more guards drove them back into line by prodding or bashing them with rifle butts. These pouncers were usually the northern group who had forced themselves on the Sergeant when he was getting his party together.

We stopped in a village which looked remarkably like one I'd known in Northumberland[292] — several rows of small, terrace houses near a coal pithead. Called Marchiennes[293], it looked a poor sort of place. A row of terrace dwellings on one side of the main street had been enclosed behind barbed-wire fencing. Through a gate we entered the enclosure and found there were no gardens behind the houses, just a long, open space inside the wire fence. There stood the primitive sanitation, comprising a long pole suspended over a trench by means of a crude tripod at each end. So, in full view of all, you and others squatted on the pole and got rid of your always-watery faeces.

Everything calculated to reduce a man to the lowest level of self-respect was provided.

About 60 of us were allotted to each dwelling: two rooms upstairs, two down, all small and furnished with two shelves, six feet wide and running wall to wall, one a foot off the floor, the other three feet higher. On each of these wooden shelves eight or ten men must lie and sleep — so, 16 or more prisoners in a space normally occupied by two people at most.

Unfortunately, I found myself in a room mainly occupied by strangers. I soon got into the habit of leaving it and them quite early in the morning to call on the Sergeant and others of the Essex Regiment. Then I stayed among them as long as I possibly could.

I eventually justified myself in spending several hours daily in the Sergeant's room by starting to carve into one of the plaster walls a large-scale copy of the Regimental badge. Below this, with a pencil lent by the Sergeant, I drew a sort of scroll. Having collected the names and numbers of all Essex men in the prison, I spent hours writing them into the scroll — my idea being that, as the British beat back the Germans when the tide of war changed in our favour, British troops could note our names and numbers and tell the War Office and relatives we were alive, though prisoners in enemy hands.

Up to that point, our captors had made no attempt to record our names and details, so our people would not know what had become of us. Correct procedure would have ensured that this information was passed on through the Red Cross organisation in a neutral country but, in my case and in many others, this did not happen.

Discomfort caused by lack of nourishment spoilt all our waking hours. The morning piece of black bread and the evening can of stewed vegetables hardly filled the belly and the can of hot water with coffee substitute was warming but lacked milk and sugar. The only dietary variant at Marchiennes I recall: for several days, *Sauerkraut* replaced stew as our main meal — nothing with it, no meat, just sour cabbage. Shitting being one of our main occupations, much discussion concerned which meal made you go oftenest, the stew or the sauerkraut, but we had no measurable means of deciding the question.

The mental effect of such deficient nutrition depended on the individual; I concluded that the men who had lived rough, hard lives before enlisting fought the hardest to grab anything which could possibly be eaten — such as cabbage stumps or potato peelings which the *Landsturm* or their cooks might throw on the ground outside their kitchen.

Despite the guards' vigilance, I heard that a woman passing outside the barbed wire at one end of the enclosure exchanged some food for a piece of cloth a Scotsman tore from his kilt. I also learned that he might as well have kept his uniform intact for little of the food passed his lips after the ravenous ones had pounced; lucky for the Scotsman they didn't devour him too, although some of them had begun to display animal looks and tendencies.

No one smiled any more; the effort required was just too much, even for the nicest fellows.

All the daylight hours had to be passed in those depressing surroundings, mooching in the stinking space behind the dwellings — and beside the latrine — or lying on the wooden shelf.

One chap in my room, which I had to return to at night, dismally sang verse after verse of a dirge about a Liverpudlian hero called, I believe, McCaffereet. After all these years, I remember only the concluding lines: "Now come my lads, just list to me/And never from your hopes do flee/For if you do you're sure to meet/With the same fate as young McCaffereet." That may not be the correct spelling of the poor bloke's name, but just put to those words the most miserable tune you can think of and imagine a young-gone-old man lying on his back on a wood shelf in a small, dingy room intoning verse after pathetic verse about Mac's equally dingy life story. Be cold and starving hungry as you listen to the tale of woe and stave off utter dejection if you can.

The most important part of each day spent in that dump — the bit that saved me from complete despair — was when I visited and talked with that Sergeant. I gained hope and strength just from being near the man. Probably about 30, he had managed to retain his safety razor and a strop of a type not seen for many years — it passed through the hinged razor holder, then a few flips back and forth re-sharpened the blade. So he looked clean and he kept his uniform in much better shape than did most prisoners. I never had reason to suspect that he received better treatment regarding food than the rest of us, yet he had so far avoided that awful, shifty, hungry look I saw in most faces there.

As to what he saw when he looked at me I had no idea. Throughout the following months I could only guess about my face by feeling around it when I managed to clean it: soft straggly hair round chin and sides; my hair, cropped pretty short when I last stayed in Arras, I judged no longer than as worn by many civilians then, but it must have been terribly dirty — hot water, not to mention soap, being unobtainable. My clothes I wore night and day, week after week; feeling cold all the time, with no means of washing them, I felt no inclination to remove them.

Oddly, though, I had no need of de-lousing. The filthy little animals had deserted me, presumably because my body yielded nothing they fancied — this being the one and only benefit I derived from captivity in the hands of people expert in the art of killing slowly those whom they considered surplus to requirements.

Eventually, after how many days or weeks I'm not sure, early one morning the guards marched half the prisoners off to a place where they could have a bath of some sort. The rest of us were supposed to go next day, but we never did. The clean ones returned that evening — worn out because they were so debilitated that it had taken them many hours to walk the necessary 11 kilometres each way, but still pleased to be clean in body, even though they'd had to don the same old filthy clothes.

Chapter Fifty-One

Shortly after that, with a few others, I was taken to a point where we joined another group of British prisoners, complete strangers — a few of them Irish, many Scots and the rest from Yorkshire, Lancashire and Staffordshire, I learned. Suddenly and permanently, I'd lost touch with the Sergeant and the Essex Regiment men around him.

Two noteworthy incidents occurred during the march that followed. The German under-officer commanding the guards who flanked our column was the first blond enemy soldier I had seen and, basing my opinion on a fallacy current at that time, I assumed that he came from Saxony. Since I was an Anglo-Saxon, I reasoned that he would be kinder to me than would a dark-skinned Prussian.

Keen to maintain a steady rate of progress, he constantly moved up and down the column, adjuring his men to urge their shambling prisoners onwards. They responded with shouts of "*Vorwärts!*" and "*Schnell!*" and "*Fester machen!*" or words which sounded like that and whose meaning was obvious. But, at least, no violence, no jabbing with rifle barrels, nor blows from their butts occurred... And the fair-haired NCO, here, there and everywhere, pleasant-faced, even exchanged a near-smile with one or other of his men while always pressing everybody to maintain a steady, forward movement. We could justifiably have slouched along, debilitated as we were, but something about that man's energy seemed to give us an obscure enthusiasm.

When we passed through a village, I observed the very first signs of interest in our plight on the part of French civilians. People stood at cottage doors, some even waved to us. We returned their salutes with gratitude, for these were the only folk who had greeted us with friendly gestures since the *Boche* had made prisoners of us. I found it reassuring that our French ally's women, though now under enemy rule, should risk their freedom by revealing sympathetic feelings for the race whom Germans appeared to hate above all others at that time.

One bold woman hurried forward carrying a long loaf of bread. She came among us, breaking off pieces and handing them round. Eager hands grabbed the pieces, holding up our march for a moment — and then the guards did weigh in with their rifle butts.

As for my Saxon under-officer, he dispelled my romantic foolishness about fair-haired Germans. With glaring eyes and red, bloated face, he dragged the woman to the roadside. His hands at her throat, yelling loudly, having lost all control of himself, he appeared to be strangling her. We who were nearby moved to help the kindly woman, but more guards rushed to support their noble leader and rifle butts battered us, bayonets prodded our sides and behinds, and they drove us onwards to shouts of "*Marschieren!*" and "*Vorwärts!*"

I looked back when able to do so and could see the swine still holding the lady by the neck although, by then, she had collapsed. He must almost certainly have killed her, having for no good reason allowed bad temper to rob him of all human decency. Curiously enough, I never saw him again; he never rejoined our column.

The other notable event on that march also illustrated the loyalty of our French ally to the common cause. We entered a fairly large town and noticed that the inhabitants — possibly because large numbers of them were out in the streets — showed no fear of the German soldiers who, fully armed, formed a line between us and the population which looked impenetrable. The women, without exception, waved and called out encouraging messages. Some men took off their hats and waved them.

All this kindness had immense value to us, restoring our morale and, to some extent, our self-respect, at least for the moment. For weeks we had been totally isolated, debased by wretched living conditions and semi-starvation; we had come to believe we were weak and of no account to anybody. I had been feeling lost and lonely for, since my departure from the Sergeant and his group, I had met no one with whom I wished to be really friendly. Rather had I found it necessary to be on my guard — if I had saved a crust of the small bread ration or had picked up some edible item.

Then, in the middle of this town, for some reason, marching was suspended. I looked around: on one side of us a fine old church and, on the other side of the street, a row of shops, the pavement packed with people. And from them came more of these greetings, these smiles, from ordinary citizens going about their occupations, living apparently similar lives to those we had enjoyed in a past which now seemed terribly distant... in truth, I had feared it was lost to me forever. Just to be allowed to stand there and look at human beings — instead of staring, glaring eyes in sunken faces — uplifted and reassured me, a tonic restoring some sort of hope for the future.

I noticed an *estaminet* to my left and saw several men in there taking their morning break from work, chatting over a glass of wine.

The door of this place opened and a man emerged, wearing an apron and carrying a large, white, enamelled jug. He hurried our way, pushed in amongst us, and we appreciated his good intention immediately. Eagerly, we held out our tin cans, receptacles of all sorts, whatever we had been able to procure that would hold liquid. He poured beer into every container he could reach.

He must have known the trouble he was bringing on himself and he worked speedily. A guard tried to get to him, but we jammed around this brave Frenchman so closely the German could not touch him. Only when the liquor had all been given away did the good man speak and his "*Bon santé!*" and "*Fini*" were well understood and a passage to the pavement cleared for him, whereupon he ran back into the *estaminet*.

I hoped he got away with his act of defiance of the enemy. I don't know because the guards set us marching again immediately.

I believe the town was Valenciennes.

This weary procession ended in a place called Sancourt[294], and our first purpose-built prisoner-of-war camp. It consisted of a number of the wooden huts familiar to all soldiers — but in his case without beds. We were each given a thin blanket made of some ersatz[295] material.

British soldiers usually expressed defiance of such sweaty and foul living conditions through blasphemous songs, often set to hymn tunes. But we who had lost touch with our nationals and who fed and fared worse than many animals, we sang no bawdy songs, made no jokes in bad taste, laughed at nothing; the energy to do any of these normal things had deserted us. To stand up required a deal of effort and walking had become a hard labour. One laid down when not under pressure to work — our work regime began here at Sancourt — and slept during the night only between lurching almost hourly to the latrine in order to avoid fouling the only clothing we possessed.

My pitch on the hut floor placed me at the mercy of a lad from Bradford, a mild, inoffensive chap, but one who droned on at all times about the pie-shop at the corner of the street where he lived. Jimmy Britten tortured and tantalised himself — and me — in his broad Yorkshire drawl with graphic descriptions of the aromas and tastes of hot pies filled with delicious chunks of meat floating in thick mouth-watering gravy... My empty, aching guts, activated by mental pictures of all this luscious grub, writhed in emptiness and agony.

Meanwhile, in the continued absence of meat pies, I cadged more potato peelings off a German guard, washed them and, on returning from work unloading coal barges on a river, stewed them over a little fire; I did the same with nettles I pulled from a roadside patch — they had an almost beefy flavour, but an unwelcome laxative effect on an already overworked bowel.

One health- and soul-destroying job which some unfortunates, me included, had to do, was shovelling lime out of railway vans. First, the big doors needed prising open, then out tumbled the lime, perhaps on to wet ground with the consequent heat and fumes arising. The large, German shovels had long shafts without the handles at the end we were used to, which made applying leverage more difficult.

After loading whatever lime had fallen on the ground into a horse-drawn box-cart, one unlucky man would have to secure a foothold just inside the door of the van and start shovelling the stuff straight on to the cart. Eyes and chest suffered. When he'd cleared a space, number two man would join him, toiling under the snarls and urgings of an impatient guard. And so on all down a long line of wagons.

Hungry, weak, and now afflicted by the lime-filled air in the enclosed wagon, it felt like day-long torture.

One morning, when I tried to stand in line while the Jerries counted the lime-shovelling group, blood and slime were oozing from me uncontrollably. I called a guard's attention to this and I was shoved into a horse-drawn wagon and taken about a mile down the road to a German

Army field hospital. Large tents housed wounded and sick soldiers, who mostly lay on straw-filled mattresses in wooden bunks. I was allotted one of them and a burly man came and looked at me, departed, then soon returned with an immaculately-dressed officer who briefly examined me, gave some instructions and left.

The German lads evinced no surprise at my presence. Soon the male nurse (a flattering description of his skills) served them with what appeared to be macaroni; he ladled it into their mess tins. Still in their field grey uniforms, most of them ate little and indicated that I could help myself to their unwanted food. I over-ate, scarcely able to believe in my good fortune.

When night came, having cleaned my rear with hay from a mattress, I crawled out to a covered latrine; over a trench stood one long seat with many round holes in it. All that night and for several more thereafter, I lay with my rear over one of these holes, enduring the stench and discomfort rather than continually rising from my bed. Meanwhile, each day, I shared the sick men's food and coffee. Rapidly, I grew stronger, until I felt able to remain in the tent overnight, perhaps only having to go out three or four times.

Now I could do little jobs to help those Germans who were confined to their bunks; perhaps push a man to the far side of his mattress, punch and work up the hay filling nearest to me, then go round the other side and repeat the process, finally making him a shade more comfortable than he had been.

These bed-bound men had leg injuries; those with arm wounds could fend for themselves. The standard of care for these wounded Germans was very poor. Most of them had body lice. I had no contact with men in the other tents, but I assumed that cases with trunk injuries were sent further back to proper hospitals.

The powerfully built man in charge of my tent, the orderly as we would say, began to notice the improvement in my condition and must have reported it to the doctor, for I was given a sort of large metal dish — the orderly, by putting it to his backside, indicated its purpose. Regret close to fear that I would be returned to the prison camp, almost made me sorry to feel so much better, but I took the bedpan to the latrine and produced the required, shall we say, sample; the officer doctor was passing, examined my stool — and the presence of blood secured me a reprieve.

The men called the orderly Adamski. He now got me to do most of the very limited nursing chores he had sometimes done for the wounded men. In return, he allowed me to keep on eating and drinking leftover items.

One day, he gave me to understand — I was acquiring a few words of German — that I would leave the hospital, such as it was, in a week's time. Then he said "*Ringen!*", which from his actions I guessed meant "rings". "*Gold Ringen,*" he said excitedly, pointing in the direction of our prison camp. "*Gefangenen* (I knew that one, of course: "prisoners") *hab' gold Ringen?*" Now I got the drift of his hopeful questioning and quickly assured him that the *Gefangenen* had lots of gold *Ringen*. So, said he — demonstrating with a pile of mess cans — I could help myself to spare food, fill as many cans as I could carry, and exchange them for my fellow prisoners' gold rings. These Jerry food cans were not wanted, he explained, their owners having died, *tot, kaput.*

I began to collect every bit of food I could lay my hands on — stewed meat and veg, macaroni, beans, soup — and hid the full cans under my bunk, hoping the stuff wouldn't go mouldy. I also collected spoons and forks.

On the day before I was to leave, I sat on a box, chatting as best I could with a young German. He spoke a little English and, by means of signs and odd words in either language, we understood each other pretty well. He had almost recovered from his wound, but he was homesick. He lived near Berlin, he said, and he handed me photographs of home and family, explaining with easily grasped German words such as *Mutter, Vater, Schwester, Haus* and *Heim*[296]. The lad had a good face, which description has nothing to do with bone structure or colour. I'd have liked to have him as a friend; he wasn't repulsed by my emaciated condition, looked straight at me, and smiled now and then.

I retain no clear memory of the many other patients in my big tent. I spoke to most of them — those I was able to do small things for and those who showed signs of tolerance or friendliness by trying to match my efforts at communication. I always listened and tried to learn or work out more words of their language.

For instance, a standard question of theirs sounded like, "*Wie lang gewesen sie hier?*", which I took to mean, "How long have you been here?", and I could reply something like "*Drei Monat Gefangene*", which

I hoped meant roughly "Three months a prisoner". Then some words on a noticeboard puzzled me, but I got one when a name beside the word "*Arzt*" at the bottom of the board made me think this must meant "doctor" or "surgeon". And so often was I told "*Bleib' du da!*" with an imperative finger pointing at my feet that I decided it must mean "Stay you there!"

The sad day came when Adamski told me to go back to the prison camp, accompanied by an elderly guard. I quickly tied a string around my waist and hung from it all the full German mess tins; I filled my pockets with the spoons, knives and forks I had accumulated, and stuffed my tunic with pieces of rye bread quickly gathered from bedsides.

The weight of all this almost defeated me, especially when Adamski kept me standing and waiting while he gave me careful instructions about handing over the gold rings I'd promised him in return for all the cans and food. He waxed very emphatic about my obligations to him; I understood his meaning and threats, not word for word but sufficiently. When we left the prison-camp to move elsewhere we should have to pass the field hospital on our way to the nearby *Bahnhof* — I guessed he was telling me — and he would be there to collect. "*Ja, ja,*" I assured him and struggled away with my load.

Back with my hungry mob, I gathered together Jimmy Britten and several others I knew and asked them to protect me should anyone try to take by force the food I'd brought; in return I would share it with them. This way we made the grub last a couple of days. I kept for myself a mess tin with a folding handle on top — it made a good drinking utensil. The knives, forks and spoons I kept hidden on my person for future trading.

I often stood hopefully near the barbed-wire fencing, knowing that front-line German fighters, men from the trenches, had no hatred for us — often a degree of sympathy, in fact — and would sometimes endeavour to converse with me when they passed by on the road (also they didn't give a damn for the older *Landsturm* men who guarded us).

One such kindly soldier gave me a German printed field card, similar to the British version I have previously described, with a series of printed statements which said "I'm well" or its opposite or "I am in hospital" and so on. I looked at his card, struck out the lines which, according to my rough translations, did not apply, addressed it to my parents in England and handed it back to the kind young German with a "*Dankeschön*", but no hopes of it ever being received at home. Probably the only way the card would get into the German postal system was if the soldier handed it to his Regimental Post Office.

Sometimes work took me over the Belgian border and I recall the drab scene when, during a rest from work, I strayed from the party of prisoners, sat on a small heap of slag, and compared the view with similar ones I'd seen around coalfields in northern England.

An old man dressed in black cloth with black leggings and heavy boots joined me. The customary exchange of words, signs by looks and hands, along with something approaching telepathy, established understanding between us and I learned that he had worked in a mine near Mons[297] "over there" — he pointed, but I couldn't see any sign of the colliery, it was too far away.

He wasn't a big man, but clearly a very tough one. Difficult though communication was, I valued those few moments spent with someone who did not have the spell of the prisoner curse upon him, who didn't stink of decay, who gave off emanations of hopefulness.

One day, the guards told 50 or so of us to get ready to leave Sancourt. I draped my thin blanket over my shoulders, hung my precious Jerry mess can on the string I used as a belt, and stuffed lots of forks and spoons into an old sack which I now carried wrapped around my body under my tunic.

The gang set off at a crawl towards the railway station.

The danger of Adamski spotting me was obvious — the road passed fairly close to the field hospital, which was sited in a hollow bounded on one side by the railway line. Explaining my difficulty to the men around me, I positioned myself in the middle of the group, asking them to conceal me as much as possible. As we approached the place, I could see the bulky figure of Adamski standing at the foot of the embankment below the road. I feared he would kill me when he discovered I had no gold rings for him, but I hoped I might escape his notice by keeping my head down and getting those around me to keep close.

We had almost passed him when he spotted me; the roar he let out must have startled the several guards who accompanied us, for one of them stopped to question him as he awkwardly scrambled up the incline. The word "*Ringen*" came over loud and clear. We continued marching so I risked a backward look and he pointed towards me, shook his fists and ranted terribly. But still the guard appeared puzzled and stood in Adamski's way.

In a few minutes, we reached the small station. The enraged villain must have given up hope of collecting his crafty fortune. I saw no more of him, though keeping a lookout from my hiding place behind other men.

We actually travelled in compartments marked "Fourth Class" — "*Vierte Klasse*" — instead of the usual goods wagons and we arrived after many delays at, of all places, the famous Bapaume[298], now in German hands. On foot, we crossed several railway tracks, passed the ruins of some buildings, then filtered through an area cluttered with wrecked tanks, lorries and guns.

Clear of all this junk, I saw a German aeroplane which had crashed; I was surprised at its general scruffy appearance, the rough finish of its fuselage. It looked like a really cheap mass-produced monoplane, so different from the gleaming red bi-planes of Richthofen's squadron which had spent a sunny afternoon photographing and shooting up our sector shortly before the big German attack. This grey-green, Spartan, single-wing plane could probably have been turned out in large numbers at low cost — and, doubtless, with little consideration for the safety of the youngsters who would fly them. Its gauntness reminded me of the remains of the horse lying by the roadside near Gavrelle. Desperate shortage of equipment as well as food seemed indicated. The huge German effort must be the last gamble, I concluded. Bad though my condition was, I felt more cheerful and hopeful of survival until fighting ceased.

Another tented field hospital loomed ahead and there we stopped. We were to work there, living in tents.

Soon after arriving, I had a brief return to the old front-line tension when a shell screamed overhead and crashed not far away. However, fear quickly turned to elation when it dawned on us that it must have been a British shell. It meant our Army was only a few miles away... and we quietly discussed hopes, dreams of escaping...

My first job there, with a group of other prisoners, was distributing food. In each large tent, the orderly or male nurse took charge of it, and then gave us our next task — usually taking covered buckets away to the latrines for emptying and cleansing. We cleared any litter from the earthen floor of each tent and dumped it by the ever-burning incinerator a few hundred yards away. Other prisoners had to carry stores from the railway siding — heavy work for such enfeebled men.

The wounded German soldiers lay in wooden bunks, many of them, for warmth, still wearing their grey tunics or draping them over their shoulders if they had arm or torso wounds. The German Army, like ours, passed serious cases back to better equipped hospitals, but returned the lightly wounded to their units after brief treatment which showed little humane consideration for their needs.

Our diet remained the same, wickedly poor and sparse. So when the blessing of a British air raid on the area furnished an opportunity, we got busy.

Anti-aircraft guns made a terrific din and set all the hospital staff running in one direction... Then they vanished. When someone yelled out the explanation — "They've gone down into dugouts!" — as one man we rushed to their tents and grabbed anything edible. After that, we headed for the hospital tents and gobbled up every bit of food we found. I saw no wounded man objecting, nor did any of them complain later to the staff about our conduct; perhaps they were glad to see us around, their own (male) nurses having left them to their fate.

No bombs fell on the hospital, so we awaited the next raid with some eagerness.

Sometimes, a brief but hellishly loud shriek, different to anything I'd heard before, would precede the arrival of a large shell. An artilleryman fellow prisoner knew what it was: "A high-velocity shell, something new we developed. You can hardly hear the gun fire because the shell arrives and bursts so quickly."

I recall an occasion when one of these shells burst and I heard a chunk of metal buzzing my way; when it hit the ground I picked it up — it was hot! — and carried it to a group of Germans crouching in a shelter and dropped it among them... to their surprised consternation, until my grin and the word "souvenir" reassured them.

On such rare occasions, I felt some self-respect briefly restored.

Their front-line men, as I have stated, seldom showed animosity towards us so, when I saw a small group of lightly wounded, young fellows sharing a newspaper, I joined them, hopeful of hearing some up-to-date information. They greeted me in friendly fashion; me, a stooping scarecrow with sunken cheeks, hardly a soldierly figure, yet they knew I had shared certain experiences common only to men who had spent time on the front line — to which, I took it, they were due to return. Now recovered from wounds or one of the active-service maladies, they would soon be back to that crashing, roaring hell. Small chance of living through it…

But the German boys helped me to understand the main news items. Thus, I learned that several places, which had been well behind our Army's front line before the Ludendorff assault, were now established as German Army staff HQs. And a depressing feature with a Berlin dateline claimed that Paris was under bombardment by a huge gun[299], its shells hitting the French capital every half-hour from a position 90 kilometres away.

The Germans had bombarded London from the air, initially from the sausage-shaped airships named after Count Zeppelin, later from aircraft, but a gun lobbing big shells into the city at intervals throughout every day and every night seemed far worse to me than the brief visitation of an air raid, during which most people could find safe shelter. There could be no warning of approaching shells. Yet people couldn't spend night and day in hiding; life must go on.

What alarmed me about that article wasn't just that enemy forces had advanced close enough to Paris to bombard it; it meant that, if they reached the French coast, they would be able to shell England. Again it became difficult to maintain faith in eventual victory for our Forces. Speculating on what our fate would be if our side were defeated caused me a spasm of deep despair.

But… to hell with it all, and when the odd group of raiding British planes came over, we cheered them on and laughed to see the Jerries diving below.

Chapter Fifty-Two

Soon, another move. The Germans put some of us on a train and, after a while, we alighted at an unidentifiable spot where we were quartered in a couple of huts. So well remembered, this place — especially because the evening stew had occasional chunks of meat among the stewed root vegetables; tough meat, undoubtedly horseflesh, but ranking as a luxury. And it meant the daybreak ersatz coffee with black bread could all be consumed as one meal now because we knew our bellies would be filled again later — until then most of us had tried to save a thin slice of the morning bread to avoid that horrible empty feeling throughout the night.

The first day there provided another surprise, for the guards did not accompany us when we set off to work. Instead, alongside us walked several Germans armed with revolvers, not rifles, and wearing uniforms of a superior cut and caps with shiny black peaks and red-and-gold bands round the crown. Their chief wandered happily here and there around and among us.

Presently, we came to an area where massive barbed-wire defences stretched right and left as far as the eye could see. They led us through a wide gap and we marched on, the barbed wire ranged on either side of us. Its great depth amazed me. I'd seen nothing so vast as this before — and the word passed quietly amongst us: "This must be the Hindenburg Line[300]".

The chief amused himself by shooting at the wood stakes securing the wire, or at the occasional can lying around. This kept him happy while demonstrating to us his good marksmanship and, possibly, the reason why the Jerries had dispensed with the usual guards.

We worked on railway construction, building a branch line through a wooded area to join a main line nearly a mile distant. We started on low ground, joining together pre-fabricated sections of light, narrow-gauge track and proceeding gradually uphill.

With competent instructors, we learned quickly, levelling the ground and packing stones under cross-members. We soon completed the uphill part, then laid more track across the higher level for about a quarter of a mile, excavating earth on each side of it and shovelling the spoil into small metal tip-trucks — about 20 of them.

When all the trucks were full, we'd begin pushing them, two men per truck, towards the downhill section. When the leading three trucks reached the start of the slope, each two-man crew mounted the small platform at the rear of their truck and applied the brakes by turning a wheel. When all appeared ready for the descent, the chief gave a signal, brakes were released, and with a push from the men waiting behind, the small train got under way. Speed increased, controlled by light touches on the brakes, and momentum carried the three trucks along a short length of level track at the bottom of the hill.

Then we tipped the earth out of the trucks, making a ridge along one side of the track. Next train down tipped on the opposite side. While we were pushing our empty trucks back up the incline and loading at the top, others removed a short section of track, levelled out the ridges of earth we'd dumped, then replaced the track on this new, flat surface. The third train down would stop short of the raised section and start a repeat process.

Repeating this operation day after day, we were lowering the higher ground and raising the lower, building a small embankment and a cutting. We grew familiar with our tasks so, on the loaded downhill run, we gradually increased speed by making less use of the handbrakes…

One day, while pushing empty trucks uphill I noticed a pink mushroom growing alongside the track. On the next down run, I asked my mate to look after the brake as I was going to jump off and collect that mushroom. Although, as we approached the spot, I felt the train going much too fast I leapt off regardless, rolled over as I landed, and picked my small mushroom…

Then I heard an awful noise down below and cries of pain. Several trucks had left the rails. Mine was at the bottom of the embankment, wheels uppermost. My mate had jumped clear as the truck ahead canted over, but several men were hurt and one badly crushed.

The little, pink mushroom appeared to have saved me from injury or, possibly, death. I didn't eat it after all, for that might have been tempting providence.

The embankment and cutting completed, we moved on into the woods and, for a change, sampled tree-felling as an occupation. Most of us proved too physically impaired to swing an effective axe, but we could work steadily on a two-man crosscut saw. Our cheerful chief acknowledged this and procured more saws — whereas the average infantry or *Landsturm* officer would have driven us on with snarls and blows to swing axes until we dropped exhausted or injured ourselves.

When a tree crashed down, we stripped off branches with hatchets and saws, trimmed the sturdier branches into useful lengths suitable for pit props etc, while the trunks would make telegraph poles or go to sawmills.

When a path of the correct width had been cleared through the wood, we debouched on to a mainline railway and, having prepared the ground, track-laying commenced — the really heavy graft. We went back to where we'd started and began to lay a full-scale, single-line railway, replacing the light, narrow-gauge track we'd used when building up the embankment and cutting.

Sleepers to be manhandled, laid, packed and secured — adding stone ballast to stabilise them — holes for bolts drilled, and finally the so-heavy lengths of steel rail to be carried and lowered into position. Experience taught us that the men carrying a rail must be placed in line with careful regard to height; a short man between two taller chaps would contribute nothing to the general effort — and effort it really was in our underfed condition.

Despite that — how it happened I don't know and I'm sure the slightly better food was only part of it — to me, the moral quality of that gang of fellow prisoners felt higher than that of most with whom I had recently lived. We responded to our engineer overseers — types superior to the *Landsturm* prison-camp guards — and especially to the sporty, cheerful officer in charge, by working to the best of our abilities and not scrounging; for the time being, our bearing returned to its former upright posture, the shrinking pariah stoop disappeared, and we began to feel like men again, instead of scruffy slaves behind barbed-wire fences.

Those weeks provided a much-appreciated break from the dismal, hopeless routine of useless living endured in small, closely guarded *Gefangenenlager*[301].

However, something appeared to go wrong with the railway plan before we had completed it, and our next outing took us and our few miserable possessions to a station on the same main line which our single-line track would have joined.

More British prisoners, strangers to us, had already assembled there and we all piled into railway wagons when ordered to do so. I managed to squat near a door which the guard kept open so that he could sit with his legs dangling out. Aged about 35, I reckoned, he took a keen interest in the passing views and, from time to time, drew a mouth organ from a tunic pocket and played or sang a tune.

His face reminded me of several brothers who had lived near us in pre-war days, the Knappers — all hard-working house decorators and general handymen. Had they also been Germans I wondered, along with the Schmidts and Schulzes and others who disappeared so suddenly as war began? When the musician gave a lively rendering of Yip-I-Addy-I-Ay[302], a song we in Britain had been singing around 1914, I wondered the more. He took little notice of us and never seemed to understand English when spoken to, so I may have been mistaken about him.

German ingenuity solved a transport problem, even in those far-off days. Goods on railway wagons often had to be offloaded from lorries then, at their destination, transferred once more to a road vehicle. The Germans had means whereby they could replace a lorry's wheels with railway wheels so that the lorry could then drive along the railway line! This I saw often in areas contiguous to the battlefield. They must have planned it pre-war, noting that their lorries fitted the width of French railway tracks too.

Around this time, we occasionally encountered the sad sight of a train of flat railway trucks each carrying a captured British tank — on their way to the Fatherland for scrap, I guessed. On the other hand, more encouragingly we passed through Cambrai[303] which, on its eastern side, was just at that moment starting to come under fire from British long-range artillery.

We first alighted from this train at a town called Saargemund[304]. The guards led us across a great mass of railway lines and it seemed fortunate that we were not run down by a train as we lumbered and stumbled over track after track.

With a few others, I found myself spending a couple of days "imprisoned" in an empty corner shop, from whose windows I scanned a dreary industrial scene, confirming we had entered that famous Saar manufacturing belt. A guard patrolled outside the shop and, twice each day, escorted us to another building to get our meagre rations.

We left that town in style, seated not in wagons, but in saloon-style railway carriages, nicely upholstered, seemingly much too posh for soiled, scruffy prisoners — but appreciated by me, anyway, although I found myself among a new lot of strangers; they looked quite young, their accents suggesting they mainly came from the Midlands and Scotland.

I'd secured a seat next to an exit and was surprised when an armed German, a *Landsturm* guard I hadn't seen before, took the seat next to me. Bearded, he looked like a nice old granddad, and gave no indication of dislike for me, nor did he shout orders or demands as they usually did.

In some comfort, we settled down for the journey — as ever with no clue as to our destination. Place names I recall passing through, though not in order I think, were Charleville, Sedan, Metz[305]; the many others don't come readily to mind. The first night we dozed through many stops and starts; the guards gave out black bread and coffee substitute during one of several long pauses in various sidings. But our train made quite a good run the following morning.

During this journey, aided by imaginative hand movements I conversed with the elderly guard. He spoke a dialect I found easier to partially understand than others I'd encountered. I gathered his home was in Heligoland[306]. Remembering that the place had belonged formerly to Britain, I thought I'd discovered a possible reason for the rapport which made me prefer his company to that of any prisoner comrade in that carriage.

However, around midday our train stopped in a large station and what happened there made me feel deeply ashamed of being a member of that gang of war prisoners. As our train moved slowly alongside the platform, we could see, placed at intervals, large containers full of steaming food. By each of these, ready with his ladle, stood a German soldier — a marvellous prospect, the quantity of hot food obviously generous indeed compared to any previous experience of mine as a prisoner.

All our chaps needed to do was queue in orderly fashion and be served. I remained seated, observing some men already pushing and shoving quite unnecessarily. When the first of them reached the container nearest to me and held out their cans, those behind did not wait, but surrounded the large, round boiler and thrust their cans, even their hands, into the steaming stew. Those behind, fearful of getting little or none, pushed and scrambled and reached over those in front who now could not get away and were pressed downwards. All in that area soon became daubed with food, thrusting hands into it, struggling to get some into their mouths, while those behind yelled and shrieked like demented baboons and tore at the clothing of the men in front of them.

The resulting filthy outcome of this shameful lack of control was that few secured any worthwhile quantity of food. Most of it finished up on the ground or on their clothes.

Looking on, the friendly face of the Heligolander guard turned to rage. He shouted at me "*Bleiben sie da!*" and sprang to the platform, battering the nearest men with his rifle butt. Other guards set upon the mob with whatever came to hand and drove them back to the carriages, some bleeding, many smeared with good-food-wasted. The scum of Birmingham, Northern England and Scotland, the conscripted scrapings of the barrel after four years of terrible warfare... Compared with the volunteers of 1914 and their close comradeship — crap.

Heligoland reappeared, took my mess-can (souvenir of Adamski's hospital tent) and returned later, my can and his own filled to the brim with delicious macaroni stew. No one dared grab mine, as I'm sure they would have done if Granddad hadn't sat beside me.

He was the kindliest German I had met — and, of course, it had to be in front of him that this disgusting behaviour occurred. His epithet, "*Schweinereien*"[307], whatever it meant, sounded well deserved by that selfish mob.

That journey, which could have been so pleasant, so different from the pauperish existence of prisoners behind bars or barbed wire, ended for me and about a dozen others when we stopped at a station — I forget where — and Heligoland told us to follow him off the train.

Outside the station, we climbed into two low-slung wagons, each drawn by a pair of horses. Time slipped away as we trotted off along a beautiful country road; memory hauled me back to 1916, the end of that year, when I had been sent to the huge base at Harfleur –leaving a Battalion much reduced in numbers and in spirit by Somme battles, but slowly being reinforced in preparation for further General Haig attempts to win the war by nibbling away (the tactics which cost so many lives to achieve so little).

I digress — that wagon set me reminiscing simply because it had no springs and a similar one at Harfleur had shaken my innards then as this one did, making frequent micturation necessary. Which further recalls Egypt in 1915 where one of our wits nicknamed a bloke who had to pee frequently Mustapha Piss...

When good old Heligoland gestured at the ascending forest rising to great heights on either side of the road and shouted "*Schwarzwald!*" I knew what the first part of the word meant, "black", so I guessed we were in the Black Forest[308]. The sun shining, the air sweet — all I then required to make life heavenly was a good meal and a return to normal strength. With neither forthcoming, the lovely surroundings nonetheless raised my hopes of better times to come.

A certain vagueness about where we went thereafter bothers me[309], but I know we eventually left the wagons, started walking and, feeling flaked out, were allowed to rest awhile by the roadside, and observe what must have been at that time a proud monument to German success in the 19th Century — a huge, grey, stone arch above the spotlessly maintained highway along which we had marched. The massive figures in the centre of the edifice hit one right in the eyeballs: "1870". A blow to French pride and a sort of threat that history might repeat itself in 1918 if the Americans didn't add the necessary punch to the Allied counter-offensive.

Grass-lined, graced by grand, towering trees on both sides, this highway at that point with that arch marked the entrance to territory known to us as Alsace-Lorraine[310], but which I later gathered the Germans regarded as two separate provinces, Elsass and Lothringen.

A short walk from there brought us to a large, ancient fort and barracks, where we spent some time and were given a drink of the familiar ersatz coffee, memorable because sweetened, albeit with sugar substitute. Our guards permitted us to rest in the cool shelter of a paved area, fronted by arches and looking out into a large, sanded parade ground... where, unexpectedly, an American soldier appeared. Immaculately-dressed, he walked up and down, presumably for exercise, without any visible supervision. He took no notice of us.

What had secured this preferential treatment for him? Mystery indeed! If this American had been captured during a front-line battle, how come his uniform remained spotless? I had plenty of time to speculate about this point as I sprawled in the shade. Back and forth he strolled, looking neither to left nor right, so perhaps he had the same worries about survival prospects as some of us.

A further rail journey of several hours gave me a view of much attractive countryside with prosperous farms and villages and occasionally a town such as Freiburg[311], certainly a place of some architectural worth; even from the train I reckoned it the sort of town I would like to explore in time of peace.

I always felt that inward ache when I looked at a beautiful town or village which had so far avoided damage by the opposing armies, and so carried on some sort of fairly steady existence which might, with luck, continue until a treaty relieved its people of the fears caused by war.

A town of considerable size called, at that time, Mülhausen[312], loomed up, but we stayed on the train. Ahead we saw a wide river and soon we crossed it by way of a bridge, which seemed endless. This, I guessed, must be the Rhine, though its width surprised me, considering how far south we had travelled.

Soon after that, we detrained and our guards conducted us through a very pleasant country town and a little way beyond it until they marched about 40 of us into a barbed-wire enclosure containing several Army huts. This turned out to be our base for two or three months. A wooden shelf sleeping ten men, with a similar shelf below it, comprised the war-prisoner accommodation we had come to expect.

As first priority, I had to seek out the latrine because the after-effects of dysentery made several night visits to that usually stinking place unavoidable. But in this small *Gefangenenlager*, instead of the standard pole-over-trench open-air outfit, we had an enclosed bog. This superior sanitary convenience gave me a sense of things looking up, that perhaps, in this lovely area, life might become more easily bearable — might there be even some hope of supplementing our meagre vegetable diet by catching a bird or a rabbit?

Chapter Fifty-Three

At daybreak, a Jerry guard shoved the hut door open, banged on the floorboards with his rifle butt, and prodded men with his bayonet, yelling, "*Los! Raus! Aufmachen du Schlavina!*"[313] — or that's how it sounded. An evil-looking swine, with a yellowish complexion, dark, beady eyes, he had a face that never had and never would smile. This part of his work was evidently his pleasure and his delight.

I had known such wretched sorts in England, but they had not had power over me like this specimen did — backed by a loaded rifle. Give your dear old working man some authority over his fellows and usually he will relish the job of asserting it; the non-commissioned officer, the bobby on the beat, the factory foreman, the traffic warden, all at times lean more heavily on their victims than is, to say the least, appropriate. Give a born bossy type like that authority over prisoners captured on the battlefield and he may swell into a bullying tyrant...

So we tumbled off those wooden sleep benches, hoping to avoid a jab from his bayonet. I was lucky.

After the black bread and coffee substitute, we were divided into working parties. I found myself in the largest group and guarded by two *Soldaten* and one *Gefreiter*[314]. A couple or so kilometres brought us near to that small town we had passed through the previous day and into a big field with several long, wooden sheds. The guards split us up three or four per shed.

I was glad to find myself in a stable housing some 40 horses of various sizes and colours on either side of a gangway. By each horse's stall hung a board giving the animal's identification number, colour, and, in large letters, its disease or injury. One word frequently occurred: *Rhaude*[315].

A man with rolled-up shirtsleeves — the groom I suppose — instructed me; he took a handful of straw, dipped it into a bucket of paraffin oil, then rubbed the horse's coat vigorously. When I took my turn, as I rubbed the oil in, I saw why treatment was needed; among the tough horsehair was a thick layer of what we had always known as scurf — dried, flaked-off skin. Hopefully, the oil would soften the unhealthy stuff and the harsh straw disperse it. That did not happen at first go; I passed on to the next stall and treated another horse, which my teacher then inspected. This one wasn't so bad and the groom handed me a currycomb — something I had seen in childhood when visiting the stable at the end of our road... I remembered the whistling noise the groom in Edmonton made as his right arm arced long sweeps through the animal's coat. And, as I went at it, I blew through my teeth with each swipe.

This German groom then gave me a brush and showed me I should hold it in my right hand, while still using the comb with my left. So, a sweep along and down with the comb, then a follow-up with the brush.

And each day thereafter, that was my main chore. Physical weakness spoilt my performance, no doubt, but I gave the job all I'd got, knowing it was worthwhile. Passing from horse to horse, I found each one different in temperament. I learned to avoid standing behind them, just in case — especially the restless horse I treated most days which had a hole in the centre of its forehead, a wound from bullet or shell fragment. Sometimes it lashed out, but I made sure I stayed alongside and, fortunately, it didn't bite me. I thought it would have been put down in England, but there must have been hopes for its recovery.

At feeding time, we led horses out, one at a time, to the water trough until all had been served. Then, back in their stalls, we tipped a bucketful of mixed hay, chaff and potatoes into their wooden mangers. Most of the horses were suffering from poor diet and neglect sustained when working around the battle area, but I must confess that out of each bucket I filched a few spuds and pushed them into that sack wrapped around my waist under my tunic — for prisoners, working in a farming area had its benefits.

Always curious to learn a few more words of the lingo — to no specific end that I recall — I'd try to comprehend when the guards talked casually to one another, leaning or squatting outside their hut, particularly on Sundays, the day off for everybody in the camp.

I'd listen to our interpreter too, whenever the Jerries called him into service. I did have doubts about him, though. An ordinary prisoner, aged about 25, so keen was he to please his masters that he frequently walked around quietly mouthing German phrases. At such times, he appeared unaware he was being observed. When passing on to any of us his interpretation of an order, he would show petty annoyance if one of us didn't grasp his meaning immediately — rather as a German guard might have done. Sometimes his behaviour came too close to preferring enemy company to that of his own nationals and I noted the potential hazards of such a role. Luckily, as it turned out.

One day at the stables, the chief officer called to an aide telling him to order me to fetch his mount from a nearby stable. I understood and, without thinking, set off before the aide had delivered the instruction. I found the already saddled horse and took it to His Highness, holding its bridle while he mounted. The puzzled looks on their faces made me realise I had acted in an unexpected way. Then, while we were marching back that afternoon, a *Gefreiter* came alongside me and spoke words among which I recognised "*Dolmetscher*" — interpreter — but I assured him, truthfully, that I spoke very little German.

Apart from the practical matter of my slight knowledge, I had not yet made up my mind whether giving orders to our chaps on behalf of enemy soldiers was correct or even decent. Memories of how indignant I felt when I saw that git Goldberg mounted on his plinth yelling directions at newly captured Britishers helped me to a decision; the *Dolmetscher* lark was out. I still wanted to chat whenever possible, though.

Around that time, a guard engaged me in conversation (the usual: a few German words, a few English words, lots of actions). He started by telling me he had been in the front line until recently. He said he felt sorry for some of us prisoners. Others though, he disliked, because they dodged work whenever possible — especially by spending too much time at the latrine. His belief that some of us would perch on a pole over a foul-smelling trench full of human excrement in preference to doing a share of the work lowered his opinion of us *Engländer Schweinereien*. Well, perhaps one or two of us did make that choice, but I presumed — although expressing the thought was beyond me — that this guard had never experienced the combined effects of malnutrition and dysentery.

He had a question too. He'd heard us using a word which he pronounced "fick" — "*Warum die Engländer immer* 'fick'?" he asked. Why do the English always day 'fick'? "*Ich weiss nicht*," I said. I don't know. Nor did I, nor do I, now that it has become so poseur popular. Bloody, bugger, sod, damn and blast all serve their purposes, but the connotations of "fuck" make it an ugly sort of curse, and those Jocks and Brummies I've mentioned befouled the air in their vicinity with their effing repetitions. Although the guard was just an ordinary bloke, not familiar with the word or its meaning, he guessed it and resented the association of swearing and the sex act[316].

On the camp's Sunday "day off", a few prisoners went out to the stables just to feed and water the horses, but nobody did any grooming, as the Germans observed the Sabbath. We could stroll around inside the barbed wire or, when the sun shone, we would lie on the ground in a space between the huts and feel free to chat, stretch luxuriously, and perhaps reminisce about life before we became captives.

Warm days — July, August, by then, I'm not sure — tempted the *Kapitän* to have a number of horses, who were nearing recovery from their ailments, released from the stables into a nearby field. The beasties went berserk. They raced about and frolicked and kicked each other, a joy to behold.

One of those horses needed its regular treatment during that afternoon and a small, but tough, British lad was told to take a rope and lead it out of the field. But, as he approached, some frisky beasts circled around him and turned their hindquarters towards him. Kicks rained on the poor boy. Grabbing pitchforks or anything handy, some of us tried to break up the ring, but it took some moments and, by the time we rescued him, his injuries were many and awful.

We blamed German callousness for sending in one lad when the horses were so excited — and it was said that some of the guards stood laughing during the incident.

On other occasions, to a lesser degree, I found myself on the receiving end from both animals and guards. They ordered me to lead a big stallion through a small gap between a stable wall and a line of young fillies tethered with their hindquarters towards me. I just had to keep going while each filly in turn lashed out at the stallion as we passed. That huge brute took fewer kicks than I did. And I definitely heard laughter behind me and assumed it was a put-up job.

Shortly after that incident, a guard took me to a stable in which I had not worked before and told me to groom an animal somewhat larger than a donkey, but smaller than the average pony. Several Germans stood around. As I went into its stall the thing commenced kicking. *"Arbeit! Fest Arbeit!"*[317] yelled the watching Germans, laughing as I tried to keep close to the mad creature to lessen the effect of its kicks. Occasionally, I made contact with the currycomb, sometimes achieved a stroke with the brush, but I directed most of my efforts towards avoidance of being kicked to death.

One morning, as we shuffled out of the compound and started to form into our usual work groups, a chap shorter even than my 5ft 8½ inches, gripped one of my cuffs and whispered "Come with my little lot today". So I stood with him and about four others and, when the boss shouted *"Vorwärts!"*, our small party turned in the opposite direction to the usual one. Accompanied by just one *Posten*[318], we set off on a longish, uphill walk.

Sheer cheek appeared to have paid off, for no complaint about my presence came from the *Posten*. In fact, as we marched along the lovely country roads the rather obese German, a country lad if ever I saw one, said the odd word to me. I learned he had worked in London for some months in a hotel.

Among the hedgerows some big fruit trees grew, and I saw one young farmhand at the top of a ladder filling a basket with those fine big plums sold, in England back then, as Christmas gifts in pretty boxes. Perhaps realising how our mouths watered, our tubby *Posten* told us we could help ourselves to any windfalls lying in our path and some sweet greengages helped to assuage hunger pangs on such days as I was able to get a place at the front of the group...

That day we started work on one of several horse hospitals — *"Pferde Lazerette"* said a notice at the entrance. Another one, where we went on to work quite regularly, was on the other side of Hügelheim[319], the village a couple of kilometres from our *Gefangenenlager*.

In charge there was a man called Kayser (pronounced as in *Kaiser* Bill, the great leader of all the Jerries). His glass eye, black beard and jackboots gave him a threatening mien, yet we found him a fair, if surly, taskmaster, and quite easily satisfied if we worked steadily.

Nonetheless, on one occasion he kicked me right in the crutch with all the strength he could muster. The pain put me down on the floor, and my groin hurt for days, but I made no complaint — it was, as they say, a fair cop. I had noticed a large apple tree in a field adjacent to the stable and, hoping I was unobserved, went scrumping. There being few windfalls, I shook the tree... my big mistake — as the furious Kayser yelled after first coming up quietly behind me and throwing that terrible kick.

All the pleasant scenery and the quietness of Hügelheim could not fill our empty bellies, so we were ever on the lookout for something to fill the awful void — hence my risky scrumping expedition, of course.

Wally, the kind friend — as he became — who had invited me to join his *Pferde Lazerette* party without asking the guard's permission, found that his job sometimes took him close to pigsties; occasionally, he managed to slide his hand into a trough and pull out some dark-coloured meat which, on close study, appeared to be liver. It smelt unsavoury, but we wiped it and ate the revolting stuff. So robbing pigs of their swill was now our aim in life — though I have since suspected we were laying up stores of health troubles for future days.

Hügelheim natives proved not unfriendly, although kept at a distance by the *Soldaten*. One morning when we passed through the village on the way to Kayser's *Pferde Lazerette*, a gorgeous aroma of frying bacon greeted us and our *Posten* certainly took special note of the cottage from which it arose. So, for the whole of that working day, we saw nothing of our fat Jerry friend — and we had a fair idea where he had been lurking. He rejoined our group only as we lined up to return to our *Lager*, but we refrained from questioning him. Each day thereafter, he disappeared as soon as he'd handed us over to Kayser.

Every day, we took the horses from the *Lazerette* to water at a trough in the village, a couple of hundred yards from the stables. One lovely hot day, I took two to water and not a sound was to be heard, even though the inn — *Gasthaus* — was close by. How peaceful it all was, I thought. Horses satisfied, I was leading them away when suddenly a door slammed and they bolted. I was hanging on to a halter rope with each hand and they dragged me all the way back to the *Pferde Lazerette* and didn't stop until they were actually inside their stable.

That was the only time I saw Kayser laugh, but I didn't join in.

Few of us liked being scruffy and dirty, and we did try to do something about it when opportunity arose. A chap at the prison camp with whom I had struck up some sort of matiness told me he had seen a Jerry shearing a horse's coat with a machine powered by a man turning a wheel. He had a good idea: "If we could get into the shearing shed, do you think some of us could cut each other's hair?"

So later that day, during the one break from work allowed, some dozen of us climbed through a window at the back of that shed and we were soon shearing as to the manner born. The finished head was near enough bald. How different a man looked to his former shaggy self.

But, before we'd finished the job, our lookout saw a Jerry approaching and gave the alarm. We rapidly scrambled back out through the window. The man who had been in mid-shear at the moment of emergency rather conspicuously sported only half a haircut — our method had been to start at the nape of the neck and proceed upwards and forwards. Of course, the guards spotted his condition, and we feared all kinds of punishments, but the actual result was that the Captain detailed one of his experts to shear the lot of us. Subsequently, we were able to douse our heads and keep them free of lice.

After that, one Sunday morning, the guards told us to take off our very soiled khaki uniforms. They handed us tunics, trousers and caps, all made of loosely woven, dark-blue material with a wide, orange stripe down each trouser-leg and round the cap. So there we were — socks and underwear unwashed for months, but brand-new uniforms. If only we could somehow have a bath...

Everything appeared to be going our way, however. Soon, they lined up half our lot in front of an officer and gave each of us several tickets, on which were printed some German words, now only partially remembered — "*Kriegsgefangenen Lager Nr. ??*", then cards of different colours printed with "*Gutschein für 5 Pfennig*"[320] (or 10 or 20). We needed no instruction on what these cards were all about, they were money substitutes. So where could we spend them?

Next, they marched us off to a railway station where we entered Fourth-Class compartments with hard, wooden seats — just like the hop-pickers' train in Kent when we were digging the outer London defences back in 1914. Britain and *Deutschland* had that much in common, I thought; the harder you worked, the harder you travelled. But I can well recall the inner pleasure I felt at this seeming return to a more normal sort of life. A clean uniform, some sort of money in my pocket, and a trip on a train to... well, I must wait and see.

In the excitement, I almost forgot my ever-present hunger. Once more, we crossed the Rhine and this time we detrained at Mülhausen, which we had passed through on our journey south. As we marched through its main street, I observed the townspeople taking a real interest in the spectacle of these shuffling, bent-kneed, sunken-cheeked beings. Meanwhile, I saw two civilian-dressed men moving among them, apparently answering enquiries about us. "English soldiers — look at the condition to which those people are reduced," I heard one say. I felt sure we were the first British prisoners-of-war seen in those parts.

A busy, prosperous town, Mülhausen impressed me most with its cleanliness. Not that English towns of those days were dirty[321], but Mülhausen had a special look in 1918, so well cared for. The housewives must have thought so too, for they, in many cases, hung feather mattresses and quilts over window sills to give them the benefit of the clean, soft air, not deterred therefrom by what the neighbours might think, as would usually be the case in England.

We entered what appeared to be a large, public building and — more by signs than by word of mouth — were told to remove all our clothing. Ahead sat a man in a white coat to whom, in turn, we each had to present ourselves. He dipped a fairly large brush into a can and painted our scrotums and armpits with blue paste. We moved on to another white coat who shaved off the blue-painted hair.

Finally, we entered a shower cubicle where the water, though cold, enabled us to make ourselves cleaner than we had been for many a day. Soap was not available, but long-handled brushes vigorously applied did the job. The Treaty of Geneva[322] was working at last, for which I was truly thankful.

We had no towels so we had to dry our bodies with our trousers or tunics, but I had no complaint, feeling so refreshed by this unexpected cleansing. Unfortunately, I then had to dress myself once more in the rank vest, shirt, pants and socks. But dismay and horror hit me when I realised that my boots had vanished. A quick search of our men's sacks and bundles failed to restore them to me, so I had to appeal to the *Postens* who were in charge of us. They said they knew nothing about the theft.

However, I suspect even they couldn't face the prospect of walking through the town in full public view with one of their prisoners barefooted. Perhaps for that reason, they reported my loss to a senior officer at the cleansing station and one of his men handed me a pair of wooden clogs the like of which I had previously seen only in pictures of Dutch working people... at school we'd been told they wore clogs and smoked cigars, even when very young; I had no cigars, but gladly shoved my feet into these hand-carved-from-a-piece-of-wood shoes; I didn't find them too uncomfortable, except that they cut into my insteps.

Now I must have really looked the genuine POW in my bright, orange stripes, socks a dirty grey with trousers tucked into them, and those heavy clogs with their pointed toes. Add sunken cheeks, staring eyes and bent knees to the picture — I would not have been recognised by my own father.

After all that, though, some of us still had to wait for others to have the cleansing treatment so we spent our *Gutschein* cards at a small stand in a corner of the large hall. I secured a tablet of *Seife*[323], as I believe it was labelled, and a packet of cigarettes. These comprised cardboard tubes with a short cigarette attached — a long holder and a short smoke, in fact. I cadged a light from the man in charge of the counter. After all those months of enforced abstinence, the first puff made me dizzy. I just smoked the one and hoped to exchange the rest for some sort of food.

One more bonus came my way as a result of that visit to Mülhausen. Back in camp, I walked past the *Postens'* hut, sniffing at my tablet of imitation soap, and one of them called me over and asked where I had procured the stuff. I told him about the *Bade* in Mülhausen and he showed me the first bit of German currency I had seen, a note for *Ein Mark*. This I accepted, because I felt my hunger more urgently than my need to wash.

The following morning, when we arrived at Hügelheim, I saw the great yard at the rear of the *Gasthaus* was full of hay-loaded wagons — packed in so tightly I couldn't imagine how they could possibly have done it.

But the sight set me a-thinking... A few days earlier, as we started on the evening walk back to the prison camp, I saw, some distance ahead, three girls lying in the long grass of the verge. In all the months of prisoner life I had never seen girls behaving so naturally and, forgetting for a moment my disgusting state and appearance, as we drew level, I ventured to look at them. First one, then all three, waved to us — risking serious trouble if our guards objected to this kindly act. Pleased beyond words, and thankful that our sad plight had not sickened them, I waved back. I had to content myself with that for, short of breaking ranks, there was no way of talking to those lovely people who, just by humane action, had given deep joy and revived some self-respect in one, or maybe more of us — captive enemies, as their fathers and brothers would rightly describe us.

Well, I don't know why, but this wagon-filled yard made me wonder whether one of those sweet young girls worked at the *Gasthaus*. This, and even some daft romantic notions, occupied my mind as we passed the inn and covered the 300 yards or so to the *Pferde Lazerette*. I decided to take a risk which might, if things went wrong, land me in solitary confinement or worse.

I waited until our supervisor, Kayser, took his lunch break, then walked boldly down the lane, dived under a wagon in the *Gasthaus* yard, crept towards the rear of the inn and… reaching up, I tapped on a window, dropped back under the nearest wagon and waited to see whether one of the charming lasses who had lain in the long grass by the roadside might appear. In a few moments, thrillingly, a girl looked out and I felt certain she was one of the three!

I showed myself carefully and said, "*Bitte, Gelt, essen*"[324]. I held up my one-mark note. She might have screamed and that would have been my lot. But she didn't. I handed the note to her, slid under the wagon and waited. Presently, she looked out again, holding in one hand a large fruit pie and in the other a roll of cured tobacco leaf. These she delivered with the loveliest smile I'd seen in many a day, then she quietly closed the window.

I still recall the excitement I felt at having made slight contact with a non-military, private, human being — one, in particular, who had taken a grave risk in order to do a good turn for a stranger with little to commend him. On several later occasions, I found it was women who would risk punishment to do something mutually helpful — even those with reason to feel hatred for their country's enemies (the British, I mean).

Casually enough, I hoped, to disarm suspicion that I was attempting to escape, I walked back to the *Lazerette*. Kayser stood just inside the first stable I came to, so I was thankful that I'd stuffed the goods away in the sack round my waist under my tunic. Even so, I feared I might once more feel his jackboot connect with my crutch and the awful pain resulting. But no. Either he hadn't noticed I'd gone missing or, perhaps, a benign after-lunch mood prevailed.

Hiding between horses in the next stall, I started to wolf the pie, but my luck ran out at that point. The face of one of those earlier-mentioned Glaswegians appeared between the horses and I was caught with the remaining hunk of pie in my mouth. "Come on, shares," demanded the unwelcome Jock and, knowing his merciless ways, I gave him a chunk — for which he didn't even have the decency to thank me.

A well-dressed, young *Unteroffizier*[325], apparently on leave from his unit, came over to the stables from his house across the road and chatted with the several German workers at our prison camp who wore the ordinary grey uniforms — the while, he slapped his fine, leather riding boots with a short horsewhip.

I saw him again later as I was being escorted — on my own for some reason — along a road through the village. This immaculate, non-commissioned officer, pale of face and rather scholarly looking, proved more kindly than his aloof manner had led me to suppose. He spoke to my tubby guard, then turned to me and told me in fair English, pointing to a cottage, that an English lady lived there.

When he walked off, I looked hopefully at my keeper. Had he understood what the *Unteroffizier* had said, and would he permit me to approach the cottage? Cut off for so long from contact with civilians, I imagined this would have been a lovely experience, merely to hear the voice of an English lady... I had no thought of involving her in anything so hopeless as an attempt to escape, just a few words, perhaps about her life in Baden before the war...

No luck, although the lad didn't hurry me off to work, and showed friendly interest when, above a small shop, I spotted an enamel advertisement which read "Thompson's *Seifenpulver*"[326]. This must surely refer to a soap powder of English manufacture, famous enough to be sold in even remote parts of Germany. Just this slight proof that some things British had once been acceptable in this now hostile country somehow provided a little reassurance. But I would dearly have prized a few words with that fellow countrywoman.

I was to spend several more hours with that ruddy, dumpy, humane chap. No soldier he, no Kaiser Wilhelm moustache with long up-pointing ends for my little *Posten*. I saw him blush more than once and wondered if bigger comrades took the mickey because he was shorter than most.

One morning, arriving at Hügelheim after our walk from the prison camp, he called me from the ranks and led me to a line of ponies tethered to a rail. He detached six of them and gave me their reins, indicating I should hold three in each hand. I'd handled four horses at a time, but six seemed a bit much. He took six himself, though, said "*Komm*", and we left the gang and set off along a lovely country road — he gave me no idea where to or why. My arms threaded through the reins, my ponies following his, we moved along at a pace I could never have maintained had not the animals almost carried me.

Looking ahead at possible hazards, I hoped that if anything scared them and they bolted, I would be able to raise my arms and allow the reins to slip off. Past farms and vineyards we proceeded. I felt the weakness of near-starvation dragging at me, but determined that my well-fed companion should see no sign of my plight for I hoped he would choose me for other such outings. To be away from the eyes and curses of the more hate-laden *Soldaten*, to feel that I was worthy of being given responsibility, if only for a few animals...

All went well. At a village en route, my boss tied up our horses in the yard of the *Gasthaus* and, to my amazement and delight, took me into the inn and sat me at a well-scrubbed deal table. A couple of minutes later, he called me over to the counter to collect a basin of stew and a hunk of rye bread. I wanted to let him know how I really appreciated this kind treatment and the fact that he paid for the food out of his own pocket but, from my limited vocabulary, I could only manage a "*Danke schön*". I believed I knew the meaning of many words, but I felt reluctant to use them, concerned about the risk of offending one whom I wished to please.

Despite this kindness, the *Posten* remained correct in his treatment of me, and this I understood, for undue chumminess might have brought rebuke from the several soldiers in the dining room.

But what particularly added to the pleasure of that day was the fact that nobody commented on my appearance or jeered at me, so obviously an enemy prisoner. They were country folk, compassionate perhaps, or maybe they simply accepted the judgment of the man in charge of me.

Yet when some of our chaps broke out of the *Lager* one night and made for nearby Switzerland, landworkers spotted them and men and women armed with pitchforks chased and eventually surrounded them. When some struggled to break away the landworkers beat them. They handed the escapees over to the military. On return to our *Gefangenenlager*, they were punished by solitary confinement and a diet of bread once a day and nothing to drink but cold water.

Chapter Fifty-Four

I didn't know it, but that was to be my last day of work in Hügelheim. Next came a three-day stint of hoeing in a vineyard. How I wished it could have been much longer...

They marched about a dozen of us up into the hills until we came to the entrance to a farm. We were handed hoes and led across fields to a vast area of rows of vines. Then our guards handed us over to a man who, although wearing military uniform, left most of his tunic buttons undone, wore his cap sort of sideways, and addressed us in fluent American. Apparently the foreman, he showed one man how he wished the work to be done while the rest of us watched and learned. When his demonstrator had done about three yards, our boss set the next man on to the row to his right, and then the next, and the next, and so on, until we were all at it, forming a diagonal line across the vineyard.

The Yankee took the lane at the head of the operation himself. We all had to keep pace with him, preserving the diagonal line. If anyone slacked, he yelled at him in a voice which put fear into the culprit, so the weakest of us still slaved as if his life depended on it — as maybe it did. You've got to work under such a gaffer to know real fear; the rasping voice, the promises of agony by pitchfork, boot, or battery, the scowls convincing one of serious intent behind the threats.

Of course, put it like that and I realise I'm not portraying a good place to work; but at mid-morning they called us all to the end of the field; we dropped our hoes, followed the Yankee and sat near a hedge, while a girl handed out pieces of black bread bearing dabs of cream cheese along with bottles of white wine — each bottle to be shared by two men. Luxurious feeding, and I could now appreciate that, in return for such generosity, our Yankee German felt entitled to extract the maximum amount of work from us because they were treating us as they would their own men.

After some months of enforced abstinence, the wine had an exhilarating effect on me. I resumed work light of head and heart, wandering ahead of the gang, I purposely took the position in the row next to the gaffer. I wanted to know more about him and the vinery. Backs bent, he and we set to with a will; I felt no end of a fellow as the alcohol-laden blood got at my brain and I kept up with the boss without pausing, as I'd had to do earlier.

When he straightened up for a short rest, I did likewise and asked him where he had learned his American. He'd lived in the States for some years, he said, but, when the war started, he had been on a homeland visit and was called to serve in the Army before he could return to the USA. When next he paused, he told me that English-based firm named Margetts[327] owned the farm and vineyard — jams and preserves their main lines. I remember hoping that, if I survived, I might sample Margetts jam at the family table back home and tell them about the kindness of the company's German employees.

We'd started work early, of course, and at *Mittag*, as the gaffer called midday even when talking to us in English, we were actually taken into the farm kitchen, which served as a small canteen. The Yankee foreman's family sat us at long tables and gave us large basins of almost black stew — on the surface floated blobs of cream! I concluded that the stew consisted of blood sausage with potatoes and swedes. Bread to mop up completed a fine meal and we returned to our toil in good spirits. The whole experience did me a lot of good.

Work, when resumed for the afternoon, still had to be done correctly and without pause. Our Yankee watched us over his shoulder and now a bearded civilian constantly scrutinised us too. He moved from row to row between the vines, checking that our hoeing was sufficiently deep and that we laid uprooted weeds on the surface (so the sun would dry and kill them).

Back-breaking work, especially for weakened men, but I felt — and I was sure that most of the men did too — that, if only we could remain in this job and consume the kind of food we'd had this day, strength would return and our work would better satisfy the good farm folk. It seemed so important, I remember, that their humane treatment of enemy prisoners would be paid for in the only currency we could offer — good work.

However, after only three days, we were all sent off on different jobs. Grievously disappointed, I found some compensation because, in a group of 10 or so, I was taken into the nearby town of Müllheim-in-Baden[328], and thence to a big farm on the outskirts. Our job was to store away a recently cut crop of hay on the second floor of a large barn. In good dry condition, the hay proved easy to handle. Like all well-planned barns — I remembered from boyhood camping days — it had an open area in the middle with two spacious floors at each end and we forked the hay from ground to first floor, then up again to the top floor.

I had no experience with a pitchfork, but had the good luck to be paired with my friend Wally. A country boy, height about 66 inches, broad of shoulder and strong of limb with admirable stamina from his former open-air life and good feeding, he had withstood the privations of these months better than most of us. And he soon showed me the knack of driving the fork in with a twist, which secured a good load, then using the handle as a lever to lift the weight in one deft movement, making easy work of it even to a weakling like me.

Awaiting another load from the fields, we had a break. We'd been working on the top deck of the barn, and when I explored I found a small door at the back. Carefully opening it, I saw down below a narrow lane. I thought what you have just thought — about possible escape. But where to? Food? And so on… Meanwhile, I scrambled out anyway, finding grips in gaps in the woodwork and finally landing in grass and weeds…

And there I was, alone in the lane. But only for a moment. Coming towards me were a girl and a young soldier — and that, it appeared, would be the end of my brief freedom.

They came close, both smiled. No screams or cries of alarm. So, nothing unusual about finding a British prisoner unguarded and alone, it seemed. "*Ich arbeit darein,*"[329] I said and pointed hopefully at the barn. They talked a while and he said, "*Bleiben sie da*". All smiles, so I trusted them completely and waited, perhaps for 20 minutes. My mate Wally's head appeared above and I gave him a reassuring nod and grin; I felt sure he would alert me if necessary. When my young friends reappeared the soldier carried a pail which he offered to me — nearly full of hot potatoes boiled in their jackets.

Again, a kindly girl had risked possible arrest to help an enemy prisoner. The lad had taken an even greater risk, being in the Army. I packed the spuds into my under-tunic sack and became fuller of figure and even fuller of gratitude to these lovely, young people.

War... to hell with it — this lad who seemed so much younger than me, would probably be in the slaughter shambles on the Western Front any day now, and what might happen to his dear sister? (I had understood one word among the several he said to me, "*Schwester*".)

Sincere thanks were all I could offer. As they disappeared round a bend in the lane, I wished to heaven I could have gone with them.

A soft whistle from me brought Wally to the door above. To help me back up, he lowered his pitchfork and lay down on the deck up there, holding it, while I hauled myself up part of the way, then I completed the rest of the climb unaided.

We two then ate spuds until, as they say, fit to bust. I now had a pal to think of, a generous soul; the months of near-starvation, of frequently being robbed of bits of food he had procured with difficulty, these souring experiences had not removed the grin from Wally's face nor the kindness of his nature. You can therefore appreciate the pleasure I had from being able to give something to him by way of a change.

I still had a few potatoes hidden under my tunic when we got back to our hut, and Wally asked if I would agree to give a couple of them to George, a friend of longer standing than I was. I can't say I felt keen on going shares with this stranger, as he was to me; but you couldn't look into Wal's open mug and big, blue eyes and refuse even such a costly request. Where the next bit of extra food would come from I had no notion, but old George got his spuds.

Let me describe George as best I can: aged about 40, although he looked rather older, black-with-some-grey hair; a face which had never been full, I'd say, but, at the moment, merely skin stretched over bone; eyes brown and bloodshot; body thin and bent forward from the waist, legs bent, feet flat — the last not a result of war's ravages, but due to long hours spent on his feet as a warehouse salesman in a well-known St Paul's Churchyard firm of merchants. One of the few chaps who had managed to retain his issued cutthroat razor, he shaved when water was available and still cultivated a thin black moustache. A manly man, as I always considered those with enough courage to maintain facial adornments — men who, in contact with their fellows, feared no criticism of their efforts to augment Nature's handiwork.

At that point, we three made a pact that all extras would be split three ways, and Wally and I, at any rate, honoured that pledge. If, as I noticed, old George slipped from strict observance once or twice, no mention was made of the matter.

But something here to be surprised about: having established a sort of family, I didn't feel so much the loner with every man's hand against me. Though not entirely sure the triple partnership would work to my benefit, I found that its existence added purpose to each day's beginning. To the issued piece of black bread I must try to add something for all to share, no matter how small.

On one occasion, a guard put me to work with a small gang just outside our camp's barbed-wire fence, filling holes in the dirt track — you couldn't call it a road. We tipped in a mixture of stones and earth and punned them down with a lump of concrete on the end of a long handle; it was so heavy it took two of us to lift the implement and let it fall. But, ever on the lookout for opportunities to secure something for our threesome, I noticed two *Soldaten* some hundred yards away off to one side of the road. They were digging and, when they noticed me watching them, they waved.

I decided I was being invited to join them — I felt sure it would be safe to obey soldiers in uniform. And they had a small pile of potatoes beside them… One handed me a garden fork and indicated that I should dig. Setting to with high hopes, I found the soil dry and light and, although they had clearly gone through it quite thoroughly, I still came up with some small, but acceptable, spuds.

On leave from the Front, I discovered, those lads, who must have risked a reprimand, at least, for aiding an enemy prisoner. Once again, they demonstrated the respect many of the fighting men on both sides felt for each other in that war.

At that late stage, most of the front-line fighters were young men. On the German side, the bitter, still-filled-with-hatred, old Kaiser-lovers had moved on to duties far behind the battlefield — such as guarding us. I encountered an occasional exception, such as the tubby *Posten* who succumbed to the aroma of frying bacon at Hügelheim… And now I recall I later saw him standing at the door of his hut, looking quite ill, with many sores around his face — I wondered if his undoing perhaps resulted from those very days of visiting the good lady and eating rich farm produce when he should really have been making sure we didn't escape... "Sores all over my body," he told me, with his hands more than words, and I felt sorry for him because he was rare and fair.

I lined up one morning with no idea as to what I should be working at that day, until Wally came over to me and said he was returning to that farm where we'd loaded hay into the barn and had permission to take me as his mate. Obviously, the Germans had recognised his skill with farm tools and could trust him to do a good day's work without strict supervision. A *Posten* had to come along with us as far as the farm, but thereafter we saw nothing of him until our working day ended.

Our job proved similar to the previous one, except that we had to move hay only from the first floor up to the top one. Wally forked the stuff up to me, I carried it to the back of the top floor and stacked it. This kept me very busy as he was so much more used to the work, although with the instruction he had given me I could just cope.

Because we finished well before the expected time, we witnessed a scene I had never thought to see in my time. As we sat gazing down into the barn from the upper deck, four men laid out a silk-type sheet, covering most of the ground floor. Then, they tipped a cartload of wheat straight from the fields on to the sheet and, one at each corner and each holding a flail, they started to flog the wheat. The flail poll was probably six feet long with a hinged wood flap at its head, about two feet in length. Up, down, thwack, thwack, the four flails beating out the grain. When they'd done, they removed the straw and replaced it with a fresh load. At intervals, they attached the flails to the corners of the sheet, raised it and skilfully tipped the grain into sacks.

I remembered seeing Biblical pictures of such a scene. At a time when harvesting was already being mechanised, surely only the most primitive people would do such work by hand, not the progressive Germans... unless desperate fuel-oil shortages compelled this return to ancient practices?At about the same time, when working in the horse hospital, I had to put my back into another surprising example of hand-operation, this time on a chaff-cutting machine[330]. In Britain, this work had for many years been powered by, at least, a steam engine, usually hired in along with an operator. But I had to turn this chaff-cutter's large wheel unaided —

terribly exhausting work, especially with a slave-driver of a *Landsturm* Regiment old soldier in charge of our work at the farm. He had other prisoners ramming straw into the machine non-stop and constantly urged me to toil harder and harder till I reached the end of my strength and could turn it no longer.

Some French soldier-prisoners stood nearby, well-clothed and sleek with good living, it seemed. They showed amusement at my plight, which did nothing for my share of the *entente cordiale*.

"*Arbeit!*" yelled the Jerry, but I just couldn't oblige, I was done for. He swung a blow at me, which caught me on the jaw and put me down. Staggering up and uncaringly berserk, I told him what he was in my book and, using some of his lingo, some French, and some English including one or two swear words descriptive of his origins and nasty habits, I brought in Napoleon, Caesar and Kaiser Wilhelm as people who had always oppressed common men like him and myself, and suggested it ill-became poor fellows like us to treat each other so cruelly.

The unexpected result: at once, by signs and words in the same sort of mixture of tongues I used, he repented of his brutality and said how sorry he was about his bad conduct. I looked in some triumph at the Froggies as he promised to share that day's bread ration with me.

He proved I did get his meaning because, when we stopped work and began the homeward march, I felt a tug at my elbow and found the now kindly fellow tendering a thick piece of rye bread — at least half of his day's ration, I thought. He urged me to accept it and, as seen over my left shoulder, his ugly, but now beaming face appeared quite attractive, even though he was puffing with the exertion of catching up with us.

Our guards took little notice of him, so I had time to thank him warmly as I tucked the welcome grub into my inner sack. I had to share it three ways, but this little contribution gave me another little bit of pride that I could do something in return for Wally's earlier kindnesses.

One morning, the only German sailor I ever saw walked into the *Pferde Lazerette* and, eavesdropping his conversation with his friends among our guards, I got the idea that he was telling them something very exciting. Later I heard the details from a friendly guard; the sailor would not return to his ship because the German Navy had mutinied and many, like him, had gone home for good.

Hardly believable, this wonderful news, but it filled us with joyful anticipation — although, next day, you would never have thought our guards knew about the mutiny for they turned us out of our huts as usual and marched us off to the stables. This must have been in August, 1918[331]. Surely, I thought, the German Army must lose heart too, now that American troops had added their strength to ours on the Western Front. I knew they had been in action having seen one of their men, already a prisoner, at the historic 1870 boundary arch and barracks... Still no local signs of the war coming to an end, though.

But, that day, the guards did tell a few of us — thankfully, including my mates Wally and George — to bring our odds and ends out of our hut and we set off to a railway station. After a short journey, followed by a march, we finished up in a village in Lorraine. There we joined about 40 Britishers, all complete strangers to us. The guards led the whole crowd of us into a village hall with no bunks.

We bedded down — if that's the right word for lying on bare floorboards — and close together to benefit from shared warmth, as the nights always seemed cold.

With no work allotted next morning, I had time to reconnoitre... A stout barbed-wire fence enclosed the hall, with quite a wide space between building and wire. The sentries patrolling outside took long rests sitting on stools, I noted. Fortunately, they rested on the opposite side of the building to a footpath where civilians passed fairly frequently. So I stood there beside a small gap in the wire I'd spotted, hopefully surveying the scene.

When a lady dressed in black came by she neither paused nor looked at me, but I heard a whisper and caught the words "*retourner*" and "*retour*", French words anyway, which made me stay put and, in addition, told me one surprising thing — namely that after all the years since the 1870 war, these good people, who became German citizens with France's defeat, had still retained their mother tongue — even though, as I later discovered, officially they spoke German at all times.

In due course, the good soul walked that way again, and again without pause or any other acknowledgment of my presence, she slipped her hand through the gap in the wire and passed a small package to me. "*Merci bien*," was the best I could manage to whisper by way of thanks, for she vanished so quickly.

Now came the test of my honesty, which I failed, being always so starving hungry. Before I could check my action, I had bitten a mouthful out of the piece of fruit pie I found in the paper wrapping. Remorse was hardly a strong enough word to describe the guilt I felt; Wally had been so generous with the oddments he scrounged when working at the piggeries — many a time he must have been tempted to gobble the lot on his way back after a day's work.

I found my two pals in the village hall, confessed, handed the rest to Wally, who broke it into three small shares, returning to me a third, less one mouthful.

Still no work for several days, so I had lots of time to think and assess my general condition; the inventory did not fill me with any sort of pleasure. Given my hope, almost belief, that the enemy was approaching his last gasp, I felt if I could stand a few more weeks of near-starvation, somehow I might at last be able to rejoin the British Forces. Physically, though, I remained in poor shape. The prisoner's bent knees and staring eyes, and now, I noticed, my once-blue war prisoner uniform had turned greyish; a sort of nap had originally given it an appearance of fair quality, but now it looked what it was — ersatz, woven from a rubbishy yarn made of paper waste. Worse, my trousers had worn through at the knees revealing my grubby, long underpants, unwashed for months, and the peak of my cap was deserting the crown — I have a big bonce, 7 and 3/8ths, a size seldom obtainable in British stores and never in German paperwear outfits.

Altogether I must have looked decrepit and far older than my 20 years. Diet right back down to the minimum now, every day nothing more than that, now I had no horses to rob of their few spuds. Survival seemed a dicey business and the fate which had befallen one of our older comrades might soon be mine — one day at the prison camp we'd found him sitting, resting against a wall, dead. Exhausted, starved. I resolved to avoid that by any conceivable ploy...

No communication from home had reached any man I knew, but we had twice been given addresses — *Stammlager*[332] Parchim and *Stammlager* Friedrichsfeld, I recall — through which, they said, we could exchange letters with our families. But we didn't know whether our people were getting our letters and nothing reached us from them.

After several months of captivity, we should have been interned in one of the larger German prison camps where we could have been registered with the Red Cross office in Switzerland. They would have brought the British War Office files on missing men up to date and they, in turn, would have informed our families. But small bands of captives like us just kept wandering around occupied territories; nobody who cared knew whether we were alive or dead.

Of course, it was common talk amongst us that the thousands of food parcels hopefully forwarded to the German authorities by our families and by the Red Cross[333] filled the enemy's meagrely fed bellies while we became walking skeletons...

Chapter Fifty-Five

A sudden change then occurred which could only be due to one wonderful cause: that the Jerries now knew the war was lost to them and they must do what they could to convince the Allies that they were nice, kind, little Germans who observed the Geneva Convention and treated war prisoners correctly. So they allowed a few Red Cross parcels to get through to the wandering groups like ours and, hallelujah, George was one of the fortunate few recipients.

He reacted understandably. He avoided Wally and me, took his prize into a corner, and hid it from our sight. We decided not to approach him. When he finally spoke to Wally, it was to suggest that, as they had been buddies before they became acquainted with me, it would be fair if the two of them shared the parcel's contents. Wally, with that ever-present aching void where his tummy used to be, could well have agreed to that arrangement, but he found and kept a contents list which he discovered among the wrappings and noted carefully the items absent after George's first uncontrolled onslaught. Then he told George he was disgusted with his dishonesty and he could stuff his parcel.

Wally rejoined me and gave me the sad details of their conversation, so we turned the trio into a duo and ignored George forthwith. In turn, George responded by remaining his own man, standing in no need of friendship's prop, apparently.

So when, that night, he joined us as we sat on the floor among our paltry possessions — mine the German mess-can and one thin, dirty, grey blanket, and Wally's equally numerous and valuable — we said nowt, just waited while George tried to describe his feelings and intentions. Weakness accounted for the tears that ran down his poor emaciated face as he told us of his dear wife and daughter whom he missed so terribly and of how important it was that he should last out until the war ended…

Well, he really was still part of *our* small family at that moment, so good old Wally did the reassuring bit and our oldest member, who just then looked more like our youngest and naughtiest, spread out on the floor what remained of his parcel's contents. Few edibles, for the interval during which we had declared the triple partnership in abeyance had enabled George to feel free to put most of the goodies under his belt. The remaining food comprised: two hard, but very attractive, biscuits; two Oxo cubes; a small tin of fish paste; and an item which I would have rejected in better times, but which seemed exquisitely delectable just then, some bully beef (corned beef to you) — George had managed to leave three-quarters of the canful.

"You have one biscuit apiece, as I've had more than my share," he said. "And we'll share the bully if you don't mind." All thoughts of how he'd diddled us vanished. Wally and I carefully ate our share. At that marvellous moment, corned beef to us must have tasted as caviar to rich people.

Thereafter, we discussed the other items. How the skein of fawn wool, the two reels of cotton — one black t'other white — a packet of needles, two khaki hankies and the half yard of Army-grey shirting could be disposed of to the best advantage. The two pairs of socks — also grey, Army — should be worn, I insisted, by the two of them, since I had procured some pieces of cotton cloth which I used as "*Fusslappen*"[334] (copying a German whom I had seen in Müllheim wrapping rags round his tootsies before pulling on his jackboots).

Now came the question: could we exchange the wool etc for food and, if so, how?

With that promising sense of change still in the air, one morning the Jerries lined us all up on a grassy area outside the barbed wire surrounding the village hall. There, they had placed a trestle table with a chair. We stood in two ranks facing the table, aware of several *Soldaten* in position behind us, rifles at the ready, while in front stood one low-ranking NCO and an impressively immaculate *Unteroffizier*.

Then two officers appeared — and you would have had to see them to appreciate the elaborate decorations which enhanced their well-cut uniforms. "Bla bla bla!" yelled the obvious senior gent and the *UO* loudly replied, ending with "*Herr Offizier*" or "*Herr Kapitän*". Everything done at the yell, far louder than our British equivalents. They appeared to hate each other, but I guess it was only "bull".

"Komm!" yelled the *UO* to our man first in line, seating himself alongside the *Kapitän*, placing paper and pen on the table and opening a briefcase which, I spotted, contained some more of those *Gutschein* tickets they had given us once before. So we have a pay parade! Our lad steps forward and, from force of habit, slams his heels together and smartly salutes. "*Name?*" — meaning plain to all, despite the "Naamuh" pronunciation — "*Vorname?*" (Tom, Dick or Harry), "*Regiment?*" (pronounced "Raygiment" with a hard "g"). Then, the *UO* announced how many marks and pfennigs the prisoner was due and pushed forward some of those coloured tickets. Our boy saluted and picked up the moola, about-turned and marched back to his place.

I could see this display of correct behaviour impressed his nibs. None of us had so far ever saluted a German officer on, as we thought, good principle. But I later learned that British officer prisoners did observe such courtesies and I regretted that I had not done so on the rare occasions when I had encountered a German commissioned officer. Each man thereafter did his best to comply with this discipline, and we felt something approaching dignity emerge from this new experience.

Some villagers had congregated at the nearby roadside and, naturally, I tried to identify the lady in black who had slipped the lovely pie through the barbed wire. Careful not to appear interested in any one person, I did see her standing behind the others. I tried to catch her eye and she nodded slightly, sufficient to tell me she knew we had seen one another previously. Without comment to anyone, I did not attempt any further communication, but told Wally about my friend and suggested that something might come of it. Bringing in George, it was agreed that I should try to effect a trade of, first, half the Red Cross wool for something to eat, no stipulation being made as to what the rate of exchange should be.

Perhaps our exemplary behaviour at "pay parade" had done us some good in the Jerries" eyes, for thereafter we paraded each morning, whether or not they had work to send us to. The villagers who happened to be around at that time of morning would stop and look and a few soon approached just a little closer. The Germans may have felt flattered by this show of interest at first for, after all, these people in Lorraine had lived under German rule for 48 years and must by now have become loyal to the chosen race...

My first transaction was carried out right under the noses of the guards, though in a straightforward manner. As I stood near the fence and displayed the hank of wool behind my back to a young lady who had come fairly close to our line of prisoners, my eyes directed hers to my offer and she smiled and nodded when I said "*Essen*" and then "*mange*". She moved off, but soon returned and, behind my back, an exchange was effected so smoothly that I swear the man next to me knew nothing about it.

At the safe moment, I slipped her package into my under-tunic sack and later we unwrapped the parcel. Though necessarily small, it contained a hambone with some nice meat still on it, a piece of rye bread, and, to us smokers who hadn't had a drag for weeks — for me, not since the trip to the showers in Mülhausen — the boon of a large screw of home-cured tobacco leaf.

I had, some time back, acquired a French prayer book I'd found in a damaged and discarded German tunic — former property, I gathered, of a soldier who had died, I knew not how (at the same time, I'd taken the opportunity to dump my heavy clogs and put on his badly worn jackboots — in such poor condition were they that no guard questioned my possession of them). Now the prayer book, which the Jerry must have pinched off a Frenchman, supplied us with fine cigarette papers.

So I was already returning something for George's contributions from his parcel. I proudly disposed of the remainder of the goods to the satisfaction of my partners, without being spotted by our captors, and they elected me official dealer and *Dolmetscher* to the organisation — an unpaid appointment, which I endeavoured to discharge effectively until events separated us.

Hindsight gives one a lovely sense of "I told you so" power, and I am no exception to that self-indulgent practice. What I saw happen then I see today taking place in Britain; although disruption of life as we know it threatens, people of necessity carry on as if all is well.

That's how the Germans behaved in autumn, 1918. They tried to maintain some sort of purpose to each day's routine and sent us off under guard to do something which, really, lacked credibility from the point of view of their national interest; we worked to clean up and re-pack the sleepers on a single-track railway for which — if, as we believed, they had near enough lost the war — they would have no further use because they would soon be scuttling back to the Fatherland as fast as their legs or their few remaining road transports would take them.

They had even had some of their wooden bunks erected in a corner of the hall in which we lived, and I found myself sleeping among men with whom I had not previously been confined, mainly from the Birmingham area as far as I could judge. Lying on the hard boards produced more wakefulness than sleep and they chatted endlessly, often mentioning the Bull Ring[335]. In my ignorance, I wondered what this Bull thing was.

Came a time when the silence on my part was not to the Brummies' liking, although up to that point no opportunity to join in had presented itself. All the usual enquiries about where I had been captured led me to tell of earlier experiences in the war, but when I said I had been an acting Sergeant on the Somme in 1916, and that even earlier I had seen active service on that misbegotten peninsula in Turkey, they finally refused to believe me. All made-up yarns, said they, adding descriptive adjectives not worth repeating.

This reaction saddened me, for I realised that here we had a new generation with no knowledge of the beginning of the war who cared nothing about those who had been engaged in it. Conscripts, they felt no concern with anything but their own survival. Well, didn't we all, if it came to that?

So, aware of this gap between these young men — the conscripts — and me, I did ask them a little about their own experiences, and added my own guesses... Apparently captured on almost their first turn in the front line... previously busy in the workshops of a manufacturing maze, making big money by the standards of those times... then suddenly called to training for war and, after a few months of NCOs shoving them around and screaming at them, they encountered the shattering horrors of artillery bombardment, then they were raked by machine-gun fire, scattered by showers of stick bombs, and finally driven from their trenches at the points of bayonets and herded into barbed-wire pens... all so rapidly they had no time to realise what was actually happening to them...

Then what hope had I of convincing them that I had, on and off, been going through that sort of thing for some years? No point in trying to enlist their sympathy, or hope they might touch the forelock when addressing such a 20-year-old veteran as myself.

For a while, I felt old and lonely and full of regret for the years I had wasted by volunteering for service when I might have stayed home and maybe made lots of money. But, on further reflection, I started to see these inner moans as the idle thoughts of an idiot who'd done what he'd done from none of the highfalutin' motives which he would sometimes cite to excuse himself his silly conduct. And I knew that, later, more deflation of my ego would follow when I tried to come to terms with a mode of life to which, after four years of Army life, I had become a complete stranger.

I only had to cope with the Brummies at night-time, but one of them stands out in memory because of his habit of kneeling on the floor by his bunk and praying for half a minute or so before turning in. He had managed to get himself employed in the cookhouse, stewing up the horse and veg and coffee substitute. Naturally, the Germans took any meat in the boiler and dished out the dregs to us, but judged by this devout son of Jesus's well-fed appearance, he also had a dip into the fleshpots before we got our meatless portions.

It reminded me that, in Malta, I had walked behind one of the Roman Catholic priests and been struck by the fatness of his neck and the immensity of his behind — whereas his skinny, scantily clothed parishioners often went barefoot. No doubt, like the priest, our mate needed extra nourishment to maintain his ability to kneel in the presence of so many sinners. Nay, I now remember he gave us even better value, for he read aloud from the Good Book before getting down to the silent prayer. I do not ridicule religious beliefs or observances, but feel they should be accompanied by Christ-like living. Too often the zealot has an undue regard for Number One.

One Sunday afternoon, as I loitered optimistically by the barbed wire, I heard singing coming from the hall and sought the source of this unusual sound. Inside I found another producer of our superb stews — his face and figure full, his voice strong, his manner confident — standing on a chair and holding forth about the virtues of the good life and humility and accepting hard times cheerfully.

The preacher chose a repertoire of popular hymns which even the least religious would have learned at school, and one had to admit the singsong served as a tonic to the men. Actually, just raising their voices in song

after all the quiet and subdued, hungry and well-nigh hopeless weeks or
months since their capture could count as a creditable achievement by the
cookhouse evangelist; his chapel friends would do him due honour when
he rejoined them after hostilities ceased. Meanwhile, he had eased himself
into the best available position to survive present, difficult conditions.

At one of the now regular morning line-ups prisoners and guards alike
were startled by the clatter of galloping horses, the rattle of metal, the
clash of wheels on bumpy road, and the roar of lorry engines — a medley
of all types of artillery and ancillary units on the move. Finally, some
cars carrying German officers appeared, the whole caboodle heading away
from the direction in which, we knew, lay the battlefield.

"*Zu Österreich!*"[336] and other shouts came from the rankers as they
rushed past; and such was the speed of their going that the considerable
column passed out of sight before our bosses could gather the full
significance of the swift departure.

Our guesses came thick and fast until all of us shared the certainty that
the enemy was cracking up. Only a matter of time, we knew. The officer
in charge of us clinched our belief that the worst war ever was nearing its
end by dismissing us without allotting any toil for the day.

Assembling in the village hall to discuss matters, we shared our
elation and developing joy. Our feelings found some outlet in singing the
marching songs we'd not dared to indulge till then, because bayonet point
or boot would have silenced us. Only one *Posten* tried to stop us — one of
the old-time Prussians who regarded a prisoner as inferior and to be kept
that way by all means available — but we disregarded his efforts and he
gave up the attempt.

This martinet, who wore a look of undying anger, cultivated a *Kaiser*
Wilhelm moustache, the ends pointed upwards at an angle of 90 degrees
to the transverse portions. Always strictly on duty, he never allowed a smile
to sully his face. On every occasion when it had been my misfortune to be
accompanied by his nibs on marches to places of work, he had managed
to create an atmosphere of oppressive misery, pushing a *Gefangene* here,
prodding another with his rifle butt there, unfailingly turning a sunny day
into one overhung with gloom. More of this haybag later.

Time on our hands now. Opportunities to compare opinions about what

was afoot and to look at possibilities from a new angle: that of free men…
What men?… Free men. Who? Us… Us… Free…

That was a laugh. Armed guards still lounging around outside the wire.
Prominent in his devotion to his *Kaiser*'s heaven-given superiority and
rightful demands for the tireless services of his loyal, if hungry, subjects,
Haybag now stood out from the ordinary *Soldaten*. The others relaxed,
stood around talking, perhaps walked around the perimeter to consult
with a mate. Visibly, they shed their soldierly bearing, yielded to a mixture
of hope and fear — victims, playthings of rumour and counter-rumour,
like us.

As the day dragged on, more and more groups of soldiers passed along
the nearby road. Frequently, our guards hurried out to question them.

That night, careless of what our bosses thought of it, our men sang
loudly parodies of songs and hymns such as had helped them on many a
route march — bawdy, filthy, derogatory to NCOs and officers, and now,
to Jerries. If ever our captors were to administer the final bashing to the
despised *Englander*, now was the justification for having a go. But nowt
happened.

Seeking a spell of relief from the noise, I went outside. Total darkness,
utter silence. Where was everybody? Where were the guards? A prowl
round the wire, not a Jerry to be seen or heard.

I went in again, found Wally and George, and took them round the
confines. We agreed: we had been deserted, at least temporarily, by our
very dear friends. Following up a little preparation Wally and I had made
in case an opportunity to recce nearby territory occurred, we went into
the privy — enclosed, in this case, because of our proximity to the road
and some houses. We had quietly loosened the nails on two boards in the
tall, outer fence which, for its length, replaced the barbed wire and would
give us access to an open field. Nobody, as far as we knew, suspected our
work; we even kept it from George.

As appointed scrounger to our group, when we moved the boards I
slipped through the gap, which Wally covered once more. Difficult to
describe the feeling of loneliness as I cautiously stepped along, came to
the wire, and realised that, if we had made a mistake and some Germans
remained on guard duty, I might be shot — particularly if Haybag spotted
me. Probably the very situation he'd been praying for. But I didn't meet
him, not just then at any rate.

In the blackness, I slowly moved away from the prison, trying to walk in a straight line so that I could turn round and return to the same place. I saw nobody, heard nothing unusual... When I came to a fence I carefully climbed over it; it was only a couple of feet high and the dim sight of a cottage ahead told me I was in a back garden. Fearful of raising an alarm, I felt around on the ground nearby, got my hands on a big, hearty cabbage, pulled it, brushed the earth off its root and stuffed it into my waist sack.

The singing, now louder than ever, aided my return to the bog. I guessed it could well continue all night for all our vanished Germans cared. I told my pals I had apparently been free to walk away without hindrance. I produced the cabbage, which delighted them, and, with no means of cooking it, we pulled off the outer leaves and chewed the pale leaves from the heart. A pinch of salt would have embellished the meal, but we weren't fussy eaters.

The night being so dark, we all decided to wait till daylight before making any move.

Chapter Fifty-Six

When dawn came, however, so did the *Soldaten*. But with differences. Gone were the black-and-white Iron Cross[337] ribbons, worn on the breast — decorations for bravery won by every man in their Army, it seemed to me. These they had replaced with bright red decorations, and Regimental buttons worn on their caps had given way to red ones.

We saw no more German officers, not at any time after that sudden move to the political left. If this was the revolution — and it looked like it — then it must, we decided, be the most peaceful ever.

The guards gave us the usual piece of bread and litre of acorn juice. Then we awaited events. Lorries hurried past, each displaying a large, red flag and filled with shouting troops. They all went one way — eastwards. "*Fertig*," occurred frequently among the excited words they called out to our guards, and even the dimmest among us knew that meant "finished".

"There is an Armistice!" one *Soldat* bellowed at us as he passed by, driving a pair of horses pulling a haywain covered with rope netting under which sat many chickens. That evoked a cheer from those of us who heard the thrilling bit of news.

Wally, George, and I found ourselves in a state of intense, excited joy, though unable to tell each other of the relief from the worry, doubt and general misery which, since becoming prisoners, had defeated most of our efforts to remain normally hopeful. Although Wally had managed to smile sometimes, I felt sure that in happier times he would have been just the cheery chappie everyone loved to have around. Now the grin, which I and my parents were to find so pleasing at a later date, began to illuminate his somewhat Punchish face — his nose was not quite so big nor quite so hookish as Punch's, but his mug nicely suggested the puppet's profile.

I certainly had benefitted from my association with that young man, whose fair dealing and lack of wile and guile put new life into my ability to trust my fellow men — which had faded because of the deplorable overall standard of behaviour and of honour among those with whom I had dwelt recently. The discomforts, food shortages and absence of any of life's pleasures had so quickly reduced them to the level of wild animals with all their snarling and violent grabbing of anything edible...

Not so, Wally, though he was nobody's fool and capable of protecting his own. His word, given to me and to George, really was his bond and he expected and got the same from me. From George — older, married with children, and therefore "been through the hoop" — Wally asked slightly less, reckoning George couldn't be expected to contribute quite as much as we youngsters. That seemed reasonable to me, even gave me a feeling of some slight superiority, walking ragbag, skeleton-with-a-skin-covering though I was. Stinking pride, as my mother used to call it, can be a morale-booster at times.

So passed Armistice Day, 1918[338], with us prisoners leaderless, but not without our well-nourished Preacher sounding off in loud prayers of thanks for deliverance. Although he and his cohort sang hymns and, later on, sober songs like Will Ye No Come Back Again and Auld Lang Syne, belting them out full-strength, no reproof came from the Germans, who seemed to spend all their time in discussion, while keeping up only the appearance of maintaining a watch over us.

Late that evening, we got the usual stewed veg dished out, not by the Jerries, but by our Preacher and several of his cronies — a further indication of our guards' loss of interest in us.

Next morning, Haybag, of all people, strode into the hall and ordered us to come outside; Wally, George and I complied quickly, being impatient to get moving, rather than lounge about when we might be spotting some opportunity to slip away towards the west. We rolled our blankets and slung them over our shoulders then tied across the chest. I had my mess-can — filled with water the night before — on a string round my waist and the remainder of the cabbage in my under-tunic sack. When Haybag counted off the first 20 of us and gave the order "Marsche!", indicating a westerly direction. We set off willingly, an unusually high-spirited platoon of skin-and-bone, bent shufflers.

After half an hour, some distance ahead a huge, black cloud of smoke appeared. As we drew nearer, we started to hear explosions, big and small, and soon we saw that a large ammunition store was on fire — some bullets, but mostly shells, blowing up at random. Looking ahead with some concern, we reckoned that, if we followed the road, we should not have to pass the conflagration at close range. But when we reached the nearest point on the road, Haybag ordered us along a path which cut off the bend in the road and took us very close to the dump — and put us in much greater danger, of course. To prove he meant it, he drew back his rifle bolt, rammed a bullet into the chamber and took aim at us.

"Let's go!" someone yelled and we did — feeling, it seemed, first, that we hadn't much to lose anyway, and second, that we'd show that ruddy Haybag we weren't scared of a few hundred whizz-bangs.

So, as Haybag went round the bend — literally, I mean — covering us most of the time with his rifle, we took the pathway and felt the heat of that fire. For some minutes, flying shrapnel and such made the scene very similar to a battlefield and we all felt some temptation to break into a gallop. But we simply couldn't, so we proceeded at our usual crawl, just hoping we'd be lucky… Which we were, no casualties, and we duly rejoined Haybag on the road, feeling we were better men than him. I hoped he didn't realise we hadn't run because of physical weakness rather than bravery, and that he felt suitably ashamed of his dirty trick. He must have hoped that some or all of us would be blown up, leaving him free to go home, if such a miserable devil had a home.

Later, when we passed a farm, many of us dived into a heap of swedes left by the roadside — we'd not eaten much that day and here was food indeed. But Haybag raised his rifle and this time pulled the trigger. The bullet went just over our heads and, as he reloaded, he told us to put down the swedes. Probably, the farmer was French and intended us to help ourselves, other freed prisoners having passed that way, no doubt. But our relentless Prussian reckoned to play his miserable role to the bitter end. And I'd bet his end was awful.

Now, more groups of German troops passed by, heading east. They carried things obviously pillaged, such as chickens, ducks, sacks full of food. Occasionally they drove one or more cows, or a goat, or led a horse. The road became thick with men, all going the opposite way to us. Then a column of Daimler lorries, each with its large, red flag and load of red-decorated men, hurried by as if trying to put as great a distance as possible between themselves and the Allied Army.

We felt tired and hungry and Haybag surprised us by allowing a rest stop. Those fortunates who had picked up anything edible ate it. Wally, George and I chewed heart of cabbage, drank some water, and talked about what might be our eventual fate amid this rabble of retreating enemy troops now bent on wholesale looting.

One man near us opened a can of some blackened foodstuff, I'm not sure what, but I noticed before he did it that the top was swollen. We discussed that, but he ate some of the contents regardless. However, an hour or so later when we rose to resume the journey, he sat looking at the half-empty can and made no attempt to rise... Up to him, he could please himself.

But, looking around for Haybag to give his usual harsh command, I was amazed to see him walking off eastwards with several of his compatriots and, at last, displaying no further interest in us.

"We're free! We can do as we please... Come on, boys, let's go and get back to our people!" and many such excitable cries were heard. At once, we fell into a far brisker rate of progress, in spite of the tide of Germans flowing towards us.

However, because of hunger, weakness and general ill health, this more strenuous pace made me feel light in the head. I responded to the odd remark from Wally, but felt increasingly detached from everything and everybody around me. Worse, with great alarm, I suddenly realised I had left my rolled blanket at our stopping place. I must have turned around and, without a word to anybody, tottered back along the road.

I recognised the place, all right, for lying in the middle of the road was the man who had eaten that black stuff out of the can. His face had a bluish look and he did not appear to be alive. I searched for my blanket and found it, then felt the chap's wrist for any sign of life before resuming the hopeful homeward journey — on my own now.

I came to a village... empty, it seemed, apart from a few retreating Germans. I sat down for a while... soon no more Germans either. I felt like the last man left on Earth.

But when I moved on — shuffled on, that is — near the village's further boundary I heard voices and traced them to a cottage. I peered in through a window and was amazed to see the Preacher and two companions sitting at a table bearing hunks of bread and a large, open can of something evidently edible. Busy talking and eating, they didn't notice me standing there, and feeling indignant because the food on the table was more than six prisoners would have received for a day's rations and they clearly had more in bags I could see.

So the ranting Christian had been stealing food which should have been shared out. No wonder he looked so much fitter than the rest of us. His mates were no skeletons either.

I slunk away, thinking about how they must have left the prison hall before my Haybag group — and they probably quit leaving other men in the hall who expected the Preacher to return and lead them homewards. Maybe they were still waiting.

I did not enter any of the deserted houses. Their owners would return one day and I did not wish to loot, supposing the Germans had left anything worth taking. (In our Army, it was forbidden to move even a brick from a wrecked building, all being the property of our French allies.)

Slowly onwards... over the next several hours I saw only two Germans, driving a cow before them.

By a farmyard well stood a bucket on a rope. Someone had left it full of water, so I drank from it and refilled my mess-can. I found a turnip and a potato among the surrounding farmyard muck, washed them in the bucket and ate them. The door of a nearby shed stood open. I went inside, laid down, wrapped my blanket around my body and slept. When I awoke it was dark. I lay there, dozing occasionally, till daylight.

In the next village not a soul did I see and when a door banged I jumped from fright. Tottering onwards, resting, losing track of time, I eventually entered a town of sorts... and there I had a strange life-saving experience. Moving along a deserted street, I heard hurrying footsteps behind me, turned and saw a woman in nurse's uniform. Not the usual hospital outfit, but everything white, and a small Red Cross on the headdress.

Hazy though recollection of that rambling journey is, I remember she took me to a house not far away. There another nurse awaited us. The first nurse had spoken to me in French, but reverted to English after I had, in my limited French, asked if she could speak my language. My faded, ragged uniform had no doubt puzzled her, as it didn't belong to any known Army...

They gave me some sort of milky soup and several square, thick, white biscuits with soft cheese — later I realised how careful and wise they had been to give me only light food. When I had eaten, they led me to an upstairs room where they left me with a pail of warm water, a piece of yellow soap, a piece of white cloth and a rough towel. For the first time in many days I removed all my clothes and had the great pleasure of washing my face and my body, finally sitting in a chair and soaking and cleaning each foot in turn.

In vest and pants, I slept that night through on a mattress on the floor with the two blankets provided keeping me wonderfully warm, while a cushion under my head completed my luxurious bed. To be clean and not to lie on hard boards was beautiful comfort and I slept till a nurse awakened me.

The two nurses gave me coffee made almost white by a powder of milky flavour, and more of the thick white biscuits spread with the soft cheese. While I ate, we talked. I told them everything about myself, but must have learned little about them for only one clear detail remains in my memory; although they both had lived in France for some considerable time, they were British and one of them had originally lived in Kensington. How they came to this small, almost deserted town, which must have been in German hands till, probably, three days earlier, I can't say — I remember them with much gratitude, but it's remained a rare mystery to me over all the years. Perhaps they didn't tell me, and I certainly hadn't the nerve to question those wonderful, kindly women.

Those good nurses had known where best they could serve those who needed them. They would have plenty of wanderers to care for during that strange period when war organisations were grinding to a halt... For who would know what to do next until those who made the top decisions fully appreciated the new situation?

They could not offer me continued shelter, so they set me off on the straight road out of the town. Once more on my own, garbed in my ragged clothes, my rolled blanket across my chest, mess-can full of sweet coffee, I headed west again — in that direction, they reassured me, I would eventually meet the French Army.

I saw no one at all on the streets, but when the buildings petered out, in a large open space around a crossroads, I encountered a cluster of men and women. As I neared and passed them, I said several times "*Bonjour, mesdames, messieurs*", and they quietly returned the greeting, but said nothing else, all gazing fixedly westwards. Free at last, probably short of food — the little they had possessed would have been stolen by retreating Germans — they simply waited for the French Army to come to their aid. That was their preoccupation: help would come from the west. Patience, patience...

Looking back from time to time, I was struck by their stillness; I could well have gone back and perhaps waited with them, for loneliness already assailed me and they were the only human beings in sight. But eventually my view of their now tiny figures was obscured. Once more the lonely trudge. At my slow pace I went on for what was probably several hours, resting only briefly, when I must.

In a deep sunken lane, THE LAST GERMAN[339] passed me. I can see him now, heading my way: an officer, riding a fine horse, galloping, sabre in hand, a Uhlan[340] if ever there was one. I stood still as he drew near, a bit scared because I feared he might ride me down as a final act of revenge for his Army's defeat. But he was in a happy and friendly mood. He smiled as he rode past, waved and called out in English, "Goodbye, goodbye!"

I was always a poor hater and that farewell cancelled memory of many a cruel experience caused by lesser men than that fine officer.

Chapter Fifty-Seven

I lay down that night in a concrete structure at a crossroads. It smelt sour, but it kept off wind and night chill. I had some food and water left. Next morning — mild for November, I recall — I cared for my wants and resumed the trudge.

Certainty, not merely hope, now sustained me and that afternoon a wrecked village set my pulse racing. Its former inhabitants would have thought my reaction cruel, but to me the damage indicated I was drawing closer to the battlefield and to our French Army friends. No curiosity delayed my progress through and out of the ruins, down a shell-hole-pocked hill — and there I saw the beginning of a trench system.

Old battlefield memories returned, along with caution and watchfulness. A misplaced foot and all my endurance of recent trials would have been wasted. I stayed on top and moved forward very slowly, examining the ground ahead for signs of trip-wires, booby-traps, and small, disturbed places which might suggest the presence of mines.

A wide, deep, support trench had to be crossed. I wondered whether to go down into it or use a narrow footbridge nearby. I had just decided to feel my way down and climb up the other side, taking care to place my feet in existing footprints... when my mind suddenly started to function clearly and it dawned on me that traps would not be set for men coming from *behind* the German lines, but t'other way round, to delay the French Army when they commenced their advance towards *Deutschland*.

I found a gap in the barbed wire and entered No Man's Land, that space between the fighters... the men of the opposing forces who bore the brunt of bloody warfare while others thought they were important and pinned medals ad nauseam on each other's breasts, and used every ploy in the book to avoid front-line duty...

And there I began to see small warning signs the Jerries had placed, recently by the look of them — thin, wooden strips, 18 inches long, black letters on a white background, secured to the ground by metal pegs. They faced me, but would have been invisible to advancing French soldiers. "*Vornung vor dem Bombe*", they read... After all these years I feel sure I have correctly remembered those words, for they were so tremendously important to me at that time[341].

As I progressed, the warnings became more numerous. I hoped that, by choosing a path halfway between them, I might avoid being blown up. Slowly and now tense almost to the point of panic, I placed one foot in front of the other...

Through all the war years, I had never heard of a man ending up in quite such a predicament. Suppose, among the rough earth and long grass, a trip-wire stretched in my direction from one of those warning signs? All right, hardly likely, unless a German had been careless, but...

I could see a ridge of humps about a hundred yards ahead. Probably the forward line of the French trench system. Practically no barbed wire in front of it...

When several heads appeared above the humps, I knew that I had as good as made it. But they just watched and said nothing. My ragged uniform of no recognisable Army may have puzzled them...

I finally slid into the trench at some distance from those onlookers and my first happy contact was with a French officer who happened to be showing a nurse round the trenches. I had stated who and what I was and, in perfect English, he bade me welcome. Then, together, he and the nurse led me through the trenches and back a short distance to a village where I was questioned briefly.

Then a small lorry conveyed me to a place farther behind the lines. In a barn, I joined other returned prisoners, strangers to me, and was told to rest on a mattress. Soon I was given one of those long French loaves and a mug of hot, sweet cocoa. Replete and secure at last, I slept... until, at some time later, I awoke, scarce able to breath.

My belly had swollen, awful pain and discomfort assailed me. Movement did get rid of a vast accumulation of wind, but then the inevitable enteritis and diarrhoea took over and had to be dealt with.

A tummy too long deprived of normal nourishment simply could not tolerate the rich, sweet chocolate drink. So, both then and later, I suffered as kind people plied me generously with food which would, of course, have been good, plain fare to fit men.

During the short period of recuperation I spent in this village near the front line, I saw vast earthworks and wooden bridges being constructed to provide a wide, raised road to transport the French Army eastwards.

One large front-line area lay in low ground, but this apparent valley did not look natural, the ground having been subjected to massive upheaval. I concluded this had resulted from underground explosions, rather than bombardment — the Armies having tunnelled under one another's trench systems and dynamited them.

I also watched French colonial troops, dark of skin and in their thousands, drilling and being inspected. Probably new recruits, their uniforms and accoutrements in perfect condition, they looked fighting fit, a fine, prospective Army Of Occupation — and the fact that they were coloured men would doubly humiliate the defeated enemy.

Soon we Britishers boarded a French Army lorry and moved on to that fine town which we call Nancy[342] and they call Nawnsee, where they billeted us in a large barracks together with many other returned prisoners.

I searched for Wally and George but, among all these men, I knew no one at all. Everybody greeted me cheerfully, though, in good spirits no matter what their physical condition, certain now of rejoining their families soon and so not bothered about having to "kip down", as the expression went, on a hard floor just as they had done as prisoners of the Germans.

Still somewhat distended below, I needed no food, so I walked out of the barracks and found myself in a street mainly occupied by shops. It was then indeed that the wonderful feeling of freedom welled up in me — although it remained difficult to feel certain that no guard would loom up and drive me back into an enclosure.

I looked into shop windows and knew the pleasure of gazing at beautiful things in a jeweller's window, but then even more so when I stopped outside a shop titled "*Boulangerie, Confiserie*"[343], if that's right. The display certainly was appetising… so reminiscent of the baker's in Le Havre in the distant days of my buying trips from the Harfleur camp when Marie-Louise Baudlet became my friend and interpreter.

I came to a sweet shop and my eyes were attracted to a bar of chocolate.

I became aware of a small woman dressed in black, whom I had noticed at my side previously, looking in the same direction. She went inside, but soon emerged and smilingly handed me the bar of chocolate and another small package too. A surprised and very grateful man, I thanked her, "*Merci bien*," and the sweet kindness, which prompted her to give me things for which she felt I longed, affected me almost to the point of tears. I held out my hand in offered handshake and as I raised our joined hands it seemed the most natural thing in the world to lean forward and kiss the back of hers. This delighted her, and therefore thrilled me, and she broke into excited talking of which I understood little. However, I *compried*, as the troops used to say, such words as "*écrivez*" and "*famille*" and my sparse French allowed me to assure her that "*ma mère et mon père*" would be hearing from me shortly.

All her wartime sufferings and losses were written in lines on her dear old face and her generosity had welled up at the sight of skinny, ragged me, whose age may have matched that of her own boy, probably long dead and buried with those thousands of our French comrades who fought to the death and held on to Verdun and other vital positions... or, perhaps, the black clothes and hat indicated a husband lost and mourned for. I know I felt deeply affected by the incident.

We parted and, after a few yards, I thought to look inside the second package; it contained writing paper and envelopes — "*Écrivez à votre famille*"...

When I raised my eyes again I found myself being observed by a tall officer. He had stopped directly in my path — in doubt as to my nationality, I soon realised, because I still wore my war-prisoner rags. When I told him I was an English former POW, he took charge of me at once. He was an American airman, he told me, in charge of a depot in Nancy.

"We'll go there and feed you, and you can dress up in one of our uniforms for the time being," he said. I could see that at last my luck was in. I set off alongside him, though matching his long strides proved difficult. What with the tummy upsets and general weakness, and now the overflowing emotions caused by two acts of kindness accorded me by two such utterly different kinds of people... I was letting my feelings get out of control — and in danger of breaking down.

"Here's our place, and up the stairs we go," he said. We entered a room furnished with a table, three hard chairs and not much else beyond a filing cabinet. He picked up a telephone, turned the handle, and told somebody to bring food which he ordered in detail. Presently, a Private, or rather Airman, came in with a tray carrying two large plates of canned meat, baked beans and bread — an enormous feed, and they both adjured me to tuck it all away. Tempted to hope my stomach had settled down enough, I went at it with a will and savoured the mug of hot coffee, *not* ground acorns, they gave me when I had finished. The immediate effect: happy satiety and more gratitude.

"Stay here while we make arrangements about your uniform," said the officer. Off he went, returning shortly with a completed form which he handed to me. He directed me to take it "down the stairway, turn left at the bottom and go through the first door you come to on the left side of the street". Offering profuse thanks and the best salute I could manage, I made my way down the worn wooden stairs, but after a few steps along the pavement I must have lost consciousness... my next memory is of being carried along, not by Americans, but by two French soldiers using a hand seat — the method of carrying someone hurt or ill we had been taught to use in Boy Scout first-aid classes. Two joined hands supported me below and they held me upright with linked arms round my shoulders.

Again my belly swelled and I felt terribly ill. After what seemed a long walk, these kind *poilus*[344] carried me up stone steps and into an entrance hall. They lowered me into a chair, talked to a blue-clad nurse, then with encouraging pats on the shoulder, stepped back and waited. The nurse drew the cork from a small, brown bottle, which she handed to me, and I drank its pleasant-tasting contents. She just waited and watched to see how I reacted to the medicine.

Whatever I may have wished to do, Nature beat me to it; I began to tremble violently, just couldn't stop shaking. To complete the display of weakness I began to blubber like a kid. Then the kind soldiers were carrying me again — upstairs and into a large square hall crowded with French soldiers, some dressed, or partly, some wearing greatcoats over underpants and vests, all wounded. Some had an arm in slings or a splinted leg, but the majority wore head and eye bandages.

The *poilus* placed me on a single iron bedstead with a mattress. My friends covered me with two blankets and bade me "*Au revoir*" and other kind words not *compried* by ignorant me. They departed to a chaffing chorus of remarks from their comrades.

To rest there was all I wished and the men around me gave understanding smiles and waves. Sleep followed. The lights were on when next I surfaced. I knew then that I was ill and confused, abdomen distended and experiencing some difficulty in breathing. And now I needed to relieve my bowels.

What to do about that? One could not ask for a bedpan; I saw no nurses and it would insult a soldier to ask him for such a thing. I was worried, deeply, and did the only thing possible — I stood up and tottered across the crowded hall by holding on to the beds I passed and, when I reached the stairs, I sat on the top step and bumped my way downwards till I reached the ground floor. I went through a small door into a big yard, dimly lit. On the other side I could see what might be the sort of place I needed, a row of cubicles with half doors... The half doors brought vividly to mind the lavatories of schooldays.

I shuffled across the yard, opened a cubicle and saw there was no seat, merely a small, circular hole in the concrete floor. The cubicles had no dividing walls, only half-partitions matching the half-doors. As I squatted, I recalled that, in Cairo, I had been taken to just such a convenience by a self-appointed guide...

My door shook and a girl's face appeared above it, then she entered the next cubicle whence audible evidence of her activities proved that the circumstances caused her no embarrassment at all. In some strange way, this felt homely and reassuring. But I was in a bad way. Great gusts of escaping wind above and fluid below... Shaking, trembling and sudden showers of tears. Briefly: in a right mess.

I crawled up the stairs and then, unable to stand, crawled again on hands and knees towards my bed... where, as always, someone I'd never met before appeared and helped me; a French soldier, he got me up on to the bed. We conversed using French, German and English words and many gestures. We knew what we were telling each other perfectly and, during the following days, that good French soldier, Paul, and I became good friends.

I was then 20 years old, he about 30. A man of infinite kindness and patience, he forbade me to leave my bed except to use the "*seau*" or bucket. I must call him when in need and say *"Portez le seau"*. A patient himself, but almost recovered from his disability, he thereafter made his care of me almost a full-time job. Except during necessary absences, Paul sat at the bottom of my bed and we exchanged thoughts in our peculiar way or looked around this large square area jammed tight with beds and wounded men, most of them mobile.

My friend did step aside when the nurse who had admitted me guided a doctor to my bed… English books and weekly magazines of that period would depict French doctors as men in long, white coats, pale of face but wearing rather full black beards. And thus I would describe this doctor who looked down at me, took my pulse, examined eyes and tongue, took my temperature, and examined my distended belly with his hands. After his visit, I was given no solid food but, four times daily, a small measure of, according to Paul, champagne and brandy.

Injured-but-convalescent *poilus* constantly arrived and departed, but I cannot recall ever seeing a nurse in that area except when with a doctor on one of their rare visits. Not a bad system, though, where mobile patients would benefit from walking to appropriate clinics… Such thoughts occur to me now, but I doubt if they did then.

However, the picture of that blue-clad crowd remains clearly in my mind; there could be but one explanation for their cheery self-help and mutual regard for one another's welfare. Under stress of warfare, general tension made men most regardful of their personal survival and available comforts. But fighting had stopped, risk of imminent injury or death had gone, and soldiers could now allow themselves to relax and enjoy all those little things which, for them, had passed unnoticed when life itself was an uncertain possibility.

While not a real member of their community, I could feel their happiness and daylong pleasure in this new way of living as they sat about or lay abed or went about their little bits of business. They'd be back in the city or down on the farm very soon; if they had survived a long and awful war, then coping with peace conditions would be simple. That sort of ease and hope pervaded the place.

Quiet Paul would mix with the crowd from time to time, then return to tell me about some detail he'd picked up. Most of this I understood from our partial language and gesture system, but if it was too difficult I would signify partial comprehension by facial expressions and he might have another go or use the familiar "sanfairyann"[345] as we British soldiers pronounced it and the French didn't. We *compried* all right.

After a few days, the doctor allowed me some sort of milk food and, believing I had regained strength, I sat up, stood up, and then fell back on the bed. But, daily, I drew away from that condition of weakness which had culminated in a breakdown. It became obvious I would soon need outer clothing — my papery prisoner's garb had vanished at some point, not to my regret, but I couldn't very well walk around in dirty vest and underpants. Paul went off to attend to this important matter and returned with a brand-new French tunic, trousers and forage cap, all in the well-known medium-blue seen in every city and village throughout France in those war years.

Voilà, I was a *poilu* who couldn't speak his people's language — and wearing a cap about two sizes smaller than I needed, so just as well we had no mirror and I couldn't see what a 'nana I looked. Still, it was good to be able to walk, if only a few paces to begin with. I thanked Paul and asked him to convey my thanks to the French Army equipment officer for giving me the uniform.

I still had to rest on my bed quite a lot and I was dozing under the blankets one afternoon when Paul roused me and I awoke to see a lady standing at the foot of the bed. Smiling like a good-looking mum, she said she was the wife of a Major So-And-So and she had been told that an English soldier was recovering in the Nancy military hospital. I gave her my name, Regiment and recent history, and she said she would make arrangements for an ambulance to take me to her husband's Royal Army Medical Corps hospital.

Off she went, and I received my last visit from the good *docteur* and thanked him for all the kindness accorded me by the French hospital. Really sorry to leave Paul without being able to walk outside and get to know him away from the medical setting, I had to say goodbye too hurriedly when the RAMC Corporal came for me. In a trice, the contact with French friends was broken and lost forever.

Our ambulance pulled up amid a forest of large tents, marquees and, on one side of the encampment, a border of Nissen huts — those long corrugated-iron arches with wooden ends and doors which served so many temporary wartime purposes, housing people warmly and protecting stores of all kinds from weather and scroungers alike.

The Major, RAMC doctor and conspicuously respected boss of the medical side of this huge casualty camp, had assembled a collection of ex-prisoners who needed hospital care after being set free by the Germans. On my arrival, a doctor examined me and an officer wearing an Air Force uniform questioned me in a general sort of way. He told me that, originally, the hospital had been set up to care for casualties of the Independent Air Force[346], a new organisation composed of specially trained Allied and British Empire flyers. Their work took them deeper into enemy territory than had previously been attempted.

The doctor ordered a light diet for me, with an additional half-pint of Guinness every day — a homely touch indeed and, though no tippler, I knew it would be good for me.

Next morning, having chatted late into the night in our marquee with some other British ex-prisoner, as ordered I went to the camp's canteen tent. There, the Major explained to a group of us newcomers that he understood some of the problems which might now worry us; we should ask for any help we might require and it would be freely given, he said — before adding an "as far as possible in the circumstances". Meanwhile, we should adapt to the changed life as quickly as possible, follow doctors' instructions, and so avoid certain possible adverse reactions — which he didn't specify.

Although we who were still at least semi-confined to bed got the same food as the patients who could walk to the mess-tent for meals, I heard many complain of feeling hungry. I'm sure they were grateful for the kind treatment they received, but living as they had done in prison camps had reduced them almost to the level of wild animals and they could not change their behaviour overnight. I would notice men prying into tents or sheds, anywhere something edible might be found and filched. They still regarded one another with suspicious eyes too; they did not smile and generally maintained, even in this pleasant hospital camp, the stale, hopeless atmosphere of the *Kriegsgefangenenlager*.

When I started to move about a little myself, I came across a number of these men robbing the hospital bakery — the limit in predatory idiocy, surely. They had opened a small window on one side of the small, brick building; one man stood on the shoulders of another, reaching in, grabbing loaves and dropping them down to those waiting below. From some short distance away, on rising ground, I saw that loaves slid past the window on trays, propelled by some means, mechanical or manual. The bakers must have been taking them from the ovens to store for the next morning's issue.

This all seemed like the dog eating his own tail and then gobbling his mate's. At this rate, there would be no food for anybody tomorrow.

Next morning, all of us were summoned to a meeting in the canteen to hear a statement by the Major. It gave further proof of his tolerance and understanding — a mild reproof about the mass larceny, followed by a surprising instruction to those who still felt hungry after eating the meals provided. They should, said the Major, go to the Quartermaster's tent at nine o'clock each morning; a ticket would be issued entitling the bearer to a packet of biscuits from the canteen (none of us had any money, and would get none till we rejoined our Regiments).

How the Major financed the free biscuits issue I couldn't begin to guess — nor how he came to have such a knowledge of degraded men's psychology.

Regular meals and ample rest worked wonders for me. One morning, without hindrance, I walked out through the camp gates and entered a village. Walking along the main street, I noticed a woman, probably about the same age as my mother, leaning from an upstairs window. For no particular reason, I continued to look her way as I walked and when she waved and signalled that I should cross the road and join her, I did so.

When I entered the open front door, I was faced by an open stairway made of rough wood and devoid of bannisters. At the top, I found myself in a large room almost without furniture, but the woman from the balcony now sat there at a sewing-machine. By signs, she indicated that I should seat myself on a box facing her machine. Having some vague idea that she had asked me into her home out of a kindly intention to perhaps offer me a cup of coffee, I sat and awaited developments. But she said nothing, resumed her machining, and thereafter ignored me.

Embarrassment kept me alternately glancing at her and looking away out of the window. Perhaps she was expecting somebody who could speak my language? Perhaps, maybe, I wonder, and such passed through my confused mind, but never a guess at what, perhaps, should have been obvious... With much relief, I heard footsteps climbing the stairs and, turning that way, I beheld a girl dressed in what seemed to be the most popular colour among French ladies at that time, namely, black. I observed that she had bare legs and feet and somewhat dirty, ragged clothes.

She stood there, silent, and then I got the shock of all shocks; the machinist indicated that I should go with the beggar-girl (such she appeared to be) to a bed in the far corner of the room. Meanwhile, she, I assumed, would get on with her work and collect cash when I had been served by the poor girl. What a set-up, what a knocking shop! And what a customer — *sans* money, *sans* desire, and lacking even the strength to raise a stand. Apart from the fact that I had never had a woman and this would not have been my choice either of place or person...

So I walked out and thus concluded my unforeseen meeting with a *Madame* and her unwashed *Mam'selle*.

I continued my walk, my bewilderment gradually subsiding as I remembered that I was wearing a French Army uniform — Madame must have assumed I was one of her lot and perhaps in search of sexual relief...

I came to a railway with a train stopped and, in absence of a station and platform, several would-be passengers being pushed aloft to board and one or two cautious disembarkations in progress. Then the predicament: a sweet, little, old lady asking me, perhaps, if that was the train to so-and-so. I should have known it was bound to happen. Standing there, enjoying the freedom to look on and to share the pleasures and anxieties of departing and arriving travellers, but in a uniform I could not live up to, since French people naturally expected their soldiery to be helpful.

Back at the hospital I asked the storekeeper whether he could give me a British uniform, but he said they had none to issue. So my intention to procure a khaki outfit of some sort set me searching in a marquee, the side curtains or brailing of which I noticed were always closed and secured by cords. I detached one cord loop from its ground-peg and slipped under the canvas.

Immediately, I saw a large, rectangular stack of clothing and kitbags, much of which had belonged to soldiers of the British Empire. Although the RAMC had established this Field Hospital to care for Independent Air Force personnel, in some emergency they must have taken in and treated ground Forces. Discovering some bundles comprising complete kits — a kitbag filled with underwear, boots, socks, tied to a uniform, greatcoat and headgear — I realised that the former owners had died.

I spread out one of these outfits, tried on the trousers and found they fitted perfectly. The quality of every item in the bundle was much superior to that of the usual Army garments — the grey socks of thick wool, plain not ribbed, the greatcoat a gem of fine, close-woven wool with shoulders somewhat padded to produce a natty squareness. No epaulettes, though, and I feared their absence might be noticed (almost unbelievably, it was never commented on).

Knowing that all this gear would be destroyed or sold off, I dressed myself in the fine, warm clothes, with a cosy cardigan under the tunic — this must have been late November or early December — and filled a kitbag with spare underwear, socks, shaving tackle, towels, and even tablets of soap. I easily found a comfortable pair of boots in my medium size, and very well-made of supple leather, not too heavy. My French blue uniform I folded neatly, laying that too-small forage cap on top before selecting a replacement with no Regimental badge, but definitely of a size large enough for my big bonce (it had ear flaps too which folded neatly round the brim when not in use). My old, dingy underwear I threw into a corner of the tent, together with those tattered German jackboots I had worn for several months past.

Donning all these fine clothes, I felt warm in a way that had been unknown to me as a war prisoner. Kitbag over my shoulder, I marched away from the marquee feeling, at last, a Britisher once more.

Nearing the end of the year, living under canvas could have been unpleasantly cold, but a huge, anthracite stove kept each marquee warm inside. Its metal chimney poked through a fire-proofed exit hole in the ridge of the tent.

Fuel was brought in by men of a nation I had previously encountered only in the pages of cheap magazines which portrayed them as rather sinister people who moved in the sleazy atmosphere of Docklands eating houses, opium dens, the cabins of mist-enshrouded ships — even sewers. Occasionally, the action took place in a London West End mansion, the interior a replica of a Chinese temple wherein the vile Fu Manchu tortured and murdered his victims. Unless, of course, the great and remorseless Mr Something Smith[347] chanced to be around to circumvent him.

Nothing sinister, though, about the two Chinese men who refilled our stove so frequently. I made friends of them and we talked for a moment or two at each of their visits. No language problem; they spoke English well enough for me to learn they belonged to the Chinese Labour Corps[348], formed to do chores for our Army and, thus, free the maximum number of British men to fight in the front line. I never heard of a similar scheme to free Staff Officers for front-line duty.

These chaps told me they did most of their work in the officers' kitchens and mess, not far from the hospital. Although well-fed, they found living in tents in winter-time very cold. They said they needed warmer clothing as the cotton garments they wore were thin and they shivered all the time — none of them knew the English for "shivering", they conveyed it by illustration.

This reminded me of the dead men's clothes tent and that pile of cardigans, one of which I had appropriated, lying spare. Soon we had devised a contract which resulted in a daily rendezvous near the entrance to the officers' quarters and the swift exchange of small parcels, a cardigan for a piece of cheese or some other tasty morsel.

This did not seem to me a terribly wicked trade, for my friends needed warm clothing and I, still weak and thin, could benefit from additions to the necessarily austere diet available to an ordinary soldier at the end of a long war. So, as long as the supply of cardigans lasted, I met my customers' requirements, conscience easily salved by averring that the transfer of unused clothing from one branch of our Service to another served the purposes of all concerned. Certainly my Chinese friends agreed with my line of argument, and their smiles and thanks and reciprocal nourishing gifts did me a power of good.

Chapter Fifty-Eight

Washing and shaving daily, showering when my turn came, and feeling comfortably warm in my new clothing, all helped to restore lost confidence. In fact, throughout my stay at the Independent Air Force Field Hospital happiness was my lot, with the generous spirit of the Major matched by the all-male staff's efforts to rehabilitate us.

But decisions made somewhere resulted in us returned prisoners being removed to an American hospital near Rouen[349]. Strange that, at the end of the war, I should spend the last of my days in France in the place where I had camped after arriving from Egypt in 1916... That seemed way back to me.

This time, I was not allowed to go into town, but such was the kindly treatment freely given by the American doctors and the lovely nurses that only an ingrate would have wished for more freedom. They told me I could be examined and treated by doctors at any time, and a cheery chap showed me round the place.

When we entered the large hall where they served meals, he told me that an order issued regarding returned prisoners gave us the privilege of going back to the service counter after finishing our first plateful — up to three times if we so wished. I did this, but not three times, two proving the limit of my greedy capacity. First the generous American Air Force officer in Nancy, now the open-handed Yanks at Rouen... I could think of no way to show my appreciation of their many kindnesses, except by thanking them on every appropriate occasion.

The hospital wards consisted of roomy Nissen huts with two rows of beds separated by a gangway — quite similar to the civilian equivalent. We had no money, but GIs welcomed us into their combined canteen and entertainment hall, curious about us because they had not met many

Britishers. Some of them had come straight to France without landing in Britain, I gathered.

When fully satisfied with regard to food and drink, one could mooch across to the rows of chairs facing a stage on which some kind of performer would be doing his stuff. Certainly the best of all the "turns", in my opinion, was the American chaplain, whose straight-faced jokes and yarns kept the troops in stitches — without, of course, using any smutty gags, he kept going for longer than any comedian I had seen before and could have converted me to whatever his religion was, had he been so inclined.

German prisoners did chores around this hospital... And how, I felt, have the tables been turned. I sometimes watched them working in the grounds and noticed that they often found reason to be in the vicinity of the kitchens. I moved closer and saw that, when the cooks dumped food waste into tubs outside the kitchen doors there, the Germans would dash to get at the swill and reach in up to their elbows, searching for solids. When all had been taken, they returned to their labours. But on one occasion — as I could see from my position on the highest point of the grounds — soon after raiding the tubs and resuming their tasks, most of them began to totter around and then collapse. Unaffected prisoners ran for help and soon stretcher-bearers were carrying sick men away.

Later, I learnt that, by some accident, a poisonous substance had found its way into the waste food. Conjecture was rife about an American taking revenge on the Jerries for the horrible treatment inflicted on some Allied prisoners. But I thought it more likely that someone who had no knowledge that the German prisoners searched the waste tubs for food had dumped the poisonous stuff there.

Lying in my bed one dark night when most of the men were asleep, I heard the voices of a man and a girl, then some quiet laughter and kissing. I realised the couple were leaning against the thin wall of our hut about six inches from my head. Your imagination can improve on what would have been my description of subsequent developments, but I recall feeling glad for them. What sort of a war had they had, I wondered. At last, the stream of bloody and broken men had dried up and they could relax and give some really leisurely attention to more attractive occupations.

With improving health and strength, I thought even I might, ere long, have opportunities to try something along similar lines. Not that

I believed war had put a stop to love-making, but thousands of couples, married or courting (that word meant going steady in those distant days), had been deprived of their oats (that meant loving in those etc) and Peace would release all their pent-up emotions...

For the first time in many a day I thought about girls and all that. Evidently nothing wrong with me that a few stouts and oysters wouldn't put right — I hadn't so far tried that diet, but had often heard it recommended for older men who had failed to rise to significant occasions.

"The bloody war is over, the ruddy war is finished..." Thoughts of that kind swirled around my nut constantly as I roamed the hospital grounds, canteen and community hall. Happy days indeed and most of those kind American guys obviously had similar joyful feelings, although some thousands of miles and a long, maybe rough, sea crossing lay between them and home — at that time, not even Alcock and Brown[350] had made an air crossing...

Then suddenly, I was joining a hospital train, off to Boulogne, across the Channel, "The white cliffs of Dover!", disembarkation and off through the lovely English countryside into Victoria station and dear old London town...

PART NINE

1918-1919

HOME AGAIN:

THE PEACE BEGINS

Chapter Fifty-Nine

Like all such hospital trains during that war, ours was met by Red Cross workers — those volunteers fortunate enough to possess cars. First they handed me that ever-welcome cuppa, then a long envelope and a tag with "Lewisham Hospital" written on it. A very nice lady looked in through the open carriage door and invited the three men nearest to her, and that included me, to go along with her.

So, off across the river in her chauffeur-driven car — my first visit to that part of London, though I recalled that a lad with the Roman name of Praetor, from pre-war office days, had lived in that area.

"Care and observation" was given as the reason for my presence there. Kindly doctors spent time going over my abdomen, fingers probing here and there and finally settling in one spot. Some slight damage, they noted, from my digestive upsets as a prisoner, and the upheavals caused by excessive kindness after my return to the Allied lines. But it seemed I had been more fortunate than some repatriated men.

They warned me to be careful about my diet; meals must be lighter than most people took — white chicken meat and eggs lightly boiled came highly recommended — fried food should be avoided, and moderation emphasised above all, specifically little or no alcoholic drink. By using common sense, he said, I could avoid the worst kind of abdominal distension I'd experienced. They gave me a letter to hand to my family doctor and told me I would be free to leave in three days.

That hospital had about it a subdued air, as though cessation of intense wartime activity had left the nursing staff drained and weary. But all treated chaps like me with special kindness and consideration. They had heard about our difficulties and read about them in the papers, which now commonly carried appeals for understanding of the mental illnesses which maltreatment had given rise to in some returning prisoners.

Such articles and official advice counselled patience to families if relatives, whom they knew to be alive though captive, did not come home for a time. Some of them remained stranded in countries like Poland, singly or in small groups, held prisoner in isolated villages where news of the Armistice had not yet penetrated. Some, though freed, were believed wandering, and faring badly, among a German population in a state of panic and blind disorder, having lost a war their Kaiser and his minions had always assured them would bring glorious victory and plunder.

I had been lucky to find my way back into Allied territory so quickly and now excitement and joy filled me to a point where it felt almost too much to bear…

They let me use a telephone. The operator found my father's office number and I phoned around 8.30am, knowing he would arrive at that time, but not realising he had no knowledge at all of my whereabouts. What a shock for him to hear my voice saying I was in London!

"I'm going to make arrangements to leave the office for the day," he said. "I shall come to the hospital as quickly as possible — it may be a couple of hours before I'll see you, but I'll hurry." His senior clerk happily took over, he told me later, and he forsook work that day without worry or misgiving.

In that happy time of victory and sudden release from war's fears and tension, even the meanest employers helped to make family reunions as joyful as possible by giving people short, paid holidays when sons or husbands returned to their families from battlefronts.

My father had never been a demonstrative man, but his greeting on that occasion was the warmest ever and added to my seething, happy excitement. The family had received only one small hint that I might be alive, he told me, just a German field card[351] with my name and number on it… that card given to me by a young German soldier who passed it through the barbed-wire fence of a prison camp near the Belgian-French frontier. As you may recall, I deleted some of the printed statements on it, leaving a line or two which, I hoped, meant that I was well. That soldier must have added it to the German military mail with his own correspondence and by some miracle it got through, via either Switzerland or Holland, both neutral countries.

Pa looked happier than I could ever remember, and when he slipped a pound note into my hand — it was black, from the wartime, replacing gold sovereigns[352] — I really knew the "war's over" spirit had gripped him. We talked on for a couple of hours, my adventures of such tremendous interest to him that I had difficulty in prizing out news of family doings and local matters. Finally, he went off, brimming with eagerness to tell Ma and the rest that I had reached England and would be coming home to them in a couple of days.

Army Records must have worked non-stop trying to catch up with the histories of chaps like me; at the hospital, I spent some time filling in a log form covering my doings over the past year — a matter of back-pay to be calculated, for one thing.

Meanwhile, they gave me an address to which I could apply for money on account, and a promise that, when the combatant nations finally declared Peace (a condition of Armistice, or truce, remained in place for months), and the Army began to demobilise, money would be available to tide discharged men over the period between leaving the Services and resuming work as civilians. This provided immediate and wonderfully reassuring relief from anxiety about one's financial position during readjustment to a life interrupted for four years and more.

Meanwhile, regular hours and good food continued the process of building me up begun by the French, British and American hospitals in France, and it showed in my appearance.

My new-found confidence suffered a slight setback though, when I, with permission, visited a barber's shop. Explaining the unkempt condition of my hair to the man brought from him assurances that he would be careful and understanding. Although I felt that washing my hair in bath or shower for some weeks had made it quite clean, he shook me more than a little by saying he had found lice in my hair. This threw me right back into the "dirty old, outcast prisoner" category for the moment. But he set to work to kill off the filthy insects and cheerfully reported them all dead and done for after several dousings in curative solutions.

His charge made only a very small inroad into the quid donated by my father, but it would have been worth the lot to get rid of the last living reminder of a now past and painful period.

I left hospital with various papers, including a warrant to travel free to my home, and a long questionnaire enquiring about what had happened to me in prison camps and who had been in charge. There was going to be trial and punishment for Germans who had been cruel to our men.

But I thought such matters could be put aside for at least a couple of weeks. I intended to devote my time to the pleasures of rejoining the family, meeting old friends — if any had survived — and, very important, welcoming dear old Wally, introducing him to my parents and having him share my bedroom for a few yarn-exchanging nights, if the two single beds were still there.

Everything seemed larger than life on my journey from Lewisham to London Bridge on the upper deck of a tram. Then, a short bus ride took me to Liverpool Street where I exchanged the travel warrant for a ticket, and in half an hour I was walking the last few hundred yards from Edmonton Green station to my home.

To me, that walk was full of significance; my first time out as a completely free man, able to go wherever I chose to go, no obligation to report my whereabouts to anyone, and about to enjoy all the pleasures of reunion with the family who would be as delighted as I was that we could all be together again, free of wartime tensions. No more air raids[353] to send them into shelter under the stairs, no more stinking trenches for me. Just peace, wonderful Peace, and happy living for all for ever after.

So I pushed the old iron gate open, closed it behind me, and looked up into the bare branches of the great sycamore tree which stood next to our house[354]. Then, turning my back to the house, I gazed across the busy main road with its tramlines and overhead wires to the shops opposite… All small businesses and only one whose owner I had known before the war… I had usually bought my shoes from him.

Looking half-right, I could see some cottages, a ladies' hairdresser's, a newsagent's and an undertaker's — the last, whose premises I now hoped not to patronise for a while yet, displaying a desirable coffin in the window. On the corner of our street, facing the funeral parlour, stood the pub, adjacent to a double-fronted dairyman's place, a ladies' and children's wear shop, a grocer's and sub-Post Office, toyshop, basket-ware emporium, and finally the watch repairer.

Now to face the front door, walk up two stone steps to the old-fashioned porch — two round pillars supporting its plaster-ornamented roof — put my finger on the bell push… and set everything in motion which would begin to shape a new and, I hoped, happy and prosperous future.

A moment later, my mother stood by the open door, surprised, almost shocked at my sudden appearance there. She greeted me warmly, without restraint, and I wasn't reticent either… when we had parted, in late 1917, we had talked with some foreboding of the expected massive German attack about which the enemy had boasted openly.

Over that first, lovely, Ma-made cuppa, we discussed everything as it came to mind. Considerable time passed before it dawned on me that my anticipated massive homecoming welcome had so far been limited to a mum-and-son reunion. I'd forgotten that the world's work must go on, in spite of what may have appeared to me the Earth-shaking event of the year, my return to our family home.

So Ma brought me up to date on the rest of the family. My elder sister now worked in a factory producing aeroplane wings, my younger brother made bits and pieces which went into the planes, and my baby sister attended a nursery school only two doors away from our house. At that time of day, Pa was at his office — and good old brother Ted remained abroad still, although our father had, with help from a friend who knew about these things, got a message through to the Observer Group of the Royal Engineers to tell him that his beloved lost brother had turned up alive after being released from captivity in enemy hands. A dispensation to allow Ted home could be granted now that hostilities had ceased.

Then Ma told me the story of the German field card in more detail. In August of 1918, Ted — home on seven days' leave — answered a knock on the door and the postman handed him a strange card printed in, of all things, German. He understood a word or two from having worked alongside a German in pre-war days, and, of course, my signature at the bottom needed no interpretation… their first intimation for many months that, although in enemy hands, I was alive.

Ma told me how the stoical, hard-hitting Ted had stood and stared, then shed tears of joy and cheered. After calming down a little, he dressed in his battle-stained, but now well-washed uniform and went off to the War Office to obtain further details about my immediate future and my return, if such was available.

That evening, he told the family that, when he finally found the appropriate office, they thanked him for giving them the first news about me they had received for some months. And soon after Ted's War Office visit, a message came to the house informing the family that I was now a prisoner in German hands. Surprise, surprise! They failed to mention that their informant was my brother.

Those were wonderfully happy days, and my joy reached a climax when, out of the blue, Ted walked through the open front door. After our affectionate reunion, he said he had been granted seven days special leave when the message arranged by our father had reached his Field Survey Company (then billeted in local people's homes in Coyghem[355]).

For hours, we sat and swapped stories about our lives in recent months. His real concern about my hard times was unexpected and soul-warming, but I found cause to feel very concerned about his health and encouraged him to tell me in detail where he had been working and how he had fared in the final German attack.

Earlier in this book[356] I gave some account of how, after an examination to test his ability in English, simple maths, and general knowledge, he had been moved out of the infantry into a new Field Survey Company which — often from the top of metal towers they constructed themselves — pinpointed enemy artillery positions to bring accurate fire to bear on them. At times, those towers would be spotted by Jerry and attract gunfire. But, provided our chaps made correct calculations, the troublesome battery would be knocked out before it found the range for the observers' tower.

Hills or trees sometimes saved Ted's group from having to build any observation post. On one occasion, he said, while working at ground level, fog obscured everybody's vision and advancing German troops bypassed them. Training for such an emergency enabled them to act quickly. With hammer and axe, they smashed their cameras and other equipment and threw the fragments into shell-holes. Then began a slow, cautious retreat to the British lines. With some skill and a lot of luck, they avoided capture and returned to their own trenches in less than 24 hours...

But, all the while Ted spoke of these things, I felt a growing ache in my heart. That quick, shallow breathing... So I told him about my experience of gas shells — one in five sent over by Jerry in that last big attack when I became a war prisoner — and how the poison had affected me. This lead elicited from him a tale of one very prolonged gas shelling he'd endured, shortly before his transfer to the Field Survey Company. It had knocked him out temporarily, but afterwards he'd professed himself well enough to attend the surveyors' school way back behind the lines, and the gas trouble was forgotten, though not by Ted.

And now, at home, there he sat, panting after each sentence, but swearing he was all right... With a pre-vision of what might happen at some future time, I was inwardly shaking. I felt as if I was the older one and ought to protect him, but neither then, nor later on, would he admit he had been seriously damaged.

During that leave of his, we shared the back bedroom on the top floor. Often I awoke in the night and listened to his quick, light breathing, and heard his occasional, dry cough and felt the sadness of the situation. He had survived all through the Somme campaign, which had brought death or serious injury to tens of thousands of Britishers, and had exposed himself to frequent risks when earning, without knowing it, a Military Medal[357] and mention in dispatches. And now, the fighting over, he was to be killed by the delayed effects of poison gas.

Perhaps our parents had similar fears, but none of us discussed them. Surely a doctor would notice his condition when he rejoined his unit. There would anyway be a medical examination before he was released from the Army...

All too soon the seven days drew to an end. Thinking ahead, Ted said he was going to ask his pre-war employer to request his early release from the Service, and he certainly hoped to avoid being made to serve in the proposed Army of Occupation. So we saw him off on his journey back to Belgium, at least feeling certain he would soon and finally come back to us.

During my first few days at home, I had visited an Army office where they handed me a form entitling me to one whole month's leave of absence, and several pounds in pay to be getting on with. So, in that sense, all seemed grand. Most days I passed in looking around and chatting with the odd acquaintance I met. Then a letter came from Wally, my provider in bad times back in *Deutschland* — they'd already begun to seem like distant days. He would visit us at any time convenient to my parents, he said, and on their invitation I asked him — in a long letter telling him about my travels since we had been so strangely separated.

He brought pleasure to all our family with his simple enjoyment of everything, including the specially prepared meals — although not costly, they contrasted marvellously with those bits of black bread and burnt-acorn ersatz coffee which barely kept us alive for much of 1918. His speech — a touch of the Essex country — and his big, blue eyes and cheery grin played their part, along with his expressive words and gestures. He described to my family the great differences between the sweetness of his life since returning home and the horrible existence from which he had recently escaped.

When I took him walking along the main road, he gazed this way and that because, seen through the eyes of a man so newly freed from a prisoner-of-war environment, ordinary houses and shops looked like marvels of architecture. I was even able to treat him to what had been a boyhood Saturday-night indulgence — a raspberry-flavoured hot drink and a French pastry taken in a little shop still run by an elderly Scot and his wife. He really liked that and, to me, it represented a rejoining of threads broken, it seemed, many years ago. So it went on, with small things of no significance to others looming large at that time.

Wally was too fond of his family to stay away for long and soon he left us, greatly to everyone's regret, but with my return visit to his home already arranged.

So, shortly, I travelled over to the small Essex town where his family lived in what had been the village store in bygone days. The wide, front window was draped with lace curtains and, when I pushed at the door, the old shop bell tinkled and brought forth a rush of young people who needed no introduction to me, nor I to them: a girl of about 19, a boy two years younger, and two more girls probably 15 and 13.

I was their brother, apparently, because I'd lived with Wally "over there". Generous must have been his account of my conduct during that mutual-help period, and I felt a bit of a fraud when they sat me at the table, plied me with a vast amount of lovely grub and, chattering happily, asked questions and repeated things Wally had told them about our ordeal. They expressed sympathy, but in a comical sort of way and had me and Wally laughing and beginning to feel it had all been a bit of a lark after all.

Fresh, bright, unsophisticated, they soon taught the pair of us the importance of enjoying the pleasures to hand. What the heck — we played with the children, or talked about our war prisoner days as if in memory of sunny happiness. Just the sort of tonic one needed when the odd moment of depression could raise doubts about one's future.

Old George, what about him? He lived only a tram ride away, so one evening I called at his home on one of the earliest of London County Council estates. It comprised streets and cross-streets of similar privet-hedge-surrounded houses, well-built from good materials, much red brick, some of it pebble-dashed.

George greeted me warmly and had me shaking hands with his blushing wife, and two daughters, aged 10 and 12, in an atmosphere of much excitement. His house-proud wife commenced a tour very soon after I turned up. On the ground floor, they had a front sitting room off the narrow entrance hall, behind that a smallish living room, and behind that a scullery — that is, the kitchen cum washhouse. One slipped outside and round the corner to the privy. Upstairs, she showed me two roomy bedrooms and one small.

No new furnishings, everything bought when they wed no doubt, but so well cared for, so spotless — worthy of the pride with which they were shown to me, the friend of good old George. Here I saw a complete, compact family household, the absolute opposite of the sort of place George and I had lived in until recently.

During the evening, he revealed himself to me as a man restored to all the things he loved and valued. His cheeks had filled out and taken on a rosy bloom, his stoop had almost gone, and he smiled easily, whereas, in *Kriegsgefangene* days, he had been the saddest of our sad mutual-help threesome. His good fortune extended beyond home life too, for the firm which had employed him since boyhood had already backed up his request for speedy discharge from the Army — his future assured, then.

Before I left, his almost reborn-through-joy wife declared she just had to meet my mother. So that was arranged for a few days later, and the two women had much to talk about, while George and I shared a bottle of ale. This Pa thoughtfully provided; much like George in temperament, he was content to listen and occasionally interject the odd remark.

We wartime pals intended to retain our friendship. Yet, after the merry party with Wally's family in Essex and that warm and friendly evening at my parents' house with George and his wife, I never saw them again

— and, indeed, they were fitting conclusions, avoiding what must have been anticlimax at a time when so much had to be done to cope with our restoration to a civilised way of life in difficult post-war circumstances. We took so long to achieve this — certainly *I* did — that we left it too late and the resolve to get together eventually faded.

We discovered our next-door neighbours around that time. I believe they and my mother had already established nodding and speaking terms, but now, with the war to end all wars ended and all this relief from tensions breaking down people's normal reserves, everybody was smiling at everybody else, greeting people they scarcely knew, and inviting new friends into their homes. Given jobs for all and everyone better off, as generally predicted, we could all relax, freely spend money saved against imagined disaster, let the future take care of itself, drink and be merry...

Accordingly, those neighbours put on a party and invited us. They had thrown open the doors dividing their front dining room and rear breakfast room to make quite a large space. But it was jammed with people.

I quickly became friendly with the husband and wife, Charlie and Hester, aged about 35, I guessed. Together, they had run the catering department at a huge Government factory throughout the war. Now, already, they planned to leave their jobs and open their own restaurant in the City of London.

They knew many of their party guests — mostly female, plus two or three foremen and tool-setters — from serving them as factory canteen customers. Fine by me in my happy state, and I recall being surrounded by half a dozen women, older than me by a few years; they questioned me closely about rumours that soldiers in France used to line up outside brothels in places like Bethune and Calais. Really, I'd never seen such goings-on but — unwilling to change their looks of randy anticipation by revealing my ignorance — with meaningful looks, nods and winks, I encouraged *them* to tell *me* more.

They'd all been earning wages many times higher than pre-war, the beer and spirits flowed freely, and I enjoyed my first, naughtily titillating contact with young women who, I learned, had often obliged hard-working men on night shifts with a bit on the side. In the early hours, during warm weather, they giggled, the factory floors stood almost deserted while the surrounding fields were both well-populated and, ultimately, productive...

Inwardly, I was shocked, and for some reason resentful, but I did my utmost to play the role of a man of the world.

The succession of parties we attended following that first gay effort made it necessary for my mother to invite lots of people to something similar at our home. In advance, she baked cakes and, on the day, prepared ample dishes of sandwiches.

I felt my part could be to provide the drinks. The ladies liked port wine, I was told, so I bought three bottles. Along with a four-quart crate of pale ale, one of brown, and about six pints of mineral water, it didn't cost the Earth. In addition, my father produced two bottles of whiskey, and on the day several guests brought bottles of mixed cocktails, adorned with beautiful labels, but recipes unknown — plenty for all, regardless.

About a hundred years old, our house had a lot of very solid woodwork, including folding shutters on all ground-floor windows and, as in next-door's place, fold-away doors separating the two ground-floor rooms. With them tucked away, Ma could bring in extra chairs from the kitchen and bedrooms, along with a small table, cushions chucked down in odd corners... and still find space for the piano she hired for the occasion.

I could see this first-time entertaining involved a deal of personal prestige for her, and I did my utmost to help things go with a swing. More used to such occasions, our new friends from next door pitched in too; Charlie played the piano and Hester sang songs popular at the time with a fair voice and a style which called for slurring from a low note to a higher one... That took a bit of getting used to.

Because of long absence, I didn't recognise much of their repertoire, but I gathered that, by then, song sheets at sixpence each brought the latest London music hall tunes to the suburbs at the height of their popularity. Bang up to date with one called Deep In The Heart Of A Rose[358], Hester put it over with great feeling and appropriate eye-play. I prolonged my handclapping beyond the general applause and won a luminous smile for myself... and a full repeat performance, which I hoped the others would enjoy. The clapping that time was not too prolonged, but next day Hester called, as was the custom, to thank Ma for "a lovely evening" and left for me — because I had evidently so enjoyed her rendering of that beautiful song — a card adorned with roses and the words of that heart-shattering number: "Deep in the heart of a rose/I'll fashion a new world for you/

With only your smile for the sunshine/Your lips for the morning dew/No hope for me but your smile/No..." But I'd better give it a rest there.

After the lady had gone, Ma read it all to me and laughed long and loud, opining that Hester had fallen for me. That made me inwardly resolve to do nothing more that might challenge Charlie's position. Great stuff though the song may have been in Hester's estimation, I never heard it again[359].

Chapter Sixty

Wonderful days with never a care for the morrow... I put on weight and felt better every day, sleeping as long as I cared to... Sometimes, when I went out around Edmonton, I even wore a black jacket and grey trousers instead of my uniform. These civilian garments I had found in a cupboard and, since no one seemed to know who they belonged to and they fitted me well enough, I adopted them and Pa lent me a white shirt too, one with a stiff collar and a bright tie he had been shy of wearing.

Strictly, as I well knew, it was wrong of me to wear civilian gear, but Military Police did not patrol the outer areas of London, so risk of detection was negligible. Totally ignorant of fashionable, or even reasonable wear, I strode through well-remembered streets with a confidence born of intense joy in just being alive in that peace-conscious period, not at all bothered that some people stared at me *more* in civvies than when I wore my khaki uniform... Perhaps they still felt all young men should wear a Service uniform.

So quickly had I become used to the life of freedom that, shortly after Christmas, it came as a heavy blow, to receive a letter ordering me to use "the enclosed travel warrant" and proceed to an Army depot at Preston Park, Sussex. Of course, I had to go.

On arrival, I was told I had been transferred to one of the Home Defence Army Regiments[360] — manned during the war by older men and those otherwise unfit for service abroad. I had thus, in the course of my youth, aged 16 to 20, run the whole gamut from too-young-to-fight to senility. They gave me a Regimental badge to prove I had been relegated to the Old Man's Brigade — as they sang after the Boer War, "Where are the boys of the Old Brigade?"

Still, after the transfer formalities at Preston Park, we were sent to Hove and quartered in one of those fine Regency houses in Palmeira Square. Everything constructed during that period still looked so strong, solid and reliable, habitable and useful — although our dormitory, of course, was unfurnished, the Spartan accommodation customary for rankers in those days. But we had mattresses on low trestles, three warm blankets and a pillow — luxury sleeping compared to POW conditions.

Wealthy folk with servants still occupied adjacent houses; we waved to white-capped girls when they leant out of back windows to shake dusters… or their pretty heads when invited to "Come over here, love" or something similar.

I found myself among men all new to me, but that proved no hindrance to friendly exchanges of experiences. Returned prisoners like myself, they cared little for having to join the ranks of the defenders of home and beauty. Still, the war hadn't officially finished yet, as some of them pointed out, and our soldiers could still be sent abroad if fighting broke out on one of the Eastern Fronts — but ole-timers like us, defenders of Merry England, could sleep soundly with no fears of being thrown again into a horrid battle in which somebody would be sure to get hurt.

A month spent by the sea with nothing to do but polish our boots and buttons, and promenade along the front, or walk out on the Palace Pier and spend pennies on "What The Butler Saw" machines, did me a power of good. In fact, I began to really appreciate the wisdom of the men at the War Office who decreed that some special care should be taken of chaps like us. So… I devoted quite some time to inspecting the structure of the Pier, trying to guess its age and concluding that, in 1919, it and its amusements looked very old-fashioned and would, doubtless, soon be replaced by an up-to-date structure representing the Great New World promised by some of our more reckless politicians[361].

One great surprise encountered there made me extra happy; walking in the centre of Brighton, I caught sight of our revered Major, the last commander of my first Battalion before it was disbanded at Rouen in 1916. I had, some time previously, been told that he was last seen at Vimy Ridge suffering from a bullet wound in his head and presumed dead[362]; but here he was, before my very eyes, driving an open car through the streets of this busy town.

I could not safely try to attract his attention, so I watched him pass and disappear up the crowded street. (When, in later years, he became a Lord, he still preferred that we few, his "old boys", address him as "Major".)[363]

Soon, our small party moved on from its enjoyable sojourn in Palmeira Square to a Sussex village. Our job there at first appeared to be not really right for us: guarding about 80 German prisoners. For one thing, we thought it strange that they should still be kept away from their homeland while we had been back in England for some weeks.

A coastal railway took us along to the village station. From there a short walk brought us to the gates of a big house[364]; the outside gave no indication of its present usage. Once inside those tall wooden gates, we saw that even the extensive outhouses had been turned into living quarters.

Strange to see the field grey uniforms and peakless caps again. As the Jerries trolled from one building to another they showed no interest in our presence. We were shown to our allocated rooms — mine, a small one high up in the old house, no doubt occupied by servants in former days. The furnishings comprised two mattresses on raised boards, but for a time I slept there alone.

We new arrivals lined up next morning on parade and the Sergeant in charge called us to attention when a Sergeant Major approached. This Warrant Officer had a special message for us, delivery of which had been ordered by Mr Winston Churchill[365]. It welcomed us on our return to the old country and said that we, with our recent experiences, should make good caretakers of ex-enemy prisoners until they could be sent back to their homes. He knew that some of us might be feeling bitter about treatment endured while in enemy hands, but we must put all that out of our minds and do our duty fairly and with no malice while in charge of Germans. He believed that, if we carried out this request, we would benefit personally because in "turning the other cheek" we would be doing a good thing and our characters would be the better for it.

The SM added his hopes and the orders to back them up. We recognised the rightness of all this and I, at any rate, hoped I would be able to forgive and forget.

Yet, later that day, a man who had been there several days told me the old Home Defence men, who had previously run the place, had allowed the Germans to slip through a gap in the barbed wire on one side of the grounds and meet girls from the village — and this immediately seemed all wrong to me and I planned to put a stop to it.

So, that evening, during my stint on guard duty, I found the carelessly repaired breaks in the wire and disentangled them, hoping to tempt some unlucky Jerry to make his exit while I awaited him with my loaded rifle, hidden nearby among some bushes.

I spent three nights there, from dusk until late, without sight of a would-be love-seeker, until my hatred or maybe sour-grapes mood vanished…

After that, I made friends with a couple of Jerries I found to be nice chaps. One of them made himself known to me when I had taken a dozen or so prisoners to do work in a plant nursery. They had to shovel and barrow the topsoil out of one greenhouse and bring in replacement soil. I sat well back behind them as they worked with their backs to me. To a youngster, I called out "You work well" in my version of German: *"Du arbeitest gut,"* probably. *"Wie heisst du?"*[366] he asked. I told him, and he said his name was Hans.

About my own age, he had a merry grin, so on the homeward trip I sat with him — as the Heligolander had sat by me, and been so kind to me, some months previously — and perhaps gave the lad something to remember kindly, in the same way that I remembered my old German mate. Talking with him several times, I chummed up with his particular pal too, another fair-haired Jerry of about our age. In the familiar fashion, with a bit of theirs and bit of ours, we understood near enough what we wished to tell each other. The ruddy war was finished so why worry about being accused of fraternising with the enemy, which might have been the charge during the bad times? However, one man in that working party hated my guts and, without a word exchanged, I reciprocated. One morning, as we walked to the nursery, we came to a flooded part of the lane and, before I could give any order, this bloke — he had a Prussian type of face, which may, in part, have caused my dislike — scrambled up an embankment and through a hedge, disappearing from view. Probably, he had done this before under similar conditions, but just in case he was trying any tricks I slipped a live round into my rifle and followed him, giving the others a sign to follow me. The blighter was waiting at a point where we could go down on to the road again, though the look on his wicked mug showed that he knew what I had suspected.

One evening, when I was off duty, I heard music coming from somewhere in the house so I followed my ears to a room on a lower floor, tapped on the door and went in. There sat a German *Unteroffizier*[367], spick and span in a fine-quality uniform. He played a mandolin and very well. I knew the tune, though I couldn't name it; something from an opera I guessed. I told him that, as a boy, I had tried to play the mandolin and he offered to let me try. I managed only a very patchy effort at an old sob-song; he kindly smiled, although a groan would have been more appropriate.

I visited him occasionally thereafter and enjoyed his music. He talked of visits to a Berlin opera house and the rather stern-looking young man smiled more frequently as we became acquainted.

One frosty morning, when I had to go around the various buildings rousing the Jerries, my bang on one window shattered the pane and a lad whom I liked quite well staggered through the door half-enraged and half-scared, perhaps fearing that I had gone berserk. It took me some time to persuade him and his companions that the frozen state of the glass caused the breakage — I showed them pieces of it and glowering faces lapsed into grins when I pointed out that I would have been the injured party had I not been wearing thick gloves.

On reflection, I realised that, when a prisoner myself, I would have been very disturbed had a window shattered one morning while the harsh cries of "*Raus! Ausmachen!*" brought us back to miserable reality. I felt rather guilty about the occurrence, although I had been as surprised as the Jerries by the crash and clatter of falling glass.

After a while, two new British ex-prisoners joined our guard detail — two men who never became friendly with any of us. But, to anyone who showed willing to listen, they repeated an account of one aspect of their own lives as prisoners... The Jerries had sent them to work in mines in Eastern Germany and they had both refused to go below. To punish them, their guards hung them by their ankles head-downwards over a pit-shaft — for hours, I don't remember how long they said it was. This awful experience had caused mental derangement, though more in one man than the other.

In their absence, the Sergeant in charge of my section told us the two had joined us late because they had been detained in a mental hospital for treatment. They were now cured, normal, he said, but we must both make allowances and keep an eye on them. This proved justified.

One night, a small party of us on standby duty were enjoying a game of cards in the rest room when we heard rifle shots. We grabbed our guns and awaited orders from our Sergeant. He said that the men on guard must first deal with the trouble and they would call for our help if necessary.

Some time later, we heard footsteps slowly climbing the stairs to our room; four or five of our men flung the door open and burst in carrying a stretcher on which one of the newcomers was strapped down. The Corporal-In-Charge slowly made his report, while the Sergeant wrote notes: "[The man on the stretcher] and his companion were heard shouting, 'Charge the swine!' I ran towards them, but was unable to stop them from charging with bayonets fixed and firing their rifles as they ran towards one of the prisoners' dormitories. Inside, the Germans ran about trying to avoid being bayoneted, but one of them got an arm wound before we overpowered the two men. The violent one we secured by strapping him to the stretcher and the other, quieter chap is being held by two men."

The Sergeant telephoned the mental hospital from which they had been released. Soon an ambulance arrived and two men in white coats took charge of their former patients. The quieter one helped to carry the stretcher down the stairway and, in the ambulance, sat with a hand resting on his pal. His role, as he saw it, was to look after his poorly chum. There was more sorrow than anger about what had occurred, even, it seemed, among the Germans.

On the railway platform one morning, I awaited a train which took my party to Arundel for one of our regular jobs, repairing the banks of the River Arun. A lady, whom I guessed to be my senior by several years, smiled at me. Thus encouraged, I wished her "Good morning" and learned that she was a schoolteacher. Soon she offered me a ticket, price sixpence, which would admit me to a whist drive in the village hall; she took my tanner and hoped we would meet there on Saturday.

That convivial affair made me several civilian friends and paved the way to several people inviting me into their homes. My teacher friend proved a happy person, though strictly correct in behaviour. She asked me to bring a pal, and call at the house next to the Roman Catholic village school around teatime the following Saturday. We didn't take out prisoner working parties at the weekend, so I could easily arrange to be free.

I found a chap of the right sort, as I judged, and he did, in fact, get on extremely well with the teacher. She taught at a Church of England school, but shared the house with a Roman Catholic colleague. As you might guess, the Catholic teacher was Irish and I've usually found Irish eyes off-putting... But a good tea preceded settling down to some general conversation, the girls having insisted that we males occupy the armchairs.

Lumbered, as I felt, with the one I assumed — being RC — was strictly religious, I applied a degree of restraint in my manner which forbade any kind of fun and games. But, surprisingly, the girls seated themselves on the arms of our large chairs. So, to converse with my Irish beauty, I had to put my head back and look upwards — thus acquiring a crick in the neck. All in all, I wasn't enjoying myself, and a tentative arm placed round her waist when she appeared to be slipping off her perch brought forth a lack of response which reminded me of her calling.

More conversation rounded off that exhilarating evening.

When free of guard duties, I began to enjoy walking along lanes and across fields. Usually, I found myself in Littlehampton[368] and making a beeline for the YMCA — opened a couple of years previously, the staff told me, to cater for the growing number of troops in the area. But the Armistice had quickly reduced the number of Servicemen using the place, especially the Americans, who seemed to vanish overnight, they said.

The good ladies who gave their time freely to run the canteen had grown noticeably cool about everything coming to a halt so suddenly. So, when the occasional Tommy like me turned up, their enthusiasm revived, they lavished much smashing grub on us — and Britishers once more became of some account, the wealthy Yanks having deserted the local birds without warning. By way of earning my corn I would sit at the piano and tinkle a two- or maybe three-fingered rendering of The Long, Long Trail or some such tearjerker, the notes of which would echo through the now deserted building and, I hoped, bring back memories of livelier, happier days, when war kept things going at a rattling good pace.

More than once, when I wandered into Littlehampton, I found myself walking behind a girl quietly dressed in a calf-length, navy blue overcoat. She usually turned right, as I did, into the High Street, at the far end of which stood the YMCA. Then, every time, she would walk straight past the building and I would climb the steps... beginning to feel curious about her and where she was going.

Everything about her suggested a degree of respectability which would preclude interruptions to her progress from a poor soldier such as myself. As she walked, her bearing regal, she looked neither right nor left. Her right arm swung sort of diagonally, finishing behind her back. Her left hand held a large handbag carried with arm fully extended and rigid. A Captain maybe could make an advance of some kind, or even a Lieutenant, but me, no. Till late one afternoon...

She must have despaired of anything coming of the haughty act and this time when I followed her along the High Street — by chance as ever — she stopped in her tracks, turned round, confronted me and smiled. "You're not going to duck into that dump again, are you?" she asked. Of course, I quickly adjusted my thinking and promised never again to do that if she was likely to be available.

Nothing exciting came of it, but we met often, walked around the district and usually called at a country inn for a couple of drinks... Something different, then, to make the fairly long walk to Littlehampton worthwhile.

I treated her with the respect due to one of her obviously high moral standards. But when, on one of our pub visits, she told me she enjoyed my company best when I'd got a couple of whiskies under my belt, I wondered if I was perhaps overdoing the gallantry.

Resting one day on my mattress in my little room just below the roof of the old mansion, I heard a knock on the door and in came our Sergeant — a boozy-faced old twit, I thought — accompanied by a tall lad. "Hope you won't mind sharing with this young man," said the gaffer and, of course, I made him welcome. I said, "Come in, George, very glad to have you for a mate after all these years!" — expecting, as I did so, a sign of recognition from him... Marvelling at the strange coincidence of it all, I was staggered when he said it was great I called him by his proper name before he'd introduced himself; at which, I realised this was a stock joke of his — he thought I'd called him George because, in the Army, everyone called you George if they didn't know your proper name.

It shook me for, as a pre-war youngster, this lad had worked, just over

Southwark Bridge from Lake & Currie's offices, in the laboratory which assayed mineral samples sent in by our firm's mining engineers. General dogsbody George trotted over to the City with the results and took back anything that needed testing. I often chatted with him while he waited in the outer office I occupied with the old "Sergeant" commissionaire; I knew him well, even knew about a kidney complaint which caused him to become drowsy and fall asleep regardless of where he happened to be. He had told me he lived in a block of flats and had to climb several flights of stairs and sometimes sat down on a step and dozed off. Unusual for a boy of 15 or so, but that was about the only result of his complaint that bothered him.

I knew all this, yet he didn't appear to remember me. Feeling sure he would suddenly recall our earlier acquaintance, I waited with pleasant anticipation for his day of awakening. It never came. At meals, we often sat together and, when duties permitted, we'd withdraw to the small room up top and chat before dozing off. Most days, I tried to say things which should have made him question me. But it just didn't happen. Quiet, kindly George would occasionally talk about his boyhood times, but I had no place in them.

In spare moments, I still spent the odd half-hour with the mandolin player. His life must have been dull because, as an *Unteroffizier*, he couldn't go out with working parties — this I assumed, at least, never having seen him outside his room. An engaging bloke, he was, always well-groomed and neatly moustached... I listened mostly, being well aware that he was older, better educated and more worldly-wise. I gained an insight into the Berlin pre-war lifestyle experienced at his level; it included frequent dinings-out and visits to theatres and opera houses.

Meanwhile, the work of reinforcing the Arun's banks continued. A repetitive routine. Rifle slung over shoulder on the walk to the station, pack my merry men into a compartment and sit with them, listen and try to understand their conversations, but not often succeed — hoping that most of the Germans knew I had a smattering of their lingo, yet not exactly how much I might *comprie*... and, at the same time, suspecting that the oddball, who resented deeply his captivity, spoke rudely about me or the British in general.

When Willi Justmann, of ruddy cheek and open smile, happened to be a member of our party, he always helped us enjoy the journey. Hans, whose surname I forget, made another good companion. Both spoke as much English as I spoke German. No hatred in them by then — like me, too young to hate anybody who did them no personal harm. I think we youngsters mistrusted the opinions of most older men, chiefly because they felt so certain of their rightness. I'd bet those German lads had many a laugh, before the war, at the prancings of Kaiser imitators with the ugly, carefully moulded moustaches, points upturned, the elaborate uniforms and high-kick marching to and fro.

Detraining at Arundel, we marched to a prearranged rendezvous with a man who supervised our unloading blocks of chalk from a barge on to the riverbank at various points. That task completed, we then rolled the lumps to the river edge and down the bank to settle in the water. Then we built up one block on top of another, and gradually constructed a new, firm riverbank.

Our boss was a genuine Sussex-by-the-sea man of about 60 years, slow-talking, comfortable, and the sort of bloke for whom people work twice as hard as they will for a bully. He wore a leather strap over his corduroy trousers, just below each knee, to guard his private parts against the marauding habits of small insects and tiny rodents. His lower regions protected and his torso massively garbed in a long poacher's coat of heavy black cloth, he faced both weather and his fellows with confidence, knew his job well and shared his consequent contentment with those around him, including our German mates. The decent ones, that is, for when I numbered among my party, for one day only, that Prussian-type nut, the foreman soon got his measure and yelled, "Work you! Stop jawing and get on with it!"

No other Jerry ever had a word of reproof from him in my hearing.

Up on a hill above the town, I could see Arundel Castle in its extensive grounds and longed to slip away and explore them, but I needlessly feared someone might escape — why should they have done so, with return to *Deutschland* probably imminent?

Weeks and months passed until June arrived with warm sunshine and news that a Peace Treaty was soon to be signed. My brother had been demobbed[369]; on the first day after he left the Army, he'd started work back in his old job with a City of London paper company, determined to forget all about the recent wasted years and bring himself up to date in everything concerning his chosen trade — which company manufactured every type of paper, where it was warehoused, who the mills' agents were and where to find them... All the information he'd had at his fingertips before the war, as he described to me in many talks before we went to war and then, lately, whenever I came home on leave from Sussex.

But Ted's return to work did bring one difficulty. His boss still thought of him as the lad of five years ago and hoped to pay him accordingly — which meant merely doubling his pre-war salary[370]. Ted could just have flown off the handle and told him to stuff the job, yet no such reckless action followed; fuming inwardly, he worked politely and industriously to relearn his trade so that, at the appropriate time, he could demand a reward commensurate with his worth to the firm — eating humble pie, he told me, for a strictly limited period.

Meanwhile, I felt that, compared with Ted, I had a life of ease. Although I realised some of us must do the necessary chores aimed at winding up the Great War (as it was beginning to be called, for reasons elusive to me), I itched to shed the uniform which five years earlier had so attracted me.

However, when I faced my situation as it would look from the moment the Army handed me my notice of discharge, the shock was sufficient to destroy all the self-confidence slowly restored since my release from the degradation of living as a war prisoner. The boy who had, without much serious thought for his long-term prospects, gone along to enlist with his brother and two somewhat older fellows and struggled so hard to stay with them when that nasty Quartermaster Sergeant had thrust him aside because he suspected the lad was too young... age-wise, five years on, that kid was about to become a Man...

After posing as one for so long, I suddenly had to understand that a wartime man and a peacetime man had quite dissimilar problems to cope with... although survival remained the eventual aim of both, I reflected. These realisations shook me. So, while I guarded the prison "camp" and accompanied parties of Germans to their compulsory labours, my thoughts often wandered far from them and their activities.

Back in the City with his old firm and, therefore, close to the offices of my former employer, Lake & Currie, Ted said he would telephone or call on them to find out about my prospects, if any. But he had become so busy picking up former threads and contacts that I felt too much time was being lost. With thousands of men released from the Forces daily, I might well miss my opportunity.

So I wrote to the man who, in those far-off days just after I had joined the Army, had treated me so generously with his gold half-sovereigns and the kindly good wishes: Company Secretary F.C. Bull — brusque at times, I recalled, but only when under pressure from one of the partners, particularly the Squire of what-d'you-call-it in Suffolk. Sad to say, though, he did not now work at that address and someone at that building forwarded my letter to a different part of the City, whence I received a reply which killed off all hope of rejoining the old firm.

Signed by, of all people, the pre-war junior typist, it informed me that Lake & Currie no longer existed; she and the former senior partner (the Squire bloke) now worked in a small office in Broad Street and required no staff. So war had put the skids under such a big and prosperous business. Like many a good soldier, it had gone over the top and vanished.

For a brief, extremely enjoyable period, I continued to take my dozen or so Jerries along to the river to push those large lumps of chalk about; those we had placed in position earlier had already combined into a smooth, strong riverbank which would last for many years.

I still walked out once or twice a week with my formerly prim, arm-swinging bird, but I sensed that my slow rate of progress towards something more intimate made her impatient — especially on one fine, warm summer's evening, when she led me to the rear of a haystack where we rested among the sweet-smelling stuff, and she encouraged me to explore so far uncharted areas by telling me about her wartime goings-on.

I learned that a coloured American soldier, one of many billeted in the district during the final months, had lived in her home and become very much one of the family — to such an extent that, as an accepted part of household routine, each morning he took a cup of tea up to my girlfriend in her bedroom. He stayed talking to her while she drank it and so subtly extended the length of his visits that no one noticed when a quarter of an hour, or sometimes even more, passed before he joined the others at breakfast.

Eventually, there came a time for him to join her between the sheets. She enjoyed this morning ceremony, and tried to get me at it — even with hay for a bed and the risk of the farmer arriving at an interesting, if awkward moment.

Difficult to put my finger on the real reason for my reluctance to co-operate... Being number two to the Alabamy bloke was one thing anti, a black man in bed; a clash of some sort there. But the teachings of my pre-war mentor, Mr Frusher, the vicar, piano teacher and Scoutmaster, still held much influence within me; never take advantage of a woman's natural urge to have the egg fertilised, he would say... I also felt chagrin about being such a rotten judge, believing that what my eyes saw was necessarily the truth. The pretty little hat, the waisted, calf-length, navy-blue coat, the white gloves the dainty step, and that swinging arm. Demure propriety personified...

At the time, without giving too much thought to any of these matters, I decided to quit. That there might have been a piccaninny in the making may also have occurred to me. I don't rightly remember.

In Sussex, the fat — even a burgeoning dewlap — which happiness and good living had prematurely bestowed on me in the months after my return to England gradually disappeared. In fact, my face partially reverted to its prisoner-of-war gauntness; food had seemed so wonderful after previous deprivations, but in time my voracious appetite waned, abdominal pains returned and irked me and, despite my efforts to bear in mind all the blessings now available, a dullness settled like a blight upon me.

I resisted it constantly, pressed it down inside me. I attempted normal conversation and persevered with laughter, but it was all difficult. The officer who regularly inspected the prisoners and premises, granted my request for an interview and was understanding when I told him about these things. He sent me to see an RAMC doctor at the local Headquarters and the results of his tests led to an appointment with a Medical Board. Doctors there probed my abdomen thoroughly and somewhat painfully, then recommended my release from the Service "having become physically impaired".

I told George everything I knew about Lotty the hotty and suggested that he might enjoy brief dalliance with her. To help things along I prepared a careful letter of introduction to her. George said he would have a go at the proposition and that concluded my mild affair.

I had a fortnight's leave due before demob, during which I was to attend a further Medical Board in Chelsea, for examination and assessment relating to pension rights. So, before setting off for home, I called on my several German friends to bid them farewell, starting with the *Unteroffizier* in his little room upstairs. The rather lonely chap was touched that I had taken the trouble and showed it; although aware that his formerly great country had fallen into horrible disarray, he spoke of his yearning to get back to the Fatherland.

A formal handshake and heel click reflected little of our mutual understanding that uncertain futures awaited both of us. He had valuable skills, I had none. There again, he had known people of position and influence, but where were they now? Revolutions destroy such connections, and he had frankly admitted that he might need good fortune to survive what would be a period of bloody conflict between the Old Guard and those who intended to grasp control of their defeated country.

I had described to him what I had seen around my prison camp near the Black Forest: the overnight disappearances of all commissioned officers, the substitution of black and white Iron Cross decorations and traditional Regimental cap badges with red ribbons and buttons, the red flags adorning every military vehicle. Like me, he doubted the turnabout was genuine. It could have been an instinctive and desperate attempt to kid the Allies that the German nation had not really wished to conquer Europe, it was just that wicked Kaiser and those terrible Prussians. Maybe, but my friend would have to find out the hard way. No "*Auf wiedersehen*" for us, not a chance of ever meeting again.

Farewell to "*Wie heisst du?*" Hans… who, I recall, had told me I was wrong in thinking that Karl was the German equivalent of my first name, Charles[371]. Farewell to smiling Willi. And farewell to short, fat, rosy-cheeked "Mitzi", the cook, so nicknamed by me because that was his cat's name and he was always calling out for her. Then, quick handshakes with other Jerries who had been nice to me and a general wave to our chaps who happened to be around — handshaking was not our custom, the casual touch suited us better.

Our boozy-faced Sergeant nearly managed a smile as I made a point of calling "Goodbye" to him. So well-loved was he that I'd heard one man leave him with a promise he'd "fuckin' do for him now I'm free", but I had no feeling of ill will towards him. Finally a hearty handshake with George. I told him I felt I'd known him for years and waited to hear him at last remember that we had indeed known each other in pre-war days, but his very friendly smile and good wishes had to suffice.

Forever after, Sussex remained my favourite English county, having been such a warm and pleasant place in which to resume living, after some very hard times in the Great War.

Chapter Sixty-One

I had to go to Warley in Essex to get my discharge from the Essex Regiment, that being the last one of the several in which I had served[372]. The place was cold and impersonal, the people too — particularly the signing-off officer, who might well have had his mind on his post-war problems. So many officers had briefly enjoyed a degree of power which would not be theirs in the keenly competitive civilian market...

In truth, the only feelings of comradeship still remaining with me after all those seemingly endless years of war were for the brotherly boys of my first volunteer Battalion. Months of hard, slogging training in the Mediterranean sunshine, living under canvas before and after the inglorious campaign on that scruffy Turkish peninsula... Our total effort, both in Egypt and later in France, near Rouen, to so build up our efficiency that the authorities must augment our numbers and restore our depleted strength to that of a Battalion... One knew affection and friendly consideration for one's mates in that mob, but not in any other[373].

Still, my discharge yielded quite a bit of money from back-pay, the war gratuity, Corporal's pay credited to me but never paid over more than two years, and a ten shillings a week pension, plus a book of coupons, each worth 29 shillings, which I could cash at the rate of one per week until I started doing some sort of work.

So I dressed in a fine, new, wool, grey suit. I felt cool and prosperous. Not a clue, at that moment, as to what I might do for a living, but free and able to pay for my keep, and even for the occasional bottle of port wine which some of us favoured in those far-off days — a large bottle, of good quality, cost about three shillings.

With peace declared and signed for[374], my brother and I went up West to view the great procession of all the victorious Armies and associated bigwigs — spectators, we, watching the men who won the war[375].

Barmy as kids, at one point, in Hyde Park, to get a good view we climbed a tree. We sat on a bough, high and happy. Below us and slightly to one side, an elderly couple picnicked. The bands played gloriously and the marchers' feet crunched on the sanded road — it was great.

Then the bough broke and down we came. Thankfully, the old couple were unhurt, only scared, as the grandpa proved via his shouted opinion that our parents had conceived us in sin.

We dashed from place to place to catch up with different parts of the show — we saw Queen Alexandra[376] close-up and confirmed what we had read about her beautiful make-up — and generally had a fine old time.

Thus, we reckoned, we had completed our long connection with the forces of war and could now consider ourselves personally at peace.

At a stroke, my brother had already translated himself from a war-stained, mentioned-in-despatches-Military-Medal-you've-done-your-bit-thankyou-very-much-goodbye ex-soldier into a City gent. Now, on work days, garbed in a blue, pin-striped, well-cut suit with plenty of shirt cuff showing below the fashionable, rather short sleeves, fawn spats, and a dark, fur Homburg hat, he carried a light, knobbly cane or, if the papers forecast rain, a rolled umbrella.

Somehow, Ted had avoided contact with Army doctors, and so left the Service with what I knew to be a serious lung condition caused by a lengthy exposure to war gas; his breathing remained quicker and shallower than it should have been... He still made nothing of it, though, and, as his work demanded no physical effort, he could cover up his disability.

Above all, he wanted no further connection with anything military. Mass murder to no observable purpose had sickened and saddened him. So he threw himself into his business activities.

Unskilled me had no high-falutin' notions as to my prospects, but I was convinced that one method of turning an honest penny would eventually provide me with the price of a crust and a cuppa — to wit, buying something cheaply, adding a modest margin to its cost price, and flogging it. Many days, many failures, and a lot of physical distress were to come my way, but youth was on my side.

It seems such a shame that one must cut loose from boyhood, but the

years of adolescence had been consumed in playing at being a soldier and
a man. And now it was all finished, I really had attained the official status
of manhood.

I was just 21.

Editor's Afterword

What happened next?

My father's aching conviction that, "the fighting over", his beloved brother Ted — Philip, really — "was to be killed by the delayed effects of poison gas" proved true. Despite the buoyant energy and optimism with which Ted approached his new life post-war, he died of tuberculosis on January 26, 1922, aged 25. The family nursed him at home, his mother and my father at his bedside when he died (and, 25 years later, my parents named me after him).

When it came to earning a living, my father did indeed pursue his notion that, unskilled and modestly educated though he was, "buying something cheaply, adding a modest margin to its cost price, and flogging it" might provide him with "the price of a crust and a cuppa". With his younger brother, Alf, he got a stall in Edmonton market, selling cloth.

Although based there, after a while they bought a van and travelled to markets as far north as Yorkshire. A Socialist of some sort, at least until about 1950 when he got cynical and turned Tory, during the '30s my father enlisted most of his fellow market traders, self-employed "barrow boys", to form a rather unusual trade union branch. The brothers' drapery business continued after World War II when they rented a small shop, still in Edmonton. And Dad never travelled abroad again after 1918...

But here I must add that the slight research induced by working on this memoir threw up a few surprises and mysteries which, at least, add questions and uncertainties to my view of my father and the family. Chiefly, two uncles I never knew existed! From what Dad told me, I thought he had four siblings, Ciss, Ted, Alf and Edie. But census, baptism and death index records show:

a) my paternal grandparents had another child who died, probably before

1911, name, boy or girl, age at death, not recorded — I'd guess a baby who didn't long survive birth, but I don't know.

b) they had another child, John Fleetwood, born April 1, 1911, died July 12, 1912 — cause "Debility from Birth Exhaustion" (a common, vague diagnosis in cases of perinatal and infant mortality then; it might today translate as "failure to thrive").

c) they had a son called Frank Sydney (or Sidney on some documents), born in Manchester, June 5, 1900, died October 9, 1912, of diphtheria at the Enfield and Edmonton Joint Isolation Hospital.

I gather this sort of thing is a normal shock to people researching their ancestors. I found myself surprised that my father, who told me so much and didn't hold back memories that embarrassed, shamed or pained him, never mentioned to me these three siblings who died young. Perhaps he did talk to my mother about them, I don't know.

Well, a shrug deals with the retrospective, personal side of it; although I thought he told me "everything", he didn't have to, it's fine. But it set me thinking about my father, aged 14, just leaving school when, within six months, a baby sister is born (Edie, that May), a toddler brother dies and his 12-year-old brother goes too... although my father hero-worshipped Ted and spent a lot of time with him, Frank must have been Dad's playmate often, whether they got on or not; and Dad never spoke of him to me and, in the memoir, Frank remained so anonymous that until recently I never realised he was there, thinking the few early "younger brother" references meant Alf.

Well, Dad's silence on these matters can only remain a mystery, a matter for clueless speculation on my part — the odd sensation of absorbing this new knowledge utterly outweighed, in due course, by thankfulness that he did tell me so much about his life, to 1919 and, in conversation, way beyond.

But it set me thinking about my grandparents too, what they went through. Three children dying one after the other. Frank 12, and presumed past "the worst", I guess. A new baby born in the middle of all that. Then, two years on, two older sons coming home from a purported normal day's work to say they'd enlisted under age and were off to a war which already, in autumn 1914, had killed and maimed tens of thousands... grief, fear, worry...

I'm imagining Dad's mild, battered father, Charles Philip, his volatile, often angry mother, Lily Emma, struggling through lives that "came down in the world" and never got back up to anything like the manner they'd been accustomed to and, still, while often ashamed or angry, never giving up, always trying to look after their children, put food on the table, clothes on their back, "maintain appearances" of some sort... and then, the war survived without further losses, their oldest boy disappears in front of their eyes, wastes away, the war still killing him. (Ted's death certificate shows "Pulmonary tubercle" as the primary cause, and "Marasmus" as the secondary — meaning emaciation usually associated with malnutrition but, in his case, the effect of poison gas and disease.)

So, apart from that, what happened next?

Ah, sex. Despite the earnest teachings of the good Scout/choirmaster Rev Mr "Frusher" — another thin alias, I never saw his real name written down, but my father pronounced it "Croosher", so that may have been a politened way of saying "Crusher" — during one chortling school-holiday chat my father did admit he finally lost his cherry, and long before he married, in the early '20s, I think; essentially, he lay ill in bed at home and his then girlfriend came round to express her sympathies in the very warmest way.

That resolved, he seems to have proceeded without further inhibition; my mother told me that, when they got together, she realised he was "very experienced"; also, that when Dad took her home for the first time, his mother glared down at her from the top of the stairs and hissed "He's *mine*!" — which puts me in mind of that day, in Chapter 11, when Ted's and my father's sort-of girlfriends came to their house and the boys' mother drove them away, calling them "Hussies" and such... but also, now, of everything she'd lost, how she kept on losing for the last 40 years of her life... Even the mild, kind, sad husband she often scorned died in late 1927.

My parents married in December, 1939, the day before Ma's 22nd birthday, when my father was 41, and the "phoney" phase of World War II in the UK had been on the go — that is, nothing much happening — for about 11 weeks. They lived in my mother's father's house on a suburban street in New Southgate, north London, a three-bedroom bungalow with garden all round it; the old man, Albert, who died when I was three, had done all right as a painter and decorator. We stayed in the bungalow until 1968.

Well before they married, my parents joined an ambulance unit of the Civil Defence. Some years earlier, my father had read *Mein Kampf*, in translation. Partly because, in the rag trade, he did business with Jewish people all the time and heard from them what was happening to their relatives in Nazi Germany, he realised Hitler meant every syllable and he started preparing himself. In accordance with his decision never to fight and kill again after his experiences in the trenches near Arras (alluded to in Part Seven, Chapter Forty-Nine, the first paragraph of the sub-section headed "Murder"), in due course, he trained to a high grade in first aid, readying himself to serve as what we'd now call a paramedic.

He'd actually known my mother (Violet Mona Irene Muir — always known as Mona — born December 18, 1917, 74, Queens Road, Bounds Green, London N11), through her family, when she was a small girl, but he lost touch with them for some years. However, when they met again in the late '30s, they fell in love for life.

She studied first aid too and joined him in the Civil Defence; throughout the Blitz, they drove ambulances, helped get people out of bombed buildings, tended their injuries and rushed them to hospital. They made music together too, as members of a Civil Defence concert party which travelled around London entertaining any local group that could organise a venue for a show and a knees-up; Dad played piano and accordion, Ma sang the hits of the day (both of them very good at it — I saw them in action during the '50s at holiday camp talent nights in Devon, Ma sounding rather like Vera Lynn, Dad the most responsive of accompanists, if blushful when she sang Mr Wonderful to him).

Then came me, in 1947. They hadn't wanted to bring a child into the war, nor into an England which might be overrun by Nazis. As a kid, I watched them regularly argue then sort it out, so blazing rows never bothered me too much. In 1955, Dad had the cancer operation mentioned in the foreword and that changed everything. An unusually old, but very fit father became limited in what he could do with me — the eternal upside being that, instead, during school holidays, we did the housework and talked (as per the Foreword).

Meanwhile, the drapery shop went down and so did our income as, I remember, the wage my father paid himself peaked at a comfortable

£14 10s, then stopped altogether, and my mother started training as a telephonist on less than £9 a week. Later, she joined the Civil Service, proud of herself for coming third nationwide in that round of exams — like my father, she'd had to leave school young, for lack of money (more like paternal meanness in her case), when her ability would have led her who knows where?

Once, because of a problem with the fading business, we had to borrow a lot of money from a family friend; we didn't have a phone at home, so Ma took me to a call box at the end of the road — she had an instinct that I should know about most things, no matter how weighty — and, feeding old pennies into the slot, she asked my "Uncle" Rick if we could borrow £350. Knowing all about my father's illness, he said yes immediately, and made her promise we would never try to pay it back (he was rich by our standards and, as you see, blindingly good-hearted).

Something else that goes to show... My father's surgery left him with a permanent colostomy and, when he came home after about two months in Barnet General Hospital, one evening my mother came into my bedroom and started explaining what had happened. The cancer, the details of the operation, what a colostomy was.

Then she said that, a day or two earlier, Dad had asked her to come into the bathroom because he needed to show her "what they've done to me". He took his clothes off and she looked and said it was all right and put her arms around him and he cried. I was eight and I hadn't seen him cry, had no idea that he ever would, though much later I did see him weep a little once or twice, probably when we talked about age and death and how Ma had cared for him through all his years of pain... But what I meant to say was that I understood what she said and acted accordingly — never had any difficulty in doing so, in fact.

I was at home in London when my mother rang to say that Dad had died, suddenly in a sense, without more than a couple of hours of distress, taken by "the old man's friend", pneumonia, aged 88. Nobody of any importance.

In memoriam, and for the record: Sam Sutcliffe died in 1987, Mona Sutcliffe 1999, Charles Philip Sutcliffe 1927, Lilly Emma Sutcliffe probably in the late '40s (I can't track her death certificate, but I have a very nice letter from her to my mother congratulating her on my birth), and their other children, Ciss probably 1972, Alf 1968, Edie probably 1985.

THANKS TO

Sam and Mona Sutcliffe for all the above — and life itself, of course.

Gay Lee, my wife, for everything, but also for supporting me in my old age — and for a lot of proofreading.

Hina Pandya, our friend, a pro freelance journo, for patiently explaining — and executing — all sorts of techie and business stuff about e-books; also for designing the cover and everything else in my father's memoir that needed designing.

Hilary and Kelsey Thornton, friends who'd done some people/ancestor tracking of their own — Kelsey's a proper historian! — and volunteered online research about my family and advice on how to pursue further enquiries. Furthermore, they both actually read the book and diligently sent me errata, now corrected. Above and beyond and their reward is... much editorial gratitude.

Melanie Geraghty, our friend in Malta, for the guided tour of my father's old haunts and some information — such as Maltese spellings — hard to find on line.

Liz Lee, my sister-in-law in Arundel, for her endeavours to find out where that nearby WWI POW camp from Part Nine was located — even though nothing definite emerged from her enquiries. Little bits of history do get oddly lost.

Ancestry.co.uk for information provided, but also for the most helpful, human support service I've ever encountered from any online operation in any sphere (hats off to Leanne).

Ian Hook, Keeper of the Essex Regiment Museum, for his remarkably prompt research in his archives to fill in several details of my father's WWI Army life which had previously remained enigmatic.

The National Union of Journalists who've always had my back.

The British Red Cross, as recipient's of all e-book author/editor royalties and print version "profits" (my father's as inherited by only-son me) for their helpful approach and kind welcome for an enterprise that will probably turn out to be worth very little money to them, but offers an association that would have been much appreciated by my father.

Phil Sutcliffe

Afterword Pictures

Mona Sutcliffe, 1938, on Beachy Head, Sussex.
(picture by Sam Sutcliffe)

Sam and Mona Sutcliffe, 1938/9 — my mother's note on the back of the photo says "1938-9, just before or just after we married".

Phil and Sam Sutcliffe, 1950/51, at home in New Southgate.(picture by Phil's cousin David Bevan)

*Phil and Sam Sutcliffe, 1955, on holiday in Brixham, Devon,
just before Sam's cancer diagnosis and surgery*

Mona and Sam Sutcliffe, 1967, near their new home in Devon.

Sam Sutcliffe circa 1975, in his seventies,
during the time when he wrote this memoir

ENDNOTES

[1] My father dated this period of his childhood memories a full four years later, but I corrected it in the text to avoid confusion; information from the 1901 census and 1902 baptism records prove his memory at fault, for once, by showing the family had moved to London by then — I guess he made this mistake because he just couldn't believe he could remember anything with such clarity from the age of two... but he did!

[2] My father was born on July 6, 1898, at 53, Great Cheetham Street, Broughton, Manchester. In this memoir, he hardly used his siblings names (except for Philip/"Ted"/"George", of whom more later), but, as of 1900, they were: Dorothy (always known as "Ciss"), born December 3, 1894, at 49, Great Cheetham Street; Philip Broughton, born October 15, 1896, at 53 Great Cheetham Street (I don't know why the street number differs for Ciss's birth — perhaps the family owned two adjacent properties in their financial heyday); Frank Sidney (or Sydney, spellings vary on official documents), born June 5, 1900, at 5, Vernon Place, West Gorton, Manchester (see Afterword for a little more about him). Their parents were Charles Philip, born April 29, 1864, at 132, Elizabeth Street, Cheetham, Manchester, and Lily Emma, née Fleetwood, born August 18, 1872, in Lincolnshire (though one record shows this as her baptism, not birth date; birth certificate not retrievable) — they married on May 2, 1894, so Dorothy/Ciss must have been born prematurely, maybe. Broughton was a prosperous part of Salford; I never heard it mentioned that my Uncle Philip's name came from his birthplace, I understood it was a "family name".

[3] The census of March 31, 1901, shows they then lived in Albert Place, Longsight, Manchester. Although these changes of address reflect the family "coming down in the world", the neighbouring districts of Gorton

and Longsight could apparently both be described as "middle-class" around that time.

[4] The Minories: a district (former parish) and street near the Tower of London.

[5] This address was probably the one shown on a baptism record for September, 1902: 24 Vale Side, Eade Road, Tottenham, London N4, between Stroud Green and Stamford Hill (London postal districts with numbers were actually introduced in 1917 and replaced by the current postcodes nationally from 1959 onwards).

[6] This is the first time my father called "the boy" (himself) "Tommy" — no doubt thinking of what was to come and the long-standing generic nickname for a British soldier, "Tommy Atkins"; Wikipedia notes its first documented appearance as in 1743, and that it seems to have gone official in 1815 when the War Office adopted it for specimen forms showing how the soldier's pocket book should be filled out (to ensure his pay came through, among other things); in 1892, Rudyard Kipling dedicated his *Barrack-Room Ballads* "To T.A." and the book included a poem called Tommy, a protest from the archetypal soldier about how civilians disrespect him until they need protection or a war's declared: "for it's Tommy this, an' Tommy that, an' 'chuck 'im out, the brute!'/But it's 'saviour of 'is country' when the guns begin to shoot;/An' it's Tommy this, an' Tommy that, an' anything you please;/An' Tommy ain't a bloomin' fool — you bet that Tommy sees!"; the following year, perhaps reacting to Kipling, lyricist Henry Hamilton and S Potter (I can't find his first name) wrote a straightforwardly patriotic music hall song called Private Tommy Atkins, see http://www.halhkmusic.com/gaietygirl/agg11.html — "By Union Jack above you!/But we're proud of you and love you".

[7] Edmonton, probably at the address shown in the 1911 census, 26, Lowden Road, Edmonton (now N9).

[8] UK "old money"; until decimalisation in 1971, the pound sterling divided into 240 pennies — symbolised by the "d" in "lsd" — and 20 shillings, ergo 12d to the shilling, but... a penny further divided into halfpennies and farthings (quarterpennies). Prices would be written out as, for example, £3 4s 6d or, for shillings and pence 2/9, spoken as "Three pounds four and six" or "two and nine"; the "lsd" tag descended somehow from the Latin, "librae solidi denarii" long before the 1940s development of the hallucinogenic gave rise to punning possibilities.

[9] Alfred Brotherton (the middle name came from his grandfather, Samuel Brotherton Sutcliffe), born 1903, at the Eade Road address; Alf hardly gets a mention in my father's memoir except as "the baby", but (in due course, don't jump the gun!) see the Afterword for more on their later, lifelong business partnership — also for more on similarly anonymous brother Sidney.

[10] A toy — except for professional use by dog trainers — spherical with a hole through the middle; when placed in the mouth it produces various notes when air is blown or sucked through it.

[11] Hertford Road, which started at Bishopsgate; later the A1010.

[12] Records for the parish of St. Olave, Woodberry Down, Middlesex, discovered via ancestry.co.uk show four children baptised on September 17, 1902: Dorothy, Philip Broughton, Charles Samuel, and Frank Sidney.

[13] The mission church movement within London began about 1880; maybe the "tin church" was what www.british-history.ac.uk/report.aspx?compid=26941 describes as the "iron room" put up in 1904 on the northern side of Malden Road, Edmonton, but there seem to have been several others in the district.

[14] The river is the Lea, probably in the vicinity of what's now known as Pickett's Lock; I can't find the name of the canal.

[15] No forests in Edmonton now, nor even woods, and I can't find any reference on "old Edmonton" sites to suggest where this one might have been.

[16] For example, backslang created "yob" by reversing "boy"; "pot of beer" became "top o' reeb", "tobacco" "occabot"; at http://www.victorianweb.org/history/slang2.html (The Victorian Web being a site which kindly states their material "may be used without prior permission for any scholarly or educational purpose") researcher Dick Sullivan points out how many words suggest backslang relates to written as well as spoken English, e.g. "talk" is "klat" where, phonetically, it would be "kwat", "knife" is "efink" rather than "fine"; no absolute rules though, given the difficulty of pronouncing an "h" at the end of a word is overcome by pronouncing and writing it "tch", so "half" is "flatch", "horse" is "esrotch", "have" is "vatch"; moreover, backslang retained the phonetics of "th" and "sh" in preference to attempting a pronunciation based on spelling, so "three" is "earth", fish is "shif" and so on.

[17] teaching.shu.ac.uk/ds/sle/altered/chronology/dates.htm says World

War I brought about the restriction of licensing hours to 9am-11pm, then 10pm — although other sources suggest that the 1914 Defence Of The Realm Act tightened the permitted hours even further. The current much looser laws came in during the 1980s with further amendments in 2005.

[18] My father doesn't name it, but this must have been Lower Edmonton station, on Edmonton Green, opened 1872; the market grew up in the late 19th century alongside the working-class influx from London's "inner suburbs".

[19] In fact, my father's memoir barely touched on his life after World War I, but I have sketched it out in the Afterword.

[20] www.gutenberg.org/files/29558/29558-h/29558-h.htm has the American *Boy Scouts Handbook* 1911, the oldest I could find online, listing the promises as: "On my honor I will do my best: 1. To do my duty to God and my country, and to obey the Scout law; 2. To help other people at all times; 3. To keep myself physically strong, mentally awake, and morally straight."

[21] Published 1908.

[22] In Poole Harbour, Dorset, August 1-8, 1907; the National Trust now owns the island.

[23] Halley's Comet became visible around April 10, 1910, and came closest to the Earth on April 20; Earth passed through its tail on May 19. Astronomical appetites may have been whetted that mid-January by the one-off appearance of what became known as The Daylight Comet because of its extreme brightness.

[24] Thomas Edison, 1847-1931, "the wizard of Menlo Park, New Jersey" invented the phonograph, which recorded sound on a cylinder of tinfoil, in 1877 — and much else after that.

[25] See http://www.dmi.me.uk/music/lyrics/misc/-/when-father-papered-the-parlour/ for the official lyrics (sometimes it shifted to "painted", as per my father's recollection, rather than "papered") — when I sang it in a holiday camp talent show circa 1957 I remember the chorus went "Ma was stuck to the ceiling/The kids were stuck to the floor/You never saw a blooming family/So stuck up before"; written in 1910 by R.P. Weston (who also co-wrote What A Mouth and I'm Henery The Eighth I Am) and Fred J. Barnes and a hit for Australian-born music hall star Billy Williams, who died in 1915, aged 37, after recording more than 500 songs and taking part in the first Royal Command Performance variety

show in 1912.

[26] That was 2s 6d or 2/6 or 30 "old" pennies.

[27] A worker in a match factory; they became a *cause célèbre* for staging a famous strike at Bryant & May's in Bow, London, in 1888, protesting 14-hour days, poor pay and unsafe conditions through handling white phosphorus which caused "phossy jaw" (a disfiguring and potentially fatal form of necrosis resulting in rotting bones and brain damage).

[28] *A Topographical Dictionary Of England, Volume 2*, written and published by Samuel Lewis, first edition in 1840 (now digitised by Google), says of this school: "A charity school for boys was founded in 1624, by Mr Edward Latymer, who bequeathed a messuage at Edmonton, and lands at Hammersmith, for clothing and educating eight poor boys, for which purpose also Mr Thomas Styles, in 1679, bequeathed £20 per annum; several similar benefactions have been consolidated, producing about £550 per annum, which is appropriated to the instruction of more than one hundred boys, of which number sixty are clothed [*I presume that meant their clothes were paid for, not that the others ran naked*]: the school-room was built in 1811, pursuant to the will of Mrs Ann Wyatt, who bequeathed £500 five per cent, Navy annuities for that purpose, and £100 to keep it in repair. A charity school for girls was established by subscription in 1778."

[29] All Saints, on Church Street, Edmonton, still occupies the site of a church built in the early 12th century and a few fragments of the Norman original remain in the west walls according to www.allsaintsedmonton. org.uk/church-history.html. Charles Lamb (1775-1834) and his sister, Mary (1764-1847) — authors of *Tales From Shakespeare*, prose versions of the plays, written for children — lived at Bay Cottage, Church Street, and other addresses during their later years when both suffered mental illness — Mary's severe (she had stabbed their mother to death in 1796); their graves can be visited still in All Saints churchyard.

[30] lower-edmonton.anidea.co.uk/buildings/pubs says the name dates from 1773, the building from 1795, probably at 17 Church Street, Edmonton; http://lower-edmonton.co.uk/local/churchst.html suggests the current building may be from the 1920s.

[31] Charles Lamb, see footnote 29.

[32] Keats was apprenticed to Dr Thomas Hammond, of Church Street (the house demolished in 1931), 1810-16 officially, but they quarrelled and he

left in 1815 by mutual consent. Even so, Keats got a good reference from Hammond and went on to work at Guy's and St Thomas' hospitals; he had grown up in Enfield and would walk to and fro through fields to see friends, study at the library or go to work — sources multiple.

[33] Here, while maintaining third-person narrative and fictionalised identities for the time being, my father decided to give a name to his older brother Phil — always nicknamed "Ted" for reasons he explains later — so he called him "George".

[34] My father told me he left school at 14, so probably 1909-1912.

[35] Present building opened 1888 as the New Court Theatre.

[36] Charles Lamb Institute, Church Street, opened 1908, now a gym according to en.wikipedia.org/wiki/Edmonton,_London#cite_note-Church-12

[37] English, red, pork sausages.

[38] Mary Anne: written by Fred W. Leigh (1871-1924) and music-hall singer George Bastow (1872-1914), who recorded it in 1911; see lyrics at http://mainlynorfolk.info/folk/songs/maryanne.html

[39] The shows, popular at the time, and the name came from Mrs Jarley's Waxworks, which appears briefly in Charles Dickens's *The Old Curiosity Shop*, 1841.

[40] http://cinematreasures.org/theaters/29413 offers pictures and information; The Alcazar, "designed like a Moorish palace", opened on June 28, 1913, so my father seems to be remembering it a little early in his narrative, so to speak; the Alcazar Cinematograph Theatre had 1,700 seats; in addition, it boasted "winter gardens" for dancing indoors, and "summer gardens" for roller-skating.

[41] Charles Ancliffe (1880-1952), born in County Kildare, but served as bandmaster with the First Battalion, South Wales Borderers, 1900-18, largely in India; he wrote Nights Of Gladness when he returned home on leave on Christmas Eve 1912 — sources Wikipedia and www.hyperion-records.co.uk/

[42] Irving Berlin, 1888-1989, wrote both Alexander's Ragtime Band and Everybody's Doing It Now in 1911 — the former his first hit and both influenced by Scott Joplin's ragtime.

[43] The first air raid of the Blitz occurred on August 22, 1940, and the Alcazar was hit the following day, then subsequently by a V1 "doodlebug" in October, 1944, after which the building had to be demolished.

[44] Probably 1911, the year before my father left school; a heat wave set temperature records not broken until 1990 and the weather held until September, says Wikipedia.

[45] John Philip Sousa: 1854-1932, American composer and conductor of marches including The Stars And Stripes Forever; of Spanish and Bavarian ancestry, he started out as an apprentice US Marine Bandsman and later ran his own band; developed the sousaphone!

[46] In fact, the Queensbury Rules then in force for boxing included three-minute rounds and a one-minute break.

[47] "The baby"? No mention of his birth in my father's memoir, but he was named John Fleetwood (from his mother's maiden name), born April 1, 1911, at 26, Lowden Road (as per footnote 7) — see the Afterword for a little more about him. Benger's Food: an earlier Complan, made in Strangeways, Manchester, originated for the sick but used by the well too — a 1914 ad in The Graphic said "with this food the digestive system, whether enfeebled by illness, overwork or advancing age, is rested and restored, and while this takes place, complete nourishment is maintained… you never tire of it, as with ordinary milk foods" — source http://www.adsandmags.com/catalog/index.php?main_page=product_info&cpath=3&products_id=198

[48] 1912, almost certainly!

[49] Dents: founded 1777, still in business; now based in Warminster, formerly Worcester, but with London offices.

[50] John Howell's office then seems to have been in Old Street, but perhaps that could be seen as "the Eastern outskirts" of London at the time — or my father may have been thinking of the outskirts of the City of London; the company was founded in 1832, according to http://canequest.com/henry-howell.asp in World War I the company lost many of its skilled craftsmen and, also afflicted by the vicissitudes of fashion, struggled until it closed in 1936.

[51] Nilgiri in Tamil Nadu, Southern India, Malacca one of the southern states of Malaysia.

[52] The Alexandra Trust Dining Rooms: built in 1898, close to the tram and bus junction at Old Street by philanthropist tea mogul Sir Thomas Lipton, 1848-1931; in three halls, capacity 500 each, it offered cheap meals to the poor working classes; six boilers heated 500 gallons of hot soup, "steam chests" boiled a ton and a half of potatoes an hour, and, in

1898, fourpence-halfpenny bought a three-course meal comprising "soup, a choice at will of a large steak-pudding, roast pork, roast or boiled beef, roast or boiled mutton, Irish stew, boiled pickled pork, stewed steak, or liver and bacon [*with*] two vegetables and bread, and a choice between pastry, or a mug of tea, coffee, or cocoa"; some 100 waitresses could serve up to 12,000 meals a day — sources http://www.secret-london.co.uk/ Old_Street.html and http://edwardianpromenade.com/research/wip-research-the-alexandra-trust-dining-rooms/ quoting Arthur H Beavan's *Imperial London*, 1901.

[53] Penang: then one of the Straits Settlements, a British territory.

[54] Writing in the '70s, my father guessed accurately; according to http:// www.measuringworth.com/ukcompare/relativevalue.php in RPI terms a 1910 £5 would be worth £60.80 in 1975 — and £417 in 2011.

[55] The enlistment age in the 19th century seems not to have been specified by law, but many accounts suggest the Army often enlisted or recruited boys of 13 to 15.

[56] The Boltons: the name referred to a street and the surrounding area; it's still "fashionable" in a sense — in 2011 Zoopla reckoned it the second most expensive street in the UK behind Kensington Palace Gardens and, the following year, a seven-bedroom Boltons house fetched £55m — source http://www.zoopla.co.uk

[57] Nigeria: not officially united as a country within the British Empire until 1914, a couple of years after Tommy/my father started work at Lake & Currie.

[58] Corps Of Commissionaires founded 1859 to offer work to ex-Servicemen; now a not-for-profit private company called Corps Security with the monarch still nominally its "head".

[59] The popular written source of the rhyme seems to be a lesser-known Dickens novel, *The Chimes* (1844). It's quoted by Lady Bowley, wife of the philanthropist MP who is the butt of the book's radical social satire; her version is slightly different to Sergeant's: "O let us love our occupations,/ Bless the Squire and his relations/Live upon our daily rations/and always know our proper stations".

[60] The Great Fire occurred in 1666. On the planning and rebuilding, Royal Institute Of British Architects website http://www. architecture.com/librarydrawingsandphotographs/onlineworkshops/ urbanadventures/01wren.aspx says that Sir Christopher Wren, 1632-1723,

submitted a plan for rebuilding the city with "wide, straight streets", but it didn't happen because "building was financed by private enterprise and the desire was to rebuild quickly", whereas more radical change would have required the Government taking control.

[61] After an experiment with electric taxis, 1897-1900, the first petrol-engined taxis, from French manufacturer Prunel, came to London in 1903, according to Wikipedia — the word "taxi" an abbreviation of the French "taximeter cabriolet". Steam-powered buses had run intercity in the UK from the 1830s until killed off by speed limits and eventually the "Red Flag Act" of 1865, which, until repealed in 1896, meant a man had to walk in front of them carrying a red flag. Thomas Clarkson, 1864-1933, associate of the Royal School Of Mines, an instructor in assaying, founded the National Steam Car Company in 1909 to run buses in London; by 1914 he had 184, but, by 1919, Clarkson had switched them all to petrol. https://www.flickr.com/photos/warsaw1948/7631289348/ features a wonderful photograph of a bus-filled London street scene, including one of Clarkson's steamers, and notes that paraffin fired his "thimble tube" engines.

[62] The Edmonton Empire, opened 1908, on New Road, often called "Empire Hill" says http://www.artstart.org.uk/; later the scene of great, comic songstress Marie Lloyd's last performance, in 1922, when she collapsed while singing One Of The Ruins That Cromwell Knocked About A Bit. She died ten days later, aged 52. Converted to a cinema in 1933, the Empire was demolished 1970.

[63] In the '30s, when my mother went round to see my father at the family home in Barnet a year or two before they married, my grandmother, Lily Sutcliffe, appeared at the top of the stairs and snarled "He's mine!"

[64] Bernard Beeches? I think my father must have misremembered/typoed Burnham Beeches, 25 miles west of London; woodland, of late frequently used as a movie setting because of the nearby Pinewood and Bray studios e.g. *Goldfinger, Robin Hood Prince Of Thieves,* and a couple of *Harry Potters.*

[65] Sweetings, in Queen Victoria Street, near the Lord Mayor of London's official residence, The Mansion House, opened in 1889 and still serves lunch (only) to the same kind of clientele today, though as a specialist fish restaurant; one review notes, "many customers first went to dine there before they even started at their chosen public school".

[66] Gin cup: gin with mint, sugar and lemon juice.

[67] Burlington Arcade: in Mayfair, off Piccadilly.

[68] Edgar Wallace, 1875-1932, creator of *Sanders Of The River, King Kong, The Four Just Men*; he also became the first British radio sports reporter when he commentated on the 1923 Derby for the then British Broadcasting Company.

[69] *The Story-Teller* was published 1907-1936; Sax Rohmer, 1983-1959, who created Fu Manchu — serialised in *The Storyteller* October, 1912-June, 1913 — was born Arthur Ward in Birmingham, UK, and died in White Plains, New York (of Asian flu!).

[70] *Pearson's Weekly*, 1890-1939, serialised Rider Haggard and H.G. Wells; founded by Sir Cyril Pearson, 1866-1921, a Liberal Party supporter and philanthropist, later launched the *Daily Express*, and — being a friend of Baden-Powell — published *The Scout*. I can't find any reference to *Pearson's* running "While England Slept" (a 1909 novel by Captain Henry Curties, 1860-1928) so my father may be wrong about the publication.

[71] Harry Wood's "Island Mentalities" article at http://invasionscares.wordpress.com/2012/07/02/be-prepared-5-2/ notes a genre of "invasion fiction" developing since 1890, including William Le Queux's *The Invasion Of 1910* (1906, a "phenomenal bestseller" says Wikipedia), P.G. Wodehouse's *The Swoop! Or How Clarence Saved England: A Tale Of The Great Invasion* (1909), and Saki's *When William Came* (1913) — not insignificantly, in Wodehouse's satire, Clarence Chugwater is a Boy Scout and Wood's "Island Mentalities" says (reproduced with Harry's kind permission) Saki "saw Scouting as a potential force for national redemption, defying enemies where the older generation had entirely failed" (a sniper's bullet killed Saki/Royal Fusiliers Lance Sergeant Hector Hugh Munro near Beaumont-Hamel, during the Battle Of the Ancre, in 1916, aged 45, he having enlisted over-age at 43).

[72] The tenth article of Scout Law, added in the 1911 fourth edition of Baden-Powell's *Scouting For Boys*.

[73] Under an 1899 Act, children then had to attend school until the age of 12.

[74] Probably the Great Cambridge Road, aka the Old North Road, now the A10.

[75] Bosnian Serb Gavrilo Princip assassinated Archduke Franz Ferdinand of Austria, heir presumptive to Austria-Hungary (which included Galicia, Croatia, Bosnia, and Herzegovina), and his wife Sophie, in Sarajevo,

Bosnia, on June 28, 1914; following Serbia's military annexation of Macedonia and Kosovo from the Ottoman Empire in 1912-13, Princip and fellow plotters wanted Greater Serbia to become independent of the Austro-Hungarian Empire.

[76] White Wings, written and sung by Banks Winter, in 1884 says one source, another says later; according to www.traditionalmusic.co.uk/songster/10-white-wings.htm it went: "Sail! home, as straight as an arrow/My yacht shoots along on the crest of the sea/Sail! Home, to sweet Maggie Darrow/In her dear little home she is waiting for me/... Heigh! ho, I long for you, Maggie/I'll spread out my white wings and sail home to thee".

[77] Founded in Bristol (1786), Imperial Tobacco manufactured Bristol, introduced in 1871, Three Castles and Gold Flake, 1878, Woodbine, 1888, and Embassy, 1914. See www.imperial-tobacco.co.uk/ Known for its family spirit and a belief that workers should enjoy themselves, Wills pioneered canteens, free medical care, sports facilities and paid holidays. In 1901, Wills amalgamated as Imperial with John Player and Lambert & Butler to fend off the acquisitive American Tobacco Company until the two sides combined under the corporate umbrella of the British American Tobacco Company (BAT), which, in 2014, still exists.

[78] The first time my father called his older brother by his real nickname, "Ted", rather than the invented alias, "George"; I don't know why he did it at this point; my impression is that he just slipped into it as part of his drift, as it soon turned out, in the direction of first-person narrative's intimacy, rather than the measure of distance expressed by the third person.

[79] "Armageddon" appears in The Bible, Revelation 16:16; in various branches of Christianity it's the war preceding the Second Coming, where Satan's armies gather and are defeated; oddly, one of the last battles of WW1, the Battle Of Megiddo, took place on the "Plain Of Armageddon" (aka Sharon), now in Israel, September 19-25, 1918, resulting in an Allied victory over Turkish forces led by Mustafa Kemal Atatürk who subsequently fought to overthrow the Ottoman Empire, moving Turkey towards democracy and independence — achieved in 1923 — and serving as President 1923-38.

[80] In Germany, Daimler built the first motor truck in 1896. An online dictionary notes the first recorded use of the word "lorry" in English as

in 1911.

[81] The Treaty Of London, 1839, between Great Britain and Prussia, but confirmed by the German Empire, guaranteed Belgium's neutrality. Via a concatenation of treaties and other considerations, between the June 28 assassination of Archduke Franz Ferdinand and August 25, nations declared war on one another: Austria-Hungary on Serbia, Russia on Austria-Hungary, Germany on Russia and Serbia, France on "The Central Powers" (Germany and the Ottoman Empire), Germany on France, Germany on Belgium, Great Britain on Germany (August 4), Austria-Hungary on Russia, Japan on Germany, Japan on Austria-Hungary.

[82] Most had been either deported or interned. http://www.nationalarchives. gov.uk/pathways/firstworldwar/first_world_war/britain_outbreak_war. htm says "The Defence Of The Realm Act (August 8, 1914) increased the state's power to control and act against 'unpatriotic' forces, categorising Germans and Austrians as 'enemy aliens'". The BBC website estimates the Government deported 23,500 and interned 32,000.

[83] The Government did not introduce conscription until January, 1916; in January, 1914, the British Army numbered 710,000, only 80,000 of them regulars; before January, 1916, 2.67 million volunteered, and subsequently 2.3 million were conscripted — source Wikipedia.

[84] King George V, 1910-36, grandson of Queen Victoria and Prince Albert, and first cousin of Tsar Nicholas II of Russia And Kaiser Wilhelm II of Germany became the first monarch of the "House of Windsor" in 1917, by renaming the House of Saxe-Coburg And Gotha because of public feeling.

[85] Answering a question of mine, my father noted that Alexandra Palace Internment Camp — "prison" he called it — was the one "only a few miles away" from where he lived in Edmonton; the conversion from entertainment centre took place soon after the war started; http://www. balh.co.uk/lhn/article.php?file=lhn-vol1iss87-6.xML says 3,000 internees slept on plank beds in three large halls and that inmates organised a football team, gardening plots, concerts and a theatrical society; about 80 per cent of interned Germans returned home after the war, although many had lived in Great Britain for years beforehand.

[86] Horatio Bottomley, born 1860; he bought the magazine, *John Bull*, a penny weekly (circulation 2 million during wartime), in 1906, having co-founded *The Financial Times*, in 1888; Liberal MP for Hackney

South from 1905; Wikipedia quotes one of his war-mongering diatribes demanding Germany "must be wiped off the map of Europe... you cannot naturalise an unnatural beast — a human abortion — a hellish fiend. But you can exterminate it."; he conducted open-air recruitment meetings for fees totalling £78,000 says http://www.spartacus.schoolnet. co.uk/FWWbottomley.htm; a 1922 conviction for defrauding £900,000 out of the *John Bull* Victory Bond Club saw him jailed for seven years; Bottomley died in 1933 after several years eking out a living as a music hall turn talking about his life.

[87] Field Marshall John French, 1852-1925, Commander-In-Chief of the British Expeditionary Force, 1914-16; Field Marshall Lord Kitchener was Secretary Of State For War.

[88] Herbert Asquith, 1852-1928, Prime Minister 1908-16, nicknamed "Squiffy" for obvious reasons; actress Helena Bonham-Carter is his great granddaughter.

[89] The full height my father grew to was 5ft 8, so maybe 5ft 4 or 5 at 16.

[90] So Ted too fell well short, his 18th birthday about a month later on October 3, yet my father, and then their parents, seem never to have considered this a difficulty — I presume because he behaved in such a confident, "adult" manner.

[91] The first Lyon's Corner House opened in 1909.

[92] Handel Street, WC1, I think.

[93] According to the Promissory Oaths Act 1868, it read: "I do swear that I will be faithful and bear true allegiance to His Majesty King George the 5th, his heirs and successors, according to law. So help me God."

[94] By 1914, London had the biggest electric tram network in Europe.

[95] Subaltern: commissioned officer below the rank of Captain, so mostly different grades of Lieutenant.

[96] The names my father gave to his officers, of whatever rank, and many of his foot soldier comrades too, were aliases — I think because of a broad instinct for discretion and, sometimes, a specific wish not to make critical remarks or tell, to various degrees, demeaning stories about people who might be identified by their descendants.

[97] The 2/1st (City of London) Battalion (Royal Fusiliers) — well, probably, given confusion/mixing/substitution at various points with the 2/2nd, the 1/2nd and possibly others.

[98] The first time my father used a name for his family, he chose this light

disguise, "Norcliffe", to go with his third-person narrator point of view, but he maintained it even when moving, a little later, to the straightforwardly autobiographical first person.

[99] Wikipedia has a picture and notes: "The Foundling Hospital was founded in 1741 by the philanthropic sea Captain Thomas Coram. It was a children's home established for the 'education and maintenance of exposed and deserted young children'... a plain brick building with two wings and a chapel, built around an open courtyard." Supporters included Handel and Hogarth. In 2014, the building is long gone (demolished 1926), but the courtyard and sheltered walkways remain, the grounds known as Coram's Fields.

[100] The price of a whore in Malta, see Part 3.

[101] Dickens lived 1812-70.

[102] Norfolk jacket: a loose, single-breasted jacket with box pleats at the back and front, and a belt or half-belt.

[103] Harley Davidson: founded 1905, Milwaukee, Wisconsin.

[104] Fred Karno, aka Westcott, 1866-1941, theatre impresario and reputed inventor of custard-pie slapstick, who worked with Charlie Chaplin and Stan Laurel before they went to Hollywood; he called his company Fred Karno's Army and the name became a song in the trenches, to the tune of The Church's One Foundation: "We are Fred Karno's Army, we are the ragtime infantry/We cannot fight, we cannot shoot, what bleeding use are we?/And when we get to Berlin, we'll hear the Kaiser say,/'Hoch, hoch! Mein Gott, what a bloody rotten lot, are the ragtime infantry'"; since 1986, his houseboat, moored on the Thames at Hampton, The Astoria, has been owned by Pink Floyd's David Gilmour and operated as a recording studio, see www.marketingreinforcements.pwp.blueyonder. co.uk/index_theastoria.html

[105] Our Lodger's Such A Nice Young Man as famously sung by Vesta Victoria, 1874-1951 (another former owner of Fred Karno's houseboat), written by Fred Murray (died 1922, also co-wrote Boiled Beef And Carrots and, with R. P. Weston, I'm Henery The Eighth, I Am — see also footnote 25) and Laurence Barclay in 1897: "At our house not long ago a lodger came to stay/... He made himself at home before he'd been with us a day/He kissed mamma and all of us, 'cos Papa was away/... He's such a good, goody, goody man/Mamma told me so"; BBC radio DJ John Peel included the Parlophone Quartet's version of the song on his *Peelenium*

compilation of recordings from 1900-2000.

[106] The British Expeditionary Force (BEF), the standing Army, suffered huge casualties during autumn, 1914, in battles both won and lost alongside the French Army, including Mons (August 23 onwards, origin of the enduring Cockney phrase "the biggest cock-up since Mons"), Le Cateau (August 26), Marne (September 5-12), Aisne (September 13-28), and Ypres (October 19-November 22); the BEF were colloquially known as "the Old Contemptibles" because of an alleged written order from Kaiser Wilhelm: "Exterminate... the treacherous English and walk over General French's contemptible little Army"; on their side, German soldiers called Ypres "the slaughter of the innocents" because their commanders were already throwing in Divisions of young, inexperienced troops.

[107] During the Second Boer War, October, 1899-May, 1902, when in defensive positions, the Afrikaners responded to the British Army's traditional tactics (cavalry charges, infantry advancing in formation) with German-manufactured heavy machine guns, says Wikipedia. Despite the British victory, the war is commonly seen as a major cause of the then UK Conservative Government's landslide defeat by the Liberals in 1906, because of a) public disgust, as the facts of British commander-in-chief Lord Kitchener's scorched-earth strategy and of the concentration camps emerged b) concern for "the state of the poor", highlighted by 40 per cent of Army volunteers proving unfit for military service. At http://www.localhistories.org/life1912.html Tim Lambert writes that, before World War I, because of low wages, 25 per cent of the British people lived in poverty, 10 per cent below subsistence level; life expectancy across the whole population in 1913 was 50 for a man, 54 for a woman; http://www.bbc.co.uk/news/uk-18854073 notes UK infant mortality 1911 as 130 per thousand births.

[108] Greatcoats: wool coats, reaching below the knee, with a cape attachment around the shoulders.

[109] Wikipedia says the London Underground opened in 1863, using steam locomotives and wooden carriages, and starting in the central area with the District and Circle lines (including Cannon Street station from 1884); the City and South London line introduced electric trains in 1890 and electrification of most of the network concluded before World War I.

[110] The Galloping Major, recorded by Walter Miller aka Stanley Kirby, 1907, written by Fred W Leigh and George Bastow (see also footnote 38

re Mary Anne), a children's favourite on BBC radio when I was a kid in the '50s because of the chorus: "Bumpity! Bumpity! Bumpity! Bump!/As if I was riding my charger/Bumpity! Bumpity! Bumpity! Bump!/As proud as an Indian Rajah/All the girls declare/That I'm a gay old stager/Hey! Hey! Clear the way/Here comes the galloping Major"; Leigh, 1871-1924, also wrote lyrics for Vesta Victoria's Waiting At The Church and Marie Lloyd's My Old Man (Said Follow The Van).

[111] According to Wikipedia, in early August, Parliament had called for 100,000 volunteers, by the end of September, 1914, 750,000 had come forward, by January, 1915, a million.

[112] I'm not clear what my father meant here; purchase of commissions in the cavalry and infantry Regiments of the British Army began in 1683 and ended in 1871; by intent and effect, this had ensured the upper classes dominated the "officer class", but after the Crimean War, 1853-56, Gladstone's Government decided that it tended to produce a degenerate inefficiency of leadership when war followed a long period of peace.

[113] To me, this is the moment when my father started to drift towards his eventual decision to go full-on into the first person — "I" instead of "he/Tommy" — perhaps no longer needing that distance the third person gives, perhaps recognising more of his adult self emerging from the child... both or neither, I can't be sure because I didn't ask him!

[114] The Great Eastern ran east from Liverpool Street, 1874 onwards.

[115] Bunbridge: Tunbridge, Kent, one of my father's more thinly disguised names; an old market town dating back beyond the 1087 Domesday Book, but also (according to Wikipedia) scene of the UK's first arrest for speeding when, in 1896, a policeman on a pedal bike overhauled a motorist doing 8mph in a 2mph zone.

[116] Tonbridge had two cinemas then: The Star, Bradford Street, opened 1910, and the Empire Picture Palace, Avebury Avenue, opened 1914.

[117] Tonbridge Castle, first built around a thousand years ago, with a mansion house added in 1793; Tonbridge Council took it over in 1900, using the building for offices and the grounds as a public park.

[118] No doubt my father bought the picture, but unfortunately it's long lost.

[119] Proctor & Gamble's Ivory brand, marketed in America from 1878, did float; the company declared it an accidental outcome of the manufacturing process, but www.snopes.com/business/origins/ivory.asp reports that in

2004 a company archivist revealed it as a planned gimmick, good for sales and economical because it involved whipping bubbles of air into the soap.

[120] Trench diagram at http://www.spartacus.schoolnet.co.uk/FWW parados.htm

[121] Specific dates in *Strong For Service: The Life Of Lord Nathan Of Churt* by H. Montgomery Hyde, published by W.H. Allen, 1968, suggest this leave period occurred a little earlier than my father recalled, probably in mid-January; Lord Nathan, as he later became, served as an officer in my father's Battalion and figures significantly a little later in this memoir.

[122] My father takes a big step towards first-person autobiographical narrative with this passage "quoted" from "Tommy"; as you'll see, in a few pages, he did retreat from it again pro tem, before taking the final leap.

[123] The "magic lantern", developed in Europe from the 15th century onwards and a forerunner of the film projector, directed light through a sheet of glass to show painted or photographic images, still or, latterly, moving.

[124] *Masterman Ready*, 1841, by Captain Frederick Marryat, who also wrote *The Children Of The New Forest*, a children's novel about a shipwreck in which a family survives thanks to the good sailor's skills and Bible-bashing morality.

[125] According to H. Montgomery Hyde's biography of Lord Nathan, the Battalion sailed on February 1, 1915.

[126] The unnamed family probably travelled from Euston to Liverpool to sail for New York.

[127] *Strong For Service* author Hyde quotes a Nathan letter home in which he writes that officers on the *Galeka* enjoyed the comforts of first-class passengers and grew "fat and sleek" on the good food provided, while the troops' "scandalous" provisions recalled the Crimean war; he added that during the storm the ship pitched and tossed so badly he couldn't believe it didn't go under, but that he threw up only once, and that not from seasickness but because he inspected the troop decks and found conditions "beyond description"; a few pages on, my father names the ship, *Galena*, another of his thin-disguise aliases. SS *Galeka*, 7,000 tons, launched in Belfast, 1899, served as a Union-Castle Line mail ship on the South Africa run pre-war, until the British Government requisitioned her as a troop transport, then refitted her as a hospital ship; a mine sank her off Le Havre in October, 1916, with the loss of 19 Royal Army Medical

Corps members (no patients were on board at the time).

[128] Marook? A mystery word. That's what it looks like in my father's handwriting, but I can't find it anywhere, though context suggests it means "anchor" or maybe "anchor chain". Kelsey Thornton (see Afterword thanks) suggest it may be Yiddish and mean "miserable sod"! No way to talk about an anchor...

[129] Hyde's biography of Lord Nathan says the Battalion disembarked at Valletta, Malta, on February 11, 1915.

[130] My father's postcard of the *Galeka* (alias *Galena*) is long since lost, unfortunately, but you can see what may well be the same image at http://www.simplonpc.co.uk/UnionCastle1.html#anchor5228

[131] In fact, a Maltese friend advises that "Mateoti" isn't a trade, but the tradesman's name.

[132] Characters from Edgar Wallace's *Smithy, Nobby & Co* published in the *Daily Mail*, 1904-18 (maybe in a weekly too, but I couldn't confirm my father's recollection on that); the fictionalised archetype Wallace called Smithy dated from his reports as a *Mail* Boer War correspondent, see http://freeread.com.au/@RGLibrary/EdgarWallace/Smithy/SmithyNobbyAnd Co.html — more on Wallace in footnote 68.

[133] Hyde's Nathan biography notes that a five-mile march brought the Battalion to St. George's Barracks: "Quite modern and fairly commodious". Wikipedia says they were built 1859-62 and so named simply because they overlooked St George's Bay.

[134] The Granaries, Fosos in Maltese, lie under Publius Square/Pjazza San Publiju in the Floriana district of Valletta.

[135] My father didn't name him at all; nothing significant I'm sure, he probably just couldn't come up with one of his aliases at that moment.

[136] Lee-Enfield supplied the main British Army rifle 1895-1926; bolt-action, ten .303 rounds in the magazine, loaded either a round at a time or in 5-round "chargers"; the First World War model was the SMLE MK III, price £3 15/-, introduced in 1907 along with the Pattern 1907 sword bayonet; however, from what my father goes on to say, it's clear that, on Malta, his Battalion got issued with the older "long" version the Boer War veteran Lance Corporal mentions (30.2-inch barrel compared to 21.2-inch shorter version); redesigns simplified the Mk III during the war, for ease of manufacture more than usage, apparently; Lee-Enfield took its name from the designer of the bolt-action system James Paris Lee and

the Royal Small Arms Factory, Enfield — adjacent to my father's district, Edmonton, North London.

[137] *The Magnet*, a weekly "story book", ran from 1908 to 1940, carrying the Greyfriars School stories featuring Billy Bunter, written by Frank Richards (real name Charles Hamilton, 1876-1961); *The Gem* ran from 1907-39, its main story about another public school, St Jim's, and hero Tom Merry, and also written by Hamilton, here nom-de-plumed Martin Clifford; Amalgamated Press published both weeklies and, according to Wikipedia, World War II killed them off, because of paper shortages.

[138] St Paul's village in St Paul's Bay, on the northeast of the island, 16 kilometres from Valletta, allegedly the spot where St Paul was shipwrecked during his voyage from Caesarea to Rome.

[139] A *karozzin* is a horse-drawn carriage.

[140] The harbour's Maltese name is Marsamxett.

[141] Strada della Fontana is now St Christopher Street.

[142] Condy's Fluid, developed and patented in 1857 by Henry Bollman Condy, English chemist and industrialist; it could be taken internally or externally, although its advertised uses, says Wikipedia, included "to purify cattle dog" and "to deprive night-chairs of offensive odours".

[143] Chapel Of Bones, built from 1612 says http://www.flickr.com/photos/mmira/5021391903/; unless replaced in 1730 as per http://www.timesofmalta.com/articles/view/20120810/letters/State-of-Nibbia-chapel-ruins.432250; the first source says it was destroyed during World War II, while the second reckons it was merely buried and may be rediscovered; neither supports my father's guide's line about the bones being the remains of "French soldiers".

[144] My father's final shift to first-person narrative — candid autobiography it is, from here to the end of his memoir.

[145] General Post Office: founded 1660 to run the mail nationally, but in the late 19th/early 20th centuries it also took charge of telegraph, telephones and radio.

[146] Boys' Brigade: an international and interdenominational Christian youth organisation, founded 1883, it emphasised military discipline and physical exercise plus religion — Baden-Powell actually served as their Vice-President in 1903, then broke away to found the Scouts after the Brownsea Island experiment.

[147] *Jean Bart* was the second Dreadnought-class battleship built for the

French Navy, launched 1911, says Wikipedia; on December 21 1914, it was hit by a torpedo which struck the wine store(!), then steamed to Malta for repairs; fought in the Mediterranean and then in the Black Sea, supporting Allied troops in the Russian Civil War where her crew mutinied in sympathy with the Bolsheviks until a Vice-Admiral acceded to their demand to go home.

[148] Back in the '70s, I asked my father if he could recall the cemetery's name and he said the nearest village was St Julian's Bay (San Gilijan); this chimes with information from Harry Nathan's letters home, quoted in Hyde's biography, about an early-May move to "Pembroke Camp" — the Battalion had to leave St George's Barracks because the Army decided to convert it into a hospital, largely for Gallipoli casualties; Pembroke Camp was close to the "musketry" range and to Pembroke Military Cemetery, laid out in the mid-19th Century.

[149] The Dead March In Saul is the popular name for the funeral march from Handel's Oratorio, *Saul* (1739) — it isn't *the* "Funeral March"; that's Chopin's *Marche Funèbre*, Piano Sonata Number 2.

[150] My father's thinking of the words to a favourite old song, Alexander's Ragtime Band, Irving Berlin's first hit, in 1911 — see http://www.sing365. com/music/lyric.nsf/Alexander's-Ragtime-Band-lyrics-Irving-Berlin/ — see also footnote 42.

[151] "Booth" is my father's alias for Harry Nathan (1889-1963), who — according to Hyde's biography (details, footnote 121) — gained promotion to Captain quite early in the Battalion's Malta sojourn; one year into a career as a London solicitor when war was declared, he'd also served as a voluntary organiser of Brady Street Club For Working Lads in Whitechapel; in *Strong For Service*, Hyde quotes an August, 1914, letter from Nathan to his mother wherein he's already noting the importance of giving the troops "green vegetables, but they are not provided by the government"; Hyde also quotes Nathan blaming the poor provision for the troops — including wounded — on Field Marshall Lord Methuen (1845-1932), the Governor of Malta and Commander of all Forces on the island (February, 1915-May, 1919); Nathan wrote that he protested about all this officially and often and sometimes hoped "my remonstrances had a momentary effect"; but author Hyde makes no mention of the near-mutiny my father watched — it may be that Nathan didn't write about it, being aware that his letters, like every other soldier's, would be read by censors.

[152] Nathan's biographer Hyde dates the move to Ghajn Tuffieha from Pembroke Camp as early June when Pembroke, like St George's Barracks before it, was requisitioned for care of the wounded. Unlike my father, Nathan found the Ghajn Tuffieha camp "indescribably... depressing" (as he wrote in a letter to his family, quoted by Hyde).

[153] They trained in Egypt, then moved to Malta, says Wikipedia, before fighting at Gallipoli — landing at Anzac Cove, July 3, 1915 — and on the Somme from August 1916; during World War I, 2,227 men served in the Battalion, 336 of them died, and 734 were wounded; in the military, "pioneer" means specialising in engineering and construction — "sapper" is the British Army equivalent.

[154] Map at http://www.myweather2.com/Holiday-Destinations/Malta/Salina-Bay/map.aspx

[155] The Knights Of Malta built many stone towers in the 17th century.

[156] The Battalion left Malta on August 27, 1915, according to http://www.1914-1918.net/london.htm; SS *Ivernia* was a Cunard liner, launched in 1899, her 60-foot funnel the tallest ever fitted to a ship, says Wikipedia (but that may well be wrong!); she was sunk by a German submarine south of Greece, on January 1, 1917, with the loss of 120 troops and crew, when under the command of Captain William Turner, previously skipper of the Cunard liner *Lusitania* when it was torpedoed and sunk off southern Ireland in May, 1915, with the loss of 1,195 lives — Captain Turner survived despite staying at his post on the bridge until the ship was under water.

[157] My father could be misremembering, or *Ivernia* may have carried Anchor Line insignia given that Cunard bought that rival company in 1911.

[158] Egypt officially abolished slavery in 1896.

[159] Four kilometres from Cairo; Heliopolis was an ancient settlement dating back to 2-3000BC, but also a new town founded in 1907 by Belgian Egyptologist/entrepreneur Baron Empain.

[160] The Great Sphinx and three pyramids, including the Great Pyramid of Giza, stand on the outskirts of current Heliopolis/Cairo.

[161] "Mudhook": anchor.

[162] The Blue Mosque: Aqsunqur Mosque or Mosque of Ibrahim Agha in the Tabbana quarter of Cairo, completed in 1347, restored 1908.

[163] Ahret El Wasser, a street in Ezbekieh quarter of Cairo; on April 2,

1915, a riot known as "The Battle Of The Wazzir" occurred, with 2,000 ANZACs allegedly involved; something similar happened again on July 31, so perhaps the Fusiliers were gossiping rather old news.

[164] Hyde's biography of Harry Nathan/"Lieutenant Booth" says the Battalion spent 10 days in the Abbasieh camp; my father's account certainly gives the impression of a longer period, though perhaps he just packed a lot in; a Nathan letter home notes them sailing from Alexandria for Gallipoli on September 17, 1915.

[165] My father wrote from experience, of course, and apparently without sarcasm here, but various sites reveal a critical consensus either abusing the Aberdeen-based victualler's stew — "An inferior grade of garbage," says one — or warning of noxious side effects: "The Maconochie stew ration gave the troops flatulence of a particularly offensive nature," writes David R. Woodward in *Hell In The Holy Land*, published by the University Press Of Kentucky, 2006 (thanks to Dr Woodward for permission to quote).

[166] Mudros: sometimes spelt Moudros, on Lemnos; the island had become Greek, and a Greek Navy base, in 1812 as a result of the Russo-Turkish War; Allied Navies used it from 1915 until the end of World War I.

[167] HMT (Her Majesty's Troopship) *Aragon*, launched in Belfast 1905, worked as a Royal Mail ship on the South American run; converted to a troopship it joined the Gallipoli Campaign from the start in April, 1915; perhaps luckily for my father's air mail attempt *Aragon* also served as Forces P.O. for the Mediterranean; *Aragon* sank off Alexandria on December 31, 1917, torpedoed by a U-boat — the destroyer HMS *Attack* was also torpedoed and sunk in the same incident and more than 600 died, see http://en.wikipedia.org/wiki/HMT_Aragon#Deaths_and_survivors

[168] My father's Battalion landed at Suvla Bay, Gallipoli, on September 25, 1915, joining the 88th Brigade of the 29th Division, see http://www.1914-1918.net/london.htm; in the Nathan biography, author Hyde refers to a "late afternoon" landing, which is not my father's recollection, as you see — but different Companies (two per ship, eight in the Battalion) landed at different times, and Hyde writes that "Nathan was the first person in the Battalion to set foot on Turkish soil"; in World War I, says Wikipedia, the 88th Brigade Comprised the 4th Battalion Worcestershire Regiment, 2nd Battalion Hampshire Regiment, 1st Battalion Essex Regiment, 1st Battalion Royal Newfoundland Regiment, 1/5th Battalion Royal Scots, 2/1st Battalion London Regiment, 2nd Battalion Leinster Regiment,

88th Machine Gun Company, and the 88th Trench Mortar Battery; esteemed in the regular Army, the 88th had earned to soubriquet "the Incomparable Division". The Allies' Gallipoli landings had begun on April 25, 1915, the objective being to capture the Turkish capital, Istanbul; the Ottoman Empire had entered the war on the German/Central Powers side on October 31, 1914; this followed a period when a group known as "the Young Turks" had overthrown the reigning Emperor and installed their own, Mehmed V, in 1908; already a veteran of the Italo-Turkish Wars (1911-12) and the Balkan Wars (1912-13), soon to be founder of the Turkish Republic, Colonel Kemal Atatürk (1881-1938) successfully commanded a Division of the Turkish Army at Gallipoli, see Wikipedia.

[169] "Extended order": opposite of close order; troops separated as widely as the situation and terrain permit — recommended for "skirmishing", says www.thefreedictionary.com/

[170] Again, for his own reasons, my father decided to not even fictionalise a name here.

[171] General Sir Ian Standish Monteith Hamilton, 1853-1947; a Liberal supporter, Wikipedia notes, whom World War I Prime Minister Herbert Asquith described as "having too much feather in his brain"; but he served in Burma, India and South Africa — in the last, he was twice recommended for the Victoria Cross, but rejected first for being "too junior" and second for being "too senior" (more to that story, no doubt); he did write a volume of poetry and his reports from Gallipoli appeared in the *London Gazette* (various items at www.1914-1918.net/) and were collected as early as 1915, titled *Sir Ian Hamilton's Despatches From The Dardanelles* and then in 1920 as *Gallipoli Diary, 1920* (just two of his 163 published works). As my father's Battalion joined the Gallipoli campaign quite late, a brief outline seems appropriate here (various sources). Kitchener appointed Hamilton to command the Allied Mediterranean Expeditionary Force (from Great Britain, Australia and New Zealand — the ANZACs — India and Newfoundland) specifically for the Gallipoli campaign, withholding him from the Western Front because of his unorthodox tendencies, such as deeming cavalry obsolete; the notorious April 25, 1915, Allied landings at six beaches on Cape Helles resulted in heavy casualties and little progress because of a) forewarning — the British Navy had bombarded on February 19 and March 18 b) lack of troop numbers (78,000, when some recommended up to 200,000) c)

lack of appropriate training d) a shortage of landing craft; the Suvla Bay landings followed from August 6 and pulled up short largely because of the Turkish Army's dominant position on the Anafarta Heights; that proved the last significant Allied attempt to gain ground in Gallipoli; by October, evacuation was already being proposed, and Hamilton's opposition to it directly led to his replacement, on October 16, by Lieutenant General Sir Charles Monro; Hamilton later distinguished himself as a pre-World War II enthusiast for the peaceful intentions of Adolf Hitler.

[172] The "adjutant" here seems to be the officer my father called "Captain Blunt", an alias I presume.

[173] Possibly a Colonel Ekin — Nathan's biographer Hyde notes that Ekin had remained in Malta because of illness, then returned to command the Battalion in Gallipoli, probably in early November, but left for good after a fortnight; Hyde quotes a Nathan letter commenting that Ekin "could not stick it at all".

[174] Probably after the South Wales Borderers 2nd Battalion who fought at both Cape Helles and Suvla Bay — where they suffered "nearly 300 casualties", says http://www.royalwelsh.org.uk/downloads/B07-02-SWB-WW1-2ndBattalion.pdf

[175] Number 9: a laxative often issued as a cure-all by Army doctors — and said to be the source of the bingo caller's somewhat mysterious "Doctor's orders, Number 9".

[176] Royal Army Medical Corps: referred to by its initials RAMC for most of the memoir.

[177] Chocolate Hill: scene of fierce fighting throughout the campaign; the soldiers named it for its colour, to distinguish it from Green Hill.

[178] *Queen Elizabeth*: probably not, as she had been Hamilton's flagship for the invasion but, according to Wikipedia, was withdrawn to "a safer position" — namely, Scapa Flow, the Orkney islands, north of Scotland — after the sinking of the battleship HMS *Goliath* by a Turkish torpedo boat on May 12, 1915, with the loss of 570 crew.

[179] Lieutenant "Booth"/Nathan was not the man referred to here, I think.

[180] Taube: monoplane fighter/bomber/surveillance aircraft, manufactured from 1910 onwards; Germany's first mass-produced military plane, says Wikipedia.

[181] Several Battalions of Royal Scots did fight at Gallipoli; from the following reference to them being involved in the earliest landings, it

seems the men who impressed my father may have been members of 1/5th Battalion (Queen's Edinburgh Rifles), part of the Royal Scots (Lothian Regiment), see http://www.1914-1918.net/royalscots.htm

[182] Maybe. Or maybe HQ was misinformed. As far as I can check, Ramadan 1915 ran from July 13 or 14 to August 12.

[183] Sources agree the Gallipoli blizzards began on November 27, 1915; Harry Nathan's biographer Hyde, notes 12,000 cases of frostbite and exposure arising and, in a letter home, Nathan wrote of "15 degrees of frost" (meaning a temperature of 17° Fahrenheit); he also reports 280 men "drowned" in the mud produced by thawing snow and rain.

[184] This suggests that, in reality, the arrangement, mentioned earlier, that the two Signallers on the hill should come under the Essex Regiment Quartermaster didn't work, although my father doesn't specifically mention any such problem.

[185] The Bishop of Croydon did exist and his name at that time was Henry Pereira, but he would have been aged 70 in late 1915, so my father probably presumed correctly that his benefactor was some other cleric.

[186] Peter Nieter from my father's trainee Signallers group on Malta — except that, first time round, he called him "Miter"; I don't know whether either version of the name is "real".

[187] General Beauvoir De Lisle (1864-1955), commissioned 1883, fought in the Second Boer War, then on the Western Front in 1914, until his transfer to Gallipoli; returned to the Western Front, including the Somme, 1916-18; www.firstworldwar.com/bio/delisle.htm suggests De Lisle wasn't popular among the troops — and did not seek to be so — and that his commander in Gallipoli, Sir William Birdwood, referred to him as "a brute"; but he did at least go ashore, in the noisily eccentric manner my father encountered, to see "every corner of Suvla" for himself.

[188] Hamilton actually departed some while earlier, as per footnote 171; but, clearly, nobody told the poor bloody infantry who commanded them at any given moment.

[189] Hyde's Nathan biography notes the Battalion's evacuation taking place on December 18-19, Saturday to Sunday overnight.

[190] In case you're wondering, I've checked and I don't think my father did mention this young man and his comment earlier.

[191] I think I remember my father saying that 147 came out "unscathed", although in the text a little earlier he refers to around 200 being still active

immediately after the late-November blizzard and, soon, he mentions that figure again; I couldn't find any official figures.

[192] One site confirms *Robin Redbreast*'s part in the evacuation; www. mareud.com/Timelines/1914-1918.htm reports a steamer called *Redbreast* sunk by a U-boat in the Aegean on July 15, 1917, while employed as "fleet messenger no. 26" — I'm not sure if this is the same ship, but it seems likely.

[193] Imbros: an Aegean island ceded to Greece by Turkey in 1913 after the Balkan War and used as an administrative base and field hospital in World War I, especially by the ANZACS; returned to Turkey in 1923.

[194] Hyde's Nathan biography reports that Harry Nathan ("Booth") became Battalion commander in mid-November 1915, as other officers fell ill.

[195] Hyde's Nathan biography quotes his letter home of December 23, 1915, saying the two-mile march to a camp called Mudros West made him realise how "worn out and 'whacked' we all are... it took me all I knew to manage it."

[196] Qantara: now officially Al Qantarah El Sharqiyya, 160 kilometres northeast of Cairo in Ismailia.

[197] The "baby sister", not mentioned before (a little more background in the Afterword when you get there): Edith "Edie" Minnie Sutcliffe, born May 22, 1912, at 26, Lowden Road (see footnote 7).

[198] Hyde's Nathan biography says that, while he was eating his Christmas dinner, Nathan received the order that the Battalion remnants must return to Gallipoli, and they shipped out on Boxing Day, December 26.

[199] According to http://1914-1918.invisionzone.com/forums/index. php?showtopic=108750 Asiatic Annie fired from a place called Tepe, aiming at V Beach (where my father's Battalion had landed) and W Beach on Cape Helles; http://www.anzacsite.gov.au/2visiting/tourasia4. html says the gun was set up in a 17th-century fort called Kumkalle, five kilometres from the site of ancient Troy.

[200] SS *River Clyde*: a collier launched in March, 1905, adapted as a landing ship in 1915; that April, she sailed from Mudros to Cape Helles V Beach; bombarded from the cliffs, she was beached to serve as a bridge for landings and then for returning wounded; six of the *River Clyde*'s crew were awarded VCs; the apparent hulk was later repaired and sold to Spanish owners who used her as a Mediterranean tramp steamer until finally scrapping her in 1966; on April 15, V Beach, only 300 yards long, became one of five main

Allied landing places on Cape Helles; it was overlooked by cliffs, a fort and an ancient castle, Sedd el Bahr Kale, occupied and defended by the Turkish Army, though captured on April 26.

[201] Charles Samson: 1883-1931, says Wikipedia, born Manchester, one of the first four Royal Navy pilots, and the first to fly an aircraft from a moving ship (1912); he won the Distinguished Service Order for activities on the Western Front, earning promotion to Commander; he was sent to Gallipoli in March, 1915; different accounts have him recalled to London either in November, 1915, or at the end of the Gallipoli campaign — if the latter, he may have been flying the plane my father saw.

[202] In fact, six days after they arrived at V Beach, according to the dates in Hyde's Nathan book.

[203] Hyde's biography of Nathan quotes one of his letters home noting that the Battalion left Cape Helles V Beach "on the night of Thursday 6th, at ten minutes' notice" and that the order came through "in the middle of tea".

[204] *Partridge*: web references call it "the second last ship to leave Gallipoli", that final voyage being on January 8, apparently — so probably the day after my father's Battalion shipped out.

[205] SS *Minneapolis*: launched 1900, regularly sailed London to New York — in 1907 conveyed Mark Twain on his last trip to Europe; requisitioned as a troopship at the start of World War I.

[206] SS *Nestor*: a Blue Funnel Line ship, launched, 1913, for the Australia run and another claimant to the "tallest ship's funnel ever" at 80 feet compared to *Ivernia*'s 60 feet (see footnote 156), allegedly; operated as a troopship by the Australian Expeditionary Force — source http://iancoombe.tripod.com/id25.html. SS *Minnewaska*, launched 1908/9, like *Minneapolis* owned by the Atlantic Transport Line and ran London to New York until requisitioned in 1915; damaged by a mine at Suda Bay, Crete, on November 29, 1916, beached and wrecked, but all 1,600 troops and 200 crew on board survived, says http://www.naval-history.net/WW1LossesBrMS1914-16.htm AND http://www.atlantictransportline.us/content/30Minneapolis.htm

[207] My father heard an inaccurate account of the *Minneapolis*'s demise — over-pessimistic too; a torpedo struck her on March 23, 1916, en route from Marseilles to Alexandria but, because her cargo then comprised 60 tonnes of horse fodder, rather than hundreds of troops, and she took two days

to sink, "only" 12 died out of 179 men on board, so the third officer may well have survived — source http://www.atlantictransportline.us/content/30Minneapolis.htm and http://www.naval-history.net/WW1LossesBrMS 1914-16.htm

[208] The USA did not "enter the conflict" until April, 1917.

[209] Hyde's biography quotes a Nathan letter home saying the *Minneapolis* sailed from Mudros on January 12, 1916, and docked at Alexandria on the 14th.

[210] Rue Des Soeurs (Sharia Saba Banat): for a lurid story of the area see www.timesofmalta.com/articles/view/20110529/life-features/A-Maltese-murder-and-the-British-occupation-of-Egypt.367869

[211] Beni Salama: in the state of Al Jizah, 30 miles northwest of Cairo; later, when excavated, provided evidence of the earliest known settlement in the Nile Valley.

[212] The five Australian Light Horse Brigades served at Gallipoli and throughout the war.

[213] "Double tooth" means it has a double crown.

[214] Going on Nathan's account in Hyde's biography, *Strong For Service*, this must have been Lieutenant Colonel A.C.H. Kennard; in a quotation which Hyde doesn't date or source, Nathan complains that Kennard was parachuted in to de facto take his command simply because he had the ear of someone powerful in London; Nathan expresses further outrage on learning from Kennard that he would be installing his own second-in-command.

[215] Semite: while "anti-semitic" has come to mean "prejudiced against Jews", my father used the root word accurately because it means "a member of the group of people who speak a Semitic language, including the Jews and Arabs as well as the ancient Babylonians, Assyrians and Phoenicians" — source *Collins Concise Dictionary Plus*.

[216] Brailings: rope loops along the bottom of the tent canvas through which pegs were hammered to hold the sides of the tent to the ground.

[217] Comrades In Arms: words by Frederic T. Cardoze, music Reginald DeKoven, possibly 1901? Hear the Barry Male Voice Choir's rendering at https://www.youtube.com/watch?v=gTx5UKZAawc — I don't know the origin of my father's loathing for male voice choirs, but he sustained it loyally until his dying day.

[218] According to *Strong For Service*, Hyde's Nathan biography, they sailed

on April 17, 1916. In a letter home on April 12, Nathan — far from impartial in the circumstances, of course — wrote that Kennard, who would now apparently be leading the Battalion on the Western Front, had failed to gain the men's respect; but, in one of his regular paeans to the men of the Battalion, he praised "those that remain" for their spirited recovery from Gallipoli, and called them "first-rate men" because they could "be relied on: and in war that is everything."

[219] SS *Transylvania*: a Cunard/Anchor liner launched in 1914; *Transylvania* took 1,379 passengers ordinarily, but 3,060 as a troopship; she was sunk on May 4, 1917, en route from Marseille to Alexandria, torpedoed close to the Italian coast near Genoa; Japanese destroyers *Matsu* and *Sakaki* serving as escorts became rescuers — out of 3,000 on board, 10 crew, 29 Army officers, and 373 ranks died; my father's four-funneller could well have been the *Aquitania*, which, at over 900 feet, was even longer than the *Titanic*, though slightly smaller in tonnage — and the only liner to serve as a troopship in both world wars.

[220] Rouen: by the Seine in north-western France, historic capital of Normandy, famous for its cathedral, Joan of Arc's execution, and as the birthplace of playwright Pierre Corneille, painter Théodore Géricault, novelist Gustave Flaubert, and President François Hollande.

[221] In *Strong For Service*, author Hyde reports the probable explanation for Nathan's absence from this event: he "was granted a month's leave" shortly after the Battalion landed in Marseilles and returned in June, 1916, to find remnants of his Battalion merged into a Reserve Corps (in the 29th Division of the 8th Army; "Reserve" didn't mean non-combatant) under General Hubert Gough's command on the left of the Somme Front.

[222] One online reference suggests that the Royal Fusiliers may have renamed the 3/1st Battalion the 2/1st, when the original 2/1st disbanded in Rouen.

[223] My father wouldn't say anything further — just his instinctive reserve/discretion about names in many circumstances I presume — and the scanty records of his service I've seen suggest no apparent change at this point; in fact, it looks as though he officially belonged to the Royal Fusiliers, then the Essex Regiment, and nothing else — but obviously some reassignment happened in between... and it seems to me quite likely he means "The Kensingtons", the 13th Battalion, the London Regiment.

[224] The right to conscientious objection had been recognised in the UK since the 18th century, but only for Quakers, says Wikipedia; it became a general

right in March, 1916, after the Government introduced conscription; the same Military Service Tribunals that heard appeals against conscription on all other grounds decided on conscientious objectors' appeals (which comprised about 2 per cent of the 750,000 cases the tribunals heard 1916-18); in all 11,500 appeals on grounds of conscience were upheld during World War I, while 6,000 appellants were refused, conscripted, then, potentially, jailed if they refused to obey orders.

[225] Trench foot: the bacterial and fungal infections associated with it can lead to necrosis (cells dying) and gangrene (death and rotting of tissue); if not treated early, the outcome may be amputation or death.

[226] Neither side used poisonous gas in Gallipoli, although both made some preparations to do so; the first use of poison gas in warfare is reckoned to have been by the French Army in August, 1914, the first use of chlorine by the Germans at Ypres in April, 1915, and the first use by the British Army at Loos (north of Lens, Pas-de-Calais department) that September; phosgene and mustard gas were introduced later; gas casualties in the war totalled 1,250,000 including 91,000 fatalities (though that count probably included only those who died 1914-18; see Afterword) — source http://www.historylearningsite.co.uk/poison_gas_and_world_war_one.htm

[227] Observation balloons: their use peaked in World War I, says Wikipedia, because artillery had been developed to fire at a range beyond sight of ground-level spotters; the observers — attached to balloons full of inflammable hydrogen — became the first aviators to use parachutes.

[228] "Verey", as my father wrote it, is a common alternative spelling despite the pistols and flares being named after their inventor, US Naval officer Edward Very.

[229] Stick bomb: the Model 24 Stielhandgranate ("stick hand grenade") used by the German Army from 1915 and then throughout both World Wars; the thrower pulled a cord to ignite a five-second fuse; because of the stick, they could be thrown 30-40 yards as compared to the British Mills bomb's 15-30 yards, but fewer could be carried because of the increased size — source Wikipedia.

[230] The Last Rose Of Summer began life in 1813 as a poem by Thomas Moore (1779-1852), Irish "National Bard" and friend to Byron and Shelley; it immediately acquired its best-known tune — probably the one "played" by my father — composed by Moore's regular collaborator Sir John Stevenson, 1761-1833, although Beethoven, Mendelssohn and

Britten all wrote or arranged later variants; the lyric begins "'Tis the last rose of summer/Left blooming alone/All her lovely companions/Are faded and gone" — source Wikipedia.

[231] British soldiers nicknamed shells fired by the German 7.7cm field gun "whizz-bangs" because they travelled faster than the speed of sound, so recipients heard the "whizz" as they sliced through the air before they heard the "bang" made by the gun firing them; this meant they offered no early warning of their arrival, unlike larger shells from a more distant howitzer — source http://www.firstworldwar.com/atoz/whizzbang.htm.

[232] "Only house owners could vote for a parliamentary candidate": that was under the Third Reform Act, 1884, though more explicitly it gave the vote to men paying annual rent of £10 or owning land valued at £10 or more — this is estimated to have still excluded 40 per cent of adult males; however, it seems that, despite the 1884 Act, many lodgers found themselves excluded from voting until a 1911 Court Of Appeal decision, which is probably what made a man of my father's Assistant Scoutmaster; women (over 30 who met minimum property qualifications) won the vote in UK via the Representation Of The People Act passed well before the end of World War I, in February, 1918, and first exercised their new right later that year in the December 14 general election.

[233] "Bandook" (or "bundook"), a Hindi word for "gun", became British infantry slang through World War I and II — sorry, editor failed to note the source and can't re-find it, but in "big" dictionaries!

[234] Online information suggests my father was wrong about lice spreading any disease — you may know better...

[235] My father never named exactly where he was on the Somme Front — in his memoir I mean, he named places in conversation, but I can't remember them, and if I suggested anywhere specific from modest researches it would be too speculative.

[236] German scientists did invent the "*Flammenwerfer*", first used in combat during 1915; they were cumbersome with a maximum range of about 20 yards; the British soon responded with the "Livens Large Gallery Flame Projector", named after its inventor — source Wikipedia.

[237] Three stripes identified a Sergeant.

[238] According to Chris Henschke responding to a question on 1914-1918. invisionzone.com/forums/index.php?showtopic=35461 "The rate of exchange for issues of cash to the troops of the Expeditionary Force was

fixed at the rate of 5 francs = three shillings and seven pence for the month of July, 1916"; but there seem to be alternative versions of theses figures.

[239] *Minenwerfer*: translates as "mine thrower"; actually what the British Army called a mortar, that is, it lobbed bombs up and over into the enemy trenches; the German version came in three sizes, light, mid-size and heavy — source Wikipedia.

[240] "Red tabs": staff officers identified by red tabs on their tunic collars, based at British Army HQ — the Château de Beaurepaire, Montreuil-sur-Mer, Pas-de-Calais department, about 60 miles from the Somme Front — and rarely or never seen at the front line.

[241] Something odd struck me, as maybe it strikes you, about my father's account of July 1, 1916, the first day of the Battle Of The Somme; it's as if he's not a participant, but a remote observer. This is very different to the way he writes about other battlefields — in Gallipoli earlier, and subsequent experiences on the Western Front, including his front-line account of fighting against the German Spring Offensive around Arras in March, 1918. When he wrote his story, back in the 1970s, and I first read it, section by section, at his request querying anything I didn't understand, one of my questions — I still have the handwritten sheets — was "[Writing about the Somme] you cover the general situation but, for once, don't say what was happening to you — were you in the... advanced trench throughout and therefore a 'spectator'?... you get personal again in the aftermath, recovering bodies etc, but there is this notable blank on what you were doing at the peak of the action... " He didn't answer that question; but then he didn't answer any of the other far more banal questions on that sheet either and I simply don't know why not. So my speculation runs from he just didn't see that sheet of questions for some reason, to the events of that day so shook him that his usual total-recall memory registered very little bar broken fragments, to he did remember but it was so terrible he couldn't bring himself to write down much of it, to he felt guilty that he could do nothing/did nothing to help his comrades. Knowing him, his strength, his capacity for bitterly candid self-criticism, and considering the one reference he made to "guilt" in writing this passage, I'd make a strong guess, you might call it, about what did happen to him: that he and his platoon, like others I've read about elsewhere, got stuck in their trench, cut off, no orders coming through, and never moved, just watched the carnage and tried to live through it — hence, the remote

onlooker point of view. Of course, the Battle Of The Somme remains a notorious episode; the British Army suffered about 60,000 casualties that first day, mainly on the front between the Albert-Bapaume Road and Gommecourt; the battle did continue until November 18, at which point the British and French Armies reckoned to have progressed six miles into formerly German-occupied territory (Wikipedia notes the total casualties, dead and wounded, for the entire Battle Of the Somme, July 1-November 18, as 623,907 Allied and 4-500,000 German); another marginal benefit of the British attack is said to be that it forced the German Army to end its attack at Verdun because they had to divert troops to the Somme.

[242] David Lloyd George: Liberal Secretary Of State For War June 9-December 5, 1916; took over from Herbert Asquith as Prime Minister, December 7, 1916 to October 22, 1922 — my father must have written this letter while Lloyd George ran the War Office.

[243] A note my father wrote on the back of the photograph of himself with brother Ted displayed at the front of this e-book suggests this leave happened "around August" 1916, which sounds too early for the leave his letter eventually produced, I think — and he specifically says, a little later in the text here, that he did not see Ted on that trip home. Hence, I just don't know when the picture was taken.

[244] Salty la Bret: I can't find any reference to this place — perhaps, my father misremembered the name, or it changed, I don't know.

[245] My father wrote his own footnote here: "I believe that affectionate name for the homeland was a corruption of a Hindu word [*Bilāyati*, meaning 'foreign land' *Collins Concise English Dictionary* confirms]. The Indian Army influence remained strong it seemed, for tea was often called 'cha', jam was 'possi', 'pahni' was water. If an old soldier wished to rouse you, he might shout something which sounded like 'Chubberowyuchoot!' These things were learnt without conscious effort as were the words sung to some bugle calls; 'Officers' wives eat puddens and pies, while Sergeants' wives have skilly' was the call to Officers' Mess (dinner); the short reveille call tune had the inspiring words, 'Charlie, Charlie, get up and dress yourself/Charlie, Charlie, get up an' shite.' When mail was to be handed out, the bugler played, 'There's a letter from Lousy Lou, boys, a letter from Poxy Kate'."

[246] Amiens: capital of Somme department in Picardy; a rail hub and British logistics centre during World War I.

[247] While my father gave no clear indications of dates after the first day of the Somme, July 1, and I have no other record to indicate exactly when he wrote to his father and when his leave came through, he referred earlier to Lloyd George as "War Minister", which post he held June 9-December 5, 1916 (as per footnote 242), whereas the "Downing Street" reference here suggests my father may have clearly remembered "L.G." as Prime Minister by the time he got home — which would date it after December 7 — but that seems wrong.

[248] Ciss: I think this is the first time my father named his older sister, always known as Ciss, proper name Dorothy — see footnote 2.

[249] Mills Bomb: actually patented by a civilian, William Mills, son of a Sunderland shipbuilder, at the Mills munitions factory, Birmingham, 1915; the British Army immediately ordered 300,000 a month, though Mills claimed he lost money on the deal; the grenade did fragment, but not along the moulded lines which were designed for grip.

[250] My father was 18 on July 6, 1916; conscription of males aged 19 upwards began in January, 1916, and, although the lower limit was further dropped to 18 that May, according to www.1914-1918.net/recruitment. htm the law still said a soldier could not be sent into battle overseas until he was 19.

[251] Harfleur: a small port on the banks of the Rivers Seine and Lézarde — back then, three miles from Le Havre, now a suburb; scene of the 1415 Anglo-French battle which inspired the "Once more unto the breach, dear friends..." speech in Shakespeare's Henry V.

[252] "The franc was then 27 to the pound": that sounds about right according to footnote 238.

[253] Saint-Omer: a small canal-side town, 30 miles south-east of Calais, close to the North Sea and the Belgian border; the British Army established its "maps GHQ" there in 1915, forming three Field Survey Companies of the Royal Engineers in 1916 with more soon added; in early 1918 the Ordnance Survey, the British national mapping authority, set up an overseas branch in Saint-Omer — sources include http://www.1914-1918.net/re_survey.htm and http://www.defencesurveyors.org.uk/Images/Historical/WWI/4th%20Field%20Survey%20Battalion.pdf.

[254] Boche: insulting French slang for "German" not used much before World War I, nor since World War II; probably abbreviated from archaic caboche, literally a cabbage, figuratively something like "stupid head".

[255] "Major Booth", you may recall, being my father's alias for Major Harry Nathan; more of these events much later.

[256] Harrogate: spa town in North Yorkshire; the Royal Pump Room dates from 1842, but declined after World War I and is now a museum.

[257] Essex Regiment: founded 1881; 30 Battalions in World War I; battle honours included Le Cateau, Ypres, Loos, Somme, Cambrai, Gallipoli; Ian Hook, Keeper of the Essex Regiment Museum, Chelmsford, kindly researched my father's Regimental records and found that he transferred to the 2/7th Essex at Harrogate on December 18, 1916, though, soon after, he moved administratively to the 4th (Reserve) Battalion at Halton, Buckinghamshire (a place he never visited, to the best of my knowledge).

[258] "The Lost Division"; or rather "The Forgotten Division" according to etheses.whiterose.ac.uk/880/2/uk_bl_ethos_347486_VOL2.pdf which adds that Horatio Bottomley — see footnote 86 — was alerted to the Division's inertia by letters from "Disappointed Yorkshiremen" i.e. an anonymous source; it seems to have been the 62nd (2nd West Riding) Division and, according to Fraser Skirrow's *Massacre On The Marne*, its entry into action was delayed by a range of missteps and coincidences until lack of action and siphoning off of the fittest men to active Divisions caused a decline in morale with many men seeking transfers; the Division's training had allegedly been botched under a Lieutenant Colonel Richard A.A. Bottomley — no relation! — so that his men not only remained unfit but many succumbed to lice too; he was replaced in March, 1916; another source suggests the Division, or part of it, did move to France and the Western Front in December, 1916, which probably preceded my father's posting to Harrogate, although timings are hard to pin down in this section given no handy mentions of fixed points such as Christmas; a tangled web and I don't pretend to be clear about the facts relating to this ancient controversy.

[259] You may think this rings bells with regard to footnote 69, but I can find no hint that Sax Rohmer ever operated in Harrogate, much less in the field of character delineation; some lesser romancer then, if the story my father heard had any basis in fact.

[260] Voluntary Aid Detachment: founded 1909 with the help of the Red Cross; 38,000 served in World War I; members famous then or later included Vera Brittain, Agatha Christie, Amelia Earhart, and Freya Stark.

[261] Probably a song called A Dream Of Delight by Horatio Nicholls and

Mabel Manson, published 1916.

[262] My father never mentions the name of this place, but I think I recall him saying it was Cramlington, Northumberland.

[263] Devised by US Army Colonel Isaac Newton Lewis in 1911, with the magazine a distinctive rotating drum holding either 47 or 97 bullets, which could be fired at 5-600 a minute; it weighed 28 pounds, half as much as a contemporary Vickers machine gun; when the American Army rejected it, Lewis sailed for Belgium, then England, where he worked on manufacture with BSA in Birmingham; the British Army approved it in October, 1915, and Lewis guns came into common use early the following year, about 50,000 of them — including a belated American model — on the Western Front by the end of the war.

[264] Clipstone: north Nottinghamshire, near Sherwood Forest; then a massive encampment of huts housing 20-30,000 men — 20 Battalions — created in 1915 on Clipstone Heath, its first occupants Royal Fusiliers; in 1918 soldiers of the Queens Royal West Surrey 4th/5th Reserve Battalion and the Yorks and Lincs Regiment rioted there over delays in their demobilisation; after the camp's closure in 1920, the village of New Clipstone established itself on part of the site, around a new coal mine — sources Wikipedia and sherwoodforestvisitor.com/2012/10/18/sherwood-pines-clipstone-heath-forest-war-time-role/

[265] Alexandra Feodorovna, 1872-1918, Empress Consort of Nicholas II, the last Emperor Of Russia; the "Tsaritsa", not "Tsarina" as the British usually called her, it seems, was Queen Victoria's granddaughter and Kaiser Wilhelm II's cousin; the hotel my father refers to was the Cathcart House, then owned by the Allen family, still standing as of 2014, but converted into flats; it bears a plaque saying Empress Alexandra stayed there in 1894 and became godmother to the owners' twin children (at her own request because she took their birth during her visit as a lucky omen) — she further asked their parents, Christopher and Emma Allen, that they be named after herself and Nicholas, the then Tsarevich (heir to the Imperial throne), to whom she was engaged; the Tsaritsa was Rasputin's chief supporter at court; when revolutionaries deposed her husband in 1917, her cousin King George V refused her permission to flee to Great Britain; after a period of imprisonment, in 1918, she and her family were murdered, probably on the orders of Lenin; in 2000, the Russian Orthodox Church canonised Alexandra as "a passion bearer" — sources Wikipedia

and www.flickr.com/photos/sgwarnog/8686383158/ and www.bbc.
co.uk/ahistoryoftheworld/objects/slH_N0WPT_ylSGuNPyX6zw

[266] Samuel Smith's of Tadcaster, established 1758, just over 16 miles from
Harrogate.

[267] I haven't been able to confirm any reference to cordite causing heart
disease, but Wikipedia says "The chewing of cordite, as a form of chewing
gum was far from unknown in the late 19th and early 20th centuries. The
sweet taste made it attractive, and it gave the user feelings similar to those
produced by alcohol."

[268] A reminder that, even after he switched to first-person autobiography, he
still used "Norcliffe" as the family name whenever it came up throughout
the memoir.

[269] My father probably stayed at Wharncliffe War Hospital, formerly
Middlewood Asylum, converted for military use 1915-20.

[270] George Robey: "The Prime Minister Of Mirth", 1869-1954, music
hall star from Kennington, London; his best-known song was If You
Were The Only Girl In The World and his catch phrase "Kindly temper
your hilarity with a modicum of reserve"; he raised £500,000 for war
charities during World War I; Nobody (the correct title), written in 1905
by Bert Williams (1874-1922, the best-selling black American recording
artist pre-1920; W.C. Fields called him the funniest and the saddest man
he knew) and lyricist Alex Rogers (no dates and little other information
on him except he was a black vaudeville performer, no references to
him after 1924), for a Broadway show, Abyssinia which featured real,
live camels; lyrics include "When all day long things go amiss,/And I go
home to find some bliss,/Who hands to me a glowin' kiss?/Nobody/... I
ain't never got nothin' from nobody, no time!/And until I get somethin'
from somebody, sometime/... I don't intend to do nothin' for nobody,
no time!"; later recorded by Bing Crosby, Nina Simone, Ry Cooder,
Johnny Cash.

[271] After some toing and froing on the rules of engagement for submarines
(Unterseeboot), says Wikipedia, on January 31, 1917, Germany lifted all
restrictions on attacking merchant vessels; new tactics of convoying with
Naval escort ships somewhat reduced their effect, but U-boats sank about
11 million tons of Allied shipping 1914-18.

[272] Farthing: legal tender until 1960 in "old money" (lsd), a quarter of a
penny, so one 960th of a pound sterling (which says something about why

the UK government eventually decimalised the currency); after 1936, this smallest coin bore the image of the country's smallest bird, the wren — before that it was Britannia on the reverse of the monarch, as per all other British coins — see also footnote 8.

[273] They moved to 317, Fore Street, Edmonton.

[274] Gregory Blaxland's *Amiens, 1918* (1968), published by W. H. Allen, says that at a meeting of the German Chiefs of Staff November 11, 1917, General Erich Ludendorff decided to prepare the *Kaiserschlacht* (Kaiser's Battle) dubbed "The Spring Offensive" by the Allies.

[275] The "British Commonwealth", as opposed to the British Empire, was talked of from 1884 when, visiting Australia, future Liberal Prime Minister Lord Rosebery spoke of a "Commonwealth of Nations"; the Commonwealth's formalisation as an intergovernmental organisation didn't take place until 1949.

[276] "On your tod" is Cockney rhyming slang — "on your own/Tod Sloan"; American jockey Sloan rode many winners in England 1897-1901, hung out with magnate and gambler Diamond Jim Brady, inspired George M. Cohan's song Yankee Doodle, and Ernest Hemingway's short story My Old Man; but his career ended with a lifelong ban imposed for betting on his own races, an apparently unproven and dubious charge — source Wikipedia.

[277] My father didn't pin any dates down with regard to his return to France, but in Part Nine he does refer back to this departure date as in "late 1917" — which fits with the war being in its "fourth year". Ian Hook, of the Essex Regiment Museum, says my father was listed as part of the 2nd Battalion when he returned to France.

[278] Arras: 68 miles southeast of Calais, population 26,080 in 1911; scene of battles throughout the war around the town and region, see map www.greatwar.co.uk/places/french-flanders-artois-towns.htm.

[279] Essex Regiment cap badge: see www.google.co.uk/search?q=essex+regiment+cap+badge+ww1&tbm=isch&tbo=u&source=univ&sa=X&ei=_RrLUpuPGcbxhQeG1oCIBw&ved=0CE0QsAQ&biw=815&bih=736

[280] Built in 1866, accommodating 226 prisoners, according to http://forum-prison.forumactif.com/t1372-etablissement-penitentiaire-maison-d-arret-arras

[281] My father attended Royal Fusiliers 2/1st Battalion reunions until the 1960s.

[282] Executions by guillotine continued in France until 1977.

[283] The 2nd Irish, 3rd Coldstream, and 4th Grenadier Guards saw action in the Arras area during this period according to Rudyard Kipling's *The Irish Guards In The Great War, Edited And Compiled From Their Diaries And Papers* (1923) at www.telelib.com/authors/K/KiplingRudyard/prose/IrishGuardsv1/1918arrasarmistice.htm

[284] Manfred Freiherr Von Richthofen: "The Red Baron" ("*Freiherr*" more or less equalled "Baron" in the Prussian aristocracy, although in Germany his soubriquet was "*Der Rote Kampfflieger*", literally "The Red Battleflyer"); born May 2, 1892, near Breslau, Germany (now Wroclaw, Poland); starting Army life in the Cavalry, he transferred to Signals, then in May, 1915, to the Imperial German Army Air Service; flew on Eastern and Western Fronts early on; from January, 1917, flew a red-painted Albatross DIII and joined elite Jasta II Squadron around Lagnicourt in September, 1916, leading it from January, 1917; in June that year became leader of Jagdgeschwader 1, the "Flying Circus"; March 18-28, 1918, he recorded nine air combat victories/kills of Allied planes around the Front in northern France; the day after his 80th kill, on April 21, 1918, he was shot down over Morlancourt Ridge near the River Somme, fatally wounded by a bullet fired from the ground (the shot has been attributed to several different Australian machine gunners); No. 3 Squadron Australian Flying Corps buried him with full honours, laying a wreath dedicated "To our gallant and worthy foe" — sources Wikipedia, www.firstworldwar.com/bio/richthofen.htm, history1900s.about.com/od/1910s/a/redbaron_4.htm and en.wikipedia.org/wiki/List_of_victories_of_Manfred_von_Richthofen

[285] *Military Operations France And Belgium, 1918 March-April: Continuation Of The German Offensives* (1937), published by IWM & Battery Press, says that, on January 21, 1918, General Erich Ludendorff, of the German High Command, decided the "Spring Offensive" should go ahead — this in anticipation of America becoming militarily active, which it did in May (having declared war on April 6, 1917), and following Russia's signing an armistice with Germany (on December 23, 1917, the Kaiser having supported Lenin's Bolshevik Revolution for his own ends) which freed 50 Divisions to march from the Eastern to the Western Front; on March 21, 1918, at 4.40am Ludendorff launched Operation Michael (aka the Second Battle Of The Somme), the first of five great attacks comprising the "Spring Offensive"; www.historyofwar.org/articles/battles_sommeII.

html says that within five hours German artillery fired 1.1 million shells (including poison gas shells) from 6,500 guns and 3,500 mortars; their 17th Army commanded by General Otto Von Below, veteran of successful World War I campaigns on the Eastern Front, in Macedonia and Italy, commanded the attack on the section of the Front east and south of Arras — a second wave of this attack, known as "Operation Mars", began on March 28.

[286] Not quite back to the Romans, probably — Wikipedia says mortars were first deployed in action by Fatih Sultan Mehmet's Army in the 1453 siege of Constantinople — which actually marked the end of the Roman Empire after 1,500 years. See also footnote 239 re the *Minenwerfer*.

[287] My father wrote this passage on a separate sheet after completing his description of his final battle; he headed it "Murder" and added a note on the main manuscript instructing me to insert it at this point; the decision he took 20 years later, when he was 41 and World War II loomed, was to join the Civil Defence in London as an ambulance driver/first-aid expert, and not to enlist in the Army again — to save life, rather than kill, he told me.

[288] Gregory Blaxland's *Amiens 1918*, referred to earlier in footnote 274, offers interesting detail on the Battle Of Arras, that March; the Allies pulled much of their strength back beyond German artillery range leaving the front line as what they called "an outpost zone" planning the most substantial resistance to the infantry attack for a "battle zone" well to the rear. According to Wikipedia, this worked because "Ludendorff continually exhausted his forces by attacking strongly entrenched British units" and consequently "At Arras on March 28, he launched a hastily-prepared attack (Operation Mars) against the left wing of the British Third Army, to try to widen the breach in the Allied lines, and was repulsed". A detailed account of the day that concluded with my father's survival (but behind enemy lines), and more generally, although my father and his fellow POWs didn't know it, a great, very costly military success can be found at www.stanwickwarmemorial.co.uk/54.html — a site dedicated to tracking all the soldiers from a village called Stanwick, Northamptonshire (1911 population 922, of whom 152 enlisted in the armed forces 1914-18, many of them Essex Regiment members, and 36 were killed); in part, reproduced with the kind permission of the site's webmaster Steve Bence aka Freddie Shawm, it reads: "On the 28th March 1918 the Essex

Regiment were holding the left sector of the whole of the 4th Division front and indeed the extreme left of the Third Army where it joined the First Army boundary. The 2nd Battalion, Essex Regiment, was the front Battalion of 12 Brigade... At 3am there was heavy enemy artillery fire (high explosive and gas) on the Front, Support and Reserve lines. At 6am the bombardment became more intense but communications were still valid. At 7.10am the communications ceased and wire was cut. At 7.20am the German assault began. There was a breakthrough on the right and the front Companies fought on until ammunition was exhausted. Battalion H.Q. withdrew along Chili Avenue to its junction with Harry and Hussar Trenches. It was here that a strong point was established in conjunction with the Lancashire Fusiliers. The enemy did not penetrate further and though the position was for some hours critical in the extreme, with troops falling back on the right and the left, the line held. In this section of the line the Germans mighty effort to capture Arras had been thwarted. They were only able to advance a distance of less than 2,000 yards. That same night the 2nd Battalion, Essex Regiment moved back to Athies [two miles east of Arras]. There were 5 officers and 75 men as survivors from the 500 men who were alive in the morning of the 28th March 1918. Stanwick's Pte J G Morris was killed on that day. A fortnight later these survivors were moved to the Ypres Salient to help stem the German advance in that sector." Ian Hook, of the Essex Regiment Museum, notes the 2nd Battalion defended trenches dubbed Chili, Harry and Hussar, and that by the end of March 28, 342 were listed as "missing". He also forwarded the official Arras Day Special Order, a description of the 2nd Battalion's role in the battle, which was read out to the Battalion every March 28 1919-39 — in part, it says: the Battalion formed part of the British Army's 4th Division, 13th Corps, 1st Army; the Battalion comprised 520 men when it entered the front line and that, on the night of March 30/31 when they were relieved, this had come down to 80 men, "all ranks"; that when the German Army launched their massive infantry attack, "almost shoulder to shoulder in 6 lines... the men in our front line who yet lived had no thought of surrender... Thus it was the great attack on Arras failed, and the XIII Corps gained a glorious victory. It was the sterling qualities of grit and endurance of the British soldier in the front line which achieved this success. Cut off from all support, away from higher control, Platoon and sections though isolated, carried out their instructions to the letter.

They held out to the last man and the Enemy were only able to advance over their dead bodies… Arras was safe, and the price, ungrudgingly given by the Battalion was 440 brave men." A timeline for the day and a list of officer casualties culled from the Battalion war diary is available at 1914-1918.invisionzone.com/forums/index.php?showtopic=118324. See also www.historyofwar.org/articles/battles_sommeII.html and Field Marshall Sir Douglas Haig's own account of the whole Spring Offensive battle at www.1914-1918.net/haigs_michael_despatch.html (search "the attack on Arras" for the wider events relating to my father's experience). A post script on Ludendorff: later a nationalist supporter of Hitler, he supported the total-war theory that peace could never be more than an interlude; his long-term strategy, if Germany had won World War I, included overrunning Britain and then the United States.

[289] Gavrelle: six miles east-north-east of Arras, 10 miles west of Douai; the British captured it on April 23, 1917, and lost it this day, March 28, 1918, before reoccupying in August.

[290] Denain: 18 miles east of Douai, 38 miles east of Arras; an industrial town which inspired Émile Zola to write *Germinal* (1885); occupied by the German Army from summer 1914 to October 19, 1918 — three weeks later French President Raymond Poincaré visited and found "*Un spectacle de désolation*" according to www.ville-denain.fr/node/92

[291] *Landsturm*: 3rd-class infantry, comprising any male aged between 17 and 42 who wasn't in the standing Army, the *Landwehr*.

[292] Cramlington, probably, winter 1916-17; see footnote 262.

[293] Marchiennes: in the Nord department, 32.5 miles east of Arras, known for it's 7th-century Benedictine abbey; over the centuries it passed back and forth between Flanders, France and Holland; the town and the mine feature extensively in Émile Zola's *Germinal*.

[294] My father may have wrongly remembered the previous town they passed through as Valenciennes because, from Denain, it is in the opposite direction to Sancourt; perhaps the brave beer carrier lived in Cambrai or Saint-Quentin, sizable towns both in the road the prisoners are likely to have marched. Sancourt: 23 miles from Arras, in Nord department, 4 miles from Cambrai; liberated on September 29, 1918, by the Canadian Corps; the site of Sancourt POW camp is shown on Google maps at https://maps.google.co.uk/maps?ie=UTF-8&gl=uk&daddr=Sancourt,+France&saddr=Valenciennes,+France&panel=1&f=d&fb=1&geocode=Kb

MJtGjH7cJHMZT0_Qvs3PS1%3BKQ_4RN8tusJHMTBXZIE-8QoE
&ei=zYblUtTgGfTZ0QX7rIHQAw&ved=0CCsQ-A8wAA

[295] Another footnote from my father about the troops' use of foreign words: "That German word, 'ersatz', by the way, had been in use in England for some time, together with the French word *Boche* when we tired of calling him Jerry (should have been 'Gerry', of course); '*matelot*' was regularly used by our sailors, and '*couchet*' for sleep, as a change from 'kip', and many others."

[296] *Mutter, Vater, Schwester, Haus*, and *Heim*: in case they're not that easily grasped, they mean mother, father, sister, house, and home.

[297] Mons, Belgium: 48 kilometres north-east of Sancourt; notoriously the scene of the British Expeditionary Force's first battle of World War I, August 23-4, 1914, the Canadian Corps liberated Mons on November 11, 1918, and, says Wikipedia, one memorial plaque in the town claims "Here was fired the last shot of the great war".

[298] Bapaume: 39 kilometres from Sancourt, 22 kilometres south of Arras; occupied by Germany August 28, 1914; one of the objectives not reached by the British attack during the 1916 Battle Of The Somme; liberated March 17, 1917, by Australian troops; recaptured by Germany during the Spring Offensive, 1918; liberated again by New Zealand soldiers on August 29, 1918, during the second Battle Of Bapaume, August 2-September 3; after the war, Sheffield "adopted" Bapaume, financing the construction of a dozen houses and, with finance from razor manufacturer George Lawrence, a school.

[299] "The Paris Gun", the largest artillery piece by barrel length (21 metres) used by either side during World War I, fired on Paris, March to August, 1918, from Coucy-Le-Chateau-Auffrique, Picardy, actually a range of 120 kilometres; developed from a Navy gun, so manned by sailors, it lacked accuracy and delivered relatively small shells, but it was seen as a "psychological" weapon; Wikipedia says the shells were the first human-made objects to reach the stratosphere, their trajectory reaching its apogee at 25 miles.

[300] Hindenburg Line: or *Siegriedstellung* built 1916-17 from Neuville Vitasse near Arras to Cerny En Laonnois near Reims (about 90 miles); its barbed-wire "fields" were up to 90 metres deep; the line remained intact until September, 1918, during the Allies' "Hundred Days Offensive", August 8-November 11.

[301] *Gefangenenlager*: prison camps.

[302] Yip-I-Addy-I-Ay: recorded by Bob Roberts on Albany Indestructible Cylinder in 1909, written by Americans Will D. Cobb (lyrics, 1876-1930, also go-wrote In The Good Old Summer Time, Goodbye Dolly Gray) and John H. Flynn (composer), but with a German-American lead character it seems: "Young Herman Von Bellow/A musical fellow/Played on a big cello each night/... And music so mellow/He sawed on his cello/ She waltzed up to him and she cried,/'Yip di ada di ay, di ay'".

[303] Cambrai: 33 miles south-east of Arras on the road from Bapaume to Valenciennes; the First Battle Of Cambrai, November 20-December 3, 1917, saw one of the first deployments of tanks by the British Army — see Sir Arthur Conan Doyle's account at www.firstworldwar.com/source/ cambrai_conandoyle.htm; the Second Battle Of Cambrai, October 8-10, 1918, was part of the Allies' conclusive Hundred Days Offensive.

[304] Saargemund: now in the Moselle department of Lorraine, France; known as Sarreguemines when French (1766-1871, 1918-present).

[305] Metz: in Lorraine now, 228 miles southwest of Arras, held by Germany 1871-1918 and again during World War II. Sedan: six miles from the Belgian border in Ardennes department, occupied by Germany throughout World War I. Charleville: birthplace of poet Arthur Rimbaud, occupied from 1914 onwards and recovered during one of the last major battles of the war, around November 1, 1918. My father and his fellow POWs probably travelled 47 miles due west from Saargemund to Metz, then 114 miles northwest to Sedan, and 11 miles northwest to Charleville.

[306] Heligoland: an archipelago in the German Bight area of the North Sea off the Elba estuary; held by Denmark or Schleswig or Hamburg from the 12th century until 1714, then Danish from 1714 to 1807, then British until 1890, and German thereafter, though evacuated during World War I and again in 1945-1952, after which it became a German holiday resort.

[307] *Schweinereien*: apparently archaic, means "rascalities" or "digusting people", according to different online dictionaries. In our long school-holiday conversations at home in London during my teens, my father told me another story about the German guard "Heligoland" which has always stayed with me, although he forgot to write it here (I don't think he would have deliberately decided to omit it). As that train rolled along and they talked in broken German/broken English about the war — and Heligoland's experiences in past wars — they reached a point where

they were struggling to say something conclusive to one another — "*Wir müssen*", "We must, *ja?*", "*Jede andere,*" "Each? Each other? Go on..." — and my father gradually realised it was something like, "*Wir müssen niemals dies zu jedem anderen tun*"... "We must never do this to each other again."

[308] The Black Forest: wooded mountains, 99 miles long, 37 miles wide, in Baden-Württemberg state, southwestern Germany, source of the Danube.

[309] Oddly, the "vagueness" my father refers to in this paragraph seems to embrace lacking any recollection of his group of prisoners parting company with Heligoland, "the kindliest German".

[310] Alsace-Lorraine: annexed by the German Empire in 1871 as one of the spoils of the Franco-Prussian War; in July, 1915, the German Government banned the French language from the region; the Allies annexed Alsace back to France in December, 1918, and, in the early '20s, deported the Germans remaining there and banned their language; Hitler re-annexed Alsace in 1940-45, then lost it again.

[311] Freiburg: in the Breisgau region of Baden-Württemberg on the western edge of the Black Forest, 380 miles southeast of Arras.

[312] Mülhausen or Mulhouse: in Alsace, 396 miles south-east of Arras; formerly known as "the French Manchester" because of its textile industry; part of the Holy Roman Empire until it joined the Swiss Confederation, 1515-1798, then transferred to France during the Revolution, until annexed by the German Empire 1870-1918, after which it returned to France until 1940-45; hometown of Alfred Dreyfus and also of Dr Karl Brandt, Hitler's personal physician and chief administrator of the "action T4" programme which exterminated 275,000 German and Austrian citizens deemed incurably ill.

[313] "*Los! Raus! Aufmachen du Schlavina!*": would translate as something like "Come on! Out!" and then "*Schlavina*" may be my father's phonetic memory of "*Sklaven*" or possibly the feminine "*Sklavinnen*" as an extra (uncomprehended) insult — so "Get up, you slaves!"?

[314] *Soldaten*: soldiers. *Gefreiter*: the equivalent of a Private First Class.

[315] *Rhaude*: probably my father misremembering the word, or maybe a local spelling for "*Räude*", meaning mange.

[316] My father's interpretation of the guard's feelings may well be correct; according to the unscientific testimony of a German friend of mine, who happens to be from the Black Forest vicinity, "*Scheisse!*" (shit) is the apogee

of cursing in her language, with no "fuck" equivalent to drag sex into it.

[317] *"Arbeit! Fest Arbeit!"* : "Work! Work fast!"

[318] *Posten*: seems to mean something like "a person in a job"; it doesn't translate specifically as "guard", but, clearly, my father heard it used as the generic for the men guarding him.

[319] Hügelheim: in the Baden-Württemberg area known as Markgräflerland.

[320] *Gutschein für 5 Pfennigs*: voucher for 5 "pennies".

[321] My father footnoted: "So many of them are in 1976, as I write".

[322] Wikipedia says a series of Geneva treaties began with Swiss businessman/social activist Henri Dunant's reaction to the battle of Solferino, in the kingdom of Lombardy-Venetia, 1859, between French/Sardinian and Austrian Armies; first the Red Cross was formed in Geneva, then in 1864 came the first Geneva Convention, aka "the Red Cross Treaty"; adopted initially by 12 nations, it codified the treatment of sick and wounded soldiers on the battlefield during declared wars, and the neutrality of medical personnel, but said of prisoners only that they should be returned to their country; the list of original signatories varies from source to source, but Wikipedia has, from *International Law: A Treatise* by Ronald Roxburgh, 1920: Baden, Belgium, Denmark, France, Hesse, Italy, Netherlands, Portugal, Prussia, Spain, Switzerland And Wurttemberg, while www.spartacus.schoolnet.co.uk/EUgeneva.htm doesn't show the German then-independent states and adds Norway (with the many later ratifiers including Britain and Turkey 1865, Russia 1867, USA 1882); a Convention covering war at sea was added in 1906, then further revisions came long after World War I, in 1929, 1949 (it removed the "declared war" limitation), 1977 and 2005; protection of POWs in World War I depended more on the Hague Regulations of 1899 and 1907 which the war proved deficient, leading in part to the 1929 Geneva Convention revision covering particularly "the prohibition of reprisals and collective penalties", says www.icrc.org/ihl/INTRO/305?OpenDocument

[323] *Seife*: soap.

[324] *"Bitte, Gelt, essen"*: "Please, money, eat."

[325] *Unteroffizier*: can mean either "Corporal", or serve as a generic for non-commissioned officers.

[326] Thompson's *Seifenpulver*: "soap powder"; the company, founded by Dr Richard Thompson in Bradford, had long since moved to Düsseldorf.

[327] According to www.kzwp.com/lyons2/margetts.htm Margetts was based

in Dalston, London, from 1869, its founder James Margetts of Hackney.
[328] Müllheim: in Baden-Württemberg, 2.3 miles south of Hügelheim, between the Black Forest and the Rhine.
[329] *"Ich arbeit darein"*: "I work in there".
[330] The manual chaff-cutter's wheel is turned via a handle mangle-style — see www.youtube.com/watch?v=-H3I3GidWfg.
[331] My father's memory may be wrong with regard to timing here. Wikipedia says the first, limited, and short-lived German Navy mutiny took place at North Sea port Wilhelmshaven, October 29-30; the second and decisive one followed shortly at Kiel, on the canal linking the Baltic to the North Sea, November 3, 1918; that triggered the German Revolution which swept aside the monarchy within a few days and eventually led to the formation of the Weimar Republic; the effects of that mutiny certainly spread rapidly down to the southern region where my father was imprisoned; I don't know, but I'm guessing either the sailor's visit to the *Pferde Lazerette* occurred some weeks later than my father reckoned, or said sailor had observed or taken part in an earlier and more minor mutiny which didn't, at that point, embrace much of the German Navy.
[332] *Stammlager*: prisoner of war camp, often abbreviated to "*Stalag*"; Parchim is a small town in the German Baltic state Mecklenburg-Vorpommern; Friedrichsfeld now seems to be part of a town called Voerde in North-Rhine-Westphalia state; both are listed among the 168 "principal POW camps in Germany" at www.1914-1918.net/soldiers/powcamps.html and Wiki says a total of 2.4 million Allied prisoners were held in Germany during World War I.
[333] Ian Hook, of the Essex Regiment Museum, notes that he has a record of the Essex Regiment Prisoner Of War Fund sending food parcels to C Sutcliffe of Edmonton. But, clearly, they didn't make it.
[334] *Fusslappen*: foot cloth.
[335] The Bull Ring: market place specialising in textiles, formally from 1154 when chartered by King Henry II; the market grew and diversified through the centuries, survived World War II bombings; redeveloped from the 1950s onwards as a shopping centre.
[336] *"Zu Österreich!"*: "To Austria!"
[337] The Iron Cross: originated in Prussia during the Napoleonic Wars, says Wikipedia, became degraded by mass awards in World War 1, during which the German Army handed out at least 5.4 million, including two

to Adolph Hitler.

[338] The final steps towards Armistice began on September 29, 1918, when General Ludendorff told the Kaiser he could not guarantee holding the line for another 24 hours; he called for an immediate ceasefire, ceding to the demands of President Woodrow Wilson's "14 Points", issued in January, 1918; soon after that, Ludendorff changed his mind about suing for peace, but by then the German Army's morale had collapsed and the Navy mutiny of October 29-30 (in Wilhelmshaven on the North Sea, then Kiel on the Baltic) incited a revolutionary spirit which rapidly spread across the country; the combatants agreed the Armistice on November 11, the day after the Kaiser's abdication, and it came into force at 11am Paris time (hence "the 11th hour of the 11th day of the 11th month" of sonorous cliché); the German soldier who my father heard shouting about it may have got the news a day or so later or perhaps he was echoing a false rumour in advance of the actual signing — although my father's assumption remained that this was indeed November 11, he hadn't kept track of dates; under the Armistice terms, Germany agreed to complete demilitarisation and the occupation of the Rhineland by American, Belgian, British and French Armies; the parties did not agree and sign the final Peace Treaty (of Versailles) until June 28, 1919; the establishment of Germany's Weimar Republic followed in August.

[339] My father's capital letters here!

[340] "Uhlan": the Polish spelling, says Wikipedia — it's "Ulan" in German — it referred to light cavalry armed with lances, sabres and pistols and sporting a uniform with a black, double-breasted jacket adorned at the front by a coloured panel called a "plastron"; French and British troops in World War I tended to describe all German cavalry as "Uhlans"; but they did comprise 26 Regiments, two of them from the then state of Württemberg, so my father may well have been right about this man being a Uhlan/Ulan.

[341] "*Vornung vor dem Bombe*": my father's memory probably did let him down slightly — the signs are likely to have read "*Warnung vor der Bombe*", "Warning/beware of the bomb".

[342] Nancy: 262 miles southeast of Arras, in the department of Meurthe-Et-Moselle, remained French after the Franco-Prussian War and throughout World War I.

[343] "*Boulangerie, Confiserie*": "Baker, Confectioner".

[344] *"Poilus"*: was French slang for their own infantrymen in World War I; meaning "hairy one", it arose from Napoleon's Army of the early 19th century largely comprising heavily bewhiskered agricultural workers.

[345] "Sanfairyann": British soldierese for "Ça ne fait rien," "It doesn't matter".

[346] Independent Air Force (IAF): a short-lived World War I strategic bombing force (founded June 6, 1918), part of the Royal Air Force (itself founded April 1, 1918), used to strike against German railways, airfields and industry; statistics don't suggest the IAF enjoyed great success — 550 tons of bombs dropped and 109 aircraft lost — and it was disbanded soon after the war ended.

[347] Mr Something Smith: that's Denis Nayland Smith who, along with his Dr Watson-style back-up and Boswell Dr Petrie, regularly foiled Fu Manchu in the Sax Rohmer "Yellow Peril" stories published from 1912 onwards — see also footnotes 69 and 259.

[348] The Chinese Labour Corps: founded 1916, after Field Marshal Haig requested 21,000 labourers; recruited in China, the first ship-load sailed in January, 1917, and arrived in France three months later; by Armistice Day, they numbered 96,000; most were given transport home in 1919-20; perhaps 10-20,000 are said to have died during the war, chiefly from Spanish Flu; other Labour Corps recruited more than 300,000 men from British colonies, including Egypt, Fiji, India, Malta, Mauritius, Seychelles, the British West Indies and South Africa.

[349] American hospital near Rouen: information at http://beckerexhibits.wustl.edu/gh21/ww1/ suggests this was probably Base Hospital 21, located on the racecourse, and staffed mainly by doctors and nurses from Washington University Hospital, St Louis; it had 1,300 beds and remained active caring for former POWs until January, 1919.

[350] Alcock and Brown: John Alcock from Manchester and Arthur Brown from Glasgow, both POWs during World War I, the former shot down in Turkey, the latter in Germany, made the first non-stop Transatlantic flight in June, 1919.

[351] See Chapter 51.

[352] In fact, private banks had issued notes since 1698, says Wikipedia, but this right was gradually eroded by law and ended in 1921; meanwhile in 1914 HM Treasury acquired wartime powers to issue £1 and 10/- bank notes and did so until 1928.

[353] German airships and planes bombed many British towns — including some strikes on north-east London — during World War I, though not on anything like the scale of the World War II blitz; among the casualties of a raid on March 7, 1918, was Lena Ford, who wrote the lyrics to Keep The Home Fires Burning (music by Ivor Novello) — an American, born 1870 in Pennsylvania, she lived in London for her last 20 years and, during the war, opened her home to soldiers passing through.

[354] The Fore Street, Edmonton, address, as per the move referred to in footnote 273.

[355] Coyghem: a small village in West-Vlaanderen province, Belgium, a few kilometres over the French-Belgian border from Lille and Roubaix, and a little further from Arras.

[356] See footnote 253.

[357] The Military Medal: established in March, 1916, as the "other ranks" equivalent to the officers' Military Cross, awarded for bravery in battle on land. I'm sure my father as right about his brother winning the medal, but I haven't found any record of it.

[358] Deep In The Heart Of A Rose (1900) written by Sir Landon Ronald (1873-1938), Principal of the Guildhall School Of Music from 1910 and composer for London West End shows, and American-born lyricist Edward Teschemacher/Lockton (1876-1940).

[359] In fact, Anne Ziegler and Webster Booth revived Deep In The Heart Of A Rose in 1949 according to http://ziegler-booth.blogspot.co.uk/2009/03/discography-anne-ziegler-and-webster.html

[360] "Home Forces" seems to have been the official title; they were launched in January, 1916; www.airfieldinformationexchange.org/community/showthread.php?6805-FIRST-WORLD-WAR-Home-Defence-(Ground-Forces) describes them as comprising "men and boys who had not yet completed even a basic military training"; however, Ian Hook, of the Essex Regiment Museum specifies from their records that, during his last Army months, my father transferred to the Royal Defence Corps — formed August, 1917, with much the same functions as the Home Forces, but comprising men too old or medically unfit for battlefield service abroad.

[361] My father added one of his own footnotes here: "Actually, some 57 years later, as I write in 1976, they have just removed the 'What the butler saw' and similar machines and sold them at fantastic profit at auction... and that old pier... is still earning money"; Palace Pier, Brighton's third

pier, opened in 1899, and remains in operation at my time of writing in 2014.

[362] See footnote 255.

[363] In *Strong For Service*, the Nathan biography, author H. Montgomery Hyde reports Nathan's own account of his wounding — in mid-July, 1916, a while after the initial Somme onslaught and massacre, a sniper shot him, his steel helmet saving his life, Nathan thought, although the bullet "went clean through the base of his head". On July 24, 1916, from hospital, he dictated a letter home saying that "very considerable pain" was decreasing. He convalesced — very slowly — at Palace Green Hospital For Officers, Kensington, and another hospital in Bournemouth, before being sent for additional psychiatric treatment for "melancholia" at Craiglockhart War Hospital, Edinburgh, under the renowned trauma specialist Dr William Rivers (while there, Nathan met another Rivers patient, the war poet and decorated hero of the Somme, Siegfried Sassoon who was officially under treatment for shell shock/neurasthenia after writing a public letter to his commanding officer titled *Finished With The War: A Soldier's Declaration*; Sassoon eventually returned to the Front, was promoted to Captain, then wounded near Arras in July, 1918, and returned to England; Dr Rivers is still renowned because of his portrayal in the *Regeneration* trilogy of novels by Pat Barker (1991-5) and the film adaptation of the same name (1997)). After 18 months convalescence, Nathan was invalided out of the Army with the permanent rank of Major. Still often in pain, but — says Hyde — more personally confident because of his treatment by Rivers, he proceeded to a career in public life (although always a working solicitor to some degree). A Liberal MP for Bethnal Green North East from 1929, he switched to Labour in 1934 and returned to Parliament for Wandsworth Central in 1937, before stepping down to make way for Ernest Bevin (then General Secretary of the Transport & General Workers' Union, shortly Minister Of Labour under PM Winston Churchill in the wartime coalition) — by way of compensation, being ennobled as Lord Nathan of Churt, and serving in the post-World War II Labour Government as Under-Secretary Of State For War and Minister For Civil Aviation; a Privy Counsellor from 1946; Hansard at http://hansard.millbanksystems.com/people/colonel-harry-nathan/ shows how he contributed in Parliament constantly down the years, until his death on July 31, 1963; his wife, Eleanor (*née* Stettauer, 1892-1972, MA economics and maths Girton

College, Cambridge), was a member of London County Council for many years — initially a Liberal, like her husband she switched to Labour (and became Chairman in 1947).

364 My father didn't name this grand house, nor the village where it was located and it's strangely difficult to trace places in England used as Prisoner Of War camps; the house may possibly have been at Slindon, aka Eartham, four miles east of Arundel — source West Sussex & The Great War Project research by Rodney Gunner (but I'm speculating from thin, contradictory information).

365 In January, 1919, the Liberal Government moved Churchill from Minister For Munitions to Secretary Of State For War And Air, so he probably composed this message to the ex-POW POW guards in the latter role.

366 "*Wie heisst du?*": "What's your name?"

367 *Unteroffizier*: non-commissioned officer.

368 Littlehampton: seaside resort in Arun district of Sussex; settlement dating back to Domesday Book of 1086; repute and population grew through the 19th century as poets and artists took a shine to it (Byron, Coleridge, Shelley, Constable) and then the railway with linking cross-channel ferry to Honfleur brought other holidaymakers.

369 Ted Sutcliffe's Medal Rolls index card suggests his effective demob date was April 1, 1919, though it's expressed as transfer to "'Z' Res"; Wikipedia says Class Z Reserve was a contingent "consisting of previously enlisted soldiers, now discharged", created by Army Order on December 3, 1918, pending potential post-Armistice resumption of hostilities; after post-war treaties secured the peace, the Army disbanded Z Reserve on March 31, 1920.

370 According to UK inflation calculator http://safalra.com/other/historical-uk-inflation-price-conversion/ prices exactly doubled between 1914 and 1919, year on year increases being 12.5% 1914-15, 18.1% 1915-16, 25.2% 1916-17, 22% 1917-18, 10.1% 1918-19 — its source credited as 2004 paper "Consumer Price Inflation Since 1750" (*Economic Trends* NO. 604) by Jim O'Donoghue, Louise Goulding, and Grahame Allen.

371 Hans was wrong as far as I can tell, although my father believed him. "Karl" meant "man" in Old Norse, "peasant" in Old English, and thence became the first name "Karl/Carl" in German, then "Charles" in English

as per www.oxforddictionaries.com/definition/english/carl

[372] I can't find any record to show it's more than four: the Royal Fusiliers 1914-16, the Regiment he didn't name who may have been "The Kensingtons" for a few months in 1916 (no records of them that I've run into), the Essex 1916-19, and the Royal Defence Corps. The Essex Regiment Museum's Ian Hook found that my father's full discharge from the Army came through on March 12, 1920, which suggests that, like brother Ted, he may have been registered to Z Reserve for those final months — see footnote 369. Warley: a military town since the 18th century and HQ barracks to the Essex Regiment from its founding in 1881 until 1960 www.forces-war-records.co.uk/unit-info/253/

[373] As editor, I would just add here that my father generalised this overall feeling he had, resulting from the bitter grief of his Royal Fusiliers Battalion's demise at the hands of remote Army decision-makers, but clearly, everywhere he served, he did form many good, trusting friendships with comrades such as McIntyre, Hackerman and, most of all, at the Arras battle, Neston (aliases all, quite likely; I don't know).

[374] Following six months of negotiation at the Paris Peace Conference, the Treaty of Versailles, ended the state of war between Germany and the Allied powers on June 28, 1919, not coincidentally the fifth anniversary of the assassination of Archduke Franz Ferdinand, the event which triggered the war.

[375] "The Peace March For The Glorious Dead" took place on July 19, 1919 — so named, at least in part, because Prime Minister Lloyd George opposed the initial proposal of a "Victory Parade" and insisted that it be couched as a tribute to the dead; Sir Edward Lutyens designed a temporary wood-and-plaster version of the present "Cenotaph" memorial which was erected in Whitehall for the occasion. Field Marshall Douglas Haig, Commander-In-Chief of the British Army, and soon to be ennobled as an Earl, led 15,000 troops on the march — sources www.forces-war-records.co.uk/blog/2013/07/19/on-this-day-19th-july-1919-peace-day-when-the-boys-came-home and www.royalmunsterfusiliers.org/zl1apece.htm; various events and entertainments followed in the Central London parks. In Hyde Park, where my father and his brother Ted ended up, an "Imperial Choir" of 10,000 voices sang, accompanied by the massed bands of the Brigade Of Guards and "The King and Queen paid a surprise visit" (George V and Queen Mary); naturally, while the nation generally enjoyed

the celebration, many demurred or even protested, with ex-Servicemen often taking the lead, see www.aftermathww1.co.uk/peaceday2.asp
[376] Queen Alexandra of Denmark, then 74, mother of George V and Consort to Edward VII, who had died in 1910.